KEY INDICATORS
FOR ASIA AND THE PACIFIC
2021

52ND EDITION

ASIAN DEVELOPMENT BANK

ADB

6 ADB Avenue, Mandaluyong City, 1550 Metro Manila, Philippines
Tel +63 2 8632 4444; Fax +63 2 8636 2444
www.adb.org

ISBN 978-92-9269-020-5 (print); 978-92-9269-021-2 (electronic); 978-92-9269-022-9 (e-book)
ISSN 0116-3000
Publication Stock No. FLS210322-3
DOI: https://dx.doi.org/10.22617/FLS210322-3

Corrigenda to ADB publications may be found at http://www.adb.org/publications/corrigenda.

Notes:
In this publication, "$" refers to US dollars.
ADB recognizes "China" as the People's Republic of China, "Korea" as the Republic of Korea, and "East Timor" as Timor-Leste.
Photos: All photos by the Asian Development Bank unless otherwise indicated.

Cover design by Rhommell Rico.

Contents

Box

Table

Sustainable Development Goals Tables

Figures

Table

People

Economy and Output

Money, Finance, and Prices

Globalization

Transport and Communication

Energy and Electricity

Environment

Government and Governance

Figures

Tables

Boxes

Figures

Boxes

Foreword

We now find ourselves a year into the Decade of Action to deliver the Sustainable Development Goals by 2030. It is a critical time to advance a shared vision and accelerate responses to development challenges in Asia and the Pacific.

In tracking development targets and identifying shortfalls, trusted data plays a vital role. This is why the Asian Development Bank continues to publish our flagship statistical publication, *Key Indicators for Asia and the Pacific*.

Now in its 52nd year, the publication presents the latest economic, financial, social, and environmental indicators for the bank's 49 members from across Asia and the Pacific. It continues to serve as a vital source of data and statistics for policymakers, government officials, development professionals, researchers, and students around the world. This year's *Key Indicators for Asia and the Pacific* has been refreshed with more analyses and new infographics.

The data stories in this year's report demonstrate that Asia and the Pacific has made substantial progress in the past two decades with respect to several development targets.

Across developing Asia, the number of people living in extreme poverty fell from 1.2 billion in 1999 to 203 million in 2017, and the prevalence of undernourishment decreased from more than 521 million people in 2001 to 316 million in 2019. Among reporting economies, completion rates for primary education have increased by 8 to 11 percentage points, on average, since 2000. The region's impressive economic growth has contributed to these gains. In 2019, Asia and the Pacific accounted for 35% of global gross domestic product (in current U.S. dollars)—exceeding the share of Europe and North America.

While progress before the pandemic varied across developing member economies, the pandemic has further widened these differences. Thus, the challenge of meeting development targets, which needed urgent attention even before the global health crisis began, has intensified.

In more than one-third of reporting economies, unemployment rates increased by at least 20% in 2020, relative to estimates recorded a year earlier, and this contributed to Asia and the Pacific losing about 8% of working hours. By the end of the year, three in every four reporting economies posted declines in gross domestic product. In turn, simulations for developing Asia show that the pandemic has pushed about 75 million to 80 million people into extreme poverty, compared with a scenario without COVID-19.

In the long run, disruptions caused by the pandemic are likely to have considerable adverse effects on human capital and productivity. Our region needs a people-centered development approach to recovery that ensures nobody is left behind.

The pandemic has also revealed two faces of global value chains (GVCs): as both an amplifier and a dampener of shocks. In a number of economies, significant GVC participation was associated with a larger negative shock to GDP, suggesting that openness exacerbated disruptions. However, at much higher rates of GVC participation, the relationship seemed to reverse.

The pandemic underscores the importance of high-quality and timely data to create effective policy. In a dynamic environment where scenarios change rapidly, appropriate data is crucial to develop suitable responses. National statistical systems across the region are responding to this challenge, harnessing digital platforms for data collection and integrating conventional and innovative data sources into the compilation of vital socioeconomic indicators.

With the pandemic intensifying society's reliance on digital platforms for remote working and learning, as well as for shopping and entertainment, the special supplement to *Key Indicators for Asia and the Pacific 2021* presents a practical framework to measure the digital economy, rooted in input-output analysis and using readily available national accounts data. The study provides a sound basis on which to assess the relative importance of the digital economy in national and global production processes.

We appreciate the continued cooperation—sometimes under especially challenging circumstances—of a number of statistical partners in our member economies, who have provided the most recently available data from their official sources, along with a host of international agencies from which the data in many tables of this publication are sourced.

We hope that *Key Indicators for Asia and the Pacific 2021* brings into focus a range of important development issues, provides evidence for new thinking on pandemic recovery, and serves as a valuable resource for data on development indicators.

Masatsugu Asakawa
President
Asian Development Bank

Acknowledgments

This 52nd annual edition of *Key Indicators for Asia and the Pacific* was prepared by the Statistics and Data Innovation Unit (EROD-SDI) within the Economic Research and Regional Cooperation Department (ERCD) at the Asian Development Bank (ADB). The publication team was led by Arturo Martinez Jr, under the overall direction of Elaine S. Tan. Joseph Albert Nino Bulan, Melissa Pascua, and Eric Suan provided technical and coordination support in preparing the publication.

The statistical tables presenting development indicators for ADB's regional member economies in Parts I and II of the printed publication (and also available online via kidb.adb.org), as well as the 49 tables for individual economies available exclusively online, were prepared by EROD-SDI staff and consultants, under the supervision of Daniel Boller, Kaushal Joshi, Mahinthan Joseph Mariasingham, Arturo Martinez Jr, and Stefan Schipper. The research team included Raymond Adofina, Vararat Atisophon, Nalwino Billones, Joseph Albert Nino Bulan, Criselda De Dios, Dennis Dizon, Madeline Dumaua-Cabauatan, Anna Marie Fernando, Karen Firshan, Pamela Lapitan, Rocky Marcelino, Melissa Pascua, Lea Rotairo, Eric Suan, Albert Kirby Tardeo, and Domini Velasquez. Proofreading of statistical tables was done by Ma. Roselia Babalo, Rose Anne Dumayas, Oth Marulou Gagni, and Aileen Gatson. The analyses of Sustainable Development Goal indicators were prepared by Vararat Atisophon, Joseph Albert Nino Bulan, Dennis Dizon, Anna Marie Fernando, Reneli Gloria, Arturo Martinez Jr, Lea Rotairo, and Domini Velasquez. Part II was written by Vararat Atisophon, Raymond Adofina, Nalwino Billones, Madeline Dumaua-Cabauatan, Anna Marie Fernando, Karen Firshan, Reneli Gloria, Arturo Martinez Jr, Albert Kirby Tardeo, and Domini Velasquez. Valuable contributions were also received from Mildred Addawe, Remedios Baes-Espineda, Ron Lester Durante, Marymell Martillan, and Christian Flora Mae Soco. Rana Hasan and Lei Lei Song also provided insightful feedback. We also thank Peter Morgan and Long Trinh, who shared microlevel data from the Asian Development Bank Institute survey on the socioeconomic impacts of the pandemic on Association of Southeast Asian Nations households.

Mahinthan Joseph Mariasingham led the team that prepared the statistical tables for Part III. The multiregional input-output table was consolidated by Michael John Barsabal, John Arvin Bernabe, Janine De Vera, Julieta Magallanes, Sarah Mae Manuel, and Ana Francesca Rosales. Part III was prepared by Angeli Grace Juani, Dale Maverenz Lim, Kenneth Anthony Luigi Reyes, and Marcus Jude San Pedro. Eric Suan and Chenying Yang provided valuable comments on the analysis of Part III, which was written by Kenneth Anthony Luigi Reyes, under the guidance of Mahinthan Joseph Mariasingham, and proofread by Julian Thomas Alvarez, Elyssa Mariel Mores, and Anna Monina Sanchez.

Vararat Atisophon, Joseph Albert Nino Bulan, Anna Marie Fernando, Reneli Gloria, Arturo Martinez Jr, Melissa Pascua, Lea Rotairo, and Domini Velasquez summarized the key findings from the survey of national statistics offices that enabled the compilation of Part IV. We appreciate the feedback provided by representatives of the national statistics offices that responded to the survey. In particular, we acknowledge Zainuddin Ahmad, Noraliza Mohamad Ali, Fuziah Md Amin, Marlini Sahul Hamid, Siti Zakiah Muhamad Isa, Mohd Uzir Mahidin, Ab. Rahman Mohamad, Sabariah Hj Salim, Shafizaermawaty Shafei, and Komathi Subramaniam from the Department of Statistics Malaysia; Claire Dennis Mapa and Benjamin Arsenio Navarro from the Philippine Statistics Authority; and technical staff and officials (whose feedback was coordinated by Sanonoi Buracharoen) from the National Statistical Office of Thailand: all provided additional insights on relevant data initiatives by their respective organizations. Kaushal Joshi, Mahinthan Joseph Mariasingham, Stefan Schipper, Pamela Lapitan, Criselda De Dios, Mel Accad, and Jude David Roque provided additional input on relevant capacity-building initiatives by ADB's Statistics and Data Innovation Unit. Mildred Addawe, Remedios Baes-Espineda, and Marymell Martillan also provided valuable research support.

We are grateful for the support and guidance of Joseph E. Zveglich Jr., and Edimon Ginting; and feedback from ERCD colleagues throughout the process. The ADB Japanese Representative Office, Pacific Liaison and Coordination Office, Philippines Country Office, and Pacific Subregional Office also provided help in the data compilation.

We are very grateful for the contributions of ERCD's statistical partners—ADB regional members and international organizations—who, in spite of the many difficulties presented by the COVID-19 pandemic, generously shared their data for the statistical tables on Sustainable Development Goal indicators (Part I), regional tables (Part II), global value chains (Part III), and individual economy tables. ADB resident missions in Afghanistan, Armenia, Azerbaijan, Bangladesh, Bhutan, Cambodia, Georgia, India, Indonesia, Kazakhstan, the Kyrgyz Republic, the Lao People's Democratic Republic, Mongolia, Nepal, Pakistan, Papua New Guinea, the People's Republic of China, Sri Lanka, Tajikistan, Thailand, Timor-Leste, Turkmenistan, Uzbekistan, and Viet Nam provided support in compiling the data for their respective economies. We greatly appreciate the continuing cooperation of the governments of ADB member economies and other international agencies.

Paul Dent edited *Key Indicators for Asia and the Pacific 2021*. The cover design was prepared by Rhommell Rico, with publication dividers based on the winning entry of Charmyne Mamador in ADB's Data Storytelling and Visualization Challenge held in 2020. Rhommell Rico also led the typesetting process and provided technical support for the preparation of all promotional and awareness materials. Joseph Manglicmot and Rommel Marilla assisted with typesetting. Infographics were prepared by Mike Cortes. Staff from ADB's Information Technology Department provided database management and technology support in coordination with the Key Indicators Database team, comprising Nikko Angelo Antonio, Ephraim Cuya, Juan Miguel Olmos De La Cruz, Pamela Lapitan, Albert San Juan, Jeffrey Napoles, and Le Kim Nguyen, under the leadership of Stefan Schipper. The Logistics Management Unit of the Corporate Services Department facilitated the timely and smooth production of the publication. Terje Langeland and Lean Alfred Santos, with the assistance of ADB's Department of Communications staff, provided general guidance on production issues and organized promotional and awareness activities.

Yasuyuki Sawada
Chief Economist and Director General
Asian Development Bank

Statistical Partners

The preparation and publication of *Key Indicators for Asia and the Pacific 2021* would not have been possible without the support, assistance, and cooperation of statistical partners in Asian Development Bank member economies throughout the Asia and Pacific region, along with the invaluable contributions of international, private, and nongovernment organizations. These partners—who shared their data, knowledge, expertise, and other information—help provide the Asian Development Bank, policymakers, and other data users with a better understanding of the performance of economies across the region, encouraging the design, formulation, and monitoring of better policies to improve the quality of life for people in this part of the world.

REGIONAL MEMBERS

Afghanistan	Da Afghanistan Bank Ministry of Finance National Statistics and Information Authority
Armenia	Central Bank of Armenia (https://www.cba.am) Ministry of Finance of the Republic of Armenia (https://www.minfin.am) Statistical Committee of the Republic of Armenia (https://www.armstat.am)
Australia	Australian Bureau of Statistics (http://www.abs.gov.au) Department of Industry, Science, Energy and Resources (https://www.industry.gov.au) Reserve Bank of Australia (https://www.rba.gov.au)
Azerbaijan	Central Bank of the Republic of Azerbaijan (https://www.cbar.az) Ministry of Finance (http://www.maliyye.gov.az) State Statistical Committee of the Republic of Azerbaijan (https://www.stat.gov.az)
Bangladesh	Bangladesh Bank (https://www.bb.org.bd) Bangladesh Bureau of Statistics (http://www.bbs.gov.bd) Ministry of Finance (https://mof.gov.bd/)
Bhutan	Ministry of Finance (https://www.mof.gov.bt) Ministry of Labour and Human Resources (https://www.molhr.gov.bt) National Statistics Bureau (http://www.nsb.gov.bt) Royal Monetary Authority of Bhutan (https://www.rma.org.bt)
Brunei Darussalam	Autoriti Monetari Brunei Darussalam (https://www.ambd.gov.bn) Department of Economic Planning and Development (http://www.deps.gov.bn) Ministry of Finance and Economy (https://www.mofe.gov.bn)

Cambodia	Electricity Authority of Cambodia (https://eac.gov.kh) Ministry of Economy and Finance (https://mef.gov.kh) National Bank of Cambodia (https://www.nbc.org.kh) National Institute of Statistics (https://nis.gov.kh)
China, People's Republic of	National Bureau of Statistics of China (http://www.stats.gov.cn) The People's Bank of China (http://www.pbc.gov.cn) State Administration of Foreign Exchange (http://www.safe.gov.cn)
Cook Islands	Cook Islands Statistics Office under Ministry of Finance and Economic Management (http://www.mfem.gov.ck)
Fiji	Bureau of Statistics (http://www.statsfiji.gov.fj) Reserve Bank of Fiji (http://www.rbf.gov.fj) Ministry of Economy (http://www.economy.gov.fj)
Georgia	Ministry of Finance of Georgia (https://www.mof.ge) National Bank of Georgia (https://www.nbg.gov.ge) National Statistics Office of Georgia (https://www.geostat.ge)
Hong Kong, China	Census and Statistics Department (http://www.censtatd.gov.hk) Financial Services and the Treasury Bureau (https://www.fstb.gov.hk)
India	Central Statistical Office under the Ministry of Statistics and Programme Implementation (http://mospi.nic.in) Ministry of Finance (http://finmin.nic.in) Reserve Bank of India (http://www.rbi.org.in)
Indonesia	Bank Indonesia (https://www.bi.go.id) Badan Pusat Statistik-Statistics Indonesia (https://www.bps.go.id) Ministry of Energy and Mineral Resources (https://www.esdm.go.id) Ministry of Finance (https://www.kemenkeu.go.id) Pertamina (https://www.pertamina.com)
Japan	Bank of Japan (http://www.boj.or.jp) Economic and Social Research Institute (http://www.esri.go.jp) Japan Customs (http://www.customs.go.jp) Japan Statistics Bureau (http://www.stat.go.jp) Ministry of Economy, Trade and Industry (http://www.meti.go.jp) Ministry of Finance (http://www.mof.go.jp) The Institute of Energy Economics, Japan (http://oil-info.ieej.or.jp)

Kazakhstan	Bureau of National Statistics, Agency for Strategic Planning and Reforms of the Republic of Kazakhstan (https://stat.gov.kz) Ministry of Finance of the Republic of Kazakhstan (http://www.gov.kz/memleket/entities/minfin?) National Bank of Kazakhstan (https://nationalbank.kz)
Kiribati	Kiribati National Statistics Office (https://nso.gov.ki/)
Korea, Republic of	Bank of Korea (https://bok.or.kr) Statistics Korea (http://kostat.go.kr)
Kyrgyz Republic	National Bank of the Kyrgyz Republic (https://www.nbkr.kg) National Statistical Committee of the Kyrgyz Republic (http://www.stat.kg)
Lao People's Democratic Republic	Bank of the Lao PDR (https://www.bol.gov.la) Lao Statistics Bureau (https://www.lsb.gov.la) Ministry of Finance (https://www.mof.gov.la)
Malaysia	Bank Negara Malaysia (https://www.bnm.gov.my) Department of Statistics Malaysia (https://www.dosm.gov.my) Ministry of Finance Malaysia (https://www.mof.gov.my)
Maldives	National Bureau of Statistics (http://www.statisticsmaldives.gov.mv) Maldives Monetary Authority (http://www.mma.gov.mv) Ministry of Finance (https://www.finance.gov.mv)
Marshall Islands	Economic Policy, Planning and Statistics Office (https://www.rmieppso.org)
Micronesia, Federated States of	Division of Statistics (http://www.fsmstatistics.fm)
Mongolia	The Bank of Mongolia (https://www.mongolbank.mn) National Statistics Office of Mongolia (https://www.en.nso.mn)
Nauru	Ministry of Finance and Economic Planning (http://www.naurugov.nr) Nauru Bureau of Statistics (https://nauru.prism.spc.int)

Nepal	Central Bureau of Statistics (https://cbs.gov.np) Ministry of Finance (https://www.mof.gov.np) Nepal Rastra Bank (https://www.nrb.org.np) Water and Energy Commission Secretariat (https://www.wecs.gov.np) Ministry of Energy, Water Resources and Irrigation (https://www.moewri.gov.np) Ministry of Industry, Commerce and Supplies (https://moics.gov.np) Ministry of Industry, Commerce and Supplies, Department of Mines and Geology (http://www.dmgnepal.gov.np)
New Zealand	Ministry of Business, Innovation and Employment (https://www.mbie.govt.nz) Reserve Bank of New Zealand (https://www.rbnz.govt.nz) Stats NZ Tatauranga Aotearoa (https://www.stats.govt.nz)
Niue	Statistics Niue Office (https://niue.prism.spc.int)
Pakistan	Ministry of Finance, Revenue and Economic Affairs - Finance Division (http://www.finance.gov.pk) Pakistan Bureau of Statistics (https://www.pbs.gov.pk) State Bank of Pakistan (https://www.sbp.org.pk)
Palau	Bureau of Budget and Planning, Ministry of Finance (https://www.palaugov.pw/mof)
Papua New Guinea	Bank of Papua New Guinea (https://www.bankpng.gov.pg) Department of Treasury (http://www.treasury.gov.pg) National Statistical Office (https://www.nso.gov.pg)
Philippines	Bangko Sentral ng Pilipinas (http://www.bsp.gov.ph) Bureau of Local Government Finance (https://blgf.gov.ph) Bureau of the Treasury (http://www.treasury.gov.ph) Department of Budget and Management (http://www.dbm.gov.ph) Department of Energy (https://www.doe.gov.ph) Philippine Statistics Authority (https://www.psa.gov.ph)
Samoa	Samoa Bureau of Statistics (https://www.sbs.gov.ws) Central Bank of Samoa (https://www.cbs.gov.ws)
Singapore	Department of Statistics (https://www.singstat.gov.sg) Enterprise Singapore (https://www.enterprisesg.gov.sg) Ministry of Finance (https://www.mof.gov.sg) Ministry of Manpower (https://www.mom.gov.sg) Ministry of Trade and Industry (https://www.mti.gov.sg) Monetary Authority of Singapore (https://www.mas.gov.sg)

Solomon Islands	Central Bank of Solomon Islands (http://www.cbsi.com.sb) Solomon Islands National Statistics Office (https://www.statistics.gov.sb)
Sri Lanka	Central Bank of Sri Lanka (https://www.cbsl.gov.lk) Department of Census and Statistics (http://www.statistics.gov.lk)
Taipei,China	Central bank of Taipei,China (https://www.cbc.gov.tw) Directorate-General of Budget, Accounting and Statistics (https://eng.dgbas.gov.tw) Ministry of Finance (https://www.mof.gov.tw)
Tajikistan	National Bank of Tajikistan (https://www.nbt.tj) Agency on Statistics under President of the Republic of Tajikistan (https://www.stat.tj)
Thailand	Bank of Thailand (https://www.bot.or.th) Ministry of Finance (http://www2.mof.go.th) National Economic and Social Development Council (https://www.nesdc.go.th) National Statistical Office (http://www.nso.go.th) Ministry of Energy, Energy Policy and Planning Office (http://www.eppo.go.th)
Timor-Leste	Central Bank of Timor-Leste (https://www.bancocentral.tl) Ministry of Finance (https://www.mof.gov.tl) General Directorate of Statistics (https://www.statistics.gov.tl)
Tonga	Ministry of Finance (http://www.finance.gov.to) National Reserve Bank of Tonga (http://www.reservebank.to) Tonga Statistics Department (https://tongastats.gov.to)
Turkmenistan	Central Bank of Turkmenistan (https://www.cbt.tm) Ministry of Finance and Economy of Turkmenistan (https://www.fineconomic.gov.tm) State Committee on Statistics of Turkmenistan (https://www.stat.gov.tm)
Tuvalu	Central Statistics Division (https://tuvalu.prism.spc.int)
Uzbekistan	Office of the Cabinet of Ministers (https://www.gov.uz) Central Bank of the Republic of Uzbekistan (https://www.cbu.uz) Ministry of Finance of the Republic of Uzbekistan (https://www.mf.uz) State Committee of the Republic of Uzbekistan on Statistics (https://www.stat.uz)

Vanuatu	Department of Finance and Treasury (https://doft.gov.vu) Reserve Bank of Vanuatu (https://www.rbv.gov.vu) Vanuatu National Statistics Office (http://www.vnso.gov.vu)
Viet Nam	General Statistics Office (https://www.gso.gov.vn) Ministry of Finance (https://www.mof.gov.vn) State Bank of Viet Nam (https://www.sbv.gov.vn)

INTERNATIONAL, PRIVATE, AND NONGOVERNMENT ORGANIZATIONS

Association of Southeast Asian Nations
Food and Agriculture Organization of the United Nations
International Labour Organization
International Monetary Fund
International Telecommunication Union
Interstate Statistical Committee of the Commonwealth of Independent States
Joint United Nations Programme on HIV/AIDS
Organisation for Economic Co-operation and Development
Secretariat of the Pacific Community
Transparency International
United Nations Children's Fund (UNICEF)
United Nations Conference on Trade and Development
United Nations Department of Economic and Social Affairs
United Nations Development Programme
United Nations Economic Commission for Europe
United Nations Economic and Social Commission for Asia and the Pacific
United Nations Educational, Scientific and Cultural Organization (UNESCO) Institute for Statistics
United Nations Environment Programme
United Nations Human Settlements Programme
United Nations Office on Drugs and Crime
United Nations Population Division
United Nations Statistics Division
United Nations World Tourism Organization
United States Agency for International Development
United States Census Bureau
United States Bureau of Economic Analysis
WHO/UNICEF Joint Monitoring Programme for Water Supply, Sanitation and Hygiene
World Bank
World Health Organization
World Trade Organization

Guide for Users

Key Indicators for Asia and the Pacific 2021 begins with a Highlights section that presents key messages from various parts of the publication.

Part I comprises data tables and data stories describing trends of select indicators for the Sustainable Development Goals (SDGs) for which data were available. The indicators are presented according to the United Nations SDG global indicator framework.

Part II presents specific indicators on social, economic, and environmental developments in member economies of the Asian Development Bank (ADB) located in Asia and the Pacific. The tables containing these indicators are grouped into eight themes: People; Economy and Output; Money, Finance, and Prices; Globalization; Transport and Communications; Energy and Electricity; Environment; and Government and Governance.

The SDGs in Part I and the themes in Part II start with data stories, complemented by figures and charts describing the status of economies with respect to key trends of select targets and indicators. The scales used in some figures and charts are adjusted to show very small numbers. In addition, figures and charts appearing in this publication are also provided with a digital object identifier to facilitate easier access to data.

The SDGs and regional tables presented in Part I and II cover 49 national economies across Asia and the Pacific, all of which are members of ADB. The term "country," used interchangeably with "economy", is not intended to make any judgment as to the legal or other status of any territory or area. The 49 economies have been broadly grouped into developing ADB member economies and developed ADB member economies. The term "developing Asia" refers to the 46 developing member economies of ADB, unless stated otherwise. The developed economies refer to the economies of Australia, Japan, and New Zealand. Based on ADB's geographic operations, the 46 developing ADB member economies are divided into five subregions within the Asia and Pacific region. These subregions are Central and West Asia, East Asia, South Asia, Southeast Asia, and the Pacific. Economies are listed alphabetically within each subregion. The term "regional members", often used interchangeably with "Asia and the Pacific", refers to all 49 ADB members, both developing and developed. Indicators are shown for the most recent year (usually 2020) or period for which data were available and, in most tables, for a starting year or period (usually 2010). Depending on available data, the starting point may be a year nearest to 2010, and the most recent year (usually the year nearest to 2020). There may, however, be some exceptions to these general principles. In the tables, aggregates for regions include economies with available data and are shown if the indicator is available for more than half of the economies and if more than two-thirds of the reference population is represented.

Part III contains select indicators for depicting participation by economies of Asia and the Pacific in global value chains, and the sector-specific comparative advantage of each economy in terms of exports. Typical indicators of international trade, which mainly refer to the value of exports and imports of goods and services, can be traced back to the traditional trading of final goods across borders. Today's globalization has made many economies more open to trade, providing opportunities for firms to scale up production and allocate their resources more efficiently by moving production chains across borders where there is comparative advantage. Analysis of global value chains provides detailed cross-border trading transactions of inputs used in different stages of production—from raw materials, to intermediate inputs, to the final products purchased by the end consumers.

Part IV provides stories behind data and focuses on initiatives of the region's national statistics offices to provide data as the basis for actionable insights on development planning and policymaking.

This publication is also available on ADB's website at adb.org/ki-2021, along with individual statistical tables for each of the 49 ADB regional members. The publication's vitally important data and time series are also accessible in digitized format via the Key Indicators Database (kidb.adb.org), which also presents longer data series (usually starting from 2000) for each indicator. Data for the SDG indicators, regional tables, and individual member tables were obtained mainly from two sources: (i) ADB's statistical partners linked to regional member economies, and (ii) international statistics agencies, particularly from the United Nations' Global SDG Indicators Database, a master set of data prepared by the Department of Economic and Social Affairs of the United Nations Secretariat. The term "economy's official source", cited as a source in some tables, refers to data provided by the statistical partners linked to the ADB regional member economies.

The data presented for indicators in Part I were derived from either economy's official sources, the Global SDG Indicators Database, or databases maintained by international agencies that, based on their areas of expertise, prepared one or more of the series of statistical indicators included in the Global SDG Indicators Database. Data for Myanmar were collected from websites of data custodians and survey conducted by ADBI from May to July 2020. The data presented in Part III were drawn mainly from the ADB Multiregional Input–Output Tables Database. The results of a survey conducted by ADB's Statistics and Data Innovation Unit informed the discussion presented in Part IV.

Data produced and disseminated by international agencies are generally based on data produced and disseminated by an individual economy (including data adjusted by the economy to meet international standards). However, it should be noted that national data may be compiled using national standards and practices and, as such, international agencies often adjust the data for international comparability. In such cases, data disseminated by the international agencies may differ from data available from national sources. In other cases, when data for a specific year, or set of years, are not available; or they are available from multiple national sources (surveys, administrative data sources, and other sources); or when there are data quality issues; the relevant international agency may estimate the data. Some indicators are regularly produced for the purpose of global monitoring by the designated agency, and there are no corresponding data at the national level (e.g., population living on less than $1.90 a day at 2011 purchasing power parity). In other cases, the differences between data from national and international agencies may be because the most recent and/or revised data available at the national level are not yet available with the relevant international agency. Some data gaps are filled by supplementing or deriving data collected through sample surveys financed and carried out by international agencies. For example, many of the health indicators are estimated using data from the Multiple

Indicator Cluster Surveys and Demographic and Health Surveys. From 2021, data on Money and Interest Rates, featured in several individual member tables, are presented based on the latest international guidelines, but there are a few economies that continue to present their data using the format applied in 2020 and prior. *Key Indicators for Asia and the Pacific* now also features additional Transport and Communications indicators from ADB's Asian Transportation Outlook database.

ADB exercises due care and caution in collecting data before publication. Nevertheless, data from international sources presented in this publication may differ from those available within individual member economies. Thus, for a detailed description of how the indicators are compiled by the international agencies, readers may refer to the metadata available from databases of the individual international agencies, or to the Global SDG Indicators Database website for metadata of SDG indicators. Modeled estimates as presented on the Global SDG Indicators Database are also identified. Comparable and standardized national data gathered through a robust data-reporting mechanism of the international agencies serve as the basis for all data in the global monitoring databases.

Data obtained from ADB member economies are comparable to the extent that the ADB members follow standard statistical concepts, definitions, and estimation methods recommended by the United Nations and other applicable international agencies. Nevertheless, member economies invariably develop and use their own concepts, definitions, and estimation methodologies to suit their individual circumstances, and these may not necessarily comply with recommended international standards. Therefore, even though attempts are made to present the data in a comparable and uniform format, the data are subject to variations in the statistical methods used by individual economies, so full comparability may not be possible. These variations are reflected in the footnotes of the statistical tables or noted in the Data Issues and Comparability sections. Information about changes in compilation methodology is also provided in the footnotes. In addition, some indicators are expressed as functions of two or more indicators (e.g., indicators expressed as a proportion of gross domestic product). Hence, a change in the compilation methodology of one component indicator might affect other indicators based upon it. Hence, readers are encouraged to refer to the footnotes before making comparisons between economies and/or over time.

Moreover, the aggregates shown in some tables for the developing ADB member economies and ADB regional members are treated as approximations of the actual total or average, or growth rates, due to missing data from the primary source. For a description of the regional aggregation method, readers may refer to the footnotes presented in the tables and/or the metadata in the Key Indicators Database (kidb.adb.org). Footnotes also provide information for earlier years (earlier than 2000), which are relevant for the longer data series presented in the Key Indicators Database. Aggregates for the World were sourced from international agencies, and readers may refer to the metadata available from databases of the individual international agencies.

The data published by ADB do not constitute any form of advice or recommendation. For answers to any questions on the data, users of this publication are requested to seek advice from the relevant data source or organization.

Fiscal Year

There are 25 regional members of the Asian Development Bank with fiscal years that do not coincide with the calendar year. Whenever statistical series (for example, national accounts or government finance) are compiled on the basis of a fiscal year, these series are presented in the column for the single-year during which most of the fiscal year occurred. The 25 fiscal year definitions for 2020 are outlined below.

Regional Member	Fiscal Year	Year Caption
Afghanistan (fiscal year beginning 2012)	21 December 2019 to 20 December 2020	2020
Brunei Darussalam (fiscal year since 2002) Hong Kong, China India Japan New Zealand Singapore	1 April 2020 to 31 March 2021	2020
Fiji	1 August 2019 to 31 July 2020	2020
Australia Bangladesh Bhutan Cook Islands Kiribati Nauru Niue Pakistan Samoa Tonga	1 July 2019 to 30 June 2020	2020
Nepal	16 July 2019 to 15 July 2020	2020
Lao People's Democratic Republic Marshall Islands Micronesia, Federated States of Myanmar Palau Thailand	1 October 2019 to 30 September 2020	2020

Key Symbols

...	data not available
–	magnitude equals zero
(-/+) 0 or 0.0	magnitude is less than half of unit employed
*	provisional/preliminary/estimate/budget figure
|	marks break in series
>	greater than
<	less than
>=	greater than or equal to
<=	less than or equal to
n.a.	not applicable
%	percentage

Units of Measurement

GWh	gigawatt-hour
kg	kilogram
kl	kiloliter
kloe	kiloliter of oil equivalent
km	kilometer
km^2	square kilometer
kWh	kilowatt-hour
kt	kiloton
ktoe	kiloton of oil equivalent
L	liter
m^3	cubic meter
mj	megajoule
PM	particulate matter
teu	twenty-foot equivalent unit
t	metric ton
$\mu g/m^3$	micrograms per cubic meter

Abbreviations

ADB	Asian Development Bank
ADBI	Asian Development Bank Institute
BPM5	Balance of Payments Manual (Fifth Edition)
BPM6	Balance of Payments and International Investment Position Manual (Sixth Edition)
BPO	business process outsourcing
CAPI	computer-assisted personal interviewing
CATI	computer-assisted telephone interviewing
CAWI	computer-assisted web interviewing
CIF	cost, insurance, and freight
CO_2	carbon dioxide
CPI	consumer price index
CSO	Central Statistical Organization
Data4Now	Data For Now
DHS	Demographic and Health Survey
DOSM	Department of Statistics Malaysia
DVA_F	domestic value-added via forward linkages
EROD-SDI	Economic Research and Regional Cooperation Department, Statistics and Data Innovation Unit
FAO	Food and Agriculture Organization of the United Nations
FDI	foreign direct investment
FOB	free on board
FVA	foreign value-added
GDP	gross domestic product
GNI	gross national income
GPS	global positioning system
GVC	global value chain
HIV	human immunodeficiency virus
ICP	International Comparison Program
ICP-APSS	International Comparison Program-Asia Pacific Software Suite
IDA	International Development Association
IHR	International Health Regulations
ILO	International Labour Organization
IMF	International Monetary Fund
ISIC	International Standard Industrial Classification
LFS	labor force survey
LGU	local government unit
MDG	Millennium Development Goal
MICS	Multiple Indicator Cluster Survey
MOF	Ministry of Finance
MRIOT	multiregional input-output table
MSMEs	micro, small, and medium-sized enterprises
NEC	National Employment Council

NPL	nonperforming loan
NRCA	new revealed comparative advantage
NSO	national statistics office; national statistical office
NSS	National Statistical System
ODA	official development assistance
OECD	Organisation for Economic Co-operation and Development
PARIS21	Partnership in Statistics for Development in the 21st Century
PLI	price level index
PPP	purchasing power parity
PRC	People's Republic of China
PSA	Philippine Statistics Authority
RCA	revealed comparative advantage
SCI	statistical capacity indicator
SDG	Sustainable Development Goal
SDMX	Statistical Data and Metadata Exchange
SNA	System of National Accounts
SPI	statistical performance indicator
TRCA	traditional revealed comparative advantage
UN	United Nations
UNDESA	United Nations Department of Economic and Social Affairs
UNESCAP	United Nations Economic and Social Commission for Asia and the Pacific
UNICEF	United Nations Children's Fund
UNSD	United Nations Statistics Division
WHO	World Health Organization

Unless otherwise indicated, "$" refers to United States dollars.

HIGHLIGHTS
PART I: SUSTAINABLE DEVELOPMENT GOALS

POVERTY AND INEQUALITY

TACKLING POVERTY REQUIRES A MULTIDIMENSIONAL APPROACH

Poverty encompasses deprivations in income, health, education, and living standards

1.2 BILLION EXTREMELY POOR IN 1999 DOWN TO 202.9 MILLION IN 2017

Source: Figure 1.2.

COVID-19 HAS PLUNGED AROUND 75 TO 80 MILLION ASIANS INTO EXTREME POVERTY

This estimate could even be higher when considering inequalities.

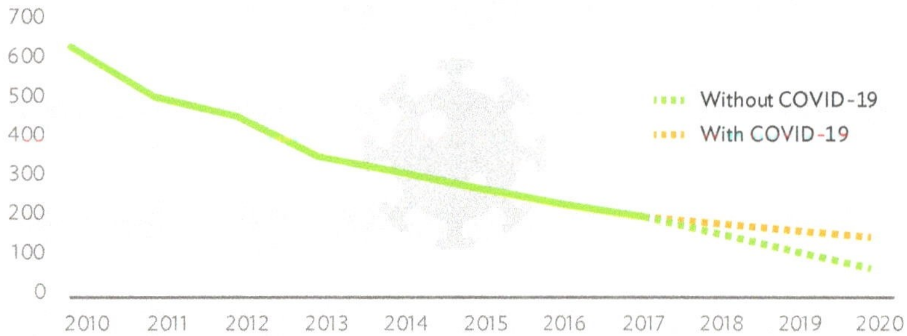

Sources: Figures 1.2 and 1.6.

LOW-SKILLED PEOPLE AND THOSE LIVING IN RURAL AREAS FACE GREATER POVERTY RISK

In some Asian economies, rural poverty rates are five to eight times higher than urban poverty rates. Poverty is also higher among those lacking in higher education.

Source: Table 1.1.1.

Access data at kidb.adb.org.

HIGHLIGHTS

PART I: SUSTAINABLE DEVELOPMENT GOALS

HUNGER, HEALTH, AND EDUCATION

PRE-COVID:

ASIA AND THE PACIFIC'S PACE OF PROGRESS FARED BEST GLOBALLY

However, a number of lower-income economies saw more modest decline in prevalence of undernourishment and other SDG 2 targets.

Source: Table 1.2.1.

PRE-COVID:

LOW AND LOWER MIDDLE-INCOME ECONOMIES STILL FALL BELOW THE GLOBAL AVERAGE FOR DENSITY OF HEALTH WORKERS

DURING COVID:

Economies with better health systems generally performed well.

Sources: Figures 1.15 and 1.17.

THE PANDEMIC THREATENS TO FURTHER IMPEDE THE REGION'S PROGRESS ON SDG 2

In some economies where food insecurity and undernourishment were already a concern prior to COVID-19, millions had to reduce food consumption due to financial difficulties caused by the pandemic.

Source: Figure 1.12.

POOR LEARNING OUTCOMES REMAIN A CHALLENGE TO EDUCATION DEVELOPMENT

Almost half of reporting economies had reading and numeracy scores below 50%.

Source: Figure 1.20.

PROGRESS HAS BEEN MADE IN OVERALL SCHOOL COMPLETION RATES

BUT THE POOREST 40% STILL STRUGGLE FOR BASIC EDUCATION

Sources: Figure 1.19 and Table 1.4.2.

SCHOOL-AGED CHILDREN IN POORER HOUSEHOLDS ARE DISADVANTAGED UNDER LEARNING MODES DURING A PANDEMIC

They are less likely to have access to schools with distance-learning programs and are deprived of remote learning resources due to lack of internet connectivity.

Source: Figure 1.22.

Access data at kidb.adb.org.

HIGHLIGHTS
PART II: REGIONAL TABLES

EMPLOYMENT AND THE ECONOMY

71% OF ASIA AND THE PACIFIC'S WORKFORCE ARE NOW IN NONAGRICULTURAL EMPLOYMENT

From 2000 to 2019, the region's nonagricultural employment grew from 52% to 71%; one of the fastest growth rates worldwide.

Source: Figure 2.1.

BEFORE THE PANDEMIC: INFORMAL EMPLOYMENT EXCEEDED 50% IN 14 OF 23 REPORTING ECONOMIES AND MILLIONS WERE UNDEREMPLOYED

There is still a need to strengthen efforts to deliver adequate employment opportunities.

Source: Figure 2.2.

IN 2020, UNEMPLOYMENT RATES INCREASED BY AT LEAST 20% IN MORE THAN ONE-THIRD OF REPORTING ECONOMIES

As businesses were disrupted, many workers lost their jobs, leading to higher unemployment and underemployment rates. The Asia and Pacific region lost an estimated 8% of working hours in 2020.

Sources: Figure 2.7 and Table 2.1.

75% OF REPORTING ECONOMIES CONTRACTED IN 2020

The economic slowdown in recent times was exacerbated by the pandemic, causing the region's first recession in 60 years.

Source: Table 2.2.11.

2000–2019: THE REGION'S ECONOMY GREW FROM 27% TO 35% OF GLOBAL GDP

Increased economic linkages with the rest of the world and strong consumption contributed to this growth. However, a number of challenges have negatively impacted growth rates in recent years.

Note: Estimates are based on current US$ terms. Based on PPP terms, the estimate is at 41%.
Source: Table 2.2.2.

Access data at kidb.adb.org.

HIGHLIGHTS
PART II: REGIONAL TABLES

INFLATION, GOVERNMENT EXPENDITURE, AND DEBT

MIXED PANDEMIC IMPACT ON PRICES OF PRODUCTS AND SERVICES ACROSS THE REGION...

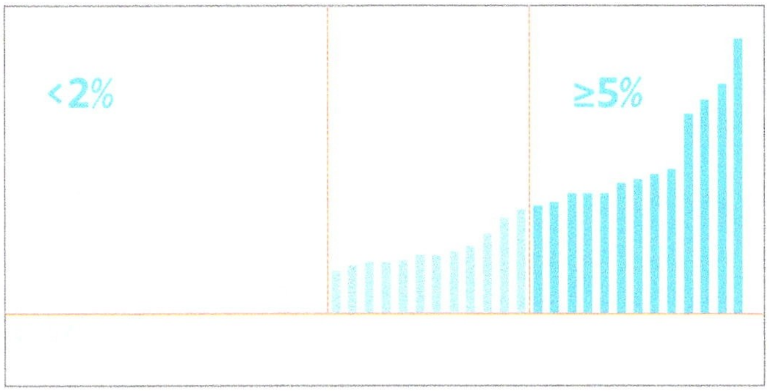

19 economies recorded inflation below 2%, while 13 recorded 5% inflation or higher.

Source: Table 2.3.1.

...BUT FOOD PRICES WENT UP IN A MAJORITY OF ECONOMIES

Food inflation increased in 29 of 41 reporting economies, affecting mainly lower-income economies. Of these, 17 economies recorded food inflation of at least 5%.

Source: Table 2.3.2.

IN 2020:

13 OF 16 ECONOMIES INCREASED SOCIAL PROTECTION TO MITIGATE THE ADVERSE IMPACTS OF THE PANDEMIC AND HELP THE MOST VULNERABLE GROUPS

Source: Table 2.8.5.

NEED TO MOBILIZE BOTH PUBLIC AND PRIVATE RESOURCES

Before the pandemic, 16 of 40 reporting economies recorded debt-gross national income ratios exceeding 40%. Record borrowing among Asian economies may result in financial challenges, highlighting the need to mobilize both public and private resources for socioeconomic recovery.

Source: Table 2.4.21.

HIGHLIGHTS
PART III: GLOBAL VALUE CHAINS
THE COVID-19 SHOCKS AND TWO FACES OF GVCs

IN 2020, THE AVERAGE ECONOMY IN ASIA AND THE PACIFIC HAD 39% OF ITS EXPORTS INVOLVED IN INDIRECT TRADING

This share goes as high as 58% for Singapore and as low as 23% for Pakistan.

Source: Figure 3.2.

GVCs HAD A VARIED EFFECT ON THE PANDEMIC SHOCK THAT ECONOMIES EXPERIENCED

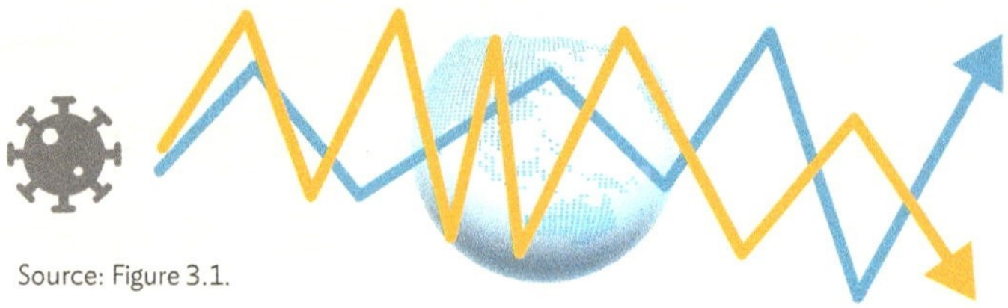

Source: Figure 3.1.

THERE IS AN OVERALL U-SHAPED RELATIONSHIP BETWEEN GVC PARTICIPATION AND THE SIZE OF THE COVID-19 SHOCK TO AN ECONOMY

Higher participation is associated with a worse shock until a participation rate of about 45%, after which point higher participation is associated with smaller shocks.

Source: Figure 3.3.

HIGHLIGHTS
PART IV: STORIES BEHIND DATA
DATA INITIATIVES IN THE COVID-19 ERA

TIMELY DATA PROVIDE ACTIONABLE INSIGHTS FOR POLICYMAKING

There is progress in Asia and the Pacific's capacity to conduct regular and timely data collection activities, but further improvements can be made.

Source: Figure 4.2.

AMID DISRUPTIONS IN OPERATIONS, STATISTICIANS ACCELERATED THE USE OF TECHNOLOGY SOLUTIONS AND DATA INTEGRATION TO DELIVER TIMELY DATA

Access data at kidb.adb.org.

Introduction

Image based on the winning entry of the ADB Data Storytelling and Visualization Challenge 2020.

Introduction

To contain the spread of COVID-19, governments have imposed some of the most extensive community lockdowns in history, sharply constraining economic activity and upending livelihoods. Airports, railways, and other public services and amenities were temporarily closed during 2020 and into 2021, while a variety of businesses, including restaurants, movie theaters, and gyms, have been shuttered for long periods. International travel has been severely restricted and human movement within localized lockdown areas has been limited to a conditional basis. Images of quiet and empty streets, even in the world's megacities, showed how the coronavirus effectively ground the world to a halt. In a bid to help health systems cope and to limit the loss of life, responses to the virus have crippled economies, left millions without jobs, and caused the deepest global recession since World War II (World Bank 2021b). Indeed, developing Asia experienced its first economic contraction in nearly 60 years (ADB 2021).

The COVID-19 pandemic has magnified long-standing social and economic inequities experienced by millions living below or near the poverty line. Estimates already suggest that, compared to a baseline scenario without COVID-19, there were approximately 75 million to 80 million more people living in extreme poverty in developing Asia by the end of 2020. There are also indications that health, education, and work disruptions due to the pandemic have had greater consequences for poorer segments of the population. As the socioeconomic impacts of responses to the virus continue to unfold, people already struggling to make ends meet are at risk of tipping over into a life of poverty.

The 2030 Agenda for Sustainable Development was launched in 2015, with the Sustainable Development Goals (SDGs) covering areas such as the eradication of extreme poverty and hunger, quality education for all, gender equality, protection of natural resources, addressing climate change, improving disaster resilience, attaining peace and security, achieving economic growth, and creating decent jobs. A global indicator framework was developed to ensure that economies can track their collective progress toward 2030 targets for inclusive and sustainable development.

The COVID-19 pandemic has created unprecedented challenges for many economies attempting to achieve development targets, including the SDGs. With 10 years to go before final SDG assessment, many economies in Asia and the Pacific are still trailing behind several critical targets set by the 2030 Agenda for Sustainable Development. The pandemic has also further highlighted the need to invest in the quality and timeliness of statistics to provide accurate data that can inform policies and interventions, especially during periods of uncertainty.

Part I of *Key Indicators for Asia and the Pacific 2021* assesses the impacts of the COVID-19 pandemic along different social gradients, such as poverty, economic inequality, hunger, health, and education. Part II covers macroeconomic impacts in the form of regional data tables. The data stories featured in Parts I and II address specific impacts of COVID-19 on select targets of the SDGs and other socioeconomic indicators, also drawing on recent data compiled by national statistical systems and international organizations. Part III discusses how the pandemic has revealed two faces of global value chain participation: as both a dampener and amplifier of shocks. In particular, a U-shaped relationship is found between an economy's value chain participation rate and the size of the shock to its gross domestic product in 2020. Part IV offers insights into the experiences of national statistics systems as they strive to provide timely data, particularly in response to the urgent need for factual evidence that can shape policymaking in the wake of the pandemic. This year's edition of *Key Indicators for Asia and the Pacific* also comes with a special supplement that presents a practical framework to measure the digital economy, which now plays a prominent role in modern life, as has been especially evident during pandemic lockdowns.

Overall, the data and associated analyses in *Key Indicators for Asia and the Pacific 2021* show how the COVID-19 pandemic has made the world's social and economic fault lines more visible than ever. The publication also shines a light on how the pace of progress toward some development targets was slowing even before the pandemic began. As policymakers seek to address these urgent development issues, it is important to harness the power of using high-quality and timely data to ensure that nobody is left behind, especially the poor and vulnerable.

PART I

Sustainable Development Goals: Trends and Tables

PART I.
Sustainable Development Goals

When the Millennium Development Goals (MDGs) concluded in 2015, Asia and the Pacific registered an impressive development scorecard. The region managed to cut the poverty rate by more than two-thirds, exceeding the initial MDG target of halving poverty between 1990 and 2015. Other MDG targets accomplished include halving the proportion of the population without access to safe drinking water, achieving universal access to primary education, promoting gender parity in education, and improving health outcomes such as reduction of tuberculosis incidence (UNESCAP, ADB, and UNDP 2015). The Sustainable Development Goals (SDGs) bank on the encouraging levels of commitment spurred by implementing the MDGs and the goodwill shown in promoting development and facilitating more sustainable and inclusive growth. The MDGs set clear, quantifiable, and time-bound targets to assess how economies fared in addressing the many and varied socioeconomic dimensions of development, and galvanized efforts targeting interventions in areas that lagged with respect to these development issues. Following this, the SDGs also set a global indicator framework comprising 231 unique indicators to track progress in meeting the 2030 Agenda for Sustainable Development.

Although Asia and the Pacific has made advances since the inception of the SDGs, progress is mixed across economies in the region. Throughout 2020, the COVID-19 pandemic further intensified the challenge of meeting development targets that needed urgent attention even before the global health crisis began. The impacts of the pandemic now threaten to reverse trends in areas where good progress has been made.

This section of *Key Indicators for Asia and the Pacific 2021* describes key trends in poverty, economic inequality, food security and hunger, health, and education.

Poverty before the pandemic. Before COVID-19 hit, there were already signs that poverty reduction was slowing in many parts of the world, including developing Asia (Composite photo).

Poverty and Inequality

The prevalence of extreme (monetary-based) poverty in developing Asia continued to decline based on pre-COVID-19 trends, but several economies had already started experiencing a slower pace of poverty reduction.[1,2]

Developing Asia made substantial progress on poverty reduction from 1990 through to 2017, contributing less and less to global poverty as the period rolled on (Figure 1.1). From 1.5 billion Asians living on less than $1.90 a day (a measure of extreme poverty) in 1990, this number dropped to 1.2 billion in 1999 and further down to 273 million when

1 Unless stated otherwise, most of the analyses for developing Asia presented in this section are based on information from 35 developing Asian Development Bank member economies for which data needed for poverty and inequality calculations are available: Armenia, Azerbaijan, Bangladesh, Bhutan, the Federated States of Micronesia, Fiji, Georgia, India, Indonesia, Kazakhstan, Kiribati, the Kyrgyz Republic, the Lao People's Democratic Republic, Malaysia, Maldives, Mongolia, Myanmar, Nauru, Nepal, Pakistan, Papua New Guinea, the People's Republic of China, the Philippines, Samoa, Solomon Islands, Sri Lanka, Tajikistan, Thailand, Timor-Leste, Tonga, Turkmenistan, Tuvalu, Uzbekistan, Vanuatu, and Viet Nam. Discussion of pre-COVID-19 pandemic trends are mostly based on data from official sources (national statistics systems and/or international organizations acting as data custodians of indicators discussed in this section). Data capturing the impacts of the COVID-19 pandemic are based on Asian Development Bank staff simulations, and/or surveys conducted by the Asian Development Bank Institute, the World Bank, and other development institutions.

2 Unless stated otherwise, "income" is used as a general term for pecuniary measures of living standards throughout this report. Monetary-based measures of poverty and inequality could be based on either household income or consumption expenditure.

Figure 1.1: Developing Asia's Contribution to Global Levels of Extreme Poverty

Developing Asia's share of the world's extremely poor is declining.

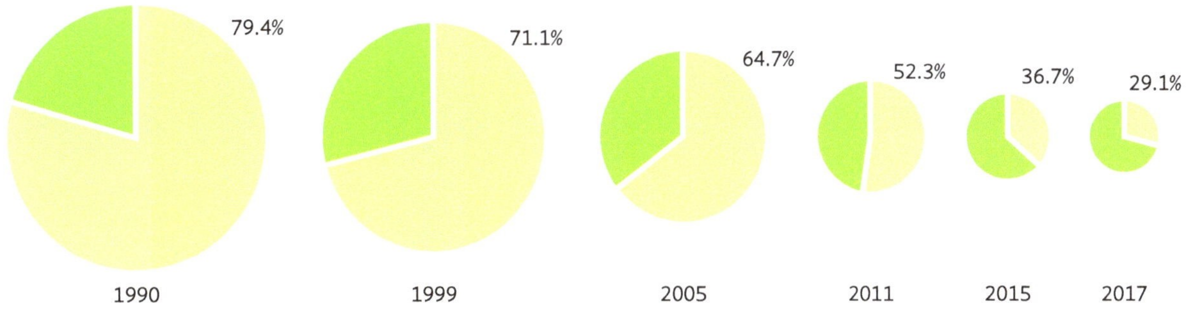

Notes: Each figure for developing Asia is calculated as the regional average of 35 developing ADB member economies with available data. Percentage of the total world population living in extreme poverty (1,912 million in 1990; 1,741 million in 1999; 1,366 million in 2005; 972 million in 2011; 744 in 2015; and 696 million in 2017). The light green slices of the pie charts represent the share of developing Asia to the global poor, while the size of each pie chart represents the size of the global poor.

Source: Asian Development Bank estimates based on the World Bank's PovcalNet database (accessed 09 July 2021).

the MDGs concluded in 2015. The reduction in the number of people living on less than $3.20 a day was equally remarkable, with more than 1.1 billion people lifted above this poverty line from 1990 to 2015.

As the figure shows, in just 2 years from the launch of the SDGs, the region's share of global extreme poverty was further reduced to 29.1% or 203 million people. Furthermore, simulations by Asian Development Bank (ADB) staff suggest that the region would have seen a steady reduction in poverty rates and the number of poor if the COVID-19 pandemic had not happened. Under a baseline scenario without COVID-19 in 2020, there would be an estimated 104 million living in extreme poverty (on less than $1.90 a day) and 732 million living in poverty (on less than $3.20 a day).

As poverty has declined, the proportion of people in higher income brackets has increased. This is particularly noteworthy among those living on between $5.50 and $15.00 a day, with the latest estimates showing that more than one in every three people from developing Asia was in this income group, a more than sevenfold increase since 1990 (Figure 1.2).

However, recent trends in poverty reduction show a relatively slower decline compared to what has been observed in the past.

Figure 1.2: Income Groups in Developing Asia

As extreme poverty in developing Asia declined, the size of the middle class has increased.

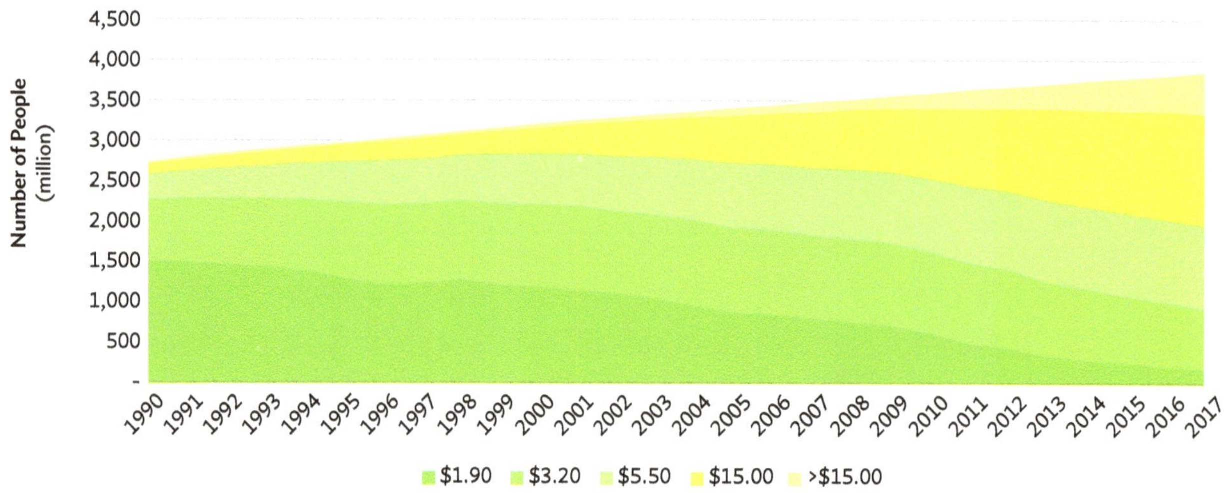

$ = United States dollars.

Note: Each figure for developing Asia is calculated as the total number of people across 35 developing ADB member economies with available data, falling under each income group.

Sources: Asian Development Bank estimates using data presented in Tables 1.1.1 and 2.1.7 of *Key Indicators for Asia and the Pacific 2021*; and the World Bank's PovcalNet database (accessed 09 July 2021).

Although it can be argued that a slower pace of reduction is natural as the incidence of extreme poverty moves to a lower base level, it is important to note that the reduction of poverty levels in developing Asia has been mainly driven by the performance of the People's Republic of China (PRC), which reduced the proportion of its population living on less than $1.90 a day from 32% in 1990 to less than 1% in 2016. A closer examination of the region's poverty reduction shows that 10 economies[3] still have at least 10% of their respective populations living on less than $1.90 a day.

Low-skilled people and those living in rural areas still face greater poverty risk.

In some developing economies of Asia and the Pacific, the incidence of poverty remains higher in rural areas than in urban areas, e.g., rural extreme poverty rates are about eight times higher than urban extreme poverty rates in Solomon Islands and Myanmar, and five times higher in Pakistan based on data compiled by the World Bank. Estimates presented in Table 1.1.1 also show significant differences between rural and urban poverty rates based on national poverty thresholds. However, some studies suggest that this gap has narrowed over time in some parts of developing Asia (Imai and Malaeb 2018). Expanding urban poverty is also a concern, with more than half of the region's population now living in urban areas.[4] The risk of falling into poverty is also much higher among younger people (Table 1.1.1) and those lacking in higher education or the job-specific skills required in the workplace.

---

3 Based on the common reference-year poverty estimates presented by the World Bank's PovcalNet database, which aligns survey-based estimates to common reference-years for the purposes of global and regional reporting. Table 1.1.1 presents poverty estimates for actual survey years, which vary from one economy to another.

4 Data on urbanization rates are presented in Part II (Table 2.1.2).

Reduction of monetary poverty does not always lower income inequality.

Addressing inequality is an important target of the SDGs. Poverty reduction does not always translate to reduced income inequality and Figure 1.3 illustrates the potential contrast between these two measures. Some of the fastest reductions in poverty since 1990 were registered by economies with widening income inequality.

One indicator used to monitor inequality is the difference between income growth of the bottom 40% of the population and the income growth of the total population. This assumes that promoting faster income growth for poorer people will allow them to catch up with the rest of their compatriots. Of the 29 ADB member economies with available data, 21 registered higher income growth for the poorest 40% since the 1990s.

Figure 1.3: Annualized Poverty Reduction in Asia and the Pacific

(%)

Monetary poverty reduction can also be accompanied by increasing income inequality.

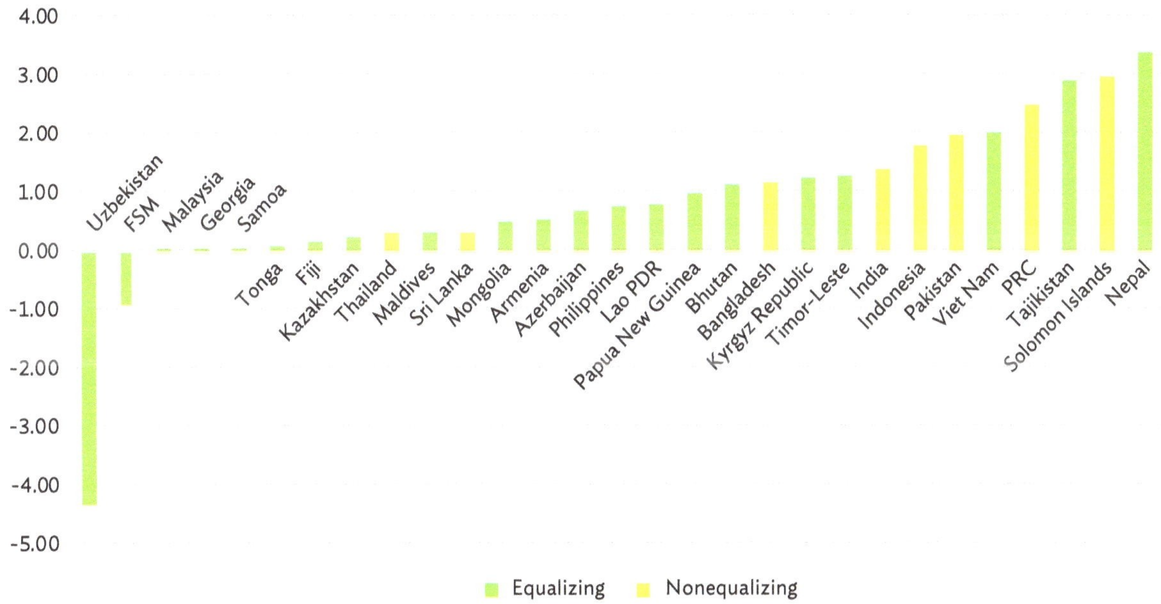

FSM = Federated States of Micronesia, Lao PDR = Lao People's Democratic Republic, PRC = People's Republic of China.

Notes: The bars represent annual poverty reduction from the 1990s to years for which the latest data are available from the World Bank's PovcalNet database. Equalizing growth is when the incomes of the bottom 40% of the population grow faster than the economy average. Nonequalizing growth is when the incomes of the bottom 40% grow more slowly than the economy average.

Sources: Asian Development Bank estimates using data presented in Tables 1.1.1 and 1.10.1 of *Key Indicators for Asia and the Pacific 2021*; and World Bank's PovcalNet database (accessed 09 July 2021).

However, as seen in the trends for some economies, income growth can be fast but poverty is reduced in a nonequalizing way—when the income of the upper 60% of the population grows faster than that of the bottom 40%. In some economies where the income growth of higher earners was not significantly faster than for lower earners (known as equalizing growth), the pace of poverty reduction is slower.

Poverty is multidimensional: it is not just about income but also deprivations in health, education, and living standards.

Developing Asia has achieved substantial reductions in monetary poverty, yet there are still significant populations disadvantaged in other ways. Socioeconomic inequality needs to be addressed, since it leads to social tensions, creates economic inefficiencies, and contributes to the intergenerational cycle of poverty. Poverty and inequality should be closely examined with a much wider perspective beyond income-based metrics. To achieve this, the SDGs aim to reduce poverty in all its dimensions and the compilation of a multidimensional poverty index has been proposed to monitor these factors.

Figure 1.4 shows the correlation between monetary-based poverty (based on the $1.90 a day threshold) and multidimensional poverty in select ADB member economies with available data. The gap from the 45-degree line highlights the economies where the disparity between the two measures is greatest.

Figure 1.4: Comparison of Monetary and Multidimensional Poverty Rates

In some economies, trends in monetary and multidimensional poverty can be quite different.

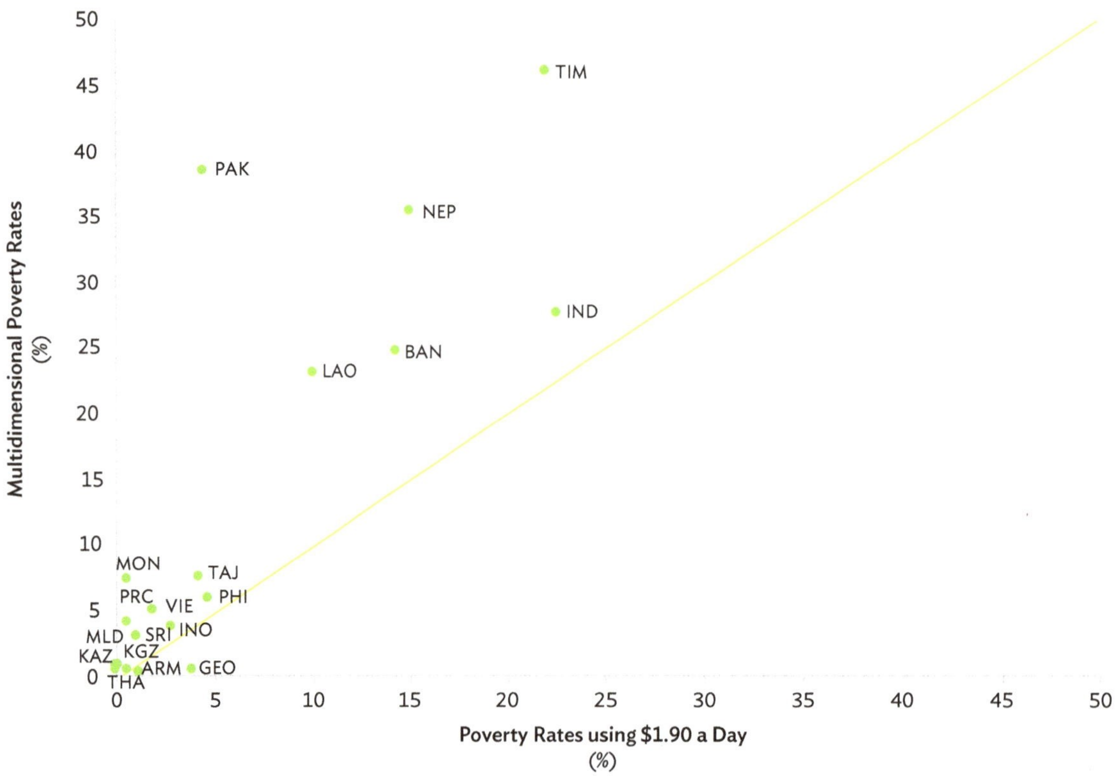

ARM = Armenia; BAN = Bangladesh; GEO = Georgia; IND = India; INO = Indonesia; KAZ = Kazakhstan; KGZ = Kyrgyz Republic ; LAO = Lao's People Democratic Republic ; MLD = Maldives; MON = Mongolia; NEP = Nepal; PAK = Pakistan; PHI = Philippines; PRC = People's Republic of China; SRI = Sri Lanka ; TAJ = Tajikistan; THA = Thailand; TIM = Timor Leste; VIE = Viet Nam.

Note: The poverty rates shown are estimates based on the most recent years for which data are available.

Sources: Asian Development Bank estimates using data presented in Table 1.1.1 of *Key Indicators for Asia and the Pacific 2021;* and Oxford Poverty & Human Development Initiative Global Multidimensional Poverty Index 2020 (accessed 09 July 2021).

:ant income during lockdown. Rickshaw drivers sit as
ey wait for customers in the streets of Dhaka, Bangladesh.

Overall, the analyses presented in this section show that, in developing Asia, monetary poverty has continued to decline, albeit at a slower rate compared to the 1990s and 2000s. There are, however, still significant levels of nonmonetary poverty in the region.

A majority of households experienced substantial reductions in income due to the COVID-19 pandemic. Interestingly, fewer households reported reduced expenditures.

Containment measures to curb the spread of COVID-19—such as lockdowns and restrictions in mobility and social interaction—have had adverse socioeconomic impacts on various segments of the population. To learn more about the impacts on households and individuals, the Asian Development Bank Institute (ADBI) administered surveys on households from select developing Asian economies.[5]

---

5 The surveys conducted by ADBI were carried out using computer-assisted telephone interviews, covering eight ADB member economies: Cambodia, Indonesia, the Lao People's Democratic Republic, Malaysia, Myanmar, the Philippines, Thailand, and Viet Nam. In each economy, approximately 1,000 households were surveyed to provide nationally representative samples (Morgan and Trinh 2021). Surveys were conducted from May to July 2020.

About 13% of households reported increased income flows, but nearly 75% of surveyed households reported a decline in household incomes and more than 50% reported a drop in their incomes by at least 26% (Morgan and Trinh 2021). Loss of household income can be attributed to temporary business closures during the pandemic, generating both unemployment and underemployment in both the formal and informal sectors. Restrictions on mobility, especially between rural and urban areas, can also hamper opportunities for migrant workers seeking nonfarm employment in urban areas during the farming off-season.

Meanwhile, 29% of respondents in the ADBI survey reported higher household expenditure and only 37% reported that their expenditure declined (Morgan and Trinh 2021). Breakdowns by socioeconomic status are shown in Figure 1.5. Data from ADBI surveys point to increased spending on health care products, household cleaning products, unexpected (higher) utility bills, and having to pay more for food as some of the reasons to explain the expenditure increases.

Figure 1.5: Changes in Household Expenditure by Socioeconomic Status

Poorer households were more likely to experience reduced consumption due to disruptions caused by the COVID-19 pandemic.

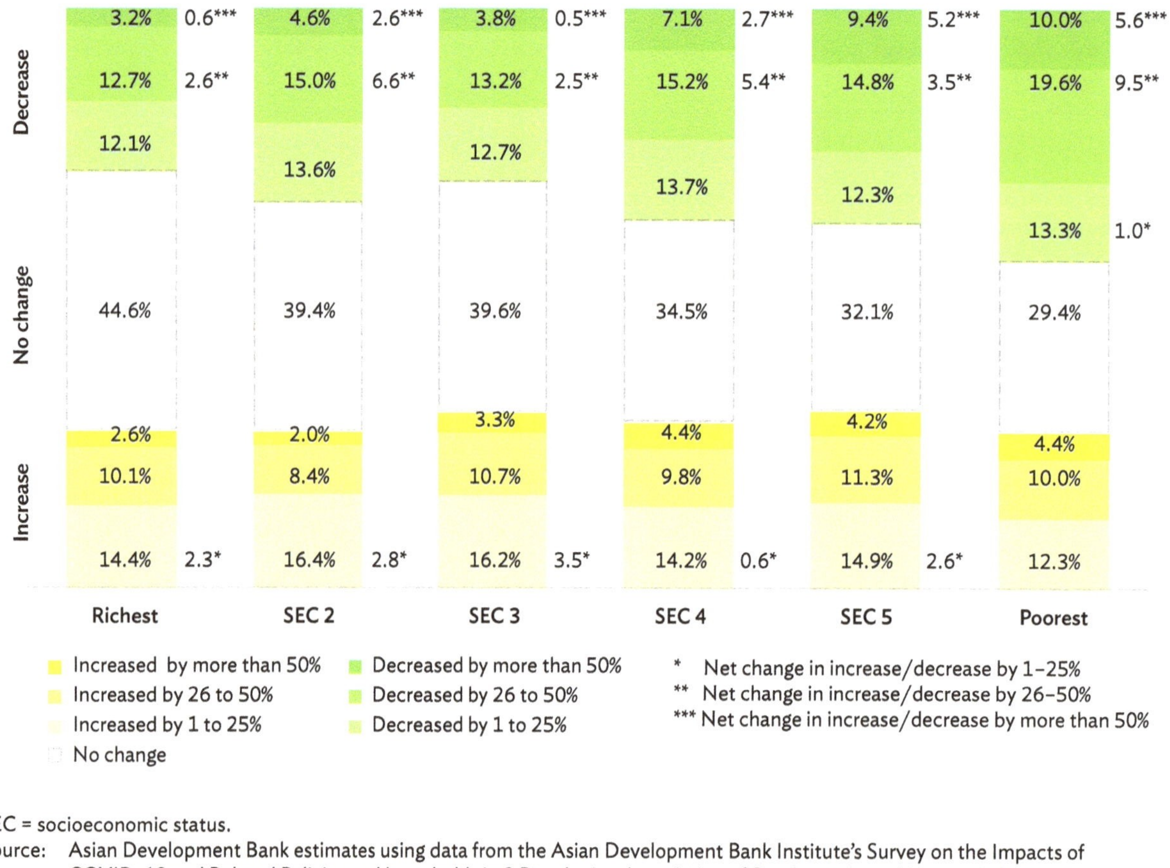

SEC = socioeconomic status.

Source: Asian Development Bank estimates using data from the Asian Development Bank Institute's Survey on the Impacts of COVID-19 and Related Policies on Households in 8 Developing Association of Southeast Asian Nations (ASEAN) Countries.

ADB data simulations suggest that the COVID-19 pandemic pushed around 75 million to 80 million extra people across developing Asia into extreme poverty in 2020, compared to a baseline scenario without COVID-19.

Since the pandemic struck, several economies have yet to conduct detailed household income and expenditure or living standards surveys, the results of which are conventionally used to compile poverty and inequality statistics.

To estimate the possible impacts of the pandemic, ADB economists and statisticians conducted a simple simulation exercise using grouped distribution data on household income or consumption expenditures per capita for 35 developing ADB member economies. This included developing an algorithm to ungroup the data and estimate the proportion of people living below different income thresholds, as well as a standard approach to extrapolating such a metric (Box 1.1).

Box 1.1: Simulating the Impact of the COVID-19 Pandemic on Monetary Poverty and Inequality

Data on household consumption expenditure and/or income were used to capture the effects of the pandemic on poverty and inequality by using gross domestic product (GDP) growth estimates for 2020. As a point of comparison, ADB economists and statisticians also considered a scenario in which COVID-19 did not strike, using GDP per capita growth numbers for 2020, as published in the Asian Development Outlook (ADO) Supplement 2019.

Specifically, the team started with the mean household expenditures and/or income levels reported in the World Bank's PovcalNet database for the most recent year available. We then extrapolated these to 2020 using the growth in mean household expenditures per capita imputed from the estimated relationship between household consumption expenditure per capita and GDP per capita.

For 2020 (without COVID-19 scenario), we used forecasts of GDP (and GDP per capita) reported in the ADO Supplement 2019. Released in December 2019, these forecasts do not take into account any pandemic-related effects and can be treated as the basis of estimating GDP per capita and, in turn, mean household expenditure per capita in a 2020 without COVID-19.

For 2020 (with COVID-19 scenario), we used published GDP (and GDP per capita) growth rates. In the initial set of simulations, a key simplifying assumption made in the analysis was that all households within an economy experience the same percentage decline in their per capita consumption expenditure and/or income as predicted based on GDP per capita growth numbers. In the second assumption, we assumed different growth rates for the mean consumption expenditure per capita of the bottom 40% of the population and the upper 60% of the population, using relevant information from the Asian Development Bank Institute household survey.

Armed with projections of mean household expenditures per capita, it is straightforward to calculate poverty using various poverty lines and our ungrouped data on the distribution of per capita household expenditures using the method described below:

As we do not observe individuals' income or consumption levels (without loss of generality, we will use the term "income" throughout), we use grouped distribution data from PovcalNet's built-in database to impute individual-level data.

Suppose grouped distribution data for a specific economy and reference time period comprise (p_k, L_k) coordinates that refer respectively to the cumulative shares in total population and in total income of income classes 1 to k, where k = 1, 2,.., m.

(continued on next page)

Box 1.1: Simulating the Impact of the COVID-19 Pandemic on Monetary Poverty and Inequality *(continued)*

The algorithm for "ungrouping" grouped data works like this. First, we fit a Lorenz parametric model L(y) using the m+1 coordinates available from PovcalNet's grouped distribution data.

$$L(y) = g(p, L, \theta) = \frac{1}{\mu_y}\int_0^x yf(y)dy \text{ (A1)}$$

where μ_y– average income, f(y) – income density curve and θ are parameters of the Lorenz function. In general, one can consider different parametric forms for the Lorenz function. Performing diagnostic tests can help identify which parametric form suits the data best. In this study, we use the Log Normal form.

Once we have estimated the parameters of the Lorenz function, Equation A3 suggests that a synthetic income quantile y_p can be imputed by multiplying the derivative of the Lorenz function (with respect to y) evaluated at $p = p_0$ by the average income. Where appropriate, we evaluate the derivative of the Lorenz function for 100,000 unique values p_0 that were uniformly distributed within [0,1] range to simulate the entire parametric Lorenz-based income distribution. This produces an individual-level income dataset with 100,000 data points. We do this for all economies and time periods of interest.

$$p = \int_0^x f(y)dy \text{ (A2)}$$

$$L'(p = p_0) * \mu_y = y(p_0) \text{ (A3)}$$

Since the distribution of imputed individual-level incomes may not exactly match the "true values" presented in PovcalNet, we implemented the adjustment procedure proposed by Shorrocks and Wan (2008) to ensure that the characteristics of the imputed incomes exactly match the actual Lorenz coordinates presented in PovcalNet. In particular, the algorithm entails adjusting the imputed individual incomes in such a way that each of the class k mean incomes are transformed into the corresponding "true" values and appropriate changes made to the intermediate values.

After following Shorrocks and Wan's algorithm, each individual-level income is compared with a pre-specified poverty line to calculate headcount poverty rates. To estimate the number of poor people, the resulting poverty rate is multiplied with published population data.

Reference:

A.F. Shorrocks and G. Wan,. 2008. Ungrouping Income Distributions: Synthesising Samples for Inequality and Poverty Analysis. Research Paper 2008/016. Helsinki: UNU-WIDER. https://www.wider.unu.edu/sites/default/files/rp2008-16.pdf

Figure 1.6 illustrates the impact of the COVID-19 pandemic on developing Asia, as represented by the 35 developing ADB member economies for which grouped distribution data on household income or consumption expenditure per capita were available. The $1.90 a day threshold measures extreme poverty, while the $3.20 a day and $5.50 a day thresholds reflect poverty lines typically found in lower middle-income economies and upper middle-income economies, respectively. The $15.00 a day threshold is commonly used to define the middle class (World Bank 2018a). All cut-off points are dollar values expressed in 2011 purchasing power parities.

The results of ADB's simulations suggest that disruption in economic activity due to the COVID-19 pandemic increased the proportion of people living below the extreme poverty line of $1.9 a day by about 2 percentage points in 2020, compared to a scenario without COVID-19. Similarly, the proportion of people living on more than $1.90 but less than $3.20 a day also increased by roughly 2.4 percentage points.

Figure 1.6: Simulated Distribution of Developing Asia's Population by Income Group, 2020

The COVID-19 pandemic has pushed millions of people into monetary poverty, relative to a baseline scenario of no pandemic.

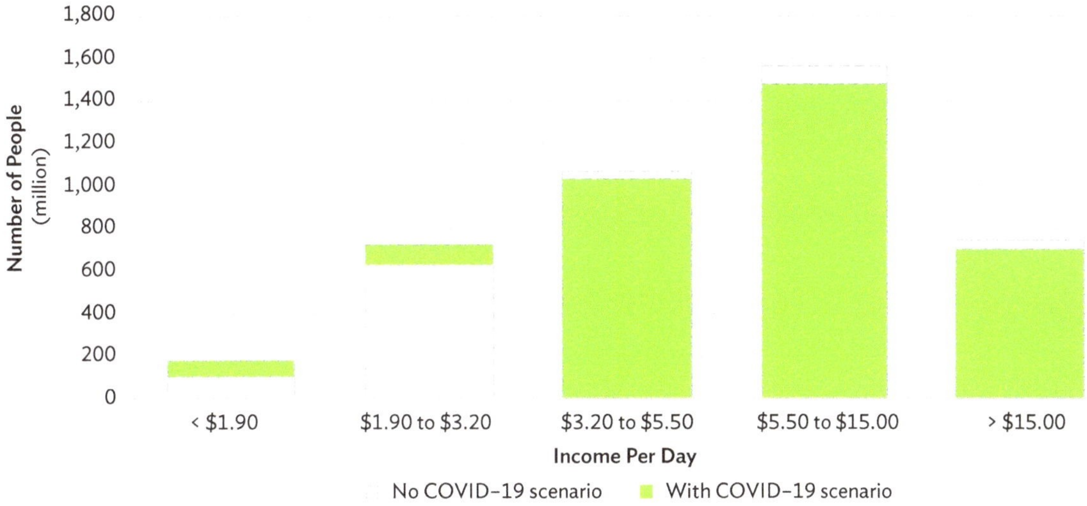

$ = United States dollars.

Note: For $1.90 and $3.20 estimates, the "with COVID-19" scenario is the sum of the white and green bars, while for higher income thresholds, the sum of the green and white bars corresponds to the "no COVID-19" scenario.

Source: Asian Development Bank estimates using simulated data derived from the World Bank's PovcalNet database (accessed 09 July 2021).

In addition to poverty, it is important to examine how the pandemic has affected inequality. In this context, total inequality can be separated into differences between economies and differences within economies.

There are a number of compelling arguments on how the COVID-19 pandemic could exacerbate inequalities between economies. Less-developed economies tend to have poorer health systems and are therefore less prepared to deal with a pandemic (Stiglitz 2020). Furthermore, a higher proportion of people in less-developed economies are not covered by social protection programs, leaving them more vulnerable to hardships caused by prolonged economic disruptions (Deaton 2021). However, a recent study also argues that a number of higher-income economies around the world are experiencing more deaths per capita and higher average income declines than some less-developed economies, despite the former having better health systems and social protection mechanisms (Deaton 2021). Therefore, at the global level, the notion that the pandemic has increased total income inequality because of wider disparities between economies warrants further scrutiny (Deaton 2021).

Figure 1.6 shows that the simulated increases in the proportion of people living on less than $1.90 or $3.20 a day is greater than the reductions in the proportion of people in higher-income segments. This is indicative of greater income inequality in the region as a result of the COVID-19 pandemic. Using the Gini coefficient as a metric of inequality, ADB economists and statisticians estimate that its value will increase by 1.6% more than the estimated value under a "no COVID-19" baseline scenario.

However, it is important to note that these numbers are mainly driven by what happened in the PRC and India, the region's two most populous economies, which contribute significantly to total economic output. Prior to the pandemic, it was estimated that the PRC had a significantly lower incidence of extreme poverty than did India. While the economies of both economies were initially expected to grow at the same pace in 2020 under a "no COVID-19" scenario[6], the negative impacts of the pandemic were more pronounced in India. The wide differences in the experiences of the region's two largest economies contribute to changes in income inequality across developing Asia in 2020.

Figure 1.7: Income Distribution

In developing Asia, income inequality between economies slightly increased when the COVID-19 pandemic struck.

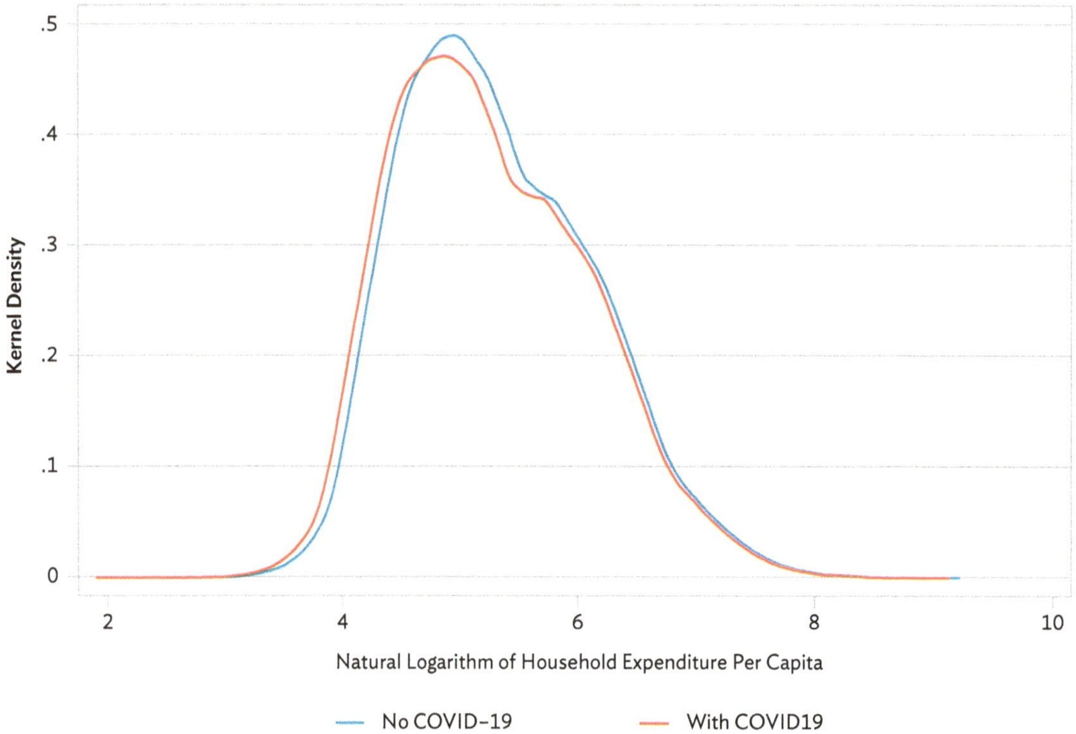

Source: Asian Development Bank estimates using simulated data derived from the World Bank's PovcalNet database (accessed 09 July 2021).

6 Estimates of GDP growth for 2020 under the "no COVID-19" scenario are available from ADB (2019a).

Low-income households were hit harder by the COVID-19 pandemic.

Up to this point, ADB simulations have been anchored on the assumption that all households within an economy experienced the same proportional decline in their per capita incomes or consumption expenditure. Therefore, the numbers stated do not capture the COVID-19 pandemic's impact on inequality within economies.

There is a tendency for income inequality to decline in the aftermath of catastrophes such as wars, earthquakes, and stock market crises as they entail massive wealth destruction (Zhuang 2020). Conversely, a basic assessment of what happened during five recent pandemics (i.e., SARS, H1N1, MERS, Ebola, and Zika) suggests that health disasters tend to increase income inequality as they involve large-scale job destruction that disproportionately affects lower-income groups (Zhuang 2020).

Amid these theoretical possibilities, providing an exact assessment of the impact of COVID-19 on income inequality within economies is difficult due to a lack of detailed and disaggregated data on household income and expenditure. Nevertheless, further insights can be gained by exploring information collected from the ADBI household survey (Figure 1.5). This further analysis included (i) reviewing the monthly expenditure of the six socioeconomic classes; (ii) calculating the net changes in monthly expenditure across three ranges of higher or lower consumption, i.e., 1% to 25%, 26% to 50%, and more than 50%; and (iii) projecting the distribution of these net changes to the data used for ADB's poverty simulations for each economy. The results are shown in Table 1.1, which outlines what income distribution in the region could look like under the impacts of the COVID-19 pandemic.

Table 1.1: Simulated Distribution of Income under Varying Inequality Scenarios

Monetary poverty rates are higher if it is assumed that the pandemic caused inequality to increase.

Scenario	$1.90 %	$3.20 %	$5.50 %	Gini Coefficient
Before COVID-19 (2017)	5.2	24.6	51.1	45.6
No COVID-19 scenario (2020)	2.6	18.5	44.7	46.4
Neutral distribution assumption (2020)	4.5	22.8	48.1	47.1
Consumption share of bottom 40% of population in each member economy decreased by 0.5 percentage point (2020)	5.3	23.5	48.6	47.5
Consumption share of bottom 40% of population in each member economy decreased by 1 percentage point (2020)	5.9	23.8	49.0	47.9
Consumption share of bottom 40% of population in each member economy increased by 0.5 percentage point (2020)	4.3	22.9	48.1	46.8
Consumption share of bottom 40% of population in each member economy increased by 1 percentage point (2020)	3.8	22.6	47.8	46.4

$ = United States dollars.

Note: "$1.90" represents those living on less than $1.90 a day; "$3.20" represents those living on less than $3.20 a day; "$5.50" represents those living on less than $5.50 a day.

Source: Asian Development Bank estimates using simulated data derived from the World Bank's PovcalNet database (accessed 09 July 2021).

The results show that the pandemic worsened developing Asia's poverty position under the neutral distribution assumption, and the simulated poverty estimates are even higher if we consider scenarios of greater inequality.[7,8]

On the other hand, if lower-income households benefited from considerable relief programs or social safety nets and, as a result, the incomes of poorer people declined at a slower rate, the poverty impacts of the COVID-19 pandemic might be lower than initially estimated.

It is important to underscore that, while the parameters used to design the simulations presented in this section were guided by relevant information such as GDP estimates and ADBI surveys, further studies based on more detailed data are needed to better understand the scope and scale of the COVID-19 pandemic's impact on developing Asia in terms of poverty and inequality.

People across developing Asia relied on various coping strategies to manage financial difficulties caused by the COVID-19 pandemic, but some of these strategies cause scarring effects in the long term and could be potentially costly.

Proper targeting of policies for the extremely poor, along with continued support from government and development institutions, is important in alleviating the long-term effects of the pandemic.

Most (55%) of households covered by ADBI's survey of developing Asia reported financial difficulties during the pandemic.[9] Furthermore, more than 80% of households who experienced financial difficulty had to reduce consumption expenditure as a coping mechanism, and 50% resorted to drawdown cash and savings. About one-third of surveyed households either borrowed from relatives or friends, deferred payments and debt reimbursements, or applied for social and/or government aid, while about 18% sold property or pawned possessions. Figure 1.8 details these coping strategies.

---

7 The simulations do not necessarily capture all possible inequality scenarios.

8 For reference, the average consumption share of the bottom 40% of the population in developing Asian economies was approximately 18% to 19% prior to the pandemic.

9 The ADBI study considers a household experiencing financial difficulty if it reported lacking financial resources for at least a week during the study period (Morgan and Trinh 2021).

Figure 1.8: Proportion of Households in Financial Difficulty and Coping Strategies Used

A considerable number of Asians used coping strategies with potential adverse consequences due to financial difficulties caused by the COVID-19 pandemic.

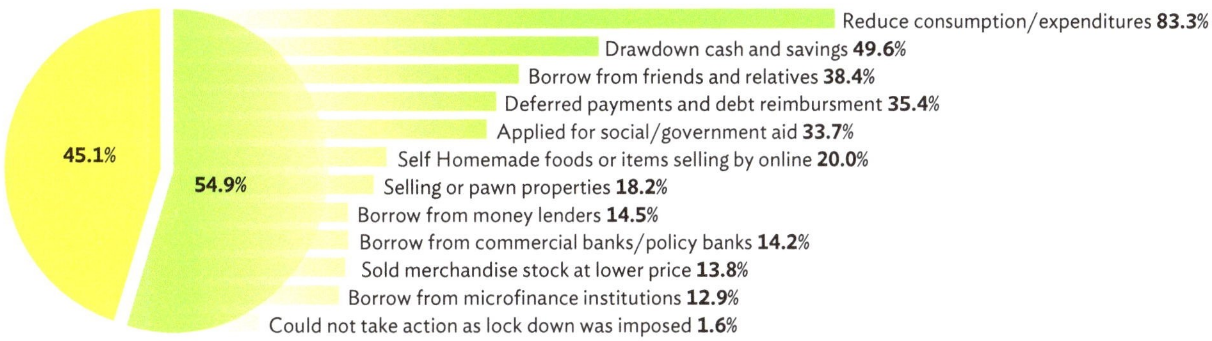

Source: Asian Development Bank estimates using data from the Asian Development Bank Institute's Survey on the Impacts of COVID-19 and Related Policies on Households in 8 Developing Association of Southeast Asian Nations (ASEAN) Countries.

Evidence from previous disasters show that some strategies commonly adopted by disadvantaged groups, such as decreasing food consumption and selling productive assets, can lead to lower accumulation of human and physical capital (Hill and Narayan 2021). These coping mechanisms may potentially have long-term harmful or scarring effects. Poor nutrition due to food poverty can impede cognitive development in children and make them less interested in going to school. Nutritional deficiencies during childhood are also associated with increased susceptibility to metabolic illnesses in adulthood (Martins et al. 2011). Loss of productive assets may drive households further into debt. Reliance on these coping mechanisms to compensate for income loss perpetuates the cycle of poverty and increases inequality.

Based on ADBI surveys, Figure 1.9 shows the proportion of households reporting difficulty and having to reduce food intake or sell or pawn possessions. While caution is warranted when making cross-economy comparisons because some economies had fewer COVID-19 infections when surveys were conducted, what stands out is that the proportion of population covered by at least one social protection benefit is considerably lower than the number of people having to resort to coping strategies that might have long-term scarring effects.

Figure 1.9: Households in Financial Distress Relative to Social Protection Benefit

In several economies, there is an urgent need to expand social protection coverage to minimize the vicious cycle of disadvantage caused by adverse coping strategies.

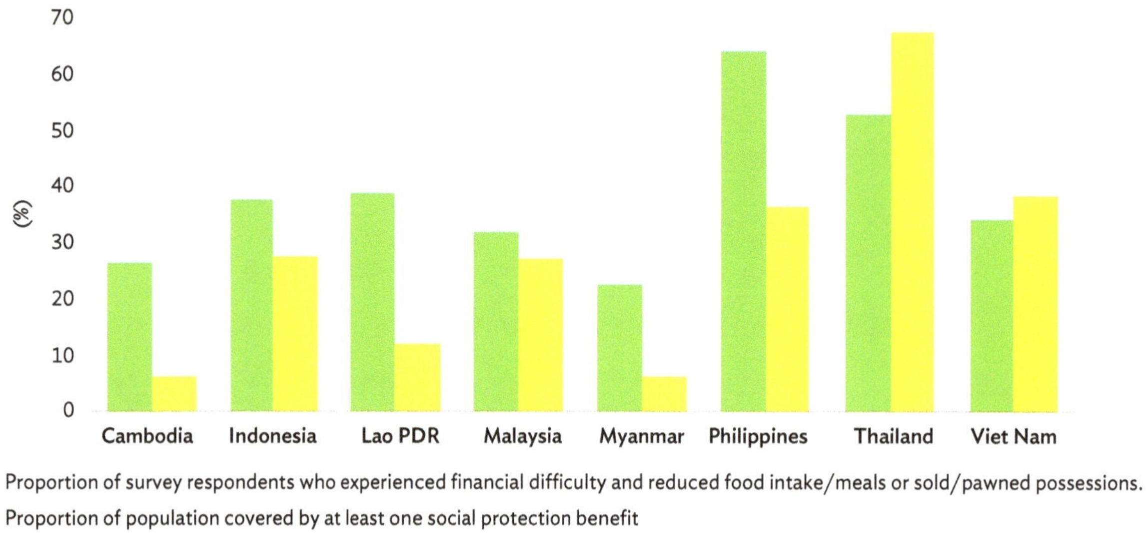

Lao PDR = Lao People's Democratic Republic.

Sources: Asian Development Bank estimates using data from the Asian Development Bank Institute's Survey on the Impacts of COVID-19 and Related Policies on Households in 8 Developing Association of Southeast Asian Nations (ASEAN) Countries; and Table 1.1.2 of *Key Indicators for Asia and the Pacific 2021*.

Hunger

There have been substantial gains in reducing hunger and food insecurity since 1990, but recent trends show that progress has slowed or, in some instances, reversed.

Since 1990, economic growth and increased agricultural productivity has contributed to substantial gains in the reduction of food insecurity and hunger in developing Asia. These advances helped economies halve their proportion of undernourished people in the period from 1990 to 2015 (FAO, IFAD, and WFP 2015). However, recent data shows a worrying trend for the SDG 2 target of eradicating hunger by 2030, as a report by the Food and Agriculture Organization of the United Nations (FAO) shows that the number of hungry people has increased worldwide since 2014.

The latest estimates from the FAO show that about 768 million people or 9.9% of the world's population were undernourished in 2020. This figure is up by more than 160 million since 2014, with almost 118 million added since 2019 (Figure 1.10). Following this peak, the number is expected to slowly decline to fewer than 660 million people or 7.7% of the world's population by 2030 (FAO, IFAD, UNICEF, WFP, and WHO 2021).

pport for vulnerable households. Distributing food as part of collaborative emergency support program from ADB and partners.

Meanwhile, malnutrition indicators show that the number of children stunted at age 5 years and below has decreased, but prevalence is still high at 22.0% in 2020. The prevalence of overweight children under 5 years increased to 38.9 million in 2020, up from 33.3 million in 2000 (UNICEF, WHO, and World Bank 2021).

Higher prices of fruits, vegetables, dairy products, and other basic food items have been caused by the adverse impacts of climate change, catastrophic weather events, and various pest infestations. The spread of infectious diseases among animals (such as the African swine fever) has also affected food production and caused food supply chain disruptions. These factors, along with poor choices of calorie sources, might have contributed to poor people having difficulty in maintaining healthy diets in recent years (World Bank 2020a).

Figure 1.10: Global Trends in Undernourishment, Malnutrition, and Child Stunting

Globally, trends with respect to SDG targets on hunger and food insecurity are mixed.

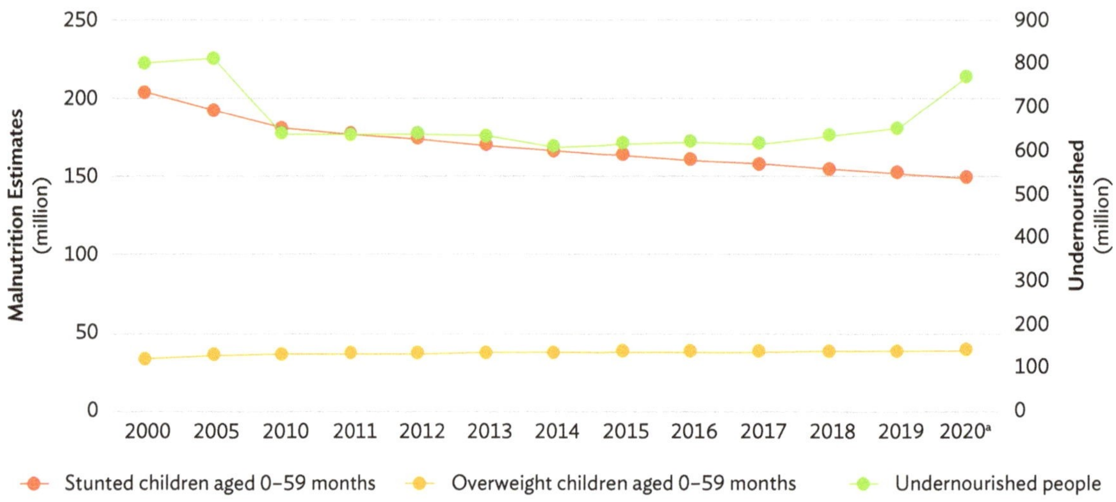

[a] The estimates for stunting and overweight prevalence for 2020 do not account for the full impact of COVID-19. Household survey data on child height, weight, and age were not collected in 2020 due to physical-distancing policies. One of the covariates used in the economy model takes the impact of COVID-19 partially into account.

Sources: For undernourishment: Food and Agriculture Organization. FAOSTAT Database. http://www.fao.org/faostat/en/#data/FS (accessed 14 July 2021). For stunting and overweight prevalence: UNICEF, WHO, World Bank Group Joint Malnutrition Estimates, April 2021 Edition. https://data.unicef.org/resources/dataset/malnutrition-data/ (accessed 6 July 2021). Table 1.2.1 of *Key Indicators for Asia and the Pacific 2021* shows prevalence of undernourishment, stunting, and overweight.

Compared to other regions, developing Asia is faring slightly better in reducing the prevalence of undernourishment. However, progress is uneven and, with high rates of child stunting and malnutrition, much needs to be done to achieve the 2030 target of ending hunger in the region.

Although home to almost half of the world's undernourished, a number of economies in developing Asia were showing progress in reducing the prevalence of undernourishment (Table 1.2.1), with numbers dropping by more than 44 million from 2010 to 2017. However, the number of undernourished in the region increased by more than 20 million from 2018 to 2019 (FAO, IFAD, UNICEF, WFP, and WHO 2021).

As shown in Figure 1.11, East Asia's performance, most notably the PRC, contributed significantly to reducing the region's prevalence of undernourishment. From 2001 to 2009, the PRC has seen an average of more than 11.6 million fewer undernourished people every year. Meanwhile, other subregions, such as South Asia and Central and West Asia, have witnessed a slower pace of reduction. In fact, the latest data suggest that the number of undernourished in Central and West Asia increased by 2.6 million in 2019, while the number grew by more than 17 million in South Asia.

Progress also varies according to economies' income levels, with upper middle-income economies showing the sharpest reductions in the prevalence of undernourishment, while low and lower middle-income economies saw more modest declines. In fact, some economies in the low-income and lower middle-income groupings reported estimates still exceeding 20%, which is twice the average for developing Asia as a whole.

Studies show that many developing economies in the region are already under stress due to changes in rainfall patterns, shortages of irrigation water, extreme weather events, and global warming—and these can affect the survival thresholds of traditional crops and agricultural produce (ADB 2019b). If these changes in weather patterns

Figure 1.11: Undernourished People in Developing Economies of Asia and the Pacific, by Subregion

Reduction in the prevalence of undernourishment has slowed since 2011, with undernourishment increasing from 2018 to 2019.

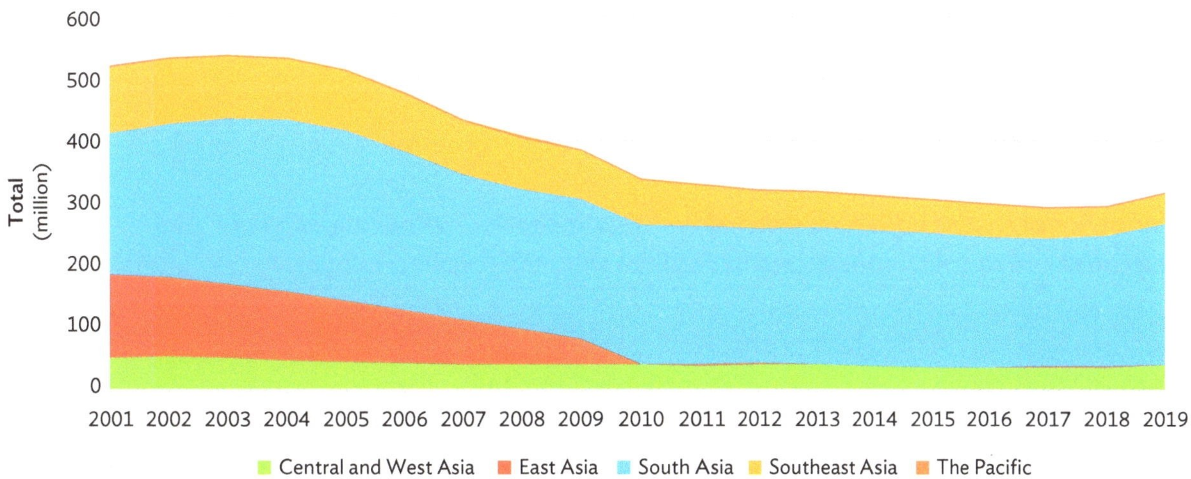

Sources: Asian Development Bank estimates using data presented in Table 1.2.1 of *Key Indicators for Asia and the Pacific 2021*; Asian Development Bank. Key Indicators Database. http://kidb.adb.org (accessed 14 July 2021); and Food and Agriculture Organization of the United Nations. FAOSTAT Database. http://www.fao.org/faostat/en/#data/FS (accessed 14 July 2021).

continue, there will be 38 million more hungry people in Asia and the Pacific by 2030, compared to the outcome if there were no further climate change impacts. Although the number of undernourished people in the region is expected to decline from 507 million in 2015 to 362 million in 2030, and the number of malnourished children from 93 million to 76 million under this climate change scenario[10], the pace of reductions would be very slow (ADB 2019b).

Changes in calorie consumption—such as increased intake of foods that are high in fats, salt, and sugar, usually from processed and packaged foods—combined with physical inactivity due to increasingly sedentary lifestyles, rapid urbanization, and changing modes of transportation, are contributing to an uptick in the number of overweight children (FAO, UNICEF, WFP, and WHO 2021; WHO 2021).

The COVID-19 pandemic threatens to further impede the region's progress in SDG 2 targets, especially in the prevalence of undernourishment.

Prior to the COVID-19 pandemic, projections on the prevalence of undernourishment indicated that most subregions in Asia and the Pacific would show significant progress in reducing undernourishment by 2030 (FAO, IFAD, UNICEF, WFP, and WHO 2020), albeit the pace of progress might be slower than what was observed in earlier decades due to impacts of climate change and other factors (ADB 2019b). Economies from East Asia and Central Asia were likely to eliminate undernourishment by 2030, but some South Asian and Southeast Asian economies need to further accelerate their efforts to achieve the 2030 targets (FAO 2020). In the latest FAO report, Asia and the Pacific is projected to have a substantial reduction in the number of undernourished, with numbers projected to drop from 418 million people in 2020 to 300 million in 2030 (FAO, IFAD, UNICEF, WFP, and WHO 2021).

The pandemic makes the goal of eradicating hunger even more challenging in several ways, although the full extent of its impact is hard to quantify due to a lack of available data. The pandemic exacerbates the vulnerabilities of people who were already suffering from undernourishment and malnutrition as these increase the chance of getting ill and dying (DIPR 2020).

The pandemic has caused both food demand and supply shocks, further magnifying food insecurity and malnutrition-related issues in developing Asian economies.

In some areas, lockdowns led to food price hikes arising from supply chain disruptions (Kim et al. 2020). Globally, a sharp increase in food insecurity and undernourishment is expected (World Bank 2020b; UNSD 2020c), fueling a worsening incidence of hunger, which was on the rise even before the pandemic began. Data available from the surveys

---

[10] This refers to the Hadley Centre Global Environmental Model (HGEM) climate change scenario, which utilizes the HGEM general circulation model together with Shared Socioeconomic Pathway 2 and Representative Circulation Pathway 8.5, which has the highest rate of climate change utilized in the Intergovernmental Panel on Climate Change Fifth Assessment Report. This scenario preserves the baseline agricultural productivity growth, economic growth, and population growth to 2030, but imposes climate change to assess its impacts.

conducted by ADBI shows the impact in select developing Asian economies. Figure 1.12 illustrates that a substantial number of households experienced financial difficulty and had to reduce food intake or number of meals.

Figure 1.12: Prevalence of Food Insecurity and Undernourishment, and Coping Measures Taken

In select economies, where the prevalence of food insecurity and undernourishment were considerable even before COVID-19 struck, a significant proportion of the population had to reduce food consumption to cope with financial difficulties caused by the pandemic.

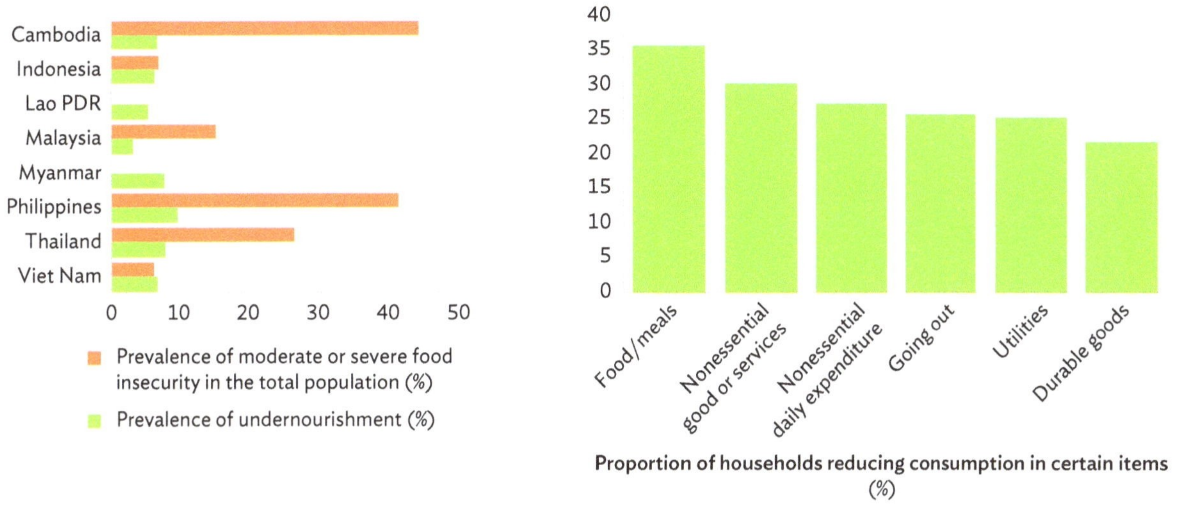

Lao PDR = Lao People's Democratic Republic.

Notes: Data on food insecurity and undernourishment are 3-year averages from 2017 to 2019. Data on prevalence of moderate or severe food insecurity are not available for the Lao PDR and Myanmar.

Sources: Asian Development Bank estimates using data from the Asian Development Bank Institute's Survey on the Impacts of COVID-19 and Related Policies on Households in 8 Developing Association of Southeast Asian Nations (ASEAN) Countries; Asian Development Bank. Key Indicators Database. http://kidb.adb.org (accessed 24 July 2021); and Food and Agriculture Organization of the United Nations. FAOSTAT Database. http://www.fao.org/faostat/en/#data/FS (accessed 24 July 2021).

Health

Prior to the COVID-19 pandemic, Asia and the Pacific had been experiencing steady progress in several SDG 3 health targets, particularly on maternal and child mortality.

From 2010 to 2017, the maternal mortality ratio across the region dropped by 28%; from an average of 164 deaths per 100,000 live births to 117 deaths per 100,000 live births (Figure 1.13). This compares well to the 15% reduction in global maternal mortality recorded during the same period. Regional trends in the under-5 mortality ratio have seen similar progress. From 2010 to 2019, the number of deaths per 1,000 live births dropped from 43 to 28. In comparison, the world's average under-5 mortality ratio was higher at 38 deaths per 1,000 live births in 2019.

If these trends continue, the region is on track to reduce maternal mortality ratio to less than 70 deaths per 100,000 live births and child mortality to 25 deaths per 1,000 live births by 2030. While some Asian economies have already met development targets for maternal and child mortality reduction, others still need to accelerate efforts to achieve the targets within SDG 3.

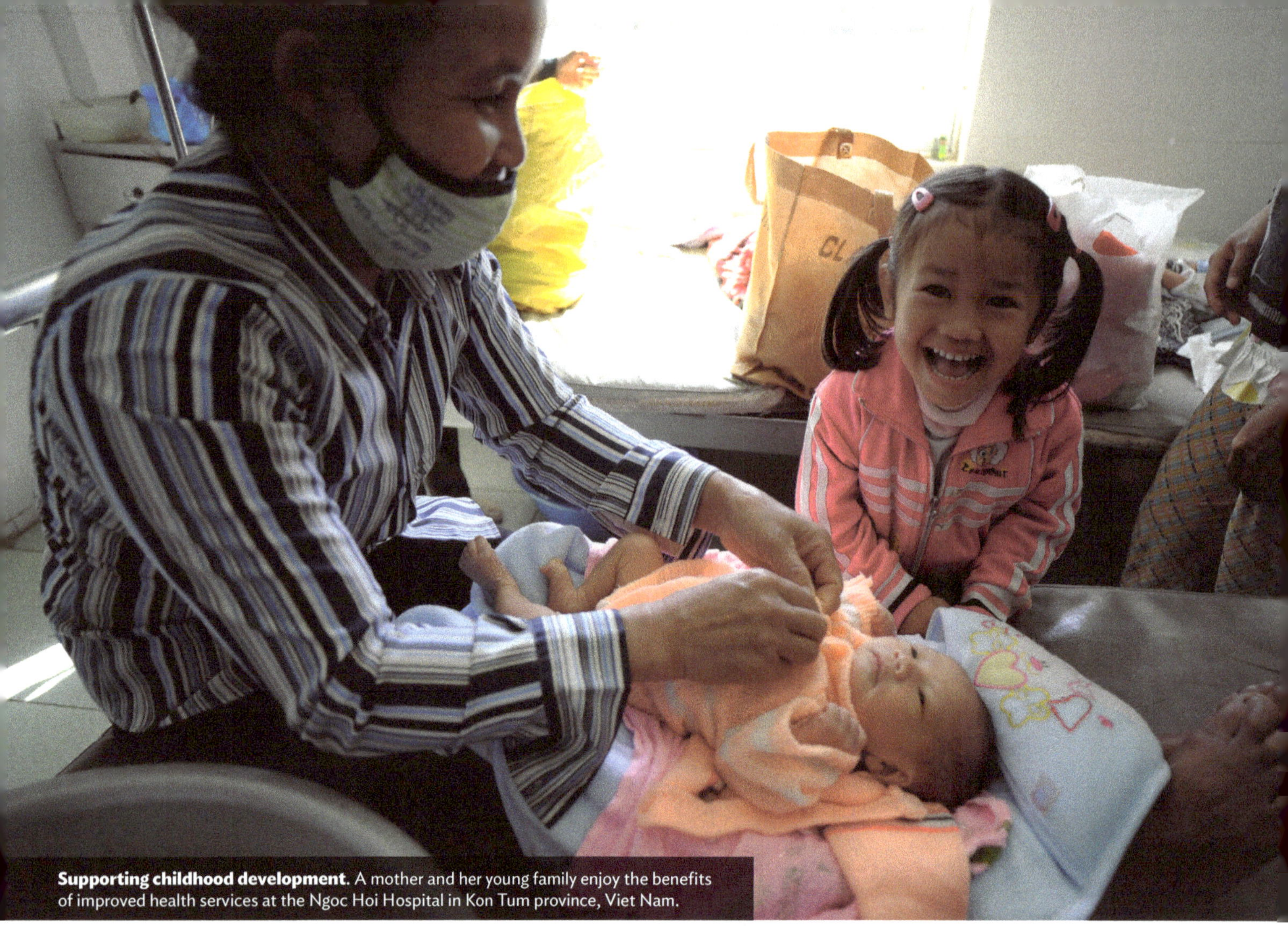

Supporting childhood development. A mother and her young family enjoy the benefits of improved health services at the Ngoc Hoi Hospital in Kon Tum province, Viet Nam.

As most maternal deaths can be prevented through appropriate management of pregnancy and care at and after birth (WHO 2020d), the progress witnessed by the region can be partly linked to enhanced provision of antenatal care by trained health personnel. Data collected prior to the COVID-19 pandemic suggest that all reporting economies of Asia and the Pacific have at least 50% of births attended by skilled health professionals compared to 87% in 2010 (Table 1.3.1). Similarly, immunization among children is regarded as a cost-effective way of protecting their health, with improved vaccination coverage contributing to lower child mortality ratios (WHO 2020d).

Despite improvements in supply of health workers, access to health services, and preparedness for national and global health risks, Asia and the Pacific needs to accelerate progress on health issues, particularly among low-income and lower middle-income economies.

Universal health coverage is critical in meeting the SDG 3 goal of ensuring healthy lives and promoting well-being. The Essential Health Services Index is used to measure the coverage of essential health services in the economies of Asia and the Pacific.
It comprises 14 tracer indicators, grouped under four categories of service coverage: (i) reproductive, maternal, newborn, and child health; (ii) infectious diseases; (iii) noncommunicable diseases; and (iii) service capacity (UNSD 2020a). The index, ranging from 0 to 100, can be viewed as performance scores, with higher values indicating better health service coverage. It does not correspond to the percentage of the population covered by universal health coverage services.

Figure 1.13: Maternal and Under-5 Mortality Ratios by Region and by Subregion of Asia and the Pacific

Before the COVID-19 pandemic struck, most parts of developing Asia were on track to meet SDG targets on maternal and under-5 mortality reduction.

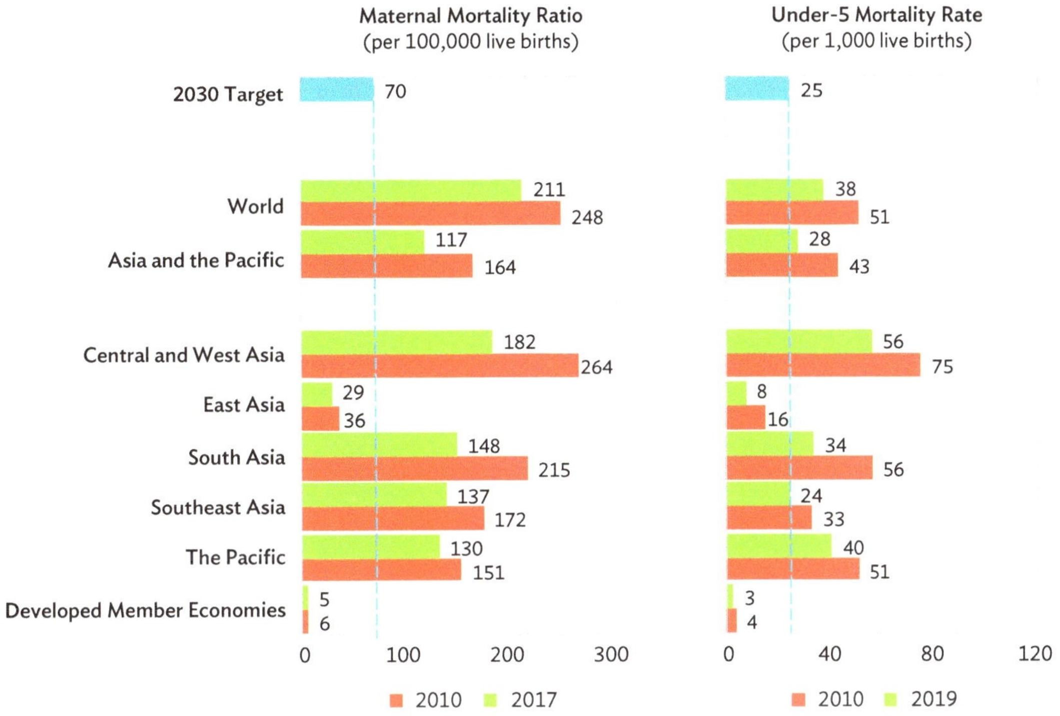

Source: Table 1.3.1 of *Key Indicators for Asia and the Pacific 2021*.

Figure 1.14 shows how various economies within Asia and the Pacific, grouped by income levels, have performed with respect to this metric, and relative to the regional and global averages. In 2010, more than half of the economies in the region (except for high-income economies) trailed behind the global average, but are now showing signs of catching up. However, the region's low and lower middle-income economies, particularly those in Central and West Asia, South Asia, and the Pacific, still lag behind the regional and global average.

Data since 2000 show that, while improvements were noted across all income groups over time, Asia and the Pacific still falls below the minimum threshold—requiring at least 4.45 doctors, nurses, and midwives per 1,000 population, based on a World Health Organization (WHO) study. This threshold represents the minimum density of health workers required to attain 80% coverage in relation to health targets of the SDGs (WHO 2016)[11].

11 The threshold is specified as the sum of doctors and nurses/midwives per 1,000 population for two reasons: (a) to be consistent with the health worker threshold from the 2006 *World health report* and previous research; and (b) due to the lack of adequate data on the numbers of other cadres of health workers (WHO 2016).

Figure 1.14: Coverage of Essential Health Services

Across Asia and the Pacific, higher-income economies enjoy better essential health services coverage.

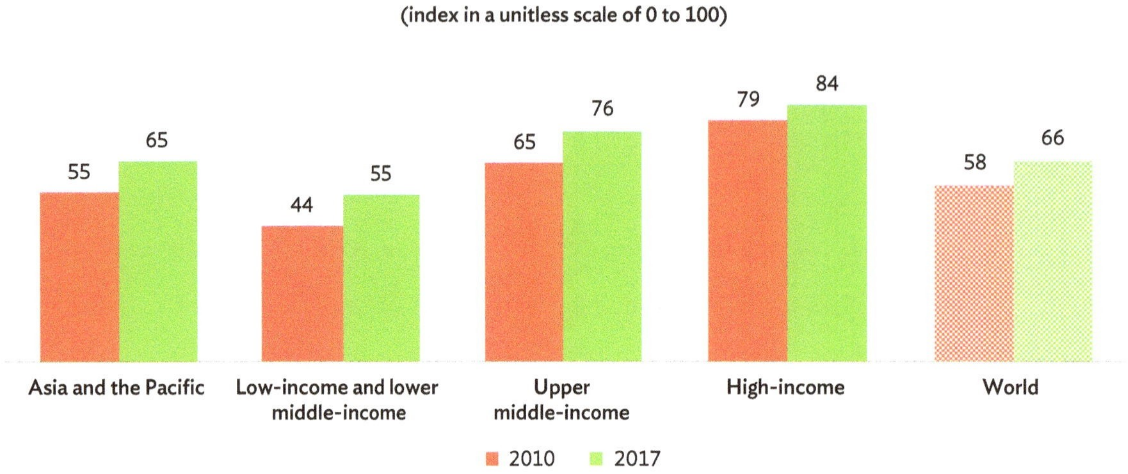

Notes: Income groupings follow the World Bank's classification as of July 2020. Aggregates are population-weighted averages estimated by Asian Development Bank staff.

Source: Asian Development Bank estimates using data presented in Table 1.3.3 of *Key Indicators for Asia and the Pacific 2021*.

Within the region, high-income economies had approximately three times more doctors than low and lower middle-income economies, and five times more personnel for nursing and midwifery (Figure 1.15). South Asia, Southeast Asia, and the Pacific remained below the regional average for density of medical doctors. East Asia and the region's developed ADB member economies have shown considerable improvement, especially for density of nursing and midwifery personnel (Table 1.3.4).

Some of the causes of nursing shortages worldwide include growing population, increasing international mobility and migration, an aging workforce, deteriorating

Figure 1.15: Density of Medical Doctors and Density of Nursing and Midwifery Personnel

Despite improvements, the region's low-income and lower middle-income economies still fall behind the global average for density of health workers.

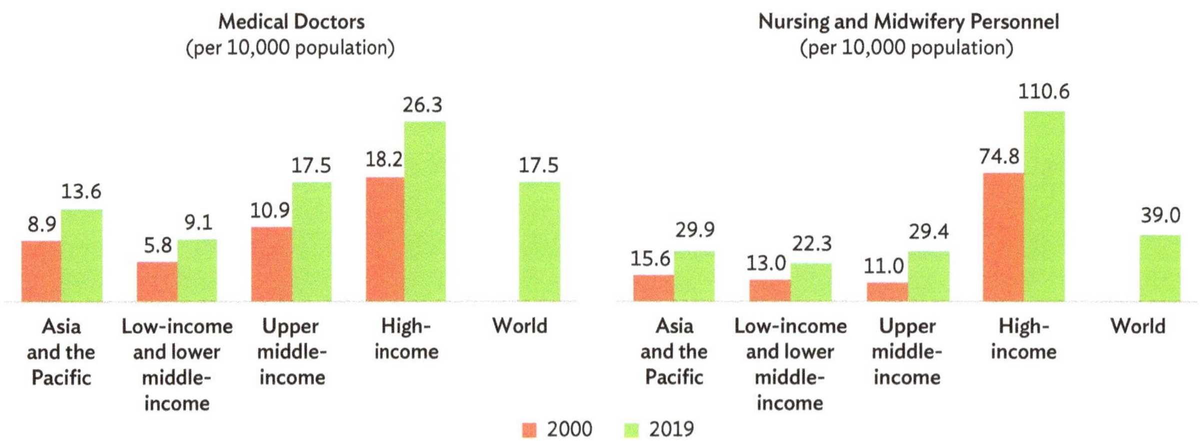

Notes: 2000 = data available for 2000 to 2009; 2019 = data available for 2010 to 2019. Income groupings follow the World Bank's classification as of July 2020. Aggregates are population-weighted averages estimated by Asian Devlopment Bank staff.

Sources: Asian Development Bank estimates using data presented in Table 1.3.4 of *Key Indicators for Asia and the Pacific 2021*; and Asian Development Bank. Key Indicators Database. http://kidb.adb.org (accessed 24 July 2021).

working conditions, poor quality of care, constrained education capacities, and limited opportunities for employment positions and clinical placement (WHO 2020c).

The capacity for preparedness for national and global health risks is also critical in achieving SDG 3. Indicator 3.d.1 was included to monitor the commitment by economies to the 2005 International Health Regulations (IHR). This requires economies to "develop and maintain minimum core capacities for surveillance and response, including at points of entry, in order to early detect, assess, notify, and respond to any potential public health events of international concern" (UNSD 2020b). Annual monitoring began in 2010, wherein economies answered and submitted a self-assessment questionnaire. In 2018, WHO introduced a new State Parties Self-Assessment Annual Reporting Tool, which reflects the revised 13 IHR core capacities on a scale scoring system.

Overall, the Asia and the Pacific region is performing well, with an average score of 67 across all 13 IHR capacities, compared to the world's average of 65. The region performs better in 9 of the 13 core capacities. Assessing the income groupings within the region, the low-income and lower middle-income grouping is performing below the regional average (Figure 1.16). The greatest deficits occur in human resources, health service provision, legislation and financing, food safety, national health emergency framework, and risk communication.

Figure 1.16: Scores for Health System Core Capacities, by Economy Income Grouping

In general, Asia and the Pacific's low-income and lower middle-income economies need to catch up in a number of core health capacities.

(SPAR score as a % for each IHR capacity in 2020)

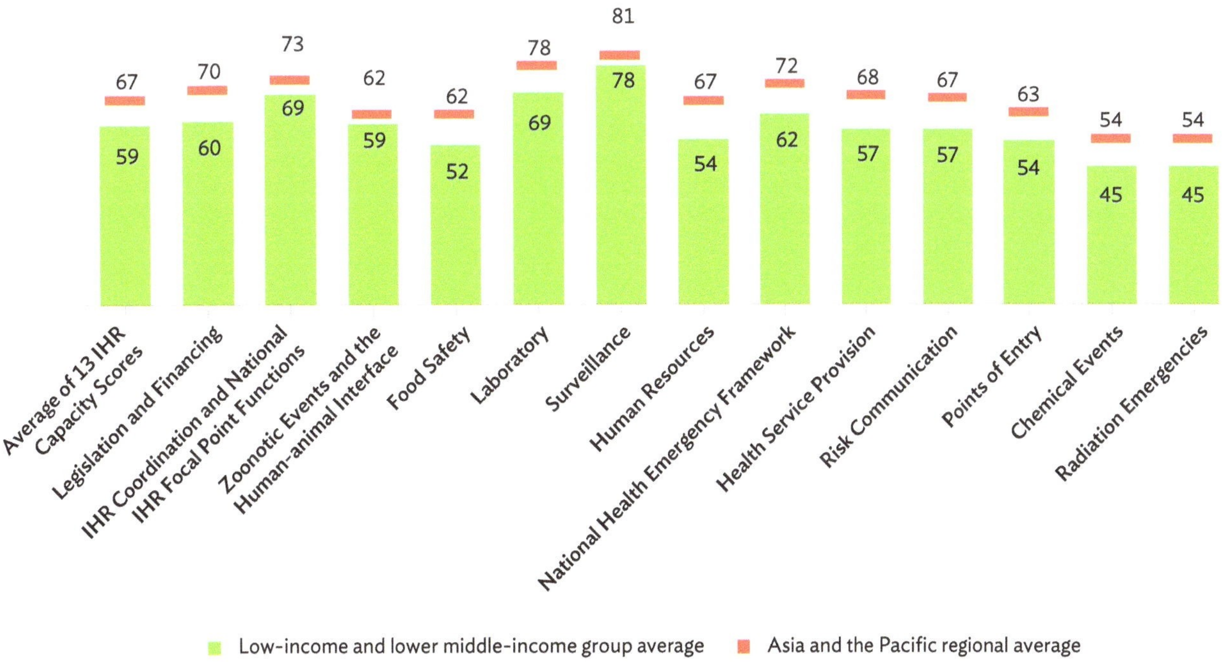

IHR = International Health Regulations, SPAR = State Parties Self-Assessment Annual Reporting Tool.

Notes: Higher scores indicate more progress made towards fully developed and functional IHR capacities. The low-income and lower middle-income grouping follows the World Bank's classifications as of July 2020.

Sources: Asian Development Bank estimates using data presented in Table 1.3.4 of *Key Indicators for Asia and the Pacific 2021*; and World Health Organization. Global Health Observatory. https://www.who.int/data/gho (accessed 12 July 2021).

Economies with higher ratings for coverage of essential health services, health workforce density, and preparedness for national and global health risks fared better during the COVID-19 pandemic.

Data presented in Figure 1.17 suggest that economies scoring higher in coverage of essential health services tended to perform better when the COVID-19 pandemic struck. The data are based on a COVID-19 Performance Index compiled by the Lowy Institute, which measures an economy's relative success in managing its pandemic situation in the 36-week period that followed its 100th confirmed case of COVID-19. Individual economies were scored from 0 to 100 based on the following indicators: (i) confirmed cases, (ii) confirmed deaths, (iii) confirmed cases per 1,000,000 people, (iv) confirmed cases as a proportion of tests, and (v) tests per 1,000 people; with higher scores representing better performance (Lowy Institute 2020). The COVID Performance Index scores are based on data available as of 13 March 2021.

Disruptions to health care systems caused by the COVID-19 pandemic could further slow the progress of SDG 3 targets or even reverse gains made.

A WHO pulse survey conducted to examine the continuity of essential health services revealed that the majority of economies covered in the study experienced disruption of essential health services during the COVID-19 pandemic (WHO 2020b). The list of health services disrupted includes "essential services for communicable diseases, noncommunicable diseases, mental health, reproductive, maternal, newborn, child and adolescent health, and nutrition" (WHO 2020b). Furthermore, other services, such as malaria prevention or immunization, were severely disrupted as these were suspended

Figure 1.17: Comparison of Essential Health Services Coverage and COVID-19 Performance

Better COVID-19 performance was noted in economies with higher scores for coverage of essential health services

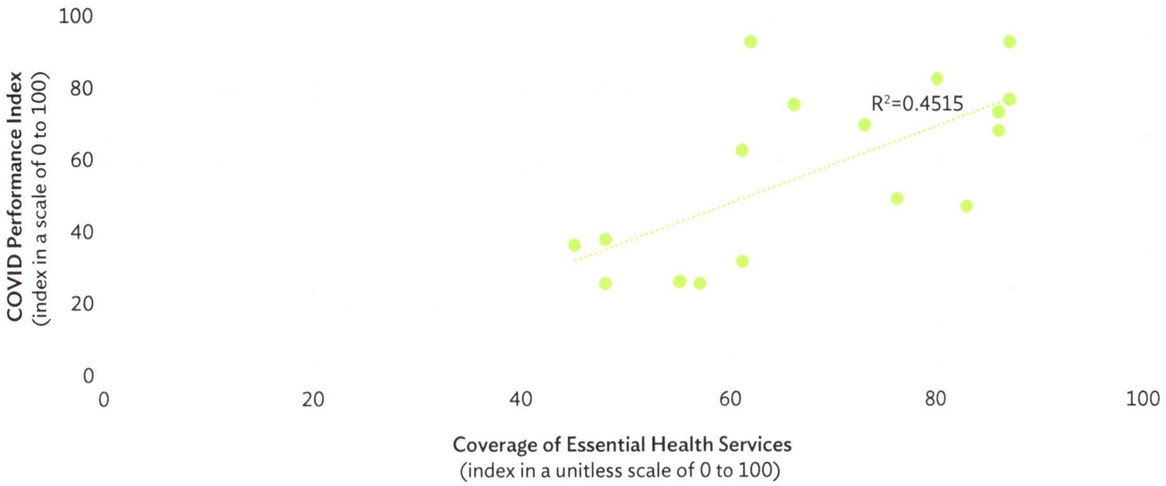

Notes: The COVID-19 Performance Index from the Lowy Institute ranges from a score of 0 (worst performing) to 100 (best performing): it is based on data available as of 13 March 2021. Coverage of Essential Health Services is an index reported on a unitless scale of 0 to 100, with 100 being the optimal value. Both indexes can be viewed as performance scores.

Sources: Asian Development Bank estimates using data presented in Table 1.3.3 of *Key Indicators for Asia and the Pacific 2021*; and Lowy Institute Covid Performance Index. https://interactives.lowyinstitute.org/features/covid-performance/ (accessed 12 July 2021).

by the respective governments. Disruptions were either partial (a change of 5% to 50% in service provision or use) or severe or complete (a change of more than 50% to 100%). WHO reports that these disruptions might have a "potentially harmful impact on population health in the short, medium, and long term", including increases in maternal, neonatal, and under-5 mortality (WHO 2020b).

Insights about the situation in Asia and the Pacific can be drawn from the World Bank's COVID-19 High-Frequency Monitoring Dashboard (World Bank 2021). Based on the dashboard data as of 30 July 2021, in only 7 of the 13 economies covered in the survey did almost all households receive medical attention when needed. The exceptions were Bangladesh (8 in every 10 households), Papua New Guinea (8 in every 10 households), Mongolia (8 in every 10 households), Pakistan (8 in every 10 households), Afghanistan (7 in every 10 households), and the Philippines (6 in every 10 households). Residents in rural areas received as much medical attention as those living in urban areas.

As in the WHO study, reasons for not receiving medical attention cited by households surveyed by the World Bank included lack of money, medical facilities at capacity, lack of transportation, and fear of catching the coronavirus. Lack of money was the most cited reason in Afghanistan, Bangladesh, Nepal, Pakistan, and Philippines.

The COVID-19 pandemic accelerated digitization and underscores its growing importance in achieving the SDG 3 targets.

The COVID-19 pandemic has fast-tracked the use of digital technology across Asia and the Pacific, emphasizing its potential as a means of achieving SDG-related health targets. For example, digital platforms were used in Viet Nam to inform citizens of proper health protocols and to raise funds for purchase of personal protective equipment for frontline workers. The Republic of Korea used global positioning system data and big data analytics to understand the spread of the virus and craft the appropriate public health response (UNESCAP, ADB, and UNDP 2021). Remote healthcare, or telemedicine, is increasingly being used in Southeast Asia to address the long queues in hospital emergency departments and to lessen the fear of getting infected (Loh 2020).

Moving forward, digital technology is expected to play a vital role in post-pandemic recovery and achievement of health-related SDG targets. The same technological tools and innovations used to manage the pandemic can also be used to significantly enhance access to, and delivery of, health services. Furthermore, given that timely, relevant, accurate, and accessible health data and reporting are necessary in tracking progress towards SDG targets, increased use of digital technology can greatly improve the availability of such data (WHO 2020a).

Education

Providing access to quality education is central to achieving the goal of ending extreme poverty.

As shown in Figure 1.18, when a higher proportion of the population has access to education (proxied by the primary education completion rate), poverty rates are lower. A study by the Education Commission estimates that, for low-income economies, a dollar invested per additional year of schooling increases gross earnings by approximately 10% in the long term (Education Commission 2016). Moreover, just by merely ensuring that all children complete school with basic reading skills, as much as 12% of the world's poor population could escape poverty (UNESCO 2016). Furthermore, if all children were learning, GDP in 2050 is forecast to be 70% higher for low-income economies, compared to outcomes under current education rates (Education Commission 2016).

Figure 1.18: Prevalence of Poverty in Relation to Primary Education Completion

Having better primary education outcomes helps to reduce the prevalence of poverty.

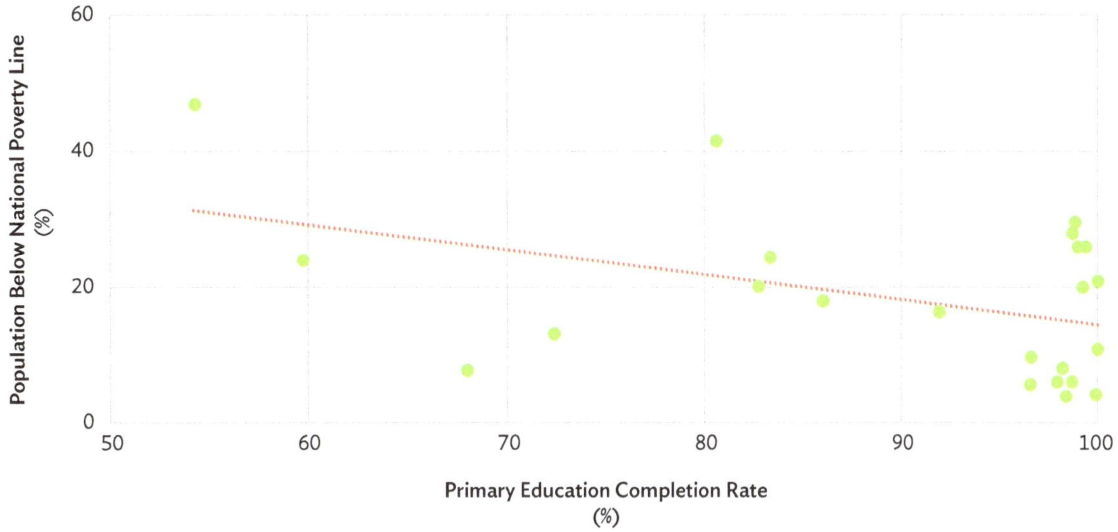

Notes: The green points represent the most recently available data on poverty and primary education completion rates for 23 economies of Asia and the Pacific with available data. The red dotted line represents the regression line.

Sources: Tables 1.1.1 and 1.4.2 of *Key Indicators for Asia and the Pacific 2021.*

Progress has been made in school attendance and education completion rates, but there is much room for improvement.

From a level of 26% in 2000, the proportion of children and youth out of primary and secondary school had declined to 19% by 2010, and dropped to 17% in 2018 (UNSD 2020c). In spite of this, 258 million children and youth around the world were still out of school in 2018. Projections also suggest that, by 2030, over 200 million children will still be out of school and that only 60% of young people will have completed upper secondary education (UNSD 2020c).

Economies in Asia and the Pacific have shown remarkable gains in primary school completion, with rates increasing by 8–11 percentage points on average, since 2000; and rates averaging around 90% by 2019 (Table 1.4.2). On average, economies in the region have sustained above 80% completion rates for primary school and above 70% for lower secondary school since 2010. However, completion rates for upper secondary levels remain below 60% and participation in organized learning has barely improved since 2016 for many economies in the region.

Students at Rita Public Elementary School during class in Majuro, Marshall Islands.

Access to education is still a challenge for poorer people.

Across Asia and the Pacific, when economy-level averages for education completion rates are compared to population wealth quintiles, a clear inequity can be seen among socioeconomic classes (Figure 1.19). Students from more affluent families continue to have significantly higher completion rates. Moreover, the gap between the bottom 20% of the population and rest of the population is not narrowing, particularly in upper secondary education completion rates.

Figure 1.19: Regional Average Education Completion Rates Compared to Two Lowest Wealth Quintiles

Learners from lower-income households have lower secondary education completion rates.

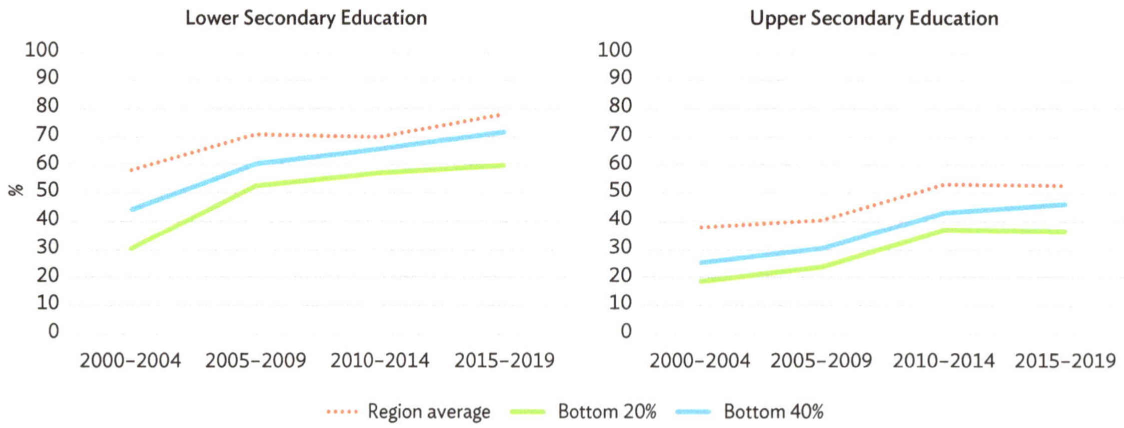

Source: Asian Development Bank estimates using data in Table 1.4.2 of *Key Indicators for Asia and the Pacific 2021*.

A focus on improving learning outcomes, not just education completion rates, is needed.

Although school attendance has increased globally, millions of children still fail to acquire even the most basic skills in their learning outcomes (World Bank 2018b; UNESCO Institute of Statistics 2019). In Asia and the Pacific, evidence of poor learning outcomes can be found in several economies, with low numbers of children and young people achieving minimum proficiency level in reading and mathematics.

Using data gathered from 2000 to 2020, Figure 1.20 shows the latest proficiency attained for reading and mathematics in select economies of the region. In about half of the economies with available data, proficiency scores were below 50% for both reading and writing at grades 2 and 3, and at the primary education levels. Moreover, more than half of the economies had proficiency scores of below 60% for both reading and writing at the lower secondary level.

Improving learning outcomes can be supported by good teaching practices.

Data from economies in Asia and the Pacific associate better teaching practices with higher proficiency in reading and mathematics. This is especially critical during primary education, where research shows that children who are lagging behind in reading proficiency in early grades are less likely to complete compulsory education (ACDP Indonesia 2014).

Figure 1.20: Proportion of Students Achieving Minimum Proficiency in Reading and Mathematics

Improving the basic reading and numeracy proficiency of students (grades 2 and 3) remains a priority, as more than half of the economies with available data had proficiency scores below 50%

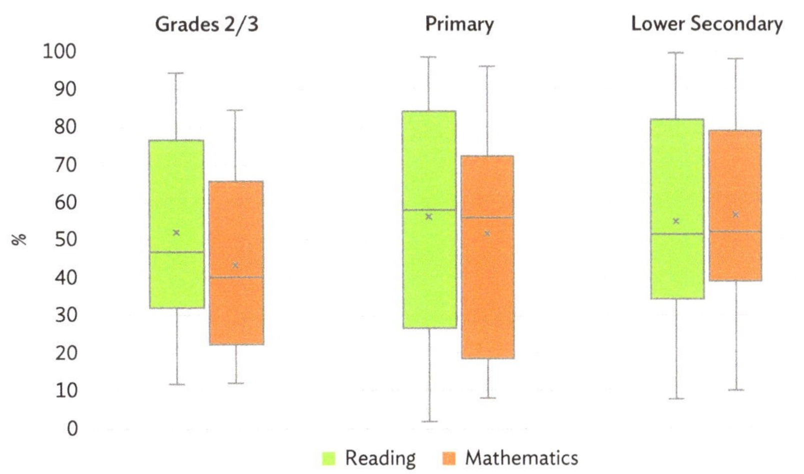

Note: Graphics based on the most recently available data for proficiency in reading and mathematics among economies of Asia and the Pacific.

Source: Table 1.4.1 of *Key Indicators for Asia and the Pacific 2021*.

Data suggest that economies of Asia and the Pacific with a lower percentage of teachers who have undergone the minimum pedagogical training at the primary level tend to deliver reduced proficiency in reading and mathematics (Figure 1.21). There also exists a positive association between prioritizing pedagogical training and proficiency of learners in reading and mathematics at the primary level, but this does not necessarily equate to better proficiency for every economy doing so.

As shown in Figure 1.21, students from lower middle-income economies usually yield lower proficiency ratings in reading and mathematics, compared to their counterparts from upper middle-income and high-income economies. This inequality in learning outcomes makes it challenging for the poor to use education as a means to escape poverty.

Figure 1.21: Proficiency in Primary-Level Reading and Mathematics, by Economy Income Level

Students from lower middle-income economies across Asia and the Pacific have exhibited relatively lower proficiency in reading and mathematics

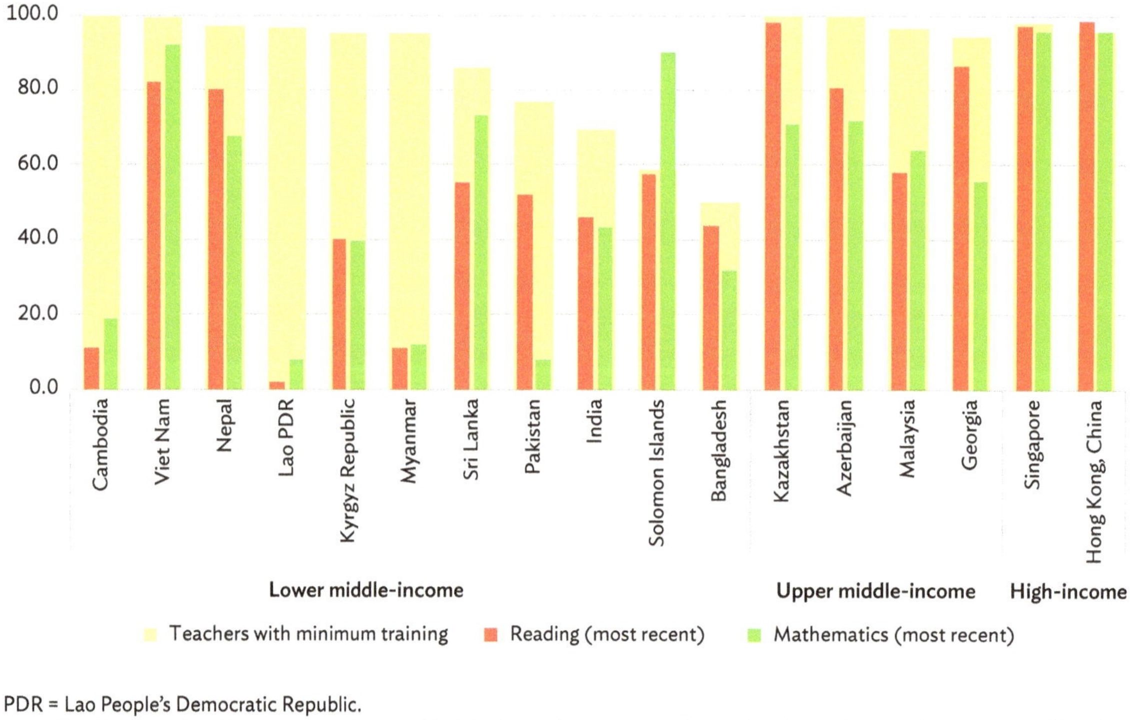

Lao PDR = Lao People's Democratic Republic.

Note: Graphics based on the most recently available data for proficiency in reading and mathematics and the proportion of teachers with minimum pedagogical training in 17 economies of Asia and the Pacific as per the World Bank's income classification system as of July 2020.

Sources: Tables 1.4.1 and 1.4.4 of *Key Indicators for Asia and the Pacific 2021*.

distance

Almost all learners in the region have been affected by school closures during the COVID-19 pandemic.

School closures, which started to be implemented within or across economies in February 2020, kept as many as 1.5 billion young students worldwide from attending face-to-face classes (UNESCO 2021).

In the Asia and Pacific region, only 5 of the 49 ADB member economies did not implement any pandemic-related school closures from pre-primary to upper secondary levels, with an estimated 825.2 million students affected.[12] This represents more than 90% of all students in Asia and the Pacific as a whole. As of April 2021, 32 of the 44 economies that implemented school closures had fully reopened their school operations. This is despite the fact that the number of COVID-19 cases recorded per month for the region had more than halved by January 2021.

12 Estimated using data on school closures and enrolment from the UNESCO Institute for Statistics database.

in Phnom Penh, Cambodia.

Despite efforts to continue school activities through remote learning, poorer students have suffered greater disruption to their education during the pandemic.

Data from the ADBI survey show that school-age children among poorer households had significantly less access to distance learning, since the schools they are enrolled in did not offer any such programs (Figure 1.22). On the other hand, where schools did offer such programs, differences in participation by children in distance learning were less evident across socioeconomic groupings.

Figure 1.22: Distance Learning Availability and Participation Rates, by Socioeconomic Grouping

In select economies, poorest households with school-age children were less likely to have access to schools that offered any type of distance learning programs.

Source: Asian Development Bank estimates using data from the Asian Development Bank Institute's Survey on the Impacts of COVID-19 and Related Policies on Households in 8 Developing Association of Southeast Asian Nations (ASEAN) Countries.

Many education systems and students in Asia and the Pacific have limited access to remote-based learning resources because of a lack of internet connectivity at home (Figure 1.23). This is generally due to a lack of infrastructure in disadvantaged communities or the inability of poor families to pay for such services (Bhattacharya 2021). In the East Asia and Pacific subregions, as much as 54% of children and youth aged 25 years and under have no home internet access, while this figure is just 13% for the same age cohort in South Asia (UNICEF and ITU 2020).

Figure 1.23: Internet Users per 100 People, by Socioeconomic Grouping

Inequality in access to information prevails, as manifested in the disparity in internet penetration rates among lower- and higher-income economies.

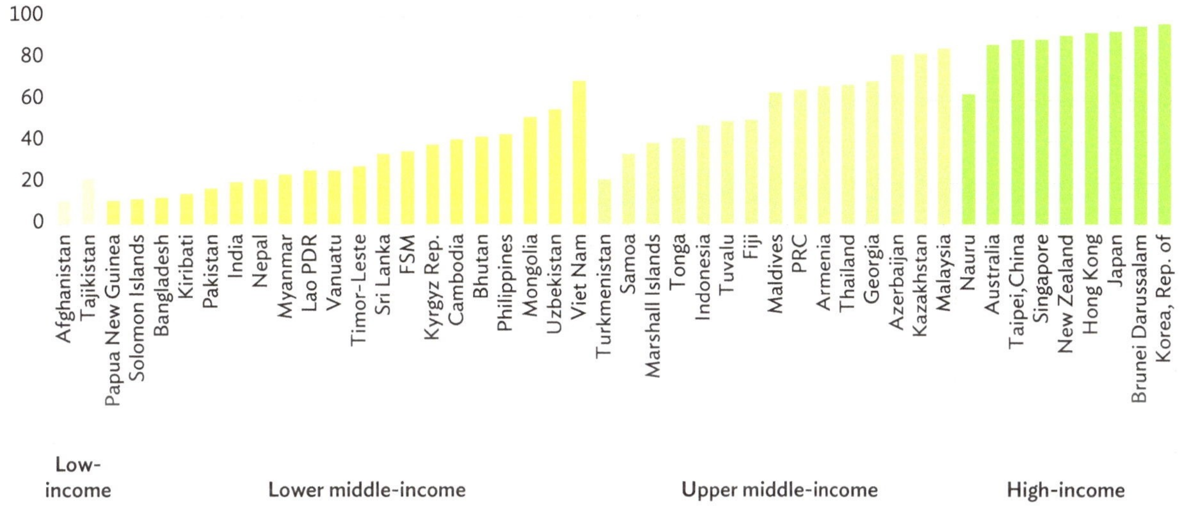

FSM = Federates States of Micronesia, Lao PDR = Lao People's Democratic Republic, PRC = People's Republic of China.

Notes: Internet users per 100 people among Asian Development Bank member economies classified using the World Bank's income classification system as of July 2020. Graphics are based on available data for the most recent year ranging from 2017 to 2020.

Source: Table 2.5.9 of *Key Indicators for Asia and the Pacific 2021*.

Disruptions arising from school closures could lead to considerable potential earning losses.

To compensate for the limitations in access to online learning resources, many economies (particularly those in the lower- and middle-income categories) resorted to other remote broadcast-based platforms, such as radio and television. However, there remain millions of students in the East Asia and Pacific subregions, along with South Asia—comprising 49% of 463 million students globally—who are beyond the reach of broadcast and digital or online-based learning approaches (UNICEF and ITU 2020).

Moreover, remote-based learning is less effective in terms of learning gains, compared to attending face-to-face classes. This is especially true among lower-income economies in the region, where learning effectiveness is expected to decline significantly (UNICEF 2020). It is estimated that learning losses may range from 8% of a learning-adjusted year of schooling in the Pacific, where schools have mostly stayed open, to 55% in South Asia, where school closures have been longest (ADB 2021b). This decline in learning effectiveness, accompanied by the increase in school dropout rates among children from poorer households, may result in a loss of $1.25 trillion for developing Asia or the equivalent of at least 5% of the region's GDP for 2020 (ADB 2021b).

References

Analytical and Capacity Development Partnership (ACDP) Indonesia. 2014. The Critical Importance of Early Grade Reading and Assessment. *ACDP Indonesia (Education Sector Analytical and Capacity Development Partnership) Working Paper December 2014*. Jakarta: ACDP. https://www.adb.org/publications/ino-early-grade-reading-and-assessment.

Asian Development Bank (ADB). 2019a. *Asian Development Outlook Supplement December 2019: Growth Slows Further in Developing Asia's Giants*. Manila: Asian Development Bank. http://dx.doi.org/10.22617/FLS190590-3.

_________. 2019b. *Ending Hunger in Asia and the Pacific by 2030: An Assessment of Investment Requirements in Agriculture*. Manila: Asian Development Bank. DOI: http://dx.doi.org/10.22617/TCS190499-2.

_________. 2021a. *Asian Development Outlook 2021: Financing a Green and Inclusive Economy*. Manila: Asian Development Bank. DOI: http://dx.doi.org/10.22617/FLS210163-3.

_________. 2021b. *Learning and Earning Losses from COVID-19 School Closures in Developing Asia. Special Topic of the Asian Development Outlook 2021*. Manila: Asian Development Bank. https://www.adb.org/sites/default/files/publication/692111/ado2021-special-topic.pdf.

_________. Key Indicators Database. https://kidb.adb.org/.

Asian Development Bank Institute (ADBI). 2020. ADBI Household Survey. https://www.adb.org/adbi/news/adbi-survey-covid-19-tests-southeast-asia-safety-nets.

A. Deaton. 2021. COVID-19 and Global Income Inequality. *NBER Working Paper Series No. 28392*. Cambridge: National Bureau of Economic Research. https://www.nber.org/papers/w28392.

S. Bhattacharya. 2021. Here's how we can get more people in Asia and the Pacific connected to the internet. Asian Development Blog. 1 February 2021. https://blogs.adb.org/blog/here-s-how-we-can-get-more-people-asia-and-pacific-connected-internet.

Development Initiatives Poverty Research Ltd (DIPR). 2020 *Global Nutrition Report: Action on Equity to End Malnutrition*. Bristol: Development Initiatives.

Education Commission. 2016. *The Learning Generation: Investing in Education for A Changing World*. New York: The International Commission on Financing Global Education Opportunity. https://report.educationcommission.org/report/.

Food and Agriculture Organization of the United Nations (FAO). FAOSTAT Database. http://www.fao.org/faostat/en/#home.

FAO, International Fund for Agricultural Development (IFAD), and World Food Programme (WFP). 2015. *The State of Food Insecurity in the World 2015: Meeting the 2015 International Hunger Targets: Taking Stock of Uneven Progress*. Rome: FAO. http://www.fao.org/3/i4646e/i4646e.pdf.

FAO, International Fund for Agricultural Development (IFAD), United Nations Children's Fund (UNICEF), World Food Programme (WFP) and World Health Organization (WHO). 2020. *The State of Food Security and Nutrition in the World 2020: Transforming Food Systems for Affordable Healthy Diets*. Rome: FAO. DOI: https://doi.org/10.4060/ca9692en.

———. 2021.The *State of Food Security and Nutrition in the World 2021: Transforming Food Systems For Food Security, Improved Nutrition and Affordable Healthy Diets for All.* Rome: FAO. https://doi.org/10.4060/cb4474en.

Lowy Institute. 2021. Covid Performance Index: Deconstructing Pandemic Responses. https://interactives.lowyinstitute.org/features/covid-performance/. 13 March.

R. Hill. and A. Narayan. 2021. What COVID-19 Can Mean for Long-Term Inequality in Developing Countries. World Bank Blogs. January 7. https://blogs.worldbank.org/voices/what-covid-19-can-mean-long-term-inequality-developing-countries.

K. Imai. and B. Malaeb. 2018. *Asia's Rural-Urban Disparity in the Context of Growing Inequality*. IFAD Research Series No. 27, Rome: IFAD. https://www.ifad.org/documents/38714170/40704142/27_research.pdf/86ff7619-8814-48d0-a232-fc694fcc55ce?eloutlink=imf2ifad.

K. Kim, S. Kim, and C.Y. Park. 2020. Food Security in Asia and the Pacific Amid the COVID-19 Pandemic. *ADB Brief No. 139*. Manila: Asian Development Bank. DOI: http://dx.doi.org/10.22617/BRF200176-2.

D. Loh. 2020. Telehealth Services Rush to Relieve ASEAN Hospitals' COVID Burden. *Nikkei Asia*, 22 December. https://asia.nikkei.com/Spotlight/Coronavirus/Telehealth-services-rush-to-relieve-ASEAN-hospitals-COVID-burden.

V.J.B. Martins, T.M.M. Toledo Florencio, L.P. Grillo, M.C.P. Franco, P.A. Martins, A.P.G. Clemente, C.D.L. Santos, M.F.A. Vireira, and A.L. Sawaya. Long-Lasting Effects of Undernutrition. *International Journal of Environmental Research and Public Health.* 2011 Jun; 8(6).pp 1817–1846.DOI: 10.3390/ijerph8061817.

P.J. Morgan and L.G. Trinh. 2021. Impacts of COVID-19 on Households in ASEAN Countries and Their Implications for Human Capital Development. *ADBI Working Paper 1226*. Tokyo: Asian Development Bank Institute.

A.F. Shorrocks and G. Wan. 2008. Ungrouping Income Distributions: Synthesising Samples for Inequality and Poverty Analysis. *Research Paper 2008/016*. Helsinki: UNU-WIDER. https://www.wider.unu.edu/sites/default/files/rp2008-16.pdf.

J.R. Stiglitz. 2020. Conquering the Great Divide. *IMF Finance and Development*, September 2020. https://www.imf.org/external/pubs/ft/fandd/2020/09/COVID19-and-global-inequality-joseph-stiglitz.htm.

United Nations Economic and Social Commission for Asia and the Pacific (UNESCAP), United Nations Development Programme (UNDP), and Asian Development Bank (ADB). 2015. *Making it Happen: Technology, Finance and Statistics for Sustainable Development in Asia and the Pacific*. Asia-Pacific Regional MDGs Report 2014/15. http://hdl.handle.net/11540/4378.

United Nations Economic and Social Commission for Asia and the Pacific (UNESCAP), Asian Development Bank (ADB), and United Nations Development Programme (UNDP). 2021. *Responding to the COVID-19 Pandemic: Leaving No Country Behind.* Bangkok: UNDP. DOI: http://dx.doi.org/10.22617/SPR210111-2.

United Nations Educational, Scientific and Cultural Organization (UNESCO). 2016. Education for people and planet: creating sustainable futures for all, Global education monitoring report, 2016. https://unesdoc.unesco.org/ark:/48223/pf0000245752.

United Nations Educational, Scientific and Cultural Organization (UNESCO). 2021. Global Education Coalition. *COVID-19 Education Response*. https://en.unesco.org/covid19/educationresponse/globalcoalition.

United Nations Educational, Scientific and Cultural Organization (UNESCO) Institute of Statistics. 2019. *Meeting Commitments: Are Countries On Track to Achieve SDG4?* Montreal: UNESCO Institute of Statistics.

United Nations Children's Fund (UNICEF) and International Telecommunications Union (ITU). 2020. *How Many Children and Young People Have Internet Access at Home? Estimating Digital Connectivity During the COVID-19 Pandemic*. New York: UNICEF. https://www.unicef.org/reports/how-many-children-and-young-people-have-internet-access-home-2020.

United Nations Children's Fund (UNICEF), World Health Organization (WHO), and World Bank. 2021. *Joint Child Malnutrition Estimates (global and regional)*. April 2021. https://data.unicef.org/resources/dataset/malnutrition-data/.

United Nations Development Program (UNDP) and Oxford Poverty and Human Development Initiative. 2020. *Global Multidimensional Poverty index 2020 – Charting Pathways out of Multidimensional Poverty: Achieving the SDGs. Report*. Report. United Nations Development Programme and Oxford Poverty and Human Development Initiative. https://ophi.org.uk/global-mpi-report-2020/.

United Nations Statistics Division (UNSD). 2020a. Metadata for Indicator 3.8.1: Coverage of Essential Health Services. *SDG Indicators Metadata Repository*. https://unstats.un.org/sdgs/metadata/.

———. 2020b. Metadata for Indicator 3.d.1: Coverage of Essential Health Services. SDG Indicators Metadata Repository. https://unstats.un.org/sdgs/metadata/.

———. 2020c. *The Sustainable Development Goals Report 2020*. https://unstats.un.org/sdgs/report/2020/The-Sustainable-Development-Goals-Report-2020.pdf.

World Bank. 2018a. *Riding the Wave: An East Asian Miracle for the 21st Century*. World Bank East Asia and Pacific Regional Report. Washington, DC: World Bank.

———. 2018b. *World Development Report 2018: Learning to Realize Education's Promise*. Washington, DC: World Bank. DOI: doi:10.1596/978-1-4648-1096-1.

———. 2020a. *Food Security*. October 20, 2020. https://www.worldbank.org/en/topic/food-security.

———. 2020b. SDG 2: Zero Hunger. Beyond Hunger: Ensuring Food Security for All. *Atlas of Sustainable Development Goals from World Development Indicators 2020*. https://datatopics.worldbank.org/sdgatlas/goal-2-zero-hunger/.

———. 2021a. "COVID-19 High-Frequency Monitoring Dashboard". The World Bank Group. Washington, D.C. https://www.worldbank.org/en/data/interactive/2020/11/11/covid-19-high-frequency-monitoring-dashboard.

———. 2021b. *Global Economic Prospects, January 2021*. Washington, DC: World Bank. DOI: 10.1596/978-1-4648-1612-3. License: Creative Commons Attribution CC BY 3.0 IGO.

———. PovcalNet Database. http://iresearch.worldbank.org/PovcalNet/home.aspx. (accessed July 2021).

World Health Organization (WHO). 2016. Health Workforce Requirements for Universal Health Coverage and the Sustainable Development Goals. Background Paper No. 1 to the Global Strategy on Human Resources for Health. *Human Resources For Health Observer Series No. 17* Geneva: World Health Organization. https://apps.who.int/iris/handle/10665/250330.

———. 2020a. *Health Data: A Critical Element to Meet the SDGs*. 13 May. https://www.who.int/data/stories/health-data-a-critical-element-to-meet-the-sdgs.

———. 2020b. *Pulse Survey on Continuity of Essential Health Services During the COVID-19 Pandemic*. Geneva: World Health Organization. https://apps.who.int/iris/handle/10665/334048.

———. 2020c. State of the World's Nursing 2020: Investing in Education, Jobs and Leadership. Geneva: World Health Organization. https://www.who.int/publications/i/item/9789240003279.

———. 2020d. World Health Statistics 2020: Monitoring Health for the SDGs, Sustainable Development Goals. Geneva: WHO. https://apps.who.int/iris/bitstream/handle/10665/332070/9789240005105-eng.pdf.

———. 2021. *Obesity and Overweight*. June 2021. https://www.who.int/news-room/fact-sheets/detail/obesity-and-overweight.

J. Zhuang. 2020. Mind the Gap in Combating COVID-19. 5 August 2020. https://www.adb.org/news/op-ed/mind-gap-combating-covid-19-juzhong-zhuang.

Table 1.1.1: Selected Indicators for Sustainable Development Goal 1—No Poverty

ADB Regional Member	Target 1.1: By 2030, eradicate extreme poverty for all people everywhere, measured as people living below the international poverty line of $1.90 a day (2011 PPP)						
	1.1.1.a: Proportion of Population Living below the $1.90 a Day (2011 PPP) Poverty Line[a,b] (%)		1.1.1.b: Proportion of Employed Population Living below the International Poverty Line, by Age Group and Sex[b,c] (%) 2019 Age Group				
			15+			15-24	25+
	2010	2019	Total	Female	Male		
Developing ADB Member Economies							
Central and West Asia							
Afghanistan	...	...	34.3	45.0	31.4	41.0	31.5
Armenia	1.0	1.1	0.3	0.4	0.3	0.4	0.3
Azerbaijan[d]	0.0 (2005)	...	0.0	0.0	0.0	0.0	0.0
Georgia	12.0	3.8	3.0	2.6	3.3	3.8	2.9
Kazakhstan	0.1	0.0 (2018)	0.0	0.0	0.0	0.0	0.0
Kyrgyz Republic	2.8	0.6	0.1	0.1	0.2	0.1	0.1
Pakistan	8.3	4.4 (2018)	1.3	1.5	1.3	1.4	1.3
Tajikistan	4.0 (2009)	4.1 (2015)	1.7	2.3	1.4	2.0	1.7
Turkmenistan	...	...	0.2	0.2	0.3	0.3	0.2
Uzbekistan[d]	61.6 (2003)	...	7.3	5.0	8.9	8.1	7.2
East Asia							
China, People's Republic of	11.2	0.5 (2016)	0.3	0.3	0.2	0.4	0.2
Hong Kong, China[f]	...	...	0.0	0.0	0.0	0.0	0.0
Korea, Republic of[f]	0.5	0.2 (2016)	0.0	0.0	0.0	0.0	0.0
Mongolia	0.7	0.5 (2018)	0.1	0.1	0.1	0.2	0.1
Taipei,China	0.0	0.0 (2016)	0.0	0.0	0.0	0.1	0.0
South Asia							
Bangladesh	19.2	14.3 (2016)	5.6	6.2	5.3	6.3	5.4
Bhutan	2.2 (2012)	1.5 (2017)	0.8	1.0	0.7	1.4	0.7
India	22.5 (2011)	...	7.7	8.6	7.4	10.4	7.3
Maldives	3.5 (2009)	0.0 (2016)	0.1	0.1	0.1	0.1	0.1
Nepal	15.0	...	4.3	4.4	4.3	4.4	4.3
Sri Lanka	2.8 (2009)	1.0 (2016)	0.4	0.4	0.4	0.5	0.4
Southeast Asia							
Brunei Darussalam	...	...	0.0	0.0	0.0	0.0	0.0
Cambodia[j]	...	...	9.9	9.2	10.6	11.8	9.4
Indonesia	13.3	2.7	3.5	3.6	3.4	3.7	3.5
Lao People's Democratic Republic	14.5 (2012)	10.0 (2018)	7.8	7.3	8.3	10.6	7.0
Malaysia	0.1 (2011)	0.0 (2015)	0.0	0.0	0.0	0.0	0.0
Myanmar	...	1.4 (2017)	1.0	1.1	1.0	1.4	1.0
Philippines	10.5 (2009)	4.7 (2018)	2.2	1.9	2.4	2.7	2.1
Singapore	...	...	0.0	0.0	0.0	0.0	0.0
Thailand	0.1	0.1	0.0	0.0	0.0	0.0	0.0
Timor-Leste	37.4 (2007)	22.0 (2014)	16.6	15.5	17.4	20.1	15.7
Viet Nam	4.0	1.8 (2018)	1.9	2.1	1.8	3.6	1.7
The Pacific							
Cook Islands	...	...	...	...	...	...	...
Fiji	1.6 (2008)	...	0.1	0.1	0.1	0.1	0.1
Kiribati	12.9 (2006)	...	...	...	...	...	...
Marshall Islands	...	...	...	...	...	...	...
Micronesia, Federated States of	15.4 (2013)	...	...	...	...	...	...
Nauru	0.9 (2012)	...	...	...	...	...	...
Niue	...	...	...	...	...	...	...
Palau	...	...	...	...	...	...	...
Papua New Guinea	38.0 (2009)	...	22.6	29.9	15.5	31.9	19.9
Samoa	0.6 (2008)	...	...	...	...	...	...
Solomon Islands	24.7 (2012)	...	20.9	19.2	22.6	25.9	19.1
Tonga	1.1 (2009)	1.0 (2015)	...	...	...	...	...
Tuvalu	3.3	...	...	...	...	...	...
Vanuatu	13.2	...	...	...	...	...	...
Developed ADB Member Economies							
Australia	...	...	...	...	...	...	...
Japan	...	...	...	...	...	...	...
New Zealand	...	...	...	...	...	...	...

Table 1.1.1: Selected Indicators for Sustainable Development Goal 1—No Poverty *(continued)*

ADB Regional Member	Target 1.2: By 2030, reduce at least by half the proportion of men, women, and children of all ages living in poverty in all its dimensions according to national definitions 1.2.1: Proportion of Population Living below the National Poverty Line, by Urban-Rural Location[a] (%)					
	2010			2019		
	Total	Urban	Rural	Total	Urban	Rural
Developing ADB Member Economies						
Central and West Asia						
Afghanistan	38.3 (2011)	...	...	47.3 (2020)	47.0 (2020)	46.7 (2020)
Armenia	35.8	35.7	36.0	26.4	22.2	33.2
Azerbaijan[d]	9.1	...	...	6.2 (2020)	...	...
Georgia	37.3 [e]	32.7 [e]	43.3 [e]	21.3 [e] (2020)	18.0 [e] (2018)	23.1 [e] (2018)
Kazakhstan	6.5	3.7	10.1	4.3	1.3 (2015)	4.4 (2015)
Kyrgyz Republic	33.7	23.6	39.5	20.1	29.3 (2015)	33.6 (2015)
Pakistan	36.8	18.2 (2013)	...	24.3 (2015)	12.5 (2015)	30.7 (2015)
Tajikistan	34.3 (2013)	...	...	26.3	...	...
Turkmenistan	...	...	...	...	...	...
Uzbekistan[d]	17.7	...	...	11.0	...	...
East Asia						
China, People's Republic of	...	...	17.2	...	...	0.6
Hong Kong, China[f]	15.7	...	...	15.8	...	...
Korea, Republic of[f]	18.6 (2011)	...	...	16.3	...	...
Mongolia	38.8	33.2	49.0	28.4 (2018)	27.2 (2018)	30.8 (2018)
Taipei,China	1.2 [g]	...	...	1.3 [g]	...	...
South Asia						
Bangladesh	31.5	21.3	35.2	20.5	...	...
Bhutan	12.0 (2012)	1.8 (2012)	16.7 (2012)	8.2 (2017)	0.8 (2017)	11.9 (2017)
India	21.9 [h] (2011)	13.7 [h] (2011)	25.7 [h] (2011)	...	...	...
Maldives	...	...	...	8.2 [i] (2016)	...	...
Nepal	25.2	15.5	27.4	...	...	...
Sri Lanka	6.7 (2012)	2.1 (2012)	7.6 (2012)	4.1 (2016)	1.9 (2016)	4.3 (2016)
Southeast Asia						
Brunei Darussalam	...	...	...	...	...	...
Cambodia[j]	21.1	17.0	22.7	...	...	...
Indonesia	13.3	9.9	16.6	9.8 [k] (2020)	7.4 [k] (2020)	12.8 [k] (2020)
Lao People's Democratic Republic	23.2 (2012)	10.0 (2012)	28.6 (2012)	18.3 (2018)	...	...
Malaysia	1.7 (2011)	1.0 (2012)	...	5.6	0.2 (2016)	1.0 (2016)
Myanmar	42.4	...	...	24.8 (2017)	11.3 (2017)	30.2 (2017)
Philippines	25.2 (2012)	13.0 (2012)	...	16.7 (2018)	9.3 (2018)	24.5 (2018)
Singapore	...	...	...	...	...	...
Thailand	16.4	...	...	6.2	...	...
Timor-Leste	41.8 (2014)	28.3 (2014)	47.1 (2014)	...	...	...
Viet Nam	14.2	6.9	17.4	5.8 (2016)	2.0 (2016)	7.5 (2016)
The Pacific						
Cook Islands	...	...	...	...	...	...
Fiji	28.1 [l] (2013)	19.8 [l] (2013)	36.7 [l] (2013)	29.9 [l]	...	...
Kiribati	...	...	...	...	...	...
Marshall Islands	...	...	...	...	...	...
Micronesia, Federated States of	41.2 [l] (2013)	...	...	...	...	...
Nauru	24.0 [l] (2013)	...	...	...	...	...
Niue	...	...	...	...	...	...
Palau	...	...	...	...	...	...
Papua New Guinea	...	...	...	37.5 [l] (2017)	...	...
Samoa	18.8 [l] (2013)	...	...	...	...	...
Solomon Islands	12.7 [m] (2012)	9.1 [m] (2012)	13.6 [m] (2012)	...	...	...
Tonga	...	...	...	27.0 [l] (2015)	...	...
Tuvalu	26.3 [l]	24.8	27.5 [l]	...	...	...
Vanuatu	12.7 [l]	... [l]	10.0 [l]	...	...	...
Developed ADB Member Economies						
Australia	...	...	...	...	...	...
Japan	...	...	...	...	...	...
New Zealand	...	...	...	...	...	...

... = data not available, 0.0 = magnitude is less than half of unit employed or true zero, $ = United States dollars, ADB = Asian Development Bank, PPP = purchasing power parity.

a For Indicator 1.1.1.a and Indicator 1.2.1, the year indicated in the table refers to the year when the household survey data were collected. For economies in which the household survey data collection period bridged 2 calendar years, the table reports the first year.

b For Indicator 1.1.1.a, data are consumption-based, except for Malaysia; the Republic of Korea; and Taipei,China, whose estimates are income-based. For Indicator 1.1.1.a and Indicator 1.1.1.b, the estimates are based on the international poverty line of $1.90 a day (2011 PPP).

c Data are taken from estimates and projections modeled by the International Labour Organization (ILO). These modeled estimates present an internationally comparable series, which consists of estimates from economy's official sources and imputations for missing data. Global and regional estimates are updated by the ILO annually.

d For Indicator 1.1.1a, the latest available estimate for Azerbaijan is for 2005: 0.0%. For Uzbekistan, the latest available estimate is for 2003: 61.6%.

e Refers to absolute poverty or the share of the population under the absolute poverty line.

f For indicator 1.2.1, for Hong Kong, China, data refer to the poverty rate after policy intervention (recurrent cash). For the Republic of Korea, data refer to the relative poverty rate.

g Refers to the percentage of the low-income population to the total population.

h Based on the Tendulkar methodology, using mixed reference period.

i Based on half the median of total consumption expenditure equivalent to Maldivian Rufiyaa 74.

j For Indicator 1.2.1, the most recent year estimate for Cambodia is for 2014: 13.5%(national), 12.8%(urban) and 12.5%(rural). The urban and rural poverty estimates refer to other areas excluding Phnom Penh.

k Reference period is March 2020.

l Data refer to the percentage of the population living below the basic-needs poverty line.

m Refers to the poverty headcount ratio using the upper poverty line, which serves as spatial deflator with respect to Honiara (the Solomon Islands capital).

Source: For indicator 1.1.1a: World Bank. PovcalNet Database. http://iresearch.worldbank.org/PovcalNet/povDuplicateWB.aspx (accessed 09 July 2021); and United Nations Statistics Division. Sustainable Development Goals (SDGs), SDG Indicators, Global Database. http://unstats.un.org/sdgs/indicators/database/ (accessed 12 July 2021). For indicator 1.1.1b: International Labour Organisation. ILOSTAT. http://www.ilo.org/ilostat (accessed 12 July 2021). For indicator 1.2.1: Economy's official sources; United Nations Statistics Division. Sustainable Development Goals (SDGs), SDG Indicators, Global Database. http://unstats.un.org/sdgs/indicators/database/ (accessed 12 July 2021); and Secretariat of the Pacific Community. National Minimum Development Indicators. https://www.spc.int/nmdi/ (accessed 12 July 2021).

Table 1.1.2: Selected Indicators for Sustainable Development Goal 1—Social Protection

ADB Regional Member	Target 1.3: Implement nationally appropriate social protection systems and measures for all, including floors, and by 2030 achieve substantial coverage of the poor and the vulnerable				
	1.3.1.a: Proportion of Population Covered by at least One Social Protection Benefit (%)		1.3.1.b: Proportion of Population above Statutory Pensionable Age Receiving a Pension (%)		
	2015	2020	2010	2015	2020
Developing ADB Member Economies					
Central and West Asia					
Afghanistan	...	7.5	10.7	...	24.7
Armenia	47.3 (2016)	54.4	87.0 (2000)	68.5 (2016)	65.2
Azerbaijan	40.3 (2016)	39.0	97.0 (2000)	81.1 (2016)	72.8
Georgia	28.6 (2016)	97.1	80.0 (2000)	91.9 (2016)	90.9
Kazakhstan	100.0 (2016)	100.0	100.0 (2000)	82.6 (2016)	99.6
Kyrgyz Republic	...	41.7	86.0 (2000)	100.0 (2016)	100.0
Pakistan	...	9.2	2.3	...	5.8
Tajikistan	...	26.6	88.0 (2005)	92.8 (2016)	93.7
Turkmenistan	...	...	...	...	...
Uzbekistan	...	42.7	98.1	100.0 (2017)	100.0
East Asia					
China, People's Republic of	63.0 (2016)	70.8	24.0 (2000)	100.0 (2016)	100.0
Hong Kong, China	...	59.7	76.0 (2000)	72.9 (2016)	73.2
Korea, Republic of	65.7 (2016)	77.3	...	100.0 (2014)	100.0
Mongolia	72.4 (2016)	100.0	80.0 (2000)	100.0 (2016)	100.0
Taipei,China	...	...	...	...	...
South Asia					
Bangladesh	28.4 (2016)	...	6.0 (2002)	33.4 (2016)	39.0
Bhutan	...	8.8	3.2 (2012)	...	18.8 (2019)
India	22.0 (2016)	24.4	7.0 (2000)	25.2 (2016)	42.5
Maldives	...	21.2	99.7 (2012)	...	100.0
Nepal	...	17.0	62.5	...	84.2
Sri Lanka	30.4 (2016)	36.4	19.0 (2000)	25.2 (2016)	35.7
Southeast Asia					
Brunei Darussalam	...	34.1	81.7 (2011)	...	100.0
Cambodia	...	6.2	1.0 (2000)	3.2 (2016)	6.6 (2018)
Indonesia	...	27.8	6.0 (2002)	14.0 (2016)	14.8
Lao People's Democratic Republic	...	12.1	5.6	...	6.3
Malaysia	...	27.3	19.8	...	18.6
Myanmar	...	6.3	...	0.9 (2016)	14.9
Philippines	47.1 (2016)	36.7	20.0 (2000)	39.8 (2016)	20.5
Singapore	...	100.0	...	...	33.1
Thailand	...	68.0	5.0 (2000)	83.0 (2016)	89.1
Timor-Leste	...	30.6	...	89.7 (2016)	100.0
Viet Nam	37.9 (2016)	38.8	16.0 (2000)	39.9 (2016)	40.9
The Pacific					
Cook Islands	...	86.3 (2019)	...	...	100.0
Fiji	...	58.9	9.0 (2000)	10.6	92.1
Kiribati	...	21.0	...	...	93.8
Marshall Islands	...	25.2	64.2	...	62.7
Micronesia, Federated States of	...	19.4	...	...	100.0
Nauru	...	45.4 (2019)	56.5	...	95.7
Niue	...	...	...	...	...
Palau	...	35.8 (2019)	48.0	...	100.0
Papua New Guinea	...	9.6	0.9	...	22.3
Samoa	...	21.1	49.5 (2011)	...	91.4
Solomon Islands	...	1.1 (2019)	13.1	...	20.5 (2019)
Tonga	...	22.2	...	...	90.0
Tuvalu	...	...	15.0 (2000)	...	...
Vanuatu	...	57.4	3.5 (2011)	...	8.5 (2019)
Developed ADB Member Economies					
Australia	82.0 (2016)	100.0	80.0 (2000)	74.3 (2016)	100.0
Japan	75.4 (2016)	98.0	74.0 (2000)	100.0 (2014)	100.0
New Zealand	66.6 (2016)	100.0	100.0 (2000)	100.0 (2016)	100.0

Table 1.1.2: Selected Indicators for Sustainable Development Goal 1—Social Protection *(continued)*

ADB Regional Member	Target 1.3: Implement nationally appropriate social protection systems and measures for all, including floors, and by 2030 achieve substantial coverage of the poor and the vulnerable					
	1.3.1.c: Proportion of Poor Population Receiving Social Assistance Cash Benefit (%)		1.3.1.d: Proportion of Vulnerable Population Receiving Social Assistance Cash Benefit (%)		1.3.1.e: Proportion of Children/ Households Receiving Child/ Family Cash Benefit (%)	
	2015	2020	2015	2020	2015	2020
Developing ADB Member Economies						
Central and West Asia						
Afghanistan	...	...	...	5.9	...	0.4
Armenia	38.2 (2016)	100.0 (2018)	16.2 (2016)	19.6	21.4 (2016)	30.2
Azerbaijan	100.0 (2016)	100.0 (2018)	12.6 (2016)	13.4	...	16.9
Georgia	100.0 (2016)	100.0 (2018)	12.0 (2016)	92.9	...	48.1
Kazakhstan	28.9 (2016)	...	100.0 (2016)	74.2	100.0 (2016)	57.4
Kyrgyz Republic	...	89.4 (2018)	...	14.1	17.8 (2016)	16.9
Pakistan	...	69.2 (2018)	...	5.0	...	5.4
Tajikistan	...	28.1 (2018)	...	7.5	6.4 (2016)	14.0
Turkmenistan	...	...	...	...	...	...
Uzbekistan	68.0 (2017)	82.5 (2018)	16.0 (2017)	15.6	22.0 (2017)	29.2
East Asia						
China, People's Republic of	51.6 (2016)	100.0	31.0 (2017)	33.2	2.2 (2016)	3.0
Hong Kong, China	...	...	...	28.3	...	...
Korea, Republic of	21.4 (2016)	...	...	48.9	...	40.0
Mongolia	94.9 (2016)	100.0 (2018)	35.1 (2016)	88.5	100.0 (2016)	85.0
Taipei,China	...	...	...	...	...	...
South Asia						
Bangladesh	11.0 (2016)	61.0 (2018)	4.3 (2016)	14.9	29.4 (2016)	29.4
Bhutan	...	60.2 (2018)	...	5.0	...	13.5
India	...	...	10.4 (2016)	16.4	...	24.1
Maldives	...	100.0 (2018)	...	8.1	...	8.2
Nepal	...	70.1 (2018)	...	14.8	...	22.9
Sri Lanka	51.5 (2016)	100.0 (2018)	4.4 (2016)	16.0	...	32.0
Southeast Asia						
Brunei Darussalam	...	...	...	14.7	...	...
Cambodia	...	48.4 (2018)	...	4.3	...	4.5
Indonesia	...	100.0 (2018)	...	16.5	...	25.6
Lao People's Democratic Republic	...	0.1 (2018)	...	7.7	...	...
Malaysia	...	100.0 (2018)	...	2.1	...	2.8
Myanmar	...	0.8 (2018)	...	1.1	...	2.1
Philippines	...	100.0 (2018)	7.8 (2016)	22.4	13.6 (2016)	31.1
Singapore	...	...	...	100.0	...	...
Thailand	...	100.0 (2019)	...	54.3	18.9 (2016)	21.0
Timor-Leste	...	94.9 (2018)	...	26.5	30.7 (2016)	38.2
Viet Nam	...	100.0 (2018)	10.0 (2016)	24.6	...	1.0 (2019)
The Pacific						
Cook Islands	...	...	...	85.8	...	100.0
Fiji	...	68.0 (2018)	...	28.2	...	2.6
Kiribati	...	15.9 (2018)	...	5.1	...	1.3
Marshall Islands	...	...	...	1.7	...	...
Micronesia, Federated States of	...	...	...	2.2	...	6.8
Nauru	...	...	...	45.4	...	...
Niue	...	...	...	...	...	...
Palau	...	56.0 (2018)	...	17.8	...	60.0 (2019)
Papua New Guinea	...	...	...	...	...	...
Samoa	...	69.2 (2018)	...	5.3	...	– (2018)
Solomon Islands	...	2.9 (2018)	...	0.4 (2019)	...	...
Tonga	...	16.7 (2018)	...	6.2	...	3.3
Tuvalu	...	...	...	...	...	...
Vanuatu	...	100.0 (2018)	...	53.3	...	12.9 (2019)
Developed ADB Member Economies						
Australia	100.0 (2016)	...	53.0 (2016)	100.0	100.0 (2016)	100.0
Japan	...	...	...	100.0	...	85.4
New Zealand	37.4 (2016)	...	9.7 (2016)	100.0	...	67.1

... = data not available, – = magnitude equals zero, ADB = Asian Development Bank

Note: The population covered by at least one social protection benefit (effective coverage) refers to the proportion of the total population receiving at least one contributory or noncontributory cash benefit, or actively contributing to at least one social security scheme. For children, older persons, and the poor and vulnerable, effective coverage is expressed as a share of the respective population.

Source: United Nations Statistics Division. Global SDG Indicators Database. https://unstats.un.org/sdgs/indicators/database/ (accessed 19 July 2021).

Goal 2. End hunger, achieve food security and improved nutrition, and promote sustainable agriculture

Table 1.2.1: Selected Indicators for Sustainable Development Goal 2—Zero Hunger

	Target 2.1: By 2030, end hunger and ensure access by all people, in particular the poor and people in vulnerable situations, including infants, to safe, nutritious, and sufficient food all year round		Target 2.2: By 2030, end all forms of malnutrition, including achieving, by 2025, the internationally agreed targets on stunting and wasting in children under 5 years of age, and address the nutritional needs of adolescent girls, pregnant and lactating women, and older persons					
ADB Regional Member	2.1.1: Prevalence of Undernourishment (%)		2.2.1: Prevalence of Stunting among Children under 5 Years of Age[a] (%)		2.2.2.c: Prevalence of Malnutrition (Overweight) among Children under 5 Years of Age[a] (%)		2.2.2.d: Prevalence of Malnutrition (Wasting) among Children under 5 Years of Age (%)	
	2010[b]	2019[c]	2010	2020	2010	2020	2010	2019
Developing ADB Member Economies								
Central and West Asia[d]	...	...	**38.9**	**30.7**	**6.1**	**4.1**	...	...
Afghanistan	23.7	25.6	47.2	35.1	5.6	3.9	8.6 (2004)	5.1 (2018)
Armenia	4.3	3.4	15.6	9.1	15.9	10.8	4.1	4.4 (2016)
Azerbaijan	<2.5	<2.5	18.4	16.3	11.3	9.4	6.6 (2011)	3.2 (2013)
Georgia	4.2	8.7	10.3	5.7	16.0	7.6	1.3 (2009)	0.6 (2018)
Kazakhstan	3.5	<2.5	12.3	6.7	12.0	8.8	4.1	3.1 (2015)
Kyrgyz Republic	8.3	7.2	17.7	11.4	8.4	5.8	1.3 (2009)	2.0 (2018)
Pakistan	15.9	12.9	44.2	36.7	4.9	3.4	14.9 (2011)	7.1 (2018)
Tajikistan	...	...	29.5	15.3	6.4	3.5	4.3 (2009)	5.6 (2017)
Turkmenistan	4.5	4.1	14.7	7.6	5.4	3.8	7.2 (2006)	4.1
Uzbekistan	5.4	<2.5	15.8	9.9	10.1	5.0	4.4 (2006)	1.8 (2017)
East Asia[d]	...	...	**8.6**	**4.7**	**7.0**	**8.3**	...	...
China, People's Republic of	<2.5	<2.5	8.7	4.7	7.0	8.3	2.3	1.9 (2017)
Hong Kong, China	<2.5	<2.5	...	...	...	...	...	...
Korea, Republic of	<2.5	<2.5	2.3	2.2	7.4	8.8	1.2 (2009)	...
Mongolia	19.1	4.3	15.2	7.1	10.1	10.1	1.6	0.9 (2018)
Taipei,China	4.6	3.3	...	...	...	...	...	...
South Asia[d]	...	...	**43.7**	**30.6**	**2.4**	**1.9**	...	...
Bangladesh	15.2	9.7	40.2	30.2	1.5	2.1	15.7 (2011)	9.8
Bhutan	...	...	33.0	22.4	6.0	5.2	5.9	...
India	16.0	15.3	44.5	30.9	2.6	1.9	20.0 (2006)	17.3 (2017)
Maldives	...	...	18.3	14.2	5.9	4.6	10.6 (2009)	9.1 (2017)
Nepal	10.5	4.8	42.8	30.4	1.3	1.8	11.2 (2011)	12.0
Sri Lanka	11.3	6.8	17.2	16.0	1.2	1.3	11.8 (2009)	15.1 (2016)
Southeast Asia[d]	...	...	**31.6**	**27.4**	**5.3**	**7.5**	...	...
Brunei Darussalam	<2.5	<2.5	18.4	12.7	8.1	9.3	2.9 (2009)	...
Cambodia	13.3	6.2	37.5	29.9	2.3	2.1	11.0	9.7 (2014)
Indonesia	13.0	6.5	35.7	31.8	7.2	11.1	12.3	10.2 (2018)
Lao People's Democratic Republic	16.0	5.3	43.2	30.2	2.2	3.0	5.9 (2011)	9.0 (2017)
Malaysia	3.2	3.2	17.9	20.9	6.0	6.1	13.2 (2006)	9.7
Myanmar	13.1	7.6	33.2	25.2	2.6	1.5	7.9 (2009)	6.7 (2018)
Philippines	13.4	9.4	32.7	28.7	3.1	4.2	7.0 (2011)	5.6 (2018)
Singapore	...	...	3.3	2.8	3.8	4.8	3.6 (2000)	...
Thailand	10.0	8.2	14.9	12.3	8.4	9.2	6.7 (2012)	7.7
Timor-Leste	32.5	22.6	54.4	48.8	3.1	2.6	18.9 (2009)	9.9 (2013)
Viet Nam	11.0	6.7	27.6	22.3	3.7	6.0	4.1	5.8 (2017)
The Pacific[d]	...	...	**40.9**	**42.1**	**7.1**	**8.1**	...	...
Cook Islands	...	...	...	...	...	...	...	...
Fiji	4.0	5.6	8.5	7.5	4.7	5.2	6.3 (2004)	...
Kiribati	5.6	4.1	16.3	14.9	2.4	2.4	...	3.5 (2018)
Marshall Islands	...	...	37.6	32.2	4.0	4.2	...	3.5 (2017)
Micronesia, Federated States of	...	...	...	...	...	...	...	...
Nauru	...	...	21.6	15.0	3.1	3.7	1.0 (2007)	...
Niue	...	...	...	...	...	...	...	...
Palau	...	...	...	...	...	...	...	...
Papua New Guinea	22.7	24.6	46.6	48.4	7.7	8.9	14.1	...
Samoa	4.2	4.6	5.6	6.8	6.6	7.1	...	3.1
Solomon Islands	13.5	16.5	33.0	29.3	3.4	4.0	4.3 (2007)	8.5 (2015)
Tonga	...	...	7.8	2.6	13.0	12.6	5.2 (2012)	1.1
Tuvalu	...	...	10.1	9.7	6.1	6.4	3.3 (2007)	...
Vanuatu	5.2	9.3	27.0	28.7	4.8	4.9	5.9 (2008)	4.7 (2013)
Developed ADB Member Economies[d]	...	...	**5.9**	**4.6**	**4.2**	**6.5**	...	...
Australia	<2.5	<2.5	2.0	2.1	13.0	18.5	– (2007)	...
Japan	2.7	<2.5	6.9	5.5	1.9	2.4	2.3	...
New Zealand	<2.5	<2.5	...	...	...	...	...	...
DEVELOPING ADB MEMBER ECONOMIES[d]	...	...	**31.8**	**23.1**	**4.6**	**4.9**	...	...
ALL ADB REGIONAL MEMBERS[d]	...	...	**31.3**	**22.8**	**4.6**	**5.0**	...	...
WORLD	**9.2**	**9.9** (2020)	**27.7**	**22.0**	**5.6**	**5.7**	...	**6.7** (2020)

... = data not available, < = less than, – = magnitude equals zero, ADB = Asian Development Bank.

a Refers to modeled estimates from the Joint Child Malnutrition Estimates Database. The estimates for 2020 do not account for the full impact of COVID-19. Household survey data on child height and age were not collected in 2020 due to physical-distancing policies. One of the covariates used in the model takes the impact of COVID-19 partially into account.
b Economy level data refer to 3-year average for 2009–2011. World estimate refers to annual value.
c Economy level data refer to 3-year average for 2018–2020. World estimate refers to annual value.
d For indicators 2.2.1 and 2.2.2.c, estimated as weighted averages using total population of children 0–5 years old from the United Nations' World Population Prospects 2019 and official communication from The Pacific Community's Statistics for Development Division as weight.

Source: For Indicator 2.1.1: Food and Agriculture Organization of the United Nations. FAOSTAT Database. http://www.fao.org/faostat/en/#data/FS (accessed 17 July 2021). For Indicator 2.2.1, Indicator 2.2.2.c, and Indicator 2.2.2.d: United Nations Statistics Division. Global SDG Indicators Database. https://unstats.un.org/sdgs/indicators/database/ (accessed 7 July 2021) and UNICEF/WHO/World Bank Joint Child Malnutrition Estimates Database. https://data.unicef.org/resources/dataset/malnutrition-data/ (accessed 24 May 2021). For total population of children 0–5 years old used as weights: United Nations. World Population Prospects 2019. https://population.un.org/wpp/Download/Standard/Interpolated/ (accessed 10 July 2021) and The Pacific Community, Statistics for Development Division. Official communication, 3 July 2019.

Table 1.2.2: Selected Indicators for Sustainable Development Goal 2—Improved Agricultural Investment

ADB Regional Member	Target 2.a: Increase investment, including through enhanced international cooperation, in rural infrastructure, agricultural research and extension services, technology development, and plant and livestock gene banks in order to enhance agricultural productive capacity in developing countries, in particular least developed countries					
	2.a.1: The Agriculture Orientation Index for Government Expenditures			2.a.2: Total Official Flows to the Agriculture Sector[a] (constant 2019 $ million)		
	2010	2015	2019	2010	2015	2019
Developing ADB Member Economies						
Central and West Asia	...	...	...	**1,163.4**	**983.8**	**1,012.9**
Afghanistan	0.2	0.2	0.1 (2017)	716.6	344.9	235.5
Armenia	0.3	0.1	0.2	87.7	38.2	18.3
Azerbaijan	0.5	0.5	0.6	16.8	53.3	13.0
Georgia	0.1	0.3	0.4	16.9	43.1	51.9
Kazakhstan	0.9	0.9	1.2	55.1	67.5	15.6
Kyrgyz Republic	0.1	0.1	0.1 (2018)	22.8	25.5	13.4
Pakistan	0.1	0.1	0.1	163.8	305.8	297.4
Tajikistan	...	...	...	50.8	34.0	40.4
Turkmenistan	...	...	...	1.1	0.1	4.0
Uzbekistan	0.2 (2011)	0.2	0.2	31.8	71.4	323.4
East Asia	...	...	...	**362.2**	**417.0**	**467.6**
China, People's Republic of	0.9	1.1	1.3	321.2	398.9	449.9
Hong Kong, China	2.7	1.8	2.5 (2018)	...	...	...
Korea, Republic of	2.1	2.1	0.8 (2018)	...	...	...
Mongolia	0.4	0.1	0.1	41.0	18.1	17.7
Taipei,China	...	...	...	...	...	...
South Asia[b]	...	...	...	**1,055.2**	**1,498.5**	**1,071.3**
Bangladesh	0.5	0.5	...	183.0	257.3	279.1
Bhutan	0.8	0.8	0.7 (2018)	6.2	7.3	17.5
India	0.5	0.4	0.5 (2018)	730.5	1,092.8	604.2
Maldives	0.2	0.0	0.1 (2018)	0.1 (2011)	0.7	14.6
Nepal	0.3	0.3	0.2	100.4	105.3	110.5
Sri Lanka	0.6	0.8	0.6	35.1	35.1	45.4
Southeast Asia	...	...	...	**1,575.2**	**954.3**	**1,173.7**
Brunei Darussalam	...	...	...	...	...	...
Cambodia	...	...	...	75.6	115.9	175.2
Indonesia	0.1	0.2	0.3	968.5	227.3	160.6
Lao People's Democratic Republic	...	...	...	52.5	68.9	89.0
Malaysia	0.3	0.4	0.3	2.3	4.8	2.4
Myanmar	0.1 (2012)	0.2	0.3	37.9	142.4	233.7
Philippines	0.5	0.4	0.3	131.6	115.5	195.8
Singapore	6.8	7.7	7.5	...	...	...
Thailand	0.4	0.9	0.8	11.8	7.6	8.1
Timor-Leste	0.1	0.1	...	25.8	25.2	25.0
Viet Nam	0.3	0.3 (2014)	...	269.2	246.7	283.9
The Pacific	...	...	...	**54.9**	**83.3**	**122.6**
Cook Islands	0.9	0.9	0.6	1.2	0.3	0.7
Fiji	0.3	0.6	0.5	3.1	20.8	12.1
Kiribati	...	...	...	2.9	2.6	4.2
Marshall Islands	0.2	0.2	0.3 (2018)	3.8	1.5	4.3
Micronesia, Federated States of	0.1	0.1	0.2 (2018)	1.1	1.9	4.3
Nauru	...	...	...	0.5	0.4	1.0
Niue	...	...	...	0.2	0.1	0.7
Palau	0.1	0.2	0.2 (2018)	0.6	0.8	3.1
Papua New Guinea	...	...	0.1	20.7	30.6	61.2
Samoa	0.2	0.4	0.4	1.5	4.0	3.2
Solomon Islands	0.2 (2011)	0.1	0.1	10.7	12.6	14.2
Tonga	...	...	...	2.1	1.8	3.5
Tuvalu	...	...	...	0.9	2.1	2.9
Vanuatu	0.1	0.1	...	5.6	3.8	7.2
Developed ADB Member Economies	...	...	...	...	...	...
Australia	0.5	0.3	0.3	...	...	...
Japan	2.1	2.0	1.8 (2018)	...	...	...
New Zealand	0.2	0.1	0.2	...	...	...
DEVELOPING ADB MEMBER ECONOMIES	...	...	...	**4,210.9**	**3,936.9**	**3,848.1**

... = data not available, 0.0 = magnitude is less than half of unit employed, $ = United States dollars, ADB = Asian Development Bank.

a Total official flows refer to official development assistance plus other official flows. Data refer to gross disbursements.
b Includes only reporting economies with data corresponding to the year heading.

Source: United Nations Statistics Division. Global SDG Indicators Database. https://unstats.un.org/sdgs/indicators/database/ (accessed 14 July 2021).

Goal 3. Ensure healthy lives and promote well-being for all at all ages

Table 1.3.1: Selected Indicators for Sustainable Development Goal 3—Maternal and Child Health

ADB Regional Member	Target 3.1: By 2030, reduce the global maternal mortality ratio to less than 70 per 100,000 live births				Target 3.2: By 2030, end preventable deaths of newborns and children under 5 years of age, with all countries aiming to reduce neonatal mortality to at least as low as 12 per 1,000 live births and under-5 mortality to at least as low as 25 per 1,000 live births			
	3.1.1: Maternal Mortality Ratio[a] (per 100,000 live births)		3.1.2: Proportion of Births Attended by Skilled Health Personnel[b] (%)		3.2.1: Under-5 Mortality Rate[a,c] (per 1,000 live births)		3.2.2: Neonatal Mortality Rate[a,c] (per 1,000 live births)	
	2010	2017	2010	2019	2010	2019	2010	2019
Developing ADB Member Economies								
Central and West Asia	**264**	**182**	…	…	**75**	**56**	**42**	**34**
Afghanistan	954	638	34.3 [d]	58.8 [d] (2018)	88	60	47	36
Armenia	32	26	99.5 [d]	99.8 [e] (2016)	19	12	10	6
Azerbaijan	31	26	99.4 [f]	99.4 [f] (2018)	37	20	20	11
Georgia	32	25	99.6 [d]	99.9 [d] (2018)	14	10	10	5
Kazakhstan	22	10	99.4 [f]	99.9 [g] (2018)	20	11	12	5
Kyrgyz Republic	79	60	98.3 [f]	99.8 [d] (2018)	30	18	17	12
Pakistan	191	140	43.0 [d] (2011)	71.0 [e]	87	67	50	41
Tajikistan	23	17	87.7 [f]	94.8 [d] (2017)	43	34	20	15
Turkmenistan	10	7	99.5 [d] (2006)	100.0 [e]	43	42	23	24
Uzbekistan	31	29	100.0 [f]	100.0 [e] (2018)	33	17	18	10
East Asia	**36**	**29**	…	…	**16**	**8**	**8**	**4**
China, People's Republic of	36	29	99.6 [f]	99.9 [f] (2016)	16	8	8	4
Hong Kong, China	1	–* (2019)	…	…	…	…	1	1
Korea, Republic of	15	11	99.9 [g] (2009)	100.0 [g] (2015)	4	3	2	2
Mongolia	66	45	98.8 [d]	99.3 [e] (2018)	30	16	12	8
Taipei,China	4	16 (2019)	…	…	…	…	3	2
South Asia	**215**	**148**	…	…	**56**	**34**	**31**	**21**
Bangladesh	258	173	26.5 [e]	59.0 [e]	49	31	28	19
Bhutan	247	183	64.5 [e]	96.3 [f]	42	29	22	17
India	210	145	52.3 [f] (2008)	81.4 [e] (2016)	58	34	32	22
Maldives	67	53	98.2 [d]	99.5 [d] (2017)	14	8	8	5
Nepal	305	186	36.0 [d] (2011)	77.2 [e]	47	31	27	20
Sri Lanka	38	36	98.6 [d] (2007)	99.5 [d] (2016)	12	7	6	4
Southeast Asia	**172**	**137**	…	…	**33**	**24**	**16**	**13**
Brunei Darussalam	28	31	99.8 [f]	99.8 [f] (2017)	10	11	5	6
Cambodia	248	160	71.0 [d]	…	44	27	21	15
Indonesia	228	177	83.1 [e] (2012)	94.7 [d]	34	24	17	12
Lao People's Democratic Republic	292	185	40.1 [d] (2012)	64.4 [d] (2017)	68	46	29	22
Malaysia	30	29	98.6 [f]	99.6 [e]	8	9	4	5
Myanmar	265	250	70.6 [e]	60.2 [e] (2016)	63	45	28	22
Philippines	144	121	72.2 [d] (2011)	84.4 [d] (2017)	32	27	15	13
Singapore	10	8	99.7 [g]	99.6 [e]	3	3	1	1
Thailand	42	37	99.4 [d] (2009)	99.1 [e]	14	9	8	5
Timor-Leste	219	142	29.3 [d]	56.7 [e] (2016)	62	44	25	20
Viet Nam	47	43	91.9 [d] (2011)	…	23	20	12	11
The Pacific	**151**	**130**	…	…	**51**	**40**	**23**	**19**
Cook Islands	…	…	100.0 [f] (2009)	…	11	8	6	4
Fiji	39	34	99.7 [f]	99.8 [f] (2016)	24	26	10	11
Kiribati	112	92	98.3 [f]	91.9 [e]	65	51	26	22
Marshall Islands	…	…	90.0 [d]	92.4 [d] (2017)	39	32	18	15
Micronesia, Federated States of	110	88	100.0 [f] (2009)	…	39	29	20	16
Nauru	…	…	97.4 [e] (2007)	…	39	31	24	20
Niue	…	…	100.0 [f]	…	30	23	16	13
Palau	…	…	99.6 [d]	100.0 [d] (2018)	23	17	13	9
Papua New Guinea	168	145	53.0 [d] (2006)	56.4 [e] (2018)	57	45	26	22
Samoa	58	43	80.8 [e] (2009)	88.9 [f] (2020)	18	15	10	8
Solomon Islands	141	104	85.5 [e] (2007)	86.2 [e] (2015)	26	20	11	8
Tonga	57	52	99.0 [f]	98.3 [e]	17	17	7	7
Tuvalu	…	…	93.1 [d] (2007)	…	32	24	21	16
Vanuatu	92	72	89.4 [e] (2013)	…	30	26	13	11
Developed ADB Member Economies	**6**	**5**	…	…	**4**	**3**	**2**	**1**
Australia	5	6	99.1 [g]	98.7 [g] (2018)	5	4	3	2
Japan	6	5	99.8 [g]	99.9 [g]	3	3	1	1
New Zealand	11	9	96.8 [g]	96.4 [g] (2018)	6	5	3	3
DEVELOPING ADB MEMBER ECONOMIES	**167**	**119**	…	…	**44**	**28**	**24**	**17**
ALL ADB REGIONAL MEMBERS	**164**	**117**	…	…	**43**	**28**	**23**	**17**
WORLD	**248**	**211**	**71.0**	**82.6 (2020)**	**51**	**38**	**22**	**18**

… = data not available, * = provisional, preliminary, ADB = Asian Development Bank.

a Regional aggregates are weighted averages estimated using population of annual live births for the respective year headings. The data for maternal, under-5, and neonatal deaths are from United Nations Statistics Division databases. For Taipei,China, maternal and neonatal deaths data are from the Government of Taipei,China's Ministry of Health and Welfare. Aggregates are derived for reporting economies only. Aggregates for East Asia exclude Hong Kong, China. For under-5 mortality rate, aggregates also exclude Taipei,China.

b Based on data from national-level household surveys and routine service statistics.

c Data are estimates as published on the Global SDG Indicators Database.

d Estimates are aligned with the standard definition of doctor, nurse, and/or midwife.

e Includes other health personnel not in alignment with the standard definition.

f Estimate provided with no clear definition of health personnel.

g Refers to institutional births, including all deliveries that occurred at a health facility.

Source: For Indicator 3.1.1 and 3.2.2: United Nations Statistics Division. Global SDG Indicators Database. https://unstats.un.org/sdgs/indicators/database/ (accessed 7 July 2021). For Hong Kong, China: Government of the Hong Kong Special Administrative Region of the People's Republic of China, Department of Health. Health Facts of Hong Kong 2020 Edition; past editions. (accessed 7 July 2021). For Taipei,China: Government of Taipei,China, Ministry of Health and Welfare. Cause of Death Statistics 2019. https://www.mohw.gov.tw/np-128-2.html (accessed 7 July 2021). For Indicators 3.1.2 and 3.2.1: United Nations Statistics Division. Global SDG Indicators Database. https://unstats.un.org/sdgs/indicators/database/ (accessed 7 July 2021).

Table 1.3.2: Selected Indicators for Sustainable Development Goal 3—Incidence of Communicable Diseases

ADB Regional Member	Target 3.3: By 2030, end the epidemics of AIDS, tuberculosis, malaria, and neglected tropical diseases; and combat hepatitis, water-borne diseases, and other communicable diseases					
	3.3.1: Number of New HIV Infections[a] (per 1,000 uninfected population)		3.3.2: Tuberculosis Incidence[b] (per 100,000 population)		3.3.3: Malaria Incidence[c] (per 1,000 population)	
	2010	2020	2010	2019	2010	2019
Developing ADB Member Economies						
Central and West Asia						
Afghanistan	0.03	0.04	189.0	189.0	12.9	14.5
Armenia	0.08	0.11	61.0	26.0	-	-
Azerbaijan	0.08	0.04	104.0	60.0	0.2	-
Georgia	0.18	0.17	127.0	74.0	-	-
Kazakhstan	0.12	0.19	144.0	68.0	-	-
Kyrgyz Republic	0.14	0.11	120.0	110.0	0.0	-
Pakistan	0.08	0.12	276.0	263.0	8.2	3.3
Tajikistan	0.15	0.09	128.0	83.0	0.0	-
Turkmenistan	...	...	79.0	45.0	-	-
Uzbekistan	0.13	0.08	97.0	67.0	0.1	-
East Asia						
China, People's Republic of	...	...	76.0	58.0	0.0	-
Hong Kong, China	...	...	81.0	63.0	...	...
Korea, Republic of	...	...	95.0	59.0	0.4	0.1
Mongolia	0.02	0.01	428.0	428.0	...	...
Taipei,China	...	...	...	...	...	...
South Asia						
Bangladesh	0.01	0.01 (2018)	221.0	221.0	4.3	1.2
Bhutan	0.17	0.09	239.0	165.0	0.9	0.0
India	...	0.04	247.0	193.0	17.5	4.3
Maldives	...	...	32.0	36.0	...	...
Nepal	0.08	0.03	311.0	238.0	3.9	0.1
Sri Lanka	0.01	<0.01	66.0	64.0	0.1	-
Southeast Asia						
Brunei Darussalam	...	0.16	70.0	64.0	...	...
Cambodia	0.14	0.07	438.0	287.0	34.9	12.0
Indonesia	0.26	0.10	342.0	312.0	8.9	2.4
Lao People's Democratic Republic	0.17	0.13	221.0	155.0	15.7	2.8
Malaysia	0.19	0.19	75.0	92.0	4.6	-
Myanmar	0.31	0.20 (2018)	500.0	322.0	67.0	2.3
Philippines	0.05	0.15	531.0	554.0	1.0	0.7
Singapore	0.14	<0.01	35.0	41.0	...	...
Thailand	0.24	0.10	181.0	150.0	1.8	0.3
Timor-Leste	0.08	0.10	498.0	498.0	99.7	-
Viet Nam	0.18	0.06	231.0	176.0	0.4	0.1
The Pacific						
Cook Islands	...	...	-	13.0	...	...
Fiji	0.08	0.16	27.0	66.0	...	...
Kiribati	...	...	347.0	436.0	...	...
Marshall Islands	...	...	428.0	483.0	...	...
Micronesia, Federated States of	...	...	199.0	100.0	...	...
Nauru	...	...	34.0	182.0	...	...
Niue	...	...	-	143.0 (2018)	...	...
Palau	...	...	122.0	38.0	...	...
Papua New Guinea	0.35	0.39	432.0	432.0	169.6	156.4
Samoa	...	...	8.7	11.0	...	...
Solomon Islands	...	...	80.0	66.0	174.9	247.9
Tonga	...	...	12.0	11.0	...	...
Tuvalu	...	...	153.0	296.0	...	...
Vanuatu	...	...	69.0	41.0	66.3	3.5
Developed ADB Member Economies						
Australia	0.05	0.03	6.5	6.9	...	...
Japan	0.01	<0.01	20.0	13.0	...	...
New Zealand	0.04	0.02	7.9	7.5	...	...

... = data not available, < = less than, - = magnitude equals zero, 0.0 = magnitude is less than half of unit employed, ADB = Asian Development Bank.

a Spectrum modelling is used on the data. Alternative methods of measures include household or key population surveys with HIV incidence-testing, or routine surveillance among key populations.

b Estimates of tuberculosis incidence are produced through a consultative and analytical process led by the World Health Organization and are published annually. These estimates are based on annual case notifications, assessments of the quality and coverage of tuberculosis notification data, national surveys of the prevalence of tuberculosis disease, and information from death (vital) registration systems.
Estimates of incidence for each economy are derived, using one or more of the following approaches, depending on available data: (i) incidence = case notifications and/or estimated proportion of cases detected; (ii) capture-recapture modelling, (iii) incidence = prevalence and/or duration of condition.

c Malaria incidence is expressed as the number of new cases per 1,000 population per year, with the population of each economy derived from projections made by the United Nations Population Division and the total proportion at risk estimated by an economy's national malaria control program.

Sources: For Indicator 3.3.1: The Joint United Nations Programme on HIV/AIDS. https://www.unaids.org/en/resources/documents/2021/HIV_estimates_with_uncertainty_bounds_1990-present/ (accessed 4 August 2021). For Indicators 3.3.2 and 3.3.3: United Nations Statistics Division. Global SDG Indicators Database. http://unstats.un.org/sdgs/indicators/database/ (accessed 16 July 2021).

Goal 3. Ensure healthy lives and promote well-being for all at all ages

Table 1.3.3: Selected Indicators for Sustainable Development Goal 3—Mortality Rates, Reproductive Health

ADB Regional Member	Target 3.4: By 2030, reduce by one-third premature mortality from noncommunicable diseases through prevention and treatment, and promote mental health and well-being					Target 3.6: By 2020, halve the number of global deaths and injuries from road traffic accidents	
	3.4.1: Mortality Rate Attributed to Cardiovascular Disease, Cancer, Diabetes, or Chronic Respiratory Disease[a] (%)		3.4.2: Suicide Mortality Rate[b,a] (per 100,000 population) 2019			3.6.1: Death Rate Due to Road Traffic Injuries[a] (per 100,000 population)	
	2010	2019	Total	Female	Male	2010	2019
Developing ADB Member Economies							
Central and West Asia							
Afghanistan	37.8	35.3	4.1	3.6	4.6	14.4	15.9
Armenia	25.0	19.9	3.3	1.3	5.6	18.0	20.0
Azerbaijan	29.8	27.2	4.1	1.6	6.6	11.4	6.7
Georgia	27.1	24.9	9.2	3.0	16.0	17.2	12.4
Kazakhstan	31.4	22.4	17.6	6.8	29.0	25.9	12.7
Kyrgyz Republic	27.9	20.3	7.4	3.2	11.7	18.0	12.7
Pakistan	31.8	29.4	8.9	4.3	13.3	14.7	13.0
Tajikistan	30.5	28.3	4.3	2.8	5.7	18.7	15.7
Turkmenistan	33.1	27.7	5.7	2.6	8.8	16.9	13.5
Uzbekistan	28.9	25.3	8.0	4.8	11.3	11.3	11.7
East Asia							
China, People's Republic of	19.0	15.9	8.1	6.2	9.8	20.3	17.4
Hong Kong, China	...	...	...	...	...	1.7	1.5
Korea, Republic of	10.6	7.3	28.6	16.9	40.2	13.7	8.6
Mongolia	41.6	35.0	17.9	5.4	30.7	18.6	21.0
Taipei,China	...	...	16.4	...	...	...	...
South Asia							
Bangladesh	21.5	18.9	3.7	1.7	5.7	16.9	15.3
Bhutan	19.4	18.5	4.6	2.7	6.3	13.6	16.2
India	23.7	21.9	12.7	11.1	14.1	17.2	15.6
Maldives	16.5	11.6	2.7	0.8	3.9	3.0	1.6
Nepal	20.2	21.5	9.0	2.7	16.4	15.8	16.3
Sri Lanka	17.0	13.2	14.0	6.2	22.3	14.2	19.7
Southeast Asia							
Brunei Darussalam	19.9	18.5	2.7	0.8	4.4	7.7	7.5
Cambodia	23.7	22.5	4.9	2.8	7.0	18.1	19.6
Indonesia	26.1	24.8	2.4	1.1	3.7	13.7	11.3
Lao People's Democratic Republic	28.3	26.8	5.4	3.2	7.6	14.3	17.9
Malaysia	18.9	18.4	5.7	2.3	8.9	25.1	22.5
Myanmar	28.3	24.9	2.9	1.1	4.9	19.1	20.4
Philippines	24.4	24.5	2.2	1.2	3.1	11.5	12.0
Singapore	11.0	9.5	11.2	7.1	15.0	5.1	2.1
Thailand	14.9	13.7	8.8	2.9	15.0	38.3	32.2
Timor-Leste	19.9	19.9	3.7	2.0	5.3	15.3	11.9
Viet Nam	22.4	21.2	7.5	4.7	10.4	25.6	30.6
The Pacific							
Cook Islands	...	...	...	...	...	...	...
Fiji	39.6	37.7	9.0	5.7	12.2	9.8	13.5
Kiribati	53.0	50.8	28.3	8.6	48.6	5.8	1.9
Marshall Islands	...	...	...	...	...	...	...
Micronesia, Federated States of	44.6	46.3	28.2	12.7	43.2	2.9	0.2
Nauru	...	30.0 (2017)	...	...	...	...	...
Niue	...	18.5 (2016)	...	...	...	...	...
Palau	...	...	...	...	...	...	...
Papua New Guinea	35.4	36.0	2.9	1.6	4.2	17.1	12.6
Samoa	32.4	31.2	12.6	6.7	18.0	12.9	13.0
Solomon Islands	40.4	39.2	14.7	1.9	27.0	17.8	16.5
Tonga	26.3	24.8	3.8	2.6	5.0	5.8	33.0
Tuvalu	...	...	...	...	...	...	...
Vanuatu	40.4	39.7	18.0	7.6	28.1	13.5	14.9
Developed ADB Member Economies							
Australia	9.9	8.6	12.5	6.4	18.6	6.5	4.9
Japan	9.5	8.3	15.3	9.2	21.8	5.3	3.6
New Zealand	11.8	10.3	11.0	5.8	16.5	9.3	9.6

Table 1.3.3: Selected Indicators for Sustainable Development Goal 3—Mortality Rates, Reproductive Health *(continued)*

	Target 3.7: By 2030, ensure universal access to sexual and reproductive health-care services, including for family planning, information, and education, and the integration of reproductive health into natural strategies and programs				Target 3.8: Achieve universal health coverage, including financial risk protection; access to quality essential health-care services; and access to safe, effective, quality, and affordable essential medicines and vaccines for all	Target 3.9: By 2030, substantially reduce the number of deaths and illnesses from hazardous chemicals and air, water, and soil pollution and contamination	
ADB Regional Member	3.7.1: Proportion of Women of Reproductive Age (Aged 15–49 Years) Who Have Their Need for Family Planning Satisfied with Modern Methods		3.7.2: Adolescent Birth Rate (Aged 15–19 Years) per 1,000 Women in That Age Group		3.8.1: Coverage of Essential Health Services[c] (index in a unitless scale of 0 to 100)	3.9.1: Mortality Rate Attributed to Household and Ambient Air Pollution (per 100,000 population)	3.9.2: Mortality Rate Attributed to Unsafe Water, Unsafe Sanitation, and Lack of Hygiene (per 100,000 population)
	2010	2018	2010	2018	2017	2016	2016
Developing ADB Member Economies							
Central and West Asia							
Afghanistan	...	42.2 (2016)	80.0 (2009)	62.0 (2017)	37.0	95.0	13.9
Armenia	39.4	40.2 (2016)	27.1	18.9	69.0	81.0	0.2
Azerbaijan	21.5 (2006)	...	60.0	43.5	65.0	55.0	1.1
Georgia	52.8	50.5	48.5	30.1	66.0	184.0	0.2
Kazakhstan	79.1 (2011)	73.2	28.3	25.6	76.0	57.0	0.4
Kyrgyz Republic	62.1 (2012)	64.6	34.1	35.9	70.0	74.0	0.8
Pakistan	47.0 (2013)	48.6	44.3 (2011)	54.0 (2017)	45.0	113.0	19.6
Tajikistan	50.9 (2012)	52.1 (2017)	47.0	54.3 (2016)	68.0	70.0	2.7
Turkmenistan	67.5 (2000)	79.6 (2019)	28.0 (2014)	22.0 (2017)	70.0	51.0	4.0
Uzbekistan	...	...	29.5	18.9 (2017)	73.0	54.0	0.4
East Asia							
China, People's Republic of	96.6 (2001)	...	5.9	...	79.0	140.0	0.6
Hong Kong, China	...	...	3.0	2.1	...	...	...
Korea, Republic of	...	...	1.8	0.9	86.0	35.0	1.8
Mongolia	65.0	63.6	18.9	32.6	62.0	97.0	1.3
Taipei,China	...	...	...	...	...	...	...
South Asia							
Bangladesh	69.7 (2011)	70.3	118.3	74.0	48.0	103.0	11.9
Bhutan	84.6	...	59.0 (2009)	...	62.0	88.0	3.9
India	64.0 (2008)	72.8 (2016)	37.2	12.2	55.0	141.0	18.6
Maldives	42.6 (2009)	29.2 (2017)	15.4	8.9 (2017)	62.0	14.0	0.3
Nepal	56.2 (2011)	61.9 (2019)	90.0	63.0	48.0	133.0	19.8
Sri Lanka	69.4 (2007)	74.3 (2016)	20.3 (2008)	...	66.0	89.0	1.2
Southeast Asia							
Brunei Darussalam	...	...	14.5 (2011)	9.9	81.0	9.0	–
Cambodia	51.6 (2011)	...	46.1 (2009)	...	60.0	87.0	6.5
Indonesia	79.0 (2012)	77.0 (2017)	48.0	36.0 (2016)	57.0	81.0	7.1
Lao People's Democratic Republic	60.5 (2012)	72.3 (2017)	94.4	83.4 (2016)	51.0	110.0	11.3
Malaysia	...	...	14.0 (2011)	8.8	73.0	35.0	0.4
Myanmar	56.0 (2001)	74.9 (2016)	33.0 (2013)	...	61.0	116.0	12.6
Philippines	54.1 (2011)	56.0 (2017)	59.0 (2011)	36.4	61.0	117.0	4.2
Singapore	...	...	4.8	2.5	86.0	39.0	0.1
Thailand	89.2 (2012)	88.2 (2019)	50.1	23.0 (2019)	80.0	85.0	3.5
Timor-Leste	38.4	45.9 (2016)	50.0	...	52.0	77.0	9.9
Viet Nam	72.8 (2011)	...	38.0	35.0 (2019)	75.0	65.0	1.6
The Pacific							
Cook Islands	76.2 (2015)	...	56.0 (2011)	41.9 (2017)	...	...	– (2012)
Fiji	74.5 (2015)	...	27.4 (2008)	23.1 (2016)	64.0	76.0	2.9
Kiribati	35.8 (2009)	53.1 (2019)	49.0	50.6 (2017)	41.0	88.0	16.7
Marshall Islands	80.5 (2007)	...	84.5 (2011)	...	...	...	7.6 (2012)
Micronesia, Federated States of	66.0 (2002)	...	44.0 (2009)	...	47.0	93.0	3.6
Nauru	42.5 (2007)	...	60.5	...	...	...	– (2012)
Niue	...	...	20.0 (2011)	...	...	...	– (2012)
Palau	39.4 (2015)	...	34.0 (2012)	33.8 (2017)	...	...	4.8 (2012)
Papua New Guinea	40.6 (2007)	49.2	65.0 (2004)	68.0 (2016)	40.0	90.0	16.3
Samoa	34.9 (2009)	...	39.2 (2011)	...	58.0	62.0	1.5
Solomon Islands	60.0 (2007)	...	61.6 (2009)	...	47.0	67.0	6.2
Tonga	47.9 (2012)	49.9 (2019)	24.0	30.0 (2016)	58.0	57.0	1.4
Tuvalu	41.0 (2007)	...	28.0 (2012)	26.6 (2016)	...	...	– (2012)
Vanuatu	50.7 (2013)	...	78.0 (2011)	...	48.0	76.0	10.4
Developed ADB Member Economies							
Australia	...	...	16.7	9.4	87.0	17.0	0.1
Japan	...	...	4.5	3.1	83.0	43.0	0.2
New Zealand	...	...	29.0	13.8	87.0	14.0	0.1

... = data not available, – = magnitude equals zero, ADB = Asian Development Bank.

a For Afghanistan, Bangladesh, Bhutan, Cambodia, India, Indonesia, the Federated States of Micronesia, Myanmar, Nepal, Pakistan, Papua New Guinea, the People's Republic of China, Samoa, Timor, Tonga, Vanuatu, and Viet Nam, the numbers shown are modeled estimates as published on the United Nations' Global SDG Indicators Database.

b Data refers to crude suicide rates (per 100,000 population).

c The universal health coverage service coverage index is calculated as the geometric mean of 14 tracer indicators of health service coverage. The index is reported on a unitless scale of 0 to 100, with 100 being the optimal value. The reported values do not directly translate to the percentage of the population covered by universal health coverage services, but they can be viewed as performance scores.

Sources: For Indicators 3.4.1, 3.4.2, 3.6.1, 3.7.1, 3.7.2, 3.8.1, 3.9.1, 3.9.2: United Nations Statistics Division. Global SDG Indicators Database. https://unstats.un.org/sdgs/indicators/database/ (accessed 10 July 2021). For Indicator 3.4.1 for Nauru and Niue: Secretariat of the Pacific Community (SPC). Pacific Data Hub, SDG Dashboard. https://stats.pacificdata.org/ (accessed 12 July 2021). For Indicator 3.4.2 for Taipei,China: Government of Taipei,China, Ministry of Health and Welfare. 2019 Cause of Death Statistics. https://www.mohw.gov.tw/lp-4964-2.html (accessed 12 July 2021). For Indicator 3.6.1 for Hong Kong, China: Government of the Hong Kong Special Administrative Region of the People's Republic of China. Road Traffic Accident Statistics. https://www.td.gov.hk/en/road_safety/road_traffic_accident_statistics/accident_trend_since_1953/index.html (accessed 12 July 2021). For Indicator 3.7.1 for the Cook Islands, the Federated States of Micronesia, Fiji, and Palau, and 2015 for Tuvalu: SPC. Pacific Data Hub, SDG Dashboard. https://stats.pacificdata.org/ (accessed 12 July 2021). For Indicator 3.9.2 for the Cook Islands, the Marshall Islands, Nauru, Niue, Palau, and Tuvalu: SPC. Pacific Data Hub, SDG Dashboard. https://stats.pacificdata.org/ (accessed 12 July 2021).

Goal 3. Ensure healthy lives and promote well-being for all at all ages

Table 1.3.4: Selected Indicators for Sustainable Development Goal 3—Health Workforce and National and Global Health Risks

ADB Regional Member	Target 3.c: Substantially increase health financing and the recruitment, development, training and retention of the health workforce in developing countries, especially in least developed countries and small island developing States						Target 3.d: Strengthen the capacity of all countries, in particular developing countries, for early warning, risk reduction, and management of national and global health risks
	3.c.1: Health Worker Density, by Type of Occupation[a] (per 10,000 population)						3.d.1: International Health Regulations Capacity and Health Emergency Preparedness[b] (%)
	Density of Medical Doctors			Density of Nursing and Midwifery Personnel			Average of 13 International Health Regulations Core Capacity Scores
	2010	2015	2019	2010	2015	2019	2020
Developing ADB Member Economies							
Central and West Asia	**13.4**	**13.7**	**...**	**26.1**	**23.9**	**...**	**65**
Afghanistan	2.4	2.9	...	6.1 (2009)	1.3	4.5 (2018)	47
Armenia	28.4	29.1	44.0 (2017)	52.4	49.5	43.7 (2018)	84
Azerbaijan	36.6	34.5 (2014)	...	73.5	64.3 (2014)	...	86
Georgia	44.5	50.1	70.8	39.5	40.2	52.2	59
Kazakhstan	39.3	39.8 (2014)	...	77.2	72.9	...	81
Kyrgyz Republic	23.4	22.1 (2014)	...	56.5	59.4 (2014)	56.0	52
Pakistan	8.1	9.3	11.2	5.6	4.8	4.8	52
Tajikistan	17.0	17.2 (2014)	...	39.5	47.5 (2014)	...	62 (2019)
Turkmenistan	22.7	22.2 (2014)	...	45.1	44.3 (2014)	...	68
Uzbekistan	25.4	23.7 (2014)	...	113.8	112.8 (2014)	...	55
East Asia	**14.6**	**17.9**	**20.0**	**...**	**24.2**	**28.3**	**92**
China, People's Republic of	14.3	17.7	19.8 (2017)	...	22.9	26.6 (2017)	94
Hong Kong, China	...	...	...	...	...	...	...
Korea, Republic of	19.8	22.5	24.1 (2018)	46.4	59.8	74.6 (2018)	98
Mongolia	27.6	32.2	38.5 (2018)	36.3	40.9	42.1 (2018)	85
Taipei,China	...	...	...	...	...	...	...
South Asia	**6.5**	**7.1**	**9.0**	**...**	**...**	**22.0**	**62**
Bangladesh	3.6	4.9	6.4	1.8	2.8	3.9	70
Bhutan	2.8 (2012)	3.4	4.6	10.5 (2012)	14.7	18.3	71
India	6.9	7.3	9.3	...	...	23.9	80
Maldives	14.4	17.7 (2014)	17.1 (2018)	51.1	65.7	64.3 (2018)	47
Nepal	5.2 (2012)	5.6 (2013)	8.1	16.0 (2012)	21.4 (2014)	33.0	39
Sri Lanka	7.2	8.6	11.5	17.5	19.6	22.6	62
Southeast Asia	**5.7**	**5.2**	**5.8**	**27.0**	**...**	**36.6**	**67**
Brunei Darussalam	14.5	17.8	16.1 (2017)	74.8	66.4	59.0 (2018)	...
Cambodia	2.3	1.9 (2014)	...	8.6	5.9	10.1	48
Indonesia	2.4	2.7	4.7	...	13.0	38.1	69
Lao People's Democratic Republic	2.0 (2009)	4.9 (2014)	3.7 (2017)	8.6	12.2	7.2	43
Malaysia	11.7	15.4	...	32.0	41.8	34.8	86
Myanmar	5.2	6.2 (2016)	7.4	8.9	10.3 (2016)	10.8	63
Philippines	12.7	...	6.0 (2017)	56.5 (2009)	...	54.4	69
Singapore	17.2	22.9 (2016)	...	57.2	60.1	62.4 (2017)	92
Thailand	3.9	4.7	9.2	20.6	23.7	31.5	85
Timor-Leste	...	6.9	7.7	11.5	14.8	17.6	42
Viet Nam	7.1	8.0	...	12.3	14.2	...	72
The Pacific	**1.3**	**...**	**...**	**9.1**	**...**	**10.4**	**56**
Cook Islands	12.9 (2009)	14.1 (2014)	...	62.4 (2009)	68.2	80.0	59
Fiji	4.4 (2009)	8.6	...	22.9 (2009)	30.2	39.6	63 (2018)
Kiribati	4.0	2.0 (2013)	...	39.3	57.5 (2013)	38.3 (2018)	70
Marshall Islands	5.7	...	...	22.5	...	33.4 (2018)	49
Micronesia, Federated States of	1.9 (2009)	...	...	...	...	21.5	49
Nauru	11.0	13.5	...	69.3 (2011)	67.3	78.5 (2018)	34 (2018)
Niue	18.8 (2008)	...	...	100.0 (2008)	...	125.0 (2018)	67 (2019)
Palau	16.1	14.2 (2014)	...	66.1	63.1 (2014)	72.6 (2018)	64
Papua New Guinea	0.5	...	0.7	5.0	...	4.5	21 (2019)
Samoa	3.4	3.4 (2016)	...	15.4	18.6 (2014)	34.4	73 (2018)
Solomon Islands	2.0 (2011)	1.9 (2016)	...	17.9 (2011)	19.9 (2013)	21.6 (2018)	47
Tonga	5.6	5.4 (2013)	...	38.5	40.1 (2013)	43.3	65
Tuvalu	11.5 (2009)	9.1 (2014)	...	62.1 (2008)	37.3 (2014)	42.6 (2018)	48
Vanuatu	1.8 (2012)	1.7 (2016)	...	18.4 (2012)	...	14.2	55
Developed ADB Member Economies	**23.8**	**25.9**	**27.1**	**103.0**	**119.9**	**124.2**	**91**
Australia	33.4	34.9	37.6 (2018)	104.0	122.0	132.4	92
Japan	22.1	24.1 (2016)	24.8 (2018)	102.7	119.5 (2016)	127.0 (2018)	95
New Zealand	26.1	30.3	34.2 (2018)	105.8	119.9	6.8	87
DEVELOPING ADB MEMBER ECONOMIES	**10.0**	**11.5**	**...**	**...**	**...**	**25.5**	**65**
ALL ADB REGIONAL MEMBERS	**10.5**	**12.1**	**13.6**	**...**	**...**	**29.3**	**67**
WORLD	**...**	**...**	**17.5** (2018)	**...**	**...**	**39.0** (2018)	**65**

... = data not available, ADB = Asian Development Bank.

a Regional aggregates are population weighted averages of the densities of the economies calculated by ADB staff. The data for number of doctors and nurses and midwifery personnel are from the World Health Organization's Global Health Observatory.

b The scores are based on self-assessment and self-reporting by each economy. In 2018, the World Health Organization introduced a new State Parties Self-Assessment Annual Reporting Tool or SPAR, which has been in use since.

Sources: For Indicator 3.c.1: United Nations Statistics Division. Global SDG Indicators Database. https://unstats.un.org/sdgs/indicators/database/ (accessed 7 July 2021). For Indicator 3.d.1: World Health Organization. Global Health Observatory. https://www.who.int/data/gho (accessed 12 July 2021).

Table 1.4.1: Selected Indicators for Sustainable Development Goal 4—Proficiency in Reading and Mathematics

ADB Regional Member	Target 4.1: By 2030, ensure that all girls and boys complete free, equitable, and quality primary and secondary education leading to relevant and effective learning outcomes					
	4.1.1.a: Proportion of Children and Young People in Grades 2 or 3 Achieving at Least a Minimum Proficiency Level (%)		4.1.1.b: Proportion of Children and Young People at the End of Primary School Achieving at Least a Minimum Proficiency Level (%)		4.1.1.c: Proportion of Children and Young People at the End of Lower Secondary School Achieving at Least a Minimum Proficiency Level (%)	
	Reading 2019	Mathematics 2019	Reading 2019	Mathematics 2019	Reading 2019	Mathematics 2019
Developing ADB Member Economies						
Central and West Asia						
Afghanistan	22.0 (2016)	24.5 (2016)	13.0 (2013)	11.0 (2013)	...	...
Armenia	...	...	...	64.0	...	50.4 (2015)
Azerbaijan	...	...	80.8 (2016)	72.0	...	...
Georgia	...	...	86.5 (2016)	56.0	35.6 (2018)	38.9 (2018)
Kazakhstan	...	...	98.1 (2016)	71.0	35.8 (2018)	50.9 (2018)
Kyrgyz Republic	38.7 (2018)	30.1 (2018)	40.3 (2017)	39.8 (2017)	48.5 (2017)	35.1 (2017)
Pakistan	35.0 (2014)	14.5 (2016)	52.1 (2016)	8.0	...	...
Tajikistan	...	...	...	...	...	...
Turkmenistan	71.0	53.0	...	...	...	...
Uzbekistan	...	...	...	...	...	...
East Asia						
China, People's Republic of	81.8 (2016)	84.6 (2015)	...	...	79.6 (2016)	78.9 (2015)
Hong Kong, China	...	...	98.6 (2016)	96.0	87.4 (2018)	90.8 (2018)
Korea, Republic of	...	...	...	95.0	84.9 (2018)	85.0 (2018)
Mongolia	44.4 (2018)	...	...	...	...	...
Taipei,China	...	...	...	...	...	...
South Asia						
Bangladesh	47.0 (2017)	34.0 (2017)	44.0 (2017)	32.0 (2017)	54.0 (2015)	57.0 (2015)
Bhutan	...	...	...	...	56.0 (2015)	...
India	47.2 (2017)	52.9 (2017)	46.3 (2017)	43.6 (2017)	38.3 (2017)	39.5 (2017)
Maldives	...	...	...	...	...	...
Nepal	...	...	80.0 (2018)	67.8 (2018)	99.5 (2017)	97.9 (2017)
Sri Lanka	...	...	55.5 (2015)	73.4 (2015)	21.3 (2016)	50.6 (2016)
Southeast Asia						
Brunei Darussalam	...	...	...	...	48.2 (2018)	52.1 (2018)
Cambodia	...	...	11.0	19.0	7.5 (2015)	9.9 (2015)
Indonesia	...	...	66.2 (2011)	17.5 (2015)	30.1 (2018)	28.1 (2018)
Lao People's Democratic Republic	83.4 (2012)	46.4 (2012)	2.0	8.0	...	...
Malaysia	...	...	58.0	64.0	54.2 (2018)	58.5 (2018)
Myanmar	...	...	11.0	12.0	...	...
Philippines	...	...	10.0	17.0	19.4 (2018)	...
Singapore	...	...	97.3 (2016)	96.0	88.8 (2018)	92.0
Thailand	...	...	...	43.4 (2011)	40.5 (2018)	47.3 (2018)
Timor-Leste	...	...	...	...	...	...
Viet Nam	...	...	82.0	92.0	86.2 (2015)	80.9 (2015)
The Pacific						
Cook Islands	...	...	...	...	...	...
Fiji	...	...	...	...	...	...
Kiribati	29.0 (2018)	12.0 (2018)	...	...	...	...
Marshall Islands	...	...	...	...	...	...
Micronesia, Federated States of	...	...	...	...	...	...
Nauru	...	...	...	...	...	...
Niue	...	...	...	...	...	...
Palau	...	...	...	...	...	...
Papua New Guinea	...	...	...	...	...	...
Samoa	11.7	21.6	...	...	...	...
Solomon Islands	71.4 (2015)	76.3 (2015)	57.8 (2015)	90.5 (2015)	...	...
Tonga	...	...	...	...	...	...
Tuvalu	...	...	...	...	...	...
Vanuatu	...	...	...	...	...	...
Developed ADB Member Economies						
Australia	94.5 (2016)	70.0	...	68.0	80.4 (2018)	77.6 (2018)
Japan	...	...	...	...	...	...
New Zealand	...	...	90.0 (2016)	56.0	81.0 (2018)	78.2 (2018)

... = data not available, ADB = Asian Development Bank.

Source: United Nations Statistics Division. Global SDG Indicators Database. https://unstats.un.org/sdgs/indicators/database/ (accessed 19 July 2021).

Table 1.4.2: Selected Indicators for Sustainable Development Goal 4—Education Completion

ADB Regional Member	Target 4.1: By 2030, ensure that all girls and boys complete free, equitable, and quality primary and secondary education leading to relevant and effective learning outcomes											
	4.1.2: Completion Rate (Primary Education, Lower Secondary Education, Upper Secondary Education)[a] (%)											
	4.1.2.a: Primary											
	2010						2019					
	Total		Q1		Q2		Total		Q1		Q2	
Developing ADB Member Economies												
Central and West Asia												
Afghanistan	40.73	(2011)	20.70	(2011)	26.24	(2011)	54.21	(2015)	44.81	(2015)	46.31	(2015)
Armenia	99.88	(2011)	99.48	(2011)	100.00	(2011)	99.27	(2016)	98.67	(2016)	99.73	(2016)
Azerbaijan	97.94	(2006)	94.76	(2006)	98.60	(2006)	...		...		...	
Georgia	...		...		...		99.91	(2018)	100.00	(2018)	100.00	(2018)
Kazakhstan	99.78	(2011)	99.36	(2011)	100.00	(2011)	99.88	(2015)	100.00	(2015)	99.86	(2015)
Kyrgyz Republic	99.58	(2012)	99.91	(2012)	99.05	(2012)	99.22	(2018)	100.00	(2018)	99.60	(2018)
Pakistan	60.90	(2012)	24.13	(2012)	49.84	(2012)	59.66	(2018)	28.44	(2018)	47.98	(2018)
Tajikistan	98.02	(2012)	97.47	(2012)	96.57	(2012)	98.86	(2017)	97.86	(2017)	99.41	(2017)
Turkmenistan	99.65	(2006)	99.67	(2006)	100.00	(2006)	99.35		98.78		99.88	
Uzbekistan	100.00	(2006)	100.00	(2006)	100.00	(2006)	...		...		...	
East Asia												
China, People's Republic of	96.69		93.16		94.76		97.21	(2014)	95.83	(2014)	98.38	(2014)
Hong Kong, China	...		...		...		...		...		...	
Korea, Republic of	...		...		...		...		...		...	
Mongolia	96.52		89.50		95.19		98.59	(2018)	96.80	(2018)	99.16	(2018)
Taipei,China	...		...		...		...		...		...	
South Asia												
Bangladesh	74.78	(2011)	47.34	(2011)	68.82	(2011)	82.61		70.44		79.88	
Bhutan	67.86		42.27		54.78		...		...		...	
India	88.35	(2011)	84.02	(2011)	85.24	(2011)	91.58	(2016)	80.48	(2016)	91.19	(2016)
Maldives	96.78	(2008)	93.97	(2008)	95.87	(2008)	98.21	(2017)	96.61	(2017)	95.97	(2017)
Nepal	75.22	(2011)	58.41	(2011)	66.78	(2011)	83.16	(2016)	81.75	(2016)	80.92	(2016)
Sri Lanka	98.38	(2006)	96.44	(2006)	98.83	(2006)	...		...		...	
Southeast Asia												
Brunei Darussalam	...		...		...		...		...		...	
Cambodia	71.07		43.38		60.83		72.28	(2014)	47.24	(2014)	62.59	(2014)
Indonesia	95.24	(2012)	87.09	(2012)	94.86	(2012)	96.60	(2017)	90.56	(2017)	97.09	(2017)
Lao People's Democratic Republic	67.14	(2012)	27.65	(2012)	54.02	(2012)	85.90	(2017)	63.15	(2017)	81.93	(2017)
Malaysia	...		...		...		...		...		...	
Myanmar	...		...		...		83.18	(2016)	64.70	(2016)	83.14	(2016)
Philippines	86.77		60.13	(2008)	82.94	(2008)	91.87	(2018)	79.27	(2018)	92.14	(2018)
Singapore	...		...		...		...		...		...	
Thailand	98.14	(2013)	97.86	(2013)	97.19	(2013)	98.68		97.37		97.42	
Timor-Leste	60.06	(2009)	39.43	(2009)	47.89	(2009)	80.48	(2016)	59.68	(2016)	70.98	(2016)
Viet Nam	95.53	(2011)	88.77	(2011)	94.66	(2011)	96.57	(2014)	90.14	(2014)	98.27	(2014)
The Pacific												
Cook Islands	...		...		...		...		...		...	
Fiji	98.74	(2007)	...		...		...		...		...	
Kiribati	...		...		...		94.09		88.40		93.22	
Marshall Islands	...		...		...		...		...		...	
Micronesia, Federated States of	...		...		...		...		...		...	
Nauru	...		...		...		...		...		...	
Niue	...		...		...		...		...		...	
Palau	...		...		...		...		...		...	
Papua New Guinea	...		...		...		61.14	(2018)	38.56	(2018)	49.45	(2018)
Samoa	...		...		...		...		...		...	
Solomon Islands	...		...		...		...		...		...	
Tonga	...		...		...		98.21		96.91		98.31	
Tuvalu	...		...		...		...		...		...	
Vanuatu	81.09	(2007)	63.88	(2007)	81.40	(2007)	...		...		...	
Developed ADB Member Economies												
Australia	...		...		...		...		...		...	
Japan	...		...		...		...		...		...	
New Zealand	...		...		...		...		...		...	

Table 1.4.2: Selected Indicators for Sustainable Development Goal 4—Education Completion *(continued)*

ADB Regional Member	Target 4.1: By 2030, ensure that all girls and boys complete free, equitable, and quality primary and secondary education leading to relevant and effective learning outcomes — 4.1.2: Completion Rate (Primary Education, Lower Secondary Education, Upper Secondary Education)[a] (%) — 4.1.2.b: Lower Secondary											
	2010						2019					
	Total		Q1		Q2		Total		Q1		Q2	
Developing ADB Member Economies												
Central and West Asia												
Afghanistan	23.38	(2011)	7.83	(2011)	12.41	(2011)	36.96	(2015)	24.71	(2015)	29.32	(2015)
Armenia	99.28	(2011)	98.32	(2011)	98.76	(2011)	96.97	(2016)	92.90	(2016)	95.48	(2016)
Azerbaijan	91.66	(2006)	84.28	(2006)	85.89	(2006)	...		...		...	
Georgia	98.65	(2013)	97.84	(2013)	96.82	(2013)	97.70	(2018)	93.17	(2018)	97.25	(2018)
Kazakhstan	99.10	(2011)	98.25	(2011)	98.45	(2011)	99.75	(2015)	99.33	(2015)	99.87	(2015)
Kyrgyz Republic	96.65	(2012)	98.14	(2012)	97.04	(2012)	98.92	(2018)	96.12	(2018)	99.67	(2018)
Pakistan	45.57	(2012)	11.30	(2012)	30.61	(2012)	49.55	(2018)	13.35	(2018)	34.38	(2018)
Tajikistan	88.63	(2012)	82.85	(2012)	85.54	(2012)	95.36	(2017)	94.69	(2017)	91.69	(2017)
Turkmenistan	98.88	(2006)	97.15	(2006)	98.38	(2006)	99.07		97.34		99.38	
Uzbekistan	97.12	(2006)	95.39	(2006)	96.32	(2006)	...		...		...	
East Asia												
China, People's Republic of	84.94		66.41		85.47		82.56	(2014)	79.43	(2014)	86.51	(2014)
Hong Kong, China	...		...		...		...		...		...	
Korea, Republic of	...		...		...		...		...		...	
Mongolia	85.13		49.46		80.10		94.87	(2018)	83.34	(2018)	93.32	(2018)
Taipei,China	...		...		...		...		...		...	
South Asia												
Bangladesh	50.63	(2011)	16.27	(2011)	36.43	(2011)	64.75		43.27		57.70	
Bhutan	38.78		16.01		19.20		...		...		...	
India	76.13	(2011)	69.65	(2011)	71.21	(2011)	80.84	(2016)	59.14	(2016)	75.27	(2016)
Maldives	77.87	(2008)	63.50	(2008)	69.93	(2008)	90.60	(2017)	81.76	(2017)	89.98	(2017)
Nepal	59.58	(2011)	35.61	(2011)	48.82	(2011)	69.68	(2016)	57.40	(2016)	61.90	(2016)
Sri Lanka	88.11	(2006)	77.02	(2006)	85.92	(2006)	...		...		...	
Southeast Asia												
Brunei Darussalam	...		...		...		...		...		...	
Cambodia	36.68		11.73		17.82		40.52	(2014)	17.05	(2014)	25.13	(2014)
Indonesia	77.17	(2012)	51.01	(2012)	66.84	(2012)	86.05	(2017)	66.41	(2017)	82.51	(2017)
Lao People's Democratic Republic	38.14	(2012)	4.21	(2012)	15.84	(2012)	52.57	(2017)	16.56	(2017)	39.30	(2017)
Malaysia	...		...		...		...		...		...	
Myanmar	...		...		...		43.81	(2016)	13.31	(2016)	24.25	(2016)
Philippines	71.10		26.77	(2008)	57.36	(2008)	80.97	(2018)	51.86	(2018)	76.24	(2018)
Singapore	...		...		...		...		...		...	
Thailand	86.33	(2013)	78.63	(2013)	84.46	(2013)	87.42		67.63		86.47	
Timor-Leste	43.87	(2009)	23.83	(2009)	28.70	(2009)	66.04	(2016)	33.55	(2016)	46.46	(2016)
Viet Nam	80.54	(2011)	67.01	(2011)	73.19	(2011)	83.43	(2014)	60.37	(2014)	84.47	(2014)
The Pacific												
Cook Islands	...		...		...		...		...		...	
Fiji	83.56	(2007)	...		...		...		...		...	
Kiribati	...		...		...		78.36		62.15		71.91	
Marshall Islands	...		...		...		...		...		...	
Micronesia, Federated States of	...		...		...		...		...		...	
Nauru	...		...		...		...		...		...	
Niue	...		...		...		...		...		...	
Palau	...		...		...		...		...		...	
Papua New Guinea	...		...		...		50.21	(2018)	25.73	(2018)	37.45	(2018)
Samoa	...		...		...		...		...		...	
Solomon Islands	...		...		...		...		...		...	
Tonga	...		...		...		92.43		87.12		88.33	
Tuvalu	...		...		...		...		...		...	
Vanuatu	38.27	(2007)	11.16	(2007)	18.49	(2007)	...		...		...	
Developed ADB Member Economies												
Australia	99.15		96.56		99.25		...		...		...	
Japan	...		...		...		...		...		...	
New Zealand	...		...		...		...		...		...	

Table 1.4.2: Selected Indicators for Sustainable Development Goal 4—Education Completion *(continued)*

ADB Regional Member	Target 4.1: By 2030, ensure that all girls and boys complete free, equitable, and quality primary and secondary education leading to relevant and effective learning outcomes — 4.1.2: Completion Rate (Primary Education, Lower Secondary Education, Upper Secondary Education)[a] (%) — 4.1.2.c: Upper Secondary											
	2010						2019					
	Total		Q1		Q2		Total		Q1		Q2	
Developing ADB Member Economies												
Central and West Asia												
Afghanistan	13.72	(2011)	2.92	(2011)	4.49	(2011)	24.08	(2015)	13.12	(2015)	15.07	(2015)
Armenia	93.05	(2011)	87.84	(2011)	88.70	(2011)	64.71	(2016)	49.60	(2016)	57.15	(2016)
Azerbaijan	74.95	(2006)	53.89	(2006)	71.18	(2006)	...		...		...	
Georgia	96.01	(2013)	89.14	(2013)	92.75	(2013)	77.27	(2018)	53.50	(2018)	68.68	(2018)
Kazakhstan	91.17	(2011)	85.38	(2011)	87.89	(2011)	93.79	(2015)	88.06	(2015)	92.17	(2015)
Kyrgyz Republic	85.29	(2012)	88.86	(2012)	84.88	(2012)	86.45	(2018)	77.61	(2018)	83.89	(2018)
Pakistan	19.51	(2012)	3.33	(2012)	8.70	(2012)	23.41	(2018)	1.62	(2018)	8.14	(2018)
Tajikistan	59.54	(2012)	50.86	(2012)	52.27	(2012)	71.63	(2017)	66.11	(2017)	67.83	(2017)
Turkmenistan	19.85	(2006)	10.29	(2006)	10.09	(2006)	95.63	(2016)	90.71	(2016)	97.69	(2016)
Uzbekistan	73.56	(2006)	64.66	(2006)	68.05	(2006)	...		...		...	
East Asia												
China, People's Republic of	43.97		26.51		34.93		60.87	(2014)	61.14	(2014)	55.57	(2014)
Hong Kong, China	...		...		...		...		...		...	
Korea, Republic of	...		...		...		...		...		...	
Mongolia	62.62		26.43		49.69		77.29	(2018)	50.50	(2018)	62.30	(2018)
Taipei,China	...		...		...		...		...		...	
South Asia												
Bangladesh	13.45	(2011)	0.24	(2011)	3.49	(2011)	29.36		12.10		20.36	
Bhutan	20.98		6.12		8.19		...		...		...	
India	34.98	(2011)	24.02	(2011)	24.12	(2011)	42.89	(2016)	13.48	(2016)	24.79	(2016)
Maldives	13.21	(2008)	4.84	(2008)	4.49	(2008)	39.65	(2017)	19.07	(2017)	27.91	(2017)
Nepal	6.87	(2007)	0.65	(2007)	1.80	(2007)	...		...		...	
Sri Lanka	25.03	(2006)	8.29	(2006)	12.68	(2006)	...		...		...	
Southeast Asia												
Brunei Darussalam	...		...		...		...		...		...	
Cambodia	16.98		0.67		3.56		21.23	(2014)	4.35	(2014)	6.38	(2014)
Indonesia	50.65	(2012)	21.76	(2012)	34.51	(2012)	63.19	(2017)	31.61	(2017)	46.39	(2017)
Lao People's Democratic Republic	24.57	(2012)	1.14	(2012)	5.51	(2012)	31.10	(2017)	4.57	(2017)	15.49	(2017)
Malaysia	...		...		...		...		...		...	
Myanmar	...		...		...		16.53	(2016)	1.73	(2016)	5.64	(2016)
Philippines	66.12		21.30	(2008)	48.96	(2008)	78.32	(2018)	47.69	(2018)	71.01	(2018)
Singapore	...		...		...		...		...		...	
Thailand	54.15	(2013)	28.66	(2013)	39.16	(2013)	66.41		39.68		60.61	
Timor-Leste	50.82	(2009)	27.12	(2009)	33.00	(2009)	51.89	(2016)	18.98	(2016)	28.40	(2016)
Viet Nam	48.39	(2011)	20.09	(2011)	32.54	(2011)	55.11	(2014)	19.76	(2014)	42.14	(2014)
The Pacific												
Cook Islands	...		...		...		...		...		...	
Fiji	34.28	(2007)	...		...		...		...		...	
Kiribati	...		...		...		16.73		–		–	
Marshall Islands	...		...		...		...		...		...	
Micronesia, Federated States of	...		...		...		...		...		...	
Nauru	...		...		...		...		...		...	
Niue	...		...		...		...		...		...	
Palau	...		...		...		...		...		...	
Papua New Guinea	...		...		...		16.89	(2018)	–	(2018)	–	(2018)
Samoa	...		...		...		...		...		...	
Solomon Islands	...		...		...		...		...		...	
Tonga	...		...		...		35.84		13.55		16.07	
Tuvalu	...		...		...		...		...		...	
Vanuatu	7.11	(2007)	–	(2007)	0.84	(2007)	...		...		...	
Developed ADB Member Economies												
Australia	85.02		73.48		77.22		...		...		...	
Japan	...		...		...		...		...		...	
New Zealand	...		...		...		...		...		...	

... = data not available, 0.0 = magnitude is less than half of unit employed, – = magnitude equals zero, ADB = Asian Development Bank, Q = wealth quintile.

a Refers to the "percentage of a cohort of children or young people aged 3–5 years above the intended age for the last grade of each level of education who have completed that grade" as defined by the UNESCO Institute for Statistics.

Source: United Nations Statistics Division. Global SDG Indicators Database. https://unstats.un.org/sdgs/indicators/database/ (accessed 12 July 2021).

Table 1.4.3: Selected Indicators for Sustainable Development Goal 4—Early Childhood Education

ADB Regional Member	Target 4.2: By 2030, ensure that all girls and boys have access to quality early childhood development, care, and preprimary education, so that they are ready for primary education. 4.2.2: Participation Rate in Organized Learning (1 Year before the Official Primary Entry Age)[a,b] (%)					
	2010			2019		
	Total	Female	Male	Total	Female	Male
Developing ADB Member Economies						
Central and West Asia						
Afghanistan	…	…	…	…	…	…
Armenia	…	…	…	49.3	50.3	48.4
Azerbaijan	30.4	29.7	30.9	74.2	81.1	68.2
Georgia	47.8 (2007)	50.5 (2007)	45.5 (2007)	…	…	…
Kazakhstan	99.2 (2011)	100.0 (2011)	98.4 (2011)	77.7 (2020)	77.5 (2020)	78.0 (2020)
Kyrgyz Republic	54.0	55.5	52.5	89.8	90.5	89.1
Pakistan	…	…	…	93.4	86.2	100.0
Tajikistan	8.0	7.4	8.6	12.5 (2017)	11.6 (2017)	13.4 (2017)
Turkmenistan	…	…	…	…	…	…
Uzbekistan	33.8	34.3	33.3	45.8	45.0	46.5
East Asia						
China, People's Republic of	…	…	…	…	…	…
Hong Kong, China	98.2 (2012)	100.0 (2012)	96.5 (2012)	97.4	100.0	95.2
Korea, Republic of	…	…	…	98.6 (2018)	98.7 (2018)	98.6 (2018)
Mongolia	98.0	99.1	96.8	96.1	95.1	97.1
Taipei,China	…	…	…	…	…	…
South Asia						
Bangladesh	36.6	36.7	36.6	…	…	…
Bhutan	4.3 (2000)	4.2 (2000)	4.4 (2000)	41.4 (2020)	41.3 (2020)	41.5 (2020)
India	…	…	…	…	…	…
Maldives	85.8 (2007)	86.1 (2007)	85.5 (2007)	93.2	94.6	92.0
Nepal	82.2 (2011)	86.9 (2011)	77.8 (2011)	87.0	82.9	91.0
Sri Lanka	…	…	…	…	…	…
Southeast Asia						
Brunei Darussalam	99.3	98.5	100.0	82.9	82.2	83.5
Cambodia	36.8	37.0	36.5	54.0	55.7	52.3
Indonesia	86.5	88.6	84.6	95.8 (2018)	100.0 (2018)	91.8 (2018)
Lao People's Democratic Republic	35.6	35.9	35.3	69.2	69.7	68.7
Malaysia	85.9	88.4	83.6	99.3 (2015)	100.0 (2015)	98.6 (2015)
Myanmar	8.8	9.0	8.5	11.8 (2018)	11.8 (2018)	11.7 (2018)
Philippines	41.5 (2009)	42.1 (2009)	40.9 (2009)	86.3	87.0	85.6
Singapore	…	…	…	…	…	…
Thailand	98.5	100.0	97.1	98.7	98.7	98.8
Timor-Leste	…	…	…	50.2	51.8	48.7
Viet Nam	90.4	…	…	99.9 (2018)	99.8 (2018)	100.0 (2018)
The Pacific						
Cook Islands	…	…	…	98.4	100.0	96.9
Fiji	49.6 (2006)	50.6 (2006)	48.7 (2006)	99.4	98.7	100.0
Kiribati	…	…	…	…	…	…
Marshall Islands	69.5 (2002)	69.7 (2002)	69.3 (2002)	68.8	69.2	68.5
Micronesia, Federated States of	…	…	…	68.0	65.6	70.3
Nauru	88.1 (2012)	76.0 (2012)	100.0 (2012)	94.5	100.0	89.2
Niue	…	…	…	81.0	61.9	100.0
Palau	…	…	…	90.9 (2014)	81.3 (2014)	100.0 (2014)
Papua New Guinea	…	…	…	71.4 (2016)	71.1 (2016)	71.8 (2016)
Samoa	25.6	28.5	22.8	35.1	35.3	34.8
Solomon Islands	…	…	…	65.6	67.0	64.3
Tonga	…	…	…	…	…	…
Tuvalu	…	…	…	93.4	100.0	87.1
Vanuatu	…	…	…	62.0 (2015)	61.9 (2015)	62.2 (2015)
Developed ADB Member Economies						
Australia	52.6	52.1	53.0	86.2 (2018)	85.8 (2018)	86.5 (2018)
Japan	…	…	…	…	…	…
New Zealand	…	…	…	93.8 (2018)	93.1 (2018)	94.4 (2018)

… = data not available, ADB = Asian Development Bank.

a According to the United Nations Educational, Scientific and Cultural Organization (UNESCO), this is the percentage of children who participate in one or more organized learning programmes, including programmes that offer a combination of education and care, 1 year before the official age for entry to primary education (varies by economy). An organized learning programme is one which consists of a coherent set or sequence of educational activities designed with the intention of achieving pre-determined learning outcomes or the accomplishment of a specific set of educational tasks.

b The figures for the following economies and years are estimates by the UNESCO Institute for Statistics (UIS) as published on the Global SDG Indicators Database: Azerbaijan (all years); Bangladesh (all years); Cambodia (2006, 2015); Hong Kong, China (all years); Indonesia (2009, 2014, 2018); Nepal (2013); Pakistan (all years); Samoa (2000, 2001); Tuvalu (2018); and Viet Nam (2013, 2014). For the purposes of estimating participation rates by age, the UIS may make one or more of the following: (i) an adjustment to account for over- or under-reporting in enrolments; (ii) an estimate of the number of enrolments in a given age group; (iii) a redistribution of enrolments of unknown age (across known ages); or (iv) an estimate of the population in the official age group for small economies. In all cases, estimates are based on evidence from the economy itself.

Source: United Nations Statistics Division. Global SDG Indicators Database. https://unstats.un.org/sdgs/indicators/database/ (accessed 7 July 2021).

Table 1.4.4: Selected Indicators for Sustainable Development Goal 4—Teacher Training and Supply

ADB Regional Member	Target 4.c: By 2030, substantially increase the supply of qualified teachers, including through international cooperation for teacher training in developing countries, especially least developed countries and small island developing states							
	Proportion of Teachers Who Have Received at Least the Minimum Organized Teacher Training, by Education Level							
	4.c.1.a: Preprimary (% of total teachers)		4.c.1.b: Primary (% of total teachers)		4.c.1.c: Lower Secondary (% of total teachers)		4.c.1.d: Upper Secondary (% of total teachers)	
	2010	2019	2010	2019	2010	2019	2010	2019
Developing ADB Member Economies								
Central and West Asia								
Afghanistan	...	...	...	...	...	...	...	...
Armenia	87.8	82.0 (2017)	77.5 (2005)	73.6	...	73.6	...	75.4
Azerbaijan[a]	90.9	93.8	100.0	99.8	...	99.6	...	70.6
Georgia	96.6 (2003)	...	94.6 (2009)	...	94.6 (2009)	...	94.8 (2009)	...
Kazakhstan[b]	...	100.0 (2014)	...	100.0 (2020)	...	...	...	...
Kyrgyz Republic[c]	42.7	...	68.4	95.4 (2017)	...	...	...	...
Pakistan[a]	...	...	84.2	76.9	...	57.5	...	...
Tajikistan	85.2	100.0 (2016)	92.9	100.0 (2017)	94.0 (2003)	...	94.3 (2003)	...
Turkmenistan	...	...	...	99.2	...	...	...	...
Uzbekistan	100.0	95.7	100.0	100.0	...	99.0 (2017)	...	93.4 (2017)
East Asia								
China, People's Republic of	...	...	...	...	...	...	...	...
Hong Kong, China	95.1	96.5	95.6	96.0	...	...	...	...
Korea, Republic of	...	...	...	...	...	...	...	...
Mongolia	89.9	95.7	97.6	88.9	100.0 (2007)	...	100.0 (2006)	...
Taipei,China	...	...	...	...	...	...	...	...
South Asia								
Bangladesh	...	...	57.7 (2011)	50.4 (2017)	58.5	55.0	40.7	66.3
Bhutan	93.8 (2000)	100.0 (2020)	91.5 (2008)	100.0 (2020)	90.2 (2008)	100.0 (2020)	72.2 (2008)	100.0 (2018)
India[a,b,d]	...	...	...	73.1	...	75.0	...	76.2
Maldives[d]	39.0	88.7 (2018)	77.0	88.8	97.6	94.1	...	91.3
Nepal	81.5	83.4	73.7	97.3	57.2	85.4	72.3	81.3
Sri Lanka[a,d]	83.1	87.0 (2018)	82.1	83.1 (2018)	...	81.5 (2018)	...	76.8 (2018)
Southeast Asia								
Brunei Darussalam[a,d]	73.0	63.7	87.1	86.6	...	89.5	...	90.6
Cambodia	98.3	98.0	99.1	100.0	99.8	100.0 (2018)	99.8 (2007)	...
Indonesia	...	...	...	...	...	...	...	...
Lao People's Democratic Republic	97.5	89.6	95.4	96.9	99.3	98.1	99.4	97.6
Malaysia	98.6 (2011)	96.6 (2018)	95.4	96.7	...	...	...	...
Myanmar	58.5	81.4 (2018)	99.9	95.3 (2018)	98.3	89.5 (2018)	100.0	87.7 (2018)
Philippines[a,b,c,d]	...	100.0	...	100.0	...	100.0	...	100.0
Singapore	...	...	98.6 (2009)	98.3 (2018)	...	...	...	...
Thailand[a,b,d]	...	...	...	100.0	...	100.0	...	100.0
Timor-Leste	...	...	...	...	...	...	...	...
Viet Nam	98.5 (2011)	99.8	98.3	99.5	99.1	99.6	...	...
The Pacific								
Cook Islands	69.7 (2011)	100.0	96.6 (2011)	100.0	...	...	...	...
Fiji	...	...	100.0 (2011)	92.3	100.0 (2012)	...	100.0 (2012)	...
Kiribati	...	...	85.4 (2008)	72.7 (2016)	79.2 (2008)	86.7 (2014)	33.6 (2008)	...
Marshall Islands	100.0 (2002)	...	...	...	...	48.4	...	...
Micronesia, Federated States of	...	99.3 (2016)	...	100.0 (2016)	...	100.0 (2016)	...	...
Nauru	82.1 (2007)	100.0 (2016)	74.2 (2007)	100.0 (2016)	...	100.0 (2016)	...	100.0 (2016)
Niue[a,b,c]	...	100.0 (2016)	...	92.3 (2016)	...	80.0 (2016)	...	100.0 (2015)
Palau	...	...	...	...	...	...	...	...
Papua New Guinea	...	...	...	...	100.0 (2012)	...	100.0 (2012)	...
Samoa[c]	...	100.0 (2018)	...	...	...	...	71.9 (2009)	79.5 (2016)
Solomon Islands	61.3 (2011)	51.2 (2013)	58.0	82.4	70.8	93.9	70.9	63.0 (2015)
Tonga[b]	100.0 (2012)	...	...	92.5 (2015)	...	...	...	...
Tuvalu[a,b,c,d]	...	100.0	...	78.3	...	67.1 (2018)	...	62.0 (2018)
Vanuatu	100.0 (2007)	46.0 (2015)	100.0 (2007)	...	...	21.5 (2015)	...	...
Developed ADB Member Economies								
Australia	...	...	...	...	...	...	...	...
Japan	...	...	...	...	...	...	...	...
New Zealand	...	...	...	...	...	...	...	...

... = data not available, ADB = Asian Development Bank.

a For Indicator 4.c.1.c, the earliest available estimate for Azerbaijan is for 2016: 91.6%. For Pakistan, the earliest available estimate is for 2015: 61.2%. For India, the earliest available estimate is for 2016: 77.0%. For Sri Lanka, the earliest available estimate is for 2013: 72.1%. For Brunei Darussalam, the earliest available estimate is for 2014: 94.0%. For the Philippines, the earliest available estimate is for 2016: 100%. For Thailand, the earliest available estimate is for 2015: 100%. For Niue, the earliest available estimate is for 2015: 100%. For Tuvalu, the earliest available estimate is for 2016: 52.4%.

b For Indicator 4.c.1.b, the earliest available estimate for Kazakhstan is for 2014: 100%. For India, the earliest available estimate is for 2016: 69.5%. For the Philippines, the earliest available estimate is for 2014: 100%. For Thailand, the earliest available estimate is for 2014: 100%. For Niue, the earliest available estimate is for 2015: 100%. For Tonga, the earliest available estimate is for 2013: 99.6%. For Tuvalu, the earliest available estimate is for 2016: 76.6%.

c For Indicator 4.c.1.a, the latest available estimate for Kyrgyz Republic is for 2011: 46.2%. For the Philippines, the earliest available estimate is for 2015: 100%. For Niue, the earliest available estimate is for 2015: 100%. For Samoa, the earliest available estimate is for 2014: 100%. For Tuvalu, the earliest available estimate is for 2014: 74.6%.

d For Indicator 4.c.1.d, the earliest available estimate is for India is for 2017: 76.4%. For Maldives, the earliest available estimate is for 2018: 99.0%. For Sri Lanka, the earliest available estimate is for 2016: 77.3%. For Brunei Darussalam, the earliest available estimate is for 2014: 90.4%. For the Philippines, the earliest available estimate is for 2016: 100%. For Thailand, the earliest available estimate is for 2015: 100%. For Tuvalu, the earliest available estimate is for 2016: 34.6%.

Source: United Nations Statistics Division. Global SDG Indicators Database. https://unstats.un.org/sdgs/indicators/database/ (accessed 7 July 2021).

Table 1.5.1: Selected Indicators for Sustainable Development Goal 5—Early Marriage and Women in Leadership

ADB Regional Member	Target 5.3: Eliminate all harmful practices such as child, early, and forced marriage, and female genital mutilation				Target 5.5: Ensure women's full and effective participation in, and equal opportunities for leadership at, all levels of decision-making in political, economic, and public life		
	5.3.1: Proportion of Women Aged 20–24 Years Who Were Married or in a Union (%)				5.5.1.a: Proportion of Seats Held by Women in National Parliaments (%)		5.5.2: Proportion of Women in Managerial Positions (%)
	Before Age 15		Before Age 18				
	2010	2018	2010	2018	2010	2020	2019
Developing ADB Member Economies							
Central and West Asia[a]					**18.7**	**22.6**	
Afghanistan	...	4.2 (2017)	...	28.3 (2017)	27.3	27.0	4.9 (2020)
Armenia	...	0.0 (2016)	...	5.3 (2016)	9.2	23.5	26.2
Azerbaijan	1.9 (2011)	...	11.0 (2011)	...	11.4	16.8	35.8
Georgia	1.1	0.3	14.0	13.9	5.1	14.1	36.7
Kazakhstan	...	0.2 (2015)	...	7.0 (2015)	17.8	27.1	41.1 (2020)
Kyrgyz Republic	0.9 (2014)	0.3	11.6 (2014)	12.9	25.6	19.2	37.8 (2018)
Pakistan	2.8 (2013)	3.6	21.0 (2013)	18.3	22.2	20.2	4.9 (2018)
Tajikistan	...	0.1 (2017)	...	8.7 (2017)	17.5	19.1	14.8 (2009)
Turkmenistan	...	0.2 (2019)	...	6.1 (2019)	16.8	25.0	...
Uzbekistan	0.3 (2006)	...	7.2 (2006)	...	22.0	32.0	...
East Asia[a]					**20.3**	**24.1**	
China, People's Republic of	...	...	...	...	21.3	24.9	...
Hong Kong, China	...	...	...	...	...	...	...
Korea, Republic of	...	...	...	...	14.7	17.3	15.7 (2020)
Mongolia	0.1 (2013)	0.9	5.2 (2013)	12.0	4.0	17.3	43.7
Taipei,China	...	...	...	...	...	...	...
South Asia[a]					**18.7**	**17.3**	
Bangladesh	22.4 (2014)	15.5 (2019)	58.6 (2014)	51.4 (2019)	18.6	20.9	10.7 (2017)
Bhutan	6.2	...	25.8	...	8.5	14.9	18.5 (2015)
India	...	6.6 (2016)	...	27.3 (2016)	10.8	14.4	14.6
Maldives	0.3 (2009)	0.0 (2017)	3.9 (2009)	2.2 (2017)	6.5	4.6	19.6 (2016)
Nepal	...	7.9 (2019)	...	32.8 (2019)	33.2	32.7	13.2 (2017)
Sri Lanka	...	0.9 (2016)	...	9.8 (2016)	5.8	5.3	26.0 (2018)
Southeast Asia[a]					**19.3**	**21.4**	
Brunei Darussalam	...	...	...	...	...	9.1	33.0
Cambodia	1.9 (2014)	...	18.5 (2014)	...	21.1	20.0	24.1 (2017)
Indonesia	...	0.6	...	11.2	18.0	20.4	29.8
Lao People's Democratic Republic	...	7.1 (2017)	...	32.7 (2017)	25.2	27.5	31.8 (2010)
Malaysia	...	...	...	...	9.9	14.4	23.3
Myanmar	...	1.9 (2015)	...	16.0 (2015)	4.3 (2011)	11.1	35.7
Philippines	...	2.2 (2017)	...	16.5 (2017)	21.0	28.0	50.5
Singapore	...	0.0 (2020)	...	0.1 (2020)	23.4	24.0	36.4 (2018)
Thailand	...	3.0 (2019)	...	20.2 (2019)	13.3	16.2	35.1
Timor-Leste	...	2.6 (2016)	...	14.9 (2016)	29.2	38.5	24.5 (2016)
Viet Nam	0.9 (2014)	...	10.6 (2014)	...	25.8	26.7	26.3 (2020)
The Pacific[a]					**2.5**	**6.2**	
Cook Islands	...	...	...	...	...	...	59.8
Fiji	...	...	...	...	8.5 (2006)	19.6	38.9 (2016)
Kiribati	2.8 (2009)	2.4 (2019)	20.3 (2009)	18.4 (2019)	4.4	6.5	37.2 (2015)
Marshall Islands	5.5 (2007)	...	26.3 (2007)	...	3.0	6.1	...
Micronesia, Federated States of	...	...	...	...	0.0	0.0	20.3 (2014)
Nauru	1.9 (2007)	...	26.8 (2007)	...	0.0	10.5	36.1 (2013)
Niue	...	...	...	...	...	...	...
Palau	...	...	...	...	0.0	12.5	29.9 (2014)
Papua New Guinea	2.1 (2006)	8.0	21.3 (2006)	27.3	0.9	0.0	18.1 (2010)
Samoa	0.7 (2014)	0.9 (2020)	10.8 (2014)	7.4 (2020)	8.2	10.0	43.1 (2017)
Solomon Islands	...	5.6 (2015)	...	21.3 (2015)	0.0	6.1	25.7 (2013)
Tonga	0.3 (2012)	0.4 (2019)	5.6 (2012)	10.1 (2019)	3.1	7.4	41.6 (2018)
Tuvalu	0.0 (2007)	...	9.9 (2007)	...	0.0	6.3	35.9 (2016)
Vanuatu	2.5 (2013)	...	21.4 (2013)	...	3.9	0.0	22.1 (2010)
Developed ADB Member Economies[a]					**18.1**	**19.2**	
Australia	...	...	...	...	27.3	30.5	37.8 (2018)
Japan	...	...	...	...	11.3	9.9	14.8
New Zealand	...	...	...	...	33.6	40.8	...
DEVELOPING ADB MEMBER ECONOMIES[a]					**18.7**	**21.1**	
ALL ADB REGIONAL MEMBERS[a]					**18.6**	**21.0**	

... = data not available, 0.0 = magnitude is less than half of unit employed, ADB = Asian Development Bank.

a Regional aggregates for proportion of seats held by women in national parliaments are estimated as a weighted average based on the number of parliament seats in reporting economies.

Source: United Nations Statistics Division. Global SDG Indicators Database. https://unstats.un.org/sdgs/indicators/database (accessed 19 July 2021). For Afghanistan, Bangladesh, and Nepal for indicator 5.5.1.a: Inter-Parliamentary Union. Women in National Parliaments. http://archive.ipu.org/wmn-e/classif-arc.htm (accessed 19 July 2021).

Goal 6. Ensure availability and sustainable management of water and sanitation for all

Table 1.6.1: Selected Indicators for Sustainable Development Goal 6—Clean Water and Sanitation

ADB Regional Member	Target 6.1: By 2030, achieve universal and equitable access to safe and affordable drinking water for all 6.1.1: Proportion of Population Using Safely Managed Drinking Water Services (%)					
	2010			2020		
	Total	Urban	Rural	Total	Urban	Rural
Developing ADB Member Economies						
Central and West Asia						
Afghanistan	19.0	28.0	16.0	28.0	36.0	24.0
Armenia	81.0	...	...	87.0	...	...
Azerbaijan	77.0	93.0	58.0	88.0	96.0	78.0
Georgia	64.0	84.0	39.0	66.0	84.0	40.0
Kazakhstan	78.0	...	...	89.0	...	...
Kyrgyz Republic	58.0	88.0	41.0	70.0	92.0	57.0
Pakistan	37.0	46.0	32.0	36.0	40.0	33.0
Tajikistan	47.0	...	...	55.0	...	...
Turkmenistan	82.0	92.0	73.0	95.0	97.0	92.0
Uzbekistan	58.0	85.0	30.0	59.0	86.0	31.0
East Asia						
China, People's Republic of	...	89.0	...	...	95.0	...
Hong Kong, China	97.2	97.2	...	100.0 (2017)	100.0 (2017)	...
Korea, Republic of	98.0	...	...	99.0	...	...
Mongolia	27.0	37.0	5.0	30.0	39.0	11.0
Taipei,China	...	...	...	...	...	...
South Asia						
Bangladesh	55.0	42.0	60.0	59.0	53.0	62.0
Bhutan	34.0	49.0	25.0	37.0	49.0	28.0
India	...	...	43.0	...	...	56.0
Maldives	...	...	...	...	...	...
Nepal	29.0	38.0	28.0	18.0	25.0	16.0
Sri Lanka	...	88.0	...	...	93.0	...
Southeast Asia						
Brunei Darussalam	...	...	...	...	...	...
Cambodia	22.0	51.0	15.0	28.0	57.0	18.0
Indonesia	...	...	...	...	...	...
Lao People's Democratic Republic	14.0	24.0	9.0	18.0	27.0	12.0
Malaysia	93.0	...	...	94.0	...	...
Myanmar	44.0	68.0	34.0	59.0	74.0	52.0
Philippines	45.0	61.0	32.0	47.0	62.0	35.0
Singapore	100.0	100.0	...	100.0	100.0	...
Thailand	...	...	...	...	...	...
Timor-Leste	...	...	...	...	...	...
Viet Nam	...	...	...	...	...	...
The Pacific						
Cook Islands	...	...	...	...	...	...
Fiji	...	...	...	...	...	...
Kiribati	12.0	19.0	6.0	15.0	21.0	7.0
Marshall Islands	...	...	...	...	...	...
Micronesia, Federated States of	...	...	...	...	...	...
Nauru	...	...	...	...	...	...
Niue	97.0	...	...	94.0	...	...
Palau	79.0	85.0	63.0	91.0	96.0	70.0
Papua New Guinea	...	...	...	...	...	...
Samoa	45.0	...	...	46.0	...	...
Solomon Islands	...	...	...	...	...	...
Tonga	29.0	50.0	23.0	30.0	51.0	23.0
Tuvalu	...	50.0	...	...	50.0	...
Vanuatu	41.8	55.0	...	44.1 (2017)	57.0	...
Developed ADB Member Economies						
Australia	...	99.0	...	...	99.0	...
Japan	98.0	...	...	99.0	...	...
New Zealand	89.0	...	...	100.0	...	...

Table 1.6.1: Selected Indicators for Sustainable Development Goal 6—Clean Water and Sanitation *(continued)*

ADB Regional Member	Target 6.2: By 2030, achieve access to adequate and equitable sanitation and hygiene for all and end open defecation, paying special attention to the needs of women and girls and those in vulnerable situations 6.2.1a: Proportion of Population Using Safely Managed Sanitation Services (%)					
	2010			2020		
	Total	Urban	Rural	Total	Urban	Rural
Developing ADB Member Economies						
Central and West Asia						
Afghanistan	...	...	...	...	...	...
Armenia	54.0	53.0	...	69.0	71.0	...
Azerbaijan	25.0	14.0	...	21.0 (2019)	9.0	...
Georgia	41.0	33.0	51.0	34.0	28.0	44.0
Kazakhstan	...	92.0	...	...	91.0	...
Kyrgyz Republic	89.0	82.0	93.0	92.0	86.0	96.0
Pakistan	...	...	...	...	...	...
Tajikistan	...	...	57.0	...	...	59.0
Turkmenistan	...	...	...	...	...	...
Uzbekistan	...	...	...	...	...	...
East Asia						
China, People's Republic of	35.0	54.0	17.0	70.0	86.0	44.0
Hong Kong, China	91.9	91.9	...	91.8 (2017)	91.8 (2017)	...
Korea, Republic of	89.0	...	...	100.0	...	...
Mongolia	41.0	45.0	34.0	56.0	59.0	49.0
Taipei,China	...	...	...	...	...	...
South Asia						
Bangladesh	28.0	31.0	27.0	39.0	34.0	42.0
Bhutan	65.0	69.0	62.0	65.0	63.0	67.0
India	25.0	29.0	24.0	46.0	37.0	51.0
Maldives	...	...	...	...	...	...
Nepal	27.0	28.0	27.0	49.0	42.0	50.0
Sri Lanka	...	...	...	...	...	...
Southeast Asia						
Brunei Darussalam	...	...	...	...	...	...
Cambodia	...	...	...	...	...	...
Indonesia	...	...	...	...	...	...
Lao People's Democratic Republic	44.0	56.0	39.0	61.0	63.0	60.0
Malaysia	69.0	...	...	77.0 (2018)	...	...
Myanmar	61.0	61.0	61.0	61.0	53.0	64.0
Philippines	49.0	48.0	50.0	61.0	55.0	66.0
Singapore	100.0	100.0	...	100.0	100.0	...
Thailand	23.0	26.0	20.0	26.0	30.0	22.0
Timor-Leste	...	...	...	...	...	...
Viet Nam	...	...	...	...	...	...
The Pacific						
Cook Islands	...	...	...	...	...	...
Fiji	...	...	...	...	...	...
Kiribati	23.0	26.0	20.0	27.0	26.0	27.0
Marshall Islands	...	...	...	...	...	...
Micronesia, Federated States of	...	...	...	...	...	...
Nauru	...	...	...	...	...	...
Niue	...	...	...	...	...	...
Palau	...	...	...	...	...	...
Papua New Guinea	...	30.0	...	...	28.0	...
Samoa	48.0	38.0	51.0	48.0	37.0	50.0
Solomon Islands	...	...	...	...	...	...
Tonga	36.0	29.0	39.0	34.0	23.0	37.0
Tuvalu	6.0	5.0	7.0	6.0 (2018)	5.0 (2018)	8.0 (2018)
Vanuatu	...	...	...	...	...	...
Developed ADB Member Economies						
Australia	65.0	...	...	74.0	...	...
Japan	77.0	...	...	81.0	...	...
New Zealand	80.0	...	...	82.0	...	...

Goal 6: Ensure availability and sustainable management of water and sanitation for all

Table 1.6.1: Selected Indicators for Sustainable Development Goal 6—Clean Water and Sanitation *(continued)*

	Target 6.4: By 2030, substantially increase water-use efficiency across all sectors and ensure sustainable withdrawals and supply of freshwater to address water scarcity and substantially reduce the number of people suffering from water scarcity			Target 6.a: By 2030, expand international cooperation and capacity-building support to developing countries in water- and sanitation-related activities and programmes, including water harvesting, desalination, water efficiency, wastewater treatment, and recycling and reuse technologies		
ADB Regional Member	6.4.2: Level of Water Stress: Freshwater Withdrawal as a Proportion of Available Freshwater Resources (%)			6.a.1: Amount of Water- and Sanitation-Related Official Development Assistance as Part of a Government-Coordinated Spending Plan ($ million)		
	2010	2015	2018	2010	2015	2019
Developing ADB Member Economies						
Central and West Asia						
Afghanistan	54.8 (2009)	54.8	54.8	105.6	75.3	142.9
Armenia	42.9	66.0	54.8	82.0	38.8	6.3
Azerbaijan	51.1	54.3	53.7	17.4	70.5	94.6
Georgia	5.9	4.7	4.2	51.9	44.7	47.2
Kazakhstan	33.0	30.0	32.7	20.9	0.2	1.1
Kyrgyz Republic	50.0	50.0	50.0	11.0	22.3	14.7
Pakistan	113.7	120.8	118.2	80.2	285.2	176.4
Tajikistan	71.6	68.7	61.5	21.8	41.7	61.8
Turkmenistan	143.6	143.6	143.6	0.0	...	0.0
Uzbekistan	143.1	158.1	168.9	31.0	107.1	149.9
East Asia						
China, People's Republic of	42.9	43.2	43.2	282.4	203.6	83.2
Hong Kong, China	...	...	...	...	...	...
Korea, Republic of	85.2	85.2	85.2	...	...	...
Mongolia	3.9	3.2	3.4	24.4	7.6	23.5
Taipei,China	...	...	...	...	...	...
South Asia						
Bangladesh	5.7	5.7	5.7	173.3	201.2	330.4
Bhutan	1.4	1.4	1.4	2.7	7.1	21.7
India	66.5	66.5	66.5	450.6	465.3	373.6
Maldives	15.7	15.7	15.7	2.0	7.5	7.9
Nepal	8.3	8.3	8.3	74.7	107.6	145.2
Sri Lanka	90.8	90.8	90.8	164.0	153.5	144.2
Southeast Asia						
Brunei Darussalam	3.5 (2009)	3.5	3.5	...	...	...
Cambodia	1.0	1.0	1.0	40.2	79.9	177.0
Indonesia	24.2	28.8	29.7	271.0	128.7	131.0
Lao People's Democratic Republic	3.8	5.1	4.8	26.7	109.2	76.5
Malaysia	4.5	3.2	3.4	58.4	71.0	28.9
Myanmar	5.8 (2009)	5.8	5.8	19.7	82.2	142.0
Philippines	25.5	26.4	28.7	45.2	28.0	92.1
Singapore	74.6	84.6	82.0	...	...	...
Thailand	23.0	23.0	23.0	7.2	8.1	3.1
Timor-Leste	28.3	28.3	28.3	17.3	16.6	3.2
Viet Nam	18.1	18.1	18.1	371.6	559.3	405.6
The Pacific						
Cook Islands	...	...	...	0.5	4.2	1.8
Fiji	0.3	0.3	0.3	1.8	3.3	18.3
Kiribati	...	...	...	0.1	6.5	5.0
Marshall Islands	...	...	...	0.2	1.0	2.0
Micronesia, Federated States of	...	...	...	0.1	1.9	1.5
Nauru	...	...	...	0.2	4.9	0.2
Niue	...	...	...	0.3	0.0 (2016)	0.0
Palau	...	...	...	0.2	1.4	7.1
Papua New Guinea	0.1	0.1	0.1	13.4	6.2	26.9
Samoa	...	...	...	14.8	19.8	7.8
Solomon Islands	...	...	...	5.6	7.7	16.2
Tonga	...	...	...	1.0	1.6	1.1
Tuvalu	...	...	...	0.0	3.0	0.0
Vanuatu	...	...	...	0.8	3.0	4.7
Developed ADB Member Economies						
Australia	5.3	6.7	4.7	...	...	...
Japan	37.3	36.7	36.5	...	...	...
New Zealand	4.2	8.1	8.1	...	...	...

... = data not available, 0.0 = magnitude is less than half of unit employed, $ = United States dollars, ADB = Asian Development Bank.

Source: United Nations Statistics Division. Global SDG Indicators Database. https://unstats.un.org/sdgs/indicators/database/ (accessed 13 July 2021).

Table 1.7.1: Selected Indicators for Sustainable Development Goal 7—Affordable and Clean Energy

ADB Regional Member	Target 7.1: By 2030, ensure universal access to affordable, reliable, and modern energy services								Target 7.2: By 2030, increase substantially the share of renewable energy in the global energy mix		Target 7.3: By 2030, double the global rate of improvement in energy efficiency	
	7.1.1: Proportion of Population with Access to Electricity (%)						7.1.2: Proportion of Population with Primary Reliance on Clean Fuels and Technology (%)		7.2.1: Renewable Energy Share in Total Final Energy Consumption (%)		7.3.1: Energy Intensity Measured in Terms of Primary Energy and GDP (MJ/$ 2011 PPP GDP)	
	Total		Urban		Rural							
	2010	2019	2010	2019	2010	2019	2010	2019	2010	2018	2010	2018
Developing ADB Member Economies												
Central and West Asia												
Afghanistan	42.7	97.7	82.8	100.0	30.2	96.9	20.0	36.0	14.9	21.4	2.2	1.8
Armenia	99.8	100.0	99.7	100.0	100.0	100.0	>95	>95	9.4	11.1	3.9	3.4
Azerbaijan	99.9	100.0	100.0	100.0	99.9	100.0	93.0	>95	4.4	2.0	3.7	4.3
Georgia	100.0	100.0	100.0	100.0	100.0	100.0	66.0	88.0	39.1	27.9	3.6	3.8
Kazakhstan	100.0	100.0	100.0	100.0	100.0	100.0	93.0	>95	1.4	1.9	8.6	6.8
Kyrgyz Republic	99.0	99.9	99.1	99.7	98.9	100.0	72.0	77.0	25.6	23.2	5.1	5.9
Pakistan	70.8	73.9	97.1	100.0	56.6	58.7	36.0	49.0	47.4	41.7	5.1	4.6
Tajikistan	98.7	99.6	99.3	99.1	98.4	99.8	70.0	82.0	61.8	39.5	5.4	5.0
Turkmenistan	100.0	99.9	100.0	99.9	100.0	99.9	>95	>95	0.1	0.1	21.7	13.3
Uzbekistan	99.8	100.0	100.0	100.0	99.6	100.0	86.0	85.0	1.3	1.5	15.5	8.7
East Asia												
China, People's Republic of	99.7	100.0	100.0	100.0	99.4	100.0	53.0	64.0	12.3	13.1	8.9	6.3
Hong Kong, China	100.0	100.0	100.0	100.0	100.0	100.0	...	...	0.2	0.2	1.6	1.3
Korea, Republic of	100.0	100.0	100.0	100.0	100.0	100.0	>95	>95	1.3	3.2	6.1	5.5
Mongolia	78.5	99.1	96.1	100.0	41.9	97.2	35.0	52.0	4.5	3.4	8.1	6.4
Taipei,China	...	...	...	...	...	...	...	...	1.6	2.1 (2015)	...	...
South Asia												
Bangladesh	55.3	92.2	90.1	97.8	40.0	88.9	13.0	23.0	41.1	30.7	3.0	2.5
Bhutan	73.3	100.0	99.3	100.0	59.4	100.0	64.0	79.0	90.8	81.1	10.1	8.3
India	76.3	97.8	94.0	100.0	68.4	96.7	35.0	64.0	41.1	31.7	5.6	4.4
Maldives	99.4	100.0	99.6	100.0	99.3	100.0	93.0	>95	1.4	1.1	2.3	2.6
Nepal	68.6	89.9	95.5	94.2	63.2	88.8	21.0	31.0	87.3	75.0	6.7	6.4
Sri Lanka	85.3	100.0	95.6	100.0	83.0	100.0	21.0	31.0	61.8	51.4	2.2	1.8
Southeast Asia												
Brunei Darussalam	100.0	100.0	100.0	100.0	100.0	100.0	>95	>95	–	0.0	5.2	6.0
Cambodia	31.1	93.0	91.3	99.7	15.8	90.9	11.0	31.0	68.5	61.8	5.7	5.1
Indonesia	94.2	98.9	99.0	99.9	89.4	97.5	42.0	82.0	34.8	20.9	4.2	3.2
Lao People's Democratic Republic	70.1	100.0	97.2	99.8	58.5	100.0	<5	8.0	64.9	41.9	3.3	5.8
Malaysia	99.0	100.0	99.8	100.0	98.1	100.0	>95	>95	2.0	5.3	5.2	4.5
Myanmar	48.8	68.4	89.0	92.7	32.5	57.5	10.0	30.0	84.9	60.1	3.7	3.7
Philippines	85.4	95.6	93.9	98.0	78.3	93.5	40.0	47.0	28.8	23.2	3.0	2.8
Singapore	100.0	100.0	100.0	100.0	100.0	100.0	>95	>95	0.5	0.7	2.5	2.9
Thailand	99.7	99.9	100.0	99.9	99.5	99.9	74.0	80.0	22.7	23.7	5.1	4.5
Timor-Leste	38.0	94.7	83.4	100.0	20.6	92.3	<5	13.0	34.8	18.4	1.4	2.0
Viet Nam	97.4	99.4	99.9	100.0	96.4	99.1	49.0	65.0	34.8	23.5	5.5	4.8
The Pacific												
Cook Islands[a]	99.0	100.0	99.0	100.0	...	...	81.0	78.0	–	4.4	...	...
Fiji	89.2	100.0	96.1	100.0	81.7	100.0	31.0	50.0	28.0	27.9	2.4	2.1
Kiribati	63.2	100.0	90.0	89.0	39.4	100.0	<5	10.0	48.5	41.1	6.7	6.0
Marshall Islands	89.2	97.4	92.4	95.9	80.5	100.0	53.0	65.0	13.3	11.7	10.4	10.1
Micronesia, Federated States of	65.0	82.0	84.6	95.8	58.8	78.1	12.0	12.0	1.8	1.8	4.1	5.6
Nauru	99.1	100.0	98.4	100.0	100.0 (2015)	100.0	>95	>95	0.1	0.7	8.7	5.1
Niue[b]	100.0 (2011)	100.0	100.0 (2011)	100.0	...	...	93.0	>95	26.7	23.3	...	...
Palau	99.0	100.0	99.4	100.0	96.4	100.0	>95	>95	–	0.1	10.7	9.2
Papua New Guinea	20.0	63.0	71.2	83.2	11.8	60.4	8.0	9.0	55.3	49.6	5.6	4.6
Samoa	96.0	99.0	99.0	100.0	95.7	99.0	27.0	36.0	41.3	36.6	3.7	4.2
Solomon Islands	34.0	70.0	65.4	76.6	26.4	68.2	8.0	9.0	45.1	48.5	7.3	4.9
Tonga	93.0	98.0	97.9	100.0	91.1	97.9	60.0	76.0	1.0	1.7	2.9	3.0
Tuvalu	97.0	100.0	98.5	100.0	95.4	100.0	50.0	69.0	–	9.9	3.9	3.0
Vanuatu	44.0	65.0	82.3	94.8	31.7	54.4	12.0	8.0	38.4	30.8	3.5	3.8
Developed ADB Member Economies												
Australia	100.0	100.0	100.0	100.0	100.0	100.0	>95	>95	8.2	9.6	5.3	4.3
Japan	100.0	100.0	100.0	100.0	100.0	100.0	>95	>95	4.8	7.4	4.4	3.4
New Zealand	100.0	100.0	100.0	100.0	100.0	100.0	>95	>95	31.7	31.0	4.8	4.2
WORLD	**83.3**	**90.1**	**95.7**	**97.3**	**72.1**	**82.5**	**57.0**	**66.0**	**16.4**	**17.1**	**5.6**	**4.8**

... = data not available, – = magnitude equals zero, 0.0 = magnitude is less than half of unit employed, < = less than, > = greater than, $ = United States dollars, ADB = Asian Development Bank, GDP = gross domestic product, MJ = megajoule, PPP = purchasing power parity.

a For 2006 (available in the Key Indicators Database) and 2011, values are economy data. Data for other years are modeled estimates.
b For access to electricity, 2011 is the earliest year for available economy data. Data for 2012–2019 are modeled estimates.

Sources: For Indicator 7.1.1: World Bank. World Development Indicators. https://data.worldbank.org/indicator (accessed 17 July 2021); and for Cook Islands and Niue: United Nations Statistics Division. Global SDG Indicators Database. http://unstats.un.org/sdgs/indicators/database/ (accessed 6 August 2021).
For Indicator 7.1.2, Indicator 7.2.1, and Indicator 7.3.1: United Nations. Global SDG Indicators Database. http://unstats.un.org/sdgs/indicators/database/ (accessed 17 July 2021); and for Taipei,China: World Bank. DataBank: Sustainable Energy for All. https://databank.worldbank.org/source/sustainable-energy-for-all# (accessed 17 July 2021).

Goal 8. Promote sustained, inclusive and sustainable economic growth; full and productive employment; and decent work for all

Table 1.8.1: Selected Indicators for Sustainable Development Goal 8—Youth Participation in Education and Work, Child Labor

ADB Regional Member	Target 8.6: By 2020, substantially reduce the proportion of youth not in employment, education, or training — 8.6.1: Proportion of Youth (Aged 15–24 Years) not in Education, Employment, or Training (%)		Target 8.7: Take immediate and effective measures to eradicate forced labor, end modern slavery and human trafficking, and secure the prohibition and elimination of the worst forms of child labor, including recruitment and use of child soldiers; and, by 2025, end child labor in all its forms — 8.7.1: Proportion of Children (Aged 5–17 Years) Engaged in Child Labor (%)		
	2010	2019	Total 2019	Female 2019	Male 2019
Developing ADB Member Economies					
Central and West Asia					
Afghanistan	...	42.0 (2017)	16.6 (2014)	12.6 (2014)	20.3 (2014)
Armenia	44.6 (2011)	31.1 (2018)	3.9 (2015)	2.7 (2015)	4.9 (2015)
Azerbaijan	...	...	...	...	...
Georgia	32.6 (2012)	26.0	1.5 (2015)	0.9 (2015)	2.1 (2015)
Kazakhstan	8.2	9.5 (2016)	...	...	...
Kyrgyz Republic	18.5	20.5 (2018)	20.1 (2018)	15.6 (2018)	24.2 (2018)
Pakistan	31.1	31.0 (2018)	9.0 (2018)	5.1 (2018)	12.4 (2018)
Tajikistan	42.2 (2009)	...	...	...	...
Turkmenistan	...	...	0.3 (2016)	0.1 (2016)	0.4 (2016)
Uzbekistan	...	...	...	...	...
East Asia					
China, People's Republic of	...	...	...	...	...
Hong Kong, China	...	...	...	...	...
Korea, Republic of	...	...	...	...	...
Mongolia	17.6	19.7	7.9 (2018)	6.5 (2018)	9.1 (2018)
Taipei,China	...	...	...	...	...
South Asia					
Bangladesh	30.1	27.4 (2017)	5.9	3.0	8.7
Bhutan	...	...	1.7 (2010)	1.7 (2010)	1.6 (2010)
India	27.9	29.5	4.3 (2012)	3.1 (2012)	5.3 (2012)
Maldives	32.5 (2009)	23.5 (2016)	...	...	...
Nepal	23.1 (2008)	35.4 (2017)	19.0 (2014)	19.3 (2014)	19.2 (2014)
Sri Lanka	26.7	24.2 (2018)	0.8 (2016)	0.6 (2016)	0.9 (2016)
Southeast Asia					
Brunei Darussalam	17.2 (2014)	20.1	...	...	...
Cambodia	0.2	6.1 (2017)	11.5 (2012)	12.2 (2012)	10.8 (2012)
Indonesia	26.7	20.5	...	...	...
Lao People's Democratic Republic	5.1	42.1 (2017)	26.3 (2017)	26.2 (2017)	26.3 (2017)
Malaysia	14.4 (2011)	12.5 (2018)	...	...	...
Myanmar	...	14.9	8.1 (2015)	7.6 (2015)	8.7 (2015)
Philippines	25.3	18.8	4.3 (2011)	3.5 (2011)	5.1 (2011)
Singapore	3.7 (2013)	4.1	...	...	...
Thailand	12.5	14.9	...	...	...
Timor-Leste	19.0	21.0 (2016)	7.2 (2016)	6.9 (2016)	7.6 (2016)
Viet Nam	8.2	14.4	12.1 (2014)	12.5 (2014)	11.9 (2014)
The Pacific					
Cook Islands	...	12.6	...	...	...
Fiji	18.4 (2011)	20.1 (2016)	...	...	...
Kiribati	...	46.9 (2015)	7.1	5.5	8.6
Marshall Islands	...	...	...	...	...
Micronesia, Federated States of	23.7 (2014)	...	...	...	...
Nauru	36.4 (2013)	...	...	...	...
Niue	...	...	...	...	...
Palau	12.9 (2014)	...	...	...	...
Papua New Guinea	27.7	...	...	...	...
Samoa	38.9 (2012)	37.9 (2017)	...	...	...
Solomon Islands	7.0 (2013)	...	13.8 (2015)	13.8 (2015)	13.8 (2015)
Tonga	...	30.3 (2018)	25.9	18.5	32.9
Tuvalu	...	29.0 (2016)	...	...	...
Vanuatu	31.0	...	15.0 (2013)	15.8 (2013)	14.2 (2013)
Developed ADB Member Economies					
Australia	11.3	8.9 (2017)	...	...	...
Japan	4.3	3.1	...	...	...
New Zealand	13.6	11.6	...	...	...

... = data not available, ADB = Asian Development Bank.

Source: United Nations Statistics Division. Global SDG Indicators Database. https://unstats.un.org/sdgs/indicators/database/ (accessed 18 July 2021).

Goal 8. Promote sustained, inclusive, and sustainable economic growth; full and productive employment; and decent work for all

Table 1.8.2: Selected Indicators for Sustainable Development Goal 8—Access to Banking, Insurance, and Financial Services, and Trade

ADB Regional Member	Target 8.10: Strengthen the capacity of domestic financial institutions to encourage and expand access to banking, insurance, and financial services for all					
	8.10.1: Number of Commercial Bank Branches and ATMs per 100,000 Adults				8.10.2: Proportion of Adults (15 Years and Older) with an Account at a Bank or Other Financial Institution or with a Mobile-Money Service Provider (%)	
	Commercial Bank Branches		ATMs			
	2010	2019	2010	2019	2011	2017
Developing ADB Member Economies						
Central and West Asia						
Afghanistan	2.4	1.9	0.5	1.6	9.0	14.9
Armenia	18.6	24.2	34.0	65.5	17.5	47.8
Azerbaijan	9.9	...	27.1	34.5	14.9	28.6
Georgia	21.2	33.6	48.3	85.1	33.0	61.2
Kazakhstan	3.3	2.5	61.4	85.9	42.1	58.7
Kyrgyz Republic	6.1	8.0	7.3	39.3	3.8	39.9
Pakistan	8.4	10.4	4.3	10.8	10.3	21.3
Tajikistan	7.0	22.9 (2018)	4.5	...	2.5	47.0
Turkmenistan	...	...	...	...	0.4	40.6
Uzbekistan	39.2	34.2	4.0	38.5	22.5	37.1
East Asia						
China, People's Republic of	7.8 (2012)	8.9	24.9	95.5	63.8	80.2
Hong Kong, China	23.8	21.0	46.9	53.2	88.7	95.3
Korea, Republic of	18.2	15.1	265.4	267.0 (2018)	93.0	94.9
Mongolia	54.6	63.9	18.5	148.8	77.7	93.0
Taipei,China	17.0 (2011)	16.4 (2020)	...	150.2 (2020)	...	...
South Asia						
Bangladesh	7.7	9.0	2.1	9.4	31.7	50.0
Bhutan	15.3	19.3	8.9	48.1	...	...
India	10.0	14.6	7.2	21.0	35.2	79.9
Maldives	11.7	13.9	16.5	35.0	...	...
Nepal	5.1	17.8	7.4 (2011)	16.5	25.3	45.4
Sri Lanka	15.9	...	13.4	...	68.5	73.6
Southeast Asia						
Brunei Darussalam	23.3	17.6	82.0	74.0	...	...
Cambodia	4.1	8.3	5.3	23.3	3.7	21.7
Indonesia	8.1	15.6	13.0	53.4	19.6	48.9
Lao People's Democratic Republic	2.5	3.2 (2018)	8.7	25.7 (2018)	26.8	29.1
Malaysia	10.9	10.1	53.5	44.7	66.2	85.3
Myanmar	1.5	5.6	0.1 (2012)	6.9	...	26.0
Philippines	7.5	9.2	15.1	29.0	26.6	34.5
Singapore	9.8	7.8	59.1	58.8	98.2	97.9
Thailand	11.0	11.2	81.9	115.1	72.7	81.6
Timor-Leste	1.8	6.2	2.4	8.9	...	...
Viet Nam	3.2	4.0	17.0	25.9	21.4	30.8
The Pacific						
Cook Islands	...	...	...	...	...	...
Fiji	11.1	11.3	33.1	53.9	...	...
Kiribati	6.0 (2011)	...	10.5 (2011)	...	...	...
Marshall Islands	17.6	13.4	2.9	5.7	...	...
Micronesia, Federated States of	15.1	12.8	9.1	12.8	...	...
Nauru	...	...	...	...	...	...
Niue	...	...	...	...	...	...
Palau	...	...	36.5	45.8 (2017)	...	...
Papua New Guinea	1.6	1.5 (2018)	5.3	8.2 (2018)	...	...
Samoa	25.3	23.7	25.3	45.7	...	...
Solomon Islands	4.5	4.2 (2017)	11.2	11.9 (2017)	...	...
Tonga	21.5	33.0 (2018)	27.7	40.5 (2018)	...	...
Tuvalu	...	...	...	...	...	...
Vanuatu	20.6	21.2	28.1	47.9	...	...
Developed ADB Member Economies						
Australia	30.8	28.2 (2018)	168.7	146.2 (2018)	99.1	99.5
Japan	33.8	33.9	130.9	124.1	96.4	98.2
New Zealand	34.5	25.4	72.2	63.5	99.4	99.2

... = data not available, ADB = Asian Development Bank.

Sources: United Nations Statistics Division. Global SDG Indicators Database. https://unstats.un.org/sdgs/indicators/database/ (accessed 13 July 2021). For indicator 8.10.1: Commercial Bank Branches for Taipei,China: Central bank of Taipei,China. https://www.cbc.gov.tw/en/cp-535-1059-E918E-2.html (accessed 13 July 2021); and ATMs for Taipei,China: Financial Supervisory Commission, Banking Bureau. https://www.banking.gov.tw/en/home.jsp?id=124&parentpath=0,100,122 (accessed 13 July 2021). For Indicator 8.10.2: World Bank. World Development Indicators. https://data.worldbank.org/indicator (accessed 31 May 2021).

Goal 9. Build resilient infrastructure, promote inclusive and sustainable industrialization, and foster innovation

Table 1.9.1: Selected Indicators for Sustainable Development Goal 9—Road and Rail Transport, Passenger and Freight Volume

	Target 9.1: Develop quality, reliable, sustainable and resilient infrastructure, including regional and transborder infrastructure, to support economic development and human well-being, with a focus on affordable and equitable access for all			
ADB Regional Member	9.1.2: Passenger Volume, by Road Transport[a] (p-km million)	9.1.2: Freight Volume, by Road Transport[b] (t-km million)	9.1.2: Passenger Volume, by Rail Transport[a] (p-km million)	9.1.2: Freight Volume, by Rail Transport[b] (t-km million)
	2019	2019	2019	2019
Developing ADB Member Economies				
Central and West Asia	**874,392.8**	**837,186.6**	**235,776.7**	**280,134.0**
Afghanistan	36,546.4	4,268.0	392.8	2,082.4
Armenia	9,567.3	5,779.2	6,648.2	1,522.8
Azerbaijan	28,941.3	24,175.6	22,518.8	14,864.4
Georgia	11,437.9	7,115.2	9,553.2	6,633.4
Kazakhstan	70,748.0	305,555.6	22,998.6	171,608.6
Kyrgyz Republic	11,583.8	7,772.6	4,661.3	1,345.4
Pakistan	583,264.5	415,801.8	104,230.6	54,089.6
Tajikistan	15,017.2	2,749.6	6,950.0	3,563.4
Turkmenistan	19,178.2	16,091.0	19,211.8	4,655.0
Uzbekistan	88,108.3	47,878.0	38,611.4	19,769.0
East Asia[b]	**5,709,458.3**	**7,055,112.6**	**1,872,553.1**	**3,631,201.6**
China, People's Republic of	5,359,866.9	6,883,712.4	1,734,503.9	3,577,208.6
Hong Kong, China	38,075.7	6,014.0	11,631.8	14,091.8
Korea, Republic of	297,260.9	96,865.6	119,610.8	25,696.0
Mongolia	14,254.8	68,520.6	6,806.6	14,205.2
Taipei,China	...	...	...	...
South Asia[b]	**5,901,892.8**	**2,217,969.4**	**3,759,081.0**	**458,053.6**
Bangladesh	858,302.1	51,903.8	87,167.8	32,599.2
Bhutan	6,117.4	339.2	1,052.6	–
India	4,872,638.6	2,143,986.2	3,576,649.0	422,069.0
Maldives	5,531.2	11.6	4,903.4	–
Nepal	41,644.5	1,520.2	5,642.4	–
Sri Lanka	117,659.0	20,208.4	83,665.8	3,385.4
Southeast Asia[b]	**2,964,059.3**	**1,033,122.8**	**269,857.5**	**89,144.6**
Brunei Darussalam	7,327.6	503.0	502.2	–
Cambodia	49,845.3	25,823.8	3,726.7	4,677.2
Indonesia	1,264,823.6	452,520.4	51,330.6	12,522.0
Lao People's Democratic Republic	28,862.5	16,786.0	2,189.1	–
Malaysia	267,724.7	120,291.8	32,190.7	24,357.6
Myanmar	90,195.8	11,896.2	6,761.1	3,935.4
Philippines	436,266.2	73,191.4	63,609.3	587.8
Singapore	91,474.4	1,788.2	15,294.4	9,916.2
Thailand	358,907.0	182,592.8	42,116.0	24,789.0
Timor-Leste	1,761.6	–	–	–
Viet Nam	366,870.7	147,729.2	52,137.4	8,359.4
The Pacific[b]	**21,561.0**	**1,194.0**	**621.6**	–
Cook Islands	45.0	–	2.0	–
Fiji	2,499.4	139.0	62.0	–
Kiribati	213.0	5.8	8.8	–
Marshall Islands	949.4	–	18.4	–
Micronesia, Federated States of	302.0	9.0	12.0	–
Nauru	21.6	–	1.0	–
Niue	2.0	–	–	–
Palau	266.2	3.8	14.4	–
Papua New Guinea	13,409.8	1,019.2	361.4	–
Samoa	734.6	–	30.4	–
Solomon Islands	1,599.4	–	48.0	–
Tonga	446.6	16.2	18.6	–
Tuvalu	32.0	1.0	1.0	–
Vanuatu	1,040.0	–	43.6	–
Developed ADB Member Economies	**1,131,016.5**	**1,432,259.4**	**293,702.4**	**318,015.6**
Australia	311,625.8	1,137,499.4	14,196.4	226,695.2
Japan	768,816.6	277,907.8	278,071.6	75,692.6
New Zealand	50,574.1	16,852.2	1,434.4	15,627.8
DEVELOPING ADB MEMBER ECONOMIES[b]	**15,471,364.2**	**11,144,585.4**	**6,137,889.9**	**4,458,533.8**
ALL ADB REGIONAL MEMBERS[b]	**16,602,380.7**	**12,576,844.8**	**6,431,592.3**	**4,776,549.4**
WORLD	**42,280,264.8**	**26,503,565.8**	**9,215,756.8**	**10,899,502.8**

... = data not available, – = magnitude equals zero, ADB = Asian Development Bank, p-km = passenger-kilometer, t-km = ton-kilometer.

Note: The numbers shown in the table are modeled estimates as published on the United Nations' Global SDG Indicators Database.

a A passenger-kilometer, abbreviated as p-km, is a unit of measurement representing the transport of 1 passenger by a defined mode of transport over 1 kilometer.

b A ton-kilometer, abbreviated as t-km, is a unit of measurement of freight transport representing the transport of 1 metric ton of goods (including packaging and tare weights of intermodal transport units) by a defined mode of transport over a distance of 1 kilometer.

c For reporting economies only.

Source: United Nations Statistics Division. Global SDG Indicators Database. http://unstats.un.org/sdgs/indicators/database/ (accessed 20 July 2021).

Table 1.9.2: Selected Indicators for Sustainable Development Goal 9—Growth in Manufacturing

ADB Regional Member	Target 9.2: Promote inclusive and sustainable industrialization; and, by 2030, significantly raise industry's share of employment and GDP, in line with national circumstances, and double its share in least developed countries					
	9.2.1: Manufacturing Value Added[a]				9.2.2: Manufacturing Employment as a Proportion of Total Employment (%)	
	As a Proportion of GDP (%)		Per Capita (at constant 2015 $)			
	2010	2020	2010	2020	2010	2019
Developing ADB Member Economies						
Central and West Asia						
Afghanistan	7.0	4.4	35.3	22.3	6.8 (2012)	7.7 (2017)
Armenia	9.0	12.3	267.4	503.3	5.7	9.9 (2018)
Azerbaijan	4.5	5.7	239.4	288.9	4.8	5.3
Georgia	8.8	7.8	252.9	325.4	5.3	5.8
Kazakhstan	11.1	10.5	1,005.1	1,153.0	7.0	6.8 (2017)
Kyrgyz Republic	17.6	13.1	170.9	152.3	7.6 (2012)	11.8 (2018)
Pakistan	13.0	12.0	158.1	176.2	13.5	16.2 (2018)
Tajikistan	20.2	18.5	157.9	221.3	5.5 (2009)	5.4 (2018)
Turkmenistan	46.4	45.1	1,994.5	3,342.6	...	...
Uzbekistan	13.1	13.9	262.1	427.9	11.5	11.9
East Asia						
China, People's Republic of	29.7	27.7	1,636.5	2,822.4	...	...
Hong Kong, China	1.3	1.0	504.3	417.3	...	...
Korea, Republic of	26.8	26.1	6,822.0	8,254.0	17.0	16.3
Mongolia	9.0	9.4	238.6	385.3	6.3	7.9
Taipei,China	28.1	34.2	5,613.9	9,710.0	27.3	26.7
South Asia						
Bangladesh	14.3	20.2	138.2	332.7	12.4	14.4 (2017)
Bhutan	8.5	7.8	193.8	243.1	3.9	...
India	15.3	15.4	194.4	284.8	11.1	12.1
Maldives	2.0	2.5	167.4	199.0	9.1 (2009)	...
Nepal	5.8	5.0	36.1	42.7	0.2 (2008)	15.1 (2017)
Sri Lanka	18.7	16.3	550.4	677.3	17.1	18.3 (2018)
Southeast Asia						
Brunei Darussalam	14.7	15.5	4,924.8	4,774.7	3.7 (2014)	4.3
Cambodia	14.3	16.8	127.2	230.8	10.7	16.7 (2017)
Indonesia	21.4	20.4	583.0	766.0	12.5	14.4
Lao People's Democratic Republic	8.0	8.1	126.5	202.2	5.1	7.9 (2017)
Malaysia	22.8	20.3	1,881.2	2,158.7	16.8	17.8
Myanmar	19.3	24.2	171.2	367.0	10.9 (2015)	10.5
Philippines	19.2	19.1	448.3	592.4	8.2	8.5
Singapore	21.1	18.0	10,136.4	10,135.1	17.7	9.6
Thailand	30.0	25.7	1,547.7	1,596.7	14.1	16.3
Timor-Leste	0.9	1.5	10.9	19.5	3.2	...
Viet Nam	11.5	17.8	189.9	470.5	14.3	22.0
The Pacific						
Cook Islands	2.5	2.2	359.3	488.3	3.9 (2011)	3.8
Fiji	11.7	11.9	436.0	559.2	9.3 (2011)	...
Kiribati	5.1	3.9	68.9	60.9	13.2	...
Marshall Islands	1.1	1.5	34.3	60.0	0.7	...
Micronesia, Federated States of	...	...	...	...	2.4 (2014)	...
Nauru	...	...	...	...	0.5 (2013)	...
Niue	...	...	...	...	...	...
Palau	0.7	1.1	94.0	154.0	3.2 (2008)	...
Papua New Guinea	2.6	1.5	57.8	42.0	1.8	...
Samoa	10.4	5.8	412.7	240.3	6.8 (2012)	6.8 (2017)
Solomon Islands	12.0	9.9	206.1	173.5	5.5 (2013)	...
Tonga	6.1	5.7	211.4	236.0	...	20.2 (2018)
Tuvalu	1.1	0.7	29.5	25.5	...	...
Vanuatu	5.0	3.0	148.5	76.6	2.3	...
Developed ADB Member Economies						
Australia	7.5	5.4	3,690.0	2,783.7	9.7	6.9
Japan	20.5	19.5	6,659.3	6,745.3	16.8	16.2
New Zealand	12.3	10.5	4,319.5	4,287.8	11.6	9.1

... = data not available, $ = United States dollars, ADB = Asian Development Bank, GDP = gross domestic product.

a United Nations Statistics Division figures calculated from GDP, manufacturing value-added, and population data.

Source: United Nations Statistics Division. Global SDG Indicators Database. https://unstats.un.org/sdgs/indicators/database/ (accessed 18 July 2021); For Taipei,China: United Nations Industrial Development Organization. Statistics Data Portal. https://stat.unido.org/SDG (accessed 18 July 2021).

Goal 9. Build resilient infrastructure, promote inclusive and sustainable industrialization, and foster innovation

Table 1.9.3: Selected Indicators for Sustainable Development Goal 9—Carbon Dioxide Emissions

ADB Regional Member	Target 9.4: By 2030, upgrade infrastructure and retrofit industries to make them sustainable, with increased resource-use efficiency and greater adoption of clean and environmentally sound technologies and industrial processes, with all countries taking action in accordance with their respective capabilities — 9.4.1: Carbon Dioxide Emissions[a]			
	Per Unit of GDP (PPP) (kg of CO_2 equivalent per constant 2017 $)		Per Unit of Manufacturing Value-Added (kg of CO_2 equivalent per constant 2015 $)	
	2010	2018	2010	2018
Developing ADB Member Economies[a]				
Central and West Asia				
Afghanistan	…	…	…	…
Armenia	0.15	0.14	0.7	0.3
Azerbaijan	0.18	0.22	0.6	0.4
Georgia	0.14	0.17	0.5	1.0
Kazakhstan	0.65	0.46	3.2	1.4
Kyrgyz Republic	0.27	0.32	0.6	0.9
Pakistan	0.18	0.19	1.3	1.4
Tajikistan	0.14	0.23	0.1 (2012)	1.1
Turkmenistan	1.30	0.80	0.2	0.1
Uzbekistan	0.90	0.48	2.3	0.8
East Asia				
China, People's Republic of	0.66	0.45	1.2	0.7
Hong Kong, China	0.12	0.09	1.6	1.8
Korea, Republic of	0.32	0.28	0.2	0.2
Mongolia	0.70	0.56	1.9	1.0
Taipei,China	…	…	0.3	0.2
South Asia				
Bangladesh	0.12	0.11	0.5	0.4
Bhutan	…	…	…	…
India	0.30	0.26	1.6	1.4
Maldives	…	…	…	…
Nepal	0.06	0.12	1.3	2.7
Sri Lanka	0.07	0.07	0.1	0.1
Southeast Asia				
Brunei Darussalam	0.26	0.28	0.2	0.2
Cambodia	0.12	0.16	0.1	0.2
Indonesia	0.20	0.18	0.9	0.5
Lao People's Democratic Republic	0.08	0.33	1.1	0.5
Malaysia	0.33	0.26	0.6	0.5
Myanmar	0.05	0.12	0.3	0.1
Philippines	0.14	0.15	0.3	0.2
Singapore	0.11	0.09	0.2	0.2
Thailand	0.23	0.19	0.5	0.4
Timor-Leste	…	…	…	…
Viet Nam	0.28	0.31	2.5	1.6
The Pacific				
Cook Islands	…	…	…	…
Fiji	…	…	…	…
Kiribati	…	…	…	…
Marshall Islands	…	…	…	…
Micronesia, Federated States of	…	…	…	…
Nauru	…	…	…	…
Niue	…	…	…	…
Palau	…	…	…	…
Papua New Guinea	…	…	…	…
Samoa	…	…	…	…
Solomon Islands	…	…	…	…
Tonga	…	…	…	…
Tuvalu	…	…	…	…
Vanuatu	…	…	…	…
Developed ADB Member Economies				
Australia	0.38	0.31	0.4	0.4
Japan	0.24	0.21	0.2	0.2
New Zealand	0.19	0.15	0.3	0.3

… = data not available, – = magnitude equals zero, $ = United States dollars, ADB = Asian Development Bank, CO_2 = carbon dioxide, GDP = gross domestic product, kg = kilogram, PPP = purchasing power parity.

a Refers to carbon dioxide emissions from fuel combustion.

Sources: United Nations Statistics Division. Global SDG Indicators Database. https://unstats.un.org/sdgs/indicators/database/ (accessed 18 July 2021); For CO_2 Manufacturing Value-Added for Taipei,China: United Nations Industrial Development Organization. Statistics Data Portal. https://stat.unido.org/SDG (accessed 18 July 2021).

Goal 9. Build resilient infrastructure, promote inclusive and sustainable industrialization, and foster innovation

Table 1.9.4: Selected Indicators for Sustainable Development Goal 9—Research and Development

ADB Regional Member	Target 9.5: Enhance scientific research, upgrade the technological capabilities of industrial sectors in all countries, in particular developing countries, including, by 2030, encouraging innovation and substantially increasing the number of research and development workers per 1 million people and public and private research and development spending			
	9.5.1: Research and Development Expenditure as a Proportion of GDP (%)		9.5.2: Researchers (Full-Time Equivalent) (per million inhabitants)	
	2010	2018	2010	2018
Developing ADB Member Economies				
Central and West Asia				
Afghanistan	...	...	...	...
Armenia	0.24	0.19	...	...
Azerbaijan	0.22	0.18	...	...
Georgia	0.08 (2013)	0.28	566 (2013)	1,464
Kazakhstan	0.15	0.12	371	667
Kyrgyz Republic	0.16	0.10	...	...
Pakistan	0.33 (2011)	0.24 (2017)	143 (2011)	336 (2017)
Tajikistan	0.09	0.10	...	...
Turkmenistan	...	...	...	...
Uzbekistan	0.16	0.13	545	476
East Asia				
China, People's Republic of	1.71	2.14	885	1,307
Hong Kong, China	0.75	0.86	3,115	4,027
Korea, Republic of	3.32	4.53	5,331	7,980
Mongolia	0.24	0.10	...	...
Taipei,China	...	...	...	...
South Asia				
Bangladesh	...	...	...	...
Bhutan	...	...	...	...
India	0.79	0.65	156	253
Maldives	...	...	...	...
Nepal	0.30	...	61 (2002)	...
Sri Lanka	0.14	0.13 (2017)	106	106 (2017)
Southeast Asia				
Brunei Darussalam	0.04 (2004)	0.28	284 (2004)	...
Cambodia	0.05 (2002)	0.12 (2015)	18 (2002)	30 (2015)
Indonesia	0.08 (2009)	0.23	89 (2009)	216
Lao People's Democratic Republic	0.04 (2002)	...	16 (2002)	...
Malaysia	1.04	1.04	1,462	2,185
Myanmar	0.16 (2002)	0.03 (2017)	18 (2002)	29 (2017)
Philippines	0.11 (2011)	0.16 (2015)	84 (2011)	106 (2015)
Singapore	1.93	1.92 (2017)	6,242	6,803 (2017)
Thailand	0.36 (2011)	1.00 (2017)	539 (2011)	1,350 (2017)
Timor-Leste	...	...	...	...
Viet Nam	0.19 (2011)	0.53 (2017)	679 (2013)	708 (2017)
The Pacific				
Cook Islands	...	...	...	...
Fiji	...	...	...	...
Kiribati	...	...	...	...
Marshall Islands	...	...	...	...
Micronesia, Federated States of	...	...	...	...
Nauru	...	...	...	...
Niue	...	...	...	...
Palau	...	...	...	...
Papua New Guinea	...	0.03 (2016)	...	35 (2016)
Samoa	...	...	...	...
Solomon Islands	...	...	...	...
Tonga	...	...	...	...
Tuvalu	...	...	...	...
Vanuatu	...	...	...	...
Developed ADB Member Economies				
Australia	2.38	1.87 (2017)	4,532	...
Japan	3.14	3.28	5,104	5,331
New Zealand	1.23 (2011)	1.35 (2017)	3,689 (2011)	5,530 (2017)

... = data not available, ADB = Asian Development Bank, GDP = gross domestic product.

Source: United Nations Educational, Scientific and Cultural Organization (UNESCO) Institute for Statistics. UIS.Stat Database. http://data.uis.unesco.org/# (accessed 10 July 2021).

Goal 9. Build resilient infrastructure, promote inclusive and sustainable industrialization, and foster innovation

Table 1.9.5: Selected Indicators for Sustainable Development Goal 9—Official International Support and Industry Value Added

ADB Regional Member	Target 9.a: Faciltate sustainable and resilient infrastructure development in developing countries through enhanced financial, technological and technical support to African countries, least developed countries, landlocked developing countries and small island developing States 9.a.1: Total Official International Support to Infrastructure[a] (constant 2019 $ million)		Target 9.b: Support domestic technology development, research, and innovation in developing countries, including by ensuring a conducive policy environment for, *inter alia*, industrial diversification and value addition to commodities 9.b.1: Proportion of Medium and High-Tech Industry Value Added in Total Value-Added[b] (%)	
	2010	2019	2010	2018
Developing ADB Member Economies				
Central and West Asia	**3,976.5**	**5,902.8**		
Afghanistan	1,291.9	554.1	9.5	9.5
Armenia	227.7	282.4	4.5	4.8
Azerbaijan	211.0	521.3	10.1	15.6
Georgia	342.7	624.5	17.2	13.4
Kazakhstan	1,143.3	845.0	12.8	14.5
Kyrgyz Republic	65.3	153.0	3.5	2.8
Pakistan	482.5	1,410.9	24.6	24.6
Tajikistan	124.0	222.8	3.7	2.8
Turkmenistan	1.6	1.6	...	...
Uzbekistan	86.5	1,287.1	19.7	19.9
East Asia[c]	**2,479.4**	**2,678.5**		
China, People's Republic of	2,386.9	2,422.3	41.4	41.5
Hong Kong, China	...	...	38.1	38.5
Korea, Republic of	...	...	61.2	63.8
Mongolia	92.5	256.2	2.1	4.7
Taipei,China	...	...	67.9	69.5 (2017)
South Asia	**6,706.0**	**10,934.0**		
Bangladesh	435.3	2,616.7	9.1	9.8
Bhutan	91.8	81.1	...	...
India	5,527.7	7,295.5	39.2	41.5
Maldives	29.2	43.4	2.6	2.6
Nepal	181.5	337.2	8.5	8.4
Sri Lanka	440.5	560.2	11.8	7.7
Southeast Asia[c]	**3,584.2**	**6,209.8**		
Brunei Darussalam	...	...	3.3	3.3
Cambodia	126.9	389.3	0.3	0.3
Indonesia	1,131.8	1,983.9	38.8	35.4
Lao People's Democratic Republic	103.2	122.2	3.8	3.8
Malaysia	25.4	1.2	42.6	44.0
Myanmar	5.3	643.7	11.7	7.6
Philippines	265.6	1,387.8	45.7	42.3
Singapore	...	...	85.2	80.5
Thailand	148.7	368.0	43.8	41.4
Timor-Leste	24.1	78.0	...	...
Viet Nam	1,753.1	1,235.7	25.4	40.7
The Pacific	**236.8**	**804.2**		
Cook Islands	1.5	9.3	...	...
Fiji	12.0	18.5	7.9	7.1
Kiribati	1.3	18.6	...	...
Marshall Islands	5.6	42.0	...	...
Micronesia, Federated States of	11.0	25.7	...	...
Nauru	0.2	37.9	...	...
Niue	3.2	4.1	...	...
Palau	6.0	7.3	...	...
Papua New Guinea	96.7	326.6	12.6	12.6
Samoa	23.7	60.1	...	...
Solomon Islands	14.1	149.1	...	...
Tonga	26.6	58.7	1.6	1.6
Tuvalu	0.8	6.0	...	...
Vanuatu	34.1	40.5	...	...
Developed ADB Member Economies	**...**	**...**		
Australia	...	...	27.8	28.1
Japan	...	...	55.6	56.6
New Zealand	...	...	17.6	18.5
DEVELOPING ADB MEMBER ECONOMIES[c]	**16,983.0**	**26,529.4**		

... = data not available, $ = United States dollars, ADB = Asian Development Bank.

a Gross disbursements of total official development assistance and other official flows from all donors in support of infrastructure.

b The numbers shown are modeled estimates as published on the Global SDG Indicators Database.

c Includes only reporting economies with data corresponding to the year heading.

Source: United Nations Statistics Division. Global SDG Indicators Database. http://unstats.un.org/sdgs/indicators/database/ (accessed 9 July 2021); and United Nations Industrial Development Organization. Statistics Data Portal. https://stat.unido.org/SDG (accessed 9 July 2021).

Goal 9. Build resilient infrastructure, promote inclusive and sustainable industrialization, and foster innovation

Table 1.9.6: Selected Indicators for Sustainable Development Goal 9—Coverage by Mobile Networks

ADB Regional Member	Target 9.c: Significantly increase access to information and communications technology and strive to provide universal and affordable access to the internet in least developed countries by 2020					
	9.c.1.a: Proportion of Population Covered by 2G Mobile Networks (%)		9.c.1.b: Proportion of Population Covered by 3G Mobile Networks (%)		9.c.1.c: Proportion of Population Covered by LTE Mobile Networks (%)	
	2010	2019	2010	2019	2012	2019
Developing ADB Member Economies						
Central and West Asia						
Afghanistan	80.0	90.0	28.0 (2013)	60.0	4.0 (2017)	22.0
Armenia	98.9	100.0	93.0	100.0	17.5	99.3
Azerbaijan	100.0	100.0	69.2	97.6	6.7	93.0
Georgia	99.0	100.0	74.4 (2012)	100.0	8.9 (2013)	99.7
Kazakhstan	95.0	98.0	45.7 (2012)	88.8	2.7	75.7
Kyrgyz Republic	96.0	99.3	32.0 (2011)	91.0	0.5 (2014)	85.0
Pakistan	75.0 (2012)	88.8	33.0 (2014)	76.6	7.0 (2014)	68.7
Tajikistan	60.0 (2015)	90.0 (2017)	60.0 (2014)	90.0 (2017)	8.4	80.0 (2017)
Turkmenistan	60.0 (2015)	95.8 (2017)	28.5 (2012)	75.8 (2017)	6.0 (2013)	67.0 (2017)
Uzbekistan	92.0 (2012)	99.2	40.0 (2012)	80.7	1.0 (2014)	47.7
East Asia						
China, People's Republic of	99.5	99.9	43.6 (2014)	99.9	10.0 (2013)	99.9
Hong Kong, China	100.0	100.0	99.0	99.0	91.7	99.0
Korea, Republic of	99.9	99.9	99.0	99.9	99.0 (2014)	99.9
Mongolia	85.0	134.0	49.8	96.0	6.9 (2016)	59.0
Taipei,China	...	...	...	...	...	...
South Asia						
Bangladesh	96.0	99.6	1.0 (2012)	95.4	59.0 (2014)	82.0
Bhutan	98.0	98.0	15.0	95.0	5.0 (2013)	78.0
India	93.5 (2013)	99.1	36.5 (2012)	98.2	2.0 (2014)	97.9
Maldives	100.0	100.0	57.1	100.0	11.4 (2013)	100.0
Nepal	35.1	92.5 (2017)	30.0 (2014)	54.1 (2017)	15.5 (2016)	15.5 (2017)
Sri Lanka	98.0	99.0	72.0 (2012)	89.0	5.0	80.0
Southeast Asia						
Brunei Darussalam	97.0 (2015)	99.0	80.8 (2012)	96.0	5.0 (2013)	95.3
Cambodia	99.0	99.0	60.0 (2014)	85.1	9.0 (2014)	80.3
Indonesia	100.0 (2011)	98.7	60.0 (2014)	97.7	5.0 (2013)	97.6
Lao People's Democratic Republic	59.0	95.0	17.0	82.0	2.0 (2014)	43.0 (2018)
Malaysia	95.0	96.7	81.1	95.5	15.0 (2013)	87.2
Myanmar	73.0 (2014)	95.2 (2018)	9.7 (2012)	94.2 (2018)	9.2 (2016)	75.0 (2018)
Philippines	99.0	99.0 (2017)	69.0	93.0 (2017)	6.0	80.0 (2017)
Singapore	100.0	100.0	100.0	100.0	99.0 (2014)	100.0
Thailand	100.0 (2011)	98.0	80.0 (2013)	98.0	21.0 (2015)	98.0
Timor-Leste	86.0	96.5	96.0 (2014)	96.5	20.0 (2017)	45.0
Viet Nam	94.0 (2015)	99.8	31.0 (2012)	99.8	5.0 (2016)	97.0
The Pacific						
Cook Islands	...	100.0 (2017)	20.2 (2014)	55.0 (2017)	55.0 (2017)	55.0 (2017)
Fiji	88.0 (2015)	98.0 (2018)	30.0 (2013)	94.0 (2018)	15.0 (2014)	75.0 (2018)
Kiribati	70.0 (2015)	72.0	15.0 (2013)	71.0	10.0 (2013)	53.0
Marshall Islands	65.0 (2015)	65.0 (2017)	...	...	...	...
Micronesia, Federated States of	80.0 (2015)	80.0 (2017)	15.0 (2015)	15.0 (2017)	...	...
Nauru	98.0	98.0 (2017)	98.0	98.0 (2017)	30.0 (2016)	30.0 (2017)
Niue	...	...	...	...	...	...
Palau	95.0	98.0 (2015)	88.0 (2015)	88.0 (2016)	...	...
Papua New Guinea	89.0 (2015)	89.0 (2017)	60.0 (2014)	64.4 (2017)	7.0 (2014)	50.0 (2017)
Samoa	97.0 (2015)	97.0 (2017)	31.4 (2012)	91.0 (2017)	37.0 (2016)	49.0 (2017)
Solomon Islands	91.0 (2015)	95.0 (2018)	27.1 (2012)	45.0 (2018)	11.5 (2015)	20.0 (2018)
Tonga	92.0 (2015)	99.0	15.0 (2013)	99.0	41.1 (2016)	96.0
Tuvalu	19.0 (2015)	48.0 (2017)	19.0 (2015)	48.0 (2017)	...	...
Vanuatu	87.0	90.0	23.0 (2011)	70.0	18.0 (2015)	50.0
Developed ADB Member Economies						
Australia	99.0	99.5	99.0	99.5	52.2	99.4
Japan	99.9	99.9	99.9 (2012)	99.9	84.0	99.0 (2017)
New Zealand	97.0	98.0 (2018)	97.0	98.0 (2018)	50.0 (2014)	97.0 (2018)

... = data not available, – = magnitude equals zero, 2G = second generation, 3G = third generation, ADB = Asian Development Bank, LTE = Long-Term Evolution.

Source: United Nations Statistics Division. Global SDG Indicators Database. http://unstats.un.org/sdgs/indicators/database/ (accessed 18 July 2021).

Goal 10. Reduce inequality within and among countries

Table 1.10.1: Selected Indicators for Sustainable Development Goal 10—Household Expenditure or Income Growth

ADB Regional Member	Target 10.1: By 2030, progressively achieve and sustain income growth of the bottom 40% of the population at a rate higher than the national average			
	10.1.1.a: Growth Rates of Household Expenditure or Income per Capita among the Bottom 40% of the Population[a,b] (%)		10.1.1.b: Growth Rates of Household Expenditure or Income per Capita[a,b] (%)	
Developing ADB Member Economies				
Central and West Asia				
Afghanistan	...		...	
Armenia[c]	1.0	(2013–2018)	2.0	(2013–2018)
Azerbaijan	...		...	
Georgia[c]	3.0	(2013–2018)	1.0	(2013–2018)
Kazakhstan[c]	–	(2012–2017)	-1.0	(2012–2017)
Kyrgyz Republic[c]	3.0	(2013–2018)	2.0	(2013–2018)
Pakistan[c]	3.0	(2010–2015)	4.0	(2010–2015)
Tajikistan	...		...	
Turkmenistan	...		...	
Uzbekistan	...		...	
East Asia				
China, People's Republic of	8.0	(2013–2016)	7.0	(2013–2016)
Hong Kong, China	...		...	
Korea, Republic of	...		...	
Mongolia[c]	1.0	(2011–2018)	1.0	(2011–2018)
Taipei,China	...		...	
South Asia				
Bangladesh[c]	1.0	(2010–2016)	2.0	(2010–2016)
Bhutan[c]	2.0	(2012–2017)	2.0	(2012–2017)
India	...		...	
Maldives	...		...	
Nepal	...		...	
Sri Lanka[c]	4.0	(2012–2016)	5.0	(2012–2016)
Southeast Asia				
Brunei Darussalam	...		...	
Cambodia	...		...	
Indonesia[c]	5.0	(2014–2018)	5.0	(2014–2018)
Lao People's Democratic Republic	...		...	
Malaysia[d]	8.0	(2012–2016)	6.0	(2012–2016)
Myanmar	...		...	
Philippines[d]	5.0	(2012–2015)	3.0	(2012–2015)
Singapore	...		...	
Thailand[c]	1.0	(2014–2018)	1.0	(2014–2018)
Timor-Leste	...		...	
Viet Nam[c]	5.0	(2012–2018)	5.0	(2012–2018)
The Pacific				
Cook Islands	...		...	
Fiji	...		...	
Kiribati	...		...	
Marshall Islands	...		...	
Micronesia, Federated States of	...		...	
Nauru	...		...	
Niue	...		...	
Palau	...		...	
Papua New Guinea	...		...	
Samoa	...		...	
Solomon Islands	...		...	
Tonga	...		...	
Tuvalu	...		...	
Vanuatu	...		...	
Developed ADB Member Economies				
Australia	...		...	
Japan	...		...	
New Zealand	...		...	

... = data not available, – = magnitude equals zero, ADB = Asian Development Bank.

a Based on real mean per capita consumption or income measured at 2011 purchasing power parity using the PovcalNet database (http://iresearch.worldbank.org/PovcalNet). Data reported are based on consumption, except for Malaysia and the Philippines, which are based on income.

b For the data collection periods in brackets, the initial year refers to the most recently conducted survey prior to the latest survey (only surveys conducted between 3 and 7 years before the latest survey are considered). The final year refers to the latest survey (those available between 2015 and 2018).

c Estimated from individual consumption data.

d Estimated from individual income data.

Source: United Nations Statistics Division. Global SDG Indicators Database. https://unstats.un.org/sdgs/indicators/database/ (accessed 17 July 2021).

Table 1.11.1: Selected Indicators for Sustainable Development Goal 11—Sustainable Cities and Environment

ADB Regional Member	Target 11.1: By 2030, ensure access for all to adequate, safe, and affordable housing and basic services, and upgrade slums — 11.1.1: Proportion of Urban Population Living in Slums, Informal Settlements, or Inadequate Housing (%)		Target 11.5: By 2030, significantly reduce the number of deaths and the number of people affected, and substantially decrease the direct economic losses relative to global gross domestic product caused by disasters, including water-related disasters, with a focus on protecting the poor and people in vulnerable situations — 11.5.2: Direct Economic Loss Attributed to Disasters[a] ($ million)		Target 11.6: By 2030, reduce the adverse per capita environmental impact of cities, including by paying special attention to air quality and municipal and other waste management — 11.6.2: Annual Mean Levels ($\mu g/m^3$) of Fine Particulate Matter (e.g., PM2.5 and PM10) in Cities[b] (population weighted)	
					Total	Urban
	2010	2018	2010	2020	2016	2016
Developing ADB Member Economies						
Central and West Asia						
Afghanistan	62.7 (2014)	70.7	...	567.7 (2019)	55.1	63.6
Armenia	14.4 (2014)	9.3	7.0	7.9	33.8	45.5
Azerbaijan	...	...	...	...	21.0	23.2
Georgia	...	34.1	...	0.2 (2019)	22.2	26.9
Kazakhstan	...	...	3.2 (2011)	106.2	17.8	25.6
Kyrgyz Republic	...	9.7	1.4 (2012)	7.0	23.9	28.2
Pakistan	46.6	40.1	3,835.8	18.2 (2018)	58.8	62.6
Tajikistan	...	26.0	28.8 (2015)	1.0 (2019)	34.9	46.5
Turkmenistan	...	...	...	...	18.2	33.3
Uzbekistan	...	52.2	...	...	28.3	33.9
East Asia						
China, People's Republic of	29.1	24.6	...	...	45.8	48.8
Hong Kong, China	...	...	...	...	...	...
Korea, Republic of	...	...	368.3	42.9 (2019)	26.4	26.5
Mongolia	42.7 (2014)	38.3	41.0	24.1	42.8	60.0
Taipei,China	...	...	...	...	...	...
South Asia						
Bangladesh	61.6	47.2	...	...	62.8	64.1
Bhutan	...	...	0.5	1.9 (2018)	37.6	36.9
India	29.4	35.2	...	...	68.8	78.2
Maldives	...	30.1	0.2 (2008)	0.3 (2017)	11.0	10.4
Nepal	58.1	49.3	301.2	82.6 (2019)	81.6	88.0
Sri Lanka	...	...	365.1 (2008)	1.3	16.5	16.8
Southeast Asia						
Brunei Darussalam	...	...	...	...	7.5	7.4
Cambodia	55.1 (2014)	45.1	125.3	0.1	25.0	27.2
Indonesia	23.0	30.6	859.9	1,285.0 (2019)	19.0	20.7
Lao People's Democratic Republic	31.4 (2014)	21.1	366.1	...	20.5	21.8
Malaysia	...	...	28.2	104.9	16.3	17.2
Myanmar	41.0 (2014)	56.1	17.7	5.5	33.1	33.7
Philippines	40.9	42.9	...	...	21.3	23.7
Singapore	...	...	...	...	17.2	17.2
Thailand	27.0	23.7	...	...	29.8	31.9
Timor-Leste	...	33.4	29.6	0.7 (2017)	16.3	17.7
Viet Nam	35.2	13.8	988.0	...	22.0	23.7
The Pacific						
Cook Islands	...	...	...	...	8.9	...
Fiji	...	11.2	24.6	24.2	10.7	11.1
Kiribati	...	...	0.3 (2014)	0.0	11.1	11.6
Marshall Islands	...	...	0.2 (2008)	1.8 (2016)	10.2	...
Micronesia, Federated States of	...	...	...	8.3 (2019)	10.5	10.8
Nauru	...	...	...	...	8.2	8.2
Niue	...	...	...	...	9.3	...
Palau	...	...	6.2 (2012)	...	8.8	8.7
Papua New Guinea	...	...	2.6 (2009)	1.6	11.1	12.2
Samoa	...	...	27.2 (2009)	...	10.8	11.0
Solomon Islands	...	...	5.8	...	11.1	11.8
Tonga	...	...	4.7	8.6 (2018)	11.0	11.1
Tuvalu	...	...	...	...	8.5	...
Vanuatu	...	...	3.1	64.5 (2018)	10.5	11.1
Developed ADB Member Economies						
Australia	...	...	106.3	167.4	7.1	7.3
Japan	...	...	2,048.0 (2015)	4,867.3 (2019)	13.4	13.7
New Zealand	...	...	42.2 (2015)	52.4 (2019)	6.6	6.7

... = data not available, $ = United States dollars, ADB = Asian Development Bank, m^3 = cubic meter, PM = particulate matter, μg = microgram.

a The data are submitted to the Global SDG Indicators Database by the United Nations Office for Disaster Risk Reduction and have been extracted from two sources: (i) the Sendai Framework Monitoring System as provided by designated national focal points; and (ii) Desinventar disaster loss databases. Some of the data have not undergone an official validation process and may be subject to revision at a later date.

b Data are estimates as published on Global SDG Indicators Database.

Source: United Nations Statistics Division. Global SDG Indicators Database. https://unstats.un.org/sdgs/indicators/database/ (accessed 14 July 2021).

Goal 12. Ensure sustainable consumption and production patterns

Table 1.12.1: Selected Indicators for Sustainable Development Goal 12—Responsible Consumption and Production

ADB Regional Member	Target 12.2: By 2030, achieve the sustainable management and efficient use of natural resources							
	12.2.1: Material Footprint[a]				12.2.2: Domestic Material Consumption[a]			
	All (t million)		Per Capita (t)		All (t million)		Per Capita (t)	
	2010	2017	2010	2017	2010	2017	2010	2017
Developing ADB Member Economies								
Central and West Asia	**1,199.0**	**1,524.7**	**...**	**...**	**1,629.1**	**2,089.7**	**...**	**...**
Afghanistan	38.7	43.4	1.3	1.2	59.7	67.9	2.1	1.9
Armenia	18.5	23.9	6.4	8.2	23.6	32.5	8.2	11.1
Azerbaijan	42.9	61.5	4.8	6.3	67.8	90.1	7.5	9.2
Georgia	28.2	35.7	6.7	9.1	20.9	26.5	4.9	6.8
Kazakhstan	273.1	330.0	16.7	18.1	418.8	530.4	25.5	29.1
Kyrgyz Republic	42.0	52.3	7.8	8.6	38.8	50.7	7.1	8.4
Pakistan	493.2	628.6	2.9	3.2	664.0	875.8	3.9	4.4
Tajikistan	16.5	33.0	2.2	3.7	20.1	31.2	2.6	3.5
Turkmenistan	90.6	124.0	17.8	21.5	72.4	95.0	14.2	16.5
Uzbekistan	155.2	192.3	5.4	6.0	243.1	289.6	8.5	9.1
East Asia	**...**	**...**	**...**	**...**	**...**	**...**	**...**	**...**
China, People's Republic of	21,825.1	29,432.1	16.1	20.9	26,182.9	35,194.1	19.3	25.0
Hong Kong, China	...	...	...	...	...	...	...	...
Korea, Republic of	1,221.5	1,456.7	24.6	28.6	789.1	808.6	15.9	15.9
Mongolia	26.8	42.6	9.9	13.9	65.5	106.2	24.1	34.5
Taipei,China	...	...	...	...	...	...	...	...
South Asia	**5,582.5**	**6,732.9**	**...**	**...**	**6,338.3**	**8,098.0**	**...**	**...**
Bangladesh	305.0	388.9	2.0	2.4	365.5	438.3	2.4	2.7
Bhutan	6.6	8.4	9.1	10.4	6.0	8.4	8.3	10.4
India	5,142.5	6,162.0	4.2	4.6	5,793.8	7,417.2	4.7	5.5
Maldives	5.2	6.3	14.2	14.5	2.2	3.0	6.1	6.8
Nepal	66.1	81.6	2.4	2.8	92.8	114.4	3.4	3.9
Sri Lanka	57.2	85.8	2.8	4.1	78.0	116.8	3.9	5.6
Southeast Asia[b]	**4,657.2**	**5,746.3**	**...**	**...**	**4,987.5**	**5,840.6**	**...**	**...**
Brunei Darussalam	7.2	8.6	18.5	20.0	6.9	9.8	17.8	22.9
Cambodia	65.6	57.9	4.6	3.6	86.9	84.7	6.1	5.3
Indonesia	1,362.3	1,649.8	5.6	6.2	1,828.4	1,974.2	7.5	7.5
Lao People's Democratic Republic	32.7	51.7	5.2	7.5	52.4	82.2	8.4	12.0
Malaysia	594.7	763.8	21.2	24.2	519.6	609.4	18.5	19.3
Myanmar	76.9	76.4	1.5	1.4	169.9	187.6	3.4	3.5
Philippines	398.7	461.4	4.3	4.4	385.1	416.5	4.1	4.0
Singapore	373.8	434.4	73.7	76.1	151.0	186.3	29.7	32.6
Thailand	809.4	1,033.1	12.0	15.0	686.5	879.1	10.2	12.7
Timor-Leste	...	...	...	...	9.6	10.0	8.7	7.7
Viet Nam	936.0	1,209.2	10.6	12.7	1,091.2	1,400.7	12.3	14.7
The Pacific[b]	**...**	**...**	**...**	**...**	**95.4**	**99.9**	**...**	**...**
Cook Islands	...	...	...	...	...	...	...	...
Fiji	5.1	6.5	6.0	7.2	5.8	5.9	6.8	6.5
Kiribati	...	...	...	...	0.5	0.7	5.2	6.3
Marshall Islands	...	...	...	...	0.1	0.1	2.7	2.0
Micronesia, Federated States of	...	...	...	...	0.2	0.2	1.8	2.3
Nauru	...	...	...	...	...	...	...	...
Niue	...	...	...	...	...	...	...	...
Palau	...	...	...	...	0.0	0.0	0.4	1.2
Papua New Guinea	19.4	21.3	2.7	2.6	81.8	84.0	11.5	10.2
Samoa	1.3	1.6	7.2	7.9	0.9	1.0	4.7	5.3
Solomon Islands	...	...	...	...	3.2	4.3	6.1	7.1
Tonga	...	...	...	...	1.3	1.8	12.0	16.9
Tuvalu	...	...	...	...	0.0	0.0	1.1	1.1
Vanuatu	1.9	2.1	7.9	7.6	1.5	1.7	6.5	6.1
Developed ADB Member Economies	**4,054.4**	**4,480.9**	**...**	**...**	**2,264.7**	**2,182.8**	**...**	**...**
Australia	903.9	1,059.9	40.9	43.3	899.6	927.4	40.7	37.9
Japan	3,054.9	3,305.9	23.8	25.9	1,267.2	1,141.6	9.9	9.0
New Zealand	95.6	115.1	21.9	24.5	98.0	113.7	22.4	24.2

... = data not available, 0.0 = magnitude is less than half of unit employed, ADB = Asian Development Bank, t = metric ton.

a Data are estimates as published on the Global SDG Indicators Database.
b Regional aggregates include reporting economies only.

Source: For Indicator 12.2.1: United Nations Environment Programme. Environment Live. https://environmentlive.unep.org/ (accessed 21 July 2021).
For Indicator 12.2.2: United Nations Statistics Division. Global SDG Indicators Database. https://unstats.un.org/sdgs/indicators/database/ (accessed 21 July 2021).

Table 1.13.1: Selected Indicators for Sustainable Development Goal 13—Impact of Disasters and Risk Reduction Strategies

ADB Regional Member	Target 13.1: Strengthen resilience and adaptive capacity to climate-related hazards and natural disasters in all countries				
	13.1.1.a: Number of Persons Affected by Disaster[a]		13.1.1.b: Number of Deaths Due to Disaster[a]		13.1.2: Countries that Adopt and Implement National Disaster Risk Reduction Strategies in Line with the Sendai Framework for Disaster Risk Reduction 2015–2030[b,c]
	2010	2020	2010	2020	2020
Developing ADB Member Economies					
Central and West Asia					
Afghanistan	...	372,261 (2019)	...	368 (2019)	0.73 (2019)
Armenia	7,640	169,950	155	3,284	0.70
Azerbaijan	...	...	...	...	– (2019)
Georgia	...	87 (2019)	...	7 (2019)	0.98 (2018)
Kazakhstan	1,401 (2011)	189,035	9	2,793	0.78
Kyrgyz Republic	188 (2011)	81,771	158	3,957	0.90 (2019)
Pakistan	1,055,502	11,614 (2018)	5,105	137 (2018)	0.43 (2018)
Tajikistan	...	2,027 (2019)	...	8	1.00 (2019)
Turkmenistan	...	...	...	...	0.75 (2019)
Uzbekistan	...	1 (2019)	...	2 (2019)	1.00 (2019)
East Asia					
China, People's Republic of	...	6,343,237 (2019)	...	816 (2019)	...
Hong Kong, China	...	...	...	...	...
Korea, Republic of	150,103	9,195 (2019)	91	100 (2019)	1.00 (2019)
Mongolia	9,085	8,310	226	255	1.00 (2019)
Taipei,China	...	...	...	...	...
South Asia					
Bangladesh	...	36,782 (2018)	96	7,840	0.95
Bhutan	1,710	242 (2018)	2,763	21 (2019)	–
India	...	53,324,677 (2019)	7,489	2,769	1.00
Maldives	132 (2008)	59 (2017)	4 (2008)	1 (2019)	– (2017)
Nepal	183,236	183,401 (2019)	1,002	489 (2019)	0.75 (2019)
Sri Lanka	1,193,504	608	50	83	– (2017)
Southeast Asia					
Brunei Darussalam	...	...	...	...	...
Cambodia	30,465	19	91	154 (2019)	0.65 (2019)
Indonesia	333,235	106,653 (2019)	1,630	478 (2019)	0.83 (2019)
Lao People's Democratic Republic	53,514	...	50	...	...
Malaysia	9,882	207,819	4	479	0.43
Myanmar	545,156	1,830	55	21	0.70 (2017)
Philippines	1,489,711	4,547,901	192	9,396	0.73
Singapore	...	...	...	...	...
Thailand	...	142,780 (2018)	...	81 (2018)	0.68
Timor-Leste	26,211	575 (2017)	10	2 (2017)	...
Viet Nam	639,291	...	60	...	...
The Pacific					
Cook Islands	4,443	...	3	...	...
Fiji	7,641	237,072	3	16	0.98
Kiribati	176 (2014)	15	...	95 (2018)	0.93
Marshall Islands	96 (2008)	56,718	...	1	–
Micronesia, Federated States of	...	30,521 (2019)	2 (2011)	521 (2019)	0.58
Nauru	...	...	...	...	0.60
Niue	...	...	...	...	...
Palau	1,325 (2012)	...	...	...	0.73
Papua New Guinea	580 (2009)	3,297	16	40	0.78
Samoa	10,434 (2009)	5,700 (2019)	369 (2009)	83 (2019)	0.73
Solomon Islands	1,456	...	4	...	0.78
Tonga	1,376	84,311 (2018)	9 (2009)	...	0.48
Tuvalu	...	4,548	...	...	0.30
Vanuatu	500	246,802	1 (2011)	3	0.65
Developed ADB Member Economies					
Australia	15,418	16,585	38 (2011)	127	0.65
Japan	...	446,061 (2018)	89	444 (2018)	1.00 (2019)
New Zealand	...	87 (2019)	186 (2011)	22 (2019)	0.88 (2019)

... = data not available, – = magnitude equals zero, ADB = Asian Development Bank.

a The data are submitted to the Global SDG Indicators Database by the United Nations Office for Disaster Risk Reduction and have been extracted from two sources: (i) the Sendai Framework Monitoring System as provided by designated national focal points; and (ii) Desinventar disaster loss databases. Some of the data have not undergone an official validation process and may be subject to revision at a later date.

b Economies displaying data in this column have adopted and implemented national disaster risk reduction strategies. Data refer to the score for adoption and implementation of national disaster risk reduction strategies in line with the Sendai Framework. The scores indicate the compliance of alignment of national strategies with the Sendai Framework, based on self-assessments of the economy using 10 criteria for monitoring the progress of national national disaster risk reduction strategies. The score ranges are as follows: 1 = comprehensive alignment, 0.75 = substantial alignment, 0.50 = moderate alignment, 0.25 = limited alignment, 0 = no alignment.

c Some of the data have not undergone an official validation process and may be subject to revision at a later date.

Source: United Nations Statistics Division. Global SDG Indicators Database. https://unstats.un.org/sdgs/indicators/database/ (accessed 15 July 2021).

Goal 14. Conserve and sustainably use the oceans, seas, and marine resources for sustainable development

Table 1.14.1: Selected Indicators for Sustainable Development Goal 14—Life Below Water

ADB Regional Member	Target 14.5: By 2020, conserve at least 10% of coastal and marine areas, consistent with national and international law and based on the best available scientific information			
	14.5.1.a: Average Proportion of Marine Key Biodiversity Areas Covered by Protected Areas (%)		14.5.1.b: Coverage of Protected Areas in Relation to Marine Areas (Exclusive Economic Zones)[a] (%)	14.5.1.c: Protected Marine Areas (Exclusive Economic Zones)[a] (km^2)
	2010	2020	2020	2020
Developing ADB Member Economies				
Central and West Asia				
Afghanistan	...	...	...	...
Armenia	...	...	...	...
Azerbaijan	...	...	0.4	345.3
Georgia	35.6	35.6	0.7	153.0
Kazakhstan	...	...	1.1	1,249.5
Kyrgyz Republic	...	...	...	...
Pakistan	14.6	14.6	0.8	1,707.4
Tajikistan	...	...	...	...
Turkmenistan	...	...	3.0	2,331.8
Uzbekistan	...	...	...	...
East Asia				
China, People's Republic of	6.8	7.1	5.5	48,125.6
Hong Kong, China	32.5	32.5	–	–
Korea, Republic of	32.6	38.7	2.5	7,979.4
Mongolia	...	...	...	...
Taipei,China	...	...	...	...
South Asia				
Bangladesh	34.4	34.5	5.4	4,530.0
Bhutan	...	...	...	...
India	19.2	19.2	0.2	3,928.3
Maldives	–	–	0.1	580.8
Nepal	...	...	...	...
Sri Lanka	46.3	50.0	0.1	398.6
Southeast Asia				
Brunei Darussalam	5.4	5.4	0.2	51.7
Cambodia	41.2	51.0	1.4	691.5
Indonesia	16.1	25.5	3.1	181,864.7
Lao People's Democratic Republic	...	...	...	...
Malaysia	13.7	13.7	1.7	7,438.0
Myanmar	9.3	19.2	0.5	2,456.8
Philippines	37.4	38.0	1.2	21,269.2
Singapore	3.3	3.3	0.0	0.1
Thailand	47.5	47.5	1.9	5,773.8
Timor-Leste	18.7	19.6	1.4	583.0
Viet Nam	18.0	23.9	0.6	3,630.3
The Pacific				
Cook Islands	19.8	44.8	100.0	1,981,931.2
Fiji	16.5	16.5	0.9	11,959.0
Kiribati	32.9	32.9	11.8	408,796.5
Marshall Islands	6.7	7.8	0.3	5,388.4
Micronesia, Federated States of	1.6	1.6	0.0	475.1
Nauru	–	– (2019)	...	...
Niue	...	...	–	4.4
Palau	56.4	72.3	100.0	608,173.3
Papua New Guinea	1.9	1.9	0.1	3,343.5
Samoa	54.2	54.2	0.1	190.5
Solomon Islands	3.1	3.2	0.1	1,879.4
Tonga	19.2	19.2	0.1	390.0
Tuvalu	...	...	0.0	213.9
Vanuatu	3.3	3.3	0.0	47.5
Developed ADB Member Economies				
Australia	54.0	64.6	40.8	3,035,629.9
Japan	60.7	67.1	8.2	332,690.6
New Zealand	46.5	47.1	30.4	1,249,398.6

... = data not available, – = magnitude equals zero, 0.0 = magnitude is less than half of unit employed, ADB = Asian Development Bank, km^2 = square kilometer.

a An Exclusive Economic Zone comprises an area that extends either from the coast, or, in federal systems, from the seaward boundaries of the constituent states (3 to 12 nautical miles, in most cases) to 200 nautical miles (370 kilometres) off the coast.

Source: United Nations Statistics Division. Global SDG Indicators Database. https://unstats.un.org/sdgs/indicators/database/ (accessed 20 July 2021).

Goal 15. Protect, restore, and promote sustainable use of terrestrial ecosystems; sustainably manage forests; combat desertification and halt and reverse land degradation; and halt biodiversity loss

Table 1.15.1: Selected Indicators for Sustainable Development Goal 15—Protection of Ecosystems and Biodiversity

ADB Regional Member	Target 15.1: By 2020, ensure the conservation, restoration, and sustainable use of terrestrial and inland freshwater ecosystems and their services, in particular forests, wetlands, mountains, and drylands, in line with obligations under international agreements					
	15.1.1: Forest Area as a Proportion of Total Land Area[a] (%)		15.1.2: Proportion of Important Sites for Terrestrial and Freshwater Biodiversity that are Covered by Protected Areas			
			Terrestrial (%)		Freshwater (%)	
	2010	2020	2010	2020	2010	2020
Developing ADB Member Economies						
Central and West Asia	**3.9**	**4.0**	...	...	...	...
Afghanistan	1.9	1.9	5.7	5.7	–	–
Armenia	11.6	11.5	21.6	22.6	26.8	30.5
Azerbaijan	12.5	13.7	36.1	36.6	12.7	14.5
Georgia	40.6	40.6	34.4	40.3	22.5	38.9
Kazakhstan	1.1	1.3	11.0	13.1	10.0	10.0
Kyrgyz Republic	6.4	6.9	23.6	23.6	35.4	35.4
Pakistan	5.3	4.8	34.8	34.8	35.9	35.9
Tajikistan	2.9	3.1	15.8	16.8	27.9	30.5
Turkmenistan	8.8	8.8	14.0	14.0	12.7	12.7
Uzbekistan	7.7	8.4	15.4	17.7	13.4	13.4
East Asia	**20.1**	**21.8**	...	...	...	...
China, People's Republic of	21.3	23.3	8.6	10.1	6.9	9.6
Hong Kong, China	...	...	48.9	48.9	16.6	16.6
Korea, Republic of	65.7	64.5	33.8	37.6	36.8	36.8
Mongolia	9.1	9.1	40.4	45.0	35.7	41.4
Taipei,China	58.1	60.7 (2019)	...	...	...	...
South Asia	**24.5**	**25.3**	...	...	...	...
Bangladesh	14.5	14.5	41.5	41.5	–	–
Bhutan	71.0	71.4	45.4	47.0	30.5	34.8
India	23.4	24.3	17.6	20.7	16.6	18.9
Maldives	2.7	2.7	–	–	...	...
Nepal	41.6	41.6	50.7	50.7	32.4	32.4
Sri Lanka	33.5	34.2	41.1	43.7	40.2	43.9
Southeast Asia	**49.7**	**47.1**	...	...	...	...
Brunei Darussalam	72.1	72.1	41.7	41.7	50.0	50.0
Cambodia	60.0	45.7	24.7	54.5	12.9	45.0
Indonesia	53.1	49.1	19.7	25.9	36.6	39.0
Lao People's Democratic Republic	73.4	71.9	44.0	44.0	29.9	29.9
Malaysia	57.7	58.2	28.5	28.5	50.0	50.0
Myanmar	48.1	43.7	21.9	25.1	27.1	27.1
Philippines	22.9	24.1	41.4	41.6	49.8	49.8
Singapore	25.3	22.0	21.1	21.1	...	...
Thailand	39.3	38.9	71.1	71.1	40.7	40.7
Timor-Leste	62.9	61.9	40.7	45.6	...	...
Viet Nam	43.2	47.2	31.1	40.0	29.2	38.2
The Pacific	**78.3**	**77.8**	...	...	...	...
Cook Islands	65.0	65.0	24.4	30.9	...	...
Fiji	58.7	62.4	11.2	11.2	0.1	0.1
Kiribati	1.5	1.5	40.0	40.0	...	...
Marshall Islands	52.2	52.2	8.4	10.1	...	...
Micronesia, Federated States of	91.6	92.0	0.0	0.0	...	...
Nauru	–	–	–	–	...	...
Niue	72.2	72.6	95.3	95.3	...	...
Palau	88.2	90.0	44.9	48.1	...	...
Papua New Guinea	79.9	79.2	7.2	7.3	...	...
Samoa	58.8	57.1	47.0	47.1	...	...
Solomon Islands	90.4	90.1	4.5	4.6	...	...
Tonga	12.4	12.4	26.1	26.1	...	...
Tuvalu	33.3	33.3	...	...	...	...
Vanuatu	36.3	36.3	2.9	2.9	...	...
Developed ADB Member Economies	**19.8**	**20.3**	...	...	...	...
Australia	16.9	17.4	45.9	56.6	30.2	37.7
Japan	68.5	68.4	61.1	65.1	64.2	64.4
New Zealand	37.4	37.6	45.7	46.5	23.4	24.6
DEVELOPING ADB MEMBER ECONOMIES	**23.5**	**24.0**	...	...	...	...
ALL ADB REGIONAL MEMBERS	**22.6**	**23.0**	...	...	...	...

Goal 15. Protect, restore, and promote sustainable use of terrestrial ecosystems; sustainably manage forests; combat desertification and halt and reverse land degradation; and halt biodiversity loss

Table 1.15.1: Selected Indicators for Sustainable Development Goal 15—Protection of Ecosystems and Biodiversity *(continued)*

ADB Regional Member	Target 15.4: By 2030, ensure the conservation of mountain ecosystems, including their biodiversity, in order to enhance their capacity to provide benefits that are essential for sustainable development 15.4.1: Coverage by Protected Areas of Important Sites for Mountain Biodiversity (%)		Target 15.5: Take urgent and significant action to reduce the degradation of natural habitats, halt the loss of biodiversity and, by 2020, protect and prevent the extinction of threatened species 15.5.1: Red List Index[b]	
	2010	2020	2010	2020
Developing ADB Member Economies				
Central and West Asia	...	...	...	...
Afghanistan	7.5	7.5	0.84	0.84
Armenia	22.3	23.4	0.83	0.83
Azerbaijan	55.5	55.5	0.91	0.91
Georgia	34.8	40.9	0.89	0.89
Kazakhstan	15.6	23.7	0.87	0.87
Kyrgyz Republic	31.5	31.5	0.99	0.98
Pakistan	35.2	35.2	0.90	0.86
Tajikistan	15.8	16.8	0.99	0.99
Turkmenistan	15.2	15.2	0.98	0.98
Uzbekistan	30.6	35.6	0.98	0.97
East Asia	...	...	...	...
China, People's Republic of	10.2	11.8	0.77	0.73
Hong Kong, China	57.0	57.0	0.84	0.84
Korea, Republic of	20.2	20.2	0.73	0.70
Mongolia	45.0	49.3	0.96	0.96
Taipei,China	...	...	...	...
South Asia	...	...	...	...
Bangladesh	–	–	0.79	0.75
Bhutan	45.4	47.0	0.80	0.80
India	22.3	28.1	0.71	0.67
Maldives	...	...	0.89	0.84
Nepal	60.6	60.6	0.83	0.83
Sri Lanka	29.4	30.4	0.61	0.57
Southeast Asia	...	...	...	...
Brunei Darussalam	69.5	69.5	0.86	0.85
Cambodia	60.8	93.8	0.81	0.78
Indonesia	21.6	27.5	0.80	0.76
Lao People's Democratic Republic	51.9	51.9	0.82	0.81
Malaysia	32.8	32.8	0.75	0.71
Myanmar	38.1	42.7	0.83	0.80
Philippines	43.5	43.9	0.71	0.68
Singapore	...	...	0.89	0.85
Thailand	89.4	89.4	0.81	0.78
Timor-Leste	45.4	50.8	0.88	0.85
Viet Nam	34.1	44.3	0.76	0.72
The Pacific	...	...	...	...
Cook Islands	–	–	0.80	0.77
Fiji	5.5	5.5	0.72	0.70
Kiribati	...	...	0.80	0.77
Marshall Islands	...	...	0.87	0.84
Micronesia, Federated States of	–	–	0.69	0.65
Nauru	...	...	0.81	0.77
Niue	...	...	0.84	0.81
Palau	...	...	0.79	0.70
Papua New Guinea	7.3	7.4	0.87	0.84
Samoa	35.6	35.7	0.77	0.76
Solomon Islands	0.0	0.1	0.79	0.76
Tonga	–	–	0.74	0.72
Tuvalu	...	...	0.87	0.83
Vanuatu	3.8	3.8	0.70	0.67
Developed ADB Member Economies	...	...	...	...
Australia	47.3	66.1	0.85	0.82
Japan	66.5	66.9	0.80	0.77
New Zealand	33.5	34.6	0.67	0.62
DEVELOPING ADB MEMBER ECONOMIES	...	...	...	...
ALL ADB REGIONAL MEMBERS	...	...	...	...

... = data not available, 0.0 = magnitude is less than half of unit employed, – = magnitude equals zero, ADB = Asian Development Bank.

a The regional aggregates are calculated by averaging the combined estimates for each economy. The aggregates for East Asia exclude Hong Kong, China. The data for forest area and land area are from the Global SDG Indicators Database and from the Directorate-General of Budget, Accounting and Statistics for Taipei,China.

b The Red List Index value ranges from 1, which means all species are categorized as "Least Concern" (no species expected to become extinct in the near future), to 0, meaning that all species are categorized as "Extinct". The index therefore indicates how far the set of species has moved overall towards extinction.

Source: United Nations Statistics Division. Global SDG Indicators Database. https://unstats.un.org/sdgs/indicators/database/ (accessed 21 July 2021).

Goal 16. Promote peaceful and inclusive societies for sustainable development; provide access to justice for all; and build effective, accountable, and inclusive institutions at all levels

Table 1.16.1: Selected Indicators for Sustainable Development Goal 16—Peace, Justice, and Strong Institutions

ADB Regional Member	Target 16.1: Significantly reduce all forms of violence and related death rates everywhere — 16.1.1: Number of Victims of Intentional Homicide (per 100,000 population)		Target 16.3: Promote the rule of law at the national and international levels and ensure equal access to justice for all — 16.3.2: Unsentenced Detainees as a Proportion of Overall Prison Population (%)		Target 16.5: Substantially reduce corruption and bribery in all their forms — 16.5.2: Proportion of Firms Experiencing at least One Bribe Payment Request (%)	Target 16.9: By 2030, provide legal identity for all, including birth registration — 16.9.1: Proportion of Children Under 5 Years of Age Whose Births have been Registered with a Civil Authority[a] (%)
	2010	2018	2015	2018	2019	2019
Developing ADB Member Economies						
Central and West Asia						
Afghanistan	3.4	6.7	29.5	27.7	46.8 (2014)	42.3 (2015)
Armenia	1.9	1.7	27.9	35.6	1.5 (2020)	99.3 (2016)
Azerbaijan	2.3	2.2	16.9	15.5	12.1	93.6 (2006)
Georgia	4.4	2.2	14.7	11.5	1.3	98.5 (2017)
Kazakhstan	8.5	5.3 (2017)	15.0	10.9	11.6	99.7 (2015)
Kyrgyz Republic	16.8	2.2	18.2	16.4	31.4	98.9 (2018)
Pakistan	7.7	3.9	69.3	66.1	30.8 (2013)	42.2 (2018)
Tajikistan	2.4	...	...	...	11.1	95.8 (2017)
Turkmenistan	4.2 (2006)	...	...	...	...	99.9
Uzbekistan	3.0 (2008)	1.1 (2017)	...	...	5.9	99.9 (2006)
East Asia						
China, People's Republic of	1.0	0.5	...	...	11.6 (2012)	...
Hong Kong, China	0.5	0.7	18.1	22.2	...	...
Korea, Republic of	1.0	0.6	35.2	35.4	...	...
Mongolia	8.8	6.2	15.6	22.9	24.7	99.6 (2018)
Taipei,China	0.8	0.8 (2015)	5.5	5.2	...	...
South Asia						
Bangladesh	2.6	2.4	75.7	84.7	47.7 (2013)	56.0
Bhutan	2.2	1.2	...	...	0.9 (2015)	99.9 (2010)
India	3.8	3.1	67.3	67.7	22.7 (2014)	79.7 (2016)
Maldives	1.6	0.7 (2013)	...	...	...	98.8 (2017)
Nepal	3.0	2.2 (2016)	...	...	14.5 (2013)	77.2
Sri Lanka	3.8	2.4	45.3	57.8	10.0 (2011)	97.2 (2007)
Southeast Asia						
Brunei Darussalam	0.3	0.5 (2013)	7.9	7.1	...	...
Cambodia	2.3	...	49.3	31.7	64.7 (2016)	73.3 (2014)
Indonesia	0.4	0.4 (2017)	35.0	30.7	30.6 (2015)	74.4
Lao People's Democratic Republic	...	...	...	...	40.3 (2018)	73.0 (2017)
Malaysia	1.9	2.1 (2013)	24.0	33.0	28.2 (2015)	...
Myanmar	1.6	2.3 (2016)	...	...	29.3 (2016)	81.3 (2016)
Philippines	9.2	6.5	66.3	73.4	17.2 (2015)	91.8 (2017)
Singapore	0.4	0.2	10.2	11.5	...	99.9 (2018)
Thailand	5.4	2.6 (2017)	20.7	18.0	9.9 (2016)	99.8
Timor-Leste	3.5	4.1 (2015)	76.1	23.2	44.2 (2015)	60.4 (2016)
Viet Nam	1.5	...	...	...	26.1 (2015)	96.1 (2014)
The Pacific						
Cook Islands	5.6 (2012)	...	16.9	14.6	...	100.0 (2017)
Fiji	2.3	2.3 (2014)	22.7	25.9	10.5 (2009)	...
Kiribati	3.9	...	9.8	5.4	...	91.6
Marshall Islands	...	...	...	...	...	83.8 (2017)
Micronesia, Federated States of	...	...	...	...	4.6 (2009)	...
Nauru	...	...	...	...	...	95.9 (2013)
Niue	...	...	...	...	...	...
Palau	...	11.2	...	...	...	...
Papua New Guinea	10.0	...	32.5	37.8	26.4 (2015)	13.4 (2018)
Samoa	8.6	3.1 (2013)	5.3	6.5	30.5 (2009)	66.9 (2020)
Solomon Islands	3.8 (2008)	...	46.7	50.4	43.8 (2015)	88.0 (2015)
Tonga	1.0	...	7.4	7.4	24.9 (2009)	97.7
Tuvalu	9.5	...	...	...	...	49.9 (2007)
Vanuatu	...	...	12.1	22.4	11.9 (2009)	43.4 (2013)
Developed ADB Member Economies						
Australia	1.0	0.9	25.3	31.6	...	100.0 (2017)
Japan	0.4	0.3	11.2	11.3	...	100.0 (2017)
New Zealand	1.0	0.7 (2017)	14.9	18.2	...	100.0 (2017)

... = data not available, ADB = Asian Development Bank.

a Changes in the definition of birth registration were made from the second and third rounds of Multiple Indicator Cluster Surveys (MICS2 and MICS3) to the fourth round (MICS4). In order to allow for comparability with the latter round, data from MICS2 and MICS3 on birth registration were recalculated according to the MICS4 indicator definition. Therefore, the recalculated data presented here may differ from estimates included in MICS2 and MICS3 national reports.

Sources: For Indicator 16.1.1: United Nations Office on Drugs and Crime. Statistics Online. https://dataunodc.un.org/ (accessed 10 July 2021). For Indicator 16.3.2: United Nations Statistics Division. Global SDG Indicators Database. https://unstats.un.org/sdgs/indicators/database/ (accessed 10 July 2021).
For Indicator 16.5.2: World Bank. World Development Indicators. https://data.worldbank.org/indicator (accessed 10 July 2021).
For Indicator 16.9.1: United Nations Children's Fund. UNICEF Data Warehouse. https://data.unicef.org/ (accessed 10 July 2021).

Goal 17. Strengthen the means of implementation and revitalize the Global Partnership for Sustainable Development

Table 1.17.1: Selected Indicators for Sustainable Development Goal 17—Financial Sustainability of Developing Economies

ADB Regional Member	Target 17.4: Assist developing economies in attaining long-term debt sustainability through coordinated policies aimed at fostering debt financing, debt relief, and debt restructuring, as appropriate, and address the external debt of highly indebted poor economies to reduce debt distress — 17.4.1: Debt Service as a Proportion of Exports of Goods and Services (%)		Target 17.9: Enhance international support for implementing effective and targeted capacity-building in developing economies to support national plans to implement all the Sustainable Development Goals, including through North-South, South-South, and triangular cooperation — 17.9.1: Dollar Value of Financial and Technical Assistance Committed to Developing Economies[a] (constant 2019 $ million)	
	2010	2019	Average, 2000–2010	Average, 2010–2019
Developing ADB Member Economies				
Central and West Asia[b]	**...**	**...**	**1,596.5**	**3,319.1**
Afghanistan	0.3	4.0 (2017)	795.8	1,285.2
Armenia	2.7	6.6	66.9	101.3
Azerbaijan	1.1	8.3	35.4	114.7
Georgia	6.3	4.8	84.7	167.4
Kazakhstan	0.5	2.1	93.3	300.7
Kyrgyz Republic	3.7	7.0	52.2	96.4
Pakistan	11.5	16.0	392.7	965.2
Tajikistan	2.7	8.7	32.6	45.1
Turkmenistan	...	...	6.1	6.2
Uzbekistan	3.4 (2016)	3.0	36.7	236.9
East Asia[b]	**...**	**...**	**409.3**	**927.6**
China, People's Republic of	0.8	0.8	366.1	745.0
Hong Kong, China	...	...	...	...
Korea, Republic of	...	...	...	...
Mongolia	4.3	11.6	43.2	182.6
Taipei,China	...	...	...	...
South Asia[b]	**...**	**...**	**1,082.1**	**1,534.2**
Bangladesh	4.6	4.2	238.8	518.3
Bhutan	14.4	10.4	16.5	26.0
India	1.7	4.2	617.8	668.2
Maldives	3.0	7.9	4.5	10.4
Nepal	10.4	7.4 (2017)	90.0	195.8
Sri Lanka	10.7	21.7	114.5	115.5
Southeast Asia[b]	**...**	**...**	**1,662.6**	**2,992.6**
Brunei Darussalam	...	...	...	...
Cambodia	1.0	1.4	91.9	134.9
Indonesia	6.6	8.5	845.4	1,359.9
Lao People's Democratic Republic	4.0	10.8	53.8	87.5
Malaysia	...	...	19.0	13.7
Myanmar	3.1	4.8	15.1	215.1
Philippines	16.0	4.5	155.7	414.1
Singapore	...	...	...	...
Thailand	0.4	0.5	45.3	65.7
Timor-Leste	0.0 (2012)	0.3	53.5	45.4
Viet Nam	2.1	1.4	382.9	656.3
The Pacific[b]	**...**	**...**	**335.8**	**383.1**
Cook Islands	...	...	2.6	4.0
Fiji	1.3	1.9	17.0	19.9
Kiribati	...	...	7.6	9.5
Marshall Islands	...	...	18.4	7.9
Micronesia, Federated States of	...	...	39.7	16.3
Nauru	...	...	10.0	7.5
Niue	...	...	2.0	6.5
Palau	...	...	1.7	3.5
Papua New Guinea	1.4	1.7	100.5	177.0
Samoa	5.3	9.8	17.2	35.0
Solomon Islands	3.1	1.3	91.1	56.1
Tonga	9.3	7.2	10.8	15.6
Tuvalu	...	...	2.9	4.6
Vanuatu	1.4	2.0 (2016)	14.4	19.5
Developed ADB Member Economies	**...**	**...**	**...**	**...**
Australia	...	...	...	...
Japan	...	...	...	...
New Zealand	...	...	...	...
DEVELOPING ADB MEMBER ECONOMIES[b]	**...**	**...**	**5,086.3**	**9,156.6**
DEVELOPING ECONOMIES WORLDWIDE[c]	**...**	**...**	**21,284.0**	**31,054.1**

... = data not available, 0.0 = magnitude is less than half of unit employed, $ = United States dollars, ADB = Asian Development Bank.

a Technical assistance includes assistance through North-South, South-South, and triangular cooperation. The United Nations Statistics Division dataset and metadata refer to this indicator as total official development assistance (gross disbursements) for technical cooperation.

b For reporting economies only.

c The figures provided refer to aggregates for all developing economies as reported in the United Nations' Global SDG Indicators Database.

Source: United Nations Statistics Division. Global SDG Indicators Database. http://unstats.un.org/sdgs/indicators/database/ (accessed 12 July 2021).

Table 1.17.2: Selected Indicators for Sustainable Development Goal 17—Statistical Capacity Building

ADB Regional Member	Target 17.18: By 2020, enhance capacity-building support to developing countries, including for least developed countries and small island developing states, to increase significantly the availability of high-quality, timely, and reliable data disaggregated by income, gender, age, race, ethnicity, migratory status, disability, geographic location, and other characteristics relevant in national contexts	Target 17.19: By 2030, build on existing initiatives to develop measurements of progress on sustainable development that complement gross domestic product and support statistical capacity-building in developing countries	
	Availability of National Statistical Plan[a]	Value of All Resources Made Available to Strengthen Statistical Capacity in Developing Countries[b] (current $)	Countries that Have Conducted at Least One Population and Housing Census in the Past 10 Years[c]
	2020	2018	2020
Developing ADB Member Economies			
Central and West Asia			
Afghanistan	B	11,502,321.9	...
Armenia	A, B, C, D	235,622.2	2011
Azerbaijan	...	886,714.5	2019
Georgia	...	75,364.9	2014
Kazakhstan	A, B, C	303,009.6	...
Kyrgyz Republic	A, B, C, D	222,040.9	...
Pakistan	A, B, C	35,261,287.1	2017
Tajikistan	C, D, E (2019)	553,985.4	2010
Turkmenistan	...	132,359.6	2012
Uzbekistan	A, B, C, D, E	426,837.0	...
East Asia			
China, People's Republic of	A, B, C	265,346.2	2010
Hong Kong, China	A, B, C	...	2016
Korea, Republic of	B, C	...	2015
Mongolia	A, B, C, D	492,648.6	2010
Taipei,China	...	...	2010
South Asia			
Bangladesh	A, B, C, D	17,775,910.9	2011
Bhutan	A, B, D	110,204.1	2017
India	B, C	484,243.1	2011
Maldives	B, C	174,524.7	2014
Nepal	B, C	366,560.1	2011
Sri Lanka	D (2019)	216,406.0	2012
Southeast Asia			
Brunei Darussalam	A, C (2019)	4,925.0	2011
Cambodia	C, D (2019)	185,225.2	2019
Indonesia	C (2019)	782,839.1	2010
Lao People's Democratic Republic	B	2,201,282.6	2015
Malaysia	...	208,799.5	2010
Myanmar	B (2019)	1,891,167.7	2014
Philippines	B	286,417.2	2015
Singapore	A, B, C	20,677.3	2010
Thailand	A, B, C	235,376.6	2010
Timor-Leste	B (2019)	515,881.2	2015
Viet Nam	B	4,355,908.0	2019
The Pacific			
Cook Islands	B, C (2019)	53,303.1	2016
Fiji	...	465,617.1	2017
Kiribati	...	1,569,407.9	2015
Marshall Islands	...	2,052,374.7	2011
Micronesia, Federated States of	...	6,950.7 (2017)	2010
Nauru	C (2019)	102,572.6	2011
Niue	...	15,919.0	2017
Palau	A, C (2019)	1,105,000.0	2015
Papua New Guinea	B	949,138.0	2011
Samoa	A, B, C, D	157,371.8	2016
Solomon Islands	B	125,624.7	2019
Tonga	A, B, C, D, E	90,638.9	2016
Tuvalu	B	122,443.2	2012
Vanuatu	C (2019)	86,278.5	2016
Developed ADB Member Economies			
Australia	A, B, C	...	2016
Japan	A, B, C	...	2015
New Zealand	A, B, C, E	47,286.1	2018

... = data not available, $ = United States dollars, ADB = Asian Development Bank.

a A = a national statistical plan fully funded, B = a national statistical plan under implementation, C = a national statistical plan with funding from government, D = a national statistical plan with funding from donors, E = a national statistical plan with funding from others.

b Data refer to the sum of economy-specific and unallocated commitments received during 2007–2018.

c Refers to the most recent year in which a population and housing census was conducted.

Source: United Nations Statistics Division. Global SDG Indicators Database. http://unstats.un.org/sdgs/indicators/database/ (accessed 19 July 2021).
For Taipei,China: Government of Taipei,China. Directorate-General of Budget, Accounting and Statistics. https://eng.stat.gov.tw/ (accessed 19 July 2021).

Data Gaps and Other Data-Related Issues

New and huge data demands. The approved global framework for monitoring the SDGs consists of 231 unique indicators with greater disaggregation and across a wider spectrum of topics than the Millennium Development Goals. With international development support, governments are strengthening their national statistical systems to address data demands across all SDG indicators.

Limited data availability for Sustainable Development Goal indicators. While there have been many improvements to data availability and timeliness since the launch of the SDGs in 2015, there is more to be done. While only 27% of SDG indicators had enough data for progress assessment in 2017, sufficient data availability had increased to 49% of indicators by 2020, but this remains well short of the mark. Significantly, the number of indicators with no data availability at all stood at 17% in 2020.

Differing priorities among national statistics offices with regard to economic data production result in disparities in data availability. Most national statistics offices across Asia and the Pacific conduct population and housing censuses every decade. Such sources provide baseline socioeconomic data that overlap SDG indicators with economic and social dimensions. Depending on the frequency of data collection, administrative reporting systems and household surveys—such as labor force surveys, household income and expenditure surveys, demographic and health surveys, establishment surveys, and agriculture surveys—can be other good sources of data for SDG indicators.

Gaps in data granularity. Many SDG indicators require disaggregation by location, sex, gender, age, income, ethnicity, migration status, disability status, and other relevant dimensions. Granular data can illustrate disparities within and across economies.

However, the extent to which specific groups are disproportionately at risk is difficult to decipher given the lack of data disaggregation and interlinkages across indicators. Sex disaggregations, even for basic indicators such as extreme poverty rates based on the $1.90 a day (at 2011 purchasing power parity) level, are not currently available. Similarly, poverty numbers are currently unavailable for vulnerable groups, such as people with disabilities or indigenous peoples, since the sample surveys these poverty calculations are based on are designed to obtain an overview of welfare conditions. Investments are needed (e.g., in special surveys) to obtain poverty data for vulnerable groups that make up only a small proportion of the total population.

Innovative data sources, such as big data and crowdsourced data, can potentially address these data gaps and strengthen the monitoring of SDG indicators. However, some types of big data may not represent the underlying groups of interest. Therefore, it is necessary to ensure that reliable statistical inferences can be made when complementing surveys and other conventional data sources with big data (Cox, Kartsonaki, and Keogh 2018).

Lack of data comparability. Differences in definitions mean that SDG indicators, such as the proportion of the population with access to safely managed drinking water services, rely on data related to housing conditions, which may not be fully comparable across economies. Likewise, comparisons of SDG indicators across economies are difficult for urban–rural disaggregation due to various definitions of "urban" and "rural" across time and economies.

Sparse data and irregular frequency. Some indicators that provide a useful description of income inequality—such as the growth in household expenditure among those in an economy's bottom 40th percentile of income distribution in relation to national averages are only currently available for a few economies. In another example, data on progress made toward addressing climate change are sparse.

Frequency is also of concern as some indicators, such as the coverage of protected areas in relation to marine areas, are not regularly collected. Indicators on material footprint and domestic material consumption, which are widely accepted as strategic sustainability indicators of production and consumption, are not produced annually.

Further, some protected areas are not assigned management categories. While access to remote sensing data has improved in recent years, forest regrowth cannot easily be detected with remote-sensing techniques.

Data limitations. The indicators included in the framework for monitoring the SDGs, while carefully chosen, may have some limitations. For example, the labor share in GDP does not include the income of the self-employed, even though a sizeable proportion of the employed population in developing Asia comprises people who are self-employed. Current measures of poverty used by economies are largely based on income or consumption data, while the SDG indicators include a multidimensional poverty measure that has yet to be tested on a wider scale.

The many challenges facing cities—pollution, traffic congestion, and inadequate housing for the poor—can be exacerbated by migration and population growth, changes in family structures, inequality of opportunity for excluded groups, and rising insecurity. Currently available data do not allow for a simple assessment of these issues.

The Red List Index is a composite index aggregated across multiple taxonomic groups. While it can be updated annually, the index does not adequately capture the deteriorating status of common species that are abundant and widespread yet declining gradually. Data on other indicators for monitoring many targets under SDG 15 are also sparsely available. The absence of a framework for monitoring terrestrial ecosystems, low data availability, and the lack of good-quality data must be carefully addressed.

Measurement errors. The quality of data for all SDG indicators needs to be considered when identifying trends and drawing inferences. For example, self-reporting of land area and production by farmers is known to have significant biases (Dillon and Rao 2018). The calculation of under-5 mortality rates requires complete counts of live births and child deaths by a precise age, which are not always available in economies of Asia and the Pacific that lack civil registration systems. Maternal deaths are likewise not always accounted for, given incomplete or inaccurate records on causes of death. The measurement of quality education across economies is hampered by the lack of standard definitions for minimum competency. Anthropometric measures of malnutrition (including stunted heights) are subject to measurement errors and issues around reference standards (i.e., local versus international standards). Access to safely managed drinking water and sanitation services, and information on hygiene all depend on more and better data, particularly administrative data sources (WHO and UNICEF 2017).

A complete stocktaking of all statistical capacity development programs cannot be guaranteed in the data compiled by PARIS21 for measuring the dollar-value support for statistics development. Double counting of projects can occur, or the data may also be inflated by the inaccurate inclusion of multisector projects. Further, donor commitments do not always lead to actual disbursements to recipient economies.

Ultimately, the reliability of data on SDG indicators depends on the quality of the underlying data sources. Governments across Asia and the Pacific need to increase investment, look for innovative data sources, and form strategic partnerships with a range of stakeholders to enhance data quality, comparability, measurement, and timeliness. Reliable and comprehensive data supports evidence-based policymaking that leads to better development outcomes.

PART II

Regional Trends and Tables

Regional Trends and Tables

The recent economic history of Asia and the Pacific chronicles how the region rapidly evolved to become one of the key drivers of the global economy. At the turn of the millennium, Asia and the Pacific accounted for just over a quarter of global gross domestic product (GDP). Through increased levels of consumption and integration into international trade, the region's contribution to global output increased to 29% by 2010 and its progress continued across the following decade. Prior to the onset of the COVID-19 pandemic, Asia and the Pacific was contributing approximately 35% of global GDP.

As in many other regions of the world, Asia and the Pacific has been hit hard by the COVID-19 pandemic. Its regional economy was beset on several fronts, the scale of the impacts unseen in several generations. Part II of *Key Indicators for Asia and the Pacific 2021* brings into focus how the region's macroeconomic performance has been affected by the greatest public health crisis in a century. It does so by revisiting data on select economic and financial indicators such as work and employment, economic output, government expenditure, inflation, interest rates, and debt.

The analyses presented here complement earlier studies that relied on scenario-based forecasts, simulations, and preliminary estimates to assess the economic toll of the pandemic. These analyses draw on the latest 2020 estimates for the nominated indicators, as compiled by national and international statistical systems. The data presented show mixed outcomes in economic performance across Asia and the Pacific, with some economies doing slightly better than earlier estimates anticipated, while others have fared much worse than initially expected.

Work and Employment

Providing greater access to adequate and quality employment remains a challenge for several of the region's economies.

Since the 1990s, structural transformation across Asia and the Pacific has been the primary driver behind the transition of employment from agricultural activities to industry and service sectors.

In 2000, about 48% of jobs across Asia and the Pacific were found in the agriculture sector. However, as individual economies have developed, the agriculture sector's share of employment has declined, with a significant fraction of the working population moving into industry and services. The latest pre-pandemic estimates show about 26% of the region's employed population working in industry and around 45% in services, up from 20% and 32%, respectively, in 2000 (Figure 2.1). This pace of increase in nonagricultural employment is among the fastest worldwide.

Figure 2.1: Employment Share in Asia and the Pacific, by Sector

Roughly 71% of the region's workforce were in nonagricultural employment by 2019.

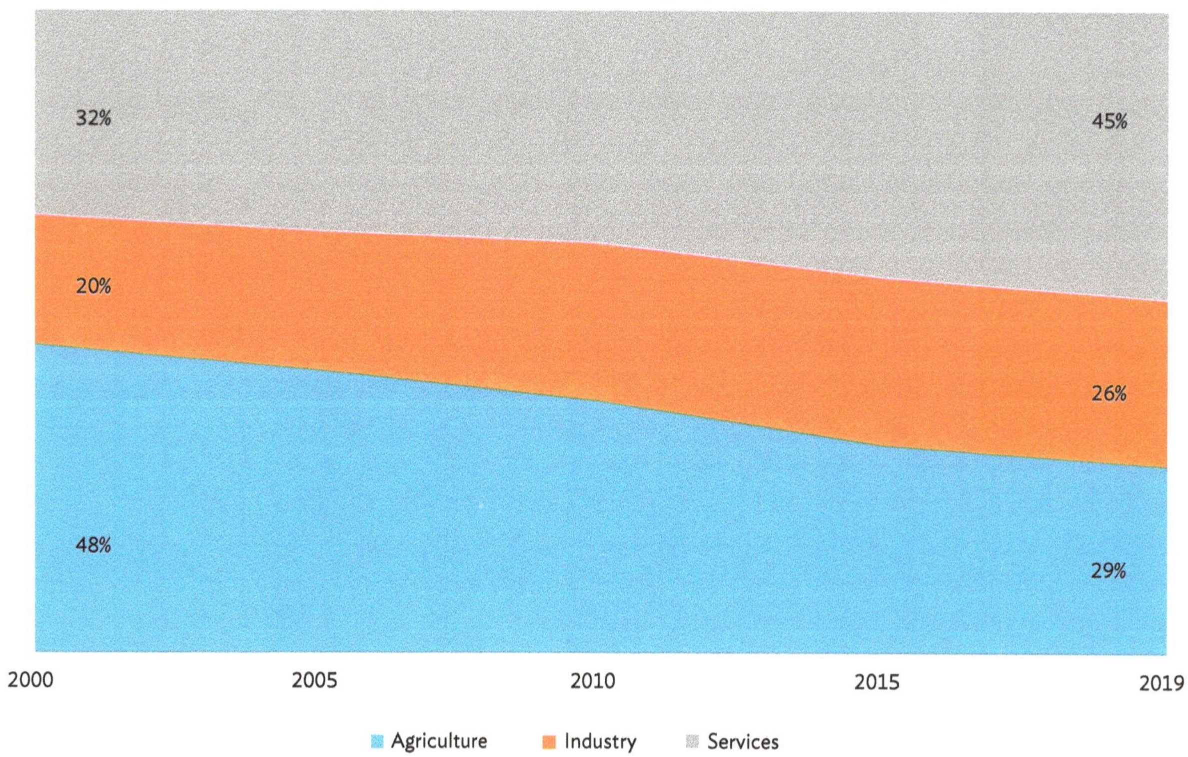

Sources: Asian Development Bank estimates using data presented in Table 2.1.5 of *Key Indicators for Asia and the Pacific 2021*; Asian Development Bank. Key Indicators Database. https://kidb.adb.org/ (accessed 15 July 2021); and International Labour Organization. ILOSTAT Database. https://ilostat.ilo.org/ (accessed 15 July 2021).

Low-income and lower middle-income economies saw their agricultural employment decline by 15 percentage points from 2000 to 2019, while the reduction for upper middle-income economies was 13 percentage points over the same period. Economies in the high-income group, coming from a small agricultural base, registered a 3-percentage point decline in employment share for the sector.

The decline in agricultural employment coincided with lower poverty rates in the region, as discussed in Part I. However, even as more workers transition to nonagricultural employment, the agriculture sector is likely to remain a significant employer, so designing policies that promote enhanced productivity of agricultural workers should continue as an important part of poverty reduction strategies.

It is also important to note that nonagricultural work does not necessarily equate to high-quality or adequate work, with considerable underemployment rates and informal employment arrangements still prevalent across Asia and the Pacific (Figure 2.2).

Figure 2.2: Prevalence of Underemployment and Informal Employment

Despite increased employment in industry and services, provision of adequate and high-quality jobs remains a challenge.

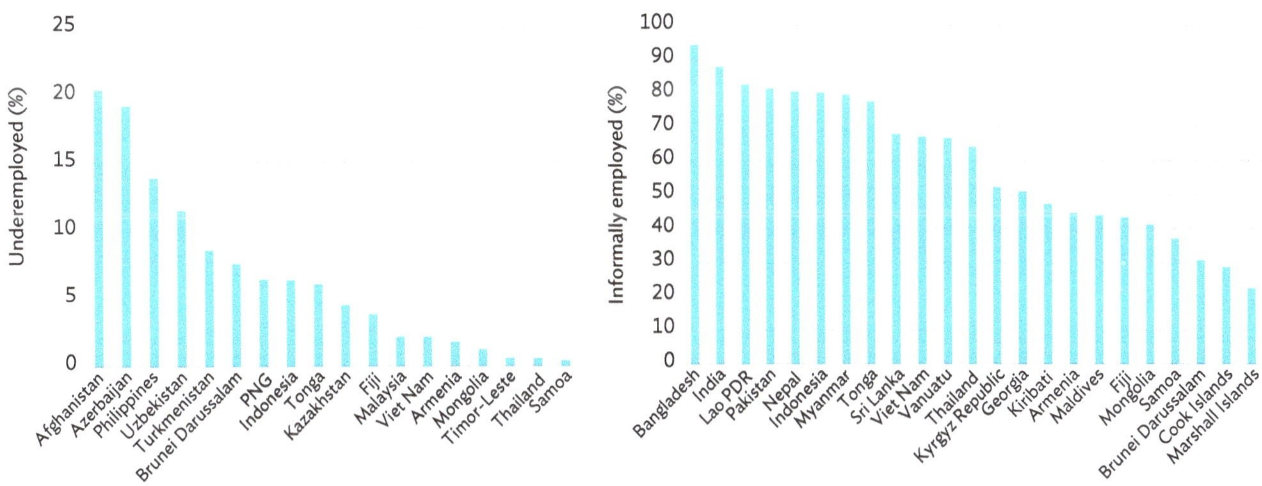

Lao PDR = Lao People's Democratic Republic, PNG = Papua New Guinea.

Notes: Underemployment and informal employment are expressed as proportions of the employed population in each economy. Data are for the most recently available year ranging from 2013 to 2019.

Sources: Asian Development Bank estimates using data available in individual economy tables for 2021 in the Key Indicators Database (https://kidb.adb.org/); and International Labour Organization. ILOSTAT Database. https://ilostat.ilo.org/ (accessed 15 July 2021).

It is of utmost importance that the lack of employment opportunities and prevalence of low-quality work in the region be addressed, especially during periods of uncertainty, as studies show that people in the informal economy are less likely to enjoy job security and social protection benefits (Figure 2.3).

Figure 2.3: Proportion of Wage Workers Who Received Benefits, by Nature of Employment (%)

People in informal employment have limited access to social protection.

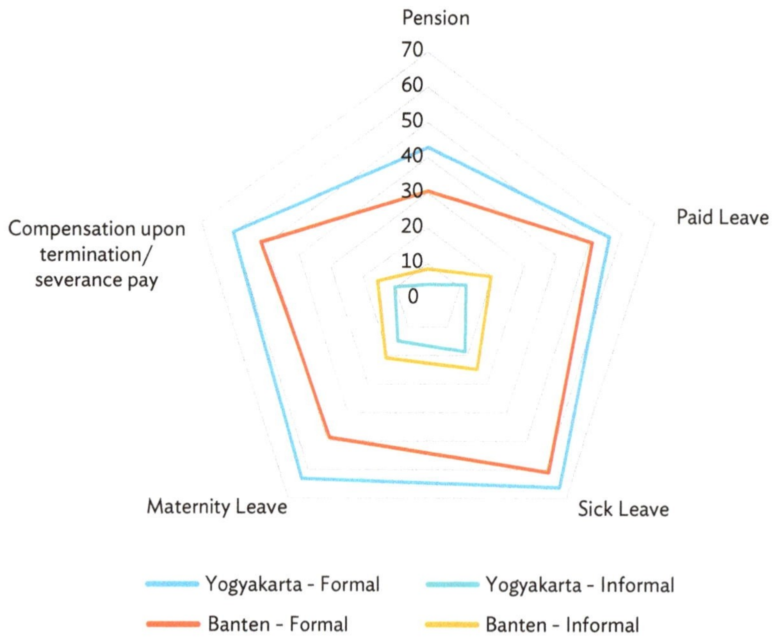

Note: The results are based on a mixed survey approach adopted by BPS-Statistics Indonesia in partnership with the Asian Development Bank. The approach was used to collect informal sector and informal employment data for two pilot provinces.

Source: Asian Development Bank. 2011. *A Handbook on Using the Mixed Survey for Measuring Informal Employment and the Informal Sector.* Manila. p. 64.

During the COVID-19 pandemic, households engaged in business activities experienced larger decreases in income than those engaged in farming or relying on wages or salary.

Some household businesses that existed before the pandemic were able to thrive in 2020 because they successfully pivoted to new business models: some traditional bricks-and-mortar stores shifted to e-commerce, while farmers groups that previously sold to restaurants and hotels began using online platforms to sell produce directly to households.

However, data collected from Asian Development Bank Institute surveys in 2020 show that a significant number of households engaged in business were severely affected by the pandemic (Figure 2.4). Almost two-thirds of survey respondents who cited business as one of their main sources of income reported seeing their incomes reduced by 26% or more, while more than one-quarter of these respondents saw their incomes reduced by over 50%.

Of households engaged in agriculture or relying on wages and salary, more than half reported either an increase, no change, or a decrease of less than 26% in their incomes. However, more than 2 in every 5 households in both categories reported reduced incomes of more than 25%, likely the result of reduced working hours or retrenchment.

Struggling to get by. A vendor selling vegetables during the COVID-19 lockdown in Pakistan.

Figure 2.4: Magnitude of Increase or Decrease in Income, by Income Source (%)

People relying on entrepreneurial activities saw their incomes decline substantially because of disruptions caused by the COVID-19 pandemic.

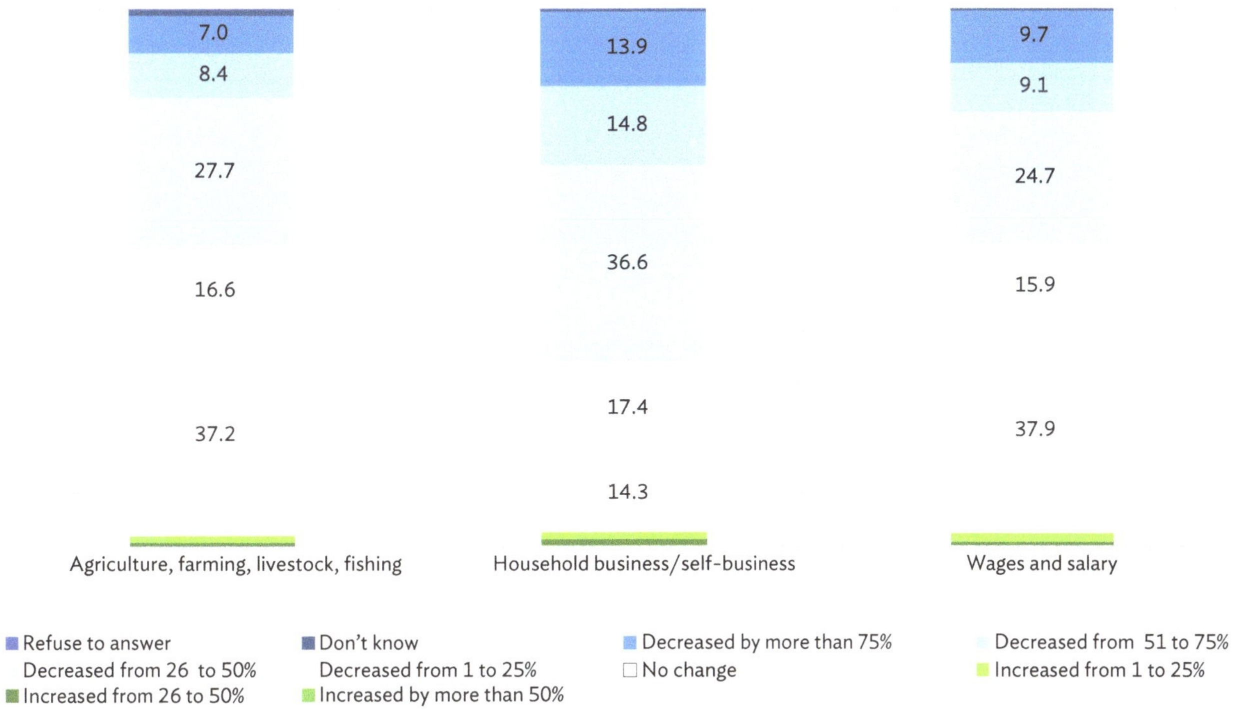

Source: Asian Development Bank estimates using data from the Asian Development Bank Institute's Survey on the Impacts of COVID-19 and Related Policies on Households in 8 Developing Association of Southeast Asian Nations (ASEAN) Countries.

Support for businesses to endure the adverse impacts of the pandemic is particularly critical for micro, small, and medium-sized enterprises (MSMEs), which account for a significant fraction of all enterprises and employ a substantial number of the labor force in Asia and the Pacific (ADB 2020a). Studies suggest that many of the region's MSMEs have limited access to bank credit, which has the potential to exacerbate the risk of bankruptcies (ADB 2020a).

It is also important that there is a favorable environment for new and innovative MSMEs to emerge to meet post-pandemic demand (and thereby deliver ongoing employment). However, an examination of the World Bank's Doing Business Report 2020 suggests that 40% of economies in the region included are in the bottom half of the list for ease of starting a business (Figure 2.5).

Figure 2.5: Scores in Ease of Starting Business, by Gross Domestic Product per Capita

A number of economies in Asia and the Pacific ranked in the bottom half for ease of starting business.

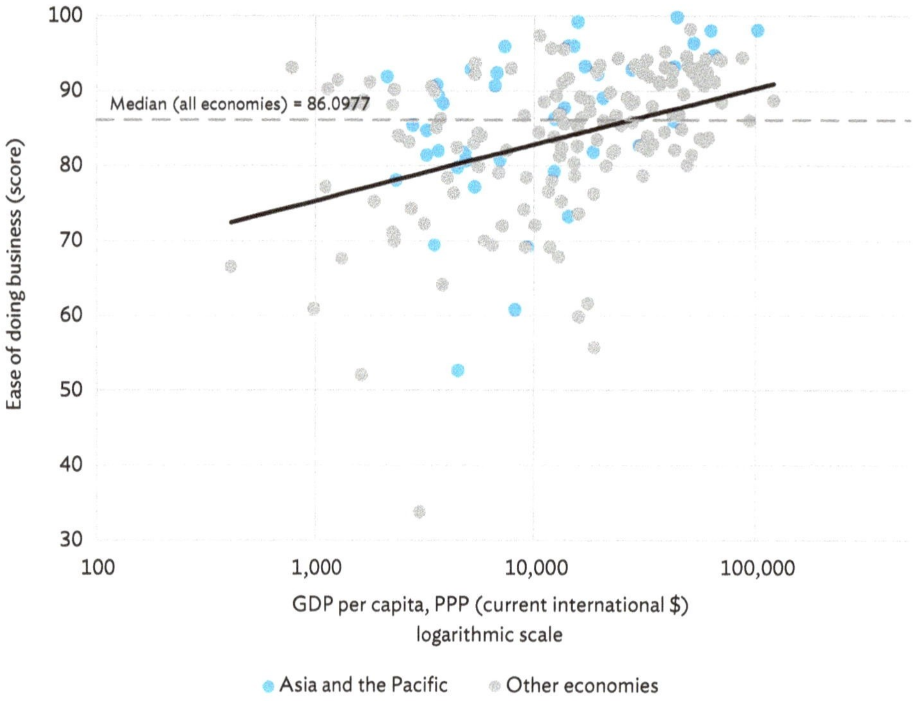

GDP = Gross Domestic Product, PPP = Purchasing Power Parity.

Note: Scores in ease of doing business range from 0 to 100 with higher values associated to greater ease in doing business.

Sources: Asian Development Bank estimates using data presented in Tables 2.2.3 and 2.8.6 of *Key Indicators for Asia and the Pacific 2021*; and World Bank. *Doing Business Report 2020*. https://www.doingbusiness.org/ (accessed 1 June 2021).

Because indications suggest that labor market outcomes for women have been adversely impacted by the pandemic, policymakers should prioritize action to address gender inequalities.

Although labor force participation in Asia and the Pacific ranged from about 40% to 75% of the working age population in 2019, a majority of ADB member economies reported faring better than the world average of 61%.

However, from 2019 to 2020, 18 of the 23 ADB member economies with available data showed a decline in labor force participation rates. The largest declines were noted in Viet Nam (–2.17 percentage points), the Philippines (–1.77 percentage points), Sri Lanka (–1.71 percentage points), and Mongolia (–1.70 percentage points) (Table 2.1.4).

While participation by women in the labor force has generally improved across the region, there are a few economies with rates for women's labor force participation that are below 40% (KIDB 2021).

From 2019 to 2020, labor force participation rates among women, on average, declined by 1.4%, while labor force participation rates among men declined by an average of 0.8% (Figure 2.6). The impact of the COVID-19 pandemic on work and employment is believed to be borne more by women, with a risk of amplifying gender inequalities in the labor market (ILO 2020). Working women across Asia and the Pacific are heavily concentrated in sectors such as manufacturing (e.g., textiles and clothing), education, public administration, wholesale and retail trade, and health and social services.

Figure 2.6: Labor Force Participation Rates Among Men and Women, 2019–2020

On average, labor force participation rates among men in reporting economies declined 0.8%, while participation by women declined 1.4%.

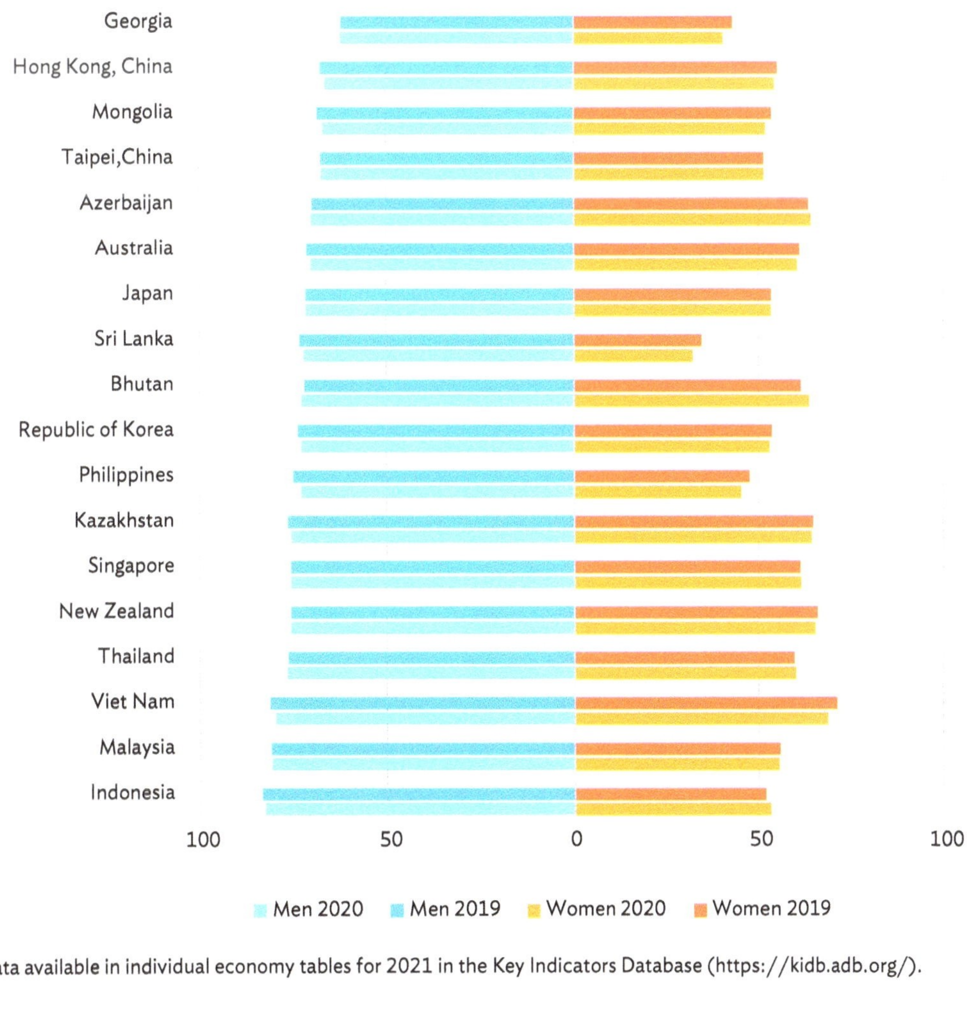

Sources: Data available in individual economy tables for 2021 in the Key Indicators Database (https://kidb.adb.org/).

They are also underrepresented in jobs that are suitable for remote work—such as professional, technical, and scientific work—and nearly two-thirds of them remain in vulnerable and informal employment (Park and Inocencio 2020). The International Labour Organization has estimated that about 40% of all women work in sectors severely affected by the pandemic (ILO 2020).

With unemployment rates soaring and the number of work hours lost approaching 8%, delivery of social protection programs for the most vulnerable should be enhanced.

Figure 2.7 shows how unemployment rates soared across Asia and the Pacific in 2020. Unemployment increased in 21 of the 23 economies with available data. Of these, 16 economies saw their unemployment rates increase by at least 10% relative to values recorded a year earlier, while more than one-third saw increases of 20% or more (Figure 2.7).

On the other hand, the highest increases in unemployment rates were noted in the Philippines (5.2 percentage points); Hong Kong, China (2.9 percentage points); Azerbaijan (2.4 percentage points); Bhutan (2.3 percentage points); and Indonesia (1.8 percentage points).

Overall, it is estimated that the region lost as much as 8% work hours in 2020. The highest among the subregions was South Asia, which recorded 13.6% of work hours lost, followed by Central and West Asia with 9.2% and Southeast Asia with 8.4%. The Pacific recorded

Figure 2.7: Unemployment Rates in Economies of Asia and the Pacific

Unemployment rates increased by at least 20% in more than one-third of economies with available data for 2020.

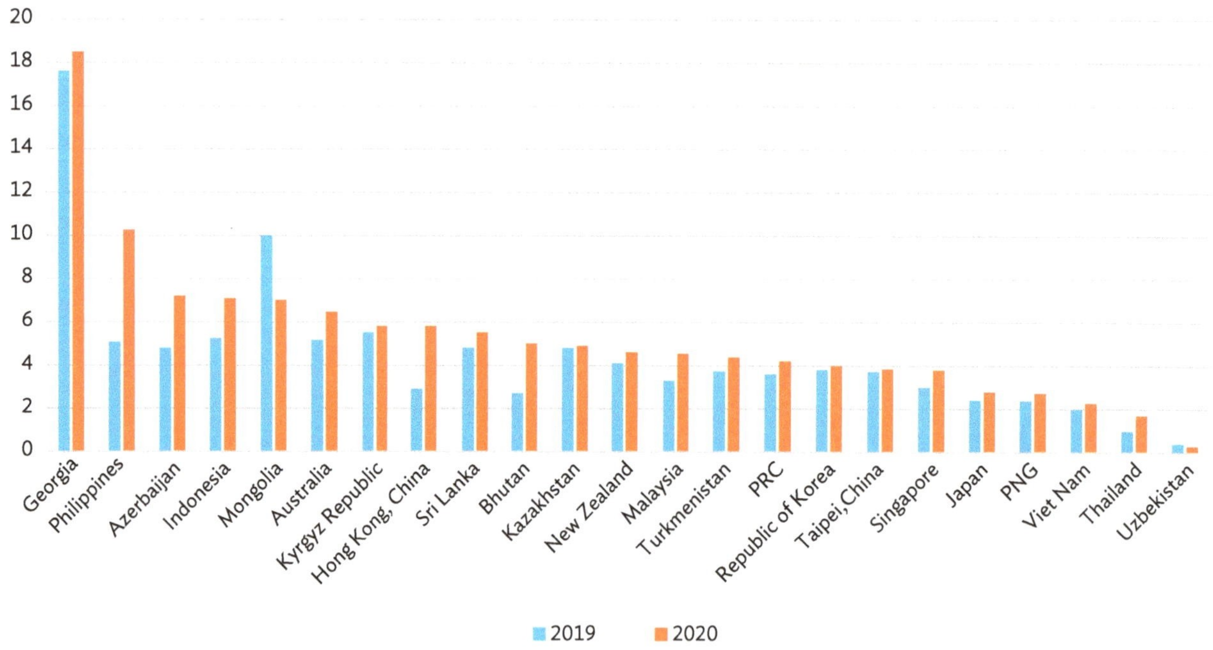

PNG = Papua New Guinea, PRC = People's Republic of China.

Sources: Data available in individual economy tables for 2021 in the Key Indicators Database (https://kidb.adb.org/); and International Labour Organization. ILOSTAT Database. https://ilostat.ilo.org/ (accessed 26 July 2021).

Table 2.1: Work Hours Lost in 2020 by Subregion of Asia and the Pacific

Hours worked fell by more than 8% in three highly populated subregions.

Region	Central and West Asia	East Asia	South Asia	Southeast Asia	The Pacific	Developed ADB Member Economies	ADB Regional Member Economies
Work hours lost expressed as number of FTE jobs (total)	11,994,737	37,376,440	85,177,662	28,314,749	94,291	3,917,484	166,875,363
Work hours lost (%)	9.2%	4.1%	13.6%	8.4%	2.4%	5.2%	8.0%

FTE = full-time employment.

Notes: Work hours lost are expressed as full-time equivalent employment losses. The estimates of working hours lost (%) are relative to no COVID-19 baseline scenario, as modeled by ILO.

Sources: Asian Development Bank estimates using data from the International Labour Organization. ILOSTAT Database. https://ilostat.ilo.org/ (accessed 15 July 2021).

the smallest change in work hours lost with only 2.4% (Table 2.1) (ILO 2021; ADB 2021a).

During 2020, the Asian Development Bank Institute conducted household surveys in several economies that are members of the Association of Southeast Asian Nations. The results of these surveys revealed that the proportion of households with at least one member losing a job, or having their working hours reduced, was significantly higher among poorer households (Figure 2.8). This corroborates the hypothesis in Part I that disruptions caused by managing the pandemic have the potential to exacerbate inequality. It also emphasizes the importance of enhancing the delivery of social protection programs, particularly for those in the informal economy who do not have adequate financial buffers

Figure 2.8: Changes in Unemployment Rates, by Income Level and Job Loss or Reduction in Working Hours, by Socioeconomic Status of Household

People in poorer households were more likely to report reduced work hours or job loss.

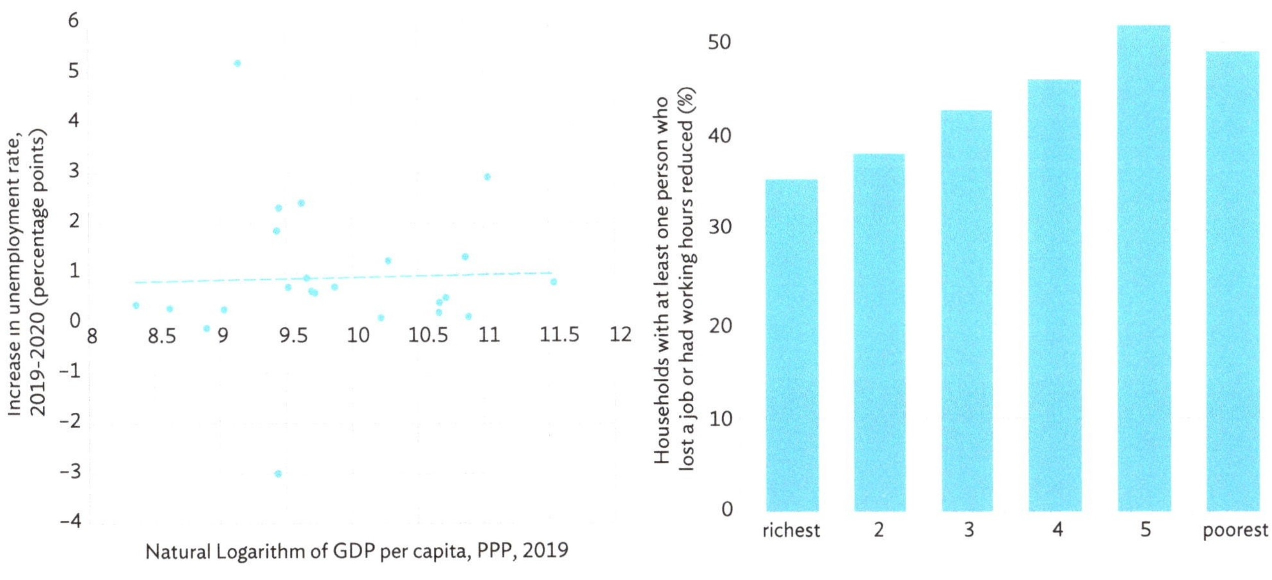

GDP = gross domestic product, PPP = purchasing power parity.

Sources: Asian Development Bank estimates using data presented in Economy Tables and Table 2.2.3 of *Key Indicators for Asia and the Pacific 2021*; the Key Indicators Database. https://kidb.adb.org/ (accessed 26 July 2021); and the Asian Development Bank Institute's Survey on the Impacts of COVID-19 and Related Policies on Households in 8 Developing ASEAN Countries.

or access to standard employment entitlements. However, changes in unemployment rates did not vary significantly based on the GDP of each economy (Figure 2.8).

Economic Output

Asia and the Pacific became one of the largest contributors to global economic output from 2010 to 2019, but growth was already slowing toward the end of the decade.

In current dollar terms, Asia and the Pacific's contribution to global economic output was about 35% before the pandemic: in purchasing power parity terms, the contribution was as much as 41%.

Within the region, East Asia's economic performance is particularly noteworthy, with its GDP doubling from 2010 to 2019 (Figure 2.9). This was mostly driven by the stellar performance of the People's Republic of China. A number of lower-middle income economies, such as Bangladesh, Cambodia, and the Lao People's Democratic Republic also experienced considerable GDP growth rates from 2010 to 2019 (Table 2.2.2).[1]

In GDP per capita terms, economies with lower incomes saw generally higher growth rates in the region from 2010 to 2019 (Table 2.2.5). Higher-income economies also experienced economic growth, albeit at a more modest pace.

Figure 2.9: Share of Global Gross Domestic Product at Current $ (%)

Asia and the Pacific [illegible] North America.

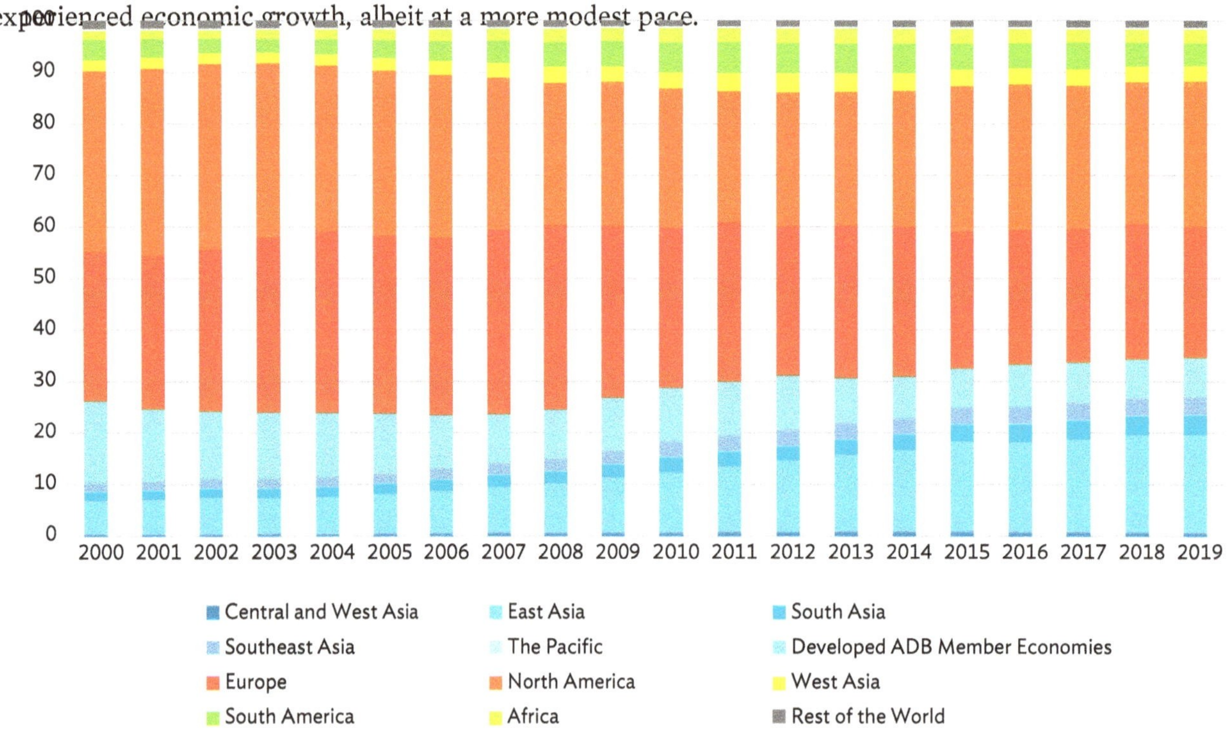

$ = United States dollars.

Sources: Asian Development Bank estimates using data presented in Table 2.2.2 of *Key Indicators for Asia and the Pacific 2021*; and World Bank. World Development Indicators. https://databank.worldbank.org/source/world-development-indicators (accessed 18 July 2021).

1 The economy income groupings follow the World Bank's classification as of July 2020.

From 2010 to 2019, economies in the region saw the agriculture sector's relative share of economic output diminish, while the industry and service sectors grew (KIDB 2021). Almost one-third of the reporting economies reported service sectors posting increases of at least 0.5 percentage point per year.

However, Asia and the Pacific's growth path was unlikely to remain linear, even without the COVID-19 pandemic. Some of the region's higher-income economies, for instance, were already encountering restricted labor supply, budget constraints associated with aging populations, impacts of international trade tensions, and significant financing needed to address climate-related disasters (ADB 2019).

In 2019, the regional economy of Asia and the Pacific grew by approximately 5%, relatively slower than in previous years (ADB 2020b; ADB 2020d). This moderated growth was posted in most subregions, with the exception of Central Asia, which showed more robust growth compared to the rest of the region. Factors such as weaker domestic investment, slowing global trade and economic activity, and protracted trade tensions triggered lower growth forecasts at the beginning of 2020 (ADB 2019).

The COVID-19 pandemic took a huge economic toll across the entire region, but some economies fared worse than others.

Under a best-case scenario, which assumed that the COVID-19 contagion could be contained quickly and disruptions kept to a minimum, it was estimated that the economic impact might amount to 0.1% of global GDP (Abiad et al. 2020).

However, as the pandemic evolved and the health responses became more extensive and protracted, it was clear that sharp declines in demand, lower tourism and business travel, production linkages and supply disruptions, and job losses would lead to falling growth unprecedented since World War II. In fact, ADB has estimated that developing Asia's economy contracted by 0.2% in 2020, the region's first recession in nearly 60 years (ADB 2021a).

Figure 2.10 measures latest 2020 estimates of economic growth, as reported by national statistical systems, against corresponding growth forecasts made in 2020, with the size of the bubble representing the size of each economy. Points below the 45-degree line represent the latest economic growth estimates that came in below the initial growth forecasts, while those above the line show latest growth estimates that were higher than the forecasts. It should be noted that initial forecasts were based on more optimistic scenarios. Over time, forecasts were recalibrated and became closer to the actual growth numbers, as shown in the figure, where most of the economies are near the 45 degree line. Complementing traditional data with innovative and more timely sources will also assist in improved forecasting.

Figure 2.10: Latest Economic Growth Estimates versus Initial Growth Forecasts

Economic growth was impacted in all economies of the region, but some were able to manage better than others.

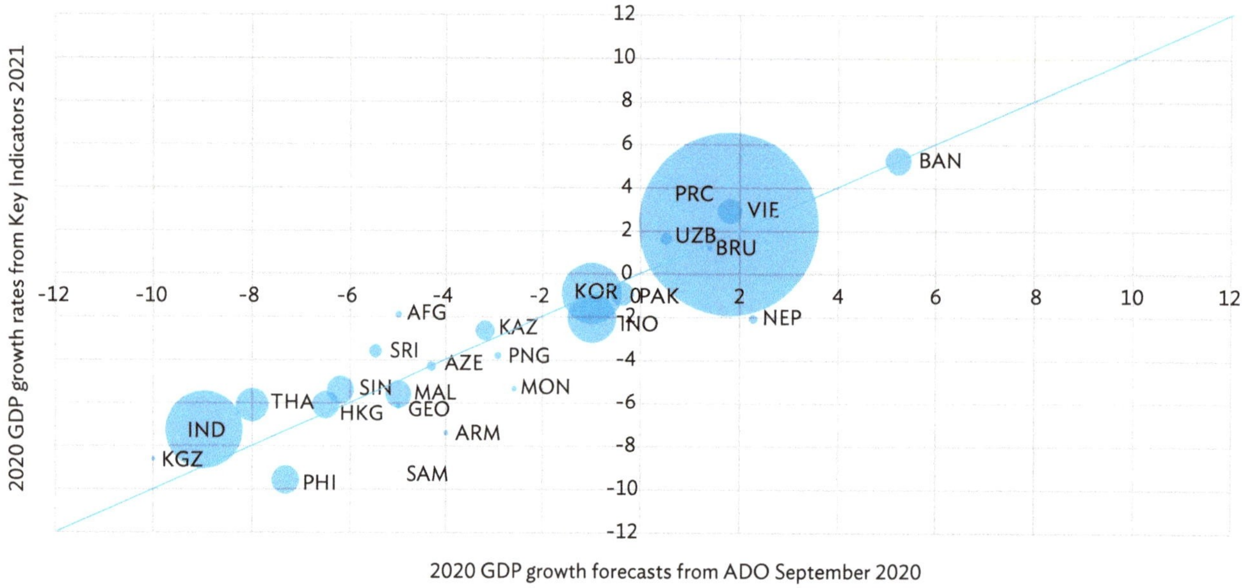

$ = United States dollars, ADO = Asian Development Outlook, AFG = Afghanistan, ARM = Armenia, AZE = Azerbaijan, BAN = Bangladesh, BRU = Brunei Darussalam, PRC = People's Republic of China, GDP = gross domestic product, GEO = Georgia, HKG = Hong Kong, China, IND = India, INO = Indonesia, KAZ = Kazakhstan, KGZ = Kyrgyz Republic, MAL = Malaysia, MON = Mongolia, NEP = Nepal, PAK = Pakistan, PNG = Papua New Guinea, PHI = Philippines, KOR = Republic of Korea, SAM = Samoa, SIN = Singapore, SRI = Sri Lanka, THA = Thailand, UZB = Uzbekistan, VIE = Viet Nam.

Note: "Key Indicators" is a shortened form of the Asian Development Bank's Key Indicators for Asia and the Pacific.

Sources: Asian Development Bank (ADB) estimates using data presented in Tables 2.2.2 and 2.2.11 of *Key Indicators for Asia and the Pacific 2021*; ADB. Key Indicators Database. https://kidb.adb.org/ (accessed 17 July 2021); and ADB. 2020. *Asian Development Outlook Update 2020*. Manila.

Overall, mixed economic performance can be seen across Asia and the Pacific, with some economies doing better than earlier economic forecasts predicted, while others fared worse than initially anticipated. Among the economies with available data, about 25% managed to post positive GDP growth in 2020, but a number of these had been expected to demonstrate much better economic progress.

For many economies in the region, the disruption in commercial activity brought about by the pandemic resulted in plummeting economic growth, particularly during the first half of 2020. The estimates suggest that around 75% of the reporting economies saw their latest 2020 economic growth scorecards in negative territory, and some contracted much more than the predictions made in September 2020, prior to release of full-year growth estimates.

The economic output of the services sector was most affected by the pandemic, with 15 of 34 reporting economies showing a reduction of 5% or more in this sector in general (KIDB 2021). Three of the hardest hit subsectors were accommodation and food services; arts, entertainment, and recreation; and transport and storage.

Economies that rely heavily on tourism and export earnings proved most vulnerable during the crisis. Those that are dependent on manufacturing were also exposed to supply chain disruptions, and even those economies specializing in commodities were affected by the drop in global demand.

However, growth in most economies strengthened during the latter part of 2020. In particular, the economic revival was especially strong in East Asia, driven by exports of electronics and products related to the pandemic (ADB 2021a).

In summary, the latest estimates for 2020 show that the economic shock from COVID-19 may be deeper and longer lasting than initially expected, but regional growth is expected to rebound (ADB 2021a). This rebound does, however, rely upon containing the ongoing spread of the virus and the effective roll-out of vaccination programs; prolonged pandemic and vaccine supply challenges in developing economies may threaten recovery and stability in some economies already seriously affected.

Inflation and Interest Rates

Since 2000, inflation across Asia and the Pacific has both surged and receded, with some significant variances by subregion.

Asia and the Pacific has experienced multiple inflation regimes since the turn of the millennium.

Figure 2.11 shows that, in 2000, prices of consumer goods and services were generally increasing in a majority of economies, but with notable variations across subregions. At that time, prices moving higher than inflation targets was seen as a major risk to the region's macroeconomic outlook (Jongwanich et al. 2016). This period can be largely attributed to structural changes in the Asia and Pacific economy, accompanied by the emergence of a sizable middle class in many of the region's developing economies, which stimulated demand and contributed to higher prices for consumer goods and services.

The inflationary surge of the early 2000s was interrupted when the global financial crisis hit and the downward trend continued through to 2015 and beyond. As well as the economic crisis caused by the stock market collapse, reduced volatility in global oil prices also led to lower inflation.

Figure 2.11: Distribution of Headline Inflation, by Subregion (%)

Inflationary pressures have varied over time and across subregions of Asia and the Pacific.

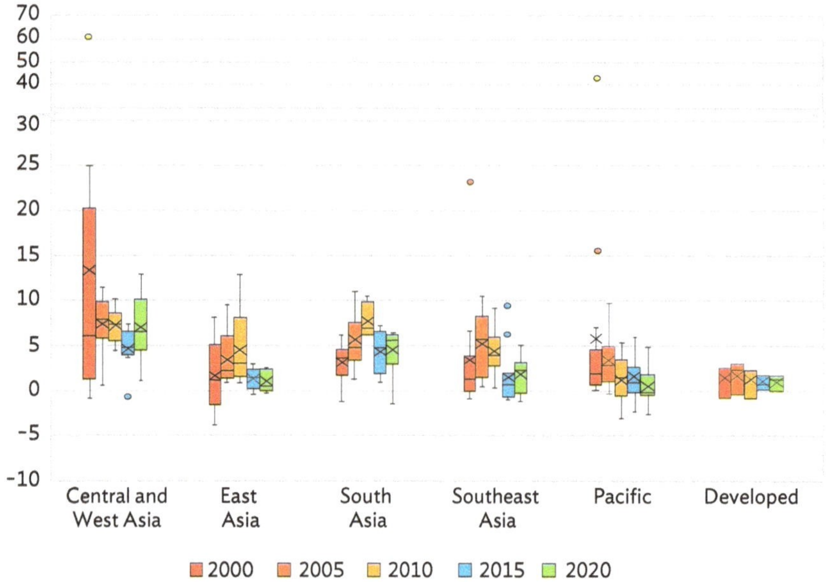

Sources: Asian Development Bank estimates using data presented in Table 2.3.1 of *Key Indicators for Asia and the Pacific 2021*; and Asian Development Bank. Key Indicators Database. https://kidb.adb.org/ (accessed 19 July 2021).

However, prior to the COVID-19 pandemic, consumer prices were again trending upward for a number of subregions, particularly Central and West Asia, East Asia, and Southeast Asia, with this inflationary phase driven mainly by increases in food prices. Natural disasters, extreme weather events, and the spread of animal disease were key contributors to food price volatility (ADB 2020b).

The impact of the COVID-19 pandemic on consumer price inflation in Asia and the Pacific is mixed, although further analysis is needed on these figures.

In anticipation of depressed demand and lower oil prices due to the pandemic, consumer price inflation in Asia and the Pacific was initially projected to decelerate from 2019 to 2020 (ADB 2020c). Latest estimates for 2020, compiled by national statistical systems, show that 19 of the 44 economies with available data had consumer price inflation falling below 2%, with 10 of these experiencing deflation. On the other hand, 13 economies reported increases in the consumer price index (CPI) of 5% or higher (Table 2.3.1).

The economies that reported the largest declines in CPI growth rates from 2019 to 2020 were Myanmar (–5.1 percentage points); Fiji (–4.4 percentage points); Turkmenistan (–3.3 percentage points); Mongolia (–2.9 percentage points); Hong Kong, China (–2.6 percentage points); and Samoa (–2.6 percentage points). The highest increases were noted in the Kyrgyz Republic (5.2 percentage points); Kiribati (4.3 percentage points); Pakistan (3.4 percentage points); Afghanistan (3.3 percentage points); and Bhutan (2.9 percentage points) as shown in Table 2.3.1.

Results are also mixed when these statistics are compared with estimates released last year, with 18 economies reporting lower consumer price inflation rates and 16 economies reporting higher rates (Figure 2.12).

Figure 2.12: Latest Consumer Price Inflation Estimates versus Initial Inflation Forecasts

The number of economies reporting either higher or lower inflation against initial forecasts is almost evenly split.

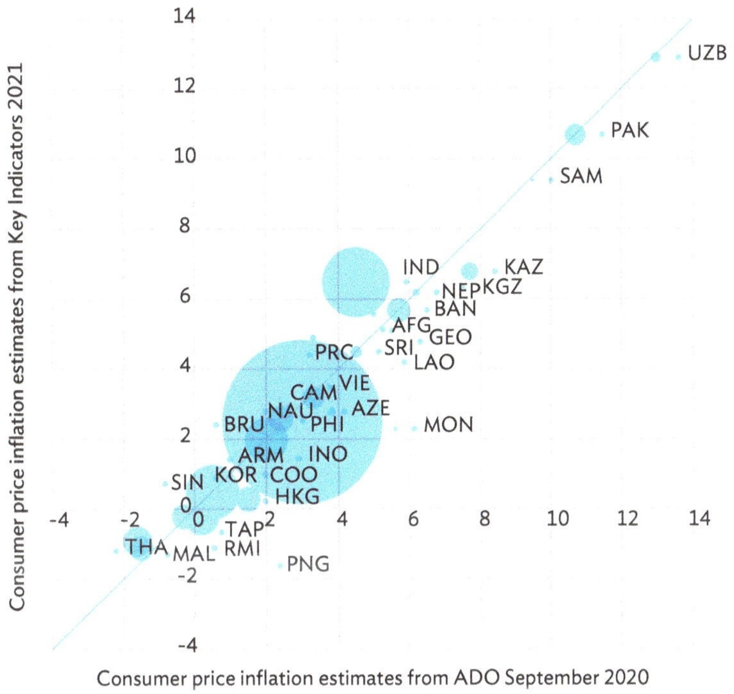

ADO = Asian Development Outlook, AFG = Afghanistan, ARM = Armenia, AZE = Azerbaijan, BAN = Bangladesh, BRU = Brunei Darussalam, CAM = Cambodia, COO = Cook Islands, GEO = Georgia, HKG = Hong Kong, China, IND = India, INO = Indonesia, KAZ = Kazakhstan, KGZ = Kyrgyz Republic, LAO = Lao PDR, MAL = Malaysia, RMI = Marshall Islands, MON = Mongolia, NAU = Nauru, NEP = Nepal, PAK = Pakistan, PHI = Philippines, PNG = Papua New Guinea, PRC = People's Republic of China, KOR = Republic of Korea, SAM = Samoa, SIN = Singapore, SRI = Sri Lanka, TAP = Taipei,China, TAJ = Tajikistan, THA = Thailand, UZB = Uzbekistan, VIE = Viet Nam.

Note: "Key Indicators" is a shortened form of the Asian Development Bank's *Key Indicators for Asia and the Pacific*.

Sources: Asian Development Bank (ADB) estimates using data presented in Table 2.3.1 of *Key Indicators for Asia and the Pacific 2021*; ADB. Key Indicators Database. https://kidb.adb.org/ (accessed 19 July 2021); and ADB. 2020. *Asian Development Outlook Update 2020*. Manila.

It must be noted that official inflation numbers might not reflect the realities of everyday life. Community lockdowns, social distancing protocols, and work disruptions have likely reduced demand for nonessentials such as travel and clothing, diverting spending toward basics such as food and housing. Such pronounced changes in spending behavior might have not been immediately reflected in the set basket of goods and services that authorities use to track movements in consumer prices. For instance, a study conducted by the International Monetary Fund, using credit and debit card data to adjust the CPI weights and match spending patterns during the pandemic, suggests that global inflation to the second quarter of 2020 could be significantly higher than initially estimated (Reinsdorf 2020) and additional discussion on this topic is provided in Part IV.

Spikes in global food prices could hit developing Asia's poor populations hard.

In developing Asia, the share of food to the total consumption basket is high, reaching approximately 50% for a number of economies. Hence, movements in food prices could have a significant impact on overall inflation in many of the region's developing economies. Moreover, sudden spikes in food prices can more severely impact the poor, as they spend a larger fraction of their incomes on food.

Figure 2.13 shows changes in food inflation from 2019 to 2020, arranged by the socioeconomic status of each economy. Almost all economies with available data showed positive food CPI growth in 2020. Comparing 2020 to 2019, food inflation increased in 29 of the 41 reporting economies, of which 17 posted food inflation of 5% or higher. The largest increases in food price inflation were observed mostly in lower-middle income economies such as Pakistan (11.3 percentage points), Sri Lanka (10.6 percentage points), the Kyrgyz Republic (10.3 percentage points), and Bhutan (7.8 percentage points).

Trends in nonfood price inflation in 2020 were mixed and ranged from as low as −10.3% to as high as 18.6% by economy.

Figure 2.13: Food Inflation, by Economy (%)

The consumer price index for food increased in majority of economies during 2020.

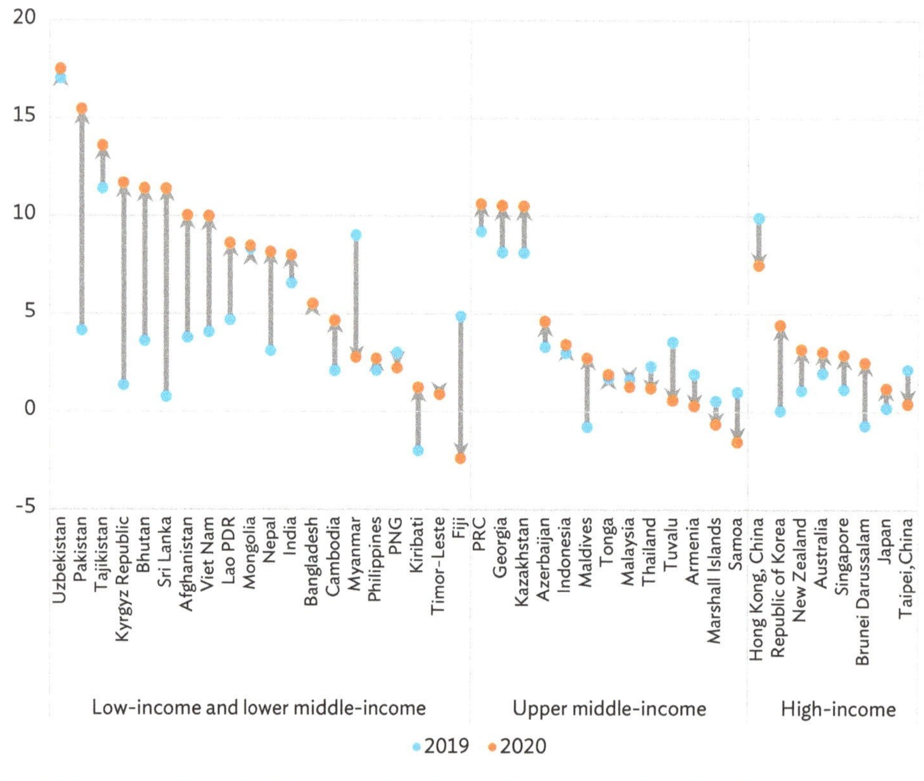

Lao PDR =Lao People's Democratic Republic, PNG = Papua New Guinea, PRC = People's Republic of China.

Note: The economy income groupings follow the World Bank's classification as of July 2020.

Sources: Asian Development Bank estimates using data presented in Table 2.3.2 of *Key Indicators for Asia and the Pacific 2021*; and Asian Development Bank. Key Indicators Database. https://kidb.adb.org/ (accessed 19 July 2021).

An assessment of the components of the nonfood CPI basket reveals that the largest decreases were seen in transport and communication. The largest declines in transport prices were seen in Viet Nam (–10.3%), Malaysia (–10%), and Afghanistan (–9.7%); while for communication, the biggest drops were seen in Sri Lanka (–10.3%), Maldives (–9.8%), and Uzbekistan (–6.4%).

However, other nonfood components saw an increase in prices in 2020, particularly for miscellaneous goods and services, and for alcoholic beverages, tobacco, and narcotics. For miscellaneous goods and services, the highest increases were seen in India (12.3%), Nepal (11.4%), and Afghanistan (11.2%). For alcoholic beverages, tobacco, and narcotics, the Philippines (16.1%), Maldives (12.4%), and Papua New Guinea (12.3%) posted the largest increases.

Details of food and nonfood inflation are provided in individual economy tables available at kidb.adb.org.

Interest rates declined as governments loosened monetary policies.

From 2019 to 2020, a number of economies of Asia and the Pacific saw lending interest rates decline by as much as 2.0 percentage points. This is because, as the COVID-19 pandemic worsened, governments aggressively loosened monetary policy to cushion broad declines in consumption, investment, and trade. In fact, 19 of the 28 reporting economies in the region observed lower lending rates in 2020 than in 2019 (Figure 2.14).

Figure 2.14: Lending Interest Rates in Economies of Asia and the Pacific (% per annum, period averages)

As monetary policies were loosened to support demand and growth, interest rates declined in a majority of economies.

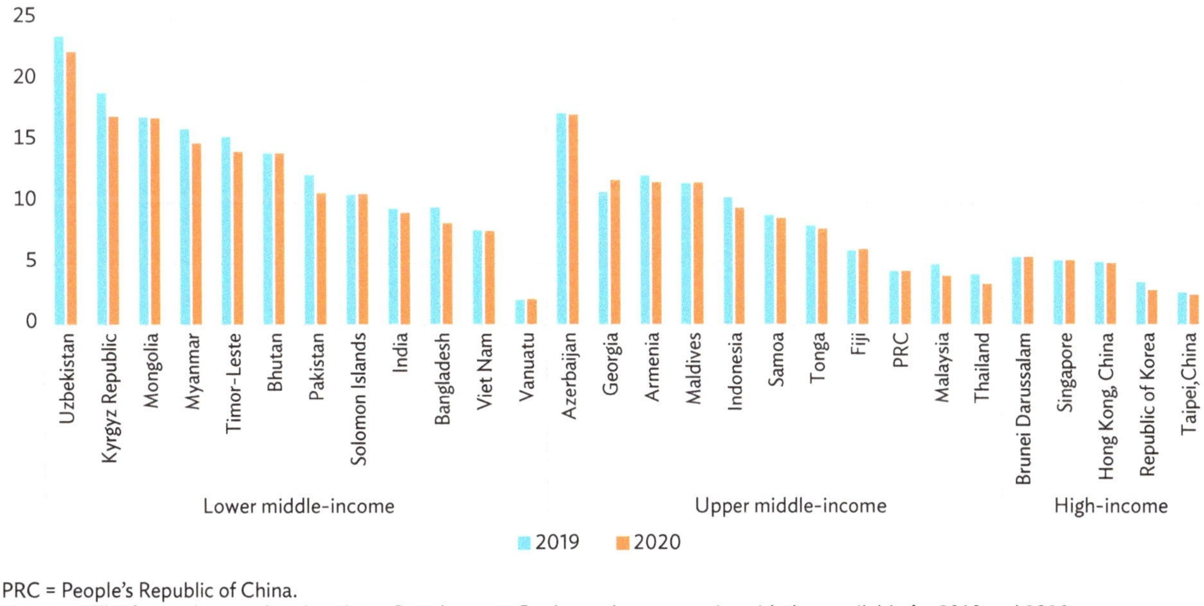

PRC = People's Republic of China.

Notes: The figure shows only select Asian Development Bank member economies with data available for 2019 and 2020. The economy income groupings follow the World Bank's classification as of July 2020.

Sources: Asian Development Bank estimates using data presented in Table 2.3.8 of *Key Indicators for Asia and the Pacific 2021*; and Asian Development Bank. Key Indicators Database. https://kidb.adb.org/ (accessed 25 July 2021).

Government Expenditure

Social sector spending still varies enormously across Asia and the Pacific, and several economies continue to fall short of recommended benchmarks.

Access to basic health care, quality education systems, and functional social safety nets are important elements of a country's or economy's strategy to accumulate human capital and reduce poverty, while letting its people live healthy and active lives. Trends since 2000 show that Asia and the Pacific still exhibits wide gaps in social sector spending. Several economies continue to lag well behind recommended expenditure benchmarks, while others have made some progress.

The expenditure benchmark laid out in the Education 2030 Framework for Action by the United Nations Educational, Scientific and Cultural Organization (UNESCO) suggests that at least 4%–6% of GDP and/or at least 15%–20% of total public expenditure should go to education (UNESCO 2015). Asia and the Pacific needs to accelerate its efforts to meet such a target. As Table 2.8.5 shows, in 2010 to 2012, only 15 of the 34 reporting economies had government expenditure on education as a proportion of GDP reaching 4% or higher. This remained relatively unchanged based on latest estimates available. Table 2.8.5 further shows that since 2010, fewer than half of the reporting economies in the region have increased government expenditure on education, and some economies even reported a decrease in government expenditure in this sector.

By 2019, or the latest year for which pre-pandemic data were available, only 5 of 35 reporting economies of Asia and the Pacific recorded expenditure on health exceeding 4% of GDP. With the exception of Kiribati, whose expenditure on health was 12% of GDP, the expenditure on health in the low-income to lower middle-income economies ranged from 0.7% to 3.4% of GDP, and 15 economies in other income brackets also reported health expenditure below 4%–5% of GDP. There is, however, some improvement being made, with three-fifths of all reporting economies showing an increase in expenditure on health as a share of GDP since 2010. The highest increases were in Samoa (3.6% to 5.0%) and Maldives (2.9% to 3.9%) as shown in Table 2.8.5.

Studies show that expenditure on social protection helps reduce poverty (Barrientos 2019; UNESCAP 2018). It has also been demonstrated that public pensions, higher levels of social assistance, and disability and unemployment benefits can improve income inequality (Cammeraat 2020). In 2019, or the latest year for which pre-pandemic data were available, expenditure on social protection averaged 4.0% of GDP across Asia and the Pacific, which is considerably lower than the world average of 11.2%. There are also considerable variations between the region's economies, with 2019 values ranging from 0.9% to 8.7% in low-income to lower middle-income economies; 1.2% to 7.0% in upper middle-income economies; and 0.7% to 10.6% in high-income economies. However, social protection expenditure across the region did improve from 2010 to 2019, with a little over three-fifths of the reporting economies showing an increase during this period (Table 2.8.5).

Government social sector spending increased during the COVID-19 pandemic.

To mitigate the impacts of the COVID-19 pandemic, governments have ramped up spending to support economic growth and help vulnerable groups by introducing fiscal stimulus packages and easing monetary policy to drive domestic demand. As of July 2021, ADB member economies had spent almost $31 trillion on relief packages (ADB 2021c). Among these many and varied initiatives, there was a marked increase in spending on health and social protection.

Among the ADB member economies with available data, health expenditure (as a proportion of GDP) increased by an average of 0.7 percentage points from 2019 to 2020. According to ADB's COVID-19 policy database, this health expenditure was channeled mainly into: (i) improving heath infrastructure, such as expanding facilities for testing and treatment; (ii) purchasing equipment such as ventilators and personal protective equipment; and (iii) providing incentives for health workers and more assistance to patients.

As the health crisis triggered an unprecedented economic contraction, social protection expenditure as a proportion of GDP increased in 13 of 16 ADB economies with available data, or by an average of 1.0 percentage point from 2019 to 2020. Among these economies, the highest increases were in Uzbekistan (2.8 percentage points), Georgia (2.8 percentage points), and Thailand (2.5 percentage points). Figure 2.15 illustrates the increase reported in 2020 relative to values recorded in 2019. This social spending largely delivered income support through cash supplements for the poor and workers affected by pandemic closures and restrictions, while businesses received direct and indirect subsidies.

In education, fiscal support was given to schools that adopted alternative learning options, including funding for increased broadband access to support remote learning. ADB estimates that, as of April 2021, only three economies in developing Asia had not implemented school closures (ADB 2021b).

Increased social sector spending may have mitigated the immediate impacts of the COVID-19 pandemic, but could also have caused long-term ramifications for public balance sheets. Estimates show that, even before the pandemic, a number of economies in Asia and the Pacific were experiencing substantial debt. In particular, data presented in Table 2.4.21 show that 16 of the 40 reporting economies recorded total external debt to gross national income ratios exceeding 40%, based on latest estimates.

Figure 2.15: Relative Changes in Health and Social Protection Expenditure, 2019–2020

A majority of reporting economies saw an increase in health and social protection expenditures as a proportion of GDP.

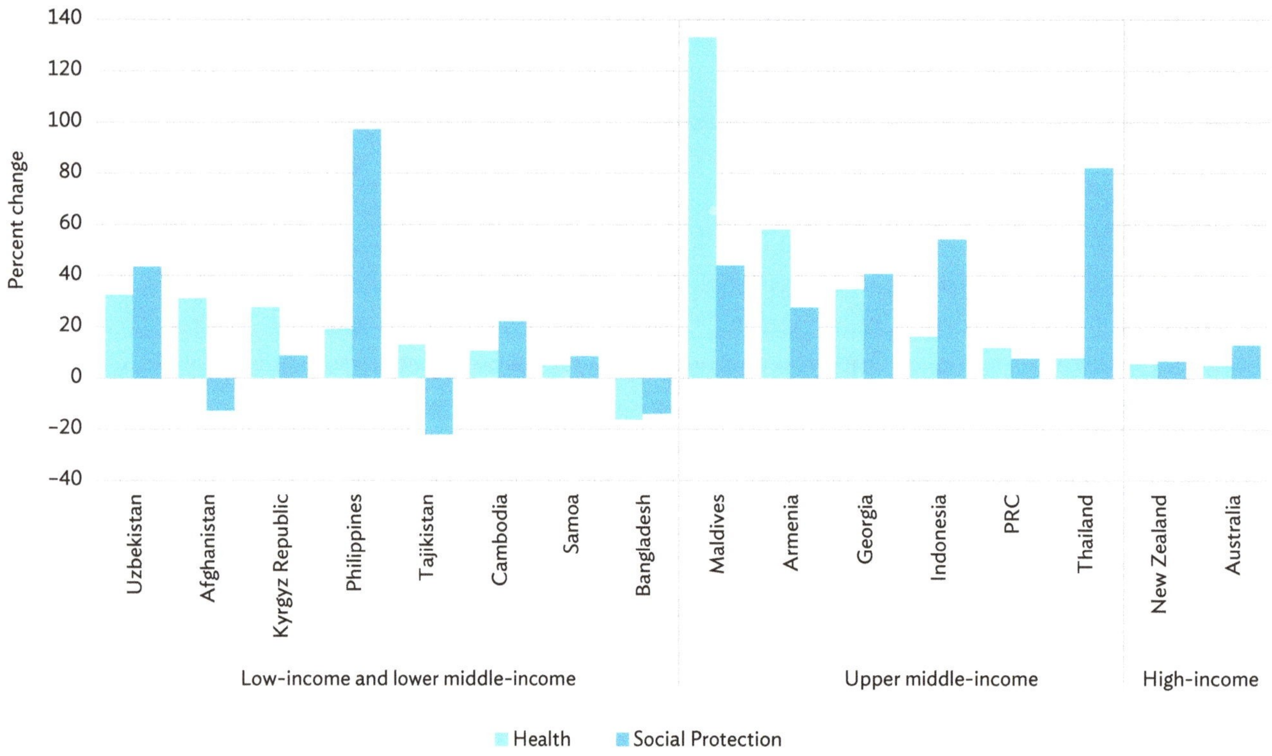

GDP = gross domestic product, PRC = People's Republic of China.

Notes: The graph shows select ADB member economies with data on health and social protection expenditure as a proportion of GDP for both 2019 and 2020. The economy income groupings follow the World Bank's classification as of July 2020.

Sources: Asian Development Bank estimates using data presented in Table 2.8.5 of *Key Indicators for Asia and the Pacific 2021*.

References

A. Abiad, M. Arao, S. Dagli, B. Ferrarini, I. Noy, P. Osewe, J. Pagaduan, D. Park and R. Platitas. 2020. The Economic Impact of the COVID-19 Outbreak in Developing Asia. *ADB Briefs No. 128.* Manila: Asian Development Bank. DOI: http://dx.doi.org/10.22617/BRF200096.

Asian Development Bank (ADB). 2011. *A Handbook Using the Mixed Survey for Measuring Informal Employment and the Informal Sector.* Manila: Asian Development Bank. http://hdl.handle.net/11540/130.

——. 2019. *Asian Development Outlook Supplement December 2019: Growth Slows Further in Developing Asia's Giants.* Manila: Asian Development Bank. http://dx.doi.org/10.22617/FLS190590-3.

——. 2020a. *Asia Small and Medium-Sized Enterprise Monitor 2020: Volume II-COVID-19 Impact on Micro, Small, and Medium-Sized Enterprises in Developing Asia.* Manila: Asian Development Bank. DOI: http://dx.doi.org/10.22617/TCS200311-2.

——. 2020b. *Asian Development Outlook 2020: What Drives Innovation in Asia?* Manila: Asian Development Bank. DOI: http://dx.doi.org/10.22617/FLS200119-3.

——. 2020c. *Asian Development Outlook Supplement December 2020: Paths Diverge in Recovery from the Pandemic.* Manila: Asian Development Bank. http://dx.doi.org/10.22617/FLS200389-3.

——. 2020d. Key Indicators for Asia and the Pacific 2020. Manila: Asian Development Bank. DOI: https://dx.doi.org/10.22617/FLS200250-3.

——. 2021a. *Asian Development Outlook 2021: Financing a Green and Inclusive Economy.* Manila: Asian Development Bank. DOI: http://dx.doi.org/10.22617/FLS210163-3.

——. 2021b. *Learning and Earning Losses from COVID-19 School Closures in Developing Asia. Special Topic of the Asian Development Outlook 2021.* Manila: Asian Development Bank. https://www.adb.org/sites/default/files/publication/692111/ado2021-special-topic.pdf.

——. 2021c. *One Year of Living with COVID-19: An Assessment of How ADB Members Fought the Pandemic in 2020.* Manila: Asian Development Bank. DOI: http://dx.doi.org/10.22617/TCS210151-2.

——. ADB COVID-19 Policy Database. https://covid19policy.adb.org/.

——. Key Indicators Database (KIDB). https://kidb.adb.org.

Asian Development Bank Institute (ADBI). 2020. ADBI Household Survey. https://www.adb.org/adbi/news/adbi-survey-covid-19-tests-southeast-asia-safety-nets.

A. Barrientos. 2019. The Role of Social Assistance in Reducing Poverty and Inequality in Asia and the Pacific. *ADB Sustainable Development Working Paper Series No. 62.* Manila: Asian Development Bank. DOI: http://dx.doi.org/10.22617/WPS190423-2.

E. Cammeraat. 2020. The Relationship Between Different Social Expenditure Schemes and Poverty, Inequality and Economic Growth. *International Social Security Review.* 70(2), pp. 101-123. DOI: https://doi.org/10.1111/issr.12236.

International Labour Organization (ILO). 2020. *ILO Monitor: COVID-19 and the World of Work. Fifth Edition. Updated Estimates and Analysis.* 30 June. Geneva: ILO. https://www.ilo.org/wcmsp5/groups/public/@dgreports/@dcomm/documents/briefingnote/wcms_749399.pdf.

——. *ILOSTAT Database.* https://ilostat.ilo.org/ (accessed 15 July 2021).

J. Jongwanich, P. Wongcharoen and D. Park. 2016. Determinants of Consumer Price Inflation Versus Producer Price Inflation in Developing Asia. *ADB Economics Working Paper Series No. 491.* Manila: Asian Development Bank. https://www.adb.org/sites/default/files/publication/188864/ewp-491.pdf.

P.J. Morgan and L.G. Trinh. 2021. Impacts of COVID-19 on Households in ASEAN Countries and Their Implications for Human Capital Development. *ADBI Working Paper 1226.* Tokyo: Asian Development Bank Institute. https://www.adb.org/publications/impacts-covid-19-households-asean-countries.

C.Y. Park and A.M. Inocencio. 2020. COVID-19 is No Excuse to Regress on Gender Equality. *ADB Brief No. 157.* Manila: Asian Development Bank. DOI: http://dx.doi.org/10.22617/BRF200317-2.

M. Reinsdorf. 2020. COVID-19 and the CPI: Is Inflation Underestimated? *IMF Working Paper No 20/224.* Washington, DC: International Monetary Fund. https://www.imf.org/en/Publications/WP/Issues/2020/11/05/COVID-19-and-the-CPI-Is-Inflation-Underestimated-49856.

United Nations Economic and Social Commission for Asia and the Pacific (UNESCAP). 2018. Social Outlook for Asia and the Pacific Poorly Protected. Bangkok: UNESCAP. https://www.unescap.org/sites/default/files/publications/SDD-SP-Social-Outlook-v14-1-E.pdf.

United Nations Educational, Scientific and Cultural Organization (UNESCO). 2015. *SDG4-Education 2030, Incheon Declaration (ID) and Framework for Action.* For the Implementation of Sustainable Development Goal 4, Ensure Inclusive and Equitable Quality Education and Promote Lifelong Learning Opportunities for All, ED-2016/WS/28. http://uis.unesco.org/sites/default/files/documents/education-2030-incheon-framework-for-action-implementation-of-sdg4-2016-en_2.pdf.

World Bank. 2020. Doing Business 2020. Washington, D.C: World Bank. https://doi.org/10.1596/978-1-4648-1440-2.

World Bank. World Development Indicators. https://data.worldbank.org.

Table 2.1.1: Midyear Population

ADB Regional Member	Population (million)					Population Growth Rates[a] (%)				
	2010	2015	2018	2019	2020	2010	2015	2018	2019	2020
Developing ADB Member Economies										
Central and West Asia[b]	**276.8**	**303.9**	**326.1**	**332.2**	**338.3***	**2.0**	**1.9**	**2.3**	**1.8**	**1.8***
Afghanistan[c]	24.5	27.1	30.1	30.7	31.4	2.1	2.1	6.6	2.2	2.2
Armenia	3.0	3.0	3.0	3.0	3.0*	-0.7	-0.3	-0.3	-0.2	-0.0*
Azerbaijan	9.1	9.6	9.9	10.0	10.1	1.2	1.2	0.9	0.8	0.4
Georgia	3.8	3.7	3.7	3.7	3.7	-0.7	0.2	-0.0	-0.2	0.1
Kazakhstan	16.3	17.5	18.3	18.5	18.8	1.4	1.5	1.3	1.3	1.3
Kyrgyz Republic[c]	5.4	5.9	6.3	6.4	6.5	1.3	2.1	1.9	2.1	2.1
Pakistan	173.5	191.7	207.1	211.2	215.3	2.1	2.0	2.0	1.9	1.8
Tajikistan	7.5	8.5	9.0	9.2	9.4	2.5	2.4	2.2	2.2	2.0
Turkmenistan	5.1	5.6	5.9	5.9	6.0	1.6	1.8	1.6	1.6	1.5
Uzbekistan	28.6	31.3	33.0	33.6	34.2*	2.9	1.8	1.7	1.8	1.9*
East Asia[b]	**1,423.3**	**1,468.0**	**1,491.2**	**1,496.2**	**1,498.0**	**0.5**	**0.5**	**0.4**	**0.3**	**0.1**
China, People's Republic of[c]	1,340.9	1,383.3	1,405.4	1,410.1	1,411.8	0.5	0.5	0.4	0.3	0.1
Hong Kong, China	7.0	7.3	7.5	7.5	7.5	0.7	0.9	0.8	0.8	-0.3
Korea, Republic of	49.6	51.0	51.6	51.7	51.8	0.5	0.5	0.5	0.2	0.1
Mongolia	2.7	3.0	3.2	3.3	3.4	1.6	2.1	1.9	1.8	1.8
Taipei,China	23.1	23.5	23.6	23.6	23.6	0.3	0.2	0.1	0.1	-0.2
South Asia[b]	**1,382.6**	**1,493.4**	**1,543.6**	**1,560.3**	**1,576.7**	**1.4**	**1.2**	**1.1**	**1.1**	**1.1**
Bangladesh	148.6	158.9	164.6	166.5	168.5	1.4	1.4	1.3	1.3	1.3
Bhutan	0.7	0.8	0.7	0.7	0.7	1.8	1.6	1.0	1.0	0.9
India[c]	1,186.0	1,284.4	1,327.0	1,341.0	1,355.0	1.4	1.2	1.1	1.1	1.0
Maldives	0.4	0.5	0.5	0.5	0.6	2.3	3.9	4.2	4.3	4.4
Nepal	26.3	28.0	29.1	29.7	30.0	1.4	1.4	1.4	2.1	2.1
Sri Lanka	20.7	21.0	21.7	21.8	21.9	1.0	0.9	1.1	0.6	0.5
Southeast Asia[b]	**589.2**	**629.0**	**650.5**	**657.2**	**664.4**	**1.2**	**1.3**	**1.1**	**1.0**	**1.1**
Brunei Darussalam	0.4	0.4	0.4	0.5	0.5	1.8	1.2	3.0	3.9	-1.3
Cambodia	14.1	15.1	15.7	16.0	16.2	1.3	1.4	1.4	1.4	1.4
Indonesia	237.6	255.6	264.2	266.9	270.2	1.4	1.4	1.1	1.0	1.2
Lao People's Democratic Republic	6.0	6.5	6.8	6.9	7.0	1.5	1.4	1.4	1.4	1.4
Malaysia	28.6	31.2	32.4	32.5	32.7	1.8	1.6	1.1	0.4	0.4
Myanmar[c]	50.2	52.5	53.9	54.3	54.8	0.7	0.9	0.9	0.9	0.9
Philippines	93.1	100.8	105.8	107.3	109.0	1.0	1.7[d]	1.5	1.5	1.4
Singapore	5.1	5.5	5.6	5.7	5.7	1.8	1.2	0.5	1.2	-0.3
Thailand	65.9	68.0	69.1	69.3	69.5	0.6	0.6	0.3	0.3	0.3
Timor-Leste	1.1	1.2	1.3	1.3	1.3	1.8	1.9	2.0	2.0	2.0
Viet Nam	87.1	92.2	95.4	96.5	97.6	1.2	1.1	1.2	1.2	1.1
The Pacific[b,e]	**9.3**	**10.6***	**11.5***	**11.8***	**12.1***	**2.7**	**2.7***	**2.7***	**2.7***	**2.7***
Cook Islands	23.7	18.4*	18.6*	20.2*	17.9	4.9	0.0*	-4.6*	8.6*	-11.4
Fiji	850.7	869.5	886.2	889.3	891.4	0.6	0.4	0.6	0.6	0.6
Kiribati[c]	103.1	110.1	114.6	116.1*	119.9*	2.2	1.3	1.3	1.3*	3.3*
Marshall Islands	52.9	54.0	54.6	54.8*	55.0*	1.1	0.4	0.4*	0.4*	0.4*
Micronesia, Federated States of[c]	102.8	103.7	104.3	104.5*	104.6*	-0.5	0.2	0.2	0.2*	0.2*
Nauru	9.7	10.8	11.4	11.6	11.7	1.9	1.7	1.6	1.6	1.6
Niue	1.6 (2011)	1.5	1.8	1.9*	1.9*	1.4[f]	1.5	–	4.4*	1.4*
Palau	18.3	17.7	17.5	17.5*	17.5*	-1.9	1.8	-2.0	-0.5*	0.4*
Papua New Guinea	7,055.4	8,225.6	9,018.9	9,300.0	9,589.9	3.1	3.1	3.1	3.1	3.1
Samoa	185.9	193.8	198.7	200.3	201.9	0.8	0.8	0.8	0.8	0.8
Solomon Islands	555.5	625.6	667.0	680.0*	694.6*	2.6[g]	2.3	2.1	1.9*	2.1*
Tonga	102.8	101.7	100.1	99.6	99.0	0.2	-0.5	-0.5	-0.5	-0.5
Tuvalu	11.1	10.7	10.6	10.6	10.6	0.5	-0.3	-0.3	-0.3	-0.3
Vanuatu	239.7	268.6	284.6	290.8	297.2	2.4	2.3	2.1	2.2	2.2
Developed ADB Member Economies[b]	**154.5**	**155.6**	**156.4**	**156.6**	**156.6**	**0.3**	**0.2**	**0.1**	**0.1**	**0.0**
Australia	22.0	23.8	25.0	25.4	25.7	1.6	1.4	1.5	1.5	1.3
Japan	128.1	127.1	126.5	126.3	125.8	0.0	-0.1	-0.2	-0.2	-0.3
New Zealand	4.4	4.6	4.9	5.0	5.1	1.1	2.1	1.8	1.6	2.3
DEVELOPING ADB MEMBER ECONOMIES[b]	**3,681.2**	**3,905.0***	**4,023.0***	**4,057.6***	**4,089.6***	**1.0**	**1.0***	**0.9***	**0.9***	**0.8***
ALL ADB REGIONAL MEMBERS[b]	**3,835.7**	**4,060.5***	**4,179.4***	**4,214.3***	**4,246.2***	**1.0**	**1.0***	**0.9***	**0.8***	**0.8***
WORLD	**6,956.8**	**7,379.8**	**7,631.1**	**7,713.5**	**7,794.8**	**1.2**	**1.2**	**1.1**	**1.1**	**1.1**

... = data not available, * = provisional or preliminary, – = magnitude equals zero, 0.0 = magnitude is less than half of unit employed, ADB = Asian Development Bank.

a The annual population growth rate is calculated as the percentage change in population when comparing the reference year with the year prior. For example, the population growth rates under the column heading "2020" refer to population growth from 2019 to 2020.

b Regional population totals include only reporting economies with data corresponding to the year heading, while regional population growth rates are estimated as a weighted average of the annual population growth rates of the reporting economies. Weights are based on the total population of the region for the years in which the reporting economies have published the annual growth rates.

c Estimates of population size are as of 1 January for the Kyrgyz Republic; 10 June for Afghanistan; 30 September for the Federated States of Micronesia; 1 October for India and Myanmar; 7 November for Kiribati; and 31 December for the People's Republic of China.

d Refers to the 2016 annual population growth rate.

e The total population for the Pacific subregion is expressed in millions, while estimates of population size for ADB developing member economies in the Pacific are expressed in thousands.

f Refers to the 2013 annual population growth rate.

g Refers to the 2011 annual population growth rate.

Sources: Economy's official sources. For Azerbaijan, Nauru (2020), Palau (2020), Papua New Guinea, Tajikistan (2020), Tuvalu (2015 onward), and Vanuatu (2020): Asian Development Bank estimates using data from economy's official sources. For Myanmar (2010): World Bank. World Development Indicators. http://databank.worldbank.org/data/reports.aspx?source=world-development-indicators# (accessed 1 July 2017). For Tuvalu (2010): Secretariat of the Pacific Community. http://www.spc.int/sdd/ (accessed 27 May 2015). For Turkmenistan and World: United Nations. World Population Prospects 2019. https://population.un.org/wpp/Download/Standard/Population/ (accessed 20 April 2021).

Table 2.1.2: Migration and Urbanization

ADB Regional Member	Net International Migration Rate[a] (per 1,000 population)		Urban Population[b] (% of total population)						
	2010-2015	2015-2020	2010	2015	2016	2017	2018	2019	2020
Developing ADB Member Economies									
Central and West Asia	**...**	**...**	**39.2**	**40.8**	**42.4**	**39.0**	**43.0**	**43.3**	**43.7***
Afghanistan[c]	3.3	-1.7	23.2	24.7	25.0	25.3	25.0	25.3	25.6
Armenia	-2.1	-1.7	63.5	63.6	63.6	63.7	63.8	63.9	63.9*
Azerbaijan	0.2	0.1	53.0	53.1	53.0	53.0	52.9	52.8	52.8
Georgia	-4.7	-2.5	56.5	57.5	57.9	58.2	58.5	58.9	59.2
Kazakhstan	1.9	-1.0	54.5	56.6	57.0	57.8	58.0	58.5	58.9
Kyrgyz Republic	-3.3	-0.6	34.1	33.7	33.7	33.8	33.9	34.0	34.2
Pakistan	-1.1	-1.1	36.9	39.2	41.7	36.4	42.7	43.2	43.7
Tajikistan	-3.4	-2.2	26.4	26.4	26.9	26.3	26.4	26.3	26.3
Turkmenistan[d]	-1.9	-0.9	48.5	50.3	50.7	51.2	51.6	52.0	52.5
Uzbekistan	-0.4	-0.3	51.5	50.8	50.6	50.6	50.6	50.5	50.6
East Asia	**...**	**...**	**51.5**	**58.5**	**59.9**	**61.2**	**62.4**	**63.5**	**64.6**
China, People's Republic of	-0.2	-0.2	50.0	57.3	58.8	60.2	61.5	62.7	63.9
Hong Kong, China[d]	2.1	4.0	100.0	100.0	100.0	100.0	100.0	100.0	100.0
Korea, Republic of[d]	1.6	0.2	81.9	81.6	81.6	81.5	81.5	81.4	81.4
Mongolia	-0.3	-0.3	69.2	68.6	68.3	67.6	67.9	68.5	69.0
Taipei,China[e]	1.5	1.3	59.3	60.9	61.0	61.1	60.9	61.0	61.1
South Asia	**...**	**...**	**29.1**	**32.4**	**32.8**	**33.1**	**33.5**	**33.9**	**35.6***
Bangladesh[d]	-3.0	-2.3	25.9	34.3	35.1	35.9	36.6	37.4	38.2
Bhutan[d]	0.1	0.4	34.8	38.9	39.4	37.8	40.9	40.9	42.3
India[d]	-0.4	-0.4	29.9	32.7	33.0	33.3	33.7	34.0	34.9
Maldives[d]	28.4	22.8	36.4	38.5	39.0	39.4	39.8	40.2	40.7
Nepal[f]	-15.1	1.5	16.6	18.5	19.6	20.1	20.8	21.4	62.4*
Sri Lanka[d]	-4.7	-4.6	18.2	18.3	18.3	18.4	18.5	18.6	18.7
Southeast Asia	**...**	**...**	**44.2**	**47.2**	**47.8**	**48.3**	**48.8**	**49.4**	**50.3**
Brunei Darussalam[d]	-0.4	–	75.0	76.7	77.0	77.3	77.6	77.9	78.3
Cambodia[d]	-2.0	-1.9	20.3	22.2	22.6	23.0	23.4	23.8	24.2
Indonesia[d]	-0.4	-0.4	49.9	53.3	54.0	54.7	55.3	56.0	56.6
Lao People's Democratic Republic[d]	-3.5	-2.1	30.1	33.1	33.7	34.4	35.0	35.6	36.3
Malaysia	1.7	1.6	71.0	74.3	74.8	75.2	75.6	76.2	76.7
Myanmar[d]	-2.0	-3.1	28.9	29.3	29.4	29.5	30.0	30.0	31.1
Philippines[d]	-1.7	-0.6	45.3	46.3	46.5	46.7	46.9	47.1	47.4
Singapore	11.8	4.7	100.0	100.0	100.0	100.0	100.0	100.0	100.0
Thailand[g]	0.5	0.3	42.0	48.6	50.0	51.0	52.3	53.6	54.8
Timor-Leste	-4.9	-4.3	27.7	29.5	29.8	30.2	30.6	30.9	31.3
Viet Nam	-0.9	-0.8	30.4	33.5	33.7	33.9	34.2	35.0	36.8
The Pacific	**...**	**...**	**18.6**	**18.7**	**18.8**	**18.9**	**18.9**	**19.0**	**19.1**
Cook Islands[d]	...	...	73.3	74.4	74.6	74.8	75.1	75.3	75.5
Fiji	-12.0	-7.0	52.2	54.7	55.2	55.9	56.2	56.8	57.2
Kiribati[d]	-7.7	-6.9	47.4	51.6	52.5	53.3	54.1	54.8	55.6
Marshall Islands[d]	...	...	73.6	75.8	76.2	76.6	77.0	77.4	77.8
Micronesia, Federated States of[d]	-5.7	-5.4	22.3	22.5	22.5	22.6	22.7	22.8	22.9
Nauru[d]	...	...	100.0	100.0	100.0	100.0	100.0	100.0	100.0
Niue[d]	...	...	38.7	42.6	43.3	44.1	44.8	45.5	46.2
Palau	...	...	77.0	78.7	...	...	...	...	...
Papua New Guinea[d]	-0.1	-0.1	13.0	13.0	13.1	13.1	13.2	13.3	13.3
Samoa	-12.8	-14.3	19.9	19.2	19.1	19.0	18.9	18.8	18.8
Solomon Islands[d]	-2.8	-2.5	20.0	22.4	22.8	23.3	23.7	24.2	24.7
Tonga	-25.4	-7.7	23.4	23.1	23.1	23.0	22.8	22.6	22.5
Tuvalu[d]	...	...	54.8	59.7	60.6	61.5	62.4	63.2	64.0
Vanuatu	1.4	0.4	24.4	24.6	24.9	24.9	25.0	25.1	25.2
Developed ADB Member Economies	**...**	**...**	**89.9**	**90.4**	**90.5**	**90.5**	**90.6**	**90.7**	**90.7**
Australia	8.6	6.4	85.7	86.4	86.5	86.7	86.8	86.9	87.0
Japan[d]	0.6	0.6	90.8	91.4	91.5	91.5	91.6	91.7	91.8
New Zealand	4.0	3.2	83.9	84.0	84.0	84.1	84.1	84.1	84.1
DEVELOPING ADB MEMBER ECONOMIES	**...**	**...**	**40.9**	**45.2**	**46.1**	**46.5**	**47.4**	**48.1**	**49.2***
ALL ADB REGIONAL MEMBERS	**...**	**...**	**42.9**	**46.9**	**47.8**	**48.1**	**49.1**	**49.7**	**50.7***
WORLD	**...**	**...**	**51.6**	**53.9**	**54.4**	**54.8**	**55.3**	**55.7**	**56.2**

... = data not available, * = provisional or preliminary, – = magnitude equals zero, ADB = Asian Development Bank.

a Refers to annual average migration over the period shown. United Nations population estimates and projections are based on all available sources of data on population size and levels of fertility, mortality, and international migration. Statistics on international migration are sourced from population registers and other administrative sources. These estimates and projections are made for 235 distinct national economies or areas comprising the total population of the world.

b In estimating the aggregates for Asia and the Pacific, imputation was done for economies with missing data by substituting available data from the nearest years. The aggregates were derived using data on total population and percentage of urban population from economy's official sources and the United Nations publications World Population Prospects 2019 and World Urbanization Prospects: The 2018 Revision.

c For urban population, refers to the share of urban population to total resident population, i.e., excluding the nomadic population.

d For urban population, refers to data from the World Urbanization Prospects 2018 Revision for: 2015–2020 for Bangladesh: 2016, 2018, and 2020 for Bhutan: 2020 for India: 2010 and 2020 for Myanmar: and the whole data series for Brunei Darussalam; Cambodia; the Cook Islands; the Federated States of Micronesia; Hong Kong, China; Indonesia; Japan; Kiribati; the Lao People's Democratic Republic; Maldives; the Marshall Islands; Nauru; Niue; Papua New Guinea; the Philippines; the Republic of Korea; Solomon Islands; Sri Lanka; Turkmenistan; and Tuvalu.

e For urban population, refers to localities of 100,000 or more inhabitants.

f For urban population, the figure for 2020 refers to 293 municipalities.

g For urban population, data for 2010 onward include non-Thai citizens who are listed in the civil registration.

Sources: For net international migration rate: United Nations. World Population Prospects 2019. https://population.un.org/wpp/Download/Standard/Migration/ (accessed 21 July 2021). For urban population: economy's official sources; and United Nations. World Urbanization Prospects: The 2018 Revision. https://population.un.org/wup/Download/ (accessed 19 July 2021).

Table 2.1.3: Proportion of Total Population by Age Bracket, and Age Dependency Ratio

ADB Regional Member	Population Aged 0–14 Years (% of total population)				Population Aged 15–64 Years (% of total population)			
	2010	2015	2019	2020	2010	2015	2019	2020
Developing ADB Member Economies								
Central and West Asia	**35.9**	**34.7**	**34.2**	**34.1**	**59.7**	**60.9**	**61.2**	**61.3**
Afghanistan	48.2	44.9	42.5	41.8	49.5	52.6	54.9	55.5
Armenia	19.5	20.1	20.8	20.8	69.5	69.0	67.8	67.4
Azerbaijan	22.8	22.9	23.4	23.5	71.3	71.4	70.1	69.7
Georgia	18.0	19.0	20.0	20.2	67.8	66.7	64.9	64.5
Kazakhstan	24.1	26.7	28.9	29.1	69.1	66.5	63.5	63.0
Kyrgyz Republic	29.9	31.5	32.5	32.6	65.6	64.2	62.9	62.6
Pakistan	37.7	35.9	35.1	34.8	58.1	59.8	60.6	60.8
Tajikistan	35.7	35.8	37.1	37.3	61.0	61.2	59.8	59.6
Turkmenistan	29.5	30.4	30.8	30.8	66.3	65.5	64.6	64.4
Uzbekistan	29.1	28.4	28.8	28.8	66.4	67.6	66.6	66.4
East Asia	**18.5**	**17.8**	**17.6**	**17.5**	**73.3**	**72.7**	**70.8**	**70.4**
China, People's Republic of	18.7	18.1	17.8	17.7	73.3	72.6	70.7	70.3
Hong Kong, China	11.9	11.2	12.3	12.7	75.1	73.6	70.2	69.1
Korea, Republic of	16.1	13.8	12.7	12.5	73.2	73.4	72.2	71.7
Mongolia	27.0	28.9	30.8	31.1	69.2	67.3	65.0	64.6
Taipei,China	15.9	13.6	12.8	12.7	73.4	73.9	72.1	71.4
South Asia	**31.0**	**28.6**	**26.7**	**26.2**	**64.0**	**65.8**	**67.0**	**67.3**
Bangladesh	32.0	29.3	27.2	26.8	63.2	65.6	67.6	68.0
Bhutan	31.2	27.4	25.3	24.9	63.7	66.9	68.6	68.9
India	30.8	28.4	26.6	26.2	64.1	65.9	67.0	67.3
Maldives	25.3	21.2	19.9	19.6	70.2	74.8	76.5	76.8
Nepal	36.3	33.4	29.6	28.8	58.7	61.1	64.7	65.4
Sri Lanka	25.4	24.8	24.0	23.7	67.2	65.8	65.2	65.1
Southeast Asia	**27.9**	**26.5**	**25.4**	**25.2**	**66.6**	**67.5**	**67.7**	**67.7**
Brunei Darussalam	26.0	24.1	22.6	22.3	70.7	71.8	72.2	72.1
Cambodia	33.3	31.6	31.1	30.9	62.9	64.3	64.2	64.2
Indonesia	28.8	27.5	26.2	25.9	66.2	67.2	67.7	67.8
Lao People's Democratic Republic	36.4	33.6	32.3	31.9	59.9	62.6	63.5	63.8
Malaysia	28.0	25.1	23.7	23.4	67.1	68.9	69.4	69.4
Myanmar	30.0	27.8	25.9	25.5	65.1	67.0	68.1	68.3
Philippines	34.0	32.3	30.5	30.0	61.9	63.1	64.2	64.4
Singapore	14.0	12.6	12.3	12.3	78.7	78.3	75.3	74.3
Thailand	19.2	18.0	16.8	16.6	71.9	71.4	70.8	70.5
Timor-Leste	42.5	39.5	37.3	36.8	53.4	56.1	58.4	58.9
Viet Nam	23.6	23.0	23.2	23.2	69.9	70.3	69.2	68.9
The Pacific	**37.5**	**36.4**	**35.3**	**35.0**	**59.0**	**60.1**	**60.9**	**61.1**
Cook Islands	27.9	27.8	25.6	25.3	63.8	62.6	63.8	64.0
Fiji	29.0	29.8	29.3	29.0	66.2	65.2	65.1	65.2
Kiribati	36.1	35.0	35.8	35.9	60.3	61.4	60.1	59.9
Marshall Islands	41.8	39.8	37.7	37.2	55.9	57.5	58.7	59.0
Micronesia, Federated States of	35.7	32.8	31.5	31.2	61.1	63.8	64.4	64.4
Nauru	35.6	39.5	40.0	40.0	63.1	58.8	57.6	57.4
Niue	24.8	24.2	21.0	20.4	63.0	63.0	64.1	64.0
Palau	20.3	19.3	19.9	19.7	73.2	70.6	70.9	70.6
Papua New Guinea	38.3	36.8	35.5	35.1	58.4	60.0	61.0	61.3
Samoa	38.3	38.8	37.9	37.2	56.7	56.7	57.2	57.7
Solomon Islands	40.8	40.4	40.1	40.0	55.9	56.0	56.2	56.3
Tonga	37.4	36.4	35.1	34.8	56.9	57.6	59.0	59.3
Tuvalu	32.0	32.7	31.3	31.4	62.7	61.7	62.1	61.8
Vanuatu	38.2	39.1	38.7	38.4	57.9	57.2	57.7	58.0
Developed ADB Member Economies	**14.4**	**14.1**	**13.9**	**13.8**	**64.7**	**61.9**	**60.4**	**60.2**
Australia	19.0	18.9	19.3	19.3	67.6	66.3	64.8	64.5
Japan	13.4	13.0	12.6	12.4	64.1	61.0	59.4	59.2
New Zealand	20.5	20.0	19.6	19.4	66.4	65.4	64.4	64.2
DEVELOPING ADB MEMBER ECONOMIES	**26.1**	**24.7**	**23.8**	**23.5**	**67.6**	**68.2**	**68.0**	**68.0**
ALL ADB REGIONAL MEMBERS	**25.6**	**24.3**	**23.4**	**23.2**	**67.5**	**68.0**	**67.7**	**67.7**
WORLD	**27.0**	**26.2**	**25.6**	**25.4**	**65.5**	**65.6**	**65.3**	**65.2**

continued on next page

Table 2.1.3: Proportion of Total Population by Age Bracket, and Age Dependency Ratio *(continued)*

ADB Regional Member	Population Aged 65 Years and Older (% of total population)				Age Dependency Ratio for Total Population			
	2010	2015	2019	2020	2010	2015	2019	2020
Developing ADB Member Economies								
Central and West Asia	**4.5**	**4.4**	**4.6**	**4.6**	**67.6**	**64.3**	**63.4**	**63.1**
Afghanistan	2.3	2.5	2.6	2.6	102.0	90.0	82.1	80.1
Armenia	11.0	10.9	11.5	11.8	43.8	44.8	47.6	48.4
Azerbaijan	5.9	5.7	6.4	6.7	40.3	40.1	42.6	43.4
Georgia	14.2	14.3	15.1	15.3	47.5	50.0	54.1	55.0
Kazakhstan	6.8	6.8	7.7	7.9	44.6	50.3	57.6	58.8
Kyrgyz Republic	4.5	4.3	4.6	4.7	52.5	55.8	59.0	59.7
Pakistan	4.2	4.3	4.3	4.3	72.2	67.4	65.0	64.4
Tajikistan	3.3	2.9	3.1	3.2	63.9	63.4	67.1	67.9
Turkmenistan	4.1	4.1	4.6	4.8	50.7	52.7	54.7	55.2
Uzbekistan	4.5	4.1	4.6	4.8	50.7	48.0	50.1	50.6
East Asia	**8.2**	**9.5**	**11.7**	**12.2**	**36.5**	**37.6**	**41.3**	**42.1**
China, People's Republic of	8.1	9.3	11.5	12.0	36.5	37.7	41.4	42.2
Hong Kong, China	12.9	15.2	17.5	18.2	33.1	35.8	42.5	44.7
Korea, Republic of	10.7	12.9	15.1	15.8	36.6	36.3	38.5	39.5
Mongolia	3.8	3.9	4.2	4.3	44.6	48.6	53.8	54.8
Taipei,China	10.7	12.5	15.1	15.8	36.2	35.4	38.7	40.0
South Asia	**5.1**	**5.6**	**6.3**	**6.5**	**56.3**	**51.9**	**49.2**	**48.6**
Bangladesh	4.8	5.1	5.2	5.2	58.1	52.4	47.9	47.0
Bhutan	5.1	5.7	6.1	6.2	57.0	49.5	45.8	45.1
India	5.1	5.6	6.4	6.6	56.0	51.6	49.2	48.7
Maldives	4.6	3.9	3.6	3.6	42.5	33.6	30.7	30.2
Nepal	5.0	5.5	5.8	5.8	70.4	63.6	54.7	53.0
Sri Lanka	7.4	9.4	10.8	11.2	48.8	51.9	53.4	53.7
Southeast Asia	**5.5**	**6.0**	**6.9**	**7.1**	**50.1**	**48.2**	**47.7**	**47.7**
Brunei Darussalam	3.4	4.1	5.2	5.6	41.5	39.2	38.6	38.7
Cambodia	3.7	4.1	4.7	4.9	58.9	55.6	55.8	55.7
Indonesia	5.0	5.4	6.1	6.3	51.0	48.9	47.6	47.5
Lao People's Democratic Republic	3.7	3.8	4.2	4.3	67.0	59.9	57.4	56.8
Malaysia	4.9	6.0	6.9	7.2	49.0	45.1	44.1	44.2
Myanmar	4.8	5.2	6.0	6.2	53.5	49.2	46.9	46.5
Philippines	4.1	4.6	5.3	5.5	61.6	58.4	55.7	55.2
Singapore	7.3	9.0	12.4	13.4	27.0	27.7	32.8	34.5
Thailand	8.9	10.6	12.4	13.0	39.0	40.0	41.3	41.9
Timor-Leste	4.0	4.4	4.3	4.3	87.2	78.2	71.2	69.8
Viet Nam	6.5	6.7	7.6	7.9	43.1	42.2	44.4	45.1
The Pacific	**3.5**	**3.5**	**3.8**	**3.8**	**69.6**	**66.5**	**64.2**	**63.6**
Cook Islands	8.2	9.6	10.6	10.8	56.7	59.8	56.7	56.3
Fiji	4.8	5.0	5.6	5.8	51.1	53.4	53.7	53.4
Kiribati	3.6	3.5	4.1	4.2	65.8	62.7	66.4	67.0
Marshall Islands	2.3	2.7	3.6	3.8	78.8	74.0	70.5	69.5
Micronesia, Federated States of	3.2	3.4	4.2	4.4	63.7	56.9	55.4	55.2
Nauru	1.3	1.7	2.4	2.6	58.5	70.0	73.6	74.2
Niue	12.1	12.8	14.9	15.6	58.7	58.8	56.0	56.3
Palau	6.5	10.1	9.2	9.6	36.7	41.7	41.0	41.6
Papua New Guinea	3.3	3.2	3.5	3.6	71.3	66.8	63.9	63.2
Samoa	5.0	4.5	4.9	5.1	76.3	76.5	74.8	73.3
Solomon Islands	3.3	3.5	3.6	3.7	78.9	78.4	77.8	77.6
Tonga	5.7	6.0	5.9	5.9	75.8	73.6	69.5	68.6
Tuvalu	5.3	5.6	6.6	6.8	59.5	61.9	61.1	61.8
Vanuatu	3.9	3.7	3.6	3.6	72.8	74.8	73.4	72.5
Developed ADB Member Economies	**20.9**	**24.0**	**25.7**	**26.0**	**54.5**	**61.5**	**65.4**	**66.2**
Australia	13.4	14.9	15.9	16.2	47.9	50.9	54.3	55.1
Japan	22.5	26.0	28.0	28.4	55.9	64.0	68.3	69.0
New Zealand	13.1	14.6	16.0	16.4	50.5	52.9	55.2	55.8
DEVELOPING ADB MEMBER ECONOMIES	**6.3**	**7.0**	**8.2**	**8.5**	**47.9**	**46.5**	**47.0**	**47.1**
ALL ADB REGIONAL MEMBERS	**6.9**	**7.7**	**8.9**	**9.1**	**48.1**	**47.1**	**47.6**	**47.8**
WORLD	**7.6**	**8.2**	**9.1**	**9.3**	**52.8**	**52.4**	**53.2**	**53.3**

ADB = Asian Development Bank.

Notes:

1 All figures presented in this table are ADB estimates using data from the United Nations' World Population Prospects 2019 and/or official communications from The Pacific Community's Statistics for Development Division.

2 United Nations population estimates are based on all available sources of data on population size and levels of fertility, mortality, and international migration for 235 distinct countries or areas comprising the total population of the world.

Sources: United Nations. World Population Prospects 2019. https://population.un.org/wpp/ (accessed 12 May 2021). For the Cook Islands, the Marshall Islands, Nauru, Niue, Palau, and Tuvalu: The Pacific Community, Statistics for Development Division. Official communication, 3 July 2019.

Table 2.1.4: Labor Force Participation Rates
(%)

ADB Regional Member	2010	2015	2016	2017	2018	2019	2020
Developing ADB Member Economies							
Central and West Asia							
Afghanistan[a,b]	49.8 (2011)	55.4 (2013)	...	53.9	...	...	41.9
Armenia[c]	61.2	62.5	61.0	60.9	58.9	59.9*	...
Azerbaijan[c]	64.8	65.4	66.0	66.2	66.3	66.5	66.9
Georgia[c]	51.5	55.5	55.0	54.5	52.9	51.8	50.5
Kazakhstan	71.2	69.7	70.0	69.7	70.0	70.1	69.5
Kyrgyz Republic	64.2	62.4	61.5	60.1	59.8	60.2	...
Pakistan	45.9	45.2	...	...	44.3	...	...
Tajikistan	50.3	47.7	46.7	46.2	45.7	45.5	...
Turkmenistan[d]	58.8	58.3	58.3	58.2	58.0	57.9	56.6
Uzbekistan[c]	70.7	71.9	72.5	73.5	74.3	74.9	73.9
East Asia							
China, People's Republic of[d]	71.3	70.0	69.6	69.2	68.7	68.2	66.8
Hong Kong, China	59.6	61.1	61.1	61.1	61.2	60.6	59.6
Korea, Republic of	61.1	62.8	62.9	63.2	63.1	63.3	62.5
Mongolia[c]	61.6	61.5	60.5	61.1	61.0	60.5	58.8
Taipei,China	58.1	58.7	58.7	58.8	59.0	59.2	59.1
South Asia							
Bangladesh	59.3	57.1 (2013)	58.5	58.2	...	...	...
Bhutan[e]	68.6	63.1	62.2	63.3	62.6	66.4	67.8
India	36.4 (2011)	...	...	36.9*	37.5*	...	...
Maldives[f]	52.1	63.8 (2014)	57.6	...	...	60.2	...
Nepal[c]	74.3 (2012)	72.2 (2014)	...	...	38.5	...	...
Sri Lanka	48.6	53.8	53.8	54.1	51.8	52.3	50.6
Southeast Asia							
Brunei Darussalam[c]	68.9 (2011)	65.6 (2014)	...	62.7	65.4	64.3	...
Cambodia	87.0	82.7	84.0	86.6	...	...	...
Indonesia	67.7	65.8	66.3	66.7	67.3	67.5	67.8
Lao People's Democratic Republic[c]	79.2	...	...	40.8	...	...	...
Malaysia[c]	63.7	67.9	67.7	68.0	68.3	68.7	68.4
Myanmar	...	64.7	...	61.2	61.5	63.2	...
Philippines	64.1	63.7	63.5	61.2	60.9	61.3	59.5
Singapore[g]	66.2	68.3	68.0	67.7	67.7	68.0	68.1
Thailand[h]	72.3	69.8	68.8	68.1	68.3	67.5	67.8
Timor-Leste[c]	24.0	30.6 (2013)	46.9	...	...	...	...
Viet Nam	77.4	77.8	77.3	76.7	76.8	76.2	74.0
The Pacific							
Cook Islands	71.0 (2011)	...	71.9	...	...	70.4	...
Fiji[i]	...	55.2 (2014)	58.3	57.1	...	...	...
Kiribati	59.3	66.0	...	...	...	...	...
Marshall Islands	41.7 (2011)	...	...	...	...	...	...
Micronesia, Federated States of	57.3	49.3 (2013)	...	...	...	...	...
Nauru[b]	64.0 (2011)	60.8 (2013)	...	...	...	...	...
Niue	68.9 (2011)	...	...	68.6	...	...	...
Palau	68.1 (2012)	77.4	...	...	...	...	...
Papua New Guinea[d]	48.3	47.2	47.1	47.0	47.2	47.0	46.7
Samoa[b]	41.3 (2011)	...	47.4	43.3	...	...	...
Solomon Islands	62.9 (2009)	73.8 (2013)	...	...	...	...	...
Tonga	94.8 (2003)	...	63.7	...	46.7	...	...
Tuvalu	59.4 (2012)	...	52.3	...	...	...	...
Vanuatu[d]	69.7	70.0	70.0	69.9	69.9	69.9	68.5
Developed ADB Member Economies							
Australia	65.4	65.0	64.9	65.2	65.6	66.0	65.0
Japan	59.6	59.6	60.0	60.5	61.5	62.1	62.0
New Zealand	67.6	68.8	70.0	70.9	70.9	70.5	70.2

... = data not available, * = provisional or preliminary, ADB = Asian Development Bank.

Note: Based on varying concepts and definitions of "labor force" across economies.

a For 2017, data cover the period from April 2016 to April 2017. For 2020, data cover the period from October 2019 to September 2020.

b Figures for different years may not be directly comparable with each other due to changes in methodology and labor concepts adopted.

c Recommendations from the 19th International Conference of Labour Statisticians were adopted by: Armenia, beginning 2018; Azerbaijan, beginning 2015; Brunei Darussalam, beginning 2017; Georgia, beginning 2010; the Lao People's Democratic Republic, for 2017; Malaysia, beginning 2019; Mongolia, beginning 2019; Nepal, for 2018; Timor-Leste, beginning 2010; and Uzbekistan, beginning 2017. Hence, data for these years may not be directly comparable with data in other years. The 19th conference provided the statistical concept of work for reference purposes; and the operational concepts, definitions, and guidelines for (i) three distinct subsets of work activities, referred to as forms of work, which include own-use production work, employment work, and volunteer work; (ii) related classifications of the population according to their labor force status and main work status; and (iii) measures of labor underutilization. The concept of employment has also been refined to refer to work for pay or profit.

d Data refer to estimates modeled by the International Labour Organization.

e For 2017, data are from the census of population. For all other years, data are from labor force surveys. Thus, data prior to and after the census year may not be directly comparable with 2017 data.

f Includes local population only.

g Refers to Singapore residents only.

h Includes seasonally inactive labor force.

i For 2017, the reported number of employed people excludes those who are engaged in unpaid employment as of end of June. Hence, data for 2014 and 2016 are not comparable with data for 2017 because the former years include unpaid employment.

Sources: Economy's official sources. For Papua New Guinea, the People's Republic of China, Turkmenistan, and Vanuatu: International Labour Organization. ILOSTAT Database. http://www.ilo.org/ilostat/ (accessed 5 July 2021). For the Federated States of Micronesia (2013), Solomon Islands (2013), and Tuvalu: Secretariat of the Pacific Community. Pacific Data Hub. PDH.Stat Data Explorer. National Minimum Development Indicators. https://stats.pacificdata.org/ (accessed 5 July 2021).

Table 2.1.5: Employment in Agriculture, Industry, and Services
(% of total employment)

ADB Regional Member	Agriculture				
	2010	2015	2018	2019	2020
Developing ADB Member Economies					
Central and West Asia					
Afghanistan[a]	69.6 (2004)	...	43.6 (2017)	...	44.5
Armenia[b]	38.6	35.3	25.9	21.9	...
Azerbaijan[b]	38.2	36.4	36.3	36.0	36.3
Georgia[b,c]	26.2	23.0	19.6	19.1	19.8
Kazakhstan	28.3	16.2	14.1	13.5	13.5
Kyrgyz Republic	31.2	29.3	20.3	18.1	18.3
Pakistan	45.0	42.3	38.5	...	...
Tajikistan	65.9	64.9	60.8	61.2	...
Turkmenistan	48.7 (2002)	...	...	...	...
Uzbekistan[b]	26.8	27.6	26.6	26.2	26.9
East Asia					
China, People's Republic of[d]	36.7	28.1	25.8	24.7	23.6
Hong Kong, China[e]	–	–	–	–	–
Korea, Republic of	6.6	5.1	5.0	5.1	5.4
Mongolia[b]	33.5	28.5	26.7	25.3	23.8
Taipei,China	5.2	5.0	4.9	4.9	4.8
South Asia					
Bangladesh	47.5	42.7 (2016)	40.6 (2017)	...	...
Bhutan	59.4	58.0	54.0	51.1	49.9
India	53.2 (2009)	...	...	...	...
Maldives[f]	4.3	9.0 (2016)	...	7.4	...
Nepal[b]	64.0 (2011)	...	21.5	...	...
Sri Lanka[g]	32.5	28.7	25.5	25.3	27.1
Southeast Asia					
Brunei Darussalam[b]	1.3 (2011)	0.5 (2014)	1.1	2.0	...
Cambodia	72.3	64.3 (2014)	...	...	...
Indonesia	38.3	32.9	29.0	27.5	29.8
Lao People's Democratic Republic[b]	72.2	...	31.3 (2017)	...	...
Malaysia[b]	13.6	12.5	10.6	10.2	10.5
Myanmar	...	51.7	48.2	45.3	...
Philippines	33.2	29.2	24.3	22.9	24.8
Singapore[h]	0.2	0.1	0.1	0.1	0.1
Thailand	38.2	32.3	32.1	31.4	31.3
Timor-Leste[b]	26.3	31.6 (2016)	...	...	...
Viet Nam[i]	49.5	44.0	37.7	34.5	32.8
The Pacific					
Cook Islands[j]	4.3 (2011)	5.3 (2016)	...	2.5	...
Fiji[k]	1.7	19.2 (2016)	3.2	...	...
Kiribati[l]	22.1	24.3	...	...	...
Marshall Islands	1.0	1.1	1.2	1.0	...
Micronesia, Federated States of	52.2 (2000)	...	...	...	...
Nauru	...	...	...	...	...
Niue	10.4 (2011)	...	8.7 (2017)	...	...
Palau[m]	7.8 (2005)	6.4	...	...	...
Papua New Guinea	...	...	...	...	...
Samoa	37.0 (2011)	41.9 (2016)	21.9 (2017)	...	...
Solomon Islands[n]	25.2 (2009)	...	...	...	...
Tonga	27.9 (2006)	24.1 (2016)	20.0	...	...
Tuvalu	...	...	...	...	...
Vanuatu	...	...	...	...	...
Developed ADB Member Economies					
Australia	3.2	2.6	2.6	2.5	2.8
Japan	4.0	3.6	3.4	3.3	3.2
New Zealand	6.7	6.2	5.9	5.8	6.0

continued on next page

Table 2.1.5: Employment in Agriculture, Industry, and Services *(continued)*
(% of total employment)

ADB Regional Member	Industry				
	2010	2015	2018	2019	2020
Developing ADB Member Economies					
Central and West Asia					
Afghanistan[a]	6.2 (2004)	...	17.8 (2017)	...	18.1
Armenia[b]	17.4	15.9	22.9	22.8	...
Azerbaijan[b]	13.7	14.1	14.7	14.8	14.6
Georgia[b,c]	10.5	10.1	19.5	19.2	18.2
Kazakhstan	18.7	21.0	19.9	19.7	19.7
Kyrgyz Republic	21.1	20.9	24.8	26.7	25.9
Pakistan	20.9	23.6	24.6	...	...
Tajikistan	7.9	6.7	8.8	8.6	...
Turkmenistan	14.2 (2002)	...	...	...	...
Uzbekistan[b]	22.7	22.9	22.7	23.2	23.1
East Asia					
China, People's Republic of[d]	28.7	29.7	28.2	28.1	28.7
Hong Kong, China[e]	11.2	11.4	11.6	11.4	11.2
Korea, Republic of	25.0	25.4	25.2	24.6	24.7
Mongolia[b]	16.2	20.3	20.6	21.6	20.7
Taipei,China	35.9	36.0	35.7	35.6	35.4
South Asia					
Bangladesh	17.6	20.5 (2016)	20.4 (2017)	...	...
Bhutan	6.6	9.6	13.1	15.5	14.9
India	21.5 (2009)	...	...	...	...
Maldives[f]	9.4	18.4 (2016)	...	18.0	...
Nepal[b]	9.5 (2011)	...	30.8	...	...
Sri Lanka[g]	24.6	25.8	27.9	27.6	26.9
Southeast Asia					
Brunei Darussalam[b]	19.6 (2011)	17.9 (2014)	19.4	20.7	...
Cambodia	9.2	9.0 (2014)	...	...	...
Indonesia	19.3	22.2	23.2	23.4	21.6
Lao People's Democratic Republic[b]	8.1	...	14.1 (2017)	...	...
Malaysia[b]	28.3	27.5	27.1	27.9	26.2
Myanmar	...	15.8	17.2	15.7	...
Philippines	15.0	16.2	19.1	19.1	18.3
Singapore[h]	21.8	17.2	15.9	14.8	14.8
Thailand	20.8	23.7	22.8	22.8	22.6
Timor-Leste[b]	14.3	17.5 (2016)	...	...	...
Viet Nam[i]	21.0	22.7	26.8	30.1	30.9
The Pacific					
Cook Islands[j]	11.7 (2011)	10.1 (2016)	...	11.3	...
Fiji[k]	23.9	14.4 (2016)	23.8	...	...
Kiribati[l]	16.1	18.2	...	...	...
Marshall Islands	22.0	14.4	15.4	16.0	...
Micronesia, Federated States of	...	...	...	...	...
Nauru	...	...	...	...	...
Niue	14.2 (2011)	...	14.2 (2017)	...	...
Palau[m]	2.6 (2005)	11.7	...	...	...
Papua New Guinea	...	...	...	...	...
Samoa	12.2 (2011)	9.1 (2016)	15.4 (2017)	...	...
Solomon Islands[n]	7.9 (2009)	...	...	...	...
Tonga	27.8 (2006)	25.6 (2016)	29.7	...	...
Tuvalu	...	...	...	...	...
Vanuatu	...	...	...	...	...
Developed ADB Member Economies					
Australia	21.0	19.4	19.7	19.1	19.2
Japan	25.4	24.6	23.9	23.7	23.5
New Zealand	20.7	21.7	20.0	19.5	20.4

continued on next page

Table 2.1.5: Employment in Agriculture, Industry, and Services *(continued)*
(% of total employment)

ADB Regional Member	Services				
	2010	2015	2018	2019	2020
Developing ADB Member Economies					
Central and West Asia					
Afghanistan[a]	24.2 (2004)	...	38.6 (2017)	...	36.7
Armenia[b]	44.0	48.8	51.2	55.3	...
Azerbaijan[b]	48.1	49.6	49.0	49.2	49.0
Georgia[b,c]	63.3	66.8	60.9	61.7	61.9
Kazakhstan	53.0	62.6	66.0	66.8	66.8
Kyrgyz Republic	47.7	49.8	54.9	55.2	55.9
Pakistan	34.2	34.2	36.9	...	...
Tajikistan	26.3	28.4	30.3	30.2	...
Turkmenistan	37.2 (2002)	...	...	...	...
Uzbekistan[b]	50.5	49.5	50.7	50.6	50.0
East Asia					
China, People's Republic of[d]	34.6	42.3	46.1	47.1	47.7
Hong Kong, China[e]	88.9	88.5	87.9	88.3	89.0
Korea, Republic of	68.4	69.5	69.8	70.3	70.0
Mongolia[b]	50.2	51.3	52.7	53.1	55.5
Taipei,China	58.8	59.0	59.4	59.6	59.8
South Asia					
Bangladesh	35.3	36.9 (2016)	38.9 (2017)	...	...
Bhutan	33.7	32.4	32.9	33.4	35.2
India	25.3 (2009)	...	...	...	...
Maldives[f]	86.3	72.6 (2016)	...	74.6	...
Nepal[b]	25.7 (2011)	...	47.7	...	...
Sri Lanka[g]	42.9	45.6	46.6	47.1	46.0
Southeast Asia					
Brunei Darussalam[b]	79.1 (2011)	81.6 (2014)	79.5	77.4	...
Cambodia	18.6	26.6 (2014)	...	...	...
Indonesia	42.3	44.9	47.8	49.0	48.7
Lao People's Democratic Republic[b]	19.7	...	54.6 (2017)	...	...
Malaysia[b]	58.1	60.0	62.3	61.9	63.4
Myanmar	...	32.5	34.6	39.0	...
Philippines	51.8	54.6	56.6	58.0	56.9
Singapore[h]	78.0	82.7	84.0	85.1	85.1
Thailand	41.0	44.0	45.1	45.7	46.1
Timor-Leste[b]	59.4	50.9 (2016)	...	...	...
Viet Nam[i]	29.5	33.2	36.2	35.4	36.3
The Pacific					
Cook Islands[j]	84.0 (2011)	84.6 (2016)	...	86.3	...
Fiji[k]	74.4	66.4 (2016)	72.9	...	...
Kiribati[l]	61.8	57.5	...	...	...
Marshall Islands	77.1	84.5	83.4	83.0	...
Micronesia, Federated States of	...	...	...	...	...
Nauru	...	...	...	...	...
Niue	75.4 (2011)	...	77.1 (2017)	...	...
Palau[m]	89.6 (2005)	82.0	...	...	...
Papua New Guinea	...	...	...	...	...
Samoa	50.9 (2011)	48.5 (2016)	62.7 (2017)	...	...
Solomon Islands[n]	66.9 (2009)	...	...	...	...
Tonga	44.3 (2006)	50.3 (2016)	50.3	...	...
Tuvalu	...	...	...	...	...
Vanuatu	...	...	...	...	...
Developed ADB Member Economies					
Australia	75.9	78.0	77.6	78.4	78.1
Japan	70.5	71.8	72.7	73.0	73.7
New Zealand	72.6	72.1	74.1	74.7	73.6

... = data not available; – = magnitude equals zero, ADB = Asian Development Bank.

Note: Data are based on varying labor force concepts and definitions adopted by different economies. Some values may not add up to 100% due to limitations on data availability.

a For 2017, data cover the period from April 2016 to April 2017. For 2020, data cover the period from October 2019 to September 2020. For 2011 onward, different methodologies were used in surveys for labor force estimation, therefore, data are not directly comparable overtime.

b Recommendations from the 19th International Conference of Labour Statisticians have been adopted by: Armenia, beginning 2018; Azerbaijan, beginning 2015; Brunei Darussalam, beginning 2017; Georgia, beginning 2010; the Lao People's Democratic Republic, for 2017; Malaysia, beginning 2019; Mongolia, beginning 2019; Nepal, for 2018; Timor-Leste, beginning 2010; and Uzbekistan, beginning 2017. Hence, data for these years may not be directly comparable with data for other years. The 19th conference provided the statistical concept of work for reference purposes; and the operational concepts, definitions, and guidelines for (i) three distinct subsets of work activities, referred to as forms of work, which include own-use production work, employment work, and volunteer work; (ii) related classifications of the population according to their labor force status and main work status; and (iii) measures of labor underutilization. The concept of employment has also been refined to refer to work for pay or profit.

c Prior to 2017, employment in services includes people who were engaged in construction industries.

d Refers to persons engaged in social labor and receiving remuneration or earning business income.

e Employment in services includes people who are engaged in: electricity and gas supply; water supply; and sewerage, waste management, and remediation activities.

f Figures include local population only. For 2010, employment in services includes people who were engaged in industries other than agriculture, forestry, and fishing; mining and quarrying; or manufacturing.

g Some data may not add up because for 2010, data exclude the northern and eastern provinces.

h Refers to Singapore residents only.

i Refers to total number of persons engaged in any activity regardless of age.

j Covers all wage and salary earners from all islands.

k For 2010 and 2018, the reported number of employed people excludes those who are engaged in unpaid employment as of end of June. For 2016, figures are not comparable with other years because they include unpaid employment.

l Refers to cash work and unpaid village work. For 2010, employment in agriculture includes people who were engaged in mining and quarrying.

m For 2005, employment in services includes people who were engaged in electricity, gas, water, and construction industries.

n For 2009, the figure refers to paid employment.

Source: Asian Development Bank estimates using data from economy's official sources.

Table 2.1.6: Poverty and Inequality

ADB Regional Member	Proportion of Population Living on Less Than $1.90 a Day (2011 PPP)[a] (%)			Proportion of Population Living on Less Than $3.20 a Day (2011 PPP)[a] (%)			Income Ratio of Highest 20% to Lowest 20%[b]			Gini Coefficient[c]		
	2010	2015	2019	2010	2015	2019	2010	2015	2019	2010	2015	2019
Developing ADB Member Economies												
Central and West Asia												
Afghanistan	...	...	...	...	...	...	...	...	...	...	...	...
Armenia	1.0	1.3	1.1	14.1	9.5	9.9	4.3	5.0	4.3	0.300	0.324	0.299
Azerbaijan[d]	0.0(2005)	...	...	0.0(2005)	...	...	3.5(2005)	...	...	0.266(2005)	...	...
Georgia	12.0	3.7	3.8	30.6	15.7	14.9	8.0	6.5	6.3	0.395	0.365	0.359
Kazakhstan	0.1	0.0	0.0(2018)	1.5	0.3	0.2(2018)	4.0	3.7	3.9(2018)	0.280	0.268	0.278(2018)
Kyrgyz Republic	2.8	1.8	0.6	19.0	18.4	9.7	4.5	4.1	4.1	0.301	0.290	0.297
Pakistan[e]	8.3	4.0	4.4(2018)	48.0	35.5	35.7(2018)	4.1	4.7	4.5(2018)	0.298	0.326	0.316(2018)
Tajikistan	4.0(2009)	4.1	...	22.5(2009)	17.8	...	4.7(2009)	5.6	...	0.308(2009)	0.340	...
Turkmenistan	...	...	...	...	...	...	...	...	...	...	...	...
Uzbekistan[f]	61.6(2003)	...	...	86.2(2003)	...	...	5.9(2003)	...	...	0.353(2003)	...	...
East Asia												
China, People's Republic of	11.2	0.7	0.5(2016)	28.6	7.0	5.4(2016)	9.6	7.1	7.0(2016)	0.437	0.386	0.385(2016)
Hong Kong, China	...	...	...	...	...	...	...	...	...	...	...	...
Korea, Republic of	0.5	0.2(2014)	0.2(2016)	0.8	0.5(2014)	0.2(2016)	5.4	5.2(2014)	5.2(2016)	0.320	0.312(2014)	0.314(2016)
Mongolia	0.7	0.2(2014)	0.5(2018)	9.6	3.0(2014)	5.0(2018)	5.3	5.0(2014)	5.2(2018)	0.331	0.320(2014)	0.327(2018)
Taipei,China[g]	0.0	0.0(2013)	0.0(2016)	0.2	0.3(2013)	0.0(2016)	4.3	3.9	3.9	0.296	0.279	0.276
South Asia												
Bangladesh	19.2	...	14.3(2016)	60.0	...	52.3(2016)	4.7	...	4.8(2016)	0.321	...	0.324(2016)
Bhutan	8.2(2007)	2.2(2012)	1.5(2017)	30.6(2007)	14.7(2012)	12.2(2017)	6.7(2007)	6.9(2012)	6.6(2017)	0.381(2007)	0.388(2012)	0.374(2017)
India[e]	22.5(2011)	...	...	61.7(2011)	...	...	5.5(2011)	...	...	0.357(2011)	...	...
Maldives[e]	3.5(2009)	...	0.0(2016)	16.6(2009)	...	0.2(2016)	7.0(2009)	...	4.8(2016)	0.384(2009)	...	0.313(2016)
Nepal[e]	15.0	...	...	50.9	...	...	5.0	...	...	0.328	...	...
Sri Lanka	2.8(2009)	1.9(2012)	1.0(2016)	19.9(2009)	16.2(2012)	11.0(2016)	5.7(2009)	6.4(2012)	6.6(2016)	0.361(2009)	0.387(2012)	0.393(2016)
Southeast Asia												
Brunei Darussalam	...	...	...	...	...	...	...	...	...	...	...	...
Cambodia	...	...	...	...	...	...	...	...	...	...	...	...
Indonesia	13.3	5.8	2.7	45.0	30.6	20.0	5.8	6.8	6.6	0.364	0.397	0.382
Lao People's Democratic Republic[e]	25.7(2007)	14.5(2012)	10.0(2018)	64.1(2007)	46.6(2012)	37.4(2018)	5.5(2007)	5.8(2012)	6.6(2018)	0.354(2007)	0.360(2012)	0.388(2018)
Malaysia	0.1(2011)	0.0	...	1.2(2011)	0.3	...	9.5(2011)	8.2	...	0.439(2011)	0.411	...
Myanmar	...	4.8	1.4(2017)	...	24.6	15.0(2017)	...	6.3	4.5(2017)	...	0.381	0.307(2017)
Philippines[h]	10.5(2009)	7.8	4.7(2018)	37.0(2009)	31.9	25.5(2018)	9.9(2009)	9.1	7.9(2018)	0.463(2009)	0.446	0.423(2018)
Singapore	...	...	...	...	...	...	...	...	...	...	...	...
Thailand	0.1	0.0	0.1	2.4	0.5	0.4	7.0	5.8	5.6	0.394	0.360	0.349
Timor-Leste	37.4(2007)	22.0(2014)	...	77.3(2007)	65.9(2014)	...	3.9(2007)	4.1(2014)	...	0.278(2007)	0.287(2014)	...
Viet Nam	4.0	2.6(2014)	1.8(2018)	16.8	11.0(2014)	6.6(2018)	7.1	5.9(2014)	6.4(2018)	0.393	0.348(2014)	0.357(2018)
The Pacific												
Cook Islands	...	...	...	...	...	...	...	...	...	...	...	...
Fiji[e]	1.6(2008)	0.5(2013)	...	10.9(2008)	7.5(2013)	...	7.2(2008)	6.0(2013)	...	0.404(2008)	0.367(2013)	...
Kiribati	12.9(2006)	...	...	34.6(2006)	...	...	6.7(2006)	...	...	0.370(2006)	...	...
Marshall Islands	...	...	...	...	...	...	...	...	...	...	...	...
Micronesia, Federated States of	8.1(2005)	15.4(2013)	...	24.6(2005)	38.7(2013)	...	8.7(2005)	8.4(2013)	...	0.424(2005)	0.401(2013)	...
Nauru	...	0.9(2012)	...	...	13.3(2012)	...	...	5.7(2012)	...	...	0.348(2012)	...
Niue	...	...	...	...	...	...	...	...	...	...	...	...
Palau	...	...	...	...	...	...	...	...	...	...	...	...
Papua New Guinea[e]	38.0(2009)	...	...	65.6(2009)	...	...	9.3(2009)	...	...	0.419(2009)	...	...
Samoa[e]	0.6(2008)	1.1(2013)	...	9.6(2008)	9.6(2013)	...	7.7(2008)	6.8(2013)	...	0.420(2008)	0.387(2013)	...
Solomon Islands	48.6(2005)	24.7(2012)	...	73.0(2005)	58.1(2012)	...	10.4(2005)	6.4(2012)	...	0.461(2005)	0.371(2012)	...
Tonga	1.1(2009)	1.0	...	8.9(2009)	7.5	...	6.7(2009)	6.7	...	0.375(2009)	0.376	...
Tuvalu	3.3	...	...	17.6	...	...	7.0	...	...	0.391	...	...
Vanuatu	13.2	...	...	39.5	...	...	6.7	...	...	0.376	...	...
Developed ADB Member Economies												
Australia	...	...	...	...	...	...	5.8	5.7(2014)	...	0.347	0.344(2014)	...
Japan	...	...	...	...	...	...	4.9	5.3(2013)	...	0.321	0.329(2013)	...
New Zealand[i]	...	...	...	...	...	...	...	...	...	0.323(2011)	0.349(2014)	...

... = Data not available, 0.0 = magnitude is less than half the unit employed or true zero value, $ = United States dollars, ADB = Asian Development Bank, PPP = purchasing power parity.

a Poverty estimates are consumption-based, except for Malaysia; the Republic of Korea; and Taipei,China, whose estimates are income-based.
b Derived from income or expenditure share of the highest 20% and lowest 20% groups by income.
c Inequality estimates are consumption-based, except for Malaysia; the Republic of Korea; and Taipei,China, whose estimates are income-based.
d The most recent year data are for 2005: 0.0% for proportion of population below $1.90 a day (2011 PPP); 0.0% for proportion of population below $3.20 a day (2011 PPP); 3.5 for income ratio of highest 20% to lowest 20%; and 0.266 for Gini coefficient.
e Household income and expenditure surveys for these economies were conducted in overlapping years. The table adopts the approach of the World Bank's World Development Indicators, i.e., using the initial year of the survey as the reference period for the poverty estimates.
f The most recent year data are for 2003: 61.6% for proportion of population below $1.90 a day (2011 PPP); 86.2% for proportion of population below $3.20 a day (2011 PPP); 5.9 for income ratio of highest 20% to lowest 20%; and 0.353 for Gini coefficient.
g The Gini coefficient reflected in the table refers to the coefficient using per capita disposable income published by the Government of Taipei,China's Directorate-General of Budget, Accounting and Statistics. The estimates using disposable income of households are 0.326 for 2000 and 0.338 for 2018. Alternative estimates for the Gini coefficient are available in the World Bank's PovcalNet Database.
h Consumption-based poverty estimates were used. However, income-based estimates are also available for $1.90 poverty line, 10.7% (2009), 6.1% (2015), and 2.7% (2018); and for $3.20 poverty line 38.1% (2009), 25.7% (2015), and 17.0% (2018).
i The Gini coefficient data are based on disposable income post taxes and transfers. Using the new income definition, the earliest available figure for the Gini coefficient is 0.323 for 2011.

Sources: World Bank. World Development Indicators. http://data.worldbank.org/data-catalog/world-development-indicators (accessed 26 July 2021). For New Zealand's Gini coefficient: Organisation for Economic Co-operation and Development. Income Distribution and Poverty. https://stats.oecd.org/index.aspx?queryid=66670# (accessed 26 July 2021). For Taipei,China's income ratio and Gini coefficient: Government of Taipei,China, Directorate-General of Budget, Accounting and Statistics. http://eng.dgbas.gov.tw/mp.asp?mp=2 (accessed 26 July 2021).

Table 2.1.7: Human Development Index

ADB Regional Member	2010	2013	2015	2016	2017	2018	2019	Rank in 2019[a]
Developing ADB Member Economies								
Central and West Asia	**0.661**	**0.679**	**0.688**	**0.691**	**0.696**	**0.699**	**0.704**	
Afghanistan	0.472	0.496	0.500	0.502	0.506	0.509	0.511	169
Armenia	0.747	0.762	0.768	0.766	0.769	0.771	0.776	81
Azerbaijan	0.726	0.735	0.744	0.751	0.754	0.754	0.756	88
Georgia	0.751	0.775	0.790	0.792	0.799	0.805	0.812	61
Kazakhstan	0.764	0.791	0.806	0.808	0.815	0.819	0.825	51
Kyrgyz Republic	0.662	0.680	0.690	0.691	0.694	0.696	0.697	120
Pakistan	0.512	0.523	0.536	0.542	0.550	0.552	0.557	154
Tajikistan	0.638	0.653	0.652	0.653	0.657	0.661	0.668	125
Turkmenistan	0.666	0.685	0.694	0.699	0.701	0.710	0.715	111
Uzbekistan	0.669	0.692	0.701	0.705	0.713	0.717	0.720	106
East Asia	**0.812**	**0.830**	**0.839**	**0.845**	**0.848**	**0.852**	**0.856**	
China, People's Republic of	0.699	0.724	0.739	0.746	0.750	0.755	0.761	85
Hong Kong, China	0.904	0.918	0.930	0.936	0.941	0.946	0.949	4
Korea, Republic of	0.889	0.901	0.907	0.910	0.912	0.914	0.916	23
Mongolia	0.696	0.727	0.735	0.729	0.728	0.735	0.737	99
Taipei,China	0.873	0.882	0.885	0.903	0.907	0.911	0.916	...
South Asia	**0.614**	**0.640**	**0.655**	**0.660**	**0.666**	**0.671**	**0.676**	
Bangladesh	0.557	0.579	0.595	0.606	0.616	0.625	0.632	133
Bhutan	0.574	0.610	0.628	0.637	0.646	0.649	0.654	129
India	0.579	0.604	0.624	0.630	0.640	0.642	0.645	131
Maldives	0.685	0.709	0.724	0.728	0.731	0.734	0.740	95
Nepal	0.537	0.568	0.583	0.586	0.588	0.596	0.602	142
Sri Lanka	0.754	0.769	0.776	0.773	0.775	0.779	0.782	72
Southeast Asia	**0.678**	**0.696**	**0.703**	**0.707**	**0.710**	**0.713**	**0.718**	
Brunei Darussalam	0.827	0.839	0.838	0.839	0.838	0.836	0.838	47
Cambodia	0.539	0.559	0.570	0.576	0.582	0.585	0.594	144
Indonesia	0.665	0.687	0.695	0.703	0.707	0.712	0.718	107
Lao People's Democratic Republic	0.552	0.582	0.598	0.605	0.608	0.609	0.613	137
Malaysia	0.772	0.785	0.796	0.800	0.805	0.805	0.810	62
Myanmar	0.515	0.543	0.557	0.563	0.572	0.579	0.583	147
Philippines	0.671	0.691	0.701	0.704	0.708	0.711	0.718	107
Singapore	0.909	0.921	0.931	0.935	0.933	0.936	0.938	11
Thailand	0.724	0.734	0.749	0.756	0.765	0.772	0.777	79
Timor-Leste	0.628	0.630	0.610	0.598	0.599	0.599	0.606	141
Viet Nam	0.661	0.681	0.688	0.693	0.696	0.700	0.704	117
The Pacific	**0.638**	**0.651**	**0.659**	**0.660**	**0.665**	**0.666**	**0.669**	
Cook Islands	...	...	...	...	...	...	...	...
Fiji	0.715	0.728	0.737	0.738	0.740	0.742	0.743	93
Kiribati	0.593	0.608	0.625	0.622	0.627	0.628	0.630	134
Marshall Islands	...	...	...	...	0.699	0.702	0.704	117
Micronesia, Federated States of	0.601	0.605	0.612	0.614	0.616	0.618	0.620	136
Nauru	...	...	...	...	...	...	...	...
Niue	...	...	...	...	...	...	...	...
Palau	0.786	0.821	0.820	0.822	0.822	0.822	0.826	50
Papua New Guinea	0.522	0.537	0.548	0.549	0.549	0.549	0.555	155
Samoa	0.698	0.700	0.707	0.710	0.710	0.709	0.715	111
Solomon Islands	0.537	0.558	0.563	0.561	0.562	0.564	0.567	151
Tonga	0.699	0.708	0.720	0.722	0.723	0.723	0.725	104
Tuvalu	...	...	...	...	...	...	...	...
Vanuatu	0.590	0.593	0.598	0.598	0.601	0.603	0.609	140
Developed ADB Member Economies	**0.908**	**0.916**	**0.922**	**0.925**	**0.927**	**0.929**	**0.931**	
Australia	0.930	0.931	0.938	0.939	0.941	0.943	0.944	8
Japan	0.887	0.902	0.908	0.912	0.915	0.917	0.919	19
New Zealand	0.906	0.914	0.921	0.924	0.926	0.928	0.931	14
DEVELOPING ADB MEMBER ECONOMIES	**0.672**	**0.690**	**0.699**	**0.702**	**0.706**	**0.709**	**0.713**	
ALL ADB REGIONAL MEMBERS	**0.688**	**0.705**	**0.714**	**0.718**	**0.721**	**0.724**	**0.728**	
WORLD[b]	**0.697**	**0.713**	**0.722**	**0.727**	**0.729**	**0.731**	**0.737**	

... = data not available, ADB = Asian Development Bank.

Notes:

1 Regional indexes are calculated as an arithmetic average of the indexes of reporting economies with data corresponding to the year heading.

2 The Human Development Index (HDI) is calculated by the Human Development Report Office of the United Nations Development Programme (UNDP) using the most recently revised historical data from national and international agencies, which continually improve their data series. Hence, the HDI values and ranks presented in this table are not comparable to those published in previous editions. For this 2021 edition, HDI data presented depict the state of human development before the COVID-19 pandemic, based on available data for 2019 and previous years. More information is available at the UNDP website, http://hdr.undp.org/en/content/human-development-report-2020-readers-guide.

a Rank in 2019 among the 189 national economies presented in the Human Development Report 2020 of the UNDP.

b Calculated by the UNDP Human Development Report Office by applying the human development index formula to the weighted group averages of component indicators. Missing values are estimated using cross-economy regression models.

Sources: United Nations Development Programme. Human Development Data (1990–2019). http://hdr.undp.org/en/data# (accessed 17 May 2021). For Taipei,China: Government of Taipei,China, Directorate-General of Budget, Accounting and Statistics. https://eng.stat.gov.tw/ct.asp?xItem=25280&ctNode=6032&mp=5 (accessed 17 May 2021).

Table 2.1.8: Life Expectancy at Birth
(years)

ADB Regional Member	Both Sexes		Female		Male	
	2010	2019	2010	2019	2010	2019
Developing ADB Member Economies						
Central and West Asia[a]	**66.0**	**68.3**	**67.8**	**69.9**	**64.3**	**66.7**
Afghanistan	61.0	64.8	62.5	66.4	59.7	63.4
Armenia	73.3	75.1	76.4	78.5	70.0	71.3
Azerbaijan	70.9	73.0	74.1	75.5	67.8	70.5
Georgia	71.5	73.8	76.0	78.1	66.9	69.3
Kazakhstan	68.5	73.2	73.4	77.3	63.6	68.8
Kyrgyz Republic	69.3	71.6	73.5	75.8	65.3	67.6
Pakistan	65.3	67.3	66.2	68.3	64.4	66.3
Tajikistan	68.7	71.1	71.2	73.4	66.5	68.9
Turkmenistan	66.7	68.2	70.2	71.7	63.2	64.7
Uzbekistan	69.7	71.7	72.5	73.8	66.9	69.6
East Asia[a]	**74.7**	**77.2**	**76.9**	**79.6**	**72.7**	**75.0**
China, People's Republic of	74.4	76.9	76.6	79.2	72.5	74.8
Hong Kong, China	83.0	85.1	86.0	88.1	80.1	82.2
Korea, Republic of	80.1	83.2	83.6	86.3	76.8	80.3
Mongolia	67.4	69.9	71.6	74.1	63.5	65.8
Taipei,China	79.2	80.9	82.5	84.2	76.1	77.7
South Asia[a]	**67.2**	**70.1**	**68.3**	**71.5**	**66.1**	**68.8**
Bangladesh	69.9	72.6	71.3	74.6	68.7	70.9
Bhutan	68.4	71.8	68.6	72.2	68.2	71.4
India	66.7	69.7	67.7	71.0	65.7	68.5
Maldives	75.9	78.9	77.4	80.8	74.7	77.5
Nepal	67.6	70.8	69.0	72.2	66.3	69.3
Sri Lanka	75.4	77.0	78.9	80.3	72.0	73.6
Southeast Asia[a]	**70.5**	**72.6**	**73.4**	**75.7**	**67.6**	**69.7**
Brunei Darussalam	74.7	75.9	75.9	77.1	73.7	74.7
Cambodia	66.6	69.8	68.6	71.9	64.3	67.5
Indonesia	69.2	71.7	71.3	74.0	67.2	69.6
Lao People's Democratic Republic	64.3	67.9	66.1	69.7	62.5	66.1
Malaysia	74.5	76.2	76.7	78.3	72.5	74.2
Myanmar	63.5	67.1	66.9	70.1	60.1	64.0
Philippines	69.8	71.2	74.0	75.5	66.0	67.3
Singapore	81.5	83.5	84.0	85.7	79.2	81.4
Thailand	74.2	77.2	77.7	80.9	70.7	73.5
Timor-Leste	67.2	69.5	68.8	71.6	65.6	67.5
Viet Nam	74.8	75.4	78.9	79.5	70.7	71.3
The Pacific[a,b]	**63.6**	**65.8**	**65.1**	**67.2**	**62.1**	**64.4**
Cook Islands	74.5	76.6 (2020)	77.4	79.6 (2020)	71.7	73.8 (2020)
Fiji	66.7	67.4	68.3	69.3	65.2	65.7
Kiribati	65.8	68.4	69.7	72.3	61.9	64.2
Marshall Islands	71.4	74.1 (2020)	73.5	76.5 (2020)	69.3	71.8 (2020)
Micronesia, Federated States of	66.5	67.9	68.2	69.6	64.9	66.2
Nauru	64.0	67.3 (2020)	67.6	71.0 (2020)	60.5	63.8 (2020)
Niue[c]	73.1[d] (2011)	73.6[e] (2016)	76.3[d] (2011)	75.7[e] (2016)	70.1[d] (2011)	71.8[e] (2016)
Palau	71.3	74.1 (2020)	74.6	77.5 (2020)	68.2	70.9 (2020)
Papua New Guinea	62.0	64.5	63.4	65.8	60.7	63.3
Samoa	71.7	73.3	74.0	75.5	69.5	71.3
Solomon Islands	70.7	73.0	72.5	74.9	69.1	71.3
Tonga	70.1	70.9	72.0	72.9	68.1	69.0
Tuvalu	64.5	67.8 (2020)	66.7	70.3 (2020)	62.3	65.4 (2020)
Vanuatu	69.1	70.5	70.8	72.2	67.6	69.0
Developed ADB Member Economies[a]	**82.6**	**84.0**	**85.9**	**86.9**	**79.5**	**81.3**
Australia	81.7	82.9	84.0	85.0	79.5	80.9
Japan	82.8	84.4	86.3	87.5	79.6	81.4
New Zealand	80.7	81.7	82.7	83.5	78.8	80.0
DEVELOPING ADB MEMBER ECONOMIES[a,b]	**70.5**	**73.0**	**72.4**	**75.0**	**68.7**	**71.0**
ALL ADB REGIONAL MEMBERS[a,b]	**71.0**	**73.4**	**73.0**	**75.5**	**69.1**	**71.4**
WORLD[f]	**70.6**	**72.7**	**72.8**	**75.0**	**68.4**	**70.6**

ADB = Asian Development Bank.

a Estimated as weighted averages using total population of appropriate sex(es) from the United Nations' World Population Prospects 2019 as weight. For the Cook Islands, Marshall Islands, Nauru, Niue, Palau, and Tuvalu, sex-disaggregated population figures were derived using total populations from World Population Prospects 2019 and the proportions of total population by sex for Pacific small island states from the World Development Indicators.

b For estimating regional aggregates, imputation was done for economies with missing data by substituting available data from the nearest years.

c Calculated directly from recorded deaths, through 5-year periods.

d Covers 2007–2011.

e Covers 2012–2016.

f Estimated by the World Bank as weighted averages using total population of appropriate sex(es) as weight.

Sources: United Nations. World Population Prospects 2019. https://population.un.org/wpp/Download/Standard/Population/ (accessed 18 May 2021). World Bank. World Development Indicators. https://databank.worldbank.org/source/world-development-indicators (accessed 17 May 2021). For the Cook Islands, the Marshall Islands, Nauru, Palau, and Tuvalu: United States Census Bureau. International Data Base. https://www.census.gov/programs-surveys/international-programs/data/tools/international-data-base.html (accessed 17 May 2021). For Niue: Statistics Niue. Vital Statistics Report 2012–2016. https://niue.prism.spc.int/ (accessed 17 May 2021). For Taipei,China: Government of Taipei,China, Directorate-General of Budget, Accounting and Statistics. https://eng.dgbas.gov.tw/mp.asp?mp=2 (accessed 17 May 2021).

Table 2.1.9: Births, Deaths, and Fertility Rates

ADB Regional Member	Crude Birth Rate (per 1,000 people)		Crude Death Rate (per 1,000 people)		Total Fertility Rate (births per woman)	
	2010	2019	2010	2019	2010	2019
Developing ADB Member Economies						
Central and West Asia[a]	**29.0**	**26.9**	**7.4**	**6.6**	**3.7**	**3.4**
Afghanistan	39.8	31.8	8.3	6.3	6.0	4.3
Armenia	15.3	13.6	9.7	9.8	1.7	1.8
Azerbaijan	18.3	14.1	5.9	5.6	1.9	1.8
Georgia	13.9	13.2	13.1	12.8	1.9	2.1
Kazakhstan	22.5	21.7	9.0	7.2	2.6	2.9
Kyrgyz Republic	26.8	26.9	6.6	5.2	3.1	3.3
Pakistan	30.1	27.8	7.6	6.9	4.0	3.5
Tajikistan	31.6	30.0	5.7	4.8	3.6	3.6
Turkmenistan	25.4	23.1	7.2	7.0	2.8	2.7
Uzbekistan	22.0	24.3	4.8	4.6	2.3	2.8
East Asia[a,b]	**11.8**	**10.3**	**7.0**	**7.1**	**1.6**	**1.7**
China, People's Republic of	11.9	10.5	7.1	7.1	1.6	1.7
Hong Kong, China	12.6	7.0	6.0	6.5	1.1	1.1
Korea, Republic of	9.4	5.9	5.1	5.7	1.2	0.9
Mongolia	24.7	23.4	6.6	6.3	2.6	2.9
Taipei,China	7.2	7.0 (2020)	6.3	7.3 (2020)	0.9	1.0 (2020)
South Asia[a]	**21.1**	**17.7**	**7.3**	**7.1**	**2.5**	**2.2**
Bangladesh	21.1	17.9	5.7	5.5	2.3	2.0
Bhutan	19.4	17.0	6.4	6.3	2.3	2.0
India	21.1	17.6	7.5	7.3	2.6	2.2
Maldives	19.6	13.6	3.5	2.8	2.2	1.8
Nepal	22.7	19.6	6.8	6.3	2.5	1.9
Sri Lanka	17.8	15.5	6.0	6.8	2.2	2.2
Southeast Asia[a]	**19.8**	**17.2**	**6.5**	**6.6**	**2.4**	**2.2**
Brunei Darussalam	17.3	14.5	3.8	4.5	1.9	1.8
Cambodia	25.5	22.0	6.5	6.0	2.9	2.5
Indonesia	20.8	17.7	6.7	6.5	2.5	2.3
Lao People's Democratic Republic	26.9	23.1	7.4	6.4	3.1	2.6
Malaysia	17.3	16.6	4.6	5.2	2.1	2.0
Myanmar	19.8	17.4	8.9	8.2	2.4	2.1
Philippines	25.0	20.2	5.6	5.9	3.2	2.5
Singapore	9.3	8.8	4.4	5.0	1.2	1.1
Thailand	11.8	10.2	7.2	7.8	1.5	1.5
Timor-Leste	30.7	29.3	6.5	5.9	4.8	3.9
Viet Nam	17.3	16.5	5.8	6.4	1.9	2.1
The Pacific[a,b]	**29.4**	**26.5**	**7.9**	**7.1**	**3.9**	**3.5**
Cook Islands	15.4	13.0 (2020)	7.2	8.8 (2020)	2.4	2.1 (2020)
Fiji	22.3	21.0	8.0	8.3	2.8	2.8
Kiribati	29.6	27.5	7.0	6.3	3.8	3.5
Marshall Islands	29.9	22.9 (2020)	4.5	4.2 (2020)	3.5	2.9 (2020)
Micronesia, Federated States of	24.1	22.7	7.2	6.6	3.5	3.0
Nauru	28.2	21.9 (2020)	6.3	6.2 (2020)	3.1	2.7 (2020)
Niue	15.8[c] (2011)	3.0[d]	8.3[c] (2011)	1.2[d]	2.8[c] (2011)	2.7[e] (2016)
Palau	11.9	11.2	8.1	10.8	2.2 (2012)	2.2 (2015)
Papua New Guinea	30.0	26.8	8.3	7.4	4.0	3.5
Samoa	28.0	24.1	5.8	5.2	4.3	3.8
Solomon Islands	34.0	32.0	4.8	4.2	4.4	4.4
Tonga	27.4	24.0	7.2	7.1	3.9	3.5
Tuvalu	23.0	23.3 (2020)	9.3	8.1 (2020)	3.1	2.9 (2020)
Vanuatu	32.3	29.2	5.5	5.2	4.1	3.7
Developed ADB Member Economies[a]	**9.4**	**8.0**	**9.0**	**10.3**	**1.5**	**1.4**
Australia	13.7	12.1	6.5	6.7	1.9	1.7
Japan	8.5	7.0	9.5	11.1	1.4	1.4
New Zealand	14.7	12.0	6.5	6.9	2.2	1.7
DEVELOPING ADB MEMBER ECONOMIES[a,b]	**17.9**	**15.7**	**7.1**	**6.9**	**2.2**	**2.1**
ALL ADB REGIONAL MEMBERS[a,b]	**17.6**	**15.4**	**7.1**	**7.1**	**2.2**	**2.1**
WORLD[f]	**19.8**	**17.9**	**7.9**	**7.5**	**2.5**	**2.4**

ADB = Asian Development Bank.

a ADB estimates using data on total population from the United Nations. World Population Prospects 2019; data on crude birth rates, crude death rates, and total fertility rates from the World Bank's World Development Indicators, the United States Census Bureau, and economy's official sources; and data on the population of women of reproductive age from the World Health Organization, World Population Prospects 2019, and official communication from The Pacific Community's Statistics for Development Division.
b For estimating aggregates, imputation was done for economies with missing data by substituting available data from the nearest years.
c Refers to a multiyear average for the intercensal years 2007–2011. Crude birth rate and crude death rate are calculated by dividing the average annual number of births and deaths of the intercensal period 2007–2011 by the midperiod population size of the intercensal period. For total fertility rate, the estimate is based on the average registered number of children born, by age of mother, of the intercensal period 2007–2011, and the estimated midperiod number of women of childbearing age.
d Refers to July–December 2019.
e Refers to a multiyear average for the intercensal years 2012–2016. Total fertility rate is estimated based on the average registered number of children born, by age of mother, of the intercensal period 2012–2016, and the estimated midperiod number of women of childbearing age.
f Estimated by the World Bank as weighted averages of the rates using the value of the denominator or, in some cases, another indicator as a weight. Aggregation is done after imputing values for missing data according to certain imputation rules by the World Bank, as described in their data compilation methodology.

Sources: Pacific Community, Statistics for Development Division. Official communication, 3 July 2019; United Nations. World Population Prospects 2019. https://population.un.org/wpp/Download/Standard/Population/ (accessed 31 May 2021); World Bank. World Development Indicators. https://databank.worldbank.org/source/world-development-indicators (accessed 28 May 2021); and World Health Organization. Maternal, Newborn, Child & Adolescent Health. https://www.who.int/data/maternal-newborn-child-adolescent/indicator-explorer-new/mca/women-of-reproductive-age-(15-49-years)-population-(thousands) (accessed 31 May 2021). For the Cook Islands, the Marshall Islands, Nauru, and Tuvalu: United States Census Bureau. International Data Base. https://www.census.gov/programs-surveys/international-programs/data/tools/international-data-base.html (accessed 28 May 2021). For Niue: Statistics Niue, Department of Finance and Planning. https://niue.prism.spc.int (accessed 28 May 2021). For Taipei,China: Government of Taipei,China, Ministry of the Interior. https://www.moi.gov.tw/english/ (accessed 14 June 2021).

Table 2.1.10: Adult (15 Years and Older) Literacy Rate
(%)

ADB Regional Member	Both Sexes 2010	Both Sexes 2018	Female 2010	Female 2018	Male 2010	Male 2018
Developing ADB Member Economies						
Central and West Asia						
Afghanistan	31.4 (2011)	43.0[a]	17.0 (2011)	29.8[a]	45.4 (2011)	55.5[a]
Armenia	99.7 (2011)	99.7 (2017)	99.7 (2011)	99.7 (2017)	99.8 (2011)	99.8 (2017)
Azerbaijan	99.8[b]	99.8 (2017)	99.7[b]	99.7 (2017)	99.9[b]	99.9 (2017)
Georgia	99.7 (2002)	99.4 (2017)	99.6 (2002)	99.3 (2017)	99.8 (2002)	99.4 (2017)
Kazakhstan	99.8[a]	99.8[a]	99.7[a]	99.7[a]	99.8[a]	99.8[a]
Kyrgyz Republic	99.2 (2009)	99.6[a]	99.0 (2009)	99.5[a]	99.5 (2009)	99.7[a]
Pakistan	55.4	59.1 (2017)	41.0	46.5 (2017)	68.9	71.1 (2017)
Tajikistan	99.5 (2000)	99.8[a] (2014)	99.2 (2000)	99.7[a] (2014)	99.7 (2000)	99.8[a] (2014)
Turkmenistan	...	99.7[a] (2014)	...	99.6[a] (2014)	...	99.8[a] (2014)
Uzbekistan	98.6 (2000)	100.0	98.1 (2000)	100.0	99.2 (2000)	100.0
East Asia						
China, People's Republic of	95.1	96.8[a]	92.7	95.2[a]	97.5	98.5[a]
Hong Kong, China	...	...	...	...	...	...
Korea, Republic of	98.0 (2008)	...	97.6 (2008)	...	98.3 (2008)	...
Mongolia	98.3	98.4[a]	98.3	98.6[a]	98.2	98.2[a]
Taipei,China	...	...	...	...	...	...
South Asia						
Bangladesh	58.8 (2011)	74.7 (2019)	55.1 (2011)	71.9 (2019)	62.5 (2011)	77.4 (2019)
Bhutan	55.3 (2012)	66.6 (2017)	45.2 (2012)	57.1 (2017)	66.0 (2012)	75.0 (2017)
India	69.3 (2011)	74.4[a]	59.3 (2011)	65.8[a]	78.9 (2011)	82.4[a]
Maldives	98.4 (2006)	97.7 (2016)	98.4 (2006)	98.1 (2016)	98.4 (2006)	97.3 (2016)
Nepal	59.6 (2011)	67.9[a]	48.8 (2011)	59.7[a]	71.7 (2011)	78.6[a]
Sri Lanka	91.2	91.7	90.0	90.8	92.6	92.8
Southeast Asia						
Brunei Darussalam	96.1 (2011)	97.2[a]	94.7 (2011)	96.3[a]	97.4 (2011)	98.1[a]
Cambodia	76.1 (2009)	80.5 (2015)	69.1 (2009)	75.0 (2015)	83.9 (2009)	86.5 (2015)
Indonesia	92.8 (2011)	95.7	90.1 (2011)	94.0	95.6 (2011)	97.3
Lao People's Democratic Republic	58.3[a] (2011)	84.7 (2015)	49.7[a] (2011)	79.4 (2015)	67.4[a] (2011)	90.0 (2015)
Malaysia	93.1	94.9	90.7	93.5	95.4	96.1
Myanmar	89.9 (2000)	75.6[a] (2016)	86.4 (2000)	71.8[a] (2016)	93.9 (2000)	80.0[a] (2016)
Philippines	95.4 (2008)	98.2 (2015)	95.8 (2008)	98.2 (2015)	95.0 (2008)	98.1 (2015)
Singapore	95.9	97.3	93.8	95.9	98.0	98.9
Thailand	96.4	93.8	96.4	92.4	96.4	95.2
Timor-Leste	58.3	68.1[a]	53.0	64.2[a]	63.6	71.9[a]
Viet Nam	93.5 (2009)	95.0[a]	91.4 (2009)	93.6[a]	95.8 (2009)	96.5[a]
The Pacific						
Cook Islands	...	...	...	...	...	...
Fiji	...	99.1 (2017)	...	99.1 (2017)	...	99.1 (2017)
Kiribati	...	...	...	...	...	...
Marshall Islands	98.3 (2011)	...	98.2 (2011)	...	98.3 (2011)	...
Micronesia, Federated States of	...	...	...	...	...	...
Nauru	...	...	...	...	...	...
Niue	...	...	...	...	...	...
Palau	...	96.6 (2015)	...	96.3 (2015)	...	96.8 (2015)
Papua New Guinea	61.6[a]	...	57.9[a]	...	65.3[a]	...
Samoa	99.0 (2011)	99.1[a]	99.1 (2011)	99.2[a]	98.9 (2011)	99.0[a]
Solomon Islands	76.6[a] (2009)	...	69.0[a] (2009)	...	83.7[a] (2009)	...
Tonga	99.4 (2011)	99.4[a]	99.4 (2011)	99.5[a]	99.3 (2011)	99.4[a]
Tuvalu	...	...	...	...	...	...
Vanuatu	78.4[a] (2004)	87.5[a]	76.2[a] (2004)	86.7[a]	80.5[a] (2004)	88.3[a]
Developed ADB Member Economies						
Australia	...	...	...	...	...	...
Japan	...	...	...	...	...	...
New Zealand	...	...	...	...	...	...
WORLD	**84.0**	**86.5** (2019)	**79.8**	**83.0** (2019)	**88.3**	**89.9** (2019)

... = data not available, ADB = Asian Development Bank.

a Refers to UNESCO Institute for Statistics estimates.
b Based on national estimation.

Source: United Nations Educational, Scientific and Cultural Organization (UNESCO) Institute for Statistics. UIS.Stat Database. http://data.uis.unesco.org/ (accessed 12 May 2021).

Table 2.1.11: Years of Schooling
(years)

ADB Regional Member	Expected[a]					
	Both Sexes		Female		Male	
	2010	2019	2010	2019	2010	2019
Developing ADB Member Economies						
Central and West Asia						
Afghanistan	9.3 (2011)	10.2[c] (2018)	7.2 (2011)	7.7[c] (2018)	11.2 (2011)	12.6[c] (2018)
Armenia	13.1 (2011)	13.1[c]	13.4[c] (2011)	13.7[d]	12.9 (2011)	12.6[d]
Azerbaijan	...	13.5[d]	...	13.6[d]	...	13.3[d]
Georgia	13.5[c] (2009)	15.3 (2018)	13.5[c] (2008)	15.9	12.8[c] (2008)	15.3
Kazakhstan	15.1 (2012)	15.8 (2020)	15.4 (2012)	16.0 (2020)	14.8 (2012)	15.5 (2020)
Kyrgyz Republic	12.7[d] (2012)	13.0	12.9[d] (2012)	13.2	12.5 (2012)	12.8
Pakistan	6.9[c] (2012)	8.3[c] (2018)	6.2[c] (2012)	7.6[c] (2018)	7.6[c] (2012)	8.9[c] (2018)
Tajikistan	11.3 (2012)	11.4 (2013)	10.6 (2012)	10.7 (2013)	12.0 (2012)	12.1 (2013)
Turkmenistan	...	12.9[c]	...	12.7[c] (2018)	...	13.2[c]
Uzbekistan	11.6 (2012)	12.5	11.5 (2012)	12.4	11.8 (2012)	12.6
East Asia						
China, People's Republic of	12.4[c]	...	12.4[c]	...	12.4[c]	...
Hong Kong, China	15.9[c] (2012)	17.2[c]	15.7[c] (2012)	17.5[c]	15.6[c] (2012)	17.0[c]
Korea, Republic of	16.7 (2012)	16.5 (2017)	15.9 (2012)	16.0 (2018)	17.5 (2012)	16.9 (2018)
Mongolia	14.6[c]	...	15.3[c]	...	13.9[c]	...
Taipei,China	16.7 (2012)	16.6 (2020)	16.8 (2012)	16.8 (2020)	16.7 (2012)	16.5 (2020)
South Asia						
Bangladesh	9.2[d] (2009)	12.0[c] (2018)	9.3 (2009)	12.4 (2018)	9.1[d] (2009)	11.7[c] (2018)
Bhutan	12.5[c] (2012)	13.1[c] (2018)	12.7[c] (2012)	13.5[c] (2018)	12.4[c] (2012)	12.8[c] (2018)
India	11.5[c] (2012)	11.5[c]	11.0[c] (2011)	11.7[c]	11.3[c] (2011)	11.3[c]
Maldives	12.2 (2003)	...	12.3 (2003)	...	12.0 (2003)	...
Nepal	12.4[c] (2011)	13.2	12.5[c] (2011)	13.4[c]	12.3[c] (2011)	12.9
Sri Lanka	13.7 (2012)	14.1 (2018)	14.1 (2012)	14.5 (2018)	13.4 (2012)	13.8 (2018)
Southeast Asia						
Brunei Darussalam	14.9 (2012)	14.1	15.3 (2012)	14.6	14.6 (2012)	13.6
Cambodia	10.6 (2008)	...	9.9 (2008)	...	11.2[c] (2008)	...
Indonesia	12.9 (2012)	13.6 (2018)	13.0 (2012)	13.7 (2018)	12.8 (2012)	13.5 (2018)
Lao People's Democratic Republic	10.5 (2012)	10.5	9.9 (2012)	10.2	11.1 (2012)	10.9 (2018)
Malaysia	13.0 (2012)	13.7 (2017)	13.4[c] (2012)	14.0 (2017)	12.6[c] (2012)	13.3 (2017)
Myanmar	8.2 (2007)	10.7 (2018)	...	10.9 (2018)	...	10.5 (2018)
Philippines	11.4 (2009)	13.1 (2017)	11.6 (2009)	13.5[c] (2017)	11.1 (2009)	12.8[c] (2017)
Singapore	...	16.5 (2018)	...	16.7[d] (2018)	...	16.4[d] (2018)
Thailand	13.3 (2012)	15.4 (2016)	13.8[c] (2012)	15.8[c] (2016)	12.8[c] (2012)	15.1[c] (2016)
Timor-Leste	12.4	...	12.0	...	12.9	...
Viet Nam	...	...	...	...	...	...
The Pacific						
Cook Islands	14.8 (2012)	...	14.2 (2012)	...	15.5 (2012)	...
Fiji	13.9 (2004)	...	14.1 (2004)	...	13.7 (2004)	...
Kiribati	11.8 (2008)	...	12.2 (2008)	...	11.4 (2008)	...
Marshall Islands	12.2[c] (2002)	10.2	12.2 (2002)	...	12.2 (2002)	10.1
Micronesia, Federated States of	...	...	...	...	...	...
Nauru	9.6 (2008)	...	9.7 (2008)	...	9.5 (2008)	...
Niue	12.2 (2005)	...	12.4 (2005)	...	12.0 (2005)	...
Palau	14.1[c] (2000)	16.6 (2013)	14.8[c] (2000)	17.2 (2013)	13.4 (2000)	16.1 (2013)
Papua New Guinea	...	...	...	...	...	...
Samoa	12.0 (2000)	...	12.4[c] (2000)	...	11.7 (2000)	...
Solomon Islands	9.2 (2007)	...	8.8 (2007)	...	9.6 (2007)	...
Tonga	14.5[c] (2003)	...	13.9[c] (2002)	...	13.4 (2002)	...
Tuvalu	10.9 (2001)	...	11.0 (2001)	...	10.8 (2001)	...
Vanuatu	10.6[c] (2004)	...	10.2[c] (2004)	...	10.9[c] (2004)	...
Developed ADB Member Economies						
Australia	...	20.5 (2018)	...	21.1 (2018)	...	19.9 (2018)
Japan	...	...	...	...	...	...
New Zealand	...	18.9 (2018)	...	19.9 (2018)	...	17.9 (2018)
WORLD	**11.8** (2012)	**12.3**[c]	**11.7**[c] (2012)	**12.3**[c]	**11.9**[c] (2012)	**12.3**[c]

continued on next page

Table 2.1.11: Years of Schooling *(continued)*
(years)

ADB Regional Member	Mean[b]					
	Both Sexes		Female		Male	
	2010	2019	2010	2019	2010	2019
Developing ADB Member Economies						
Central and West Asia						
Afghanistan	...	...	...	...	...	...
Armenia	11.2 (2011)	11.2 (2017)	11.2 (2011)	11.2 (2017)	11.2 (2011)	11.2 (2017)
Azerbaijan	10.5 (2012)	10.5 (2017)	10.2 (2012)	10.2 (2017)	10.8 (2012)	10.9 (2017)
Georgia	12.5 (2012)	12.9 (2017)	12.4 (2012)	12.9 (2017)	12.6 (2012)	12.8 (2017)
Kazakhstan	11.0 (2009)	12.2 (2018)	11.0 (2009)	12.2 (2018)	11.0 (2009)	12.2 (2018)
Kyrgyz Republic	10.9 (2009)	...	10.9 (2009)	...	10.8 (2009)	...
Pakistan	4.8 (2012)	5.1 (2017)	3.4 (2012)	3.9 (2017)	6.2 (2012)	6.4 (2017)
Tajikistan	10.8 (2000)	11.4 (2017)	10.3 (2000)	10.8 (2017)	11.3 (2000)	12.0 (2017)
Turkmenistan	...	...	...	...	...	...
Uzbekistan	...	11.8 (2018)	...	11.6 (2018)	...	12.0 (2018)
East Asia						
China, People's Republic of	6.7	...	6.2	...	7.2	...
Hong Kong, China	11.6 (2011)	12.2	11.2 (2011)	11.8	12.1 (2011)	12.7
Korea, Republic of	11.6	12.1 (2015)	10.9	11.4 (2015)	12.5	12.9 (2015)
Mongolia	10.1	...	10.4	...	9.8	...
Taipei,China	...	...	...	...	...	...
South Asia						
Bangladesh	5.3 (2012)	6.5	4.5 (2012)	6.0	6.1 (2012)	7.1
Bhutan	2.2 (2012)	4.1 (2017)	1.5 (2012)	3.3 (2017)	3.0 (2012)	4.8 (2017)
India	5.3 (2011)	...	4.0 (2011)	...	6.5 (2011)	...
Maldives	3.5 (2006)	...	...	...	...	...
Nepal	3.5 (2011)	...	2.3 (2011)	...	4.9 (2011)	...
Sri Lanka	10.2 (2009)	10.6 (2018)	10.1 (2009)	11.1 (2018)	10.4 (2009)	11.0 (2018)
Southeast Asia						
Brunei Darussalam	11.6 (2011)	...	11.3 (2011)	...	11.8 (2011)	...
Cambodia	3.9 (2009)	3.7 (2015)	3.1 (2009)	2.8 (2015)	5.0 (2009)	4.8 (2015)
Indonesia	7.5 (2011)	8.2 (2018)	7.3 (2011)	7.8 (2018)	8.0 (2011)	8.6 (2018)
Lao People's Democratic Republic	...	...	...	...	...	...
Malaysia	9.7	10.4 (2016)	9.4	10.3 (2016)	10.0	10.5 (2016)
Myanmar	...	...	...	...	...	...
Philippines	8.9	8.4 (2017)	9.0	8.7 (2017)	8.8	8.2 (2017)
Singapore	11.3 (2012)	11.7 (2018)	10.8 (2012)	11.3 (2018)	11.7 (2012)	12.2 (2018)
Thailand	7.6	8.4 (2018)	7.4	8.2 (2018)	7.8	8.6 (2018)
Timor-Leste	...	...	...	...	...	...
Viet Nam	7.6 (2009)	...	7.1 (2009)	...	8.2 (2009)	...
The Pacific						
Cook Islands	9.9 (2006)	...	9.8 (2006)	...	10.0 (2006)	...
Fiji	9.2 (2007)	10.6 (2017)	9.2 (2007)	10.7 (2017)	9.3 (2007)	10.6 (2017)
Kiribati	...	...	...	...	...	...
Marshall Islands	10.9 (2011)	...	10.7 (2011)	...	11.1 (2011)	...
Micronesia, Federated States of	...	...	...	...	...	...
Nauru	...	...	...	...	...	...
Niue	...	...	...	...	...	...
Palau	...	12.8 (2013)	...	12.9 (2013)	...	12.8 (2013)
Papua New Guinea	...	...	...	...	...	...
Samoa	11.7 (2011)	...	11.8 (2011)	...	11.6 (2011)	...
Solomon Islands	...	...	...	...	...	...
Tonga	10.9 (2011)	...	10.9 (2011)	...	10.9 (2011)	...
Tuvalu	...	...	...	...	...	...
Vanuatu	...	...	...	...	...	...
Developed ADB Member Economies						
Australia	12.3 (2012)	12.6 (2018)	12.3 (2012)	12.6 (2018)	12.3 (2012)	12.5 (2018)
Japan	12.5	...	12.2	...	12.9	...
New Zealand	13.4 (2012)	13.3 (2016)	13.3 (2012)	13.3 (2016)	13.4 (2012)	13.4 (2016)
WORLD	...	...	...	...	...	...

... = data not available, ADB = Asian Development Bank.

a Refers to the expected number of years of schooling from primary to tertiary level of education.

b Refers to the average number of completed years of education among population aged 25 years and older by highest level of education attained, excluding years spent repeating individual grades.

c UNESCO Institute for Statistics estimate.

d National estimate.

Source: United Nations Educational, Scientific and Cultural Organization (UNESCO) Institute for Statistics. UIS.Stat Database. http://data.uis.unesco.org/ (accessed 27 May 2021). For expected years of schooling, for Taipei,China: Government of Taipei,China, Ministry of Education. https://english.moe.gov.tw/cp-87-14508-95005-1.html (accessed 27 May 2021).

Table 2.1.12: Education Resources

ADB Regional Member	Pupil/Trained Teacher Ratio[a]				Pupil/Qualified Teacher Ratio[b]			
	Primary		Secondary		Primary		Secondary	
	2010	2020	2010	2020	2010	2020	2010	2020
Developing ADB Member Economies								
Central and West Asia								
Afghanistan	...	...	...	...	...	61.7 (2018)	...	42.1 (2018)
Armenia	27.4 (2005)	...	...	13.3 (2019)	...	21.4 (2019)	...	9.9 (2019)
Azerbaijan	11.9 (2012)	15.8 (2019)	...	...	...	15.8 (2019)	...	7.9 (2019)
Georgia	9.4 (2009)	...	8.0 (2009)	...	...	...	...	...
Kazakhstan	...	16.8	...	8.3	...	16.8	...	8.3
Kyrgyz Republic	33.2 (2012)	26.1 (2017)	16.2 (2012)	14.0 (2017)	48.8 (2002)	...	...	...
Pakistan	49.3 (2012)	59.6 (2019)	...	...	...	...	...	...
Tajikistan	24.5 (2012)	22.3 (2017)	17.0 (2004)	...	...	23.0 (2017)	...	...
Turkmenistan	...	25.9 (2019)	...	9.3 (2019)	...	25.7 (2019)	...	9.3 (2019)
Uzbekistan	15.6 (2011)	21.1 (2019)	13.3 (2011)	11.0 (2019)	15.4 (2012)	21.1 (2019)	13.1 (2012)	10.9 (2019)
East Asia								
China, People's Republic of	...	...	...	...	...	17.1 (2019)	...	14.2 (2019)
Hong Kong, China	15.1 (2012)	13.7 (2019)	16.0 (2012)	11.4 (2019)	...	13.2 (2019)	...	11.0 (2019)
Korea, Republic of	...	...	...	...	...	...	...	...
Mongolia	29.0 (2012)	34.2 (2019)	14.8	15.3 (2019)	...	32.3 (2019)	...	14.1 (2019)
Taipei,China	...	...	...	...	...	...	...	...
South Asia								
Bangladesh	78.3 (2009)	59.6 (2017)	57.4 (2012)	63.4 (2019)	...	30.1 (2018)	...	35.1 (2018)
Bhutan	32.7 (2008)	32.0	28.5 (2008)	10.8 (2018)	...	32.0	...	10.8 (2018)
India	...	37.8 (2019)	...	28.4 (2019)	...	30.1 (2019)	...	24.7 (2019)
Maldives	14.7 (2012)	10.9 (2019)	18.4 (2002)	5.8 (2019)	...	21.9 (2019)	...	7.2 (2019)
Nepal	29.7 (2012)	20.3 (2019)	43.0 (2011)	33.9 (2019)	...	20.4 (2019)	...	31.8 (2019)
Sri Lanka	29.2 (2011)	26.5 (2018)	21.0 (2011)	22.1 (2018)	...	26.5 (2018)	...	22.3 (2018)
Southeast Asia								
Brunei Darussalam	12.0 (2012)	11.3 (2019)	10.9 (2012)	9.0 (2019)	...	9.8 (2019)	...	8.9 (2019)
Cambodia	45.7 (2012)	41.9 (2019)	29.1 (2007)	...	...	41.9 (2019)	...	...
Indonesia	...	...	...	...	...	19.0 (2018)	...	15.8 (2018)
Lao People's Democratic Republic	27.9 (2012)	22.2 (2019)	18.7 (2012)	17.6 (2019)	...	24.8 (2018)	...	22.4 (2017)
Malaysia	12.4 (2012)	11.8 (2017)	14.0 (2012)	12.2 (2018)	...	11.7 (2017)	...	12.0 (2019)
Myanmar	28.3	25.6 (2018)	34.5	30.6 (2018)	...	26.7 (2018)	...	28.1 (2018)
Philippines	...	25.7 (2019)	...	25.2 (2019)	...	25.8 (2019)	...	25.2 (2019)
Singapore	18.5 (2009)	14.6 (2018)	16.3 (2009)	11.5 (2018)	18.2 (2009)	14.3 (2018)	16.2 (2009)	11.3 (2018)
Thailand	...	13.0 (2019)	...	26.2 (2019)	...	13.0 (2019)	...	26.2 (2019)
Timor-Leste	...	...	...	...	...	34.8 (2019)	...	32.3 (2019)
Viet Nam	19.5 (2012)	21.9 (2019)	...	...	...	...	...	...
The Pacific								
Cook Islands	15.5 (2012)	16.7 (2019)	15.6 (2011)	14.8 (2019)	...	16.7 (2019)	...	14.8 (2019)
Fiji	28.0 (2012)	21.2 (2019)	19.3 (2012)	19.3 (2012)	...	19.6 (2019)	...	...
Kiribati	29.3 (2008)	35.4 (2016)	28.1 (2008)	...	...	25.6 (2017)	...	...
Marshall Islands	...	...	...	...	...	...	...	...
Micronesia, Federated States of	...	22.6 (2016)	...	...	...	24.9 (2019)	...	...
Nauru	26.8 (2007)	40.2 (2016)	57.4 (2007)	...	...	28.1 (2019)	...	60.2 (2019)
Niue	...	43.4 (2019)	...	39.8 (2019)	...	16.7 (2019)	...	6.2 (2019)
Palau	...	...	...	...	...	...	...	...
Papua New Guinea	...	...	27.4 (2012)	27.4 (2012)	...	...	...	...
Samoa	...	...	...	...	...	...	...	...
Solomon Islands	35.2 (2012)	29.9 (2019)	37.1 (2012)	37.1 (2012)	...	29.9 (2019)	...	...
Tonga	...	23.4 (2015)	...	24.8 (2015)	...	23.4 (2015)	...	18.3 (2015)
Tuvalu	...	20.3 (2019)	...	13.4 (2019)	...	15.9 (2019)	...	8.1 (2019)
Vanuatu	23.8 (2007)	...	...	...	...	37.0 (2015)	...	26.1 (2015)
Developed ADB Member Economies								
Australia	...	...	...	...	...	...	...	...
Japan	...	...	...	...	...	...	...	...
New Zealand	...	...	...	...	...	...	...	...
WORLD[c]	**...**	**27.9** (2019)	**...**	**21.1** (2019)	**...**	**24.7** (2019)	**...**	**17.9** (2019)

... = data not available, ADB = Asian Development Bank.

a The UNESCO Institute for Statistics (UIS) defines a trained teacher as one who has received at least the minimum organized pedagogical teacher training pre-service and in-service required for teaching at the relevant level in a given economy in a given academic year.

b The UIS defines a qualified teacher as one who has at least the minimum academic qualifications required for teaching their subjects at the relevant level in a given economy in a given academic year.

c UIS estimation.

Source: United Nations Educational, Scientific and Cultural Organization (UNESCO) Institute for Statistics Database. UIS.Stat. http://data.uis.unesco.org/ (accessed 10 June 2021).

Table 2.1.13: Health Care Resources
(per 1,000 population)

ADB Regional Member	Physicians[a]		Hospital Beds[b]	
	2000	2019	2000	2017
Developing ADB Member Economies				
Central and West Asia				
Afghanistan	0.24	0.28 (2016)	0.4	0.4 (2017)
Armenia	2.84	4.40 (2017)	3.7	4.2 (2015)
Azerbaijan	3.66	3.45 (2014)	5.1	4.8 (2014)
Georgia	4.45	7.08 (2019)	3.0	2.9 (2014)
Kazakhstan	3.93	3.98 (2014)	7.3	6.1 (2014)
Kyrgyz Republic	2.34	2.21 (2014)	4.8	4.4 (2014)
Pakistan	0.81	1.12 (2019)	0.6	0.6 (2017)
Tajikistan	1.70	1.72 (2014)	5.1	4.7 (2014)
Turkmenistan	2.27	2.22 (2014)	4.1	4.0 (2014)
Uzbekistan	2.54	2.37 (2014)	4.4	4.0 (2014)
East Asia				
China, People's Republic of	1.43	1.98 (2017)	2.5	4.3 (2017)
Hong Kong, China	...	...	...	...
Korea, Republic of	1.98	2.41 (2018)	8.7	12.4 (2018)
Mongolia	2.76	3.85 (2018)	6.0	8.0 (2017)
Taipei,China[c]	1.91	2.40 (2019)	6.9	7.1 (2019)
South Asia				
Bangladesh	0.36	0.64 (2019)	0.3 (2005)	0.8 (2016)
Bhutan	0.02	0.46 (2019)	1.7 (2006)	1.7 (2012)
India	0.69	0.93 (2019)	0.5	0.5 (2017)
Maldives	1.44	1.71 (2018)	4.3 (2009)	...
Nepal	0.21 (2004)	0.81 (2019)	5.0 (2006)	0.3 (2012)
Sri Lanka	0.72	1.15 (2019)	3.5	4.2 (2017)
Southeast Asia				
Brunei Darussalam	1.45	1.61 (2017)	2.5	2.9 (2017)
Cambodia	0.23	0.19 (2014)	0.8	0.9 (2016)
Indonesia	0.24	0.47 (2019)	0.6	1.0 (2017)
Lao People's Democratic Republic	0.78	0.37 (2017)	0.7	1.5 (2012)
Malaysia	1.17	1.54 (2015)	1.8	1.9 (2017)
Myanmar	0.52	0.74 (2019)	0.6 (2006)	1.0 (2017)
Philippines	1.27	0.60 (2017)	1.1	1.0 (2014)
Singapore	1.72	2.29 (2016)	3.1 (2008)	2.5 (2017)
Thailand	0.39	0.92 (2019)	2.1	2.1 (2010)
Timor-Leste	0.08	0.77 (2019)	5.9	5.9 (2010)
Viet Nam	0.71	0.83 (2016)	2.9	2.6 (2014)
The Pacific				
Cook Islands	1.29 (2009)	1.41 (2014)	...	...
Fiji	0.43	0.86 (2015)	2.1 (2009)	2.0 (2016)
Kiribati	0.40	0.20 (2013)	1.4	1.9 (2016)
Marshall Islands	0.57	0.42 (2012)	2.7	2.7 (2010)
Micronesia, Federated States of	0.18	0.18 (2010)	3.2 (2009)	...
Nauru	1.10	1.35 (2015)	5.0	5.0 (2010)
Niue	1.88 (2008)	...	...	...
Palau	1.61	1.42 (2014)	4.8	4.8 (2010)
Papua New Guinea	0.05	0.07 (2019)	...	...
Samoa	0.34	0.34 (2016)	1.0 (2007)	...
Solomon Islands	0.22	0.19 (2016)	1.4 (2005)	1.4 (2012)
Tonga	0.56	0.54 (2013)	2.6	2.6 (2010)
Tuvalu	1.09	0.91 (2014)	5.6 (2001)	...
Vanuatu	0.12	0.17 (2016)	1.7 (2008)	...
Developed ADB Member Economies				
Australia	3.34	3.76 (2018)	3.8	3.8 (2016)
Japan	2.21	2.48 (2018)	13.5	13.0 (2018)
New Zealand	2.61	3.42 (2018)	2.8	2.6 (2019)
WORLD	**1.33**	**1.57** (2017)	**2.6**	**2.9** (2017)

... = data not available, ADB = Asian Development Bank.

a Main source of data is the United Nations Statistics Division's Global SDG Indicators Database.
b Main source of data is the World Health Organization's Global Health Observatory.
c Physicians include doctors of Chinese medicine.

Sources: World Bank. World Development Indicators. https://databank.worldbank.org/source/world-development-indicators (accessed 31 May and 1 June 2021); World Health Organization. Global Health Observatory. https://www.who.int/data/gho (accessed 31 May and 1 June 2021); and United Nations Statistics Division. Global SDG Indicators Database. https://unstats.un.org/sdgs/indicators/database/ (accessed 31 May 2021). For Taipei,China: Government of Taipei,China, Directorate-General of Budget, Accounting and Statistics. https://eng.dgbas.gov.tw/mp.asp (accessed 31 May and 1 June 2021).

Table 2.1.14: Adults Aged 15 Years and Older Living with HIV
('000)

ADB Regional Member	All Adults		Women	
	2010	2019	2010	2019
Developing ADB Member Economies				
Central and West Asia				
Afghanistan	4.3	10.0	1.2	3.0
Armenia	3.2	3.5	1.1	1.2
Azerbaijan	9.3	9.6	3.2	3.3
Georgia	2.8	9.0	1.0	2.9
Kazakhstan	13.0	33.0	4.0	11.0
Kyrgyz Republic	4.0	9.7	1.2	3.3
Pakistan	67.0	180.0	20.0	53.0
Tajikistan	4.9	13.0	1.1	3.3
Turkmenistan	...	...	...	...
Uzbekistan	19.0	44.0	6.6	16.0
East Asia				
China, People's Republic of	...	...	...	...
Hong Kong, China	...	...	...	...
Korea, Republic of	...	...	...	...
Mongolia	0.5	1.0	0.1	0.2
Taipei,China	...	...	...	...
South Asia				
Bangladesh	...	...	...	...
Bhutan	...	...	...	...
India	...	...	...	...
Maldives	...	...	...	...
Nepal	30.0	28.0	9.6	11.0
Sri Lanka	3.9	3.6	1.1	1.0
Southeast Asia				
Brunei Darussalam	...	...	...	...
Cambodia	79.0	70.0	40.0	36.0
Indonesia	...	...	...	...
Lao People's Democratic Republic	8.4	13.0	3.6	5.5
Malaysia	71.0	87.0	12.0	15.0
Myanmar	220.0	230.0	83.0	88.0
Philippines	17.0	96.0	1.0	5.8
Singapore	6.5	7.9	1.0	1.0
Thailand	570.0	470.0	250.0	210.0
Timor-Leste	...	...	...	...
Viet Nam	210.0	220.0	61.0	70.0
The Pacific				
Cook Islands	...	...	...	...
Fiji	0.5	1.0	0.2	0.5
Kiribati	...	...	...	...
Marshall Islands	...	...	...	...
Micronesia, Federated States of	...	...	...	...
Nauru	...	...	...	...
Niue	...	...	...	...
Palau	...	...	...	...
Papua New Guinea	30.0	48.0	17.0	28.0
Samoa	...	...	...	...
Solomon Islands	...	...	...	...
Tonga	...	...	...	...
Tuvalu	...	...	...	...
Vanuatu	...	...	...	...
Developed ADB Member Economies				
Australia	21.0	29.0	2.3	3.5
Japan	...	...	...	...
New Zealand	2.3	3.5	0.5	1.0
WORLD	28,300.0	36,200.0	14,900.0	19,200.0

... = data not available, 0.0 = magnitude is less than half of unit employed, ADB = Asian Development Bank.

Note: Figures reported in this table are based on modelled HIV estimates. According to the Joint United Nations Programme on HIV/AIDS, modelled HIV estimates provide a scientifically appropriate way of describing HIV epidemic levels and trends, and are required because it is impossible to count the exact number of people living and newly infected with HIV, or people who have died from AIDS-related causes in any economy. Doing so would require regularly testing every person for HIV and investigating all deaths, which is logistically impossible and ethically problematic.

Source: Joint United Nations Programme on HIV/AIDS (UNAIDS). AIDSInfo. https://aidsinfo.unaids.org/ (accessed 2 June 2021).

Data Issues and Comparability

Demographic data are based on vital registration records, censuses, and surveys. Since vital registration records in many developing ADB member economies are incomplete, they cannot be used for statistical purposes. In most economies, population censuses, which are used to provide more accurate estimates of population sizes, are conducted every 10 years. Population numbers in between census years are products of imputation methods that use various population distributional assumptions.

The United Nations (UN) Department of Economics and Social Affairs' Population Division uses future trends on fertility, mortality, and international migration to project population numbers through to 2100. The medium-fertility variant included in the UN's World Population Prospects 2019 assumes, over the remainder of the century, a decline of fertility in economies where large families are still prevalent, a slight increase of fertility in several economies where women have fewer than two live births on average over a lifetime, and continued reductions in mortality at all ages.

Urban population statistics are compiled according to each economy's national definition, as there is no agreed international standard for defining an urban area, which poses constraints in comparability of urban and city indicators across economies. Data from World Urbanization Prospects were used when national estimates were not available.

Household surveys, which are the best source of labor force data, are not carried out in all economies on a regular basis. Some economies rely on census data supplemented by enterprise surveys and unemployment registration records, which are often incomplete and may refer only to formal employment. Furthermore, a breakdown by economic activities also may not be available. An initiative is underway to adopt new standards for work and employment statistics, following the recommendations of the 19th International Conference of Labour Statisticians in 2013. These recommendations were adopted by Armenia, beginning 2018; Azerbaijan, beginning 2015; Brunei Darussalam, beginning 2017; Georgia, beginning 2010; the Lao People's Democratic Republic, beginning 2017; Malaysia, beginning 2019; Mongolia, beginning 2019; Nepal, beginning 2018; Timor-Leste, beginning 2010; and Uzbekistan, beginning 2017. Hence, data for these years may not be directly comparable with data in other years. For all other economies, the conceptual definitions used are based on the old framework.

Table 2.2.1: Gross Domestic Product at Purchasing Power Parity
(current international dollars, million)

ADB Regional Member	2010	2015	2016	2017	2018	2019	2020
Developing ADB Member Economies							
Central and West Asia	**1,479,140**	**1,898,465**	**1,950,987**	**2,052,148**	**2,204,929**	**2,315,143**	**...**
Afghanistan	51,342	74,020	70,098	74,712	77,416	81,880	81,268
Armenia	21,598	29,167	31,429	35,677	38,433	41,927	39,351
Azerbaijan	135,151	144,146	140,230	139,153	144,632	150,865	146,111
Georgia	28,643	45,036	47,930	50,663	54,391	58,121	55,201
Kazakhstan	313,789	407,416	423,833	448,473	478,069	508,501	505,424
Kyrgyz Republic	16,810	25,107	28,459	31,280	33,235	35,385	32,728
Pakistan	698,014	872,097	898,016	950,382	1,030,000	1,061,931	1,072,812
Tajikistan	17,527	26,634	26,986	28,887	31,829	34,794	35,914
Turkmenistan	49,909	76,309	78,493	81,788	88,944	96,235	...
Uzbekistan	146,357	198,534	205,512	211,135	227,980	245,505	252,573
East Asia	**15,207,591**	**21,275,951**	**22,304,490**	**23,611,519**	**25,639,605**	**27,428,226**	**28,315,496**
China, People's Republic of	12,378,809	17,796,747	18,712,097	19,887,033	21,739,076	23,443,654	24,273,360
Hong Kong, China	345,487	411,294	419,811	442,388	465,904	466,255	443,204
Korea, Republic of	1,573,258	1,933,589	2,026,968	2,103,651	2,192,613	2,215,708	2,243,095
Mongolia	20,621	32,285	32,833	35,222	38,682	41,404	39,669
Taipei,China	889,416	1,102,036	1,112,781	1,143,224	1,203,330	1,261,205	1,316,167
South Asia	**5,823,154**	**8,053,216**	**8,699,731**	**9,326,945**	**10,175,923**	**10,804,965**	**...**
Bangladesh	359,947	555,570	608,047	664,404	733,857	807,855	852,325
Bhutan	4,588	6,915	7,704	8,307	8,767	9,411	...
India	5,229,334	7,159,798	7,735,002	8,276,934	9,029,376	9,562,006	8,979,567
Maldives	4,649	7,628	8,279	8,930	9,978	10,809	...
Nepal	58,606	80,943	81,509	98,516	108,571	117,866	116,802
Sri Lanka	166,030	242,361	259,190	269,854	285,374	297,019	289,888
Southeast Asia	**5,058,508**	**6,618,089**	**6,936,347**	**7,364,097**	**7,931,070**	**8,444,463**	**...**
Brunei Darussalam	31,199	25,949	23,633	25,891	26,526	28,045	28,726
Cambodia	34,739	52,598	57,942	62,891	69,211	75,416	73,932
Indonesia	2,056,981	2,647,707	2,744,897	2,894,126	3,116,959	3,331,808	3,302,377
Lao People's Democratic Republic	22,601	41,583	46,850	50,464	54,904	58,446	59,741
Malaysia	578,512	750,777	783,874	829,297	889,715	944,564	902,586
Myanmar	164,098	227,959	213,835	225,517	243,827	264,138	...
Philippines	528,684	733,864	798,601	854,095	930,065	1,004,590	919,424
Singapore	382,249	481,405	501,388	535,131	567,145	585,034	560,200
Thailand	886,663	1,087,189	1,146,014	1,205,866	1,286,547	1,339,162	1,272,883
Timor-Leste	2,148	3,484	3,817	3,911	3,962	4,788	...
Viet Nam	370,634	565,575	615,496	676,910	742,209	808,472	842,042
The Pacific[a]	**32,548**	**48,296**	**50,920**	**53,810**	**55,493**	**58,629**	**...**
Cook Islands	...	...	...	...	...	...	...
Fiji	6,805	10,782	11,020	11,784	12,527	12,694	...
Kiribati	177	234	248	255	267	282	...
Marshall Islands	183	201	203	215	227	247	...
Micronesia, Federated States of	336	365	372	389	399	...	...
Nauru	62	157	143	137	149	152	...
Niue	...	...	...	...	...	...	...
Palau	238	313	320	319	344	345	...
Papua New Guinea	21,314	32,162	34,283	36,162	36,927	39,789	38,712
Samoa	1,019	1,188	1,241	1,265	1,301	1,346	...
Solomon Islands	1,225	1,476	1,579	1,694	...	...	...
Tonga	479	582	627	660	677	695	...
Tuvalu	30	40	47	49	53	60	...
Vanuatu	680	798	837	880	927	...	...
Developed ADB Member Economies	**5,528,933**	**6,475,077**	**6,492,453**	**6,658,563**	**6,833,852**	**6,964,906**	**...**
Australia	865,877	1,102,403	1,145,197	1,192,763	1,255,451	1,324,171	1,349,040
Japan	4,527,143	5,199,915	5,158,900	5,262,255	5,363,113	5,416,301	5,242,080
New Zealand	135,912	172,759	188,356	203,545	215,288	224,433	...
DEVELOPING ADB MEMBER ECONOMIES[a]	**27,600,941**	**37,894,017**	**39,942,475**	**42,408,518**	**46,007,020**	**49,051,426**	**...**
ALL ADB REGIONAL MEMBERS[a]	**33,129,874**	**44,369,094**	**46,434,927**	**49,067,081**	**52,840,872**	**56,016,331**	**...**

... = data not available, ADB = Asian Development Bank.

Note: Gross domestic product figures in local currency units are obtained from economy's official sources and converted into a common currency using the purchasing power parity (PPP) from the World Bank's World Development Indicators. For years prior to 2011 (as featured in the Key Indicators Database), the PPP figures are extrapolated from the revised 2011 International Comparison Program (ICP). For 2012–2016, PPP estimates are interpolated from the two ICP reference years 2011 and 2017. For 2017 onward, the PPP figures are extrapolated from the 2017 ICP PPPs or imputed based on a regression model. Moreover, PPP figures for 2011 and 2017 are based on results from the ICP benchmark rounds. For Taipei,China, the PPP figures for 2000–2010 (available in the Key Indicators Database) and 2018–2020 are Asian Development Bank estimates using data from economy's official sources and the World Bank, while the PPP conversion factor used for 2011–2017 was from the World Bank's ICP 2017 database.

a For estimating aggregates, imputation was done for economies with missing data by substituting available data from the nearest years.

Source: Asian Development Bank estimates.

Table 2.2.2: Gross Domestic Product
(current $ million)

ADB Regional Member	2010	2015	2016	2017	2018	2019	2020
Developing ADB Member Economies							
Central and West Asia	**492,970**	**683,266**	**628,128**	**669,374**	**666,273**	**653,819**	**...**
Afghanistan	16,078	20,607	18,020	18,896	18,419	18,904	19,793
Armenia	9,260	10,553	10,546	11,527	12,458	13,619	12,641
Azerbaijan	52,906	53,076	37,867	40,867	47,112	48,174	42,607
Georgia	12,243	14,954	15,142	16,243	17,600	17,477	15,892
Kazakhstan	148,047	184,388	137,278	166,806	179,340	181,667	171,240
Kyrgyz Republic	4,794	6,678	6,813	7,703	8,271	8,871	7,736
Pakistan	174,508	267,035	277,521	302,710	284,150	253,847	256,777
Tajikistan	5,642	8,271	6,992	7,536	7,765	8,301	7,997
Turkmenistan	22,582	35,855	36,169	37,926	40,765	45,231	...
Uzbekistan	46,909	81,847	81,779	59,160	50,393	57,727	57,707
East Asia	**7,911,047**	**13,383,417**	**13,608,226**	**14,877,030**	**16,604,422**	**16,920,607**	**17,388,963**
China, People's Republic of	6,087,192	11,061,573	11,233,315	12,310,490	13,894,907	14,279,968	14,722,801
Hong Kong, China	228,639	309,386	320,840	341,242	361,692	363,016	346,584
Korea, Republic of	1,143,672	1,466,039	1,499,680	1,623,074	1,725,373	1,651,423	1,637,896
Mongolia	7,189	11,750	11,187	11,426	13,109	13,997	13,137
Taipei,China	444,354	534,670	543,205	590,798	609,342	612,203	668,546
South Asia	**1,861,270**	**2,451,609**	**2,624,651**	**2,994,020**	**3,158,768**	**3,317,417**	**...**
Bangladesh	114,508	194,466	220,837	245,633	269,628	301,051	329,484
Bhutan	1,548	2,004	2,159	2,450	2,447	2,531	...
India	1,669,620	2,146,759	2,290,587	2,624,329	2,761,676	2,889,934	2,664,748
Maldives	2,588	4,109	4,379	4,736	5,327	5,642	...
Nepal	16,281	23,667	24,288	29,443	31,726	34,268	33,079
Sri Lanka	56,726	80,604	82,401	87,428	87,963	83,991	80,677
Southeast Asia	**1,999,422**	**2,480,721**	**2,598,226**	**2,800,455**	**2,998,366**	**3,171,824**	**...**
Brunei Darussalam	13,707	12,930	11,400	12,128	13,567	13,469	12,016
Cambodia	11,242	18,050	20,017	22,177	24,572	27,089	25,291
Indonesia	755,094	860,854	931,877	1,015,619	1,042,272	1,119,091	1,058,424
Lao People's Democratic Republic	6,747	14,426	15,913	17,071	18,142	18,741	19,082
Malaysia	255,018	301,355	301,255	319,109	358,712	364,684	336,664
Myanmar	...	62,543	60,100	60,793	64,896	69,329	...
Philippines	208,369	306,446	318,627	328,481	346,842	376,823	361,489
Singapore	239,808	307,999	318,753	343,332	375,970	374,398	339,988
Thailand	341,105	401,282	413,357	456,367	506,620	544,261	501,795
Timor-Leste	882	1,594	1,651	1,599	1,560	2,018	...
Viet Nam	115,932	193,241	205,276	223,780	245,214	261,921	271,158
The Pacific[a]	**21,198**	**31,065**	**30,600**	**33,329**	**35,070**	**35,778**	**...**
Cook Islands	241	302	310	346	362	379	284
Fiji	3,140	4,682	4,930	5,353	5,581	5,496	...
Kiribati	156	171	178	187	197	198	...
Marshall Islands	162	185	201	213	221	240	244
Micronesia, Federated States of	297	316	332	367	402	...	...
Nauru	51	90	102	111	120	115	117
Niue	18	24	25	26	30	31	...
Palau	184	279	297	288	285	280	...
Papua New Guinea	14,251	21,723	20,759	22,743	24,110	24,829	23,592
Samoa	692	787	822	825	835	847	772
Solomon Islands	903	1,307	1,379	1,484	...	...	...
Tonga	371	403	421	461	480	508	...
Tuvalu	31	35	41	45	48	54	...
Vanuatu	701	760	804	880	915	...	...
Developed ADB Member Economies	**7,099,186**	**5,843,499**	**6,427,156**	**6,488,514**	**6,630,276**	**6,719,108**	**...**
Australia	1,193,597	1,220,504	1,234,535	1,350,726	1,381,159	1,357,436	1,366,360
Japan	5,759,072	4,444,931	5,003,678	4,930,837	5,036,892	5,148,781	5,048,688
New Zealand	146,518	178,064	188,943	206,951	212,226	212,891	...
DEVELOPING ADB MEMBER ECONOMIES[a]	**12,285,907**	**19,030,078**	**19,489,831**	**21,374,209**	**23,462,898**	**24,099,445**	**...**
ALL ADB REGIONAL MEMBERS[a]	**19,385,093**	**24,873,577**	**25,916,987**	**27,862,723**	**30,093,175**	**30,818,553**	**...**

... = data not available, $ = United States dollars, ADB = Asian Development Bank.

Note: Gross domestic product figures in local currency units are obtained from economy's official sources and converted to United States dollars using the official exchange rates from the International Monetary Fund. The exchange rates used are expressed as the average rate for a period of time (average of period), calculated as annual averages based on the monthly averages (local currency units relative to the United States dollar). For Myanmar, the 2010 figure for GDP in US dollars was converted from the domestic currency using the World Bank's alternative conversion factor to calculate the aggregate for Southeast Asia.

a For estimating aggregates, imputation was done for economies with missing data by substituting available data from the nearest years.

Source: Asian Development Bank estimates.

Table 2.2.3: Gross Domestic Product per Capita at Purchasing Power Parity
(current international dollars)

ADB Regional Member	2010	2015	2016	2017	2018	2019	2020
Developing ADB Member Economies							
Central and West Asia	**5,344**	**6,246**	**6,235**	**6,341**	**6,761**	**6,969**	**...**
Afghanistan	2,097	2,731	2,535	2,647	2,574	2,665	2,589
Armenia	7,093	9,707	10,503	11,974	12,945	14,153	13,286
Azerbaijan	14,927	14,938	14,371	14,121	14,551	15,050	14,514
Georgia	7,564	12,089	12,858	13,590	14,596	15,623	14,828
Kazakhstan	19,225	23,224	23,819	24,863	26,158	27,466	26,948
Kyrgyz Republic	3,103	4,259	4,728	5,094	5,312	5,538	5,035
Pakistan	4,023	4,549	4,517	4,576	4,974	5,029	4,984
Tajikistan	2,331	3,151	3,121	3,269	3,531	3,777	3,817
Turkmenistan	9,811	13,712	13,862	14,205	15,202	16,196	...
Uzbekistan	5,126	6,343	6,453	6,517	6,919	7,318	7,385
East Asia	**10,685**	**14,493**	**15,096**	**15,894**	**17,193**	**18,332**	**18,902**
China, People's Republic of	9,232	12,866	13,440	14,204	15,468	16,626	17,193
Hong Kong, China	49,185	56,409	57,221	59,849	62,529	62,106	59,238
Korea, Republic of	31,748	37,902	39,575	40,957	42,487	42,849	43,319
Mongolia	7,637	10,762	10,591	11,362	12,088	12,547	11,667
Taipei,China	38,435	46,969	47,320	48,533	51,032	53,450	55,808
South Asia	**4,212**	**5,393**	**5,758**	**6,104**	**6,592**	**6,925**	**...**
Bangladesh	2,422	3,496	3,781	4,084	4,458	4,852	5,059
Bhutan	6,594	9,135	10,024	11,425	11,938	12,689	...
India	4,409	5,575	5,953	6,300	6,804	7,131	6,627
Maldives	11,813	16,786	17,525	18,165	19,486	20,243	...
Nepal	2,232	2,896	2,877	3,431	3,731	3,968	3,894
Sri Lanka	8,039	11,560	12,224	12,584	13,169	13,623	13,225
Southeast Asia	**8,585**	**10,522**	**10,903**	**11,442**	**12,192**	**12,850**	**...**
Brunei Darussalam	80,659	62,922	56,638	60,282	59,959	61,033	63,329
Cambodia	2,459	3,485	3,786	4,053	4,398	4,726	4,571
Indonesia	8,656	10,359	10,619	11,073	11,799	12,483	12,222
Lao People's Democratic Republic	3,741	6,405	7,113	7,552	8,099	8,499	8,563
Malaysia	20,236	24,074	24,780	25,897	27,475	29,043	27,638
Myanmar	3,272	4,346	4,041	4,224	4,527	4,861	...
Philippines	5,677	7,278	7,789	8,199	8,795	9,362	8,432
Singapore	75,295	86,975	89,417	95,350	100,581	102,573	98,526
Thailand	13,450	15,993	16,793	17,505	18,617	19,320	18,312
Timor-Leste	1,965	2,913	3,131	3,145	3,125	3,703	...
Viet Nam	4,257	6,132	6,600	7,179	7,781	8,379	8,629
The Pacific[a]	**3,504**	**4,559**	**4,682**	**4,816**	**4,845**	**4,993**	**...**
Cook Islands	...	...	...	...	...	...	...
Fiji	7,999	12,401	12,620	13,317	14,135	14,273	...
Kiribati	1,714	2,122	2,225	2,256	2,333	2,431	...
Marshall Islands	3,455	3,721	3,751	3,949	4,164	4,509	...
Micronesia, Federated States of	3,268	3,516	3,578	3,737	3,828	...	...
Nauru	6,361	14,516	12,976	12,263	13,115	13,134	...
Niue	...	...	...	...	...	...	...
Palau	13,035	17,713	17,874	17,823	19,620	19,736	...
Papua New Guinea	3,021	3,910	4,042	4,135	4,094	4,278	4,037
Samoa	5,479	6,132	6,352	6,420	6,549	6,721	...
Solomon Islands	2,205	2,359	2,469	2,594	...	...	...
Tonga	4,664	5,724	6,196	6,557	6,769	6,978	...
Tuvalu	2,726	3,701	4,421	4,637	4,945	5,620	...
Vanuatu	2,838	2,972	3,071	3,157	3,258	...	...
Developed ADB Member Economies	**35,797**	**41,623**	**41,645**	**42,628**	**43,691**	**44,495**	**...**
Australia	39,301	46,288	47,340	48,483	50,253	52,203	52,497
Japan	35,349	40,899	40,623	41,505	42,386	42,896	41,658
New Zealand	31,239	37,480	39,956	42,285	43,931	45,074	...
DEVELOPING ADB MEMBER ECONOMIES[a]	**7,498**	**9,704**	**10,116**	**10,624**	**11,436**	**12,089**	**...**
ALL ADB REGIONAL MEMBERS[a]	**8,637**	**10,927**	**11,314**	**11,829**	**12,643**	**13,293**	**...**

... = data not available, ADB = Asian Development Bank.

Note: The figures in the table are calculated as gross domestic product (GDP) at purchasing power parity (PPP) divided by the midyear population. GDP figures in local currency units are obtained from economy's official sources and converted into a common currency using the purchasing power parity (PPP) from the World Bank's World Development Indicators. For years prior to 2011 (as featured in the Key Indicators Database), the PPP figures are extrapolated from the revised 2011 International Comparison Program (ICP). For 2012–2016, PPP estimates are interpolated from the two ICP reference years 2011 and 2017. For 2017 onward, the PPP figures are extrapolated from the 2017 ICP PPPs or imputed based on a regression model. Moreover, PPP figures for 2011 and 2017 are based on results from the ICP benchmark rounds. For Taipei,China, the PPP figures for 2000–2010 (available in the Key Indicators Database) and 2018–2020 are Asian Development Bank estimates using data from economy's official sources and the World Bank, while the PPP conversion factor used for 2011–2017 was from the World Bank's ICP 2017 database.

a For estimating aggregates, imputation was done for economies with missing data by substituting available data from the nearest years.

Source: Asian Development Bank estimates.

Table 2.2.4: Gross National Income per Capita, Atlas Method
(current $)

ADB Regional Member	2010	2015	2016	2017	2018	2019	2020
Developing ADB Member Economies							
Central and West Asia[a]	**1,577**	**2,200**	**2,013**	**1,960**	**1,990**	**1,986**	**...**
Afghanistan	510	600	550	530	520	530	500
Armenia	3,470	4,010	3,760	3,950	4,250	4,680	4,220
Azerbaijan	5,370	6,570	4,760	4,090	4,060	4,490	4,450
Georgia	3,210	4,410	4,080	4,040	4,460	4,690	4,290
Kazakhstan	7,440	11,380	8,770	8,040	8,070	8,820	8,680
Kyrgyz Republic	850	1,180	1,110	1,110	1,220	1,240	1,160
Pakistan	970	1,260	1,310	1,400	1,480	1,410	1,280
Tajikistan	920	1,260	1,110	1,030	1,030	1,070	1,060
Turkmenistan	4,070	7,030	6,830	6,380	6,740	7,220	...
Uzbekistan	1,390	2,600	2,650	2,350	2,020	1,800	1,670
East Asia[a]	**5,358**	**9,078**	**9,413**	**9,917**	**10,865**	**11,663**	**11,849**
China, People's Republic of	4,340	7,940	8,270	8,740	9,600	10,390	10,610
Hong Kong, China	33,620	41,180	42,970	46,390	50,060	50,480	48,630
Korea, Republic of	22,290	28,720	29,330	30,300	32,730	33,790	32,860
Mongolia	2,000	3,820	3,500	3,230	3,630	3,790	3,670
Taipei,China	19,903	23,316	23,440	24,473	26,239	27,473	28,686
South Asia[a]	**1,182**	**1,582**	**1,666**	**1,807**	**1,995**	**2,113**	**1,927**
Bangladesh	800	1,220	1,370	1,520	1,750	1,940	2,010
Bhutan	2,040	2,520	2,650	2,800	2,970	3,140	2,860
India	1,220	1,600	1,680	1,820	2,010	2,120	1,900
Maldives	5,960	7,650	8,070	8,600	9,210	9,670	6,830
Nepal	540	890	880	990	1,120	1,230	1,190
Sri Lanka	2,410	3,760	3,810	3,870	4,040	4,010	3,720
Southeast Asia[a]	**3,004**	**3,994**	**3,983**	**4,086**	**4,411**	**4,672**	**...**
Brunei Darussalam	33,300	38,850	33,170	29,800	29,390	32,230	...
Cambodia	750	1,060	1,140	1,230	1,380	1,530	1,490
Indonesia	2,530	3,430	3,400	3,530	3,840	4,050	3,870
Lao People's Democratic Republic	1,000	1,970	2,120	2,240	2,450	2,490	2,480
Malaysia	8,260	10,680	10,150	9,950	10,650	11,230	10,580
Myanmar	900	1,160	1,150	1,200	1,280	1,360	1,260
Philippines	2,370	3,380	3,450	3,530	3,710	3,850	3,430
Singapore	44,930	53,160	53,060	54,460	56,900	58,390	54,920
Thailand	4,580	5,710	5,700	5,970	6,610	7,260	7,050
Timor-Leste	2,850	2,200	1,750	1,780	1,800	2,020	1,830
Viet Nam	1,250	1,970	2,080	2,130	2,380	2,590	2,660
The Pacific[b]	**2,039**	**3,122**	**3,010**	**2,928**	**3,005**	**3,137**	**...**
Cook Islands	9,349	17,157	18,347	17,360	19,709	19,160	17,482
Fiji	3,650	5,100	5,280	5,370	5,910	5,800	4,720
Kiribati	2,050	3,470	2,920	3,020	3,080	3,340	3,010
Marshall Islands	3,550	4,250	4,200	4,390	4,780	5,010	...
Micronesia, Federated States of	2,900	3,490	3,410	3,450	3,400	4,010	...
Nauru	5,810	13,690	12,730	12,370	14,320	16,630	...
Niue	10,896 (2011)	...	...	14,016	...	...	...
Palau	11,400	15,860	16,680	16,650	17,810	16,500	...
Papua New Guinea	1,740	2,860	2,710	2,590	2,600	2,750	2,660
Samoa	3,240	3,960	4,110	4,070	4,030	4,200	4,070
Solomon Islands	1,470	2,130	2,150	2,220	2,360	2,370	2,300
Tonga	3,370	4,440	4,410	4,590	4,800	5,000	...
Tuvalu	4,400	5,440	5,060	4,810	5,440	5,620	5,820
Vanuatu	2,600	2,780	2,750	2,860	3,110	3,360	2,780
Developed ADB Member Economies[a]	**43,504**	**42,206**	**40,430**	**40,564**	**43,092**	**43,806**	**...**
Australia	46,630	60,500	54,140	51,560	53,190	55,100	53,730
Japan	43,440	38,840	37,860	38,490	41,150	41,580	...
New Zealand	29,680	40,650	39,440	38,910	41,680	42,610	...
DEVELOPING ADB MEMBER ECONOMIES[b]	**3,089**	**4,798**	**4,926**	**5,167**	**5,628**	**5,990**	**...**
ALL ADB REGIONAL MEMBERS[b]	**4,690**	**6,221**	**6,266**	**6,493**	**7,021**	**7,387**	**...**
WORLD	**9,426**	**10,672**	**10,415**	**10,492**	**11,162**	**11,553**	**...**

... = data not available, $ = United States dollars, ADB = Asian Development Bank.

Note: The Atlas method refers to a conversion factor that averages the exchange rate for a given year and the 2 preceding years, adjusted for differences in rates of inflation between the member economy and the G5 economies.

a Aggregates are weighted averages estimated using midyear population.

b Aggregates are weighted averages estimated using midyear population. For estimating aggregates, imputation was done for economies with missing data by substituting available data from the nearest years.

Sources: World Bank. World Development Indicators. https://databank.worldbank.org/source/world-development-indicators (accessed 25 June 2021). For the Cook Islands; Niue; and Taipei,China: Asian Development Bank estimates using the Atlas method based on economy's official sources.

Table 2.2.5: Gross Domestic Product per Capita
(current $)

ADB Regional Member	2010	2015	2016	2017	2018	2019	2020
Developing ADB Member Economies							
Central and West Asia	**1,781**	**2,290**	**2,007**	**2,068**	**2,043**	**1,968**	**...**
Afghanistan	657	776	652	670	612	615	631
Armenia	3,041	3,502	3,524	3,869	4,196	4,597	4,268
Azerbaijan	5,843	5,566	3,881	4,147	4,740	4,806	4,232
Georgia	3,233	4,020	4,062	4,357	4,723	4,698	4,269
Kazakhstan	9,070	10,666	7,715	9,248	9,813	9,813	9,130
Kyrgyz Republic	885	1,156	1,132	1,255	1,322	1,388	1,190
Pakistan	1,006	1,420	1,396	1,458	1,372	1,202	1,193
Tajikistan	750	1,002	809	853	862	901	850
Turkmenistan	4,439	6,559	6,388	6,587	6,967	7,612	...
Uzbekistan	1,643	2,662	2,568	1,826	1,529	1,721	1,687
East Asia	**5,558**	**9,161**	**9,210**	**10,015**	**11,135**	**11,309**	**11,608**
China, People's Republic of	4,540	8,036	8,068	8,793	9,887	10,127	10,429
Hong Kong, China	32,550	42,795	43,731	46,166	48,543	48,354	46,324
Korea, Republic of	23,079	28,889	29,280	31,601	33,433	31,937	31,631
Mongolia	2,663	3,917	3,609	3,686	4,096	4,241	3,864
Taipei,China	19,202	22,846	23,099	25,081	25,841	25,945	28,348
South Asia	**1,346**	**1,663**	**1,737**	**1,960**	**2,046**	**2,126**	**...**
Bangladesh	771	1,240	1,373	1,510	1,638	1,808	1,956
Bhutan	2,225	2,689	2,809	3,370	3,332	3,412	...
India	1,408	1,693	1,763	1,997	2,081	2,155	1,967
Maldives	6,576	9,392	9,269	9,634	10,404	10,567	...
Nepal	620	858	857	1,025	1,090	1,154	1,103
Sri Lanka	2,747	3,881	3,886	4,077	4,059	3,852	3,681
Southeast Asia	**3,393**	**3,989**	**4,084**	**4,351**	**4,609**	**4,827**	**...**
Brunei Darussalam	35,437	31,723	27,322	28,238	30,667	29,313	26,490
Cambodia	796	1,213	1,308	1,429	1,561	1,698	1,564
Indonesia	3,177	3,414	3,605	3,886	3,946	4,193	3,917
Lao People's Democratic Republic	1,117	2,254	2,416	2,555	2,676	2,725	2,735
Malaysia	8,920	9,813	9,523	9,965	11,077	11,213	10,309
Myanmar	...	1,203	1,136	1,139	1,205	1,276	...
Philippines	2,237	3,068	3,108	3,153	3,280	3,512	3,315
Singapore	47,237	56,310	56,846	61,175	66,677	65,643	59,796
Thailand	5,174	5,939	6,057	6,625	7,331	7,852	7,219
Timor-Leste	806	1,358	1,354	1,286	1,230	1,561	...
Viet Nam	1,332	2,119	2,201	2,373	2,571	2,715	2,779
The Pacific[a]	**2,276**	**3,006**	**2,809**	**2,978**	**3,056**	**3,041**	**...**
Cook Islands	10,160	16,422	17,773	17,725	19,477	18,767	15,840
Fiji	3,691	5,409	5,646	6,050	6,298	6,180	...
Kiribati	1,515	1,574	1,598	1,656	1,717	1,701	...
Marshall Islands	3,065	3,431	3,700	3,913	4,053	4,373	4,445
Micronesia, Federated States of	2,887	3,056	3,197	3,522	3,854	...	...
Nauru	5,275	8,468	9,280	9,951	10,515	9,944	9,973
Niue	13,021 (2011)	15,575	15,656	14,644	16,885	16,548	...
Palau	10,044	16,065	16,601	16,062	16,265	16,064	...
Papua New Guinea	2,020	2,723	2,447	2,600	2,673	2,670	2,460
Samoa	3,723	4,095	4,206	4,188	4,202	4,230	3,822
Solomon Islands	1,625	2,137	2,156	2,271	...	...	...
Tonga	3,612	3,945	4,162	4,585	4,795	5,107	...
Tuvalu	2,816	3,266	3,869	4,253	4,531	5,116	...
Vanuatu	2,923	2,893	2,952	3,157	3,215	...	...
Developed ADB Member Economies	**45,964**	**37,635**	**41,226**	**41,539**	**42,390**	**42,903**	**...**
Australia	54,176	51,990	51,033	54,903	55,285	53,515	53,171
Japan	44,968	34,924	39,401	38,891	39,808	40,778	40,121
New Zealand	33,677	39,425	40,080	42,993	43,306	42,756	...
DEVELOPING ADB MEMBER ECONOMIES[a]	**3,337**	**4,922**	**4,936**	**5,354**	**5,832**	**5,939**	**...**
ALL ADB REGIONAL MEMBERS[a]	**5,054**	**6,185**	**6,314**	**6,717**	**7,200**	**7,313**	**...**
WORLD	**9,558**	**10,251**	**10,293**	**10,830**	**11,372**	**11,417**	**10,926**

... = data not available, $ = United States dollars, ADB = Asian Development Bank.

Note: The figures in the table are calculated as gross domestic product (GDP) in current United States (US) dollars divided by the midyear population. GDP figures in local currency units are obtained from economy's official sources and converted to US dollars using the official exchange rates from the International Monetary Fund. The exchange rates used are expressed as the average rate for a period of time (average of period), calculated as annual averages based on the monthly averages (local currency units relative to the US dollar). For Myanmar, the 2010 figure for GDP in US dollars was converted from the domestic currency using the World Bank's alternative conversion factor to calculate the aggregate for Southeast Asia.

a For estimating aggregates, imputation was done for economies with missing data by substituting available data from the nearest years.

Sources Asian Development Bank estimates using economy's official sources. For "World": World Bank. World Development Indicators. https://databank.worldbank.org/source/world-development-indicators (accessed 22 July 2021).

Table 2.2.6: Agriculture, Industry, and Services Value-Added
(% of GDP)

ADB Regional Member	Agriculture Value-Added			Industry Value-Added			Services Value-Added		
	2010	2015	2020	2010	2015	2020	2010	2015	2020
Developing ADB Member Economies									
Central and West Asia									
Afghanistan	28.8	22.7	28.3	21.3	22.7	13.1	49.8	54.7	58.7
Armenia	18.8	18.9	12.3	36.3	28.2	29.6	45.0	52.9	58.1
Azerbaijan	5.9	6.8	7.7	64.1	49.3	45.8	30.0	43.9	46.5
Georgia	9.6	8.8	8.4	19.1	21.5	24.7	71.4	69.7	66.9
Kazakhstan	4.7	5.0	5.6	41.9	32.5	35.5	53.4	62.5	58.9
Kyrgyz Republic	18.8	15.4	14.6	28.2	27.5	31.8	53.1	57.1	53.6
Pakistan	24.3	25.1	24.4	20.6	20.1	18.7	55.1	54.9	56.9
Tajikistan	21.8	23.7	24.9	27.9	33.2	27.4	50.3	43.1	47.8
Turkmenistan	11.5	9.3	...	60.0	56.9	...	28.5	33.8	...
Uzbekistan	32.9	34.1	28.2	25.9	26.2	35.5	41.1	39.7	36.3
East Asia									
China, People's Republic of	9.6	8.7	8.0	46.7	41.0	38.0	43.7	50.3	54.0
Hong Kong, China	0.1	0.1	0.1 (2019)	7.0	7.3	6.5 (2019)	93.0	92.7	93.4 (2019)
Korea, Republic of	2.4	2.2	2.0	37.5	37.2	35.6	60.1	60.6	62.4
Mongolia	11.6	13.3	11.9	36.1	33.7	41.7	52.4	53.1	46.4
Taipei,China	1.6	1.8	1.7	33.4	36.3	36.8	65.0	62.0	61.5
South Asia									
Bangladesh	17.8	15.5	13.0	26.1	28.2	31.1	56.0	56.4	55.9
Bhutan	14.8	14.4	15.8 (2019)	43.8	42.5	36.1 (2019)	41.4	43.1	48.1 (2019)
India	18.4	17.7	20.2	33.1	30.0	25.9	48.5	52.3	53.9
Maldives	6.1	6.3	6.0 (2019)	10.2	12.1	13.5 (2019)	83.8	81.7	80.5 (2019)
Nepal	35.4	29.4	26.2	15.1	14.6	13.4	49.5	56.0	60.4
Sri Lanka	9.5	8.8	8.9	29.7	29.3	27.8	60.9	61.9	63.3
Southeast Asia									
Brunei Darussalam	0.7	1.1	1.2	67.4	60.2	58.1	31.9	38.7	40.8
Cambodia	36.0	28.2	24.4	23.3	29.4	37.0	40.7	42.3	38.6
Indonesia	14.3	13.9	14.2	43.9	41.4	39.7	41.8	44.7	46.1
Lao People's Democratic Republic	30.6	19.7	18.5	29.8	31.0	37.2	39.6	49.4	44.3
Malaysia	10.2	8.4	8.3	40.9	38.9	36.3	48.9	52.7	55.4
Myanmar	36.9	26.8	21.4 (2019)	26.5	34.5	38.0 (2019)	36.7	38.8	40.7 (2019)
Philippines	13.7	11.0	10.2	32.3	30.5	28.4	53.9	58.5	61.4
Singapore	0.0	0.0	0.0	28.2	25.8	25.6	71.8	74.2	74.4
Thailand[a]	10.5	8.9	8.6	37.1	33.4	30.4	52.4	57.7	61.0
Timor-Leste	24.7	17.8	14.1 (2019)	8.8	18.4	29.3 (2019)	66.5	63.8	56.6 (2019)
Viet Nam	21.0	18.9	14.9	36.7	37.0	33.7	42.2	44.2	41.6
The Pacific									
Cook Islands	3.4	3.2	3.2	7.9	11.3	12.0	88.7	85.4	84.8
Fiji	11.0	10.0	14.6 (2019)	20.9	19.3	19.1 (2019)	68.1	70.6	66.3 (2019)
Kiribati	24.2	22.1	28.3 (2019)	11.9	15.6	10.9 (2019)	63.9	62.3	60.8 (2019)
Marshall Islands	11.2	12.5	22.1	14.5	12.9	13.0	76.8	77.3	68.2
Micronesia, Federated States of	26.7	27.8	23.9 (2018)	7.8	6.5	5.2 (2018)	65.5	65.7	70.9 (2018)
Nauru	6.3	4.0	...	32.7	6.1	...	61.0	89.9	...
Niue	23.0	21.0	19.1 (2018)	4.0	1.6	3.7 (2018)	73.0	77.5	77.2 (2018)
Palau	4.2	3.3	3.4 (2019)	11.0	8.9	10.4 (2019)	84.8	87.8	86.2 (2019)
Papua New Guinea	20.2	18.3	19.4	34.2	36.4	34.4	45.5	45.3	46.2
Samoa	9.1	8.9	10.5	18.1	18.1	15.2	72.8	73.0	74.3
Solomon Islands	34.8	33.3	...	13.8	15.6	...	51.4	51.1	...
Tonga	18.7	19.7	23.4 (2019)	20.5	18.1	18.0 (2019)	60.9	62.3	58.6 (2019)
Tuvalu	27.3	21.4	8.4 (2019)	5.7	12.7	18.5 (2019)	67.0	65.9	73.2 (2019)
Vanuatu	21.9	23.1	21.2 (2018)	13.0	11.5	10.1 (2018)	65.0	65.4	59.8 (2018)
Developed ADB Member Economies									
Australia	2.4	2.5	2.0	27.0	25.3	27.4	70.6	72.1	70.5
Japan	1.1	1.0	1.0 (2019)	28.3	28.8	29.0 (2019)	70.6	70.2	70.0 (2019)
New Zealand	7.1	4.9	6.2 (2018)	23.0	23.1	22.3 (2018)	69.9	72.0	71.5 (2018)

... = data not available, 0.0 = magnitude is less than half of the unit employed, ADB = Asian Development Bank, GDP = gross domestic product.

a Value-added for construction is included under services.

Source: Economy's official sources.

Table 2.2.7: Household and Government Consumption Expenditure
(% of GDP)

ADB Regional Member	Household Consumption			Government Consumption		
	2010	2015	2020	2010	2015	2020
Developing ADB Member Economies						
Central and West Asia[a]	**59.8**	**64.6**	**64.0 (2019)**	**11.1**	**11.8**	**11.6 (2019)**
Afghanistan	97.4	82.9	86.6	14.0	12.1	18.0
Armenia[b]	82.0	77.9	75.4	13.1	13.1	16.0
Azerbaijan	38.9	56.3	57.1 (2019)	10.9	12.4	11.1 (2019)
Georgia	79.5	73.6	75.9	15.3	14.3	14.4
Kazakhstan[b]	45.4	53.7	52.9	10.8	11.6	12.8
Kyrgyz Republic[b]	84.6	90.5	76.4 (2019)	18.1	17.8	16.4 (2019)
Pakistan[b]	79.7	79.8	79.3	10.3	11.0	12.8
Tajikistan[b]	84.7	71.2	76.2 (2019)	11.3	11.6	11.2 (2019)
Turkmenistan[b]	5.0	9.3 (2013)	...	9.3	9.1 (2013)	...
Uzbekistan[b]	57.0	61.4	55.4	13.3	14.3	17.6
East Asia	**38.3**	**40.0**	**39.7**	**14.4**	**15.8**	**16.7**
China, People's Republic of	34.3	37.8	38.1	14.6	16.2	16.7
Hong Kong, China[b]	61.4	66.4	66.5	8.9	9.6	12.7
Korea, Republic of	49.1	46.9	44.6	14.2	15.1	18.1
Mongolia[b]	55.2	59.1	56.8	12.7	13.5	14.6
Taipei,China[b]	53.2	51.5	48.6	15.1	13.9	14.0
South Asia	**56.5**	**60.6**	**61.6 (2019)**	**10.6**	**10.0**	**10.7 (2019)**
Bangladesh	74.1	72.4	68.5	5.1	5.4	6.2
Bhutan[b]	45.3	59.6	60.1 (2019)	20.5	18.3	18.3 (2019)
India[b]	54.7	59.0	58.6	11.0	10.4	12.5
Maldives	...	...	...	...	...	...
Nepal[b]	78.6	85.8	89.2	10.0	9.0	9.5
Sri Lanka	68.5	67.4	70.7	8.5	9.0	10.4
Southeast Asia	**52.0**	**54.1**	**54.8 (2019)**	**10.5**	**11.4**	**10.9 (2019)**
Brunei Darussalam[b]	14.7	19.8	24.1	22.2	25.1	25.4
Cambodia[b]	81.3	76.8	71.1	6.3	5.4	5.5
Indonesia[b]	55.2	56.3	57.7	9.0	9.7	9.3
Lao People's Democratic Republic	...	...	...	...	...	...
Malaysia[b]	48.1	54.0	60.9	12.6	13.1	13.0
Myanmar[c]	67.3	74.0	70.4 (2019)	...	...	...
Philippines[b]	70.2	72.5	75.1	9.7	10.9	15.3
Singapore	36.3	37.2	33.0	9.7	10.2	12.4
Thailand	51.2	50.3	52.0	15.8	17.1	17.7
Timor-Leste	68.7	55.2	63.5 (2019)	103.2	58.8	57.1 (2019)
Viet Nam	66.6	68.0	67.9	6.0	6.3	6.7
The Pacific	**...**	**...**	**...**	**...**	**...**	**...**
Cook Islands	...	...	...	...	...	...
Fiji[d]	70.5	54.2	58.7 (2019)	15.0	20.2	19.8 (2019)
Kiribati	...	...	...	...	...	...
Marshall Islands	72.2	73.3	62.9	53.8	53.5	49.0
Micronesia, Federated States of	...	...	...	...	...	...
Nauru	...	...	...	...	...	...
Niue	...	...	...	...	...	...
Palau	67.8	64.5	64.5 (2019)	37.4	28.7	33.4 (2019)
Papua New Guinea[b]	48.0 (2005)	...	...	16.1 (2005)	...	...
Samoa	...	...	...	...	...	...
Solomon Islands	61.6	59.4	56.2 (2017)	31.4	29.6	29.3 (2017)
Tonga	89.1	94.3	89.4 (2019)	18.7	21.3	20.3 (2019)
Tuvalu	...	...	...	...	...	...
Vanuatu	60.6	64.4	57.5 (2018)	17.5	15.8	16.9 (2018)
Developed ADB Member Economies	**55.8**	**55.1**	**53.7 (2019)**	**19.0**	**19.3**	**19.6 (2019)**
Australia	56.2	57.2	53.6	18.0	18.1	20.2
Japan[b]	56.9	55.8	53.5	19.2	19.6	21.1
New Zealand	57.8	57.4	57.7 (2019)	19.7	18.5	18.8 (2019)
DEVELOPING ADB MEMBER ECONOMIES[a]	**44.2**	**45.4**	**46.4 (2019)**	**13.1**	**14.4**	**14.9 (2019)**
ALL ADB REGIONAL MEMBERS[a]	**48.4**	**47.7**	**48.0 (2019)**	**15.2**	**15.5**	**15.9 (2019)**
WORLD	**57.2**	**57.7**	**57.6 (2019)**	**17.6**	**17.2**	**17.1 (2019)**

... = data not available, ADB = Asian Development Bank, GDP = gross domestic product.

Note: Figures in the table are calculated as a percentage of GDP at current prices.

a For estimating aggregates, GDP figures in domestic currencies were converted to United States dollars using official exchange rates, and imputation was done for economies with missing data by substituting available data from the nearest years.

b Data for household consumption includes nonprofit institutions serving households.

c Data refers to total final consumption expenditure.

d For years prior to 2005 (as featured in the Key Indicators Database), data for household consumption includes nonprofit institutions serving households.

Sources: Economy's official sources. For "World": World Bank. World Development Indicators. https://databank.worldbank.org/source/world-development-indicators (accessed 18 July 2021).

Table 2.2.8: Gross Capital Formation and Changes in Inventories
(% of GDP)

ADB Regional Member	Gross Capital Formation			Changes in Inventories		
	2010	2015	2020	2010	2015	2020
Developing ADB Member Economies						
Central and West Asia[a]	**22.3**	**24.2**	**24.6 (2019)**	...	...	...
Afghanistan[b,c]	17.5	19.0	11.9	5.3	28.1	...
Armenia	32.9	20.7	17.9	-0.6	0.1	1.4
Azerbaijan	18.1	27.9	20.3 (2019)	-0.1	0.1	-0.8 (2019)
Georgia	20.5	26.3	26.2	1.6	1.9	1.6
Kazakhstan	25.4	27.9	28.5	1.0	5.0	3.8
Kyrgyz Republic[d]	28.1	33.0	31.1 (2019)	-0.7	1.7	4.3 (2019)
Pakistan	15.8	15.7	15.3	1.6	1.6	1.6
Tajikistan	23.8	44.7	35.4 (2019)	-0.6	6.0	3.9 (2019)
Turkmenistan	51.9	50.3 (2013)	...	...	...	...
Uzbekistan	26.5	26.1	37.5	2.4	2.8	0.4
East Asia	**42.7**	**40.4**	**41.2**	...	...	...
China, People's Republic of	46.6	43.2	43.5	2.6	1.1	0.7
Hong Kong, China	23.9	21.5	19.0	2.1	-0.9	1.8
Korea, Republic of	32.6	29.5	31.9	2.3	0.5	0.7
Mongolia	42.1	26.4	24.3	7.6	6.0	-4.0
Taipei,China	25.1	21.7	23.7	1.4	0.3	-0.1
South Asia	**38.7**	**31.8**	**32.1 (2019)**	...	...	...
Bangladesh[b,e]	26.2	28.9	31.8	...	...	...
Bhutan	63.2	55.5	38.0 (2019)	0.5	-0.3	0.4 (2019)
India[f]	39.8	32.1	32.2 (2019)	4.4	1.9	1.0
Maldives	...	...	...	...	...	...
Nepal[g]	38.3	32.1	29.9	16.1	3.8	-0.0
Sri Lanka	30.4	31.2	25.2	5.9	5.1	-0.4
Southeast Asia	**28.2**	**27.9**	**27.9 (2019)**	...	...	...
Brunei Darussalam	23.7	35.2	40.6	0.2	0.2	0.2
Cambodia	17.4	22.5	25.5	1.2	1.0	0.9
Indonesia	32.9	34.1	32.4	1.9	1.3	0.6
Lao People's Democratic Republic	...	...	...	...	...	...
Malaysia[h]	23.4	25.4	19.7	1.0	-0.4	-1.3
Myanmar	23.2	34.8	30.6 (2019)	0.3	0.2	0.7 (2019)
Philippines	20.4	21.3	17.4	0.0	-0.9	-3.9
Singapore	27.7	25.4	22.6	2.1	-1.9	1.1
Thailand	25.4	22.4	23.9	1.4	-2.2	0.8
Timor-Leste	42.7	36.8	27.2 (2019)	0.0	1.3	1.6 (2019)
Viet Nam	35.7	27.7	27.0	3.0	3.0	2.6
The Pacific	...	...	...	...	...	...
Cook Islands	...	...	...	...	...	...
Fiji	18.7	21.0	15.8 (2019)	2.9	2.4	– (2019)
Kiribati	...	...	...	...	...	...
Marshall Islands	39.4	17.2	19.3	-2.1	-0.8	1.2
Micronesia, Federated States of	...	...	...	...	...	...
Nauru	...	...	...	...	...	...
Niue	...	...	...	...	...	...
Palau	24.5	25.4	30.4 (2019)	0.7	-1.9	– (2019)
Papua New Guinea	17.5 (2005)	...	...	1.0 (2005)	...	...
Samoa	...	...	...	...	...	...
Solomon Islands	...	...	...	-1.4 (2012)	1.3 (2016)	...
Tonga	29.6	25.4	25.4 (2019)	0.5	2.0	1.0 (2019)
Tuvalu	...	...	...	...	...	...
Vanuatu	34.7	33.7	26.3 (2018)	0.8	0.8	0.4 (2018)
Developed ADB Member Economies	**23.3**	**25.3**	**25.2 (2019)**	...	...	...
Australia	26.9	26.3	22.3	-0.2	0.1	-0.3
Japan	22.6	25.2	25.5	-0.0	0.2	0.2
New Zealand	20.2	23.2	23.6 (2019)	0.4	0.3	0.0 (2019)
DEVELOPING ADB MEMBER ECONOMIES[a]	**38.8**	**37.0**	**37.5 (2019)**	...	...	...
ALL ADB REGIONAL MEMBERS[a]	**33.1**	**34.3**	**34.8 (2019)**	...	...	...
WORLD	**24.2**	**24.3**	**24.5 (2019)**	...	...	...

... = data not available, -0.0 or 0.0 = magnitude is less than half of unit employed, – = magnitude equals zero, ADB = Asian Development Bank, GDP = gross domestic product.

Note: Figures in the table are calculated as a percentage of GDP at current prices.

a For estimating aggregates, GDP figures in domestic currencies were converted to United States dollars using official exchange rates, and imputation was done for economies with missing data by substituting available data from the nearest years.
b Refers to gross fixed capital formation.
c Changes in inventories include statistical discrepancy.
d Refers to gross fixed capital formation and acquisitions less disposals of valuables.
e Includes data on changes in inventories.
f Refers to gross capital formation, which refers to the sum of gross fixed capital formation, valuables, increases in stocks, and errors and omissions.
g Changes in inventories were derived residually; hence, statistical discrepancies or errors are included in this entry.
h Changes in inventories includes valuables and statistical discrepancy.

Sources: Economy's official sources. For "World": World Bank. World Development Indicators. https://databank.worldbank.org/source/world-development-indicators (accessed 22 July 2021).

Table 2.2.9: Exports and Imports of Goods and Services
(% of GDP)

ADB Regional Member	Exports of goods and services			Imports of goods and services		
	2010	2015	2020	2010	2015	2020
Developing ADB Member Economies						
Central and West Asia[a]	**32.4**	**22.9**	**28.2 (2019)**	**27.0**	**24.9**	**30.3 (2019)**
Afghanistan	9.8	6.9	13.4	43.9	49.0	32.5
Armenia	20.8	29.7	30.2	45.3	42.0	39.6
Azerbaijan	54.3	37.8	49.1 (2019)	20.7	34.8	36.8 (2019)
Georgia	33.0	40.9	37.4	49.9	57.9	55.9
Kazakhstan	44.2	28.5	30.1	29.9	24.5	26.0
Kyrgyz Republic	51.6	35.2	35.2 (2019)	81.7	75.8	64.1 (2019)
Pakistan	13.5	10.6	10.0	19.4	17.1	17.4
Tajikistan	26.8	9.8	15.0 (2019)	59.0	40.1	41.1 (2019)
Turkmenistan	76.3	74.8 (2013)	...	44.5	44.1 (2013)	...
Uzbekistan	27.9	15.3	26.3	19.7	15.1	36.7
East Asia	**38.2**	**29.8**	**25.0**	**34.4**	**25.8**	**24.0**
China, People's Republic of	27.2	21.4	18.6	23.5	18.1	16.0
Hong Kong, China[b]	205.3	195.9	176.7	199.4	193.5	174.9
Korea, Republic of	47.1	43.0	36.4	44.3	36.1	32.8
Mongolia	46.7	45.6	58.4	56.7	44.6	54.0
Taipei,China	79.6	71.3	58.6	73.0	58.4	44.9
South Asia	**21.8**	**19.6**	**18.2 (2019)**	**26.7**	**22.7**	**21.5 (2019)**
Bangladesh	16.0	17.3	13.4	21.8	24.8	19.4
Bhutan	43.5	34.4	34.0 (2019)	72.4	67.8	50.4 (2019)
India	22.4	19.8	18.7	26.9	22.1	19.2
Maldives	...	...	...	...	...	...
Nepal	9.6	10.5	7.1	36.4	37.4	35.7
Sri Lanka	19.6	21.0	16.6	26.8	28.5	22.9
Southeast Asia	**64.4**	**60.8**	**58.9 (2019)**	**57.8**	**55.4**	**54.6 (2019)**
Brunei Darussalam	67.4	52.2	57.3	28.0	37.7	52.9
Cambodia	54.1	61.7	62.4	59.5	66.1	63.9
Indonesia	24.3	21.2	17.2	22.4	20.8	16.0
Lao People's Democratic Republic	...	...	...	...	...	...
Malaysia	86.9	69.4	61.5	71.0	61.9	55.0
Myanmar	19.6	17.4	30.4 (2019)	15.1	27.9	30.3 (2019)
Philippines	32.9	27.2	25.2	33.2	31.9	33.0
Singapore	198.0	178.4	176.2	171.7	151.1	144.3
Thailand	66.5	67.6	51.4	60.8	57.2	46.5
Timor-Leste	8.6	3.0	2.4 (2019)	125.8	56.9	52.2 (2019)
Viet Nam	72.0	89.8	105.5	80.2	89.0	102.7
The Pacific	**...**	**...**	**...**	**...**	**...**	**...**
Cook Islands	...	...	...	...	...	...
Fiji	57.4	48.8	48.1 (2019)	63.8	52.4	58.4 (2019)
Kiribati	...	...	...	...	...	...
Marshall Islands	36.9	43.9	34.9	103.9	89.9	68.2
Micronesia, Federated States of	...	...	...	...	...	...
Nauru	...	...	...	...	...	...
Niue	...	...	...	...	...	...
Palau	49.7	58.6	41.9 (2019)	77.0	76.0	78.8 (2019)
Papua New Guinea	74.5 (2005)	...	...	56.1 (2005)	...	...
Samoa	...	...	...	...	...	...
Solomon Islands	35.0	40.4	38.3 (2017)	60.7	47.9	43.1 (2017)
Tonga	12.5	17.0	22.0 (2019)	58.3	64.5	65.2 (2019)
Tuvalu	...	...	...	...	...	...
Vanuatu	46.6	44.3	56.6 (2018)	52.7	64.5	60.0 (2018)
Developed ADB Member Economies	**16.1**	**18.3**	**19.0 (2019)**	**15.1**	**19.0**	**18.6 (2019)**
Australia	19.8	20.0	23.9	20.8	21.5	20.0
Japan	14.9	17.4	15.5	13.6	18.0	15.7
New Zealand	30.3	27.9	27.1 (2019)	28.0	27.0	27.2 (2019)
DEVELOPING ADB MEMBER ECONOMIES[a]	**39.7**	**32.2**	**29.0 (2019)**	**36.7**	**29.2**	**27.8 (2019)**
ALL ADB REGIONAL MEMBERS[a]	**31.1**	**28.9**	**26.8 (2019)**	**28.8**	**26.8**	**25.8 (2019)**

... = data not available, ADB = Asian Development Bank, GDP = gross domestic product.

Note: Figures in the table are calculated as a percentage of GDP at current prices.

a For estimating aggregates, imputation was done for economies with missing data by substituting available data from the nearest years.

b The statistics for trade in goods and services are compiled based on the change of ownership principle in recording goods sent abroad for processing and merchanting under the standards stipulated in the System of National Accounts 2008.

Source: Economy's official sources.

Table 2.2.10: Gross Domestic Saving
(% of GDP)

ADB Regional Member	2010	2015	2016	2017	2018	2019	2020
Developing ADB Member Economies							
Central and West Asia[a]	**28.6**	**23.6**	**21.4**	**22.1**	**23.4**	**22.8**	**...**
Afghanistan	-11.4	5.0	-3.2	5.1	-8.4	-19.9	-7.1
Armenia	4.9	9.0	10.2	7.7	8.7	4.0	8.6
Azerbaijan	49.8	30.9	28.5	31.1	35.4	31.4	...
Georgia	3.5	9.3	14.9	16.3	17.5	16.3	7.6
Kazakhstan	43.8	34.6	33.8	36.9	39.6	38.6	...
Kyrgyz Republic	-2.7	-8.3	-0.2	0.8	0.3	7.2	...
Pakistan	10.0	9.3	8.7	6.8	6.2	5.5	7.9
Tajikistan	4.0	17.2	8.5	8.2	12.4	12.6	...
Turkmenistan	85.6	81.6 (2013)	...	...	...	...	...
Uzbekistan	29.6	24.3	22.1	26.9	30.0	28.9	27.0
East Asia	**46.4**	**44.4**	**43.1**	**43.0**	**42.8**	**42.5**	**44.3**
China, People's Republic of	50.2	46.5	44.9	44.8	44.6	44.4	46.2
Hong Kong, China	29.8	23.9	23.8	23.1	21.8	19.7	20.8
Korea, Republic of	35.4	36.4	36.8	37.0	35.9	34.3	35.5
Mongolia	32.1	27.4	30.5	33.7	34.0	33.2	27.9
Taipei,China	31.5	34.4	34.1	34.7	33.8	33.5	36.5
South Asia	**...**	**...**	**...**	**...**	**...**	**...**	**...**
Bangladesh	20.8	22.2	25.0	25.3	22.8	25.0	25.3
Bhutan	31.8	22.1	30.8	29.3	22.5	21.6	...
India	...	...	...	...	...	...	...
Maldives	...	...	...	...	...	...	...
Nepal	11.5	7.6	3.6	13.0	14.8	15.3	6.3
Sri Lanka	23.1	23.6	20.6	24.4	22.4	20.7	18.9
Southeast Asia	**37.0**	**34.7**	**34.9**	**35.5**	**...**	**...**	**...**
Brunei Darussalam	63.1	55.2	52.6	53.0	56.3	54.5	50.5
Cambodia	14.5	19.6	20.4	23.2	26.0	27.2	25.0
Indonesia	34.8	32.8	32.7	33.6	...	...	...
Lao People's Democratic Republic	...	...	...	...	...	...	...
Malaysia	39.3	33.0	32.6	32.4	30.6	28.5	26.1
Myanmar	32.7	23.4	22.6	22.3	24.2	28.3	...
Philippines	...	...	...	...	...	...	...
Singapore	54.0	52.7	52.6	53.8	53.8	52.9	54.5
Thailand	32.0	29.3	31.6	32.6	30.7	30.7	28.8
Timor-Leste	-74.6	-17.0	-14.1	-17.8	-23.2	-1.8	...
Viet Nam	27.4	25.7	24.9	25.5	26.0	25.4	25.0
The Pacific	**...**	**...**	**...**	**...**	**...**	**...**	**...**
Cook Islands	...	...	...	...	...	...	...
Fiji	12.7	22.7	19.7	19.9	19.2	18.6	...
Kiribati	...	...	...	...	...	...	...
Marshall Islands	-30.9	-30.7	-28.0	-29.5	-29.9	...	...
Micronesia, Federated States of	...	...	...	...	...	...	...
Nauru	...	...	...	...	...	...	...
Niue	...	...	...	...	...	...	...
Palau[b]	-7.5	5.0	4.7	0.9	-1.8	-0.9	...
Papua New Guinea	35.9 (2005)	...	...	...	...	...	...
Samoa	...	...	...	...	...	...	...
Solomon Islands	...	...	...	...	...	...	...
Tonga	-15.1	-22.3	-17.1	-16.4	-20.3	-15.8	...
Tuvalu	...	...	...	...	...	...	...
Vanuatu	27.0	24.0 (2014)	...	...	...	...	...
Developed ADB Member Economies	**25.2**	**25.6**	**26.1**	**26.7**	**26.3**	**26.6**	**...**
Australia	25.8	24.7	23.1	24.6	24.9	25.7	26.2
Japan	25.1	25.9	27.0	27.3	26.8	27.0	26.9
New Zealand	22.5	24.1	23.9	24.6	24.0	23.7	...

... = data not available, ADB = Asian Development Bank, GDP = gross domestic product.

Note: Figures in the table are calculated as a percentage of GDP at current prices.

a For estimating aggregates, GDP figures in domestic currencies were converted to United States dollars using official exchange rates, and imputation was done for economies with missing data by substituting available data from the nearest years.

b Estimated as the difference between GDP by industrial origin at producer's prices and final consumption expenditure.

Source: Economy's official sources.

Table 2.2.11: Growth Rates of Real Gross Domestic Product
(%)

ADB Regional Member	2010	2015	2016	2017	2018	2019	2020
Developing ADB Member Economies							
Central and West Asia							
Afghanistan	3.2	-1.8	3.5	2.6	1.2	3.9	-1.9
Armenia	2.2	3.2	0.2	7.5	5.2	7.6	-7.4
Azerbaijan	5.0	1.1	-3.1	0.2	1.5	2.5	-4.3
Georgia	6.2	3.0	2.9	4.8	4.8	5.0	-6.2
Kazakhstan	7.3	1.2	1.1	4.1	4.1	4.5	-2.6
Kyrgyz Republic	-0.5	3.9	4.3	4.7	3.8	4.6	-8.6
Pakistan	1.6	4.7	5.5	5.6	5.8	1.1	-0.9
Tajikistan	6.5	6.0	6.9	7.1	7.6	7.4	...
Turkmenistan	9.2	6.5	6.2	6.4	6.2	6.3	...
Uzbekistan	7.3	7.4	6.1	4.5	5.4	5.8	1.6
East Asia							
China, People's Republic of	10.6	7.0	6.8	6.9	6.7	6.0	2.3
Hong Kong, China	6.8	2.4	2.2	3.8	2.8	-1.7	-6.1
Korea, Republic of	6.8	2.8	2.9	3.2	2.9	2.2	-0.9
Mongolia	17.3 (2011)	2.4	1.2	5.3	7.2	5.2	-5.3
Taipei,China	10.3	1.5	2.2	3.3	2.8	3.0	3.1
South Asia							
Bangladesh	5.6	6.6	7.1	7.3	7.9	8.2	5.2
Bhutan	11.9	6.6	8.1	4.7	3.1	5.5	...
India	8.5	8.0	8.3	6.8	6.5	4.0	-7.3
Maldives	7.3	2.9	6.3	6.8	6.9	8.6	...
Nepal	4.8	4.0	0.4	9.0	7.6	6.7	-2.1
Sri Lanka	8.0	5.0	4.5	3.6	3.3	2.3	-3.6
Southeast Asia							
Brunei Darussalam	3.7 (2011)	-0.4	-2.5	1.3	0.1	3.9	1.2
Cambodia	6.0	7.0	7.0	7.0	7.5	6.8	-3.1
Indonesia	6.2	4.9	5.0	5.1	5.2	5.0	-2.1
Lao People's Democratic Republic	8.1	7.3	7.0	6.9	6.2	5.5	3.3
Malaysia	7.4	5.1	4.4	5.8	4.8	4.3	-5.6
Myanmar	9.6	7.0	5.9	5.8	6.4	6.8	3.3
Philippines	7.3	6.3	7.1	6.9	6.3	6.1	-9.6
Singapore	14.5	3.0	3.3	4.5	3.5	1.3	-5.4
Thailand	7.5	3.1	3.4	4.2	4.2	2.3	-6.1
Timor-Leste	9.5	2.9	3.4	-4.1	-1.1	...	...
Viet Nam	6.4	6.7	6.2	6.8	7.1	7.0	2.9
The Pacific							
Cook Islands	-4.9	5.7	4.9	9.5	5.7	4.8	-14.6
Fiji	3.0	4.5	2.4	5.4	3.8	-0.4	...
Kiribati	-0.9	10.4	5.1	0.9	2.3	5.4	...
Marshall Islands	7.6	1.6	1.3	4.1	3.6	5.3	-2.1
Micronesia, Federated States of	2.3	4.6	0.9	2.7	0.2	1.1	-5.6
Nauru	13.6	2.8	3.0	-5.5	5.7	1.0	0.6
Niue	0.6	4.0	3.5	2.4	6.5	...	...
Palau	0.1	5.0	-0.4	-2.0	5.8	-1.8	...
Papua New Guinea	10.1	6.6	5.5	3.5	-0.3	5.9	-3.8
Samoa	2.4	6.7	3.7	-0.6	0.7	2.4	-9.2
Solomon Islands	9.7	1.4	5.9	5.3	3.0	1.2	-4.5
Tonga	0.8	1.2	6.6	3.3	0.3	0.7	...
Tuvalu	-3.3	9.2	...	...	...	...	...
Vanuatu	1.6	0.2	3.5	4.4	2.9	...	...
Developed ADB Member Economies							
Australia	2.1	2.2	2.8	2.3	2.9	2.2	-0.2
Japan	4.1	1.6	0.8	1.7	0.6	0.3	-4.8
New Zealand	1.5	3.7	3.7	3.6	3.2	1.6	...

... = data not available, ADB = Asian Development Bank.

Source: Economy's official sources.

Table 2.2.12: Growth Rates of Real Gross Domestic Product per Capita
(%)

ADB Regional Member	2010	2015	2016	2017	2018	2019	2020
Developing ADB Member Economies							
Central and West Asia							
Afghanistan	1.2	-3.8	1.5	0.6	-5.0	1.7	-4.0
Armenia	2.9	3.6	0.6	8.0	5.6	7.9	-7.4
Azerbaijan	3.8	-0.1	-4.2	-0.8	0.6	1.6	-4.7
Georgia	7.0	2.9	2.8	4.8	4.9	5.2	-6.2
Kazakhstan	5.7	-0.3	-0.3	2.7	2.7	3.2	-3.9
Kyrgyz Republic	-1.8	1.8	2.2	2.7	1.8	2.4	-10.5
Pakistan	-0.5	2.7	3.4	3.1	3.8	-0.8	-2.7
Tajikistan	3.9	3.5	4.5	4.8	5.3	5.1	...
Turkmenistan	7.5	4.6	4.4	4.7	4.5	4.7	...
Uzbekistan	4.3	5.5	4.3	2.7	3.6	3.9	-0.3
East Asia							
China, People's Republic of	10.1	6.5	6.1	6.3	6.3	5.6	2.2
Hong Kong, China	6.0	1.5	1.6	3.0	2.0	-2.5	-5.8
Korea, Republic of	6.3	2.3	2.5	2.9	2.4	2.0	-1.0
Mongolia	15.2 (2011)	0.3	-0.8	3.4	5.2	3.3	-7.0
Taipei,China	10.0	1.3	1.9	3.1	2.7	2.9	3.3
South Asia							
Bangladesh	4.2	5.1	5.6	5.9	6.4	6.7	3.9
Bhutan	9.9	5.0	6.5	3.3	2.0	4.4	...
India	7.0	6.7	7.0	5.6	5.4	2.9	-8.2
Maldives	4.9	-0.9	2.3	2.6	2.6	4.2	...
Nepal	3.4	2.6	-0.9	7.5	6.2	4.5	-4.1
Sri Lanka	7.0	4.0	3.3	2.4	2.2	1.7	-4.1
Southeast Asia							
Brunei Darussalam	2.0 (2011)	-1.6	-3.6	-1.6	-2.9	0.0	2.5
Cambodia	4.6	5.6	5.5	5.5	6.0	5.4	-4.4
Indonesia	4.8	3.5	3.9	3.9	4.1	3.9	-3.3
Lao People's Democratic Republic	6.6	5.7	5.5	5.4	4.7	4.0	1.8
Malaysia	5.5	3.5	3.0	4.5	3.6	3.9	-6.0
Myanmar	8.9	6.1	4.9	4.8	5.5	5.8	2.4
Philippines	6.3	4.6 (2014)	5.4	5.2	4.7	4.6	-10.8
Singapore	12.5	1.8	2.0	4.4	3.0	0.1	-5.1
Thailand	6.9	2.5	3.0	3.2	3.9	2.0	-6.4
Timor-Leste	7.5	1.0	1.4	-6.0	-3.0	...	...
Viet Nam	5.1	5.5	5.0	5.6	5.8	5.8	1.7
The Pacific							
Cook Islands	-9.3	5.7	...	...	10.8	-3.5	-3.7
Fiji	2.3	4.1	2.0	4.8	3.2	-1.0	...
Kiribati	-3.0	8.9	3.8	-0.4	1.0	4.0	...
Marshall Islands	6.3	1.2	0.9	3.7	3.2	4.9	-2.5
Micronesia, Federated States of	2.8	4.4	0.7	2.5	0.0	0.9	-5.8
Nauru	11.4	1.1	1.3	-7.0	4.0	-0.6	-1.0
Niue	...	2.4	1.7	...	6.5	...	...
Palau	2.0	3.2	-1.6	-2.1	8.0	-1.3	...
Papua New Guinea	6.8	3.4	2.3	0.4	-3.3	2.7	-6.7
Samoa	1.6	5.8	2.8	-1.4	-0.1	1.6	-9.9
Solomon Islands	4.7 (2011)	-0.9	3.6	3.1	0.9	-0.7	-6.5
Tonga	0.6	1.7	7.1	3.9	0.8	1.3	...
Tuvalu	-3.8	9.5	...	...	...	...	...
Vanuatu	-0.8	-2.1	2.0	2.1	0.8	...	...
Developed ADB Member Economies							
Australia	0.5	0.7	1.2	0.6	1.4	0.6	-1.5
Japan	4.1	1.7	0.9	1.8	0.8	0.5	-4.5
New Zealand	0.4	1.6	1.4	1.5	1.4	0.0	...

... = data not available, ADB = Asian Development Bank.

Source: Asian Development Bank estimates using economy's official sources.

Table 2.2.13: Growth Rates of Agriculture Real Value-Added
(%)

ADB Regional Member	2010	2015	2016	2017	2018	2019	2020
Developing ADB Member Economies							
Central and West Asia							
Afghanistan	-18.0	-16.9	12.4	6.4	-4.4	17.5	5.3
Armenia	-16.0	13.2	-5.0	-5.1	-6.9	-5.8	-4.1
Azerbaijan	-4.7	6.6	2.6	4.2	4.6	7.3	1.9
Georgia	-4.2	-0.1	-2.8	-7.7	13.8	0.7	3.6
Kazakhstan	-12.9	3.5	5.4	3.2	3.8	-0.1	5.6
Kyrgyz Republic	-2.6	6.2	2.9	2.2	2.6	2.5	1.1
Pakistan	0.2	2.1	0.2	2.2	4.0	0.6	3.3
Tajikistan	6.8	3.4	5.2	7.6	7.0	7.0	...
Turkmenistan	17.7	1.7 (2014)	...	...	...	...	...
Uzbekistan	6.1	6.1	6.2	1.2	0.3	3.1	3.0
East Asia							
China, People's Republic of	4.3	3.9	3.3	4.0	3.5	3.1	3.0
Hong Kong, China[a]	3.9	-6.8	-2.0	-5.2	-1.8	-0.8	4.8
Korea, Republic of	-3.6	-0.2	-5.6	2.3	0.2	3.9	-4.0
Mongolia	-0.3 (2011)	10.7	6.2	1.8	4.5	8.4	6.2
Taipei,China	2.1	-7.7	-9.7	8.3	4.5	-1.8	1.3
South Asia							
Bangladesh	6.2	3.3	2.8	3.0	4.2	3.9	3.1
Bhutan	0.8	4.7	4.2	2.9	4.2	1.3	...
India	8.8	0.6	6.8	6.6	2.6	4.3	3.6
Maldives	-3.5	-0.4	1.5	8.3	4.8	5.0	...
Nepal	2.0	1.2	-0.1	5.2	2.6	5.2	2.2
Sri Lanka	7.0	4.7	-3.7	-0.4	5.8	1.0	-2.4
Southeast Asia							
Brunei Darussalam	-2.6 (2011)	6.4	-3.6	-1.6	-1.6	-1.4	11.7
Cambodia	4.0	0.2	1.3	1.7	1.2	-0.7	0.4
Indonesia	3.0	3.8	3.4	3.9	3.9	3.6	1.8
Lao People's Democratic Republic	3.2	3.6	2.8	2.9	1.3	1.2	1.2
Malaysia	2.4	1.4	-3.7	5.9	0.1	2.0	-2.2
Myanmar	4.7	3.4	-0.5	-1.5	0.1	1.6	1.8
Philippines	1.3	0.7	-1.0	4.2	1.1	1.2	-0.2
Singapore[a]	2.7	-0.5	-0.4	2.9	3.2	6.4	-10.0
Thailand	-0.5	-6.5	-1.2	4.8	5.8	-0.6	-3.4
Timor-Leste	4.4	-4.4	-1.3	-3.0	2.9	...	...
Viet Nam	0.5	2.4	1.4	2.9	3.8	2.0	2.7
The Pacific							
Cook Islands	0.4	-2.2	-3.1	3.2	-2.5	-3.0	-5.7
Fiji	-2.6	2.9	-10.9	10.8	3.7	4.4	...
Kiribati	-3.9	1.3	10.7	9.0	0.3	4.8	...
Marshall Islands	11.1	6.1	-1.6	1.8	4.2	32.9	0.7
Micronesia, Federated States of	-3.1	9.5	-4.8	-0.9	0.1	1.7	-0.8
Nauru	3.7	5.2	10.6	43.4	-8.7	24.9	0.6
Niue	-0.4	2.0	1.2	3.5	1.7	...	...
Palau	-5.0	-3.7	7.7	8.4	-5.2	-4.2	...
Papua New Guinea	2.8	-2.6	2.7	2.4	4.6	0.1	2.1
Samoa	-9.0	1.9	7.1	7.1	-12.4	2.4	-5.8
Solomon Islands	13.0	1.8	5.7	3.6	2.1	-2.9	-4.5
Tonga	4.7	-1.7	-1.3	-2.5	0.4	3.6	...
Tuvalu	12.8	-1.8	...	...	...	...	...
Vanuatu	4.8	-15.8	5.1	0.4	0.9	...	...
Developed ADB Member Economies							
Australia	-0.8	1.5	-9.2	10.5	-3.3	-10.8	-9.5
Japan	-5.2	-4.2	-8.1	0.7	-6.5	1.4	...
New Zealand	-7.9	2.2	0.5	-4.1	6.8	-3.2	...

... = data not available, ADB = Asian Development Bank.

a Refers to other goods industries comprising agriculture, forestry, and fishing; and mining and quarrying.

Source: Economy's official sources.

Table 2.2.14: Growth Rates of Industry Real Value-Added
(%)

ADB Regional Member	2010	2015	2016	2017	2018	2019	2020
Developing ADB Member Economies							
Central and West Asia							
Afghanistan	6.3	4.5	-1.8	9.2	11.1	4.8	-4.2
Armenia	5.7	2.8	-0.3	9.0	3.7	10.5	-2.9
Azerbaijan	3.7	-1.9	-5.7	-3.1	-0.7	1.0	-5.6
Georgia[a]	8.2	2.6	6.7	4.4	-0.5	2.7	-2.8
Kazakhstan	9.5	-0.4	1.1	7.7	4.4	4.1	-0.4
Kyrgyz Republic	2.5	2.9	7.1	8.6	5.9	8.0	-10.3
Pakistan	3.4	5.2	5.7	4.6	4.6	-1.6	-3.8
Tajikistan	2.8	16.3	22.2	7.3	14.4	8.1	...
Turkmenistan	6.0	11.6 (2014)	...	...	...	...	...
Uzbekistan	5.5	8.3	5.9	5.4	11.5	8.3	2.2
East Asia							
China, People's Republic of	12.7	5.9	6.0	5.9	5.8	4.9	2.6
Hong Kong, China[a,b]	7.7	2.4	3.0	-0.7	2.5	-6.4	-7.1
Korea, Republic of[a]	...	...	...	...	...	...	...
Mongolia	8.8 (2011)	9.9	-0.4	0.7	7.9	3.1	-6.2
Taipei,China[a]	21.5	0.9	3.7	4.8	2.6	1.6	6.1
South Asia							
Bangladesh	7.0	9.7	11.1	10.2	12.1	12.7	6.5
Bhutan	12.5	8.2	6.9	2.5	-5.0	2.0	...
India	7.9	9.6	7.7	5.9	5.3	-1.2	-7.0
Maldives	7.3	18.1	8.9	10.7	10.5	8.4	...
Nepal	4.0	2.0	-4.1	17.1	10.4	7.4	-3.7
Sri Lanka	8.4	2.2	5.7	4.7	1.3	2.6	-6.9
Southeast Asia							
Brunei Darussalam	3.2 (2011)	-0.0	-2.9	1.5	-0.4	4.2	2.9
Cambodia	13.6	11.7	10.9	9.8	11.6	10.7	-1.4
Indonesia	4.9	3.0	3.8	4.1	4.3	3.8	-2.8
Lao People's Democratic Republic	17.5	7.0	12.0	11.6	7.8	5.6	9.2
Malaysia	8.4	5.2	4.3	4.7	3.3	2.3	-6.1
Myanmar	18.6	8.3	8.9	8.7	8.3	8.4	5.1
Philippines	9.8	6.5	8.2	7.0	7.3	5.5	-13.2
Singapore[a,b]	24.0	-2.7	2.6	6.9	5.5	-0.8	-0.4
Thailand[a,c]	10.6	1.9	2.2	2.1	2.9	0.0	-5.9
Timor-Leste	7.9	22.2	7.6	-26.5	5.3	...	...
Viet Nam	-9.9	9.6	7.6	8.0	8.9	8.9	4.0
The Pacific							
Cook Islands	-8.9	25.4	-13.5	19.1	7.0	10.5	-30.7
Fiji	6.5	6.9	7.2	4.2	5.5	-0.5	...
Kiribati	9.5	23.6	-2.4	-15.1	8.0	-2.0	...
Marshall Islands	20.1	-12.9	-5.6	2.7	13.0	6.6	-4.7
Micronesia, Federated States of	18.0	-6.1	5.1	4.0	-7.3	15.8	-5.2
Nauru	39.4	-17.1	77.3	-26.8	-37.9	-21.0	-1.9
Niue	14.4	0.9	2.3	-4.7	90.4	...	...
Palau	5.2	40.2	0.2	-5.8	2.3	5.9	...
Papua New Guinea	12.0	26.4	12.1	4.7	-7.5	11.4	-7.6
Samoa	7.7	8.7	-2.5	-9.4	-4.9	12.2	-15.6
Solomon Islands	13.2	-4.1	4.3	10.5	9.0	5.6	-6.1
Tonga	4.1	-0.6	12.7	9.7	-14.4	4.6	...
Tuvalu	-41.6	36.7	...	...	...	...	...
Vanuatu	12.6	35.3	4.3	7.1	4.9	...	...
Developed ADB Member Economies							
Australia[a]	...	...	...	...	...	...	...
Japan[a]	...	...	...	...	...	...	...
New Zealand[a]	...	...	...	...	...	...	...

... = data not available, -0.0 or 0.0 = magnitude is less than half of unit employed, ADB = Asian Development Bank.

a National accounts are compiled using chain volume measures.
b Industry refers to manufacturing, construction, and utilities comprising electricity, gas, steam, and air-conditioning supply; water supply; and sewerage, waste management, and remediation activities.
c Industry refers to mining and quarrying; manufacturing; electricity, gas, steam, and air-conditioning supply; water supply; and sewerage, waste management, and remediation activities.

Source: Economy's official sources.

Table 2.2.15: Growth Rates of Services Real Value-Added
(%)

ADB Regional Member	2010	2015	2016	2017	2018	2019	2020
Developing ADB Member Economies							
Central and West Asia							
Afghanistan	18.1	1.4	2.3	-0.7	1.9	-1.4	-4.8
Armenia	4.7	1.0	3.4	10.4	9.2	9.8	-8.8
Azerbaijan	8.8	4.4	-0.8	3.2	3.8	3.8	-3.9
Georgia[a]	8.2	3.8	2.8	6.4	5.8	6.1	-7.4
Kazakhstan	6.0	3.1	0.9	2.5	3.9	4.4	-5.6
Kyrgyz Republic	-1.3	3.5	3.2	3.3	2.9	3.3	-9.3
Pakistan	3.2	4.4	5.7	6.5	6.3	3.8	-0.6
Tajikistan	7.3	1.9	-1.5	6.2	2.6	8.6	...
Turkmenistan	13.8	-13.2 (2014)	...	...	...	...	...
Uzbekistan	10.6	8.3	6.3	6.4	5.5	6.3	0.1
East Asia							
China, People's Republic of	9.7	8.8	8.1	8.3	8.0	7.2	2.1
Hong Kong, China[a,b]	6.9	1.7	2.3	3.5	3.1	-0.7	-6.6
Korea, Republic of[a]	5.1	3.1	2.9	2.6	3.8	3.4	-1.0
Mongolia	17.8 (2011)	0.6	1.1	7.7	4.7	5.8	-7.1
Taipei,China[a]	6.4	1.2	1.3	2.9	3.0	3.5	1.2
South Asia							
Bangladesh	5.5	5.8	6.3	6.7	6.4	6.8	5.3
Bhutan	15.2	5.6	10.3	7.1	10.3	9.2	...
India	7.8	9.4	8.5	6.3	7.2	7.2	-8.4
Maldives	7.3	2.4	6.7	6.0	6.5	9.0	...
Nepal	5.8	5.4	1.2	8.4	9.3	6.8	-4.0
Sri Lanka	8.0	6.0	4.8	3.6	4.6	2.2	-1.5
Southeast Asia							
Brunei Darussalam	4.9 (2011)	-1.1	-1.7	1.1	0.8	3.4	-1.9
Cambodia	3.3	7.1	6.8	7.0	6.7	6.2	-6.3
Indonesia	8.4	5.5	5.7	5.7	5.8	6.4	-1.4
Lao People's Democratic Republic	7.6	8.0	4.7	4.5	6.8	6.9	-1.2
Malaysia	7.4	5.3	5.7	6.5	6.9	6.1	-5.7
Myanmar	9.5	8.7	8.1	8.1	8.7	8.3	2.5
Philippines	7.6	7.4	8.2	7.4	6.7	7.2	-9.2
Singapore[a,c]	10.9	4.3	2.7	3.6	3.2	2.3	-6.7
Thailand[a,d]	6.9	5.6	4.8	5.2	4.7	3.9	-6.5
Timor-Leste	10.5	4.6	5.7	3.2	-2.5	...	...
Viet Nam	-7.7	6.3	7.0	7.4	7.0	7.3	2.3
The Pacific							
Cook Islands	-5.8	2.4	12.3	6.6	5.1	6.4	-8.5
Fiji	2.9	3.0	0.1	3.6	1.7	0.2	...
Kiribati	-0.1	7.2	6.6	3.5	0.7	6.3	...
Marshall Islands	3.2	3.7	2.2	5.0	2.6	1.6	-2.2
Micronesia, Federated States of	2.4	3.0	2.8	2.9	0.9	0.0	-7.2
Nauru	4.2	11.6	-7.0	3.1	13.4	-3.3	-0.1
Niue	0.4	4.6	4.2	2.4	4.7	...	...
Palau	-0.3	8.9	-0.7	-2.8	9.3	0.6	...
Papua New Guinea	12.4	-2.3	2.3	1.4	5.1	2.5	-0.3
Samoa	3.0	6.9	4.8	0.4	3.9	0.5	-8.2
Solomon Islands	5.1	2.8	6.7	4.9	2.0	2.5	-4.1
Tonga	0.7	1.4	5.5	1.8	3.3	0.8	...
Tuvalu	2.3	7.1	...	...	...	...	...
Vanuatu	3.0	2.0	2.9	2.9	0.8	...	...
Developed ADB Member Economies							
Australia[a]	...	...	...	...	...	...	...
Japan[a]	...	...	...	...	...	...	...
New Zealand[a]	...	...	...	...	...	...	...

... = data not available, ADB = Asian Development Bank.

a National accounts are compiled using chain volume measures.
b Services refers to import, export, wholesale, and retail trades; accommodation and food services; transportation, storage, postal, and courier services; information and communications; financing and insurance; real estate, professional, and business services; public administration, social services, and personal services; and ownership of premises.
c Services refers to services-producing industries, including ownership of dwellings.
d Services includes construction.

Source: Economy's official sources.

Table 2.2.16: Growth Rates of Real Household Final Consumption
(%)

ADB Regional Member	2010	2015	2016	2017	2018	2019	2020
Developing ADB Member Economies							
Central and West Asia							
Afghanistan	...	...	...	-6.2	26.2	11.3	-6.5
Armenia[a]	3.9	-7.5	-2.1	14.0	4.8	11.5	-13.9
Azerbaijan[a]	10.8	10.3	1.7	0.8	4.7	5.9	...
Georgia[a]	9.0 (2011)	3.8	-5.7	7.4	5.8	7.2	5.4
Kazakhstan[a]	11.5	1.8	1.2	1.5	6.1	6.1	...
Kyrgyz Republic[a]	2.7	-0.9	-0.6	6.3	5.0	0.8	...
Pakistan[a]	2.2	2.9	7.6	8.5	6.2	3.1	-4.1
Tajikistan[a]	10.5	-15.1	13.2	4.6	4.0	5.0	...
Turkmenistan[a]	-61.4	...	...	...	...	...	...
Uzbekistan[a]	10.6	11.9	9.4	3.9	5.9	5.6	3.0
East Asia							
China, People's Republic of	...	...	...	...	...	...	...
Hong Kong, China[a]	6.1	4.8	2.0	5.5	5.3	-0.8	-9.9
Korea, Republic of	4.6	2.2	2.3	2.8	3.1	2.1	-5.2
Mongolia[a]	15.8 (2011)	8.1	-2.6	5.4	12.4	9.9	2.7
Taipei,China	3.7	3.1	2.7	2.7	1.7	2.5	-2.3
South Asia							
Bangladesh	4.6	5.8	3.0	7.4	11.0	3.9	4.0
Bhutan[a]	5.7	13.8	-4.9	5.1	14.7	6.1	...
India[a]	6.7	7.9	8.1	6.2	7.6	5.5	-9.1
Maldives	...	...	...	...	...	...	...
Nepal[a]	6.2	2.6	4.2	0.8	6.2	8.1	3.6
Sri Lanka	9.9 (2011)	7.5	7.4	3.6	4.0	3.0	-3.0
Southeast Asia							
Brunei Darussalam[a]	5.4 (2011)	5.2	-1.3	4.7	2.2	5.9	7.3
Cambodia[a]	8.8	6.0	6.8	4.6	4.6	5.6	-1.9
Indonesia[a]	4.7	5.0	5.0	4.9	5.1	5.0	-2.6
Lao People's Democratic Republic	...	...	...	...	...	...	...
Malaysia[a]	6.9	6.0	5.9	6.9	8.0	7.6	-4.3
Myanmar[b]	2.6	4.7	2.2	4.1	4.5	1.5	...
Philippines[a]	3.6	6.4	7.1	6.0	5.8	5.9	-7.9
Singapore	4.4	5.2	3.3	3.1	4.0	3.3	-14.1
Thailand[a]	5.5	2.6	2.9	3.1	4.6	4.0	-1.0
Timor-Leste	5.2	1.7	3.0	6.5	2.0	3.5	...
Viet Nam	8.2	9.3	7.3	7.3	7.3	7.4	0.5
The Pacific							
Cook Islands	...	...	...	...	...	...	...
Fiji	...	...	...	...	...	...	...
Kiribati	...	...	...	...	...	...	...
Marshall Islands	-0.4	-1.2	3.1	10.5	-0.8	8.2	-19.4
Micronesia, Federated States of	...	...	...	...	...	...	...
Nauru	...	...	...	...	...	...	...
Niue	...	...	...	...	...	...	...
Palau	-3.1	4.2	6.0	-0.5	5.2	-2.9	...
Papua New Guinea[a]	9.8 (2005)	...	...	...	...	...	...
Samoa	...	...	...	...	...	...	...
Solomon Islands	8.7	2.5	3.5	0.0	...	...	...
Tonga	2.3	8.2	6.5	1.0	4.2	0.5	...
Tuvalu	...	...	...	...	...	...	...
Vanuatu	2.6	1.3	8.9	-1.9	3.4	...	...
Developed ADB Member Economies							
Australia	3.3	2.3	2.7	2.3	2.8	1.8	-3.0
Japan	2.3	-0.3	-0.6	1.0	0.5	-0.4	-6.3
New Zealand	2.2	4.2	6.5	5.0	4.4	2.8	...

... = data not available, 0.0 = magnitude is less than half of unit employed, ADB = Asian Development Bank.

a Includes expenditure of nonprofit institutions serving households.
b Data refers to total final consumption expenditure.

Source: Economy's official sources.

Table 2.2.17: Growth Rates of Real Government Consumption Expenditure
(%)

ADB Regional Member	2010	2015	2016	2017	2018	2019	2020
Developing ADB Member Economies							
Central and West Asia							
Afghanistan	...	...	...	-6.4	-5.6	28.4	-24.6
Armenia	3.9	4.7	-2.4	-2.1	-3.0	12.9	15.2
Azerbaijan	3.4	1.5	6.8	1.1	-3.9	2.2	...
Georgia	-3.3 (2011)	4.4	10.9	1.1	1.6	5.7	5.7
Kazakhstan	2.7	2.4	2.3	2.1	-14.1	15.5	...
Kyrgyz Republic	-1.1	0.9	1.5	1.3	1.3	0.5	...
Pakistan	-0.6	8.1	8.2	5.3	8.6	0.8	6.8
Tajikistan	0.9	3.3	1.7	5.7	4.5	0.7	...
Turkmenistan	3.7	...	...	...	...	...	...
Uzbekistan	7.0	6.7	2.7	1.5	4.8	5.7	2.0
East Asia							
China, People's Republic of	...	...	...	...	...	...	...
Hong Kong, China	3.4	3.4	3.4	2.8	4.2	5.1	8.1
Korea, Republic of	5.6	3.8	4.4	3.9	5.3	6.4	5.0
Mongolia	15.3 (2011)	-4.7	10.6	-1.8	0.5	13.6	16.0
Taipei,China	1.2	-0.1	3.7	-0.4	4.0	0.7	2.6
South Asia							
Bangladesh	6.8	8.8	8.4	7.8	15.4	9.0	7.3
Bhutan	7.5	10.8	4.2	4.4	3.0	10.8	...
India	5.2	7.5	6.1	11.9	6.3	7.9	2.9
Maldives	...	...	...	...	...	...	...
Nepal	1.3	11.5	-12.0	21.4	2.1	9.8	3.8
Sri Lanka	-2.1 (2011)	10.2	2.3	-6.0	-5.1	13.0	4.4
Southeast Asia							
Brunei Darussalam	5.3 (2011)	-3.6	-6.5	7.4	1.6	1.8	-9.6
Cambodia	12.5	4.4	5.7	6.5	6.5	5.8	15.2
Indonesia	0.3	5.3	-0.1	2.1	4.8	3.3	1.9
Lao People's Democratic Republic	...	...	...	...	...	...	...
Malaysia	3.4	4.5	1.1	5.7	3.2	2.0	4.1
Myanmar	...	...	...	...	...	...	...
Philippines	4.2	7.9	9.4	6.5	13.4	9.1	10.5
Singapore	10.2	8.9	3.8	3.1	3.2	3.4	12.6
Thailand	8.9	2.5	2.2	0.3	2.6	1.7	0.8
Timor-Leste	2.1	3.6	-1.2	-5.8	-0.3	3.2	...
Viet Nam	12.3	7.0	7.5	7.4	6.3	5.8	6.2
The Pacific							
Cook Islands	...	...	...	...	...	...	...
Fiji	...	...	...	...	...	...	...
Kiribati	...	...	...	...	...	...	...
Marshall Islands	-0.7	4.8	9.9	0.4	5.6	6.3	-12.3
Micronesia, Federated States of	...	...	...	...	...	...	...
Nauru	...	...	...	...	...	...	...
Niue	...	...	...	...	...	...	...
Palau	-1.5	1.3	4.1	-0.9	4.4	0.3	...
Papua New Guinea	1.1 (2005)	...	...	...	...	...	...
Samoa	...	...	...	...	...	...	...
Solomon Islands	10.0	4.9	4.2	4.8	...	...	...
Tonga	-8.3	3.1	-1.4	2.4	1.1	9.7	...
Tuvalu	...	...	...	...	...	...	...
Vanuatu	4.3	16.9	-1.4	19.5	4.5	...	...
Developed ADB Member Economies							
Australia	1.7	2.4	4.3	5.0	3.7	5.0	6.5
Japan	1.9	1.9	1.6	0.1	1.0	1.9	2.7
New Zealand	2.0	2.3	2.2	3.4	3.7	6.1	...

... = data not available, ADB = Asian Development Bank.

Source: Economy's official sources.

Table 2.2.18: Growth Rates of Real Gross Capital Formation
(%)

ADB Regional Member	2010	2015	2016	2017	2018	2019	2020
Developing ADB Member Economies							
Central and West Asia							
Afghanistan	...	...	...	8.2	14.7	-17.3	30.4
Armenia	0.5	-3.2	-8.7	10.3	34.5	-14.3	-9.6
Azerbaijan	2.0	-8.2	-19.0	1.2	-4.3	1.1	...
Georgia	14.3 (2011)	7.5	13.3	-2.3	6.5	-5.9	-3.4
Kazakhstan	2.0	5.5	2.5	3.1	2.9	12.2	...
Kyrgyz Republic	-5.2	-2.3	8.1	6.9	16.0	7.9	...
Pakistan	-6.5	14.6	7.3	9.8	10.7	-11.3	-1.0
Tajikistan	7.5	25.2	-6.6	-12.0	25.5	8.9	...
Turkmenistan	21.5	...	...	...	...	...	...
Uzbekistan	...	...	...	...	...	...	...
East Asia							
China, People's Republic of	...	...	...	...	...	...	...
Hong Kong, China	11.3	-8.1	4.0	5.4	1.8	-16.9	-2.0
Korea, Republic of	17.1	6.5	6.3	10.9	-1.3	-1.9	0.5
Mongolia	62.8 (2011)	-26.5	2.1	34.6	18.6	30.5	-42.5
Taipei,China	35.6	2.6	1.7	-0.8	6.9	6.4	5.3
South Asia							
Bangladesh	8.6	7.1	8.9	10.1	10.5	8.4	6.7
Bhutan	46.1	16.5	12.0	-2.2	-5.3	-16.5	...
India	20.1	7.0	9.8	14.5	2.3	5.4	...
Maldives	...	...	...	...	...	...	...
Nepal	34.4	7.0	-7.6	55.2	12.2	11.1	-29.5
Sri Lanka	20.2 (2011)	3.8	5.0	6.7	3.6	-10.5	-10.1
Southeast Asia							
Brunei Darussalam	37.0 (2011)	6.6	-11.1	8.0	28.1	-4.4	-9.3
Cambodia	-7.9	9.9	10.0	6.0	6.0	6.5	12.8
Indonesia	8.8	3.0	5.0	5.7	8.5	2.4	-6.9
Lao People's Democratic Republic	...	...	...	...	...	...	...
Malaysia	25.3	6.7	4.4	6.3	-1.7	-3.9	-12.2
Myanmar	34.6	16.1	4.3	8.1	-1.5	1.6	...
Philippines	30.5	13.4	20.8	10.9	11.3	3.5	-34.4
Singapore	22.5	-9.8	9.5	11.3	-2.8	-1.5	-15.1
Thailand	32.0	2.1	-3.8	11.0	16.1	-3.5	...
Timor-Leste	2.8	-5.0	15.7	-16.0	-1.9	-15.8	...
Viet Nam	10.4	9.0	9.7	9.8	8.2	7.9	4.1
The Pacific							
Cook Islands	...	...	...	...	...	...	...
Fiji	...	...	...	...	...	...	...
Kiribati	...	...	...	...	...	...	...
Marshall Islands	18.8	-12.2	20.8	30.6	3.3	130.4	-63.2
Micronesia, Federated States of	...	...	...	...	...	...	...
Nauru	...	...	...	...	...	...	...
Niue	...	...	...	...	...	...	...
Palau	3.3	0.3	9.8	12.0	-10.0	8.5	...
Papua New Guinea	-9.8 (2005)	...	...	...	...	...	...
Samoa	...	...	...	...	...	...	...
Solomon Islands	85.2	19.9	4.9	13.4	...	...	...
Tonga	4.7	11.1	9.6	18.9	-23.2	7.9	...
Tuvalu	...	...	...	...	...	...	...
Vanuatu	-5.2	33.2	-21.5	15.9	14.9	...	...
Developed ADB Member Economies							
Australia	...	...	...	...	...	...	...
Japan	2.9	2.9	-0.9	3.5	0.5	1.5	4.4
New Zealand	7.4	2.3	3.1	8.4	5.1	-1.2	...

... = data not available, ADB = Asian Development Bank.

Source: Economy's official sources.

Table 2.2.19: Growth Rates of Real Exports of Goods and Services
(%)

ADB Regional Member	2010	2015	2016	2017	2018	2019	2020
Developing ADB Member Economies							
Central and West Asia							
Afghanistan	...	...	...	46.5	-24.7	-21.5	5.9
Armenia	26.5	4.9	21.3	19.3	5.0	16.0	-32.4
Azerbaijan	9.1	-0.2	-2.0	-2.2	0.5	-4.3	...
Georgia	16.6 (2011)	4.2	8.7	11.7	10.1	9.8	-38.2
Kazakhstan	3.1	-4.1	-4.5	8.0	9.6	2.0	...
Kyrgyz Republic	-11.7	-5.6	-3.8	6.1	-2.7	16.2	...
Pakistan	15.7	-6.3	-1.6	-0.6	12.7	14.5	2.5
Tajikistan	23.0	–	15.1	6.8	-5.2	21.5	...
Turkmenistan	11.7	...	...	...	...	...	...
Uzbekistan	2.0	2.3	11.1	1.3	9.3	20.7	-18.7
East Asia							
China, People's Republic of	...	...	...	...	...	...	...
Hong Kong, China[a]	17.6	-1.4	0.7	5.8	3.7	-6.1	-5.9
Korea, Republic of	13.0	0.2	2.4	2.5	4.0	1.7	-2.5
Mongolia	18.2 (2011)	0.1	13.8	14.8	24.0	9.1	-0.1
Taipei,China	27.6	0.4	-0.9	4.5	0.2	1.3	1.1
South Asia							
Bangladesh	0.9	-2.8	2.2	-2.3	8.1	10.9	-8.5
Bhutan	7.5	-3.2	-5.3	6.5	4.6	14.4	...
India	19.5	-5.6	5.0	4.6	12.3	-3.3	-4.7
Maldives	...	...	...	...	...	...	...
Nepal	-10.4	2.3	-17.3	8.9	7.7	5.5	-15.9
Sri Lanka	10.2 (2011)	4.7	-0.7	7.6	0.5	7.2	-9.6
Southeast Asia							
Brunei Darussalam	-3.0 (2011)	-9.9	-1.9	-5.3	5.7	14.9	7.5
Cambodia	20.6	7.2	8.6	5.3	5.3	7.8	1.1
Indonesia	15.3	-2.1	-1.7	8.9	6.5	-0.9	-7.7
Lao People's Democratic Republic	...	...	...	...	...	...	...
Malaysia	11.1	0.3	1.3	8.7	1.9	-1.3	-8.8
Myanmar	10.9	15.1	-0.4	13.5	12.0	11.3	...
Philippines	20.3	10.0	9.2	17.4	11.8	2.6	-16.3
Singapore	17.8	5.0	-0.1	7.1	7.7	0.1	-4.3
Thailand	14.2	1.3	2.7	5.2	3.4	-3.0	-19.4
Timor-Leste	28.0	-28.3	8.5	-39.1	16.6	-17.2	...
Viet Nam	14.6	12.6	13.9	16.7	14.3	6.7	5.0
The Pacific							
Cook Islands	...	...	...	...	...	...	...
Fiji	...	...	...	...	...	...	...
Kiribati	...	...	...	...	...	...	...
Marshall Islands	44.3	-2.9	-11.3	-2.3	8.6	8.3	-3.3
Micronesia, Federated States of	...	...	...	...	...	...	...
Nauru	...	...	...	...	...	...	...
Niue	...	...	...	...	...	...	...
Palau	5.7	12.7	-3.9	-9.3	-5.4	-13.1	...
Papua New Guinea	6.8 (2005)	...	...	...	...	...	...
Samoa	...	...	...	...	...	...	...
Solomon Islands	32.7	-6.5	10.7	5.2	...	...	...
Tonga	-9.4	7.9	27.2	-5.8	1.3	-3.3	...
Tuvalu	...	...	...	...	...	...	...
Vanuatu	0.4	4.9	19.5	-1.1	3.5	...	...
Developed ADB Member Economies							
Australia	4.7	6.8	6.8	5.5	4.1	4.0	-1.8
Japan	24.9	3.2	1.6	6.6	3.8	-1.4	-12.3
New Zealand	2.8	6.4	1.6	3.6	3.3	-0.3	...

... = data not available, – = magnitude equals zero, ADB = Asian Development Bank.

a The statistics for trade in goods and services are compiled based on the change of ownership principle in recording goods sent abroad for processing and merchanting under the standards stipulated in the System of National Accounts 2008.

Source: Economy's official sources.

Table 2.2.20: Growth Rates of Real Imports of Goods and Services
(%)

ADB Regional Member	2010	2015	2016	2017	2018	2019	2020
Developing ADB Member Economies							
Central and West Asia							
Afghanistan	...	...	...	-0.5	40.3	16.5	-15.8
Armenia	12.8	-15.3	6.3	24.6	13.3	11.6	-31.7
Azerbaijan	12.4	8.4	-3.2	-0.8	-0.2	-3.2	...
Georgia	15.6(2011)	7.2	2.4	8.1	10.3	6.6	-17.4
Kazakhstan	2.9	-0.1	-2.0	1.0	6.6	14.9	...
Kyrgyz Republic	-6.9	-13.2	-1.1	7.4	7.4	6.1	...
Pakistan	4.3	-1.6	16.0	21.2	17.6	4.3	-7.9
Tajikistan	8.0	–	-7.5	-6.5	9.3	6.4	...
Turkmenistan	7.3	...	...	...	...	...	...
Uzbekistan	-2.8	-11.2	-2.2	15.5	38.5	25.0	-12.9
East Asia							
China, People's Republic of	...	...	...	...	...	...	...
Hong Kong, China[a]	18.2	-1.8	0.9	6.6	4.5	-7.2	-6.2
Korea, Republic of	17.5	2.1	5.2	8.9	1.7	-0.6	-3.8
Mongolia	49.5(2011)	-11.4	12.7	24.8	30.9	22.3	-8.9
Taipei,China	30.1	1.3	-1.0	1.6	0.8	1.1	-3.9
South Asia							
Bangladesh	0.7	3.2	-7.1	2.9	27.0	-2.0	-6.9
Bhutan	28.7	17.2	-9.3	-1.0	8.2	-6.6	...
India	15.8	-5.9	4.4	17.4	8.6	-0.8	-13.6
Maldives	...	...	...	...	...	...	...
Nepal	28.3	9.6	3.2	28.2	19.0	5.8	-15.2
Sri Lanka	23.6(2011)	10.6	7.9	7.1	1.8	-5.8	-11.4
Southeast Asia							
Brunei Darussalam	33.7(2011)	-8.9	-10.8	1.3	28.1	13.8	-2.1
Cambodia	16.8	6.5	8.6	4.1	4.1	6.0	7.3
Indonesia	17.3	-6.2	-2.4	8.1	12.1	-7.4	-14.7
Lao People's Democratic Republic	...	...	...	...	...	...	...
Malaysia	15.6	0.8	1.4	10.2	1.5	-2.5	-8.3
Myanmar	51.9	21.6	-11.4	10.0	-2.2	-7.7	...
Philippines	20.7	15.0	18.8	15.1	14.6	2.3	-21.6
Singapore	16.3	3.4	0.1	7.8	7.5	0.2	-7.1
Thailand	23.0	0.0	-1.0	6.2	8.3	-5.2	-13.3
Timor-Leste	-1.9	-7.6	8.2	-8.7	2.8	-6.5	...
Viet Nam	13.7	18.1	15.3	17.5	12.8	8.3	3.3
The Pacific							
Cook Islands	...	...	...	...	...	...	...
Fiji	...	...	...	...	...	...	...
Kiribati	...	...	...	...	...	...	...
Marshall Islands	9.5	-0.9	0.5	10.9	3.1	37.3	-31.4
Micronesia, Federated States of	...	...	...	...	...	...	...
Nauru	...	...	...	...	...	...	...
Niue	...	...	...	...	...	...	...
Palau	0.9	2.5	8.3	-1.5	-3.6	0.6	...
Papua New Guinea	4.7(2005)	...	...	...	...	...	...
Samoa	...	...	...	...	...	...	...
Solomon Islands	52.2	0.8	4.1	-2.9	...	...	...
Tonga	3.0	22.6	16.9	3.5	-1.4	4.8	...
Tuvalu	...	...	...	...	...	...	...
Vanuatu	-2.2	26.2	2.3	3.3	10.4	...	...
Developed ADB Member Economies							
Australia	7.1	1.0	-0.1	4.8	7.3	0.2	-7.4
Japan	11.3	0.4	-1.2	3.3	3.8	-0.4	-6.8
New Zealand	11.5	2.6	5.6	7.8	4.4	1.2	...

... = data not available, 0.0 = magnitude is less than half of unit employed, – = magnitude equals zero, ADB = Asian Development Bank.

a The statistics for trade in goods and services are compiled based on the change of ownership principle in recording goods sent abroad for processing and merchanting under the standards stipulated in the System of National Accounts 2008.

Source: Economy's official sources.

Table 2.2.21: Growth Rates of Agriculture Production Index
(%)

ADB Regional Member	2010	2015	2016	2017	2018	2019	2020
Developing ADB Member Economies							
Central and West Asia							
Afghanistan	-0.7	-5.3	6.7	-3.3	-2.9	15.5	...
Armenia	-13.4	8.3	-10.1	-1.2	-12.0	-2.0	...
Azerbaijan	-2.1	6.5	3.9	5.8	5.6	7.9	...
Georgia	-4.5	1.9	-4.4	-8.7	16.4	1.1	...
Kazakhstan[a]	-10.4	3.4	5.4	3.0	3.5	-0.1	5.6
Kyrgyz Republic[b]	-2.6	6.2	3.1	2.4	2.7	2.6	...
Pakistan	-1.9	-4.8	2.6	11.5	5.8	-13.4	1.1
Tajikistan	5.0	6.6	0.3	34.9	7.6	7.2	...
Turkmenistan	4.7	2.2	-3.1	-2.0	-4.6	3.3	...
Uzbekistan	...	6.1	6.3	1.0	0.2	3.3	2.8
East Asia							
China, People's Republic of	2.5	2.8	0.5	1.5	1.5	-0.1	...
Hong Kong, China	-	-	-	6.3	5.9	-	-
Korea, Republic of	-4.5	-2.4	-1.2	-1.1	1.7	1.5	...
Mongolia	-23.3	31.9	-4.4	1.3	22.6	6.9	...
Taipei,China[c]	2.1	-3.4	-3.7	5.7	2.6	-3.8	-1.1
South Asia							
Bangladesh	6.1	2.5	-0.6	7.6	-0.2	1.0	...
Bhutan	4.0	-1.5	8.7	0.3	-9.7	4.1	...
India	8.7	-1.6	4.2	6.0	4.2	1.0	...
Maldives	-4.0	1.4	2.1	-0.8	-0.4	4.2	...
Nepal	1.0	-	2.4	4.5	0.6	5.4	...
Sri Lanka	10.6	13.5	-1.9	-17.0	21.6	2.1	...
Southeast Asia							
Brunei Darussalam	4.7	-2.2	4.3	-3.5	1.0	-2.1	...
Cambodia	7.7	4.1	6.9	6.3	4.8	2.3	...
Indonesia	-22.0	2.5	2.9	-2.4	22.5	8.1	...
Lao People's Democratic Republic	9.6	16.0	1.4	-7.1	-0.1	4.0	...
Malaysia	1.8	6.3	-5.9	8.3	-3.4	2.5	...
Myanmar[d]	-3.5 (2011)	2.3	-0.8	0.1	-3.9	-3.3	...
Philippines	-1.1	-0.1	-1.0	4.5	0.7	-0.3	...
Singapore	3.2	4.2	8.5	26.2	-16.4	-0.3	...
Thailand	0.9	-3.5	0.2	6.4	7.2	-1.0	-4.1
Timor-Leste	-0.3	9.7	-3.5	-1.3	-4.1	4.1	...
Viet Nam	2.0	2.2	-0.1	1.6	3.4	-0.7	...
The Pacific							
Cook Islands	-2.0	-1.9	-9.7	-7.5	-5.3	-2.4	...
Fiji	-19.6	1.7	-24.2	35.6	4.5	-3.1	...
Kiribati	0.5	0.8	0.6	0.4	-7.9	0.1	...
Marshall Islands	-5.0	8.0	40.7	-	-36.8	-6.4	...
Micronesia, Federated States of	-1.0	0.5	1.1	0.1	0.0	0.4	...
Nauru	0.9	0.6	0.6	-0.9	0.3	0.6	...
Niue	-0.6	-4.5	-2.0	-1.4	-1.3	-1.1	...
Palau	...	...	...	...	...	...	...
Papua New Guinea	-1.7	1.1	1.2	1.4	1.4	1.4	...
Samoa	1.5	1.4	-0.0	2.2	1.0	0.5	...
Solomon Islands	-25.4	1.5	0.9	1.8	1.5	1.0	...
Tonga	-0.8	-1.4	-7.0	0.8	-2.1	-2.9	...
Tuvalu	-1.4	1.5	0.2	0.8	0.8	0.6	...
Vanuatu	28.5	-5.0	0.7	0.3	0.2	0.6	...
Developed ADB Member Economies							
Australia	-0.2	-1.2	-0.7	6.0	-8.1	-8.1	...
Japan	-2.3	-1.1	-0.4	0.4	-0.3	0.3	...
New Zealand	-	2.1	-0.3	-3.4	2.2	1.5	...

... = data not available, -0.0 or 0.0 = magnitude is less than half of unit employed, - = magnitude equals zero, ADB = Asian Development Bank.

Note: Data refer to gross production index (2014–2016 = 100), except for Hong Kong, China; Indonesia; Kazakhstan; the Kyrgyz Republic; Myanmar; Pakistan; Taipei,China; Thailand; and Uzbekistan.

a Refers to the index of physical volume of the gross production (services) of agriculture.

b Refers to volume indices of agriculture, hunting, and forestry.

c Refers to the index of agricultural, forestry, and fishery production.

d For 2010–2015, fiscal year is April–March. For 2016 onward, fiscal year is October–September.

Sources: Food and Agriculture Organization of the United Nations. FAOSTAT Database. http://www.fao.org/faostat/en/#home (accessed 20 July 2021). For Hong Kong, China; Indonesia; Kazakhstan; the Kyrgyz Republic; Myanmar; Pakistan; Taipei,China; Thailand; and Uzbekistan: Economy's official sources.

Table 2.2.22: Growth Rates of Manufacturing Production Index
(%)

ADB Regional Member	2010	2015	2016	2017	2018	2019	2020
Developing ADB Member Economies							
Central and West Asia							
Afghanistan	...	...	...	...	...	...	...
Armenia	...	...	...	...	...	...	...
Azerbaijan	18.5	4.7	-5.6	-3.0	10.2	3.2	-1.0
Georgia	18.5	-12.6	3.7	1.5	4.8	0.8	0.5
Kazakhstan	13.9	0.2	0.6	5.6	4.5	5.8	3.9
Kyrgyz Republic	10.1	-7.8	5.4	7.6	5.0	8.3	-7.2
Pakistan	0.5	3.4	3.1	5.8	5.2	-2.3	-9.9
Tajikistan	-6.2 (2009)	...	...	...	...	...	...
Turkmenistan	...	...	...	...	...	...	...
Uzbekistan	8.9	5.9	6.7	4.2	7.9	6.6	7.1
East Asia							
China, People's Republic of	16.6	7.0	6.8	7.2	6.5	6.0	3.4
Hong Kong, China	3.5	-1.6	-0.4	0.4	1.3	0.4	-5.8
Korea, Republic of	7.9	-0.3	2.3	2.3	1.3	0.5	-0.3
Mongolia	...	...	...	...	...	...	...
Taipei,China	29.7	-1.2	1.9	5.3	3.9	-0.4	7.6
South Asia							
Bangladesh	6.3	10.7	13.5	11.2	15.0	14.7	1.4
Bhutan	...	...	...	...	...	...	...
India	9.0	3.0	4.1	4.6	3.9	-1.4	...
Maldives	...	...	...	...	...	...	...
Nepal	-2.7	0.3	-9.8	17.1	10.0	7.2	...
Sri Lanka	...	...	...	...	...	...	...
Southeast Asia							
Brunei Darussalam	...	...	...	...	...	...	...
Cambodia	...	...	...	...	...	...	...
Indonesia	4.4	4.8	4.0	4.7	4.0	4.1	...
Lao People's Democratic Republic	...	...	...	...	...	...	...
Malaysia	11.1	4.8	4.3	6.1	4.8	3.6	-2.7
Myanmar[a]	10.1 (2011)	10.2	9.1	9.8	9.7	7.3	...
Philippines	23.2	0.5	13.1	11.3	7.1	-8.9	-40.5
Singapore[b]	29.7	-5.1	3.7	10.4	7.0	-1.5	7.3
Thailand	14.2	0.1	1.4	1.7	3.9	-3.4	-9.3
Timor-Leste	...	...	...	...	...	...	...
Viet Nam	...	1.6	0.8	2.9	-2.0	-1.6	-5.1
The Pacific							
Cook Islands	...	...	...	...	...	...	...
Fiji	7.6	-17.2	2.1	1.5	3.6	-4.6	-6.6
Kiribati	...	...	...	...	...	...	...
Marshall Islands	...	...	...	...	...	...	...
Micronesia, Federated States of	...	...	...	...	...	...	...
Nauru	...	...	...	...	...	...	...
Niue	...	...	...	...	...	...	...
Palau	...	...	...	...	...	...	...
Papua New Guinea	...	...	...	...	...	...	...
Samoa[b]	15.2	...	...	...	...	...	...
Solomon Islands	...	...	...	...	...	...	...
Tonga	...	...	...	...	...	...	...
Tuvalu	...	...	...	...	...	...	...
Vanuatu	...	...	...	...	...	...	...
Developed ADB Member Economies							
Australia	0.5	-1.6	-2.5	-0.3	2.0	-0.7	-1.7
Japan	15.6	-1.1	–	3.1	1.1	-3.0	-10.4
New Zealand	4.6	1.8	3.1	1.9	2.0	1.4	-3.1

... = data not available, – = magnitude equals zero, ADB = Asian Development Bank.

a For 2010–2015, fiscal year is April–March. For 2016 onward, fiscal year is October–September.
b Refers to volume indices of industrial production.

Source: Economy's official sources.

Data Issues and Comparability

Indicators in this theme were derived from national accounts statistics compiled in accordance with the UN System of National Accounts. As national statistical offices gradually adopt the latest 2008 System of National Accounts framework with regard to data compilation and methodologies, these indicators will become more consistent across economies. Currently, economies in the region have varying reference periods (e.g., calendar year versus fiscal year) and price valuation methods. Due to a lack of reliable data and limited technical and financial resources dedicated for national accounts compilation, some economies with small statistical offices are not able to provide timely estimates, while some are dependent upon the estimates of external institutions.

Table 2.3.1: Growth Rates of Consumer Price Index
(%)

ADB Regional Member	2010	2015	2016	2017	2018	2019	2020
Developing ADB Member Economies							
Central and West Asia							
Afghanistan	4.9	-0.7	4.4	5.0	0.6	2.3	5.6
Armenia	8.2	3.7	-1.4	1.0	2.5	1.4	1.2
Azerbaijan	5.7	4.0	12.4	12.9	2.3	2.6	2.8
Georgia	7.1	4.0	2.1	6.0	2.6	4.9	5.2
Kazakhstan	7.1	6.6	14.6	7.4	6.0	5.3	6.8
Kyrgyz Republic	8.0	6.5	0.4	3.2	1.5	1.1	6.3
Pakistan	10.1	4.5	2.9	4.2	3.9	7.3	10.7
Tajikistan	9.8	5.1	6.1	6.7	5.4	8.0	9.4
Turkmenistan	4.4	7.4	3.6	8.0	13.0	13.3	10.0
Uzbekistan[a]	7.6	5.5	9.5	13.9	17.5	14.5	12.9
East Asia							
China, People's Republic of	3.3	1.4	2.0	1.6	2.1	2.9	2.5
Hong Kong, China	2.4	3.0	2.4	1.5	2.4	2.9	0.3
Korea, Republic of	2.9	0.7	1.0	1.9	1.5	0.4	0.5
Mongolia	12.9	1.9	1.3	6.4	8.1	5.2	2.3
Taipei,China	1.0	-0.3	1.4	0.6	1.4	0.6	-0.2
South Asia							
Bangladesh	6.8	6.4	5.9	5.4	5.8	5.5	5.7
Bhutan	7.0	4.6	3.2	5.0	2.7	2.7	5.6
India	10.4	4.9	4.6	3.7	3.4	4.8	6.5
Maldives	6.1	1.0	0.5	2.8	-0.1	0.2	-1.4
Nepal	9.6	7.2	9.9	4.5	4.2	4.6	6.2
Sri Lanka[b]	6.2	2.2	4.0	6.5	4.3	4.4	4.5
Southeast Asia							
Brunei Darussalam	0.4	-0.5	-0.3	-1.3	1.0	-0.4	1.9
Cambodia[b]	4.0	1.2	3.0	2.9	2.5	1.9	2.9
Indonesia[c]	5.1	6.4	3.5	3.8	3.2	2.8	2.0
Lao People's Democratic Republic	6.0	1.3	1.6	0.8	2.0	3.3	5.1
Malaysia	1.7	2.1	2.1	3.7	1.0	0.6	-1.1
Myanmar	7.7	9.5	6.9	4.6	6.8	8.9	3.8
Philippines	3.8	0.7	1.3	2.9	5.2	2.5	2.6
Singapore	2.8	-0.5	-0.5	0.6	0.4	0.6	-0.2
Thailand	3.3	-0.9	0.2	0.7	1.1	0.7	-0.9
Timor-Leste	5.2	0.6	-1.5	0.5	2.3	0.9	0.5
Viet Nam	9.2	0.6	2.7	3.5	3.5	2.8	3.2
The Pacific							
Cook Islands	1.5	1.1	-0.4	-0.3	0.1	0.4	1.0
Fiji	3.7	1.4	3.9	3.3	4.1	1.8	-2.6
Kiribati[b]	-3.0	0.6	1.9	0.4	0.6	-1.8	2.5
Marshall Islands[b]	1.8	-2.2	-1.5	0.1	0.8	-0.1	-0.7
Micronesia, Federated States of	3.6	0.0	-1.0	...	1.4	...	...
Nauru	-3.1	9.8	8.2	5.1	0.5	3.9	2.8
Niue	5.3	1.8	1.3	5.0	10.1	1.9	...
Palau	1.4	0.9	-1.0	0.7	2.1	0.2	...
Papua New Guinea	4.4 (2011)	6.0	6.7	5.4	4.4	3.9	4.9
Samoa	0.8	0.7	1.3	1.8	4.2	1.0	-1.6
Solomon Islands[b]	0.9	-0.6	0.5	0.5	3.5	1.6	...
Tonga	3.5	-1.1	2.6	7.5	6.1	1.2	-0.3
Tuvalu	-1.9	3.1	3.5	4.1	2.2	3.5	1.6
Vanuatu	3.1	2.5	0.8	3.3	5.0	3.0	...
Developed ADB Member Economies							
Australia	2.3	1.7	1.4	1.7	1.9	1.6	1.3
Japan	-0.7	0.8	-0.1	0.5	1.0	0.5	-0.0
New Zealand	2.3	0.3	0.6	1.9	1.6	1.6	1.7

... = data not available, 0.0 = magnitude is less than half of unit employed, ADB = Asian Development Bank.

Note: Data refer to the whole of each economy, unless otherwise indicated.

a Prior to 2016, values were calculated based on variable weights. From 2016 onward, values were calculated based on fixed weights.

b Data refer to capital city.

c In the longer time series featured in the Key Indicators Database (and relevant years in the table), data refers to consumer price indexes for 43 cities for 2000–2002, 45 cities for 2003–2007, 66 cities for 2008–2013, 82 cities for 2014–2018, and 90 cities for 2019–2020.

Source: Economy's official sources.

Table 2.3.2: Growth Rates of Food and Nonalcoholic Beverages Consumer Price Index
(%)

ADB Regional Member	2010	2015	2016	2017	2018	2019	2020
Developing ADB Member Economies							
Central and West Asia							
Afghanistan	3.5	-0.8	5.7	6.9	-1.1	3.8	10.0
Armenia	9.4	3.1	-3.3	4.1	2.3	1.9	0.3
Azerbaijan	7.5	4.8	13.7	17.2	2.0	3.3	4.6
Georgia	11.7	4.2	1.6	6.8	2.2	8.1	10.5
Kazakhstan	5.9	5.7	12.9	8.5	4.7	8.1	10.5
Kyrgyz Republic[a]	6.5	3.7	-6.5	2.5	-2.2	1.3	11.7
Pakistan[b]	12.6	2.6	1.0	3.3	2.8	4.2	15.5
Tajikistan	...	3.8	6.5	7.8	4.9	11.4	13.6
Turkmenistan	...	...	...	...	...	...	...
Uzbekistan	4.9	2.7	7.9	18.1	20.1	17.0	17.5
East Asia							
China, People's Republic of[c]	7.2	2.3	4.6	-1.4	1.8	9.2	10.6
Hong Kong, China	3.5	3.3	3.6	1.1	4.3	9.9	7.5
Korea, Republic of	6.4	1.6	2.3	3.4	2.8	0.0	4.4
Mongolia	18.6	-6.1	1.7	7.3	9.1	8.3	8.5
Taipei,China	1.1	3.9	7.9	-1.8	0.6	2.2	0.4
South Asia							
Bangladesh[d]	7.7 (2012)	6.7	4.9	6.0	7.1	5.5	5.5
Bhutan	9.4	3.3	4.0	7.5	5.0	3.6	11.4
India	...	4.7	4.4	1.9	0.4	6.6	8.0
Maldives[e]	7.5	0.5	0.6	5.6	-1.1	-0.8	2.7
Nepal[f]	15.5	9.6	10.9	1.9	2.7	3.1	8.2
Sri Lanka[g]	6.9	5.5	6.1	9.3	3.4	0.8	11.4
Southeast Asia							
Brunei Darussalam	-0.0 (2011)	1.0	-0.5	0.3	1.9	-0.7	2.5
Cambodia[g]	4.3	4.0	5.6	3.4	2.5	2.1	4.6
Indonesia[h]	9.4	7.2	7.2	2.1	4.2	3.0	3.4
Lao People's Democratic Republic	5.6 (2012)	4.5	4.3	-0.1	1.2	4.7	8.6
Malaysia	2.5	3.6	3.8	3.9	1.7	1.6	1.3
Myanmar	7.4	13.1	9.2	4.4	6.6	9.0	2.8
Philippines	4.0	1.8	1.6	3.0	6.8	2.1	2.7
Singapore	2.3	1.2	2.3	1.3	1.3	1.1	2.9
Thailand	5.4	1.1	1.6	...	0.4	2.3	1.2
Timor-Leste	6.4	0.3	-2.1	0.9	1.7	0.9	0.9
Viet Nam	10.7	1.5	2.4	-1.1	3.2	4.1	10.0
The Pacific							
Cook Islands[g,i]	2.6	0.1	1.0	0.6	0.6	1.3	2.7
Fiji	4.1	4.7	6.0	-2.1	3.4	4.9	-2.4
Kiribati[j]	-4.6	-0.6	1.7	1.8	-1.1	-2.0	1.2
Marshall Islands[g,k]	-1.5	2.3	-1.4	-0.5	1.3	0.5	-0.6
Micronesia, Federated States of	2.2	0.8	-1.2	...	-1.5	...	...
Nauru	-0.4	0.6 (2013)	...	...	...	...	...
Niue[l]	8.2	2.7	-0.2	3.4	0.6	5.1	...
Palau	1.8	1.7	-3.0	1.6	4.0	0.6	...
Papua New Guinea	-1.0 (2011)	4.9	5.1	2.8	0.8	3.0	2.2
Samoa	-6.6	3.3	5.9	1.4	5.6	1.0	-1.5
Solomon Islands[g,m]	-2.9	-3.0	0.5	-0.9	1.9	-0.4	...
Tonga	3.0	1.8	1.3	8.5	6.7	1.7	1.9
Tuvalu	-5.9	4.0	3.4	4.5	3.3	3.5	0.6
Vanuatu	4.5	3.6	2.3	6.8	3.5	6.0	...
Developed ADB Member Economies							
Australia[n]	1.6	2.1	0.1	1.8	-0.0	2.0	3.1
Japan	-0.3	3.6	2.1	0.7	1.6	0.2	1.2
New Zealand	1.0	-0.1	-0.6	2.2	-0.2	1.1	3.2

... = data not available, - = magnitude equals zero, -0.0 or 0.0 = magnitude is less than half of unit employed, ADB = Asian Development Bank.

Note: Data refer to the whole of each economy, unless otherwise indicated.

a In the longer time series featured in the Key Indicators Database, data for 2000–2002 refer to food and drinks, which includes alcoholic beverages.

b In the longer time series featured in the Key Indicators Database, growth rates for 2002–2008 were calculated using price indexes with base year 2000/2001 = 100 for food, nonalcoholic beverages, alcoholic beverages, tobacco, and narcotics. Growth rates were calculated using price indexes with base year 2007/2008 = 100 for 2009–2019, and base year 2015/2016 = 100 for 2020, for food and nonalcoholic beverages only.

c For 2016 onward, excludes nonalcoholic beverages.

d Refers to food, nonalcoholic and alcoholic beverages, and tobacco.

e Refers to food (including fish) and nonalcoholic beverages. Data prior to 2004, featured in the Key Indicators Database, also includes tobacco and narcotics.

f Includes alcoholic beverages, tobacco, and narcotics; and restaurants and hotels.

g Refers to capital city.

h In the longer time series featured in the Key Indicators Database (and relevant years in the table), data refer to consumer price indexes for 43 cities for 2000–2002, 45 cities for 2003–2007, 66 cities for 2008–2013, 82 cities for 2014–2018, and 90 cities for 2019–2020. For 2000–2018, data refer to Indonesia's index group "Foodstuff" consisting of cereals, cassava, and related products; meat and related products; fresh fish; preserved fish; eggs, milk, and related products; vegetables; beans and nuts; fruits; spices; fats and oils; and other food items (the group does not include nonalcoholic and alcoholic beverages). For 2019–2020, data refer to food, beverages, and tobacco.

i Refers to fruits and vegetables; meat, poultry, and fish; cereal products; soft drink and sweets; farm products; fats and oils; other food; and prepared food.

j In the longer time series featured in the Key Indicators Database (and relevant years in the table), data for 2006 onward refer to the Tarawa Retail Price Index, which is based on data for South Tarawa to represent all of Kiribati. Data refer to the weighted average of food and nonalcoholic drinks price indexes.

k Refers to food.

l In the longer time series featured in the Key Indicators Database (and relevant years in the table), data for 2003–2011 refer to food.

m In the longer time series featured in the Key Indicators Database (and relevant years in the table), data for 2008–2017 exclude nonalcoholic beverages.

n Includes restaurants and hotels.

Source: Economy's official sources.

Table 2.3.3: Growth Rates of Wholesale and/or Producer Price Indexes
(%)

ADB Regional Member	2010	2015	2016	2017	2018	2019	2020
Developing ADB Member Economies							
Central and West Asia							
Afghanistan	...	...	...	...	...	...	...
Armenia	22.6	-0.8	1.5	3.9	1.6	0.5	2.4
Azerbaijan	30.5	-30.6	27.5	36.8	26.0	3.2	-24.8
Georgia	11.3	7.5	-0.1	11.0	6.1	7.2	11.8
Kazakhstan	25.2	-20.5	16.8	15.3	19.0	5.1	-8.0
Kyrgyz Republic	22.8	8.8	6.4	1.7	1.5	4.3	21.3
Pakistan	13.8	-0.3	-1.1	4.0	3.5	12.0	10.2
Tajikistan	27.2	3.0	14.7	1.6	1.8	1.1	5.4
Turkmenistan	...	...	...	...	...	...	...
Uzbekistan	15.6	13.5	14.8	17.5	31.8	43.2	14.9
East Asia							
China, People's Republic of	5.5	-5.2	-1.4	6.3	3.5	-0.3	-1.8
Hong Kong, China	6.0	-2.7	1.3	3.8	2.0	1.0	2.3
Korea, Republic of	3.8	-4.0	-1.8	3.5	1.9	0.0	-0.5
Mongolia	...	...	11.3	17.5	-8.1	23.9	-2.8
Taipei,China	5.5	-8.9	-3.0	0.9	3.6	-2.3	-7.8
South Asia							
Bangladesh[a]	8.9 (2006)	...	...	...	...	...	...
Bhutan	5.8 (2012)	0.6	1.2	5.8	4.7	-3.7	2.3
India	9.6	-3.7	1.7	2.9	4.3	1.8	...
Maldives	3.9	-2.4	...	...	...	...	...
Nepal	12.2	6.1	6.3	2.7	1.7	6.2	6.9
Sri Lanka	2.6	1.0	4.2	7.4	3.4	3.4	5.4
Southeast Asia							
Brunei Darussalam	...	...	...	...	...	...	...
Cambodia	...	...	...	...	...	...	...
Indonesia	4.9	4.4	7.9	4.6	5.5	0.9	...
Lao People's Democratic Republic	...	...	...	...	...	...	...
Malaysia	12.3 (2011)	-7.4	-1.1	6.7	-1.1	-1.4	-2.7
Myanmar	...	...	...	...	...	...	...
Philippines	5.9	1.6	0.9	1.9	1.9	1.6	2.5
Singapore	4.7	-15.3	-6.9	7.0	6.4	-3.3	-8.7
Thailand	9.4	-4.1	-1.2	0.7	0.5	-0.7	-1.6
Timor-Leste	...	...	...	...	...	...	...
Viet Nam	12.6	-0.6	-0.6	2.8	3.1	1.3	...
The Pacific							
Cook Islands	...	...	...	...	...	...	...
Fiji	...	...	...	...	...	...	...
Kiribati	...	...	...	...	...	...	...
Marshall Islands	...	...	...	...	...	...	...
Micronesia, Federated States of	...	...	...	...	...	...	...
Nauru	...	...	...	...	...	...	...
Niue	...	...	...	...	...	...	...
Palau	...	...	...	...	...	...	...
Papua New Guinea	...	...	...	...	...	...	...
Samoa	...	...	...	...	...	...	...
Solomon Islands	...	...	...	...	...	...	...
Tonga	...	...	...	...	...	...	...
Tuvalu	...	...	...	...	...	...	...
Vanuatu	...	...	...	...	...	...	...
Developed ADB Member Economies							
Australia	-0.1	1.0	1.5	1.0	1.6	2.0	1.0
Japan	-0.1	-3.0	-3.5	2.3	2.6	-0.2	-1.0
New Zealand	2.3	-1.3	0.8	4.8	3.4	2.1	1.0

... = data not available, 0.0 = magnitude is less than half of unit employed, ADB = Asian Development Bank.

a For agricultural and industrial products only.

Source: Economy's official sources.

Table 2.3.4: Growth Rates of Gross Domestic Product Deflator
(%)

ADB Regional Member	2010	2015	2016	2017	2018	2019	2020
Developing ADB Member Economies							
Central and West Asia							
Afghanistan	14.3	5.1	5.2	2.4	2.1	6.5	5.5
Armenia[a]	7.8	1.2	0.3	2.1	2.8	1.0	2.0
Azerbaijan	13.6	-8.9	14.7	16.2	12.2	-0.2	-7.6
Georgia	8.5	5.8	2.6	8.5	4.4	5.2	6.9
Kazakhstan	19.6	1.9	13.6	8.4	9.2	7.6	4.4
Kyrgyz Republic	10.0	3.4	6.1	6.3	3.4	-0.8	5.8
Pakistan	10.9	4.1	0.4	4.0	2.5	8.8	10.1
Tajikistan	12.4	5.5 (2014)	...	...	2.5	3.6	...
Turkmenistan	2.3	-4.9	-5.0	-1.5	1.2	4.3	...
Uzbekistan	18.9	10.4	8.7	19.4	27.5	18.6	11.9
East Asia							
China, People's Republic of	6.9	0.1	1.4	4.2	3.5	1.3	0.6
Hong Kong, China	0.3	3.6	1.6	2.9	3.7	2.0	0.6
Korea, Republic of	2.7	3.2	2.0	2.2	0.5	-0.8	1.3
Mongolia	15.1 (2011)	1.7	2.2	10.5	8.4	9.4	4.7
Taipei,China	-1.3	3.4	0.8	-0.8	-0.6	0.1	1.3
South Asia							
Bangladesh	7.1	5.9	6.7	6.3	5.6	4.5	4.5
Bhutan	6.0	3.6	4.4	5.1	1.8	1.0	...
India	10.5	2.3	3.2	4.0	3.7	3.6	4.6
Maldives	2.9	7.9	0.2	1.4	5.3	-2.6	...
Nepal	14.4	4.5	7.1	7.0	3.1	4.3	5.6
Sri Lanka	7.3	0.6	4.8	7.3	3.9	2.7	3.4
Southeast Asia							
Brunei Darussalam	5.3	-17.6	-9.2	5.0	9.2	-3.3	-10.8
Cambodia	3.1	1.7	3.4	3.3	3.1	3.4	-2.9
Indonesia	7.3	4.0	2.4	4.3	3.8	1.6	-0.5
Lao People's Democratic Republic	3.1	2.3	3.0	1.9	1.9	1.2	2.8
Malaysia	5.4 (2011)	-0.4	1.7	3.8	0.7	0.1	-0.8
Myanmar	7.0	4.1	...	5.4	5.4	6.3	5.7
Philippines	4.4	-0.7	1.3	2.3	3.7	0.7	1.6
Singapore	1.2	3.1	0.6	3.0	3.3	-0.6	-2.9
Thailand	4.1	0.7	2.6	1.9	1.4	0.9	-1.0
Timor-Leste	10.8	7.0	0.2	1.0	-1.4	9.0	...
Viet Nam	12.1	-0.2	1.1	4.1	3.4	1.8	1.3
The Pacific							
Cook Islands	1.9	6.4	-2.1	-0.2	4.2	2.5	1.9
Fiji	2.5	2.4	2.5	1.6	0.9	...	...
Kiribati	1.2	3.5	0.2	1.0	5.3	2.4	...
Marshall Islands	-0.7	-1.6	7.2	2.0	0.3	2.8	4.2
Micronesia, Federated States of	3.6	-5.3	4.0	7.5	9.4	...	...
Nauru	-18.1	-8.3	...	11.8	4.2	2.3	2.4
Niue	7.6	-0.3	0.5	1.9	11.2	...	...
Palau	-0.1	8.9	6.9	-1.1	-6.2	0.1	...
Papua New Guinea	9.9	-1.2	2.5	7.7	9.8	0.1	0.9
Samoa	-0.0	3.7	0.9	0.6	1.7	1.5	0.9
Solomon Islands	1.7	3.6	0.0	1.4	...	...	...
Tonga	7.8	5.3	3.1	5.6	5.1	7.7	...
Tuvalu	2.5	4.6	...	2.9	7.3	6.3	...
Vanuatu	2.6	4.5	1.8	4.2	...	...	...
Developed ADB Member Economies							
Australia	1.2	-0.5	-0.5	3.7	1.9	3.4	1.9
Japan	-1.9	2.1	0.4	-0.1	0.0	0.6	0.9
New Zealand	3.7	0.8	2.4	2.8	1.1	2.9	...

... = data not available, -0.0 or 0.0 = magnitude is less than half of unit employed, ADB = Asian Development Bank.

a In the longer time series featured in the Key Indicators Database (and relevant years in the table), estimates for 2000–2012 are based on the 1993 System of National Accounts. For 2013 onward, estimates are based on the 2008 System of National Accounts.

Source: Economy's official sources.

Table 2.3.5: Growth Rates of Money Supply
(%)

ADB Regional Member	2010	2015	2016	2017	2018	2019	2020
Developing ADB Member Economies							
Central and West Asia							
Afghanistan	39.3	3.7	9.7	4.1	2.6	5.7	12.1
Armenia	11.8	10.8	17.5	18.5	7.4	11.2	9.0
Azerbaijan[a]	24.3	-1.3	-1.9	9.0	5.7	20.0	1.1
Georgia[a]	30.1	17.3	21.1	14.6	13.9	17.6	24.6
Kazakhstan	23.1	8.0	46.2	7.5	7.1	11.0	19.2
Kyrgyz Republic	21.1	14.9	14.6	17.9	5.5	12.8	23.9
Pakistan	13.0	12.8	14.5	13.9	9.5	10.8	18.3
Tajikistan	17.6	12.2	56.7	36.6	10.0	23.1	18.8
Turkmenistan[a]	74.2	18.0	9.4	11.4	8.4	8.6	...
Uzbekistan	52.4	24.3	23.6	41.0	13.2	13.8	17.9
East Asia							
China, People's Republic of	19.7	13.3	11.3	9.0	8.1	8.7	10.1
Hong Kong, China	8.1	5.5	7.7	10.0	4.3	2.8	5.8
Korea, Republic of	6.0	8.2	7.1	5.1	6.7	7.9	9.8
Mongolia	62.5	-5.5	21.0	30.5	22.8	7.0	16.3
Taipei,China	5.5	5.8	3.6	3.6	2.7	4.5	9.4
South Asia							
Bangladesh	22.4	12.4	16.3	10.9	9.2	9.9	12.6
Bhutan	16.5	3.8	23.0	17.4	6.5	13.1	27.7
India[a]	16.1	10.1	10.1	9.2	10.5	8.9	11.7
Maldives	14.6	12.1	-0.2	5.2	3.4	9.5	14.2
Nepal	14.1	19.9	19.5	15.5	19.4	15.8	18.1
Sri Lanka	18.0	17.2	18.9	17.5	13.5	7.6	22.9
Southeast Asia							
Brunei Darussalam	4.8	-1.8	1.5	-0.4	2.8	4.3	-0.4
Cambodia	21.3	17.0	21.0	23.1	26.6	18.2	15.3
Indonesia	15.4	9.0	10.0	8.3	6.3	6.5	12.4
Lao People's Democratic Republic	39.5	14.7	10.9	12.2	8.4	18.9	17.0
Malaysia[a]	6.8	3.0	3.2	4.9	9.1	3.5	4.0
Myanmar	42.5	30.7	17.4	20.5	14.6	15.5	...
Philippines[a]	10.0	9.4	12.8	11.9	9.5	11.5	9.6
Singapore	8.6	1.5	8.0	3.2	3.9	5.0	13.2
Thailand	10.9	4.4	4.2	5.0	4.7	3.6	10.1
Timor-Leste	18.2	7.1	14.2	12.1	3.1	-7.1	3.1
Viet Nam	33.3	16.2	18.4	15.0	12.4	14.8	13.9
The Pacific							
Cook Islands	0.1	9.5	0.1	6.4	9.9	7.9	...
Fiji[a]	3.5	13.9	4.8	8.3	2.8	2.7	1.2
Kiribati	...	...	...	...	...	...	...
Marshall Islands	9.4	28.6	19.9	23.9	-3.3	-4.9	21.8
Micronesia, Federated States of	...	...	...	...	...	...	...
Nauru	...	...	...	...	...	...	...
Niue	...	...	...	...	...	...	...
Palau	12.0 (2011)	30.9	17.4	0.3	0.3	-3.2	...
Papua New Guinea[a]	11.4	8.0	10.9	-0.7	-4.0	4.4	7.0
Samoa	6.4	6.0	9.2	15.2	8.8	4.6	5.4
Solomon Islands[a]	13.3	15.5	13.4	3.5	6.8	-3.1	6.6
Tonga	5.1	9.3	16.7	13.7	7.6	4.4	1.1
Tuvalu	...	...	...	...	...	...	...
Vanuatu	1.3	11.4	10.6	9.3	13.1	7.0	-0.7
Developed ADB Member Economies							
Australia[a]	4.5	6.7	5.8	7.8	1.9	4.0	8.5
Japan[b]	1.9	2.5	3.2	2.9	2.2	2.1	7.7
New Zealand[c]	3.2	8.1	7.7	7.3	6.4	4.7	12.2

... = data not available, ADB = Asian Development Bank.

Note: Data are based on money supply M2 (M2), unless otherwise stated.
a Refers to money supply M3 (M3).
b In the longer time series featured in the Key Indicators Database (and relevant years in the table), data refer to M3, except for 2000–2002 (M2).
c In the longer time series featured in the Key Indicators Database (and relevant years in the table), data refer to M3, except for 2016–2020 (M2).

Source: Economy's official sources.

Money and Finance

Table 2.3.6: Money Supply
(% of GDP)

ADB Regional Member	2010	2015	2016	2017	2018	2019	2020
Developing ADB Member Economies							
Central and West Asia							
Afghanistan	30.3	29.7	37.2	36.9	36.6	35.0	37.9
Armenia	26.3	36.8	43.0	46.4	46.1	47.2	54.4
Azerbaijan[a]	24.8	39.1	34.6	32.4	30.0	35.2	40.3
Georgia[a]	28.4	38.7	44.3	44.7	46.5	49.5	61.5
Kazakhstan	30.1	21.0	26.8	24.9	23.4	23.1	27.3
Kyrgyz Republic	31.4	33.3	34.4	36.5	35.8	37.2	47.7
Pakistan	37.7	40.2	43.5	45.1	45.5	46.0	49.5
Tajikistan	12.0	12.8	18.7	21.7	21.6	24.5	27.3
Turkmenistan[a]	17.3	48.2	52.3	55.5	56.0	54.8	...
Uzbekistan	18.9	19.3	20.7	23.4	19.7	17.9	18.5
East Asia							
China, People's Republic of	176.1	202.1	207.7	203.1	198.7	201.4	215.2
Hong Kong, China	401.7	484.4	502.2	517.2	506.1	518.4	580.5
Korea, Republic of	125.5	135.5	138.3	137.8	142.3	151.4	165.5
Mongolia	48.0	43.4	50.8	56.9	60.1	55.9	64.9
Taipei,China	220.2	233.9	235.3	237.8	238.9	242.4	253.8
South Asia							
Bangladesh	45.5	52.0	52.9	51.4	49.3	48.0	49.1
Bhutan	72.2	59.2	64.6	68.9	70.0	79.2	94.9
India[a]	85.2	84.4	83.1	81.7	81.3	82.6	95.5
Maldives	47.9	48.3	45.2	43.9	40.4	41.8	71.4
Nepal	60.3	77.5	86.1	84.2	89.5	92.8	107.3
Sri Lanka	28.3	37.1	40.2	42.5	45.0	46.0	56.7
Southeast Asia							
Brunei Darussalam	67.3	80.8	92.6	86.7	81.6	84.7	93.5
Cambodia	41.6	72.4	79.2	88.2	100.7	107.7	131.9
Indonesia	36.0	39.5	40.4	39.9	38.8	38.8	44.7
Lao People's Democratic Republic	38.0	51.2	51.5	53.1	53.1	59.1	65.2
Malaysia[a]	132.2	136.3	132.5	126.5	130.9	129.8	144.2
Myanmar	23.6	46.4	53.4	57.7	58.9	60.0	...
Philippines[a]	47.7	60.5	62.8	64.2	63.7	66.5	79.3
Singapore	123.3	122.9	127.6	122.4	118.8	123.8	152.6
Thailand	109.0	127.7	125.4	124.1	123.2	123.2	146.2
Timor-Leste	33.5	40.3	44.5	51.5	54.4	39.1	...
Viet Nam	129.3	143.6	158.3	163.7	166.2	175.1	182.5
The Pacific							
Cook Islands	83.1	59.3	57.7	56.2	57.3	56.3	...
Fiji[a]	67.6	73.3	73.0	73.8	72.1	72.6	...
Kiribati	...	...	...	...	...	...	...
Marshall Islands	63.0	82.9	91.4	106.7	99.3	87.2	104.1
Micronesia, Federated States of	...	...	...	...	...	...	...
Nauru	...	...	...	...	...	...	...
Niue	...	...	...	...	...	...	...
Palau	46.2	72.2	79.7	82.4	83.4	82.1	...
Papua New Guinea[a]	34.0	33.6	34.5	30.7	26.9	26.5	29.3
Samoa	44.2	43.1	45.0	51.8	55.0	55.4	63.7
Solomon Islands[a]	28.5	40.4	43.3	41.9	41.5	39.2	43.5
Tonga	41.2	47.5	50.5	52.6	53.6	51.6	...
Tuvalu	...	...	...	...	...	...	...
Vanuatu	83.3	78.6	82.5	82.9	88.3	...	...
Developed ADB Member Economies							
Australia[a]	94.4	109.4	113.2	115.0	111.7	110.0	117.4
Japan[b]	218.8	235.5	241.0	243.4	248.1	250.3	276.8
New Zealand[c]	111.6	121.6	102.2	102.0	102.8	102.2	113.6

... = data not available, ADB = Asian Development Bank, GDP = gross domestic product.

Note: Data are based on money supply M2 (M2), unless otherwise stated.
a Refers to money supply M3 (M3).
b In the longer time series featured in the Key Indicators Database (and relevant years in the table), data refer to M3, except for 2000–2002 (M2).
c In the longer time series featured in the Key Indicators Database (and relevant years in the table), data refer to M3, except for 2016–2020 (M2).

Source: Economy's official sources.

Table 2.3.7: Interest Rates on Savings and Time Deposits
(% per annum, period averages)

ADB Regional Member	Savings Deposits							Time Deposits[a]						
	2010	2015	2016	2017	2018	2019	2020	2010	2015	2016	2017	2018	2019	2020
Developing ADB Member Economies														
Central and West Asia														
Afghanistan	5.4	3.1	1.6	1.3	1.6	1.5	0.8	8.2	5.2	4.4	3.1	2.3	3.4	2.4
Armenia	...	...	...	...	...	...	...	10.7	15.4	12.5	9.6	9.4	9.3	9.2
Azerbaijan	...	...	...	...	...	...	...	11.0	8.2	5.5	12.1	9.8	9.4	8.6
Georgia[b]	8.7	5.3	4.5	4.0	4.3	4.7	5.2	11.6	7.0	6.7	6.1	5.8	5.7	6.6
Kazakhstan[c]	...	...	...	...	...	...	...	9.8	7.5	11.4	11.2	10.5	9.1	8.6
Kyrgyz Republic	...	...	...	...	...	...	...	11.5	14.5	13.3	10.8	10.3	9.5	9.8
Pakistan	5.0	4.7	3.7	3.5	4.1	8.6	5.9	7.2	5.9	4.7	4.3	4.6	8.0	6.2
Tajikistan	3.8	0.9	1.2	1.4	1.1	0.6	...	17.8	15.6	16.4	14.6	12.8	11.6	...
Turkmenistan	...	...	...	...	...	...	...	11.3 (2004)	...	...	...	...	...	...
Uzbekistan[d]	...	16.5	18.1	18.0	15.9	18.3	18.6	...	18.3	18.7	18.5	16.4	18.6	19.2
East Asia														
China, People's Republic of	0.4	0.4	0.4	0.4	0.4	0.4	0.4	2.3	2.1	1.5	1.5	1.5	1.5	1.5
Hong Kong, China	0.0	0.0	0.0	0.0	0.0	0.1	0.0	0.2	0.1	0.1	0.2	0.2	0.3	0.2
Korea, Republic of[e]	3.2	1.7	1.5	1.5	1.8	1.7	1.0	3.9	1.8	1.6	1.7	2.0	1.9	1.2
Mongolia[f]	10.7	13.0	12.4	13.0	11.2	10.5	8.4	...	...	...	12.8	11.8	10.9	8.8
Taipei,China	0.2	0.3	0.3	0.2	0.2	0.2	0.1	1.0	1.3	1.1	1.1	1.1	1.1	0.8
South Asia														
Bangladesh[g]	4.9	4.5	3.6	3.2	3.3	3.3	2.8	9.0	9.0	7.3	6.4	7.4	8.2	6.5
Bhutan[h]	4.8	5.3	5.3	5.5	5.3	5.4	5.4	6.8	6.8	7.0	7.0	7.8	7.8	7.6
India	3.5	4.0	4.0	...	...	...	...	7.5	6.2	5.5	...	...	...	...
Maldives[i]	2.3	2.2	1.7	1.5	1.5	1.5	1.5	4.3	4.0	3.4	3.5	3.7	3.3	3.8
Nepal	7.0	2.9	2.2	4.0	4.6	5.0	4.2	8.1	6.5	5.8	10.4	10.4	9.8	9.0
Sri Lanka	5.0	5.0	4.3	4.0	4.0	4.0	3.5	8.5	7.3	11.0	11.0	10.5	9.8	5.3
Southeast Asia														
Brunei Darussalam	0.4	0.3	0.3	0.3	0.3	0.3	0.1	0.7	0.8	0.7	0.7	0.8	0.8	0.3
Cambodia	1.2	1.2	1.5	1.2	0.6	0.6	0.6	6.6	7.4	7.4	6.4	6.2	6.3	6.3
Indonesia	3.9	1.7	1.5	1.5	1.3	1.1	0.8	7.9	8.5	7.3	6.8	6.5	6.8	5.7
Lao People's Democratic Republic	3.4	2.6	1.8	1.7	1.8	1.8	1.7	9.1	7.6	5.6	5.4	5.4	5.4	5.4
Malaysia	0.9	1.1	1.0	1.0	1.0	1.0	0.6	2.8	3.3	3.2	3.1	3.3	3.2	2.1
Myanmar[j]	...	...	...	...	...	...	...	...	...	...	...	...	...	...
Philippines[k]	1.6	0.7	0.7	0.7	0.9	1.2	...	2.1	3.1	3.0	2.8	3.5	4.6	...
Singapore	0.1	0.1	0.1	0.2	0.2	0.2	0.1	0.5	0.3	0.4	0.3	0.4	0.6	0.5
Thailand[l]	0.5	0.5	0.5	0.5	0.5	0.5	0.3	1.6	1.4	1.4	1.4	1.4	1.3	0.5
Timor-Leste	0.8	0.8	0.8	0.4	0.4	0.5	0.5	1.3	1.3	1.2	0.7	0.7	0.7	0.6
Viet Nam[m]	3.0	0.7	0.6	0.6	0.5	0.5	0.2	11.5	6.3	6.8	6.9	7.1	7.3	6.8
The Pacific														
Cook Islands	...	...	...	...	...	...	...	...	...	...	...	...	...	...
Fiji	1.0	0.9	0.9	1.2	1.3	1.1	0.9	5.6	2.6	2.9	3.2	3.4	4.6	3.3
Kiribati	...	...	...	...	...	...	...	...	...	...	...	...	...	...
Marshall Islands	0.5	0.3	0.2	0.2	0.2	0.2	0.2	3.5	1.5	1.5	1.3	1.1	0.9	0.8
Micronesia, Federated States of	...	...	...	...	...	...	...	...	...	...	...	...	...	...
Nauru	...	...	...	...	...	...	...	...	...	...	...	...	...	...
Niue	...	...	...	...	...	...	...	...	...	...	...	...	...	...
Palau	0.9	0.1	0.1	0.1	0.1	0.1	...	0.8	0.2	0.2	0.2	0.4	0.4	...
Papua New Guinea	1.0	0.4	0.6	0.5	0.7	1.0	...	4.8	2.1	2.0	2.0	2.0	1.3	...
Samoa[n]	1.0	1.0	1.0	1.0	1.0	1.0	1.0	2.9	2.9	2.9	2.9	2.9	2.9	2.9
Solomon Islands	0.3	0.3	0.3	0.3	0.4	0.6	0.5	5.0	0.7	0.9	1.0	1.3	1.5	1.6
Tonga	1.5	2.5	2.5	2.4	2.4	2.5	2.6	3.0	4.9	5.3	5.4	5.2	4.8	4.8
Tuvalu	...	...	...	...	...	...	...	...	...	...	...	...	...	...
Vanuatu	...	...	...	...	...	...	...	...	...	...	...	...	...	...
Developed ADB Member Economies														
Australia[o]	4.5	2.0	1.6	1.7	1.0	0.6	0.2	6.0	2.5	2.4	2.3	2.2	1.8	0.8
Japan[p]	0.0	0.0	0.0	0.0	0.0	0.0	0.0	0.1	0.1	0.0	0.0	0.0	0.0	0.0
New Zealand[q]	...	...	...	...	...	...	...	4.7	3.3	3.3	3.3	3.3	2.6	0.8

... = data not available, – = magnitude equals zero, 0.00 = magnitude is less than half of unit employed, ADB = Asian Development Bank.

a Refers to interest rate on time deposits of 12 months, unless otherwise indicated.
b Refers to deposits allocated with maturity of more than 1 year.
c Refers to interest rates on deposits of more than 12 months.
d Refers to weighted average interest rate on all time household savings deposits and time deposits from 181 to 365 days.
e Refers to weighted averages of interest rates on newly extended time and savings deposits of commercial and specialized banks.
f Includes both demand and time deposits.
g Refers to savings bank accounts with checking facilities.
h For savings deposits, actual range of rates for 2000–2001 (as featured in the Key Indicators Database) is 5.0%–7.0%; for 2012, 4.5%–5.0%; for 2013, 5.0%–5.5%; for 2014–2016, 5.0%–7.0%; for 2017, 5.0%–6.0%; and for 2019–2020, 5.0%–5.75%. For time deposits, rate refers to fixed deposits of 1 year to less than 3 years for 2000–2001 (as featured in the Key Indicators Database) and actual range of rates is 9.0%–10.0%. For 2010–2016, rate refers to fixed deposits of 1 year to less than 2 years and actual range of rates for 2010 is 4.5%–6.5%; for 2011, 6.0%–7.0%; for 2012, 7.0%–7.3%; for 2013–2014, 7.0%–7.5%; for 2015–2017, 6.5%–7.5%; for 2018-2019, 6.0%–9.5%; and for 2020, 6.0%–9.1%.
i Refers to time deposits of 6 months to 1 year (local currency). Figures from 2000 to 2009 (as featured in the Key Indicators Database) represent an average of the minimum and maximum rate. Figures from 2010 onward represent a weighted average.
j For 2007–2011 (as featured in the Key Indicators Database and relevant years in the table) data include savings, time, and other deposits.
k Rates for savings deposits refer to the annual percentage equivalent of commercial banks' actual monthly interest expenses on peso-savings deposits to the total outstanding levels of these deposits. Rates for time deposits refer to rates charged on interest-bearing deposits with maturities of over 1 year.
l For 2001 (as featured in the Key Indicators Database), actual range of rates on time deposits is 2.75%–3.00%.
m For 2000–2010 (as featured in the Key Indicators Database), data on time deposits refer to maximum interest per annum for state enterprise deposits.
n In the longer time series featured in the Key Indicators Database, actual range of rates for savings deposits is 2.50%–3.00% for 2007, 2.50%–3.00% for 2008, and 1.00%–2.50% for 2009: actual range of rates for time deposits is 7.00%–7.50% for 2007, 4.75%–5.50% for 2008, and 2.25%–3.50% for 2009.
o Refers to interest rates of online savings deposits.
p Refers to savings deposits of at least ¥0.3 million, calculated as the arithmetic average of weekly figures. Refers to time deposits from 12 months to less than 2 years, calculated as the arithmetic average of the monthly figures.
q Refers to interest rate on time deposits of 6 months.

Sources: Economy's official sources. For the People's Republic of China: CEIC Database. https://www.ceicdata.com/en (accessed 23 July 2021).

Table 2.3.8: Yield on Short-Term Treasury Bills and Lending Interest Rates
(% per annum, period averages)

ADB Regional Member	Yield on Short-Term Treasury Bills[a]				Lending Interest Rates			
	2010	2015	2019	2020	2010	2015	2019	2020
Developing ADB Member Economies								
Central and West Asia								
Afghanistan	...	...	...	...	15.6	15.0	...	...
Armenia[b]	10.6	12.9	6.0	5.8	19.2	17.6	12.1	11.6
Azerbaijan	1.8	13.0 (2016)	...	...	20.7	17.5	17.3	17.2
Georgia	9.6	8.8	7.2	8.6	15.8	12.5	10.8	11.8
Kazakhstan	...	...	...	...	...	...	...	...
Kyrgyz Republic	10.4	12.8	5.1	5.9	23.7	23.6	19.0	17.0
Pakistan[c]	12.5	7.1	13.3	8.6	14.0	10.2	12.2	10.8
Tajikistan[d]	6.7	0.8	...	...	23.4	25.8	23.5	...
Turkmenistan	...	...	...	...	...	...	...	...
Uzbekistan	...	...	13.2	13.9	...	13.8	23.6	22.3
East Asia								
China, People's Republic of[e]	2.6	4.8 (2014)	...	...	5.8	4.4	4.4	4.4
Hong Kong, China[f]	0.2	0.0	1.7	0.4	5.0	5.0	5.1	5.0
Korea, Republic of[g]	2.7	1.8	1.7	0.9	5.5	3.5	3.4	2.8
Mongolia[h]	12.9 (2012)	14.5	...	...	20.1	19.6	17.0	16.9
Taipei,China[i]	0.3	0.4	0.4	0.3	2.7	2.8	2.6	2.4
South Asia								
Bangladesh[d]	4.5	5.8	5.7	4.8	12.2	11.7	9.6	8.3
Bhutan[d]	2.0	0.1	4.3	2.1	13.9	14.9	14.0	14.0
India[d,j]	6.2	7.4	5.5	3.3	8.3	10.0	9.5	9.2
Maldives[k]	4.9	6.8	3.5	3.5	10.4	11.1	11.5	11.6
Nepal[d]	6.9	0.7	3.3	1.9	...	...	...	...
Sri Lanka[l]	8.6	6.7	9.1	...	10.2	7.0	11.2	...
Southeast Asia								
Brunei Darussalam	...	...	...	...	5.5	5.5	5.5	5.5
Cambodia	...	...	...	...	...	...	...	...
Indonesia	7.0	8.3	6.7	5.5	13.3	12.7	10.4	9.5
Lao People's Democratic Republic[m]	8.0	...	...	...	22.6	...	...	...
Malaysia	2.6	3.1	...	...	5.0	4.6	4.9	3.9
Myanmar	...	...	...	...	20.9	16.0	16.0	14.8
Philippines[d]	3.5	1.7	4.3	2.0	7.7	5.6	7.1	...
Singapore	0.3	0.3 (2013)	...	...	5.4	5.4	5.3	5.3
Thailand[d]	1.4	1.6	1.6	0.6	4.3	4.7	4.1	3.3
Timor-Leste	...	...	...	...	11.0 (2011)	13.5	15.4	14.1
Viet Nam[n]	11.1	4.2	...	...	13.1	7.1	7.7	7.6
The Pacific								
Cook Islands	...	...	...	...	...	...	...	...
Fiji[d]	3.4	1.2	2.5	1.8	7.5	5.8	6.0	6.2
Kiribati	...	...	...	...	...	...	...	...
Marshall Islands	...	...	...	...	...	...	...	...
Micronesia, Federated States of	...	...	...	...	15.1	15.7	15.7 (2018)	...
Nauru	...	...	...	...	...	...	...	...
Niue	...	...	...	...	...	...	...	...
Palau	...	...	...	...	...	...	...	...
Papua New Guinea[o]	4.6	5.3	6.1	...	10.4	8.7	8.7	...
Samoa	...	...	...	...	10.7	9.5	8.9	8.7
Solomon Islands[d]	3.7	0.5	0.5	0.5	14.4	10.5	10.6	10.7
Tonga	...	...	...	...	9.9 (2012)	8.2	8.1	7.8
Tuvalu	...	...	...	...	...	...	...	...
Vanuatu	...	...	...	...	5.5	3.6	2.0	2.1
Developed ADB Member Economies								
Australia[p]	4.7	2.3	1.3	0.3	7.3	5.6	5.1	...
Japan	0.4	0.2	0.0	-0.0	1.6	1.1	...	...
New Zealand	2.8	3.0	1.3	0.4	6.3	5.8	- (2018)	...

... = data not available, 0.0 = magnitude is less than half of unit employed, ADB = Asian Development Bank.

a Refers to 3-month Treasury bills, unless otherwise indicated.
b Refers to average yield on 9-month to 12-month Treasury bills since March 2001.
c Refers to weighted average yield on 6-month Treasury securities.
d Refers to 91-day Treasury bills.
e Refers to 3-month Treasury bonds trading rate.
f Refers to annualized yields on 91-day Exchange Fund bills.
g Refers to 91-day certificates of deposit.
h Refers to weighted average rate on Treasury bills of all maturities. From December 2012 onward, refers to yield on 12-week Treasury bills.
i Refers to prime lending rates.
j Figures are for fiscal year ending March.
k Refers to rate on 28-day Treasury bills.
l Refers to weighted average rate on the last monthly issuance of 364-day Treasury bills since December 2001.
m Refers to weighted average auction rate for 12-month Treasury bills.
n Refers to average monthly yield on 360-day Treasury bills sold at auction.
o Refers to rate on 182-day Treasury bills.
p Refers to estimated closing yield in the secondary market on 13-week Treasury notes.

Sources: International Monetary Fund. International Financial Statistics. http://data.imf.org/ (accessed 5 July 2021); and Organisation for Economic Co-operation and Development. Main Economic Indicators. https://stats.oecd.org/ (accessed 5 July 2021). For Bhutan; India; and Taipei,China: Economy's official sources.

Table 2.3.9: Domestic Credit Provided by Banking Sector and Bank Nonperforming Loans

ADB Regional Member	Domestic Credit Provided by Banking Sector[a] (% of GDP)						Bank Nonperforming Loans[b] (% of total gross loans)					
	2010	2015	2016	2017	2018	2019	2010	2015	2016	2017	2018	2019
Developing ADB Member Economies												
Central and West Asia												
Afghanistan	...	...	...	...	...	...	49.9	12.1	11.1	12.2	8.9	...
Armenia	27.8	48.3	54.4	58.3	62.4	65.2	3.0	7.9	6.7	5.4	4.8	5.5
Azerbaijan	...	...	28.1	13.9	13.1	14.6	...	...	...	...	...	...
Georgia	33.8	53.8	62.1	60.9	66.3	70.9	5.9	2.7	3.4	2.8	2.7	1.9
Kazakhstan	...	45.7	43.3	40.1	36.3	35.0	20.9	8.0	6.7	9.3	7.4	8.1
Kyrgyz Republic	...	...	...	...	...	...	14.8	6.7	8.5	7.4	7.3	7.7
Pakistan	...	...	...	...	...	...	14.7	11.4	10.1	8.4	8.0	8.6
Tajikistan	7.6	19.7	25.0	14.9	15.3	15.5	7.4	20.4 (2014)	...	...	...	...
Turkmenistan	...	...	...	...	...	...	...	...	...	...	...	...
Uzbekistan	...	...	...	...	...	...	1.0	1.5	0.7	1.2	1.3	1.5
East Asia												
China, People's Republic of	...	...	...	...	...	...	1.1	1.7	1.7	1.7	1.8	1.9
Hong Kong, China	...	...	...	...	...	...	0.8	0.7	0.9	0.7	0.5	0.6
Korea, Republic of	...	...	...	...	...	...	0.6	0.5	0.5	0.4	0.3	...
Mongolia	...	...	...	...	...	...	...	...	...	...	...	...
Taipei,China	0.9	...	...	...	...	...	0.6	0.2	0.3	0.3	0.2	0.2
South Asia												
Bangladesh	...	...	...	...	...	...	5.8 (2011)	8.4	8.9	8.9	9.9	8.9
Bhutan	...	...	...	...	...	...	5.2	6.6	7.2	8.4	7.0	8.4
India	...	...	...	...	...	...	2.7 (2011)	5.9	9.2	10.0	9.5	9.2
Maldives	76.9	61.3	68.7	66.1	64.7	64.5	20.9 (2012)	14.1	10.6	10.5	8.9	9.4
Nepal	...	...	...	...	...	...	...	...	1.7	1.7	1.6	...
Sri Lanka	...	...	...	...	...	...	3.8 (2011)	3.2	2.6	2.5	3.4	4.7
Southeast Asia												
Brunei Darussalam	22.7	40.0	35.5	28.6	27.7	29.5	6.9	4.0	4.7	3.7	4.7	3.9
Cambodia	...	...	...	...	...	...	3.1	1.6	2.1	2.1	2.0	1.6
Indonesia	34.2	46.8	48.0	47.0	47.2	46.5	2.5	2.4	2.9	2.6	2.3	2.4
Lao People's Democratic Republic	...	...	...	...	...	...	...	...	...	...	...	...
Malaysia	...	...	...	...	...	...	3.4	1.6	1.6	1.5	1.5	1.5
Myanmar	...	...	...	...	...	...	...	...	...	...	...	...
Philippines	...	...	...	82.3	82.9	86.5	3.4	1.9	1.7	1.6	1.7	2.0
Singapore	...	...	...	...	...	...	1.4	0.9	1.2	1.4	1.3	1.3
Thailand	133.4	171.2	169.9	169.3	166.5	169.0	3.9	2.7	3.0	3.1	3.1	3.1
Timor-Leste	...	...	...	...	...	...	...	...	...	...	...	...
Viet Nam	...	...	...	...	...	...	2.1	2.3	2.3	1.8	1.8	1.5
The Pacific												
Cook Islands	...	...	...	...	...	...	...	...	...	...	...	...
Fiji	131.7	111.4	114.7	114.8	124.7	135.3	4.4	1.4	2.2	2.4	3.1	3.8
Kiribati	...	...	...	...	...	...	...	...	...	...	...	...
Marshall Islands	...	...	...	...	...	...	...	...	...	...	...	...
Micronesia, Federated States of	...	...	...	...	...	...	...	2.0	...	...	...	...
Nauru	...	...	...	...	...	...	...	...	...	...	...	...
Niue	...	...	...	...	...	...	...	...	...	...	...	...
Palau	...	...	...	...	...	...	...	...	...	...	...	...
Papua New Guinea	23.7	40.5	44.6	41.0	36.5	37.2	1.9	3.1	2.5	2.8	3.7	3.8
Samoa	61.5	75.8	77.7	79.5	80.2	82.5	4.7	5.3	3.7	5.3	3.6	4.0
Solomon Islands	21.5	21.5	26.1	25.0	25.0	26.4	9.3	4.1	3.8	...	...	...
Tonga	...	...	...	...	...	...	–	7.7	4.3	3.7	3.6	3.2
Tuvalu	...	...	...	...	...	...	...	...	...	...	...	...
Vanuatu	...	...	...	...	...	...	4.8	12.3	10.8	15.0	...	...
Developed ADB Member Economies												
Australia	...	...	...	...	...	...	2.1	0.9	0.9	0.9	0.9	1.0
Japan	314.5	343.5	350.7	355.1	354.6	364.4	...	...	...	...	...	...
New Zealand	...	160.1	164.9	162.9	163.3	167.9	...	...	...	...	...	...

... = data not available, ADB = Asian Development Bank, GDP = gross domestic product.

a Domestic credit provided by the financial sector includes all credit to various sectors on a gross basis, with the exception of credit to the central government, which is net. The financial sector includes monetary authorities and deposit money banks, as well as other financial corporations where data are available (including corporations that do not accept transferable deposits, but do incur such liabilities as time and savings deposits). Examples of other financial corporations are finance and leasing companies, money lenders, insurance corporations, pension funds, and foreign exchange companies.

b Bank nonperforming loans to total gross loans are the value of nonperforming loans divided by the total value of the loan portfolio (including nonperforming loans before the deduction of specific loan-loss provisions). The loan amount recorded as nonperforming should be the gross value of the loan as recorded on the balance sheet, not just the amount that is overdue.

Sources: World Bank. World Development Indicators. https://databank.worldbank.org/source/world-development-indicators (accessed 15 July 2021).
For Taipei,China: Central bank of Taipei,China. http://www.cbc.gov.tw (accessed 15 July 2021).

Table 2.3.10: Growth Rates of Stock Market Price Index
(%)

ADB Regional Member	2010	2015	2016	2017	2018	2019	2020
Developing ADB Member Economies							
Central and West Asia							
Afghanistan	...	...	...	...	...	...	...
Armenia	...	...	...	...	...	...	...
Azerbaijan	...	...	...	...	...	...	...
Georgia	...	...	...	...	...	...	...
Kazakhstan	...	...	...	...	...	...	...
Kyrgyz Republic	...	...	...	...	...	...	...
Pakistan[a]	28.2	2.1	45.7	...	...	...	...
Tajikistan	...	...	...	...	...	...	...
Turkmenistan	...	...	...	...	...	...	...
Uzbekistan	...	...	...	-0.5	0.7	-42.7	8.6
East Asia							
China, People's Republic of	3.4	66.0	-19.0	6.7	...	...	...
Hong Kong, China	19.3	4.8	-12.0	22.3	10.2	-4.3	-8.4
Korea, Republic of	23.6	1.4	-1.2	16.5	0.5	-9.4	5.4
Mongolia	88.7	-14.6	-14.0	33.5	30.5	-0.8	-13.0
Taipei,China	23.1	-0.4	-2.2	16.5	4.0	1.6	11.9
South Asia							
Bangladesh[a]	82.8	-4.8	8.8	24.0	-13.8	-17.3	21.3
Bhutan	...	...	...	...	...	...	...
India	29.8	10.9	-3.6	8.6	...	...	...
Maldives	-20.4	8.9	4.8	7.4	6.8	5.2	7.7
Nepal	...	...	...	...	...	...	...
Sri Lanka[a]	96.0	-5.5	-9.7	2.3	-5.0	1.3	...
Southeast Asia							
Brunei Darussalam	...	...	...	...	...	...	...
Cambodia	...	...	...	...	...	...	...
Indonesia[a]	46.1	-12.1	15.3	20.0	-2.5	1.7	-5.1
Lao People's Democratic Republic	...	...	...	...	...	...	...
Malaysia	27.1	-6.1	-3.8	5.0	2.2	-8.4	-7.3
Myanmar	...	...	...	...	...	...	...
Philippines	43.1	5.5	0.9	8.0	0.1	2.8	-21.1
Singapore	30.3	-2.5	-11.6	10.3	...	...	...
Thailand	45.6	0.2	-2.1	12.7	6.6	-4.7	-18.1
Timor-Leste	...	...	...	...	...	...	...
Viet Nam[a]	12.2	6.1	14.8	...	...	...	...
The Pacific							
Cook Islands	...	...	...	...	...	...	...
Fiji	-11.1	22.0	26.4	22.4	57.6	45.0	1.5
Kiribati	...	...	...	...	...	...	...
Marshall Islands	...	...	...	...	...	...	...
Micronesia, Federated States of	...	...	...	...	...	...	...
Nauru	...	...	...	...	...	...	...
Niue	...	...	...	...	...	...	...
Palau	...	...	...	...	...	...	...
Papua New Guinea	26.2	-6.3	...	...	7.5	-2.9	...
Samoa	...	...	...	...	...	...	...
Solomon Islands	...	...	...	...	...	...	...
Tonga	...	...	...	...	...	...	...
Tuvalu	...	...	...	...	...	...	...
Vanuatu	...	...	...	...	...	...	...
Developed ADB Member Economies							
Australia[a]	-2.6	-2.1	7.0	7.0	-6.9	...	...
Japan	2.0	22.7	-12.6	...	...	...	...
New Zealand	9.7	12.7	17.4	11.1	14.8	18.0	12.3

... = data not available, ADB = Asian Development Bank.

Note: All data in the table refer to growth rates of stock market prices (period average), unless otherwise indicated.
a Refers to growth rates of end of period stock market prices.

Sources: Asian Development Bank estimates using data from the International Monetary Fund. International Financial Statistics. http://data.imf.org/IFS (accessed 17 July 2021). For Taipei,China: Annual statistics from the stock exchange corporation in Taipei,China. http://www.twse.com.tw/en/statistics/ (accessed 17 July 2021).

Table 2.3.11: Stock Market Capitalization

ADB Regional Member	Stock Market Capitalization ($ million)							Stock Market Capitalization (% of GDP)						
	2010	2015	2016	2017	2018	2019	2020	2010	2015	2016	2017	2018	2019	2020
Developing ADB Member Economies														
Central and West Asia														
Afghanistan	...	...	...	...	...	...	...	...	...	...	...	...	...	...
Armenia	...	...	...	...	...	...	...	...	...	...	...	...	...	...
Azerbaijan	...	...	...	...	...	...	...	...	...	...	...	...	...	...
Georgia	...	...	...	...	...	...	...	...	...	...	...	...	...	...
Kazakhstan	26,672.7	34,891.9	40,161.2	45,558.3	37,005.3	44,972.4	45,202.4	18.0	18.9	29.3	27.3	20.6	24.8	26.6
Kyrgyz Republic	...	...	...	...	...	...	...	...	...	...	...	...	...	...
Pakistan	38,007.2	...	...	...	...	...	...	21.5	...	...	...	...	...	...
Tajikistan	...	...	...	...	...	...	...	...	...	...	...	...	...	...
Turkmenistan	...	...	...	...	...	...	...	...	...	...	...	...	...	...
Uzbekistan	...	...	...	...	...	...	...	...	...	...	...	...	...	...
East Asia														
China, People's Republic of	4,027,840.3	8,188,019.3	7,320,738.4	8,711,267.2	6,324,879.8	8,515,504.4	12,214,465.6	66.2	74.0	65.2	70.8	45.5	59.6	83.0
Hong Kong, China	2,711,316.2	3,184,874.2	3,193,235.5	4,350,514.6	3,819,215.4	4,899,234.6	6,130,420.4	1,185.9	1,029.4	995.3	1,274.9	1,055.9	1,349.6	1,768.8
Korea, Republic of	1,091,911.5	1,231,199.8	1,254,541.2	1,771,767.9	1,413,716.5	1,484,840.3	2,176,189.5	95.4	84.0	83.6	109.1	82.0	90.2	133.5
Mongolia	...	...	...	...	...	...	...	...	...	...	...	...	...	...
Taipei,China	752,520.1	768,179.4	843,120.6	1,045,758.6	972,241.3	1,177,469.7	1,518,132.7	169.4	143.7	155.2	177.0	159.6	192.3	227.1
South Asia														
Bangladesh	41,616.9	65,484.9	70,419.4	86,178.8	77,390.5	64,416.5	89,773.7	36.1	33.6	31.8	34.5	28.2	21.3	27.7
Bhutan	219.0	374.0	338.5	392.8	515.1	730.1	...	14.1	18.7	15.7	16.0	21.1	28.9	...
India	1,762,461.9	1,745,169.2	1,746,297.4	2,555,988.8	2,282,310.5	2,286,924.5	2,595,465.6	105.2	83.0	76.1	96.4	84.5	79.7	99.0
Maldives	...	...	...	...	...	...	...	...	...	...	...	...	...	...
Nepal	...	...	...	...	...	...	...	...	...	...	...	...	...	...
Sri Lanka	19,923.9	20,804.1	18,678.8	18,959.5	15,575.0	15,720.5	15,981.9	35.1	25.8	22.7	21.7	17.7	18.7	19.8
Southeast Asia														
Brunei Darussalam	...	...	...	...	...	...	...	...	...	...	...	...	...	...
Cambodia	...	...	...	...	...	...	...	...	...	...	...	...	...	...
Indonesia	360,388.1	353,271.0	425,767.8	520,686.7	486,765.9	523,321.9	496,086.1	47.7	41.0	45.7	51.3	46.7	46.8	46.9
Lao People's Democratic Republic	...	...	...	...	...	...	...	...	...	...	...	...	...	...
Malaysia	408,689.1	382,976.7	359,788.3	455,772.5	398,018.7	403,957.4	436,537.9	160.3	127.1	119.4	142.8	111.0	110.8	129.7
Myanmar	...	...	...	...	...	...	...	...	...	...	...	...	...	...
Philippines	157,320.5	238,819.9	239,738.0	290,401.4	258,155.7	275,302.2	272,790.3	75.5	77.9	75.2	88.4	74.4	73.1	75.5
Singapore	647,226.4	639,955.9	640,427.5	787,255.3	687,257.2	697,271.3	652,614.7	269.9	207.8	200.9	229.3	182.8	186.2	191.9
Thailand	277,731.7	348,798.0	432,956.2	548,795.4	500,741.0	569,228.3	543,164.6	81.4	86.9	104.7	120.3	98.8	104.6	108.2
Timor-Leste	...	...	...	...	...	...	...	...	...	...	...	...	...	...
Viet Nam	36,855.0	58,734.0	73,222.2	125,310.0	132,653.0	149,817.3	186,008.5	31.8	30.4	35.7	56.0	54.1	57.2	68.6
The Pacific														
Cook Islands	...	...	...	...	...	...	...	...	...	...	...	...	...	...
Fiji	...	...	...	...	...	...	...	...	...	...	...	...	...	...
Kiribati	...	...	...	...	...	...	...	...	...	...	...	...	...	...
Marshall Islands	...	...	...	...	...	...	...	...	...	...	...	...	...	...
Micronesia, Federated States of	...	...	...	...	...	...	...	...	...	...	...	...	...	...
Nauru	...	...	...	...	...	...	...	...	...	...	...	...	...	...
Niue	...	...	...	...	...	...	...	...	...	...	...	...	...	...
Palau	...	...	...	...	...	...	...	...	...	...	...	...	...	...
Papua New Guinea	11,027.3	1,718.9	1,643.1	1,681.6	...	...	...	77.4	7.9	7.9	7.4	...	...	...
Samoa	...	...	...	...	...	...	...	...	...	...	...	...	...	...
Solomon Islands	...	...	...	...	...	...	...	...	...	...	...	...	...	...
Tonga	...	...	...	...	...	...	...	...	...	...	...	...	...	...
Tuvalu	...	...	...	...	...	...	...	...	...	...	...	...	...	...
Vanuatu	...	...	...	...	...	...	...	...	...	...	...	...	...	...
Developed ADB Member Economies														
Australia	1,454,490.6	1,187,083.5	1,268,493.5	1,508,462.8	1,262,800.3	1,487,598.5	1,720,556.2	126.9	87.8	104.9	113.5	88.1	106.5	129.3
Japan	3,827,774.2	4,894,919.1	4,955,299.7	6,222,825.2	5,296,811.1	6,191,073.3	6,718,219.6	67.2	111.5	100.7	127.9	106.9	122.2	...
New Zealand	35,506.9 (2009)	74,350.5	80,048.5	94,691.3	86,132.6	107,879.8	132,198.5	29.3 (2009)	41.8	42.4	45.8	40.6	51.6	62.2

... = data not available, $ = United States dollars, ADB = Asian Development Bank, GDP = gross domestic product.

Sources: World Bank. World Development Indicators. https://databank.worldbank.org/source/world-development-indicators (accessed 17 July 2021). For Bhutan and Taipei,China: Asian Development Bank estimates using data from economy's official sources.

Table 2.3.12: Official Exchange Rates
(local currency units per $, period averages)

ADB Regional Member	2010	2015	2016	2017	2018	2019	2020
Developing ADB Member Economies							
Central and West Asia							
Afghanistan	46.5	61.1	67.9	68.0	72.1	77.7	76.8
Armenia	373.7	477.9	480.5	482.7	483.0	480.4	489.0
Azerbaijan	0.8	1.0	1.6	1.7	1.7	1.7	1.7
Georgia	1.8	2.3	2.4	2.5	2.5	2.8	3.1
Kazakhstan	147.4	221.7	342.2	326.0	344.7	382.7	413.0
Kyrgyz Republic	46.0	64.5	69.9	68.9	68.8	69.8	77.3
Pakistan	85.2	102.8	104.8	105.5	121.8	150.0	161.8
Tajikistan	4.4	6.2	7.8	8.5	9.2	9.5	10.3
Turkmenistan	2.9	3.5	3.5	3.5	3.5	3.5	3.5
Uzbekistan[a]	1,578.4	2,568.0	2,965.3	5,113.9	8,069.6	8,836.8	10,054.3
East Asia							
China, People's Republic of	6.8	6.2	6.6	6.8	6.6	6.9	6.9
Hong Kong, China	7.8	7.8	7.8	7.8	7.8	7.8	7.8
Korea, Republic of	1,156.5	1,131.0	1,160.8	1,131.0	1,100.2	1,165.4	1,180.3
Mongolia	1,357.1	1,970.3	2,140.3	2,439.8	2,472.5	2,663.5	2,813.3
Taipei,China	31.6	31.9	32.3	30.4	30.2	30.9	29.6
South Asia							
Bangladesh	69.6	77.9	78.5	80.4	83.5	84.5	84.9
Bhutan	45.7	64.2	67.2	65.1	68.4	70.4	74.1
India	45.7	64.2	67.2	65.1	68.4	70.4	74.1
Maldives	12.8	15.4	15.4	15.4	15.4	15.4	15.4
Nepal	73.3	102.4	107.4	104.5	108.9	112.6	118.3
Sri Lanka	113.1	135.9	145.6	152.4	162.5	178.7	185.6
Southeast Asia							
Brunei Darussalam	1.4	1.4	1.4	1.4	1.3	1.4	1.4
Cambodia	4,184.9	4,067.8	4,058.7	4,050.6	4,051.2	4,061.1	4,092.8
Indonesia	9,090.4	13,389.4	13,308.3	13,380.8	14,236.9	14,147.7	14,582.2
Lao People's Democratic Republic	8,254.2	8,127.6	8,124.4	8,244.8	8,401.3	8,679.4	9,045.8
Malaysia	3.2	3.9	4.1	4.3	4.0	4.1	4.2
Myanmar[b]	5.6	1,162.6	1,234.9	1,360.4	1,429.8	1,518.3	1,381.6
Philippines	45.1	45.5	47.5	50.4	52.7	51.8	49.6
Singapore	1.4	1.4	1.4	1.4	1.3	1.4	1.4
Thailand	31.7	34.2	35.3	33.9	32.3	31.0	31.3
Timor-Leste[c]	1.0	1.0	1.0	1.0	1.0	1.0	1.0
Viet Nam	18,612.9	21,697.6	21,935.0	22,370.1	22,602.1	23,050.2	23,208.4
The Pacific							
Cook Islands[d]	1.4	1.4	1.4	1.4	1.4	1.5	1.5
Fiji	1.9	2.1	2.1	2.1	2.1	2.2	2.2
Kiribati	1.1	1.3	1.3	1.3	1.3	1.4	1.5
Marshall Islands[c]	1.0	1.0	1.0	1.0	1.0	1.0	1.0
Micronesia, Federated States of[c]	1.0	1.0	1.0	1.0	1.0	1.0	1.0
Nauru	1.1	1.3	1.3	1.3	1.3	1.4	1.5
Niue[d]	1.4	1.4	1.4	1.4	1.4	1.5	1.5
Palau[c]	1.0	1.0	1.0	1.0	1.0	1.0	1.0
Papua New Guinea	2.7	2.8	3.1	3.2	3.3	3.4	3.5
Samoa	2.5	2.6	2.6	2.6	2.6	2.6	2.7
Solomon Islands	8.1	7.9	7.9	7.9	8.0	8.2	8.2
Tonga	1.9	2.1	2.2	2.2	2.2	2.3	2.3
Tuvalu[e]	1.1	1.3	1.3	1.3	1.3	1.4	1.5
Vanuatu	96.9	109.0	108.5	107.8	110.2	114.7	115.4
Developed ADB Member Economies							
Australia	1.1	1.3	1.3	1.3	1.3	1.4	1.5
Japan	87.8	121.0	108.8	112.2	110.4	109.0	106.8
New Zealand	1.4	1.4	1.4	1.4	1.4	1.5	1.5

$ = United States (US) dollars, ADB = Asian Development Bank.

a Data show weighted averages of the official, bank, and parallel market rates.
b Beginning 1 April 2012, the Central Bank of Myanmar adopted the managed float exchange rate regime for kyat vis-à-vis the US dollar.
c Unit of currency is the US dollar.
d Unit of currency is the New Zealand dollar.
e Unit of currency is the Australian dollar.

Sources: International Monetary Fund. International Financial Statistics. http://data.imf.org/ (accessed 15 July 2021). For Turkmenistan for 2000–2009 (available in the Key Indicators Database): United Nations Statistics Division. UN National Accounts Main Aggregates Database. https://unstats.un.org/unsd/snaama/countryprofile (accessed 20 April 2021), and for 2010–2020: Interstate Statistical Committee of the Commonwealth of Independent States. http://www.cisstat.org/eng/index.htm (accessed 20 April 2021). For Uzbekistan for 2000–2012 (available in the Key Indicators Database): United Nations Statistics Division. UN National Accounts Main Aggregates Database. https://unstats.un.org/unsd/snaama/countryprofile (accessed 8 April 2021), and for 2013–2020: Central Bank of Uzbekistan. https://cbu.uz/en/statistics/e-gdds/data/111573/ (accessed 8 April 2021). For the Republic of the Marshall Islands: Economic Policy, Planning and Statistics Office. Official communication, 8 April 2021.

Table 2.3.13: Purchasing Power Parity Conversion Factor
(local currency units per $, period averages)

ADB Regional Member	2010	2011	2015	2016	2017	2018	2019	2020
Developing ADB Member Economies								
Central and West Asia								
Afghanistan	14.55	16.61	17.02	17.45	17.21	17.15	17.95	18.71
Armenia	160.21	163.65	172.92	161.23	155.97	156.56	156.06	157.09
Azerbaijan	0.31	0.38	0.38	0.43	0.51	0.55	0.54	0.50
Georgia	0.76	0.81	0.75	0.75	0.80	0.82	0.85	0.90
Kazakhstan	69.52	82.09	100.35	110.82	121.25	129.31	136.74	139.91
Kyrgyz Republic	13.11	15.73	17.15	16.74	16.96	17.13	17.50	18.28
Pakistan	21.30	24.96	31.47	32.38	33.59	33.61	35.87	38.74
Tajikistan	1.41	1.56	1.91	2.03	2.23	2.23	2.27	2.30
Turkmenistan	1.29	1.43	1.64	1.61	1.62	1.60	1.65	...
Uzbekistan	505.90	602.00	1,058.68	1,179.96	1,432.91	1,783.70	2,077.83	2,297.17
East Asia								
China, People's Republic of	3.33	3.52	3.87	3.99	4.18	4.23	4.21	4.19
Hong Kong, China	5.14	5.23	5.83	5.93	6.01	6.09	6.10	6.07
Korea, Republic of	840.68	854.59	857.48	858.81	872.62	865.72	868.57	861.82
Mongolia	473.14	533.53	717.07	729.22	791.44	837.89	900.42	931.67
Taipei,China	15.81	15.15	15.48	15.78	15.73	15.27	15.01	15.02
South Asia								
Bangladesh	22.16	23.41	27.28	28.50	29.74	30.67	31.47	32.81
Bhutan	15.43	16.40	18.59	18.83	19.21	19.09	18.94	20.11
India	14.60	15.55	19.24	19.90	20.65	20.92	21.28	21.99
Maldives	7.13	7.86	8.28	8.13	8.16	8.22	8.03	8.35
Nepal	20.35	25.25	29.94	32.00	31.23	31.83	32.74	33.52
Sri Lanka	38.63	39.29	45.18	46.28	49.39	50.08	50.55	51.65
Southeast Asia								
Brunei Darussalam	0.60	0.71	0.69	0.67	0.65	0.69	0.66	0.58
Cambodia	1,354.32	1,371.24	1,395.92	1,402.13	1,428.35	1,438.27	1,458.76	1,400.09
Indonesia	3,336.99	3,512.75	4,353.33	4,518.10	4,695.66	4,760.65	4,751.94	4,673.65
Lao People's Democratic Republic	2,464.26	2,666.53	2,819.73	2,759.43	2,789.11	2,776.01	2,783.05	2,889.36
Malaysia	1.42	1.47	1.57	1.59	1.65	1.63	1.60	1.57
Myanmar	242.40	261.78	318.98	347.07	366.71	380.55	398.50	417.35
Philippines	17.78	18.10	19.00	18.95	19.39	19.64	19.43	19.51
Singapore	0.86	0.85	0.88	0.88	0.89	0.89	0.87	0.84
Thailand	12.19	12.39	12.64	12.73	12.84	12.72	12.62	12.34
Timor-Leste	0.41	0.45	0.46	0.43	0.41	0.39	0.42	0.41
Viet Nam	5,822.00	6,915.34	7,413.46	7,315.61	7,395.34	7,467.35	7,467.60	7,473.67
The Pacific								
Cook Islands	...	...	...	...	...	...	...	...
Fiji	0.89	0.95	0.91	0.94	0.94	0.93	0.94	0.91
Kiribati	0.96	0.96	0.97	0.97	0.96	0.98	1.01	1.00
Marshall Islands	0.89	0.94	0.92	0.99	0.99	0.97	0.97	...
Micronesia, Federated States of	0.88	0.88	0.87	0.89	0.94	1.01	0.99	...
Nauru	0.90	1.00	0.76	0.96	1.06	1.07	1.09	...
Niue	...	...	...	...	...	...	...	...
Palau	0.77	0.75	0.89	0.93	0.90	0.83	0.81	...
Papua New Guinea	1.82	1.86	1.87	1.90	2.01	2.15	2.11	2.11
Samoa	1.69	1.66	1.70	1.70	1.67	1.66	1.67	...
Solomon Islands	5.94	6.37	7.01	6.94	6.91	6.94	6.91	7.08
Tonga	1.48	1.45	1.46	1.49	1.54	1.58	1.68	...
Tuvalu	1.13	1.11	1.18	1.18	1.20	1.23	1.31	1.29
Vanuatu	99.83	100.51	103.74	104.28	107.84	108.69	109.54	110.17
Developed ADB Member Economies								
Australia	1.50	1.51	1.47	1.45	1.48	1.47	1.47	1.47
Japan	111.67	107.45	103.47	105.52	105.10	103.71	103.63	102.84
New Zealand	1.50	1.49	1.48	1.44	1.43	1.42	1.44	1.45

... = data not available, $ = United States dollars, ADB = Asian Development Bank.

Note: For 2011 and 2017, purchasing power parity (PPP) figures are based on results from the 2011 and 2017 benchmark cycles of the International Comparison Program (ICP). For 2010 (and years prior featured in the Key Indicators Database), PPPs are extrapolated from the revised 2011 ICP PPP estimates. For 2012–2016, figures are interpolated from the two ICP reference years 2011 and 2017. For 2017 onward, figures are extrapolated from the 2017 ICP PPPs or imputed based on a regression model.

Sources: World Bank. World Development Indicators. https://databank.worldbank.org/source/world-development-indicators (accessed 17 July 2021). For Taipei,China: for 2000–2010 (available in the Key Indicators Database) and 2018–2020, Asian Development Bank estimates using data from economy's official sources and World Bank data; for 2011–2017, World Bank. DataBank: ICP 2017. https://databank.worldbank.org/source/icp-2017 (accessed 17 July 2021).

Table 2.3.14: Price Level Indexes
(PPPs to official exchange rates, period averages, United States = 100)

ADB Regional Member	2010	2011	2015	2016	2017	2018	2019	2020
Developing ADB Member Economies								
Central and West Asia								
Afghanistan	31.8	34.8	27.7	25.7	25.3	23.7	23.6	24.4
Armenia	42.9	43.9	36.2	33.6	32.3	32.4	32.5	32.1
Azerbaijan	39.1	48.6	36.8	27.0	29.4	32.6	31.9	29.2
Georgia	42.7	48.1	33.2	31.6	32.1	32.4	30.1	28.8
Kazakhstan	47.2	56.0	45.3	32.4	37.2	37.5	35.7	33.9
Kyrgyz Republic	28.5	34.1	26.6	23.9	24.6	24.9	25.1	23.6
Pakistan	25.4	29.2	31.0	31.0	32.0	30.5	26.3	24.5
Tajikistan	32.2	33.9	31.1	25.9	26.1	24.4	23.9	22.3
Turkmenistan	45.2	50.0	47.0	46.1	46.4	45.8	47.0	...
Uzbekistan	31.9	35.1	41.2	39.8	28.0	22.1	23.5	22.8
East Asia								
China, People's Republic of	49.2	54.5	62.2	60.0	61.9	63.9	60.9	60.7
Hong Kong, China	66.2	67.2	75.2	76.4	77.1	77.6	77.9	78.2
Korea, Republic of	72.7	77.1	75.8	74.0	77.2	78.7	74.5	73.0
Mongolia	34.9	42.2	36.4	34.1	32.4	33.9	33.8	33.1
Taipei,China	50.0	51.4	48.5	48.8	51.7	50.6	48.5	50.8
South Asia								
Bangladesh	32.0	32.9	35.1	36.4	37.6	37.3	37.5	38.7
Bhutan	33.7	35.1	29.0	28.0	29.5	27.9	26.9	27.1
India	32.0	32.4	29.4	29.7	32.0	29.9	30.0	29.4
Maldives	55.7	53.8	53.9	52.9	53.0	53.4	52.2	54.2
Nepal	27.3	34.9	30.1	30.1	29.4	30.5	29.0	28.8
Sri Lanka	34.2	35.5	33.3	31.8	32.4	30.8	28.3	27.8
Southeast Asia								
Brunei Darussalam	43.9	56.1	49.8	48.2	46.8	51.1	48.0	41.8
Cambodia	32.4	33.8	34.3	34.5	35.3	35.5	35.9	34.2
Indonesia	36.7	40.1	32.5	33.9	35.1	33.4	33.6	32.1
Lao People's Democratic Republic	29.8	33.2	34.6	33.7	33.4	32.7	31.0	31.9
Malaysia	44.1	47.9	40.1	38.4	38.5	40.3	38.6	37.3
Myanmar	31.4	30.6	25.9	25.8	26.5	24.8	27.9	29.2
Philippines	39.4	41.8	41.8	39.9	38.5	37.3	37.5	39.3
Singapore	62.7	67.3	64.0	63.6	64.2	66.3	64.0	60.7
Thailand	38.5	40.6	36.9	36.1	37.8	39.4	40.6	39.4
Timor-Leste	41.0	45.5	45.8	43.2	40.9	39.4	42.1	41.2
Viet Nam	31.3	33.7	34.2	33.4	33.1	33.0	32.4	32.2
The Pacific								
Cook Islands	...	...	...	...	...	...	...	...
Fiji	46.2	52.9	43.4	44.7	45.4	44.6	43.3	42.1
Kiribati	88.4	99.2	73.2	71.8	73.4	73.6	69.9	69.1
Marshall Islands	88.7	93.9	91.9	98.6	99.1	97.3	97.0	...
Micronesia, Federated States of	88.4	87.9	86.8	89.4	94.3	100.7	99.2	...
Nauru	79.6	98.5	63.5	70.0	79.8	83.2	77.9	...
Niue	...	...	...	...	...	...	...	...
Palau	77.1	74.9	89.1	92.9	90.1	82.9	81.4	...
Papua New Guinea	66.9	78.4	67.5	60.6	62.9	65.3	62.4	60.9
Samoa	66.5	69.6	70.0	65.0	65.7	64.7	63.7	...
Solomon Islands	73.7	83.4	88.6	87.3	87.6	87.3	84.5	86.2
Tonga	76.5	79.3	75.1	67.1	69.8	72.2	73.8	...
Tuvalu	103.3	114.5	88.5	87.5	91.7	91.6	91.0	89.0
Vanuatu	103.0	112.3	95.2	96.1	100.0	98.7	95.5	95.5
Developed ADB Member Economies								
Australia	132.4	149.0	122.6	105.6	111.4	114.1	105.5	98.7
Japan	127.2	134.6	85.5	97.0	93.7	93.9	95.1	96.3
New Zealand	109.5	119.8	100.0	102.2	102.2	97.0	93.2	94.4

... = data not available, ADB = Asian Development Bank, PPP = purchasing power parity.

Sources: World Bank. World Development Indicators. https://databank.worldbank.org/source/world-development-indicators (accessed 17 July 2021). For Taipei,China: Asian Development Bank estimates using data from economy's official sources and World Bank. Databank: ICP 2017. https://databank.worldbank.org/source/icp-2017 (accessed 17 July 2021).

Data Issues and Comparability

Not all reporting economies meet the standards and classifications of the International Monetary Fund (IMF) on the compilation of monetary and financial statistics available on the fund's Dissemination Standards Bulletin Board.[2]

Consumer price index coverage differs across economies. Most economies try to follow the Classification of Individual Consumption by Purpose guidelines, but the implementation varies across economies. In some instances, the basket of goods and services in the index is outdated or represents only urban areas (or the capital city). Other price measurements, such as the wholesale price index and the producer price index, are not available in Pacific economies.

Broad money supply in most economies relates to M2, which includes cash, checking deposits, savings deposits, money market securities, mutual funds, and other time deposits. However, 11 of the 44 economies with available data reported M3, thereby posing limits to comparability as M3 also includes less liquid financial assets. Not all economies publish the same types of aggregates, and even when aggregates have the same name (i.e., M1, M2, M3, etc.), their asset composition often differs significantly. For example, the definition of M2 in one economy may include time deposits with maturities of 1 year or less, whereas another economy's M2 definition may include time deposits with maturities of 2 years or less.

Finally, some economies use the central bank policy rate, while others use commercial bank rates in measuring banks' average deposit and lending rates.

2 For more information on the IMF's standards and classifications on the compilation of monetary and financial statistics, go to http:// dsbb.imf.org/Pages/SDDS/StatMethod.aspx.

Table 2.4.1: Trade in Goods Balance
(% of GDP)

ADB Regional Member	2010	2015	2016	2017	2018	2019	2020
Developing ADB Member Economies							
Central and West Asia							
Afghanistan	-27.3	-32.4	-31.1	-31.4	-31.1	-28.0	-25.8
Armenia	-22.3	-11.2	-9.3	-12.2	-14.1	-13.2	-10.5
Azerbaijan	37.3	11.0	11.1	15.0	20.9	17.7	5.9
Georgia	-21.5	-26.4	-25.6	-23.4	-23.4	-21.4	-19.8
Kazakhstan	19.3	6.3	6.7	10.0	14.3	10.0	6.1
Kyrgyz Republic	-25.2	-34.3	-31.1	-30.9	-36.7	-29.6	-18.4*
Pakistan	-6.5	-6.4	-6.9	-8.5	-9.8	-9.9	-8.0
Tajikistan	-43.9	-27.7	-27.0	-20.1	-24.3	-23.7	-18.1
Turkmenistan	9.9	-5.3	-15.6	-6.3	10.2	5.0*	...
Uzbekistan	1.9	-2.6	-2.9	-3.7	-13.6	-12.6	-10.8
East Asia							
China, People's Republic of	3.9	5.2	4.4	3.9	2.7	2.8	3.5
Hong Kong, China	1.4	-7.4	-5.2	-6.7	-8.9	-4.4	-1.7
Korea, Republic of	4.2	8.2	7.8	7.0	6.4	4.8	5.0
Mongolia	-2.4	4.8	12.0	13.0	5.2	8.4	13.5
Taipei,China	8.3	13.7	13.1	13.8	11.0	9.4	11.2
South Asia							
Bangladesh	-4.5	-3.6	-2.9	-3.8	-6.6	-5.2	-5.4*
Bhutan	-20.5	-22.3	-27.6	-21.6	-17.5	-16.9	-9.8
India	-7.6	-6.2	-4.9	-6.0	-6.7	-5.5	-3.2*
Maldives[a]	-40.9 |	-40.4	-42.1	-40.4	-45.6	-42.4	-38.6*
Nepal[b]	-25.5	-27.4	-26.1	-29.1	-32.9	-33.3	-26.9
Sri Lanka[a]	-8.5 |	-10.4	-10.8	-11.0	-11.7	-9.5	-7.4
Southeast Asia							
Brunei Darussalam	45.3	22.4	18.9	19.8	17.4	16.4	...
Cambodia	-23.9	-21.9	-19.2	-19.3	-23.8	-26.8	-14.2
Indonesia	4.1	1.6	1.6	1.9	-0.0	0.3	2.7
Lao People's Democratic Republic[a]	-4.7 |	-14.0	-7.1	-4.7	-5.0	-2.5	4.0
Malaysia	15.1	9.3	8.2	8.5	7.9	8.2	9.8
Myanmar[a]	0.1 |	-6.1	-5.9	-9.5	-6.3	...	...
Philippines	-8.1	-7.6	-11.2	-12.2	-14.7	-13.1	-8.8*
Singapore	26.4	30.1	28.2	29.4	27.0	25.9	27.5
Thailand	7.8	6.5	8.7	7.1	4.4	4.9	7.9
Timor-Leste[a]	-31.8 |	-39.9	-33.1	-38.4	-37.7	-28.1	...
Viet Nam[a]	-4.4 |	3.8	5.4	4.8	6.7	8.2*	...
The Pacific							
Cook Islands	-25.2	-43.3	-44.9	-46.3	-43.6	-46.2	...
Fiji	-23.5	-19.5	-20.2	-20.4	-24.2	-25.2	...
Kiribati	-40.9	-52.4	-53.5	-52.4	-46.7*	...	...
Marshall Islands	-49.4	-28.6	-24.6	-25.6	-28.6	-55.2	...
Micronesia, Federated States of	-43.2	-40.4	-33.2	-32.8	-32.0	...	...
Nauru	33.6 (2012)	-47.9	-21.1	-30.8	-40.8*	-47.0*	-46.1*
Niue	-60.3	-40.2	-35.7	-43.6	-41.4*	...	...
Palau	-45.7	-49.1	-45.3	-48.5	-48.4	-51.7*	...
Papua New Guinea[b]	15.5	27.0	29.5	30.3	29.0	31.1	27.9*
Samoa	-37.0	-33.6	-33.6	-34.4	-34.8	-36.2	-32.0
Solomon Islands	-15.1	-1.3	1.0	0.5	0.2	-2.5	-1.7
Tonga[c]	-53.0 |	-70.4	-71.9	-74.5	-80.5	-83.5	...
Tuvalu[c]	-54.3 |	-121.5	-46.8	-44.0	-38.4	-66.3	...
Vanuatu	-27.1	-35.5	-33.3	-28.9	-26.2	...	...
Developed ADB Member Economies							
Australia	-0.7	-0.8	-1.7	0.8	0.7	2.7	3.6
Japan	1.9	-0.2	1.0	0.9	0.2	0.0	0.6
New Zealand	1.4	-1.0	-1.1	-1.0	-1.5	-0.9	...

... = data not available, | = marks break in series due to change in compilation methodology, -0.0 or 0.0 = magnitude is less than half of unit employed, * = provisional or preliminary, ADB = Asian Development Bank, GDP = gross domestic product.

a Change in compilation methodology from the International Monetary Fund's Balance of Payments Manual (fifth edition) [BPM5] to the International Monetary Fund's Balance of Payments and International Investment Position Manual (sixth edition) [BPM6].

b Based on BPM5.

c Change in compilation methodology from BPM4 to BPM6.

Source: Economy's official sources.

Table 2.4.2: Trade in Services Balance
(% of GDP)

ADB Regional Member	2010	2015	2016	2017	2018	2019	2020
Developing ADB Member Economies							
Central and West Asia							
Afghanistan	6.0	-1.8	-3.3	-4.6	-3.5	-3.0	-2.0
Armenia	-2.8	-0.9	0.7	1.4	0.5	-0.2	1.2
Azerbaijan	-3.3	-8.0	-8.3	-8.3	-4.4	-5.4	-6.7
Georgia	4.5	9.4	10.4	12.5	12.7	12.4	0.8
Kazakhstan	-4.9	-2.6	-2.7	-2.1	-2.6	-2.0	-1.8
Kyrgyz Republic	-4.2	-3.1	-3.0	-1.2	-1.6	0.7	-2.0*
Pakistan	-1.0	-1.1	-1.3	-1.5	-2.3	-2.0	-1.3
Tajikistan	-0.5	-2.5	-2.0	-1.6	-2.8	-3.0	-3.4
Turkmenistan	...	...	...	...	...	...	...
Uzbekistan	-2.7	-0.9	-1.9	-3.1	-4.8	-3.9	-3.1
East Asia							
China, People's Republic of	-0.2	-2.0	-2.1	-2.1	-2.1	-1.8	-1.0
Hong Kong, China	4.4	9.8	7.5	7.7	8.7	6.1	3.7
Korea, Republic of	-1.2	-1.0	-1.2	-2.3	-1.7	-1.6	-1.0
Mongolia	-4.2	-6.1	-12.0	-10.6	-15.1	-14.2	-11.3
Taipei,China	-2.5	-2.0	-1.9	-1.5	-1.1	-0.8	0.5
South Asia							
Bangladesh	-1.1	-1.6	-1.2	-1.3	-1.6	-1.1	-0.8*
Bhutan	-4.6	-3.5	-2.8	-2.2	-1.6	-2.0	-2.9
India	2.6	3.2	3.0	3.0	3.0	2.9	2.4*
Maldives[a]	34.8 |	49.4	40.8	36.4	35.8	36.2	21.3*
Nepal[b]	-1.3	1.2	0.4	0.1	0.0	-0.4	-0.0
Sri Lanka[a]	1.2 |	2.9	3.5	3.8	4.3	3.4	1.0
Southeast Asia							
Brunei Darussalam	-5.9	-7.8	-9.8	-5.7	-7.4	-8.8	...
Cambodia	9.0	9.5	8.0	8.4	9.7	10.4	-0.5
Indonesia	-1.3	-1.0	-0.8	-0.7	-0.6	-0.7	-0.9
Lao People's Democratic Republic[a]	2.4 |	-1.6	-1.2	-2.0	-1.5	-0.4	-0.5
Malaysia	0.8	-1.8	-1.5	-1.7	-1.2	-0.7	-3.4
Myanmar[a]	-0.0 |	2.2	2.1	1.5	1.8	...	...
Philippines	2.8	1.8	2.2	2.6	3.3	3.5	3.6*
Singapore	-0.1	-2.8	-2.1	-3.0	1.8	2.4	4.4
Thailand	-2.1	3.9	4.9	5.3	4.4	4.5*	-3.0*
Timor-Leste[a]	-107.7 |	-36.5	-34.4	-21.5	-22.4	-17.7	...
Viet Nam[a]	-2.1 |	-2.5	-2.1	-1.8	-1.6	-0.9*	...
The Pacific							
Cook Islands	41.4	62.5	70.8	73.4	71.7	89.5	...
Fiji[a]	14.7	16.0	16.3	15.5	16.6	14.9	...
Kiribati[a]	-25.4	-39.4	-36.8	-35.7	-30.1*	...	...
Marshall Islands	-19.9	-18.0	-16.6	-19.0	-17.2	-20.4	...
Micronesia, Federated States of	-15.2	-10.8	-12.1	-8.3	2.1	...	...
Nauru	-13.5 (2012)	-15.9	-21.5	-15.6	-12.5*	-12.5*	-12.2*
Niue	-40.5	13.0	13.6	16.5	21.1*	...	...
Palau	19.1	32.5	25.9	21.4	19.8	16.1*	...
Papua New Guinea[b]	-17.2	-5.4	-4.6	-5.7	-5.1	-4.9	-4.3*
Samoa	10.6	15.8	15.1	18.6	17.1	22.0	-1.5
Solomon Islands	-10.6	-5.8	-6.6	-6.0	...	...	...
Tonga[c]	-2.1 |	1.2	4.1	5.8	6.7	6.3	...
Tuvalu[c]	-4.1 |	-93.7	-81.8	-63.5	-67.6	-52.5	...
Vanuatu	21.4	13.0	19.2	19.0	23.3	...	...
Developed ADB Member Economies							
Australia	-0.3	-0.7	-0.6	-0.2	-0.3	-0.2	0.3
Japan	-0.5	-0.4	-0.2	-0.1	-0.2	-0.2	-0.7
New Zealand	0.9	1.8	1.7	1.7	1.1	0.8	...

... = data not available, | = marks break in series due to change in compilation methodology, -0.0 or 0.0 = magnitude is less than half of unit employed, * = provisional or preliminary, ADB = Asian Development Bank, GDP = gross domestic product.

a Change in compilation methodology from the International Monetary Fund's Balance of Payments Manual (fifth edition) [BPM5] to the International Monetary Fund's Balance of Payments and International Investment Position Manual (sixth edition) [BPM6].

b Based on BPM5.

c Change in compilation methodology from BPM4 to BPM6.

Source: Economy's official sources.

Table 2.4.3: Current Account Balance
(% of GDP)

ADB Regional Member	2010	2015	2016	2017	2018	2019	2020
Developing ADB Member Economies							
Central and West Asia							
Afghanistan	-4.7	-20.3	-15.0	-18.8	-21.2	-20.1	-15.8
Armenia	-13.6	-2.7	-1.0	-1.5	-6.9	-7.2	-3.1
Azerbaijan	28.4	-0.4	-3.6	4.1	12.8	9.1	-0.5
Georgia	-9.8	-11.8	-12.5	-8.0	-6.8	-5.5	-12.4
Kazakhstan	0.9	-3.3	-5.9	-3.1	-0.1	-4.0	-3.7
Kyrgyz Republic	-6.5	-16.4	-11.5	-6.3	-12.1	-12.1	4.5*
Pakistan	-2.2	-1.0	-1.8	-4.0	-6.1	-4.8	-1.7
Tajikistan	-10.3	-5.8	-4.2	2.1	-4.9	-2.3	4.2
Turkmenistan	-12.9	-15.6	-20.2	-10.4*	5.5*	1.3*	...
Uzbekistan	5.4	1.1	0.3	2.5	-7.1	-5.8	-5.4
East Asia							
China, People's Republic of	3.9	2.6	1.7	1.5	0.2	0.7	1.9
Hong Kong, China	7.0	3.3	4.0	4.6	3.7	6.0	6.7
Korea, Republic of	2.4	7.2	6.5	4.6	4.5	3.6	4.6
Mongolia	-12.3	-8.1	-6.3	-10.1	-16.8	-15.6	-4.4
Taipei,China	8.3	13.6	13.1	14.1	11.6	10.6	14.1
South Asia							
Bangladesh	3.2	1.8	1.9	-0.5	-3.5	-1.5	-1.4*
Bhutan	-24.3	-28.6	-32.2	-25.1	-19.5	-21.2	-12.2
India	-2.9	-1.1	-0.6	-1.8	-2.1	-0.9	1.7*
Maldives[a]	-13.8 |	-7.4	-23.7	-21.7	-28.3	-26.4	-29.8*
Nepal[b]	-2.3	4.5	5.4	-0.3	-7.1	-6.8	-0.9
Sri Lanka[a]	-1.9 |	-2.3	-2.1	-2.6	-3.2	-2.2	-1.3
Southeast Asia							
Brunei Darussalam	36.5	16.6	12.9	16.4	6.9	6.6	...
Cambodia	-8.7	-8.9	-8.7	-8.1	-11.8	-15.0	-12.1
Indonesia	0.7	-2.0	-1.8	-1.6	-2.9	-2.7	-0.4
Lao People's Democratic Republic[a]	0.4 |	-15.7	-8.7	-7.4	-9.1	-7.0	-0.6
Malaysia	10.1	3.0	2.4	2.8	2.2	3.4	4.3
Myanmar[a]	0.0 |	-4.9	-3.0	-7.9	-3.6	...	...
Philippines	3.4	2.4	-0.4	-0.7	-2.6	-0.8	3.6*
Singapore	22.9	18.7	17.6	17.3	15.4	14.3	17.6
Thailand	3.4	6.9	10.5	9.6	5.6	7.0*	3.3*
Timor-Leste[a]	180.2 |	12.8	-33.0	-17.7	-12.3	6.6	...
Viet Nam[a]	-3.7 |	-1.1	0.3	-0.7	2.4	4.8*	...
The Pacific							
Cook Islands	15.5	29.4	36.4	35.9	32.6	50.1	...
Fiji	-7.1	-3.5	-3.6	-6.7	-8.4	-12.7	...
Kiribati	0.1	32.8	10.5	37.6	39.2*	...	...
Marshall Islands	-14.8	17.2	16.1	7.5	6.5	-23.9	...
Micronesia, Federated States of	-17.5	4.5	7.2	10.3	21.0	24.8*	21.6*
Nauru	38.1 (2012)	-18.5	2.0	12.7	-4.6*	5.0*	-4.2*
Niue	-53.9	11.1	17.6	14.9	15.7*	...	...
Palau	-9.3	-8.8	-13.7	-19.0	-15.5	-26.9*	...
Papua New Guinea[b]	-4.4	20.2	25.0	23.5	22.9	22.4	23.5*
Samoa	-8.7	-1.6	-4.7	-1.1	2.8	4.0	-9.7
Solomon Islands	-16.0	-2.7	-3.9	-4.1	-3.3	-8.9	-1.6
Tonga[c]	-8.7 |	-9.0	5.0	7.0	4.4	-0.5	...
Tuvalu[c]	-3.8 |	-74.0	13.9	11.5	53.9	-16.9	...
Vanuatu	-5.4	-1.6	0.7	-6.4	9.4	...	...
Developed ADB Member Economies							
Australia	-5.0	-3.7	-4.7	-2.2	-2.8	-0.7	1.8
Japan	3.8	3.1	3.9	4.1	3.5	3.4	3.3
New Zealand	-2.8	-2.5	-2.7	-3.1	-4.0	-2.8	...

... = data not available, | = marks break in series due to change in compilation methodology, -0.0 or 0.0 = magnitude is less than half of unit employed, * = provisional or preliminary, ADB = Asian Development Bank, GDP = gross domestic product.

a Change in compilation methodology from the International Monetary Fund's Balance of Payments Manual (fifth edition) [BPM5] to the International Monetary Fund's Balance of Payments and International Investment Position Manual (sixth edition) [BPM6].

b Based on BPM5.

c Change in compilation methodology from BPM4 to BPM6.

Source: Economy's official sources.

Table 2.4.4: Total Remittances, Inflows—Dollar Amounts
($ million)

ADB Regional Member	2010	2015	2016	2017	2018	2019	2020*
Developing ADB Member Economies							
Central and West Asia	**21,317**	**32,975**	**34,043**	**37,562**	**39,846**	**41,920**	**43,485**
Afghanistan	378	349	628	823	804	829	789
Armenia	1,669	1,491	1,382	1,539	1,488	1,528	1,327
Azerbaijan	1,410	1,270	643	1,133	1,226	1,275	1,403
Georgia	1,184	1,459	1,521	1,794	2,034	2,258	2,110
Kazakhstan	226	294	384	560	618	506	374
Kyrgyz Republic	1,266	1,688	1,995	2,486	2,689	2,411	2,200
Pakistan	9,690	19,306	19,819	19,856	21,193	22,245	26,105
Tajikistan	2,021	2,259	1,867	2,237	2,183	2,322	2,187
Turkmenistan	35	16	9	4	2	1	1
Uzbekistan	3,438	4,843	5,795	7,130	7,610	8,546	6,989
East Asia	**59,419**	**71,964**	**69,180**	**72,295**	**76,904**	**78,423**	**69,825**
China, People's Republic of	52,460	63,938	61,000	63,876	67,414	68,398	59,507
Hong Kong, China	340	387	399	437	425	451	458
Korea, Republic of	5,854	6,464	6,524	6,526	7,125	7,166	7,413
Mongolia	266	261	260	273	441	561	549
Taipei,China	500	915	997	1,183	1,500	1,846	1,898
South Asia	**71,929**	**97,958**	**90,231**	**96,635**	**109,756**	**116,755**	**120,228**
Bangladesh	10,850	15,296	13,574	13,502	15,566	18,364	21,750
Bhutan	8	20	34	43	58	57	83
India	53,480	68,910	62,744	68,967	78,790	83,332	83,149
Maldives	3	4	4	4	4	4	4
Nepal	3,464	6,730	6,612	6,928	8,294	8,250	8,102
Sri Lanka	4,123	7,000	7,262	7,190	7,043	6,749	7,140
Southeast Asia	**43,120**	**63,438**	**65,738**	**69,364**	**74,784**	**77,977**	**75,227**
Brunei Darussalam	...	...	...	...	...	...	...
Cambodia	557	1,185	1,199	1,287	1,431	1,525	1,272
Indonesia	6,916	9,659	8,907	8,990	11,215	11,666	9,651
Lao People's Democratic Republic	42	189	189	243	240	297	265
Malaysia	1,103	1,644	1,604	1,649	1,686	1,638	1,454
Myanmar	115	2,005	2,346	2,578	2,840	2,421	2,250
Philippines	21,557	29,799	31,142	32,810	33,809	35,167	34,913
Singapore	...	...	...	...	...	...	...
Thailand	4,433	5,895	6,270	6,720	7,466	8,162	8,067
Timor-Leste	137	62	80	87	96	100	155
Viet Nam	8,260	13,000	14,000	15,000	16,000	17,000	17,200
The Pacific[a]	**479**	**705**	**699**	**689**	**752**	**804**	**837**
Cook Islands	...	...	...	...	...	...	...
Fiji	176	251	269	274	285	287	312
Kiribati	16	14	16	18	20	20	19
Marshall Islands	22	27	28	30	31	31	31
Micronesia, Federated States of	18	23	23	23	23	23	23
Nauru	...	...	...	...	...	...	...
Niue	...	...	...	...	...	...	...
Palau	2	2	2	2	2	2	2
Papua New Guinea	4	4	3	4	4	3	2
Samoa	139	130	130	136	147	147	150
Solomon Islands	14	19	20	16	20	25	28
Tonga	74	129	126	159	183	190	194
Tuvalu	4	4 (2013)	...	...	...	...	...
Vanuatu	12	105	81	26	35	75	76
Developed ADB Member Economies	**3,919**	**6,031**	**6,415**	**6,985**	**6,751**	**6,623**	**6,464**
Australia	1,864	2,175	2,057	2,002	1,861	1,752	1,192
Japan	1,684	3,325	3,830	4,443	4,369	4,374	4,875
New Zealand	371	532	528	540	520	497	397
DEVELOPING ADB MEMBER ECONOMIES[a]	**196,264**	**267,040**	**259,890**	**276,545**	**302,041**	**315,879**	**309,602**
ALL ADB REGIONAL MEMBERS[a]	**200,183**	**273,071**	**266,306**	**283,530**	**308,793**	**322,502**	**316,066**
WORLD[a]	**472,946**	**601,867**	**597,129**	**639,749**	**693,996**	**719,410**	**701,931**

... = data not available, * = provisional or preliminary, $ = United States dollars, ADB = Asian Development Bank.

Note: Figures are based on the International Monetary Fund's Balance of Payments and International Investment Position Manual (sixth edition).
a Includes only reporting economies with data corresponding to the year heading.

Source: World Bank. Migration and Remittances Data. https://www.worldbank.org/en/topic/migrationremittancesdiasporaissues/brief/migration-remittances-data (accessed 14 June 2021). For Taipei,China: Central bank of Taipei,China. Official communication, 21 April 2021; past communication.

Table 2.4.5: Total Remittances, Inflows—Proportion of Economic Activity
(% of GDP)

ADB Regional Member	2010	2015	2016	2017	2018	2019	2020*
Developing ADB Member Economies							
Central and West Asia[a]	**4.3**	**4.8**	**5.4**	**5.6**	**6.0**	**6.4**	**7.3**
Afghanistan	2.4	1.7	3.5	4.4	4.4	4.4	4.0
Armenia	18.0	14.1	13.1	13.3	11.9	11.2	10.5
Azerbaijan	2.7	2.4	1.7	2.8	2.6	2.6	3.3
Georgia	9.7	9.8	10.0	11.0	11.6	12.9	13.3
Kazakhstan	0.2	0.2	0.3	0.3	0.3	0.3	0.2
Kyrgyz Republic	26.4	25.3	29.3	32.3	32.5	27.2	28.4
Pakistan	5.6	7.2	7.1	6.6	7.5	8.8	10.2
Tajikistan	35.8	27.3	26.7	29.7	28.1	28.0	27.3
Turkmenistan	0.2	0.0	0.0	0.0	0.0	0.0	...
Uzbekistan	7.3	5.9	7.1	12.1	15.1	14.8	12.1
East Asia	**0.8**	**0.5**	**0.5**	**0.5**	**0.5**	**0.5**	**0.4**
China, People's Republic of	0.9	0.6	0.5	0.5	0.5	0.5	0.4
Hong Kong, China	0.1	0.1	0.1	0.1	0.1	0.1	0.1
Korea, Republic of	0.5	0.4	0.4	0.4	0.4	0.4	0.5
Mongolia	3.7	2.2	2.3	2.4	3.4	4.0	4.2
Taipei,China	0.1	0.2	0.2	0.2	0.2	0.3	0.3
South Asia[a]	**3.9**	**4.0**	**3.4**	**3.2**	**3.5**	**3.5**	**3.9**
Bangladesh	9.5	7.9	6.1	5.5	5.8	6.1	6.6
Bhutan	0.5	1.0	1.6	1.8	2.4	2.2	...
India	3.2	3.2	2.7	2.6	2.9	2.9	3.1
Maldives	0.1	0.1	0.1	0.1	0.1	0.1	...
Nepal	21.3	28.4	27.2	23.5	26.1	24.1	24.5
Sri Lanka	7.3	8.7	8.8	8.2	8.0	8.0	8.9
Southeast Asia[a]	**2.5**	**2.9**	**2.9**	**2.8**	**2.9**	**2.8**	**2.8**
Brunei Darussalam	...	...	...	...	...	...	...
Cambodia	5.0	6.6	6.0	5.8	5.8	5.6	5.0
Indonesia	0.9	1.1	1.0	0.9	1.1	1.0	0.9
Lao People's Democratic Republic	0.6	1.3	1.2	1.4	1.3	1.6	1.4
Malaysia	0.4	0.5	0.5	0.5	0.5	0.4	0.4
Myanmar	...	3.2	3.9	4.2	4.4	3.5	...
Philippines	10.3	9.7	9.8	10.0	9.7	9.3	9.7
Singapore	...	...	...	...	...	...	...
Thailand	1.3	1.5	1.5	1.5	1.5	1.5	1.6
Timor-Leste	15.6	3.9	4.9	5.4	6.2	5.0	...
Viet Nam	7.1	6.7	6.8	6.7	6.5	6.5	6.3
The Pacific[a]	**2.3**	**2.3**	**2.3**	**2.1**	**2.2**	**...**	**...**
Cook Islands	...	...	...	...	...	...	...
Fiji	5.6	5.4	5.5	5.1	5.1	5.2	...
Kiribati	10.0	8.2	9.1	9.6	10.2	10.2	...
Marshall Islands	13.7	14.8	14.1	14.3	14.2	13.1	12.7
Micronesia, Federated States of	6.1	7.4	7.0	6.4	5.8	...	...
Nauru	...	...	...	...	...	...	...
Niue	...	...	...	...	...	...	...
Palau	0.9	0.8	0.8	0.8	0.8	0.8	...
Papua New Guinea	0.0	0.0	0.0	0.0	0.0	0.0	0.0
Samoa	20.0	16.6	15.8	16.4	17.7	17.3	19.4
Solomon Islands	1.6	1.4	1.5	1.1	...	...	...
Tonga	19.9	32.1	30.0	34.4	38.2	37.4	...
Tuvalu	12.5	10.9 (2013)	...	...	...	...	...
Vanuatu	1.7	13.8	10.0	3.0	3.8	...	...
Developed ADB Member Economies[a]	**0.1**	**0.1**	**0.1**	**0.1**	**0.1**	**0.1**	**0.1**
Australia	0.2	0.2	0.2	0.1	0.1	0.1	0.1
Japan	0.0	0.1	0.1	0.1	0.1	0.1	0.1
New Zealand	0.3	0.3	0.3	0.3	0.2	0.2	...
DEVELOPING ADB MEMBER ECONOMIES[a]	**1.6**	**1.4**	**1.4**	**1.3**	**1.3**	**1.3**	**1.3**
ALL ADB REGIONAL MEMBERS[a]	**1.0**	**1.1**	**1.0**	**1.0**	**1.0**	**1.1**	**1.0**

... = data not available, 0.0 = magnitude is less than half of unit employed, * = provisional or preliminary, ADB = Asian Development Bank, GDP = gross domestic product.

a Aggregate percentages calculated using only reporting economies with data available for both remittances and GDP in the years specified in the column headings.

Source: Economy's official sources; and World Bank. Migration and Remittances Data. https://www.worldbank.org/en/topic/migrationremittancesdiasporaissues/brief/migration-remittances-data (accessed 14 June 2021). For Taipei,China: Central bank of Taipei,China. Official communication, 21 April 2021; past communication.

Table 2.4.6: Foreign Direct Investment, Net Inflows—Dollar Amounts
($ million)

ADB Regional Member	2010	2015	2016	2017	2018	2019	2020
Developing ADB Member Economies							
Central and West Asia[a]	**20,334**	**20,069**	**31,149**	**16,259**	**7,832**	**13,651**	**12,085**
Afghanistan	191	169	94	52	119	23	13
Armenia	529	184	334	251	254	254	47
Azerbaijan	3,353	4,048	4,500	2,867	1,403	1,504	507
Georgia	921	1,735	1,658	1,918	1,260	1,341	426
Kazakhstan	7,456	6,578	17,221	4,713	83	3,321	7,265
Kyrgyz Republic	473	1,144	619	-107	144	279	...
Pakistan	2,022	1,673	2,576	2,496	1,737	2,234	2,105
Tajikistan	94	454	242	186	221	213	107
Turkmenistan	3,632	3,043	2,243	2,086	1,985	2,166	...
Uzbekistan	1,663	1,041	1,663	1,797	625	2,316	1,616
East Asia	**340,093**	**430,126**	**325,649**	**314,609**	**353,649**	**265,787**	**337,231**
China, People's Republic of	243,703	242,489	174,750	166,084	235,365	187,170	212,476
Hong Kong, China	82,709	181,047	133,259	125,717	97,036	58,299	105,011
Korea, Republic of	9,497	4,104	12,104	17,913	12,183	9,634	9,224
Mongolia	1,691	94	-4,156	1,494	1,952	2,443	1,719
Taipei,China	2,492	2,391	9,692	3,401	7,114	8,240	8,802
South Asia[a]	**29,486**	**47,877**	**48,263**	**43,787**	**46,800**	**54,437**	**65,978**
Bangladesh	1,232	2,831	2,333	1,810	2,422	1,908	1,143
Bhutan	75	6	12	-17	3	13	-3
India	27,397	44,009	44,459	39,966	42,117	50,611	64,362
Maldives	216	298	457	458	576	961	348
Nepal	88	52	106	196	68	186	127
Sri Lanka	478	680	897	1,373	1,614	758	...
Southeast Asia[a]	**108,413**	**132,976**	**116,834**	**173,067**	**155,863**	**190,744**	**132,013**
Brunei Darussalam	481	171	-151	468	516	373	566
Cambodia	1,404	1,823	2,476	2,788	3,213	3,663	3,625
Indonesia	15,292	19,779	4,542	20,510	18,910	24,994	18,685
Lao People's Democratic Republic	279	1,078	935	1,693	1,358	756	...
Malaysia	10,886	9,857	13,470	9,368	8,304	9,101	4,313
Myanmar	901	4,084	3,278	4,804	1,768	1,736	...
Philippines	1,070	5,639	8,280	10,256	9,949	8,671	6,542
Singapore	55,322	69,775	67,912	100,786	83,111	120,439	87,445
Thailand	14,747	8,928	3,486	8,285	13,186	4,817	-5,034
Timor-Leste	30	43	5	7	48	75	72
Viet Nam	8,000	11,800	12,600	14,100	15,500	16,120	15,800
The Pacific[a]	**433**	**545**	**540**	**668**	**1,733**	**752**	**...**
Cook Islands	...	...	...	...	...	...	...
Fiji	178	205	392	388	469	322	239
Kiribati	-7	-1	2	1	-1	-1	...
Marshall Islands	-9	-5	-3	6	10	4	...
Micronesia, Federated States of	0	1	...	...	...	...	...
Nauru	0	0	0	0	0	...	...
Niue	...	...	...	...	...	...	...
Palau	3	35	35	27	22	22	...
Papua New Guinea	36	214	19	161	1,135	334	...
Samoa	-1	27	3	9	17	1	...
Solomon Islands	166	32	37	43	25	33	9
Tonga	5	6	6	-6	20	2	4
Tuvalu	0	0	0	0	0	0	...
Vanuatu	63	31	49	38	38	35	25
Developed ADB Member Economies	**42,938**	**52,072**	**85,799**	**68,178**	**89,430**	**82,774**	**91,921**
Australia	35,211	46,893	42,970	47,282	61,527	39,897	21,786
Japan	7,441	5,252	40,954	18,802	25,289	39,933	65,983
New Zealand	286	-73	1,875	2,094	2,614	2,943	4,151
DEVELOPING ADB MEMBER ECONOMIES[a]	**498,759**	**631,593**	**522,434**	**548,389**	**565,877**	**525,371**	**547,585**
ALL ADB REGIONAL MEMBERS[a]	**541,697**	**683,665**	**608,233**	**616,567**	**655,307**	**608,145**	**639,506**
WORLD[a]	**1,926,405**	**2,680,119**	**2,750,079**	**2,213,224**	**1,091,559**	**1,744,100**	**...**

... = data not available, -0 or 0 = magnitude is less than half of unit employed, $ = United States dollars, ADB = Asian Development Bank.

a Includes only reporting economies with data corresponding to the year heading.

Sources: World Bank. World Development Indicators. http://data.worldbank.org/indicator/BX.KLT.DINV.CD.WD?locations=MH (accessed 29 July 2021); and International Monetary Fund. Balance of Payments Analytic Presentation. https://data.imf.org/regular.aspx?key=62805741 (accessed 3 August 2021). For Taipei,China: Central bank of Taipei,China. https://www.cbc.gov.tw/ct.asp?xItem=1061&ctNode=535&mp=2 (accessed 29 July 2021).

Table 2.4.7: Foreign Direct Investment, Net Inflows—Proportion of Economic Activity
(% of GDP)

ADB Regional Member	2010	2015	2016	2017	2018	2019	2020
Developing ADB Member Economies							
Central and West Asia[a]	**4.1**	**2.9**	**5.0**	**2.4**	**1.2**	**2.1**	**2.1**
Afghanistan	1.2	0.8	0.5	0.3	0.6	0.1	0.1
Armenia	5.7	1.7	3.2	2.2	2.0	1.9	0.4
Azerbaijan	6.3	7.6	11.9	7.0	3.0	3.1	1.2
Georgia	7.5	11.6	11.0	11.8	7.2	7.7	2.7
Kazakhstan	5.0	3.6	12.5	2.8	0.0	1.8	4.2
Kyrgyz Republic	9.9	17.1	9.1	-1.4	1.7	3.1	...
Pakistan	1.2	0.6	0.9	0.8	0.6	0.9	0.8
Tajikistan	1.7	5.5	3.5	2.5	2.8	2.6	1.3
Turkmenistan	16.1	8.5	6.2	5.5	4.9	4.8	...
Uzbekistan	3.5	1.3	2.0	3.0	1.2	4.0	2.8
East Asia	**4.3**	**3.2**	**2.4**	**2.1**	**2.1**	**1.6**	**1.9**
China, People's Republic of	4.0	2.2	1.6	1.3	1.7	1.3	1.4
Hong Kong, China	36.2	58.5	41.5	36.8	26.8	16.1	30.3
Korea, Republic of	0.8	0.3	0.8	1.1	0.7	0.6	0.6
Mongolia	23.5	0.8	-37.2	13.1	14.9	17.5	13.1
Taipei,China	0.6	0.4	1.8	0.6	1.2	1.3	1.3
South Asia[a]	**1.6**	**2.0**	**1.8**	**1.5**	**1.5**	**1.6**	**2.2**
Bangladesh	1.1	1.5	1.1	0.7	0.9	0.6	0.3
Bhutan	4.9	0.3	0.6	-0.7	0.1	0.5	...
India	1.6	2.1	1.9	1.5	1.5	1.8	2.4
Maldives	8.4	7.3	10.4	9.7	10.8	17.0	...
Nepal	0.5	0.2	0.4	0.7	0.2	0.5	0.4
Sri Lanka	0.8	0.8	1.1	1.6	1.8	0.9	...
Southeast Asia[a]	**5.5**	**5.4**	**4.5**	**6.2**	**5.2**	**6.0**	**4.5**
Brunei Darussalam	3.5	1.3	-1.3	3.9	3.8	2.8	4.7
Cambodia	12.5	10.1	12.4	12.6	13.1	13.5	14.3
Indonesia	2.0	2.3	0.5	2.0	1.8	2.2	1.8
Lao People's Democratic Republic	4.1	7.5	5.9	9.9	7.5	4.0	...
Malaysia	4.3	3.3	4.5	2.9	2.3	2.5	1.3
Myanmar	...	6.5	5.5	7.9	2.7	2.5	...
Philippines	0.5	1.8	2.6	3.1	2.9	2.3	1.8
Singapore	23.1	22.7	21.3	29.4	22.1	32.2	25.7
Thailand	4.3	2.2	0.8	1.8	2.6	0.9	-1.0
Timor-Leste	3.4	2.7	0.3	0.4	3.1	3.7	...
Viet Nam	6.9	6.1	6.1	6.3	6.3	6.2	5.8
The Pacific[a]	**2.1**	**1.8**	**1.8**	**2.1**	**5.2**	**...**	**...**
Cook Islands	...	...	...	...	...	...	...
Fiji	5.7	4.4	7.9	7.2	8.4	5.9	...
Kiribati	-4.2	-0.5	1.0	0.4	-0.6	-0.3	...
Marshall Islands	-5.8	-2.9	-1.5	2.7	4.4	1.7	...
Micronesia, Federated States of	0.0	0.3	...	...	...	...	...
Nauru	0.0	0.0	0.0	0.0	0.0	...	...
Niue	...	...	...	...	...	...	...
Palau	1.5	12.4	11.9	9.6	7.5	7.8	...
Papua New Guinea	0.2	1.0	0.1	0.7	4.7	1.3	...
Samoa	-0.2	3.4	0.3	1.1	2.0	0.1	...
Solomon Islands	18.4	2.5	2.7	2.9	...	...	...
Tonga	1.3	1.6	1.4	-1.2	4.1	0.3	...
Tuvalu	1.4	0.9	0.7	0.7	0.6	0.6	...
Vanuatu	9.0	4.1	6.1	4.3	4.1	...	...
Developed ADB Member Economies[a]	**0.6**	**0.9**	**1.3**	**1.1**	**1.3**	**1.2**	**1.4**
Australia	2.9	3.8	3.5	3.5	4.5	2.9	1.6
Japan	0.1	0.1	0.8	0.4	0.5	0.8	1.3
New Zealand	0.2	-0.0	1.0	1.0	1.2	1.4	...
DEVELOPING ADB MEMBER ECONOMIES[a]	**4.1**	**3.3**	**2.7**	**2.6**	**2.4**	**2.2**	**2.3**
ALL ADB REGIONAL MEMBERS[a]	**2.8**	**2.7**	**2.3**	**2.2**	**2.2**	**2.0**	**2.1**

... = data not available, -0.0 or 0.0 = magnitude is less than half of the unit employed, ADB = Asian Development Bank, GDP = gross domestic product.

a Aggregate percentages calculated using only reporting economies with data available for both foreign direct investment and GDP in the years specified in the column headings.

Sources: Economy's official sources; World Bank. World Development Indicators. http://data.worldbank.org/indicator/BX.KLT.DINV.CD.WD?locations=MH (accessed 29 July 2021); and International Monetary Fund. Balance of Payments Analytic Presentation. https://data.imf.org/regular.aspx?key=62805741 (accessed 3 August 2021). For Taipei,China: Central bank of Taipei,China. https://www.cbc.gov.tw/ct.asp?xItem=1061&ctNode=535&mp=2 (accessed 29 July 2021).

Table 2.4.8: Merchandise Exports
($ million)

ADB Regional Member	2010	2015	2016	2017	2018	2019	2020
Developing ADB Member Economies							
Central and West Asia[a]	**134,666**	**116,373**	**97,399**	**113,340**	**136,008**	**136,757**	**115,604**
Afghanistan	388	571	596	832	875	864	777
Armenia	1,041	1,485	1,792	2,238	2,412	2,649	2,544
Azerbaijan	26,374	15,586	13,211	15,152	20,794	19,868	12,588
Georgia	1,677	2,204	2,117	2,746	3,380	3,798	3,342
Kazakhstan	60,271	45,956	36,737	48,503	61,111	58,066	46,950
Kyrgyz Republic	1,756	1,483	1,573	1,764	1,837	1,986	1,964
Pakistan	19,261	23,526	20,859	20,566	21,296	21,222	21,234
Tajikistan	1,195	891	899	1,198	1,073	1,174	1,407
Turkmenistan	9,679	12,164	7,520	7,788	9,239	9,670	...
Uzbekistan	13,023	12,508	12,095	12,554	13,991	17,459	15,128
East Asia	**2,713,944**	**3,552,563**	**3,338,638**	**3,656,154**	**3,962,930**	**3,887,151**	**3,961,910**
China, People's Republic of	1,577,754	2,273,468	2,097,631	2,263,345	2,486,682	2,499,029	2,590,646
Hong Kong, China	390,134	465,092	462,269	497,340	530,472	509,026	506,303
Korea, Republic of	466,384	526,757	495,426	573,694	604,860	542,233	512,498
Mongolia	2,909	4,669	4,916	6,201	7,012	7,620	7,576
Taipei,China	276,763	282,577	278,396	315,573	333,905	329,244	344,887
South Asia	**274,793**	**310,212**	**320,174**	**346,730**	**386,558**	**368,227**	**334,855**
Bangladesh	16,099	30,588	33,352	33,462	35,691	39,404	32,797
Bhutan	535	561	488	566	574	610	635
India	248,648	267,550	275,233	300,440	337,439	315,229	290,389
Maldives	62	144	139	199	206	178	162
Nepal	830	833	653	699	747	862	826
Sri Lanka	8,618	10,536	10,309	11,364	11,901	11,943	10,046
Southeast Asia[a]	**1,048,353**	**1,172,177**	**1,151,655**	**1,311,960**	**1,446,426**	**1,422,398**	**1,393,458**
Brunei Darussalam	8,887	6,338	4,915	5,585	6,577	7,248	6,611
Cambodia	3,903	9,336	10,273	11,224	12,963	14,987	17,457
Indonesia	157,779	150,366	145,134	168,828	180,013	167,683	163,307
Lao People's Democratic Republic	1,746	3,653	4,245	4,873	5,295	5,764	6,143
Malaysia	198,325	199,041	189,708	217,403	248,712	240,212	233,373
Myanmar	8,872	11,432	11,837	13,878	16,704	18,110	...
Philippines	51,498	58,827	57,406	68,713	69,307	70,927	65,215
Singapore	352,553	357,730	337,963	372,939	411,957	390,361	373,725
Thailand	192,511	213,397	213,431	233,376	251,155	242,685	226,599
Timor-Leste	42	38	162	24	46	154	264
Viet Nam	72,237	162,017	176,581	215,119	243,697	264,267	282,655
The Pacific[a]	**7,003**	**10,040**	**9,823**	**11,674**	**12,300**	**13,140**	**10,659**
Cook Islands	5	14	14	20	17	18	19
Fiji	837	982	922	985	1,016	1,032	826
Kiribati	4	9	10	15	8	12	9
Marshall Islands	34 (2009)	...	...	...	...	...	...
Micronesia, Federated States of	30	40	49	46	47	...	...
Nauru	32	14	36	19	12	4	4
Niue	1	1	1	2	2	2	1
Palau	16	18	13	14	14	11	...
Papua New Guinea	5,737	8,417	8,204	9,953	10,495	11,401	9,224
Samoa	23	34	36	37	43	51	38
Solomon Islands	227	421	432	468	536	461	379
Tonga	8	18	21	19	13	20	...
Tuvalu	1	0	0	0	0	0	0
Vanuatu	48	39	50	61	63	48	46
Developed ADB Member Economies	**1,011,217**	**846,359**	**869,646**	**967,003**	**1,034,971**	**1,016,264**	**929,376**
Australia	212,027	187,525	192,140	230,950	257,480	271,069	249,911
Japan	767,826	624,681	643,753	697,951	737,877	705,733	640,606
New Zealand	31,365	34,152	33,753	38,102	39,613	39,463	38,859
DEVELOPING ADB MEMBER ECONOMIES[a]	**4,178,758**	**5,161,366**	**4,917,689**	**5,439,859**	**5,944,221**	**5,827,673**	**5,816,486**
ALL ADB REGIONAL MEMBERS[a]	**5,189,975**	**6,007,724**	**5,787,334**	**6,406,863**	**6,979,192**	**6,843,936**	**6,745,863**
WORLD[b]	**15,207,400**	**16,377,577**	**15,829,474**	**17,501,793**	**19,253,318**	**18,736,978**	**17,330,627**

... = data not available, 0 = magnitude is less than half of unit employed, $ = United States dollars, ADB = Asian Development Bank.

a For estimating aggregates, imputation was done for economies with missing data by substituting available data from the nearest years.
b The world aggregate includes estimates derived from reports of partner economies for nonreporting and slow-reporting economies.

Sources: Economy's official sources; and International Monetary Fund. International Financial Statistics. http://data.imf.org/ (accessed 17 July 2021). For Nauru: for 2002–2015 (available in the Key Indicators Database), Nauru Bureau of Statistics. 2016. Media Release on International Merchandise Trade Statistics (IMTS Release No. 01/2016), 3 November 2016; and for 2016–2020, International Monetary Fund. 2020. Article IV Staff Country Reports for the Republic of Nauru. For "World": International Monetary Fund. Direction of Trade Statistics. http://data.imf.org/?sk=9D6028D4-F14A-464C-A2F2-59B2CD424B85 (accessed 29 June 2021).

Table 2.4.9: Growth Rates of Merchandise Exports
(%)

ADB Regional Member	2010	2015	2016	2017	2018	2019	2020
Developing ADB Member Economies							
Central and West Asia[a]	**25.3**	**-33.3**	**-16.3**	**16.4**	**20.0**	**0.6**	**-15.5**
Afghanistan	-3.7	0.2	4.4	39.5	5.2	-1.3	-10.1
Armenia	46.6	-4.0	20.6	24.9	7.8	9.8	-3.9
Azerbaijan	25.3	-44.8	-15.2	14.7	37.2	-4.5	-36.6
Georgia	48.0	-23.0	-3.9	29.7	23.1	12.4	-12.0
Kazakhstan	39.5	-42.2	-20.1	32.0	26.0	-5.0	-19.1
Kyrgyz Republic	5.0	-21.3	6.1	12.1	4.1	8.1	-1.1
Pakistan	12.0	-8.5	-11.3	-1.4	3.6	-0.3	0.1
Tajikistan	18.3	-8.9	0.9	33.3	-10.4	9.5	19.8
Turkmenistan	3.8	-38.5	-38.2	3.6	18.6	4.7	...
Uzbekistan	10.6	-7.7	-3.3	3.8	11.4	24.8	-13.4
East Asia	**29.8**	**-4.3**	**-6.0**	**9.5**	**8.4**	**-1.9**	**1.9**
China, People's Republic of	31.3	-2.9	-7.7	7.9	9.9	0.5	3.6
Hong Kong, China	22.5	-1.8	-0.6	7.6	6.7	-4.0	-0.5
Korea, Republic of	28.3	-8.0	-5.9	15.8	5.4	-10.4	-5.5
Mongolia	54.3	-19.1	5.3	26.1	13.1	8.7	-0.6
Taipei,China	35.1	-11.2	-1.5	13.4	5.8	-1.4	4.8
South Asia	**38.2**	**-12.2**	**3.2**	**8.3**	**11.5**	**-4.7**	**-9.1**
Bangladesh	3.7	2.6	9.0	0.3	6.7	10.4	-16.8
Bhutan	6.5	4.1	-13.0	16.0	1.3	6.3	4.1
India	42.3	-13.9	2.9	9.2	12.3	-6.6	-7.9
Maldives	-63.6	-0.6	-3.2	43.0	3.6	-13.6	-8.8
Nepal	-4.9	-11.6	-21.6	7.0	6.9	15.5	-4.3
Sri Lanka	21.7	-5.3	-2.2	10.2	4.7	0.4	-15.9
Southeast Asia[a]	**29.7**	**-9.7**	**-1.8**	**13.9**	**10.2**	**-1.7**	**-2.0**
Brunei Darussalam	23.9	-40.2	-22.4	13.6	17.8	10.2	-8.8
Cambodia	24.4	14.3	10.0	9.3	15.5	15.6	16.5
Indonesia	35.4	-14.6	-3.5	16.3	6.6	-6.8	-2.6
Lao People's Democratic Republic	65.9	11.5	16.2	14.8	8.7	8.9	6.6
Malaysia	26.5	-14.9	-4.7	14.6	14.4	-3.4	-2.8
Myanmar	32.4	-0.2	3.5	17.2	20.4	8.4	...
Philippines	34.0	-5.3	-2.4	19.7	0.9	2.3	-8.1
Singapore	30.5	-13.8	-5.5	10.3	10.5	-5.2	-4.3
Thailand	27.2	-5.8	0.0	9.3	7.6	-3.4	-6.6
Timor-Leste	20.7	-1.7	321.2	-85.1	91.5	232.0	71.7
Viet Nam	26.5	7.9	9.0	21.8	13.3	8.4	7.0
The Pacific[a]	**30.2**	**-6.2**	**-2.2**	**18.8**	**5.4**	**6.8**	**-18.9**
Cook Islands	88.0	-20.3	-2.9	48.9	-14.3	0.7	10.8
Fiji	25.1	-19.5	-6.1	6.8	3.1	1.6	-19.9
Kiribati	-38.0	-11.0	16.3	45.2	-46.3	49.3	-24.2
Marshall Islands	5.6 (2009)	...	...	...	...	...	...
Micronesia, Federated States of	63.5	23.0	23.3	-5.6	1.7	...	...
Nauru	249.5	-39.4	...	-45.4	-38.7	-64.9	-1.0
Niue	1.0	-20.2	8.8	22.0	17.5	-7.7	-66.5
Palau	15.9	-5.3	-26.0	5.5	-1.9	-18.5	...
Papua New Guinea	30.9	-4.2	-2.5	21.3	5.4	8.6	-19.1
Samoa	114.4	23.8	6.3	3.1	14.1	18.9	-24.3
Solomon Islands	37.4	-7.6	2.7	8.3	14.5	-14.0	-17.7
Tonga	7.1	-6.5	21.1	-12.1	-31.2	56.1	...
Tuvalu	76.5	-12.0	7.2	-8.1	-11.3	51.6	-83.0
Vanuatu	-14.8	-38.0	28.8	22.1	2.9	-24.6	-3.2
Developed ADB Member Economies	**33.6**	**-12.9**	**2.8**	**11.2**	**7.0**	**-1.8**	**-8.5**
Australia	38.3	-21.8	2.5	20.2	11.5	5.3	-7.8
Japan	32.6	-9.5	3.1	8.4	5.7	-4.4	-9.2
New Zealand	26.6	-17.8	-1.2	12.9	4.0	-0.4	-1.5
DEVELOPING ADB MEMBER ECONOMIES[a]	**30.2**	**-7.0**	**-4.7**	**10.6**	**9.3**	**-2.0**	**-0.2**
ALL ADB REGIONAL MEMBERS[a]	**30.8**	**-7.9**	**-3.7**	**10.7**	**8.9**	**-1.9**	**-1.4**
WORLD[b]	**22.6**	**-12.9**	**-3.3**	**10.6**	**10.0**	**-2.7**	**-7.5**

... = data not available, 0.0 = magnitude is less than half of unit employed, ADB = Asian Development Bank.

Note: Growth rates are based on the value of exports in United States dollars.

a For estimating aggregates, imputation was done for economies with missing data by substituting available data from the nearest years.

b The world aggregate includes estimates derived from reports of partner economies for nonreporting and slow-reporting economies.

Sources: Economy's official sources; and International Monetary Fund. International Financial Statistics. http://data.imf.org/ (accessed 17 July 2021).

Table 2.4.10: Merchandise Imports
($ million)

ADB Regional Member	2010	2015	2016	2017	2018	2019	2020
Developing ADB Member Economies							
Central and West Asia[a]	**109,356**	**138,059**	**128,541**	**142,796**	**154,519**	**162,772**	**146,135**
Afghanistan	5,154	7,723	6,534	7,793	7,407	6,777	6,538
Armenia	3,749	3,239	3,273	4,097	4,976	5,538	4,559
Azerbaijan	6,662	9,774	9,004	9,037	10,952	11,335	10,077
Georgia	5,236	7,304	7,342	8,057	9,362	9,517	8,011
Kazakhstan	31,127	30,568	25,377	29,600	33,659	39,709	38,081
Kyrgyz Republic	3,223	4,154	4,000	4,495	5,292	4,989	3,684
Pakistan	34,169	45,394	44,665	52,742	55,189	49,869	43,466
Tajikistan	2,657	3,436	3,031	2,775	3,151	3,349	3,151
Turkmenistan	8,204	14,051	13,177	10,189	5,094	7,397	...
Uzbekistan	9,176	12,417	12,138	14,012	19,439	24,292	21,172
East Asia	**2,512,911**	**2,876,629**	**2,742,411**	**3,143,062**	**3,563,907**	**3,435,757**	**3,364,673**
China, People's Republic of	1,396,244	1,679,565	1,587,926	1,843,793	2,135,734	2,077,097	2,055,612
Hong Kong, China	433,102	522,001	516,395	559,074	602,335	563,487	550,421
Korea, Republic of	425,212	436,499	406,193	478,478	535,202	503,343	467,633
Mongolia	3,200	3,798	3,358	4,337	5,875	6,127	5,294
Taipei,China	255,153	234,768	228,539	257,380	284,761	285,702	285,713
South Asia	**409,681**	**455,084**	**452,941**	**537,469**	**616,970**	**569,139**	**472,360**
Bangladesh	21,245	37,528	39,795	42,779	53,571	55,159	50,636
Bhutan[b]	810	977	1,017	1,045	971	1,012	872
India	368,166	388,189	383,609	460,836	525,618	477,270	392,692
Maldives	909	1,890	2,121	2,355	3,179	3,156	2,019
Nepal	5,110	7,565	7,204	9,474	11,430	12,597	10,113
Sri Lanka	13,441	18,935	19,195	20,982	22,200	19,945	16,029
Southeast Asia[a]	**934,617**	**1,089,778**	**1,071,163**	**1,233,059**	**1,405,578**	**1,369,146**	**1,249,807**
Brunei Darussalam	2,536	3,235	2,671	3,083	4,168	5,100	5,319
Cambodia[b]	6,588	13,285	14,119	15,502	18,807	22,242	21,050
Indonesia	135,663	142,695	135,653	156,986	188,711	171,276	141,569
Lao People's Democratic Republic[b]	2,060	5,675	5,372	5,667	6,164	6,252	5,374
Malaysia	164,177	175,593	168,459	194,497	218,036	205,049	189,413
Myanmar	4,866	16,913	15,706	19,253	19,355	18,607	...
Philippines	54,933	71,067	84,108	96,093	112,841	111,593	89,812
Singapore	312,669	307,968	291,923	327,390	370,832	358,985	328,661
Thailand	165,988	187,079	177,662	200,820	228,857	216,052	186,677
Timor-Leste	298	491	512	554	565	597	625
Viet Nam	84,839	165,776	174,978	213,215	237,242	253,393	262,701
The Pacific[a]	**7,091**	**7,008**	**6,596**	**7,760**	**8,613**	**9,086**	**6,517**
Cook Islands	91	110	117	135	135	136	104
Fiji	1,806	2,268	2,301	2,402	2,729	2,782	1,731
Kiribati	73	103	111	108	103	112	109
Marshall Islands	158 (2009)	...	...	...	...	...	...
Micronesia, Federated States of	168	160	186	183	198	...	...
Nauru	13	93	57	54	61	58	58
Niue	9	13	13	15	18	14	12
Palau	103	156	169	174	171	171	...
Papua New Guinea	3,522	2,551	2,070	3,060	3,512	3,933	2,637
Samoa	280	298	312	321	333	357	285
Solomon Islands	405	485	465	516	593	553	452
Tonga	158	209	229	238	228	267	...
Tuvalu	22	37	23	27	25	33	34
Vanuatu	284	367	382	370	350	313	300
Developed ADB Member Economies	**915,836**	**885,006**	**832,052**	**933,113**	**1,020,015**	**977,235**	**874,333**
Australia	193,071	200,643	189,074	220,954	227,172	213,797	202,049
Japan	692,242	647,744	607,043	672,032	748,967	721,032	635,330
New Zealand	30,523	36,619	35,935	40,128	43,876	42,405	36,954
DEVELOPING ADB MEMBER ECONOMIES[a]	**3,973,656**	**4,566,558**	**4,401,652**	**5,064,146**	**5,749,588**	**5,545,901**	**5,239,492**
ALL ADB REGIONAL MEMBERS[a]	**4,889,492**	**5,451,563**	**5,233,703**	**5,997,260**	**6,769,603**	**6,523,136**	**6,113,825**
WORLD[c]	**15,465,280**	**16,586,392**	**16,146,475**	**17,733,831**	**19,533,353**	**18,981,297**	**17,567,591**

... = data not available, $ = United States dollars, ADB = Asian Development Bank.

a For estimating aggregates, imputation was done for economies with missing data by substituting available data from the nearest years.
b The Key Indicators Database features a longer time series on merchandise imports. The compilation methodology shifted from cost, insurance, and freight to free on board from 2004 onward for Bhutan; from 2005 onward for Cambodia; and from 2017 onward for the Lao People's Democratic Republic.
c The world aggregate includes estimates derived from reports of partner economies for nonreporting and slow-reporting economies.

Sources: Economy's official sources; and International Monetary Fund. International Financial Statistics. http://data.imf.org/ (accessed 17 July 2021). For Nauru: for 2002–2015 (available in the Key Indicators Database), Nauru Bureau of Statistics. 2016. Media Release on International Merchandise Trade Statistics (IMTS Release No. 01/2016), 3 November 2016; and for 2016–2020, International Monetary Fund. 2020. Article IV Staff Country Reports for the Republic of Nauru. For "World": International Monetary Fund. Direction of Trade Statistics. http://data.imf.org/?sk=9D6028D4-F14A-464C-A2F2-59B2CD424B85 (accessed 29 June 2021).

Table 2.4.11: Growth Rates of Merchandise Imports
(%)

ADB Regional Member	2010	2015	2016	2017	2018	2019	2020
Developing ADB Member Economies							
Central and West Asia[a]	**6.0**	**-12.5**	**-6.9**	**11.1**	**8.2**	**5.3**	**-10.2**
Afghanistan	54.5	-0.1	-15.4	19.3	-5.0	-8.5	-3.5
Armenia	12.9	-26.8	1.1	25.2	21.4	11.3	-17.7
Azerbaijan	6.9	4.7	-7.9	0.4	21.2	3.5	-11.1
Georgia	17.0	-15.1	0.5	9.7	16.2	1.7	-15.8
Kazakhstan	9.6	-26.0	-17.0	16.6	13.7	18.0	-4.1
Kyrgyz Republic	6.0	-27.6	-3.7	12.4	17.7	-5.7	-26.2
Pakistan	2.5	-0.9	-1.6	18.1	4.6	-9.6	-12.8
Tajikistan	3.4	-20.1	-11.8	-8.4	13.6	6.3	-5.9
Turkmenistan	-8.8	-15.5	-6.2	-22.7	-50.0	45.2	...
Uzbekistan	-2.8	-11.2	-2.2	15.4	38.7	25.0	-12.8
East Asia	**35.5**	**-13.2**	**-4.7**	**14.6**	**13.4**	**-3.6**	**-2.1**
China, People's Republic of	38.8	-14.1	-5.5	16.1	15.8	-2.7	-1.1
Hong Kong, China	24.7	-4.1	-1.1	8.3	7.7	-6.4	-2.3
Korea, Republic of	31.6	-16.9	-6.9	17.8	11.9	-6.0	-7.1
Mongolia	49.7	-27.5	-11.6	29.2	35.5	4.3	-13.6
Taipei,China	44.4	-16.2	-2.7	12.6	10.6	0.3	0.0
South Asia	**29.1**	**-11.6**	**-0.5**	**18.7**	**14.8**	**-7.8**	**-17.0**
Bangladesh	5.1	2.5	6.0	7.5	25.2	3.0	-8.2
Bhutan	40.7	4.5	4.1	2.8	-7.0	4.2	-13.9
India	30.7	-13.4	-1.2	20.1	14.1	-9.2	-17.7
Maldives	-5.6	-4.9	12.2	11.1	35.0	-0.7	-36.0
Nepal	39.3	3.3	-4.8	31.5	20.7	10.2	-19.7
Sri Lanka	31.8	-2.5	1.4	9.3	5.8	-10.2	-19.6
Southeast Asia[a]	**31.1**	**-11.0**	**-1.7**	**15.1**	**14.0**	**-2.6**	**-8.7**
Brunei Darussalam	5.6	-10.0	-17.4	15.4	35.2	22.4	4.3
Cambodia	35.0	10.5	6.3	9.8	21.3	18.3	-5.4
Indonesia	40.1	-19.9	-4.9	15.7	20.2	-9.2	-17.3
Lao People's Democratic Republic	41.0	14.1	-5.3	5.5	8.8	1.4	-14.0
Malaysia	33.1	-15.9	-4.1	15.5	12.1	-6.0	-7.6
Myanmar	11.0	4.3	-7.1	22.6	0.5	-3.9	...
Philippines	27.5	8.7	18.3	14.2	17.4	-1.1	-19.5
Singapore	26.9	-18.5	-5.2	12.1	13.3	-3.2	-8.4
Thailand	38.2	-10.7	-5.0	13.0	14.0	-5.6	-13.6
Timor-Leste	1.0	-11.3	4.2	8.2	2.1	5.6	4.8
Viet Nam	21.3	12.1	5.6	21.9	11.3	6.8	3.7
The Pacific[a]	**19.5**	**-17.9**	**-5.9**	**17.7**	**11.0**	**5.5**	**-28.3**
Cook Islands	11.2	-9.3	7.1	15.0	-0.2	1.2	-23.4
Fiji	17.0	-14.6	1.5	4.4	13.6	2.0	-37.8
Kiribati	5.4	-3.7	7.6	-3.0	-4.8	8.7	-2.4
Marshall Islands	15.0 (2009)	...	...	...	...	...	...
Micronesia, Federated States of	-1.8	-0.3	16.0	-1.4	7.9	...	...
Nauru	-47.3	-18.0	...	-5.9	13.2	-4.1	-0.1
Niue	28.5	-15.4	5.2	13.1	17.8	-23.7	-13.9
Palau	9.3	4.4	8.8	2.7	-1.9	0.3	...
Papua New Guinea	23.0	-30.2	-18.9	47.8	14.8	12.0	-32.9
Samoa	36.6	-12.7	4.8	2.7	3.8	7.2	-20.1
Solomon Islands	51.2	-4.1	-4.1	11.1	14.8	-6.7	-18.3
Tonga	10.3	-4.4	9.5	3.7	-4.0	17.2	...
Tuvalu	59.2	66.4	-36.2	13.1	-4.3	28.1	3.9
Vanuatu	-2.5	17.0	4.0	-3.1	-5.3	-10.6	-4.2
Developed ADB Member Economies	**25.1**	**-18.2**	**-6.0**	**12.1**	**9.3**	**-4.2**	**-10.5**
Australia	23.4	-11.9	-5.8	16.9	2.8	-5.9	-5.5
Japan	25.8	-20.1	-6.3	10.7	11.4	-3.7	-11.9
New Zealand	21.5	-13.9	-1.9	11.7	9.3	-3.4	-12.9
DEVELOPING ADB MEMBER ECONOMIES[a]	**32.7**	**-12.5**	**-3.6**	**15.1**	**13.5**	**-3.5**	**-5.5**
ALL ADB REGIONAL MEMBERS[a]	**31.2**	**-13.5**	**-4.0**	**14.6**	**12.9**	**-3.6**	**-6.3**
WORLD[b]	**21.4**	**-12.4**	**-2.7**	**9.8**	**10.1**	**-2.8**	**-7.4**

... = data not available, 0.0 = magnitude is less than half of unit employed, ADB = Asian Development Bank.

Note: Growth rates are based on the value of imports in United States dollars.

a For estimating aggregates, imputation was done for economies with missing data by substituting available data from the nearest years.

b The world aggregate includes estimates derived from reports of partner economies for nonreporting and slow-reporting economies.

Source: Economy's official sources; and International Monetary Fund. International Financial Statistics. http://data.imf.org/ (accessed 17 July 2021).

Table 2.4.12: Trade in Goods
(% of GDP)

ADB Regional Member	2010	2015	2016	2017	2018	2019	2020
Developing ADB Member Economies							
Central and West Asia[a]	**49.5**	**37.2**	**36.0**	**38.3**	**43.6**	**45.8**	**...**
Afghanistan	34.5	40.2	39.6	45.6	45.0	40.4	37.0
Armenia	51.7	44.8	48.0	55.0	59.3	60.1	56.2
Azerbaijan	62.4	47.8	58.7	59.2	67.4	64.8	53.2
Georgia	56.5	63.6	62.5	66.5	72.4	76.2	71.4
Kazakhstan	61.7	41.5	45.2	46.8	52.8	53.8	49.7
Kyrgyz Republic	103.8	84.4	81.8	81.3	86.2	78.6	73.0
Pakistan	30.6	25.8	23.6	24.2	26.9	28.0	25.2
Tajikistan	68.3	52.3	56.2	52.7	54.4	54.5	57.0
Turkmenistan	79.2	73.1	57.2	47.4	35.2	37.7	...
Uzbekistan	47.3	30.5	29.6	44.9	66.3	72.3	62.9
East Asia	**66.1**	**48.0**	**44.7**	**45.7**	**45.3**	**43.3**	**42.1**
China, People's Republic of	48.9	35.7	32.8	33.4	33.3	32.0	31.6
Hong Kong, China	360.1	319.0	305.0	309.6	313.2	295.4	304.9
Korea, Republic of	78.0	65.7	60.1	64.8	66.1	63.3	59.8
Mongolia	85.0	72.1	74.0	92.2	98.3	98.2	98.0
Taipei,China	119.7	96.8	93.3	97.0	101.5	100.4	94.3
South Asia[a]	**36.8**	**31.2**	**29.5**	**29.5**	**31.8**	**28.3**	**...**
Bangladesh	32.6	35.0	33.1	31.0	33.1	31.4	25.3
Bhutan[b]	86.9	76.7	69.7	65.7	63.1	64.1	...
India	36.9	30.5	28.8	29.0	31.3	27.4	25.6
Maldives	37.5	49.5	51.6	53.9	63.6	59.1	...
Nepal	36.5	35.5	32.3	34.6	38.4	39.3	33.1
Sri Lanka	38.9	36.6	35.8	37.0	38.8	38.0	32.3
Southeast Asia[a]	**99.2**	**91.2**	**85.6**	**90.9**	**95.1**	**88.0**	**...**
Brunei Darussalam	83.3	74.0	66.5	71.5	79.2	91.7	99.3
Cambodia[b]	93.3	125.3	121.9	120.5	129.3	137.4	152.3
Indonesia	38.9	34.0	30.1	32.1	35.4	30.3	28.8
Lao People's Democratic Republic[b]	56.4	64.7	60.4	61.7	63.2	64.1	60.4
Malaysia	142.1	124.3	118.9	129.1	130.1	122.1	125.6
Myanmar	...	45.3	45.8	54.5	55.6	53.0	...
Philippines	51.1	42.4	44.4	50.2	52.5	48.4	42.9
Singapore	277.4	216.1	197.6	204.0	208.2	200.1	206.6
Thailand	105.1	99.8	94.6	95.1	94.7	84.3	82.4
Timor-Leste	38.5	33.2	40.8	36.1	39.2	37.2	...
Viet Nam	135.5	169.6	171.3	191.4	196.1	197.6	201.1
The Pacific[a]	**66.5**	**54.9**	**53.7**	**58.3**	**59.6**	**62.1**	**...**
Cook Islands	39.8	40.9	42.3	44.9	42.0	40.6	43.7
Fiji	84.2	69.4	65.4	63.3	67.1	69.4	...
Kiribati	49.3	65.6	68.2	65.7	56.3	62.7	...
Marshall Islands	126.9 (2009)	...	...	...	...	...	...
Micronesia, Federated States of	66.6	63.1	70.6	62.6	60.9	...	...
Nauru	86.3	118.4	90.5	65.6	60.8	54.3	53.2
Niue	56.5	58.7	59.7	63.9	65.2	49.6	...
Palau	64.7	62.3	61.6	65.4	64.6	65.1	...
Papua New Guinea	65.0	50.5	49.5	57.2	58.1	61.8	50.3
Samoa	43.7	42.2	42.4	43.4	45.0	48.1	41.9
Solomon Islands	70.0	69.3	65.0	66.3	...	...	...
Tonga	44.9	56.3	59.5	55.6	50.2	56.5	...
Tuvalu	72.7	105.7	57.4	59.1	53.2	60.6	...
Vanuatu	47.4	53.4	53.7	49.0	45.2	...	...
Developed ADB Member Economies[a]	**27.1**	**29.6**	**26.5**	**29.3**	**31.0**	**29.7**	**...**
Australia	33.9	31.8	30.9	33.5	35.1	35.7	33.1
Japan	25.4	28.6	25.0	27.8	29.5	27.7	25.3
New Zealand	42.2	39.7	36.9	37.8	39.3	38.5	...
DEVELOPING ADB MEMBER ECONOMIES[a]	**66.4**	**51.1**	**47.8**	**49.1**	**49.8**	**47.2**	**...**
ALL ADB REGIONAL MEMBERS[a]	**52.0**	**46.1**	**42.5**	**44.5**	**45.7**	**43.4**	**...**

... = data not available, ADB = Asian Development Bank, GDP = Gross Domestic Product.

Note: Trade in goods is calculated as the sum of merchandise exports and imports in United States dollars.

a For estimating aggregates, imputation was done for economies with missing data by substituting available data from the nearest years.

b The Key Indicators Database features a longer time series on trade in goods. The compilation methodology shifted from cost, insurance, and freight to free on board from 2004 onward for Bhutan; from 2005 onward for Cambodia; and from 2017 onward for the Lao People's Democratic Republic.

Sources: Economy's official sources; and International Monetary Fund. International Financial Statistics. http://data.imf.org/ (accessed 17 July 2021).

Table 2.4.13: Direction of Trade: Merchandise Exports
(% of total merchandise exports)

To / From ADB Regional Member	Asia and the Pacific		Europe		North and Central America		Middle East		South America		Africa		Rest of the World	
	2010	2020	2010	2020	2010	2020	2010	2020	2010	2020	2010	2020	2010	2020
Developing ADB Member Economies														
Central and West Asia[a]	**27.7**	**31.3**	**53.3**	**52.1**	**8.7**	**5.2**	**8.3**	**4.2**	**0.4**	**0.3**	**1.2**	**1.7**	**0.4**	**5.2**
Afghanistan	63.7	87.8	21.6	4.2	1.1	0.5	13.6	7.4	0.0	0.0	0.0	0.0	0.0	0.0
Armenia	10.4	17.7	67.1	63.9	11.5	2.8	9.5	15.4	0.3	0.0	0.1	0.0	1.1	0.2
Azerbaijan	19.7	14.6	59.9	79.0	9.5	0.2	10.7	3.8	0.0	0.1	0.3	2.3	0.0	0.0
Georgia	33.8	40.0	42.0	51.8	18.6	2.6	4.6	3.7	0.4	0.8	0.6	1.0	0.0	0.0
Kazakhstan	24.2	32.1	64.5	63.2	6.0	2.0	4.5	2.2	0.1	0.1	0.1	0.4	0.7	0.0
Kyrgyz Republic	19.5	27.9	52.2	70.9	7.2	0.1	21.1	1.1	0.0	0.0	0.0	0.0	0.0	0.0
Pakistan	29.9	24.0	28.5	38.6	19.1	20.4	15.1	10.1	1.7	1.0	5.7	5.9	0.0	0.0
Tajikistan	43.5	21.9	45.0	70.3	0.0	0.0	8.6	3.2	0.0	0.2	2.9	4.4	0.0	0.0
Turkmenistan	52.0	84.2	38.4	14.2	1.9	0.4	7.1	0.0	0.0	1.1	0.7	0.1	0.0	0.0
Uzbekistan	60.2	31.4	30.6	20.2	0.0	1.2	9.0	2.1	0.1	0.0	0.0	0.0	0.0	45.1
East Asia[a]	**52.9**	**53.9**	**18.9**	**18.1**	**18.3**	**18.8**	**4.1**	**3.9**	**2.8**	**2.4**	**2.5**	**2.8**	**0.4**	**0.1**
China, People's Republic of	43.5	45.1	23.2	21.4	21.7	21.6	4.6	4.9	3.4	3.3	3.3	3.8	0.3	0.0
Hong Kong, China	72.2	73.9	12.6	13.7	12.4	8.4	1.4	2.3	0.9	0.8	0.5	0.8	0.1	0.0
Korea, Republic of	57.6	63.5	14.8	13.2	15.1	18.0	5.7	2.7	3.4	1.3	2.6	1.3	0.8	0.0
Mongolia	86.1	94.3	6.5	4.6	6.9	0.2	0.4	0.7	0.0	0.0	0.1	0.0	0.0	0.1
Taipei,China	71.1	72.9	10.6	8.2	13.0	16.2	2.3	1.4	1.3	0.6	0.8	0.5	1.0	0.3
South Asia[a]	**31.7**	**31.3**	**23.6**	**23.7**	**13.7**	**20.3**	**19.4**	**12.9**	**2.4**	**2.7**	**6.4**	**7.6**	**2.7**	**1.6**
Bangladesh	9.1	12.4	49.6	52.6	23.4	16.0	2.1	2.3	0.4	0.9	0.7	0.6	14.7	15.2
Bhutan	99.7	98.8	0.1	1.1	0.1	0.0	0.0	0.0	0.0	0.0	0.1	0.1	0.0	0.0
India	33.6	33.5	21.3	20.0	12.7	20.5	21.2	14.4	2.6	2.9	7.1	8.6	1.5	0.0
Maldives	59.5	56.4	36.1	35.4	0.7	7.5	3.1	0.3	0.0	0.0	0.6	0.5	0.0	0.0
Nepal	77.3	77.1	12.6	9.8	7.5	9.6	0.5	1.0	0.2	0.0	0.1	0.1	1.9	2.3
Sri Lanka	20.6	21.5	35.8	37.0	21.7	28.6	9.9	7.9	1.0	1.8	0.8	2.1	10.2	1.2
Southeast Asia[a]	**69.4**	**65.1**	**12.7**	**12.9**	**11.7**	**17.5**	**3.1**	**2.3**	**1.0**	**0.9**	**1.9**	**1.3**	**0.1**	**0.0**
Brunei Darussalam	99.6	98.3	0.2	0.1	0.2	1.2	0.0	0.0	0.0	0.0	0.0	0.3	0.0	0.0
Cambodia	41.6	28.4	17.6	27.7	39.7	41.9	0.3	0.5	0.4	0.6	0.1	0.5	0.2	0.4
Indonesia	70.9	71.4	12.5	10.1	10.2	12.2	3.2	3.3	1.5	1.1	1.7	1.9	0.0	0.0
Lao People's Democratic Republic	85.0	90.3	11.4	6.8	3.5	2.6	0.0	0.2	0.0	0.0	0.0	0.1	0.0	0.0
Malaysia	70.3	71.8	11.8	11.1	11.1	12.6	4.3	2.1	0.7	0.6	1.7	1.8	0.0	0.0
Myanmar	95.4	71.1	1.4	19.3	0.1	6.2	1.7	1.0	0.1	0.2	1.3	1.9	0.0	0.2
Philippines	67.3	68.0	14.8	11.7	16.0	17.9	1.1	1.5	0.5	0.6	0.4	0.2	0.0	0.0
Singapore	74.9	73.9	10.7	11.2	9.8	11.8	2.1	1.8	0.5	0.5	1.9	0.7	0.1	0.0
Thailand	62.9	63.5	14.6	13.1	12.1	16.8	5.0	3.1	2.1	1.4	3.0	1.9	0.3	0.2
Timor-Leste	56.6	75.0	22.8	3.2	0.3	9.2	8.6	0.3	0.1	11.5	11.6	0.9	0.0	0.0
Viet Nam	50.8	48.1	22.2	17.0	22.4	30.6	1.7	2.3	1.1	1.3	1.5	0.8	0.4	0.0
The Pacific[a]	**75.2**	**76.6**	**18.2**	**15.1**	**4.7**	**5.3**	**0.1**	**0.4**	**1.1**	**1.8**	**0.6**	**0.7**	**0.1**	**0.1**
Cook Islands	78.9	79.6	0.0	0.0	2.0	0.3	0.0	0.0	0.0	0.0	0.0	0.0	19.1	20.1
Fiji	71.8	64.0	7.5	9.7	18.7	25.8	0.3	0.3	0.0	0.0	0.8	0.2	0.8	0.0
Kiribati	97.8	99.4	2.2	0.5	0.0	0.1	0.0	0.0	0.0	0.0	0.0	0.0	0.0	0.0
Marshall Islands	0.3	21.8	89.3	65.5	10.4	4.0	0.0	4.6	0.0	0.9	0.0	3.3	0.0	0.0
Micronesia, Federated States of	88.3	81.0	2.4	0.1	9.0	2.0	0.0	0.6	0.0	16.3	0.0	0.0	0.2	0.0
Nauru	69.9	74.9	0.2	0.3	0.5	9.0	0.8	0.1	0.0	0.0	28.5	15.6	0.1	0.0
Niue	...	...	...	...	...	...	...	...	...	...	...	...	...	...
Palau	91.0	46.4	2.0	0.0	6.6	27.6	0.2	1.1	0.2	24.4	0.0	0.3	0.1	0.2
Papua New Guinea	80.3	84.2	17.5	11.8	2.0	1.9	0.0	0.0	0.0	2.0	0.2	0.0	0.0	0.1
Samoa	96.0	54.1	0.3	1.0	3.2	8.4	0.0	0.1	0.0	0.1	0.5	36.2	0.0	0.1
Solomon Islands	81.8	78.6	17.8	20.5	0.4	0.7	0.0	0.0	0.0	0.2	0.0	0.1	0.0	0.0
Tonga	95.0	83.8	0.0	0.0	5.0	16.1	0.0	0.0	0.0	0.0	0.0	0.0	0.0	0.0
Tuvalu	75.2	23.9	13.8	39.9	5.4	7.3	0.6	0.0	1.9	0.0	1.8	26.6	1.3	2.2
Vanuatu	31.6	31.9	1.8	2.6	20.5	63.3	0.4	0.0	45.4	1.9	0.3	0.3	0.0	0.0
Developed ADB Member Economies[a]	**63.5**	**63.6**	**12.8**	**13.1**	**16.9**	**18.4**	**3.4**	**2.6**	**1.6**	**0.9**	**1.4**	**1.1**	**0.3**	**0.3**
Australia	80.1	72.8	8.9	13.4	5.0	9.7	2.9	1.8	1.0	0.6	1.3	0.9	0.8	0.8
Japan	58.9	59.9	13.9	13.2	20.5	21.9	3.5	2.8	1.8	1.0	1.3	1.1	0.1	0.0
New Zealand	65.9	69.0	12.3	10.0	11.2	13.3	4.8	4.2	1.7	0.8	2.6	2.0	1.5	0.8
DEVELOPING ADB MEMBER ECONOMIES[a]	**55.2**	**54.7**	**18.6**	**17.9**	**16.1**	**18.3**	**4.9**	**4.1**	**2.3**	**2.1**	**2.5**	**2.7**	**0.5**	**0.2**
ALL ADB REGIONAL MEMBERS[a]	**56.8**	**55.9**	**17.5**	**17.3**	**16.2**	**18.3**	**4.6**	**3.9**	**2.1**	**1.9**	**2.3**	**2.5**	**0.5**	**0.2**
WORLD[a]	**31.0**	**33.3**	**40.2**	**38.8**	**17.3**	**18.6**	**4.6**	**3.9**	**2.9**	**2.2**	**2.7**	**2.6**	**1.4**	**0.7**

... = data not available, 0.0 = magnitude is less than half of unit employed, ADB = Asian Development Bank.

a Aggregates include estimates derived from reports of partner economies for nonreporting and slow-reporting economies.

Source: International Monetary Fund. Direction of Trade Statistics. http://data.imf.org/?sk=9D6028D4-F14A-464C-A2F2-59B2CD424B85 (accessed 29 June 2021). For the Cook Islands and Taipei,China: Economy's official sources.

Table 2.4.14: Direction of Trade: Merchandise Imports
(% of total merchandise imports)

From / To	Asia and the Pacific		Europe		North and Central America		Middle East		South America		Africa		Rest of the World	
ADB Regional Member	2010	2020	2010	2020	2010	2020	2010	2020	2010	2020	2010	2020	2010	2020
Developing ADB Member Economies														
Central and West Asia[a]	**36.2**	**41.5**	**41.3**	**41.3**	**4.9**	**4.7**	**14.7**	**9.2**	**1.6**	**1.5**	**1.3**	**1.8**	**0.0**	**0.1**
Afghanistan	70.7	71.8	15.6	6.7	2.2	1.0	10.6	19.4	0.5	0.1	0.4	0.6	0.0	0.4
Armenia	21.9	23.7	64.4	61.3	3.8	2.5	7.4	7.8	2.0	1.9	0.4	0.8	0.1	2.0
Azerbaijan	24.1	24.7	64.8	63.2	3.8	6.9	3.7	3.6	3.2	1.4	0.3	0.2	0.0	0.0
Georgia	26.4	27.2	62.6	59.2	3.9	7.2	4.6	2.4	1.9	3.8	0.6	0.2	0.0	0.0
Kazakhstan	27.2	35.2	62.7	58.8	7.0	4.2	1.2	0.8	1.4	0.6	0.4	0.4	0.0	0.0
Kyrgyz Republic	41.9	43.4	50.3	51.2	6.6	3.5	0.9	1.0	0.3	0.3	0.1	0.6	0.0	0.0
Pakistan	40.4	48.6	13.8	14.0	5.7	7.2	35.5	22.7	1.2	2.4	3.3	5.2	0.1	0.0
Tajikistan	30.5	30.0	50.8	61.4	9.3	0.7	7.3	6.2	2.0	1.6	0.0	0.0	0.0	0.0
Turkmenistan	24.7	25.3	73.4	72.3	1.1	1.2	0.7	0.1	0.1	1.1	0.0	0.0	0.0	0.0
Uzbekistan	43.1	51.2	47.5	45.7	1.5	1.2	5.0	1.1	2.7	0.6	0.1	0.1	0.0	0.0
East Asia[a]	**57.2**	**58.3**	**13.4**	**15.7**	**9.2**	**9.1**	**8.4**	**5.8**	**3.9**	**4.9**	**2.8**	**2.4**	**5.1**	**3.9**
China, People's Republic of	50.1	50.4	15.2	18.2	9.1	8.6	6.6	6.1	5.7	7.1	4.2	3.5	9.2	6.2
Hong Kong, China	82.4	84.9	9.2	7.6	6.1	4.5	1.4	1.8	0.6	0.7	0.3	0.5	0.0	0.0
Korea, Republic of	52.8	54.9	13.1	16.4	11.2	14.9	18.9	9.3	2.7	2.7	1.2	1.2	0.0	0.7
Mongolia	55.1	51.6	37.4	43.6	7.2	4.4	0.1	0.1	0.2	0.1	0.0	0.1	0.0	0.0
Taipei,China	60.8	66.8	10.5	12.9	11.5	12.6	12.3	5.5	2.2	1.4	2.7	0.8	0.0	0.0
South Asia[a]	**37.3**	**46.9**	**19.3**	**15.0**	**6.2**	**8.4**	**25.5**	**19.3**	**3.3**	**3.5**	**7.5**	**6.2**	**1.0**	**0.7**
Bangladesh	67.6	62.1	9.8	9.8	3.8	6.7	8.4	6.9	2.5	4.9	1.0	3.4	6.9	6.1
Bhutan	93.2	96.9	5.5	2.3	0.5	0.2	0.8	0.2	0.0	0.0	0.1	0.0	0.0	0.3
India	33.1	42.3	20.4	16.2	6.5	8.9	27.6	21.9	3.4	3.6	8.4	7.0	0.6	0.0
Maldives	59.7	64.4	9.7	10.2	8.9	2.8	19.9	21.4	0.6	0.6	1.2	0.6	0.0	0.0
Nepal	86.4	86.1	4.8	3.4	1.7	4.5	5.0	1.9	1.9	1.6	0.1	0.8	0.0	1.7
Sri Lanka	64.7	71.0	16.1	12.7	4.2	4.5	13.4	9.6	0.9	0.4	0.4	1.7	0.4	0.1
Southeast Asia[a]	**67.1**	**73.4**	**12.5**	**10.3**	**9.9**	**8.4**	**7.6**	**4.5**	**1.7**	**1.8**	**0.8**	**1.3**	**0.5**	**0.2**
Brunei Darussalam	77.8	64.5	10.8	17.9	10.2	5.7	0.5	8.6	0.1	1.1	0.1	2.2	0.6	0.1
Cambodia	90.0	93.0	6.7	4.9	2.7	1.3	0.2	0.3	0.2	0.4	0.1	0.1	0.0	0.0
Indonesia	72.6	75.1	9.4	9.0	8.0	6.4	6.0	4.9	2.3	2.3	1.7	2.2	0.1	0.1
Lao People's Democratic Republic	95.0	94.4	4.5	5.1	0.5	0.4	0.0	0.0	0.0	0.0	0.0	0.0	0.0	0.0
Malaysia	68.7	72.2	11.5	9.9	12.2	9.4	3.8	4.8	1.8	2.2	1.5	1.4	0.5	0.1
Myanmar	77.7	86.0	1.7	10.2	0.6	0.6	2.1	2.5	0.2	0.4	0.1	0.1	17.6	0.1
Philippines	69.4	76.6	8.9	9.6	11.6	9.9	8.5	2.4	1.4	1.1	0.2	0.3	0.0	0.0
Singapore	60.2	64.1	15.8	14.7	12.7	12.0	9.6	7.1	1.4	1.1	0.3	1.0	0.0	0.0
Thailand	65.2	69.7	12.8	10.8	6.7	8.0	11.6	6.6	1.6	1.7	0.9	1.7	1.3	1.4
Timor-Leste	96.0	71.2	2.9	26.8	0.6	0.8	0.1	0.1	0.0	0.9	0.4	0.0	0.0	0.0
Viet Nam	80.1	80.0	10.6	7.8	5.0	6.2	1.8	1.8	2.1	2.8	0.4	1.3	0.0	0.0
The Pacific[a]	**81.6**	**83.5**	**11.4**	**11.2**	**5.6**	**2.4**	**0.1**	**1.0**	**0.1**	**0.3**	**0.6**	**1.2**	**0.5**	**0.5**
Cook Islands	91.8	89.5	0.0	0.1	2.8	3.1	0.0	0.0	0.0	0.0	0.0	0.0	5.4	7.3
Fiji	91.4	92.4	2.6	4.0	3.9	2.5	0.3	0.5	0.2	0.1	0.5	0.1	1.2	0.4
Kiribati	80.9	65.8	5.1	2.3	13.2	1.3	0.0	0.1	0.4	6.0	0.5	24.5	0.0	0.0
Marshall Islands	0.1	81.8	99.7	15.5	0.0	1.2	0.0	1.4	0.0	0.0	0.1	0.1	0.0	0.0
Micronesia, Federated States of	48.1	57.4	1.2	0.4	38.1	24.2	0.1	0.0	0.0	0.8	0.3	0.3	12.1	16.9
Nauru	80.3	93.0	3.6	4.8	16.0	1.9	0.0	0.0	0.0	0.0	0.0	0.2	0.0	0.0
Niue	...	...	...	...	...	...	...	...	...	...	...	...	...	...
Palau	63.7	57.2	0.6	6.9	34.9	35.7	0.0	0.0	0.0	0.2	0.3	0.0	0.5	0.0
Papua New Guinea	88.3	93.6	5.6	3.3	5.1	1.6	0.0	0.6	0.2	0.7	0.8	0.2	0.0	0.0
Samoa	87.0	65.6	1.3	29.2	11.4	4.6	0.0	0.0	0.0	0.2	0.0	0.0	0.2	0.3
Solomon Islands	97.2	93.1	1.1	4.5	1.7	1.3	0.0	0.0	0.0	0.0	0.1	1.1	0.0	0.0
Tonga	84.4	86.8	1.9	1.7	13.1	10.6	0.1	0.0	0.2	0.8	0.1	0.0	0.2	0.0
Tuvalu	95.3	12.5	0.1	0.1	3.4	1.4	0.4	0.1	0.0	0.0	0.9	85.9	0.0	0.0
Vanuatu	91.7	69.0	5.0	26.8	2.3	3.4	0.1	0.2	0.1	0.1	0.8	0.3	0.1	0.2
Developed ADB Member Economies[a]	**54.4**	**58.9**	**14.9**	**17.0**	**12.3**	**13.8**	**13.5**	**6.4**	**2.6**	**2.3**	**1.6**	**1.2**	**0.7**	**0.3**
Australia	59.6	61.7	20.0	20.1	12.7	13.8	2.3	1.5	1.1	0.9	1.4	1.1	3.0	1.0
Japan	52.6	57.8	13.3	15.8	12.2	14.0	17.1	8.3	3.2	2.9	1.6	1.3	0.0	0.0
New Zealand	62.9	62.5	16.7	20.0	12.3	11.7	6.2	3.9	0.7	1.4	0.8	0.4	0.2	0.1
DEVELOPING ADB MEMBER ECONOMIES[a]	**57.1**	**60.6**	**14.5**	**15.1**	**8.9**	**8.7**	**10.0**	**6.7**	**3.3**	**4.0**	**2.8**	**2.4**	**3.4**	**2.6**
ALL ADB REGIONAL MEMBERS[a]	**56.6**	**60.3**	**14.6**	**15.4**	**9.6**	**9.4**	**10.7**	**6.6**	**3.1**	**3.7**	**2.5**	**2.3**	**2.9**	**2.3**
WORLD[a]	**33.5**	**37.9**	**39.1**	**38.4**	**13.1**	**13.2**	**6.0**	**3.9**	**3.5**	**2.9**	**2.9**	**2.3**	**2.0**	**1.4**

... = data not available, 0.0 = magnitude is less than half of unit employed, ADB = Asian Development Bank.

a Aggregates include estimates derived from reports of partner economies for nonreporting and slow-reporting economies.

Source: International Monetary Fund. Direction of Trade Statistics. http://data.imf.org/?sk=9D6028D4-F14A-464C-A2F2-59B2CD424B85 (accessed 29 June 2021). For the Cook Islands and Taipei,China: Economy's official sources.

Table 2.4.15: International Reserves and Ratio to Imports

ADB Regional Member	International Reserves[a] ($ million)				Ratio to Imports[b] (months)			
	2010	2015	2019	2020	2010	2015	2019	2020
Developing ADB Member Economies								
Central and West Asia[c]	**77,894**	**93,691**	**100,349**	**116,919**	**8.7**	**8.4**	**7.6**	**10.8**
Afghanistan	5,147	6,990	8,467	9,687	12.9	11.6	16.5	19.8
Armenia	1,866	1,775	2,850	2,616	6.9	7.6	6.8	7.8
Azerbaijan	6,409	7,910	7,043	7,634	11.5	9.7	7.5	9.1
Georgia	2,264	2,521	3,506	3,913	5.4	4.3	4.8	6.3
Kazakhstan	28,275	27,871	28,958	35,638	10.3	10.1	8.7	16.2
Kyrgyz Republic	1,720	1,778	2,425	2,810	6.9	5.5	6.2	9.9
Pakistan	17,210	20,045	16,463	18,251	6.6	5.8	3.8	5.0
Tajikistan	403	494	1,466	...	1.7	2.1	6.0	...
Turkmenistan	...	...	...	...	...	...	...	...
Uzbekistan	14,600	24,307	29,172	34,904	18.0	25.2	16.5	22.0
East Asia	**3,825,703**	**4,564,136**	**4,560,345**	**4,830,581**	**20.0**	**19.7**	**16.5**	**17.8**
China, People's Republic of	2,875,894	3,405,385	3,222,900	3,357,028	27.8	26.1	19.4	20.3
Hong Kong, China	268,743	358,773	441,349	491,775	8.4	8.2	9.4	10.6
Korea, Republic of	291,571	367,944	408,500	441,907	8.4	10.4	10.3	12.2
Mongolia	2,288	1,323	4,356	4,542	8.9	4.1	8.7	10.4
Taipei,China	387,207	430,711	483,240	535,327	18.5	19.4	21.2	23.8
South Asia	**320,425**	**395,972**	**510,954**	**648,465**	**9.0**	**10.2**	**10.8**	**22.6**
Bangladesh	11,178	27,493	32,692	43,164	6.3	8.8	7.1	10.2
Bhutan	1,002	1,103	1,238	1,510	15.1	13.1	14.7	20.4
India	297,746	351,551	460,209	586,045	9.3	10.6	11.6	26.5
Maldives	364	576	763	995	3.5	3.6	3.3	7.0
Nepal	2,939	7,945	8,407	11,085	7.2	12.5	8.1	13.1
Sri Lanka	7,196	7,304	7,645	5,666	6.4	4.6	4.6	4.2
Southeast Asia[c]	**688,196**	**731,611**	**934,780**	**1,105,558**	**9.3**	**8.5**	**8.7**	**12.1**
Brunei Darussalam	1,563	3,367	4,273	3,997	7.3	12.6	10.3	...
Cambodia	3,802	7,376	18,762	21,333	6.9	6.7	10.1	12.2
Indonesia	96,211	105,929	129,183	135,897	9.7	9.4	9.4	12.1
Lao People's Democratic Republic	817	1,072	1,068	1,393	4.8	2.3	2.0	3.1
Malaysia	106,525	95,287	103,613	107,636	8.6	7.8	7.4	8.5
Myanmar	5,729	4,599	5,822	7,670	16.0	4.0	4.5 (2018)	...
Philippines	62,373	80,667	87,840	110,117	14.0	14.6	10.3	16.7
Singapore	225,715	247,746	279,451	362,300	8.7	9.8	9.7	13.7
Thailand	172,129	156,514	224,322	258,128	12.4	10.0	12.5	16.6
Timor-Leste	406	438	656	657	15.9	8.0	13.3	14.9
Viet Nam	12,926	28,616	78,810	95,452	2.0	2.2	3.9	6.4
The Pacific[c]	**4,595**	**3,883**	**5,247**	**...**	**8.1**	**7.0**	**7.2**	**...**
Cook Islands	...	...	...	...	...	...	...	...
Fiji	721	919	1,043	...	5.6	5.9	5.2	...
Kiribati	8	7	7	8	1.3	0.7	0.6	...
Marshall Islands	5	5	5 (2017)	...	0.5	0.5	0.5 (2017)	...
Micronesia, Federated States of	56	135	397	...	4.2	9.7	13.9 (2018)	...
Nauru	...	1 (2016)	1 (2018)	...	...	0.2 (2016)	0.2 (2018)	...
Niue	...	...	...	...	...	...	...	...
Palau	5	4	4 (2018)	...	0.6	0.3	0.3 (2018)	...
Papua New Guinea	3,092	1,738	2,309	...	10.5	8.2	7.5	...
Samoa	173	112	177	277	7.4	4.5	6.0	11.7
Solomon Islands	266	534	571	661	8.9	14.6	13.8	19.6
Tonga	105	156	218	302	6.0	6.2	5.9	8.7
Tuvalu	3	2	2 (2017)	...	1.8	0.7	1.4 (2017)	...
Vanuatu	161	269	512	614	8.1	10.5	19.1	...
Developed ADB Member Economies[c]	**1,155,175**	**1,293,632**	**1,400,305**	**1,451,419**	**16.3**	**17.9**	**17.5**	**20.3**
Australia	42,268	45,718	58,742	43,006	2.6	2.7	3.2	2.4
Japan	1,104,680	1,233,153	1,322,443	1,394,680	21.0	23.5	22.9	27.8
New Zealand	16,723	14,700	17,814	13,733	6.5	5.1	5.2	...
DEVELOPING ADB MEMBER ECONOMIES[c]	**4,916,814**	**5,789,292**	**6,111,674**	**6,704,836**	**15.8**	**15.7**	**13.7**	**16.7**
ALL ADB REGIONAL MEMBERS[c]	**6,071,990**	**7,082,924**	**7,511,979**	**8,156,255**	**15.9**	**16.1**	**14.3**	**17.2**

... = data not available, 0 or 0.0 = magnitude is less than half of the unit employed, $ = United States dollars, ADB = Asian Development Bank.

a Data refer to international reserves with gold at national valuation, unless otherwise specified, as of the end of the year. For Afghanistan (prior to 2008 on the Key Indicators Database), Bhutan, Kiribati, Nauru, Palau, Samoa, Solomon Islands (prior to 2012), Tonga, Turkmenistan, and Vanuatu, data refer to international reserves without gold. For estimating regional aggregates, imputation was done for economies with missing data using available data from the nearest years.

b Merchandise imports from the balance of payments were used in the calculation. Aggregate ratios calculated using only reporting economies with data available for both reserves and imports in the years specified in the column headings.

c Aggregates include only reporting economies with data corresponding to the year heading.

Sources: For International Reserves: International Monetary Fund. International Financial Statistics. http://data.imf.org/ (accessed 18 July 2021); for Taipei,China: economy's official sources. For the reserves-to-imports ratio: Asian Development Bank estimates using data from the International Monetary Fund's International Financial Statistics and economy's official sources.

Table 2.4.16: Net Official Development Assistance from All Sources to Developing Economies
($ million)

ADB Regional Member	2010	2015	2016	2017	2018	2019
Developing ADB Member Economies						
Central and West Asia[a]	**11,448**	**10,667**	**9,384**	**8,524**	**7,998**	**9,216**
Afghanistan	6,235	4,274	4,069	3,812	3,792	4,140
Armenia	320	347	326	258	142	417
Azerbaijan	156	70	79	124	87	119
Georgia	589	449	463	447	589	492
Kazakhstan	212	82	63	59	80	53
Kyrgyz Republic	372	775	519	465	439	443
Pakistan	2,933	3,764	2,961	2,364	1,387	2,013
Tajikistan	388	432	360	328	404	361
Turkmenistan	44	23	32	28	20	25
Uzbekistan	198	451	511	639	1,058	1,152
East Asia[a]	**959**	**-70**	**-466**	**-224**	**-372**	**-299**
China, People's Republic of	672	-306	-791	-990	-705	-609
Hong Kong, China	...	...	...	...	...	...
Korea, Republic of	...	...	...	...	...	...
Mongolia	287	236	326	766	334	311
Taipei,China	...	...	...	...	...	...
South Asia[a]	**5,670**	**7,558**	**6,724**	**8,731**	**6,951**	**8,706**
Bangladesh	1,327	2,593	2,533	3,782	3,045	4,382
Bhutan	97	97	52	119	108	179
India	2,831	3,174	2,679	3,198	2,462	2,551
Maldives	88	24	23	46	131	71
Nepal	767	1,224	1,065	1,270	1,452	1,333
Sri Lanka	559	445	373	316	-247	192
Southeast Asia[a]	**6,365**	**6,243**	**6,146**	**6,180**	**5,992**	**4,814**
Brunei Darussalam	...	...	...	...	...	...
Cambodia	681	679	728	856	783	966
Indonesia	1,324	-28	-108	280	963	-667
Lao People's Democratic Republic	389	471	399	480	589	622
Malaysia	-6	-1	-52	-29	-35	-3
Myanmar	355	1,169	1,537	1,542	1,712	2,044
Philippines	582	515	284	160	547	886
Singapore	...	...	...	...	...	...
Thailand	-20	59	228	250	-419	-352
Timor-Leste	290	212	224	232	208	230
Viet Nam	2,770	3,167	2,906	2,407	1,645	1,088
The Pacific[a]	**1,435**	**1,576**	**1,345**	**1,579**	**1,899**	**1,742**
Cook Islands	14	26	17	19	34	29
Fiji	76	102	117	146	121	129
Kiribati	24	65	61	77	80	57
Marshall Islands	25	57	13	73	54	66
Micronesia, Federated States of	64	81	51	98	99	93
Nauru	28	31	23	26	38	54
Niue	15	20	14	15	19	19
Palau	29	14	18	22	85	25
Papua New Guinea	514	591	532	533	790	649
Samoa	124	94	89	136	128	124
Solomon Islands	333	190	176	187	196	224
Tonga	66	68	83	87	97	108
Tuvalu	14	50	24	29	27	36
Vanuatu	109	187	129	133	131	131
DEVELOPING ADB MEMBER ECONOMIES[a]	**25,876**	**25,974**	**23,134**	**24,790**	**22,468**	**24,180**
DEVELOPING ECONOMIES WORLDWIDE[b]	**129,264**	**146,742**	**158,811**	**165,090**	**167,560**	**163,504**

... = data not available, $ = United States dollars, ADB = Asian Development Bank.

Note: Net official development assistance refers to concessional flows to developing economies and multilateral institutions provided by official agencies, including state and local governments, or by their executing agencies, administered with the objective of promoting the economic development and welfare of developing economies, and containing a grant element of at least 25%. Net flow takes into account principal repayments for loans, offsetting entries for forgiven debt, and recoveries made on grants.

a For reporting economies only.

b Includes data for all developing economies as reported in the OECD.Stat database.

Source: Organisation for Economic Co-operation and Development. OECD.Stat Database. http://stats.oecd.org (accessed 20 July 2021).

Table 2.4.17: Net Other Official Flows from All Sources to Developing Economies
($ million)

ADB Regional Member	2010	2015	2016	2017	2018	2019
Developing ADB Member Economies						
Central and West Asia[a]	**4,070.1**	**5,251.1**	**5,540.1**	**2,663.7**	**1,869.2**	**3,028.3**
Afghanistan	71.2	127.4	97.2	56.1	0.2	14.8
Armenia	288.3	111.1	197.2	157.6	156.7	225.3
Azerbaijan	179.9	801.8	1,114.7	1,738.5	490.7	343.6
Georgia	250.2	342.4	486.6	262.1	218.9	411.9
Kazakhstan	2,247.2	1,256.7	441.4	-853.7	-586.6	-53.5
Kyrgyz Republic	18.3	0.4	-43.2	-6.0	51.2	33.4
Pakistan	345.3	-343.9	1,102.3	378.2	-137.1	755.9
Tajikistan	6.4	68.1	13.6	15.6	48.2	75.4
Turkmenistan	647.4	2,356.6	926.1	532.3	127.6	-811.1
Uzbekistan	16.0	530.5	1,204.2	383.0	1,499.5	2,032.6
East Asia[a]	**3,355.5**	**1,429.0**	**896.3**	**1,036.2**	**818.7**	**1,086.2**
China, People's Republic of	3,196.3	1,215.8	139.9	1,227.3	645.4	664.0
Hong Kong, China	...	...	...	...	...	...
Korea, Republic of	...	...	...	...	...	...
Mongolia	159.3	213.3	756.4	-191.1	173.3	422.2
Taipei,China	...	...	...	...	...	...
South Asia[a]	**6,175.1**	**2,531.9**	**3,653.6**	**3,636.7**	**2,831.4**	**3,289.3**
Bangladesh	35.1	417.9	1,421.5	2,337.4	938.4	1,208.9
Bhutan	24.0	-2.8	8.0	3.1	-5.2	6.4
India	5,967.5	1,811.5	1,935.6	1,190.1	1,650.9	1,899.4
Maldives	-33.9	-8.1	-24.7	-23.8	18.0	-6.6
Nepal	-6.9	-7.4	0.7	-2.3	-0.2	51.2
Sri Lanka	189.3	320.8	312.6	132.3	229.5	130.0
Southeast Asia[a]	**3,916.6**	**8,205.9**	**3,110.3**	**60.5**	**4,789.0**	**5,858.8**
Brunei Darussalam	...	...	...	...	...	...
Cambodia	-5.0	84.6	-12.3	84.1	-24.8	86.5
Indonesia	1,783.7	3,775.4	3,708.7	2,963.1	3,793.7	1,804.8
Lao People's Democratic Republic	-120.5	73.1	38.6	74.7	34.1	20.6
Malaysia	159.2	-231.8	-1,494.5	-739.8	-963.0	1,971.0
Myanmar	30.9	427.5	100.6	96.4	16.3	130.4
Philippines	-680.3	1,148.5	203.1	-32.2	956.5	456.8
Singapore	...	...	...	...	...	...
Thailand	-71.5	138.7	-39.3	-1,051.6	-614.0	718.6
Timor-Leste	4.6	7.8	24.8	11.8	26.5	38.3
Viet Nam	2,815.4	2,782.1	580.6	-1,345.9	1,563.7	631.8
The Pacific[a]	**4,982.0**	**18.1**	**-144.7**	**-164.0**	**-2.7**	**62.5**
Cook Islands	9.7	-0.6	-1.2	1.8	0.6	3.4
Fiji	14.2	-11.4	40.6	48.3	27.0	10.9
Kiribati	0.5	0.2	0.3	0.1	0.3	0.3
Marshall Islands	-0.6	7.6	36.7	17.1	58.7	144.5
Micronesia, Federated States of	0.8	0.2	2.3	1.5	0.2	0.1
Nauru	0.3	-0.1 (2013)	62.5	19.4	0.4	0.1
Niue	...	...	-	...	...	0.1
Palau	6.4 (2011)	0.3	6.6	9.9	8.7	4.9
Papua New Guinea	4,892.3	19.4	-320.7	-267.2	-120.7	-181.4
Samoa	4.1	-1.3	5.6	1.3	-0.2	0.7
Solomon Islands	59.2	0.7	19.1	0.5	10.9	73.0
Tonga	0.3	2.1	2.5	1.2	2.3	2.0
Tuvalu	-0.1	0.2	0.2	0.1	0.2	0.2
Vanuatu	1.3	0.7	0.9	2.1	8.8	3.9
DEVELOPING ADB MEMBER ECONOMIES[a]	**22,499.2**	**17,436.0**	**13,055.7**	**7,233.0**	**10,305.5**	**13,325.1**
DEVELOPING ECONOMIES WORLDWIDE[b]	**70,855.8**	**50,604.3**	**29,290.3**	**21,548.1**	**29,703.0**	**19,873.6**

... = data not available, 0.0 = magnitude is less than half of unit employed, $ = United States dollars, ADB = Asian Development Bank.

Note: Net other official flows refer to official sector transactions with economies on the Development Assistance Committee List of Official Development Assistance Recipients, which do not meet the conditions for eligibility as official development assistance, either because they are not primarily aimed at development or because they have a grant element of less than 25%. The Development Assistance Committee List of Official Development Assistance Recipients is available at http://www.oecd.org/dac/financing-sustainable-development/development-finance-standards/daclist.htm. Also includes net export credits. Net flow takes into account principal repayments for loans, offsetting entries for forgiven debt, and recoveries made on grants.

a For reporting economies only.

b Includes data for all developing economies as reported in the OECD.Stat database.

Source: Organisation for Economic Co-operation and Development. OECD.Stat Database. http://stats.oecd.org (accessed 20 July 2021).

Table 2.4.18: Net Private Flows from All Sources to Developing Economies
($ million)

ADB Regional Member	2010	2015	2016	2017	2018	2019
Developing ADB Member Economies						
Central and West Asia[a]	**-822**	**5,055**	**1,243**	**-1,184**	**-6,680**	**30**
Afghanistan	-21	-5	-5	3	1	2
Armenia	-69	57	179	88	88	107
Azerbaijan	798	436	404	146	205	482
Georgia	22	1,249	190	361	334	224
Kazakhstan	-1,511	3,090	-86	-3,000	-7,575	-1,023
Kyrgyz Republic	23	6	-23	15	12	-1
Pakistan	-75	131	192	703	-86	94
Tajikistan	18	-8	-2	-42	43	-18
Turkmenistan	-46	-11	285	107	-26	-230
Uzbekistan	39	110	108	436	323	394
East Asia[a]	**46,322**	**17,370**	**42,731**	**38,835**	**31,500**	**42,913**
China, People's Republic of	46,301	17,154	42,145	38,767	31,290	42,324
Hong Kong, China	...	...	...	...	...	...
Korea, Republic of	...	...	...	...	...	...
Mongolia	22	216	586	68	210	589
Taipei,China	...	...	...	...	...	...
South Asia[a]	**20,237**	**7,900**	**14,937**	**19,632**	**14,914**	**20,320**
Bangladesh	-3	100	-380	225	30	331
Bhutan	18	16	-0	-1	-7	0
India	19,976	7,288	14,812	18,961	13,980	19,552
Maldives	38	112	17	-1	148	148
Nepal	-11	-3	6	53	25	30
Sri Lanka	218	387	482	394	739	259
Southeast Asia[a]	**21,463**	**16,972**	**23,520**	**25,424**	**21,095**	**69,591**
Brunei Darussalam	...	...	...	...	...	...
Cambodia	256	380	403	412	457	644
Indonesia	3,348	9,678	10,353	11,225	6,429	13,829
Lao People's Democratic Republic	172	-19	44	72	27	97
Malaysia	6,573	3,689	2,133	2,961	79	9,103
Myanmar	260	865	356	452	415	556
Philippines	2,424	1,908	2,738	4,251	3,049	31,544
Singapore	...	...	...	...	...	...
Thailand	6,394	-2,337	2,762	1,497	6,647	7,477
Timor-Leste	-3	17	-42	15	4	5
Viet Nam	2,038	2,790	4,772	4,537	3,989	6,336
The Pacific[a]	**978**	**179**	**925**	**1,211**	**-2,063**	**-1,091**
Cook Islands	-0	-2	-1	0	-18	-1
Fiji	-3	53	-15	45	40	9
Kiribati	-0	3	-9	-1	9	5
Marshall Islands	974	2,245	9	572	-515	30
Micronesia, Federated States of	3	798	714	453	-1,641	-1,215
Nauru	-0 (2011)	...	-0	0	-0	-0
Niue	-0 (2012)	–	0	0	0	0
Palau	3	7	9	10	9	8
Papua New Guinea	-40	-2,931	211	134	8	61
Samoa	17	3	8	6	54	-3
Solomon Islands	3	11	-1	-8	-0	3
Tonga	-10	-1	-0	0	0	4
Tuvalu	1 (2011)	0	0	0	...	...
Vanuatu	31	-5	1	-1	-10	9
DEVELOPING ADB MEMBER ECONOMIES[a]	**88,177**	**47,476**	**83,357**	**83,916**	**58,766**	**131,763**
DEVELOPING ECONOMIES WORLDWIDE[b]	**324,145**	**116,530**	**128,540**	**235,108**	**96,422**	**216,535**

... = data not available, -0 or 0 = magnitude is less than half of unit employed, $ = United States dollars, ADB = Asian Development Bank.

Note: Net private flows refer to the sum of direct investments and portfolio investments.

a For reporting economies only.

b Includes data for all developing economies as reported in the OECD.Stat database.

Source: Organisation for Economic Co-operation and Development. OECD.Stat Database. http://stats.oecd.org (accessed 20 July 2021).

Table 2.4.19: Aggregate Net Resource Flows from All Sources to Developing Economies
($ million)

ADB Regional Member	2010	2015	2016	2017	2018	2019
Developing ADB Member Economies						
Central and West Asia[a]	**14,696**	**20,973**	**16,168**	**10,004**	**3,188**	**12,274**
Afghanistan	6,285	4,396	4,162	3,871	3,794	4,156
Armenia	539	515	703	503	386	750
Azerbaijan	1,135	1,308	1,598	2,008	783	945
Georgia	861	2,040	1,139	1,070	1,142	1,128
Kazakhstan	948	4,429	419	-3,794	-8,081	-1,023
Kyrgyz Republic	413	781	453	474	502	474
Pakistan	3,203	3,551	4,255	3,445	1,164	2,863
Tajikistan	413	492	371	302	494	418
Turkmenistan	645	2,369	1,244	667	122	-1,016
Uzbekistan	253	1,092	1,823	1,458	2,880	3,579
East Asia[a]	**50,636**	**18,729**	**43,162**	**39,647**	**31,947**	**43,700**
China, People's Republic of	50,169	18,063	41,494	39,004	31,230	42,379
Hong Kong, China	...	...	...	...	...	...
Korea, Republic of	...	...	...	...	...	...
Mongolia	468	665	1,668	642	716	1,321
Taipei,China	...	...	...	...	...	...
South Asia[a]	**32,082**	**17,990**	**25,315**	**31,999**	**24,696**	**32,316**
Bangladesh	1,360	3,111	3,574	6,345	4,013	5,922
Bhutan	140	110	60	121	95	185
India	28,774	12,274	19,427	23,349	18,093	24,002
Maldives	93	128	15	22	297	212
Nepal	749	1,215	1,071	1,321	1,477	1,414
Sri Lanka	966	1,153	1,168	842	721	581
Southeast Asia[a]	**31,744**	**31,420**	**32,776**	**31,664**	**31,876**	**80,264**
Brunei Darussalam	...	...	...	...	...	...
Cambodia	932	1,144	1,120	1,353	1,215	1,697
Indonesia	6,456	13,425	13,953	14,468	11,186	14,966
Lao People's Democratic Republic	441	526	482	627	650	739
Malaysia	6,726	3,457	587	2,192	-918	11,071
Myanmar	646	2,460	1,993	2,090	2,143	2,731
Philippines	2,326	3,571	3,225	4,379	4,552	32,887
Singapore	...	...	...	...	...	...
Thailand	6,302	-2,139	2,951	696	5,614	7,843
Timor-Leste	292	238	207	259	238	273
Viet Nam	7,623	8,739	8,258	5,599	7,197	8,056
The Pacific[a]	**7,395**	**1,773**	**2,126**	**2,626**	**-167**	**713**
Cook Islands	23	23	15	21	17	31
Fiji	87	144	143	239	188	149
Kiribati	24	68	52	77	90	62
Marshall Islands	998	2,309	58	661	-402	240
Micronesia, Federated States of	68	879	767	552	-1,542	-1,122
Nauru	28	31	85	45	38	54
Niue	15	20	14	15	19	19
Palau	32	21	33	42	102	37
Papua New Guinea	5,366	-2,320	422	400	678	528
Samoa	145	95	103	143	182	121
Solomon Islands	395	202	194	179	206	300
Tonga	57	70	85	88	100	114
Tuvalu	14	50	25	29	28	37
Vanuatu	142	182	131	134	130	143
DEVELOPING ADB MEMBER ECONOMIES[a]	**136,553**	**90,885**	**119,547**	**115,940**	**91,540**	**169,268**
DEVELOPING ECONOMIES WORLDWIDE[b]	**524,265**	**313,876**	**316,641**	**421,746**	**293,684**	**399,913**

... = data not available, $ = United States dollars, ADB = Asian Development Bank.

Note: Aggregate net resource flows refer to the sum of net official development assistance, net other official flows, and net private flows.
a For reporting economies only.
b Includes data for all developing economies as reported in the OECD.Stat database.

Source: Organisation for Economic Co-operation and Development. OECD.Stat Database. http://stats.oecd.org (accessed 20 July 2021).

Table 2.4.20: Total External Debt of Developing Economies—Dollar Amounts
($ million)

ADB Regional Member	Total External Debt			External Debt, Public and Publicly Guaranteed		
	2010	2015	2019	2010	2015	2019
Developing ADB Member Economies						
Central and West Asia[a]	**223,046**	**286,678**	**342,065**	**67,203**	**101,013**	**143,163**
Afghanistan	2,436	2,597	2,662	1,976	1,990	1,944
Armenia	6,307	8,831	11,887	2,560	3,998	5,655
Azerbaijan	7,251	13,319	15,840	3,812	8,712	13,976
Georgia	8,790	14,875	17,312	3,274	5,721	6,993
Kazakhstan	119,151	153,180	156,263	3,845	20,114	24,716
Kyrgyz Republic	4,118	7,720	8,339	2,446	3,431	3,720
Pakistan	63,098	66,691	100,819	43,700	49,119	71,113
Tajikistan	3,561	5,144	6,631	1,806	2,093	2,830
Turkmenistan	531	367	568	362	231	427
Uzbekistan	7,802	13,955	21,745	3,423	5,605	11,790
East Asia[a]	**2,083,992**	**3,211,077**	**4,472,607**	**112,111**	**151,179**	**326,841**
China, People's Republic of	742,756	1,333,777	2,114,163	102,293	146,070	318,065
Hong Kong, China	879,034	1,300,348	1,783,099 (2020)	...	...	...
Korea, Republic of	354,693	396,058	542,448 (2020)	...	...	...
Mongolia	5,928	21,940	31,442	1,782	3,993	8,147
Taipei,China	101,581	158,954	189,873 (2020)	8,035	1,116	1,446 (2020)
South Asia[a]	**344,317**	**565,871**	**685,114**	**143,188**	**220,302**	**280,487**
Bangladesh	26,567	35,960	57,088	21,140	24,370	41,037
Bhutan	935	2,011	2,703	919	1,945	2,616
India	290,428	478,826	560,035	100,563	162,305	191,797
Maldives	917	1,006	2,679	628	685	2,228
Nepal	3,787	4,143	6,513	3,507	3,543	5,845
Sri Lanka	21,684	43,925	56,095	16,430	27,453	36,964
Southeast Asia[a]	**569,451**	**816,482**	**826,656**	**273,833**	**355,749**	**395,221**
Brunei Darussalam	...	...	...	...	...	...
Cambodia	3,999	9,424	15,318	3,049	5,626	7,551
Indonesia	198,278	307,749	402,084	102,748	159,571	233,505
Lao People's Democratic Republic	6,554	11,642	16,701	3,751	6,689	10,329
Malaysia	133,800	190,951	...	61,858	66,385	...
Myanmar	10,164	10,293	11,114	8,607	9,787	10,681
Philippines	65,358	76,266	83,661	45,094	38,860	41,679
Singapore	...	...	...	...	...	...
Thailand	106,358	132,209	180,230	15,929	22,420	39,497
Timor-Leste	76 (2012)	117	203	0 (2012)	46	191
Viet Nam	44,940	77,831	117,344	32,798	46,365	51,788
The Pacific[a]	**7,991**	**22,728**	**21,475**	**2,066**	**2,954**	**6,014**
Cook Islands	99	75	71	...	...	...
Fiji	731	889	1,020	353	617	701
Kiribati	14	33	47	...	...	...
Marshall Islands	105	95	73	...	...	...
Micronesia, Federated States of	86	81	65 (2020)	...	...	...
Nauru	...	...	...	...	...	...
Niue	...	...	...	...	...	...
Palau	66	64	87	...	...	...
Papua New Guinea	5,987	20,387	18,740	1,042	1,501	4,309
Samoa	325	437	409	299	408	388
Solomon Islands	231	207	350	125	81	98
Tonga	154	184	186	144	175	177
Tuvalu	15	19	16 (2017)	...	...	...
Vanuatu	178	257	421	103	172	341
DEVELOPING ADB MEMBER ECONOMIES[a]	**3,228,798**	**4,902,836**	**6,347,917**	**598,401**	**831,198**	**1,151,727**
DEVELOPING ECONOMIES WORLDWIDE[a,b]	**5,770,981**	**8,387,017**	**10,465,591**	**1,668,524**	**2,372,134**	**3,100,057**

... = data not available, 0 = magnitude is less than half of unit employed, $ = United States dollars, ADB = Asian Development Bank.

Note: Refers to the sum of public and publicly guaranteed long-term debt, private nonguaranteed long-term debt, use of International Monetary Fund credit, and estimated short-term debt.

a Regional aggregates include only reporting economies with data corresponding to the year heading.

b Refers to all low- and middle-income economies as classified by the World Bank. For developing member economies not covered by the World Bank, data are from economy's official sources.

Sources: World Bank. International Debt Statistics Online. http://data.worldbank.org/data-catalog/international-debt-statistics (accessed 14 July 2021); and Asian Development Bank estimates using economy's official sources.

Table 2.4.21: Total External Debt of Developing ADB Member Economies—Proportion of Income
(% of GNI)

ADB Regional Member	Total External Debt			External Debt, Public and Publicly Guaranteed		
	2010	2015	2019	2010	2015	2019
Developing ADB Member Economies						
Central and West Asia						
Afghanistan	15.3	12.9	13.6	12.4	9.9	9.9
Armenia	64.9	80.4	85.5	26.3	36.4	40.7
Azerbaijan	14.7	26.1	34.4	7.7	17.1	30.4
Georgia	73.1	101.8	101.6	27.2	39.1	41.0
Kazakhstan	92.6	88.7	98.3	3.0	11.6	15.5
Kyrgyz Republic	91.7	120.3	106.4	54.5	53.5	47.5
Pakistan	36.3	25.1	37.0	25.1	18.5	26.1
Tajikistan	51.1	54.8	70.2	25.9	22.3	30.0
Turkmenistan	2.6	1.1	2.3 (2018)	1.7	0.7	1.2 (2018)
Uzbekistan	16.7	16.8	37.0	7.3	6.7	20.1
East Asia						
China, People's Republic of	12.3	12.1	14.8	1.7	1.3	2.2
Hong Kong, China[a]	384.5	420.2	514.5 (2020)	...	...	...
Korea, Republic of	31.0	26.9	33.0 (2020)	...	...	...
Mongolia	89.7	203.4	253.1	27.0	37.0	65.6
Taipei,China	22.2	29.0	27.6 (2020)	1.8	0.2	0.2 (2020)
South Asia						
Bangladesh	21.3	17.3	18.0	17.0	11.7	12.9
Bhutan	64.0	108.1	117.5	63.0	104.5	113.7
India	17.5	23.0	19.7	6.1	7.8	6.8
Maldives	40.3	26.6	52.7	27.6	18.1	43.8
Nepal	23.5	19.0	21.0	21.8	16.3	18.9
Sri Lanka	38.6	55.9	68.8	29.3	34.9	45.3
Southeast Asia						
Brunei Darussalam	...	...	...	...	...	...
Cambodia	37.3	55.6	60.0	28.4	33.2	29.6
Indonesia	27.0	37.0	37.0	14.0	19.2	21.5
Lao People's Democratic Republic	98.2	84.7	94.1	56.2	48.6	58.2
Malaysia	54.2	66.3	...	25.1	23.0	...
Myanmar	20.5	15.6	15.2	17.4	14.9	14.6
Philippines	28.2	22.3	20.2	19.5	11.4	10.1
Singapore	...	...	...	...	...	...
Thailand	32.5	34.7	34.4	4.9	5.9	7.5
Timor-Leste	1.8 (2012)	4.2	7.5	0.0 (2012)	1.6	7.1
Viet Nam	40.3	42.5	47.6	29.4	25.3	21.0
The Pacific						
Cook Islands[a]	41.0	24.8	18.7	...	...	...
Fiji	24.0	20.2	20.2	11.6	14.0	13.9
Kiribati[a]	8.5	20.0	23.0	...	...	...
Marshall Islands[a]	62.7	52.2	28.0	...	...	...
Micronesia, Federated States of[a]	28.9	25.6	18.8 (2018)	...	...	...
Nauru	...	...	...	...	...	...
Niue	...	...	...	...	...	...
Palau[a]	36.2	23.1	31.1	...	...	...
Papua New Guinea	45.4	95.6	78.8	7.9	7.0	18.1
Samoa	50.5	56.6	50.1	46.5	52.8	47.6
Solomon Islands	28.7	16.2	22.3	15.6	6.3	6.2
Tonga	40.6	41.8	34.7	37.9	39.7	33.0
Tuvalu[a]	49.1	53.5	...	...	...	...
Vanuatu	26.2	33.7	44.6	15.1	22.6	36.2

... = data not available, 0.0 = magnitude is less than half of unit employed, ADB = Asian Development Bank, GNI = gross national income.

a For total external debt as a percentage of GNI, gross domestic product is used in lieu of GNI.

Sources: World Bank. International Debt Statistics Online. http://data.worldbank.org/data-catalog/international-debt-statistics (accessed 14 July 2021); and Asian Development Bank estimates using economy's official sources.

Table 2.4.22: Total External Debt of Developing ADB Member Economies—Proportion of Exports
(% of exports of goods, services, and primary income)

ADB Regional Member	2010	2015	2016	2017	2018	2019
Developing ADB Member Economies						
Central and West Asia						
Afghanistan	88.7	152.4	188.7	189.5	141.1	142.5
Armenia	193.5	219.6	223.5	188.5	184.4	180.7
Azerbaijan	25.1	62.6	78.9	72.4	59.8	62.8
Georgia	191.5	213.9	230.1	189.0	170.2	158.6
Kazakhstan	174.7	287.6	373.0	282.6	225.0	228.3
Kyrgyz Republic	181.2	314.6	327.7	312.1	294.3	265.1
Pakistan	219.6	227.9	265.1	284.9	297.2	324.0
Tajikistan	158.4	200.6	230.3	223.2	224.5	229.9
Turkmenistan	...	...	...	...	...	...
Uzbekistan	...	100.7	123.1	111.9	101.2	109.0
East Asia						
China, People's Republic of	42.5	51.6	58.3	62.7	67.7	73.4
Hong Kong, China[a]	149.2	168.8	177.6	190.5	190.6	219.0 (2020)
Korea, Republic of[a]	62.4	59.5	60.4	58.9	57.7	84.5 (2020)
Mongolia	173.2	422.4	433.6	406.4	373.9	356.9
Taipei,China[a]	30.0	38.8	45.3	43.1	44.0	44.7 (2020)
South Asia						
Bangladesh	122.1	102.4	101.9	119.2	117.1	126.5
Bhutan	154.0	268.8	343.4	349.4	313.5	329.9
India	81.1	108.0	102.1	100.7	93.3	98.4
Maldives	45.6	31.9	38.7	45.5	64.9	71.6
Nepal	212.7	154.5	166.9	165.9	163.1	187.7
Sri Lanka	189.8	257.3	265.5	263.6	257.9	285.2
Southeast Asia						
Brunei Darussalam	...	...	...	...	...	...
Cambodia	65.6	69.1	68.4	70.0	71.2	70.3
Indonesia	117.6	176.7	185.6	177.0	171.6	193.8
Lao People's Democratic Republic	284.0	251.7	259.8	254.3	237.9	235.9
Malaysia	57.2	86.0	94.5	...	...	...
Myanmar	129.5	70.6	72.2	72.6	62.6	58.9
Philippines	106.7	93.3	89.5	75.5	77.2	77.6
Singapore	...	...	...	...	...	...
Thailand	45.7	47.8	49.1	51.6	51.1	53.7
Timor-Leste	1.9 (2012)	8.3	12.3	14.2	15.7	15.5
Viet Nam	56.1	44.8	45.2	45.5	41.1	41.5
The Pacific						
Cook Islands[a]	61.3	23.8	20.0	17.9	16.8	14.1
Fiji	38.7	37.8	39.5	39.6	35.8	37.7
Kiribati[a]	14.9	15.8	23.5	21.0	22.1	20.5
Marshall Islands[a]	94.1	57.2	55.5	47.7	42.7	39.2
Micronesia, Federated States of[a]	91.3	51.1	49.0	42.6	34.2	...
Nauru	...	...	...	...	...	...
Niue	...	...	...	...	...	...
Palau[a]	62.8	35.1	43.1	48.7	55.8	60.3
Papua New Guinea	98.2	236.6	231.2	167.6	166.7	159.4
Samoa	161.1	182.6	162.7	155.8	137.4	122.1
Solomon Islands	68.9	35.9	44.2	59.3	44.7	54.7
Tonga	283.9	208.5	142.8	138.3	120.0	111.1
Tuvalu[a]	64.1	48.8	40.1	36.6	...	...
Vanuatu	48.9	72.7	70.8	90.0	71.5	86.5

... = data not available, ADB = Asian Development Bank.

a External debt as a percentage of exports of goods, services, and primary income was derived using balance-of-payments data.

Sources: World Bank. International Debt Statistics Online. http://data.worldbank.org/data-catalog/international-debt-statistics (accessed 14 July 2021); and Asian Development Bank estimates using economy's official sources.

Table 2.4.23: Total Debt Service Paid by Developing ADB Member Economies

ADB Regional Member	Debt Service Payment ($ million)				Debt Service Payment (% of exports of goods, services, and primary income)			
	2010	2015	2018	2019	2010	2015	2018	2019
Developing ADB Member Economies								
Central and West Asia[a]	**48,016**	**46,659**	**48,721**	**69,602**				
Afghanistan	10	57	63	134	0.4	3.3	3.3	3.0
Armenia	969	1,546	1,667	1,900	29.7	38.4	28.7	31.5
Azerbaijan	414	1,907	2,682	1,856	1.4	9.0	9.9	8.6
Georgia	803	2,158	2,435	4,430	17.5	31.0	23.9	21.6
Kazakhstan	39,475	34,846	33,643	39,568	57.9	65.4	48.2	47.9
Kyrgyz Republic	557	413	564	1,446	24.5	16.8	20.3	18.0
Pakistan	4,319	4,108	6,024	15,781	15.0	14.0	19.1	35.4
Tajikistan	695	314	585	949	30.9	12.2	22.0	19.3
Turkmenistan	155	55	54	75	...	...	...	...
Uzbekistan	618	1,256	1,004	3,462	...	9.1	5.8	13.2
East Asia[a]	**58,805**	**134,639**	**257,931**	**175,609**				
China, People's Republic of	52,104	126,687	240,940	161,185	3.0	4.9	8.3	9.6
Hong Kong, China	...	...	...	...	...	...	...	...
Korea, Republic of[b,c]	2,843	...	...	...	0.5	...	...	...
Mongolia	239	1,833	7,774	7,207	7.0	35.3	97.9	133.1
Taipei,China[b,c]	3,620	6,119	9,217	7,217	1.1	1.5	2.1	1.7 (2020)
South Asia[a]	**27,283**	**55,341**	**74,684**	**70,700**				
Bangladesh	1,106	1,634	2,869	4,001	5.1	4.7	6.4	12.8
Bhutan	87	129	87	433	14.4	17.2	10.7	7.5
India	24,413	49,662	63,647	57,770	6.8	11.2	11.4	9.0
Maldives	81	139	442	408	4.0	4.4	12.3	12.2
Nepal	188	226	244	355	10.6	8.4	7.2	8.2
Sri Lanka	1,408	3,551	7,396	7,732	12.3	20.8	36.1	31.7
Southeast Asia[a]	**62,061**	**111,229**	**104,080**	**136,067**				
Brunei Darussalam	...	...	...	...	...	...	...	...
Cambodia	65	691	1,279	1,708	1.1	5.1	6.7	6.9
Indonesia	31,569	60,273	55,469	88,934	18.7	34.6	25.1	39.4
Lao People's Democratic Republic	302	421	869	2,809	13.1	9.1	13.4	7.2
Malaysia	5,575	13,503	10,385 (2016)	...	2.4	6.1	4.9 (2016)	...
Myanmar	244	524	839	994	3.1	3.6	4.9	3.8
Philippines	11,461	10,576	8,799	7,588	18.7	12.9	8.6	9.7
Singapore	...	...	...	...	...	...	...	...
Thailand	10,965	18,610	18,630	16,389	4.7	6.7	5.5	8.0
Timor-Leste	0 (2012)	1	3	11	0.0 (2012)	0.1	0.3	0.5
Viet Nam	1,880	6,631	18,192	17,636	2.3	3.8	7.0	5.8
The Pacific[a]	**913**	**1,501**	**2,963**	**5,490**				
Cook Islands[b,c]	3	5	6	4 (2019)	2.0	1.6	1.4	0.8
Fiji	41	335	60	320	2.2	14.3	2.2	6.7
Kiribati[c]	1	1	1	2 (2019)	0.9	0.5	0.5	0.9
Marshall Islands[c]	9	8	7	8 (2019)	7.7	4.6	3.9	4.1
Micronesia, Federated States of[c]	5	7	6	...	5.2	4.2	2.9	...
Nauru	...	...	...	...	...	...	...	...
Niue	...	...	...	...	...	...	...	...
Palau	...	...	...	...	...	...	...	...
Papua New Guinea	812	1,098	2,782	5,038	13.3	12.7	26.2	20.1
Samoa	11	21	30	31	5.3	8.8	9.8	9.1
Solomon Islands	21	14	40	63	6.2	2.4	5.6	2.6
Tonga	5	6	10	16	9.3	7.3	6.6	3.3
Tuvalu	...	...	...	...	...	...	...	...
Vanuatu	6	7	20	21	1.6	2.0	3.6	4.8
DEVELOPING ADB MEMBER ECONOMIES[a]	**197,078**	**349,370**	**488,380**	**457,468**				

... = data not available, 0 or 0.0 = magnitude is less than half of unit employed, $ = United States dollars; ADB = Asian Development Bank.

a Aggregates include only reporting economies with data corresponding to the year heading.

b Refers to principal repayments on long-term debt plus interest on short-term and long-term debt.

c Debt service payment as a percentage of exports of goods, services, and primary income was derived using balance-of-payments data.

Sources: World Bank. International Debt Statistics Online. http://data.worldbank.org/data-catalog/international-debt-statistics (accessed 14 July 2021); economy's official sources; and Asian Development Bank estimates.

Table 2.4.24: International Tourist Arrivals
('000)

ADB Regional Member	2010	2015	2016	2017	2018	2019	2020
Developing ADB Member Economies							
Central and West Asia[a]	**9,288**	**12,458**	**12,825**	**15,707**	**22,370**	**25,095**	**...**
Afghanistan	...	...	...	...	...	...	...
Armenia	684	1,192	1,260	1,495	1,652	1,894	375
Azerbaijan	1,280	1,922	2,044	2,454	2,633	2,864	...
Georgia	1,067	3,012	3,297	4,069	4,757	5,080	1,089
Kazakhstan	2,991	...	...	...	...	...	...
Kyrgyz Republic	1,224	4,000	3,853	4,568	6,947	8,508	...
Pakistan	907	...	...	...	...	...	...
Tajikistan	160	414	344	431	1,035	...	...
Turkmenistan	...	...	...	...	...	...	...
Uzbekistan	975	1,918	2,027	2,690	5,346	6,749	1,504
East Asia	**90,570**	**107,630**	**114,159**	**113,169**	**119,106**	**119,396**	**...**
China, People's Republic of	55,664	56,886	59,270	60,740	62,900	65,700	...
Hong Kong, China	20,085	26,686	26,553	27,884	29,263	23,752	1,359
Korea, Republic of	8,798	13,232	17,242	13,336	15,347	17,503	2,519
Mongolia	456	386	404	469	529	577	59
Taipei,China	5,567	10,440	10,690	10,740	11,067	11,864	1,378
South Asia	**8,169**	**17,136**	**19,052**	**20,481**	**22,955**	**23,363**	**...**
Bangladesh	303	126	182	237	267	323	...
Bhutan	41	155	210	255	274	316	...
India	5,776	13,284	14,570	15,543	17,423	17,910	...
Maldives	792	1,234	1,286	1,390	1,484	1,703	555
Nepal	603	539	753	940	1,173	1,197	230
Sri Lanka	654	1,798	2,051	2,116	2,334	1,914	508
Southeast Asia[a]	**70,471**	**104,243**	**110,771**	**120,569**	**128,620**	**138,592**	**...**
Brunei Darussalam	214	218	219	259	278	333	62
Cambodia	2,508	4,775	5,012	5,602	6,201	6,611	1,306
Indonesia[b]	7,003 |	9,963	11,072	12,948	13,396	15,455	...
Lao People's Democratic Republic	1,670	3,543	3,315	3,257	3,770	4,384	...
Malaysia	24,577	25,721	26,757	25,948	25,832	26,101	4,333
Myanmar	792	4,681	2,907	3,443	3,551	4,364	...
Philippines	3,520	5,361	5,967	6,621	7,168	8,261	1,483
Singapore	9,161	12,052	12,913	13,903	14,673	15,119	...
Thailand	15,936	29,923	32,530	35,592	38,178	39,874	6,702
Timor-Leste	40	62	66	74	75	81	18
Viet Nam	5,050	7,944	10,013	12,922	15,498	18,009	3,837
The Pacific[a]	**1,310**	**1,570**	**1,619**	**1,660**	**1,694**	**1,688**	**...**
Cook Islands	104	125	146	161	169	172	25
Fiji	632	755	792	843	870	894	147
Kiribati	5	4	6	6	7	8	...
Marshall Islands	5	6	5	6	7	6	...
Micronesia, Federated States of	45	31	30	27	19	18	...
Nauru	...	...	...	...	...	...	...
Niue	6	8	9	10	11	10	...
Palau	85	162	138	123	106	94	18
Papua New Guinea	140	183	179	139	140	160	...
Samoa	122	128	134	146	164	172	21
Solomon Islands	21	22	23	26	28	29	4
Tonga	47	54	59	63	54	...	...
Tuvalu	2	2	3	3	3	4	...
Vanuatu	97	90	95	109	116	121	22
Developed ADB Member Economies	**16,931**	**30,225**	**35,679**	**41,061**	**44,124**	**45,050**	**...**
Australia	5,790	7,449	8,269	8,815	9,246	9,466	1,828
Japan	8,611	19,737	24,040	28,691	31,192	31,882	4,116
New Zealand	2,530	3,039	3,370	3,555	3,686	3,702	...
DEVELOPING ADB MEMBER ECONOMIES[a]	**179,808**	**243,037**	**258,425**	**271,560**	**294,744**	**308,134**	**...**
ALL ADB REGIONAL MEMBERS[a]	**196,739**	**273,262**	**294,104**	**312,621**	**338,868**	**353,184**	**...**
WORLD[c]	**955,675**	**1,197,427**	**1,240,866**	**1,332,972**	**1,413,000**	**1,466,000**	**399,000**

... = data not available, | = marks break in the series, ADB = Asian Development Bank.

Note: For Australia; Japan; the Kyrgyz Republic; New Zealand; the Republic of Korea; Taipei,China; Tajikistan; Uzbekistan: and Viet Nam: Data refer to international visitor arrivals at frontiers (including tourists and same-day visitors). For the rest of the economies: Data refer to international tourist arrivals at frontiers (overnight visitors only, i.e., excluding same-day visitors).

a Includes only reporting economies with data corresponding to the year heading.

b Prior to 2015, data refer to international tourist arrivals at frontiers (overnight visitors only, i.e., excluding same-day visitors). For 2015 onward, data refer to international visitor arrivals at frontiers (including tourists and same-day visitors).

c Aggregations were done by the United Nations World Tourism Organization with approximations based on trends in the economies with available data.

Sources: United Nations World Tourism Organization. UNWTO.eLibrary. https://www.e-unwto.org/action/showLogin?uri=%2F& (accessed 25 July 2021); and United Nations World Tourism Organization. World Tourism Barometer. Statistical Annex. July 2021. Vol 19.

Table 2.4.25: International Tourism Receipts
($ million)

ADB Regional Member	2010	2015	2016	2017	2018	2019	2020
Developing ADB Member Economies							
Central and West Asia[a]	**3,631**	**7,568**	**8,916**	**10,451**	**11,351**	**11,757**	**2,603**
Afghanistan	75	79	49	2	28	72	65
Armenia	646	936	968	1,120	1,208	1,528	293
Azerbaijan	657	2,309	2,714	3,012	2,634	1,792	304
Georgia	659	1,868	2,111	2,704	3,222	3,269	542
Kazakhstan	1,005	1,632	1,858	2,135	2,255	2,463	459
Kyrgyz Republic	160	426	432	429	460	644	151
Pakistan	305	317	322	352	391	494	438
Tajikistan	3	1	4	8	9	14	6
Turkmenistan	...	...	...	...	...	...	...
Uzbekistan	121	...	458	689	1,144	1,481	345
East Asia	**86,731**	**110,195**	**106,407**	**97,977**	**109,968**	**100,536**	**29,478**
China, People's Republic of	45,814	44,969	44,432	38,559	40,386	35,832	14,233
Hong Kong, China	21,689	35,795	31,398	33,339	36,866	28,913	2,842
Korea, Republic of	10,263	14,798	16,886	13,368	18,567	20,867	10,528
Mongolia	244	246	316	396	445	513	29
Taipei,China	8,721	14,387	13,375	12,315	13,704	14,411	1,846
South Asia[a]	**17,244**	**27,290**	**29,203**	**35,117**	**37,074**	**38,676**	**14,129**
Bangladesh	81	150	214	341	353	388	217
Bhutan	40	94	92	103	103	120	...
India	14,490	21,013	22,427	27,365	28,568	30,720	13,036
Maldives	1,713	2,569	2,506	2,744	3,028	3,134	...
Nepal	344	483	446	639	641	707	194
Sri Lanka	576	2,981	3,518	3,925	4,381	3,607	682
Southeast Asia[a]	**68,484**	**105,091**	**112,991**	**126,145**	**138,158**	**146,899**	**31,254**
Brunei Darussalam	254 (2009)	147	144	177	190	217	16
Cambodia	1,519	3,137	3,212	3,636	4,352	4,769	1,015
Indonesia	6,958	10,761	11,206	13,139	16,426	16,911	3,312
Lao People's Democratic Republic	382	724	716	648	734	935	...
Malaysia	18,152	17,666	18,085	18,357	19,622	19,829	2,988
Myanmar	72	2,120	2,197	1,969	1,652	2,483	...
Philippines	2,645	5,272	5,143	6,988	8,240	9,781	2,010
Singapore	14,178	16,617	18,944	19,892	20,418	20,302	5,189
Thailand	20,104	41,246	44,786	52,376	56,366	59,810	14,198
Timor-Leste	24	51	58	73	78	70	26
Viet Nam	4,450	7,350	8,500	8,890	10,080	11,792	2,500
The Pacific[a]	**1,256**	**819**	**1,677**	**1,780**	**...**	**...**	**...**
Cook Islands	111	116	137	153	...	...	...
Fiji	635	816	878	940	972	963	154
Kiribati	4	2	3	4	3	...	...
Marshall Islands	4	1	5	7	9	...	...
Micronesia, Federated States of	24	25	...	...	...	...	...
Nauru	1	2	3	4	...	...	...
Niue	...	...	7	8	...	...	...
Palau	73	149	141	116	...	...	...
Papua New Guinea	2	2	1	2	3	2	1
Samoa	123	142	148	166	191	207	24
Solomon Islands	44	51	59	67	81	71	...
Tonga	16	43	51	48	48	57	...
Tuvalu	2	2 (2013)	...	...	...	...	...
Vanuatu	217	228	243	265	295	278	...
Developed ADB Member Economies[a]	**48,219**	**68,701**	**77,544**	**86,390**	**98,006**	**102,263**	**42,813**
Australia	28,472	34,269	37,019	41,732	45,035	45,709	25,821
Japan	13,224	24,968	30,752	34,054	42,096	46,054	10,700
New Zealand	6,523	9,464	9,773	10,604	10,875	10,500	6,292
DEVELOPING ADB MEMBER ECONOMIES[a]	**177,599**	**251,721**	**259,193**	**271,470**	**298,153**	**299,446**	**77,643**
ALL ADB REGIONAL MEMBERS[a]	**225,818**	**320,422**	**336,737**	**357,860**	**396,159**	**401,709**	**120,456**
WORLD[b]	**979,163**	**1,221,823**	**1,246,391**	**1,347,047**	**1,456,664**	**1,465,000**	**535,000**

... = data not available, $ = United States dollars, ADB = Asian Development Bank.

a Includes only reporting economies with data corresponding to the year heading.

b Aggregations were done by the United Nations World Tourism Organization with estimates made for nonreporting economies based on the previous year's values and the trend in neighboring economies.

Sources: United Nations World Tourism Organization. UNWTO.eLibrary. https://www.e-unwto.org/action/showLogin?uri=%2F& (accessed 20 July 2021); and United Nations World Tourism Organization. World Tourism Barometer. Statistical Annex. July 2021. Vol 19.

Data Issues and Comparability

Most of the data on international transactions presented in this section were taken from balance-of-payments statistics as reported by individual economies. IMF guidelines are followed by most governments in compiling these statistics. However, authorities have difficulty accurately recording nonofficial transactions such as migrant workers' remittances and private capital flows, which is one of the reasons that the IMF's Balance of Payments Manual (BPM) was updated to the sixth edition (BPM6) in 2009. All economies in the region have adopted BPM6 in recent years except two economies, which still rely on BPM5. However, there is not a single framework for an extended time series available for all economies. There are 20 economies reporting a mix of BPM5 and BPM6, and three economies reporting a mix of BPM4 and BPM6. This therefore affects the comparability of data across economies.

The World Trade Organization and other international agencies closely monitor international trade statistics. Common definitions are used by all economies, with the larger economies throughout Asia and the Pacific using standard forms and procedures for data processing.

Data on official development assistance, other official flows, and private direct investment and other private capital are compiled by the Organisation for Economic Co-operation and Development's Development Assistance Committee. These data are standardized on a calendar-year basis for all donors, but may have discrepancies for some economies owing to the fiscal-year data available in budget documents. Commitments from donors do not necessarily translate to actual disbursements to recipient economies of official development assistance.

Table 2.5.1: Road Indicators—Total Network, Passenger Kilometers Travel, Freight Kilometers Travel

ADB Regional Member	Road Indicators Network, Total (km)			Road Passenger Travel (passenger-km million)			Road Freight Travel (t-km million)		
	2010	2015	2019	2010	2015	2019	2010	2015	2019
Developing ADB Member Economies									
Central and West Asia									
Afghanistan	19,138 (2011)	37,090	44,870 (2017)	...	...	...	6,796.0 (2011)	4,423.0	...
Armenia	9,125	10,368	10,828	2,344.3	2,395.9	2,284.2	235.8	479.4	995.7
Azerbaijan	18,977	19,016	19,176	16,633.0	23,825.0	25,950.0	11,728.0	16,038.0	18,115.0
Georgia	19,040	20,553	20,964	...	...	...	619.7	664.3	702.3
Kazakhstan	96,018	96,529	96,246 (2018)	...	...	...	80,300.0	161,864.0	185,197.3 (2018)
Kyrgyz Republic	...	...	...	7,209.5	9,005.6	11,391.0	1,281.5	1,401.7	1,841.9
Pakistan	260,040	263,942	268,935 (2018)	...	...	...	...	...	...
Tajikistan	...	...	...	...	510.1 (2017)	510.1 (2017)	50,745.7	68,304.1	84,257.6 (2018)
Turkmenistan	...	...	...	27,657.0	...	...	11,399.0	...	...
Uzbekistan	...	...	...	78,400.0	109,100.0	124,141.2	24,464.2	12,800.0	15,879.3
East Asia									
China, People's Republic of	4,008,200	4,577,300	5,012,500	1,502,080.0	1,074,270.0	885,710.0	4,338,970.0	5,795,570.0	5,963,640.0
Hong Kong, China	2,076	2,101	2,127	...	...	...	...	...	...
Korea, Republic of	...	99,024	103,192	104,671.0	385,018.1	393,196.0 (2017)	103,898.0	132,382.0	...
Mongolia	...	113,200 (2017)	111,900	1,480.2	1,940.5	2,925.1	1,834.0	2,374.0	6,203.8
Taipei,China	40,335	41,952	43,122	...	...	...	29,631.6	37,805.3	44,370.0
South Asia									
Bangladesh	21,269	21,365	21,128 (2018)	...	...	...	...	...	...
Bhutan	4,661	11,177	18,264	...	...	...	...	...	...
India	4,582,439	4,572,144	6,204,426 (2017)	8,409,000.0	15,428,000.0	...	1,287,300.0	2,027,400.0	...
Maldives	...	...	...	...	...	...	...	...	...
Nepal	11,636 (2011)	12,898	13,448 (2017)	...	...	...	...	...	...
Sri Lanka	29,119	31,280	...	...	...	...	...	...	...
Southeast Asia									
Brunei Darussalam	3,127 (2011)	3,355	3,714	...	...	...	...	...	...
Cambodia	44,709 (2009)	...	61,534	...	...	...	...	...	...
Indonesia	487,314	529,073	544,474	...	...	...	...	...	...
Lao People's Democratic Republic	47,491	56,332	58,264	2,556.0	3,202.1	3,979.8	513.0	434.7	517.2
Malaysia	144,403	214,813	245,499 (2018)	...	...	...	...	...	...
Myanmar	...	...	133,277	...	40,840.0	28,581.8	507.9	419.4	158.4
Philippines	31,242	32,633	32,933 (2018)	...	...	...	...	...	...
Singapore	8,895	9,246	9,509	...	...	...	...	...	...
Thailand	...	...	702,210 (2020)	452,040.0	663,561.0	735,051.0	...	193,911.0	192,075.0 (2018)
Timor-Leste	...	8,701	8,811 (2018)	...	...	...	...	...	...
Viet Nam	...	309,969 (2016)	277,167	69,197.4	105,382.2	145,612.6	36,179.0	51,514.9	78,964.1
The Pacific									
Cook Islands	...	...	...	...	...	...	...	...	...
Fiji	...	...	...	...	...	...	...	...	...
Kiribati	...	...	...	...	...	...	...	...	...
Marshall Islands	...	...	...	...	...	...	...	...	...
Micronesia, Federated States of	...	...	...	...	...	...	...	...	...
Nauru	...	...	...	...	...	...	...	...	...
Niue	...	...	...	...	...	...	...	...	...
Palau	...	...	...	...	...	...	...	...	...
Papua New Guinea	...	30,000 (2016)	30,000 (2017)	...	...	...	...	...	...
Samoa	1,152 (2012)	...	...	...	...	...	...	...	...
Solomon Islands	...	...	...	...	...	...	...	...	...
Tonga	...	...	...	...	...	...	...	...	...
Tuvalu	...	120 (2017)	120 (2017)	...	...	...	...	...	...
Vanuatu	1,776 (2012)	2,241 (2014)	2,048 (2018)	...	...	...	...	...	...
Developed ADB Member Economies									
Australia	872,292	874,143	877,651 (2018)	320,040.0	343,200.0	361,580.0 (2018)	186,100.0	207,300.0	218,900.0
Japan	1,210,000	1,221,000	1,225,000 (2018)	77,677.0	71,443.5	70,101.0 (2018)	243,150.0	204,316.0	210,467.0 (2018)
New Zealand	94,126	94,822	96,848 (2020)	...	...	...	21,452.0	23,295.0	25,293.0 (2017)

... = data not available; ADB = Asian Development Bank; km = kilometer; t = metric ton.

Source: Asian Development Bank. Asian Transport Outlook Database. https://data.adb.org/dataset/asian-transport-outlook-database (accessed 23 March 2021).

Table 2.5.2: Road Indicators—Registered Vehicles

ADB Regional Member	2010	2015	2016	2017	2018	2019
Developing ADB Member Economies						
Central and West Asia						
Afghanistan	1,238,332 (2011)	1,887,263	1,906,938	1,936,686	1,951,428	1,980,033
Armenia	...	...	...	...	...	...
Azerbaijan	...	...	...	...	...	...
Georgia	702,700	1,081,400	1,167,200	1,228,100	1,289,100	1,339,300
Kazakhstan	...	...	...	...	...	...
Kyrgyz Republic	...	...	...	...	...	...
Pakistan	7,853,002	17,826,048	21,057,912	23,869,867	26,570,320	...
Tajikistan	...	...	...	...	...	...
Turkmenistan	...	...	...	...	...	...
Uzbekistan	...	...	...	...	...	...
East Asia						
China, People's Republic of	...	...	...	...	...	...
Hong Kong, China	664,726	798,316	818,316	840,597	865,661	879,154
Korea, Republic of	...	23,151,659	23,984,039	24,724,770	25,410,979	25,981,535 (2020)
Mongolia	608,274 (2012)	789,720	841,552	900,145	970,880	1,043,028
Taipei,China	22,226,684	21,510,650	21,704,365	21,871,240	22,111,807	...
South Asia						
Bangladesh	1,509,028	2,463,298	2,879,708	3,300,094	3,797,466	4,301,596
Bhutan	53,382	75,190	84,297	92,008	100,544	...
India	127,745,972	210,023,289	230,030,598	253,311,000	...	...
Maldives	46,028	77,776	87,126	97,213	108,532	...
Nepal	1,178,911	2,339,169	2,783,428	3,221,042	3,539,519	...
Sri Lanka	3,954,311	6,302,141	6,795,469	7,247,122	7,727,921	8,095,224
Southeast Asia						
Brunei Darussalam	113,655	267,281	277,332	277,200	282,265	289,978
Cambodia	...	...	...	...	...	...
Indonesia	76,907,127	120,786,914	128,069,103	130,562,687	140,785,726	126,416,772
Lao People's Democratic Republic	1,008,788	1,717,144	1,850,020	1,979,606	2,105,207	2,233,685
Malaysia	20,188,565	26,301,952	27,613,259	28,738,176	29,956,525	31,214,871
Myanmar	2,147,404	5,077,699	5,541,361	6,337,002	6,853,995	7,092,843
Philippines	6,634,855	8,706,607	9,251,565	10,410,814	11,595,434	11,851,192 (2020)
Singapore	945,829	957,246	956,430	961,842	957,006	973,990 (2020)
Thailand	28,484,829	36,731,023	39,124,339	38,308,763	...	41,388,896 (2020)
Timor-Leste	10,940	17,801	19,498	21,969	23,974	...
Viet Nam	1,274,000	2,107,000	2,516,000	2,902,000	...	...
The Pacific						
Cook Islands	...	...	...	...	...	...
Fiji	81,926	101,425	110,763	117,623	119,960	...
Kiribati	...	...	...	...	...	...
Marshall Islands	2,464 (2008)	...	...	...	...	...
Micronesia, Federated States of	7,662	8,509	9,160	8,584	9,777	11,807
Nauru	1,737 (2011)	...	...	...	...	...
Niue	926 (2011)	1,785 (2014)	...	...	...	...
Palau	5,643	5,832 (2014)	...	...	...	...
Papua New Guinea	...	...	...	...	...	...
Samoa	16,394 (2011)	17,449 (2013)	...	...	...	...
Solomon Islands	...	...	...	...	...	...
Tonga	19,432	...	...	...	...	...
Tuvalu	...	...	...	...	...	...
Vanuatu	5,368 (2009)	...	...	...	...	...
Developed ADB Member Economies						
Australia	16,061,100	18,007,600	18,387,200	18,781,100	19,173,300	19,505,100
Japan	78,473,135	80,670,393	80,900,730	81,260,206	81,563,101	81,849,782 (2020)
New Zealand	3,414,904	3,811,378	3,971,485	4,137,704	4,275,026	4,403,690

... = data not available, ADB = Asian Development Bank.

Source: Asian Development Bank. Asian Transport Outlook Database. https://data.adb.org/dataset/asian-transport-outlook-database (accessed 23 March 2021).

Table 2.5.3: Road Indicators—Safety

ADB Regional Member	Estimated Road Traffic Deaths, 2016		Road User Deaths, 2016 (%)				
	Total	Death Rate (per 100,000 population)	Four-Wheeled Vehicles	Two- and Three-Wheeled Vehicles	Cyclists	Pedestrians	Others
Developing ADB Member Economies							
Central and West Asia	**44,846**	**14.3**					
Afghanistan	5,230	15.1	...	...	...	...	...
Armenia	499	17.1	59.6	1.5	0.4	34.8	3.7
Azerbaijan	845	8.7	51.8	0.9	0.9	42.0	4.3
Georgia	599	15.3	44.9	0.5	0.7	26.5	27.4
Kazakhstan	3,158	17.6	59.8	4.3	1.7	30.9	3.3
Kyrgyz Republic	916	15.4	27.6	2.1	0.2	40.0	30.0
Pakistan	27,582	14.3	...	...	...	...	...
Tajikistan	1,577	18.1	57.4	...	2.3	40.3	–
Turkmenistan	823	14.5	...	...	...	...	...
Uzbekistan	3,617	11.5	...	...	...	...	...
East Asia[a]	**261,669**	**17.9**					
China, People's Republic of	256,180	18.2	...	...	...	...	...
Hong Kong, China	...	...	...	...	...	...	...
Korea, Republic of	4,990	9.8	...	20.5	5.9	39.9	33.7
Mongolia	499	16.5	39.3	18.6	1.2	28.7	12.2
Taipei,China	...	...	...	...	...	...	...
South Asia	**331,906**	**21.6**					
Bangladesh	24,954	15.3	...	...	...	...	...
Bhutan	139	17.4	...	...	...	...	...
India	299,091	22.6	17.9	39.6	1.7	10.4	30.4
Maldives	4	0.9	–	75.0	–	25.0	–
Nepal	4,622	15.9	...	...	...	...	...
Sri Lanka	3,096	14.9	6.2	50.8	8.1	29.2	5.7
Southeast Asia[a]	**114,030**	**17.8**					
Brunei Darussalam	...	...	...	...	...	...	...
Cambodia	2,803	17.8	6.2	73.5	2.3	9.6	8.4
Indonesia	31,726	12.2	4.9	73.6	3.2	15.5	2.7
Lao People's Democratic Republic	1,120	16.6	...	...	...	...	...
Malaysia	7,374	23.6	...	...	...	...	...
Myanmar	10,540	19.9	10.8	64.8	3.1	14.2	7.1
Philippines	12,690	12.3	0.3	4.7	0.1	1.0	93.9
Singapore	155	2.8	7.8	44.0	14.2	33.3	0.7
Thailand	22,491	32.7	12.3	74.4	3.5	7.6	2.3
Timor-Leste	161	12.7	...	...	...	...	...
Viet Nam	24,970	26.4	...	...	...	...	...
The Pacific[a]	**1,428**	**13.7**					
Cook Islands	3	17.3	20.0	80.0	–	–	–
Fiji	86	9.6	63.3	...	...	36.7	–
Kiribati	5	4.4	40.0	20.0	–	40.0	–
Marshall Islands	...	...	...	...	...	...	...
Micronesia, Federated States of	2	1.9	50.0	–	–	50.0	–
Nauru	...	...	...	...	...	...	...
Niue	...	...	...	...	...	...	...
Palau	...	...	...	...	...	...	–
Papua New Guinea	1,145	14.2	52.5	...	...	47.5	–
Samoa	22	11.3	41.2	–	5.9	47.1	5.9
Solomon Islands	104	17.4	...	...	...	...	...
Tonga	18	16.8	66.7	–	–	27.8	5.6
Tuvalu	...	...	...	...	...	...	...
Vanuatu	43	15.9	...	...	...	...	...
Developed ADB Member Economies	**6,939**	**4.4**					
Australia	1,351	5.6	60.9	19.3	2.2	14.0	3.5
Japan	5,224	4.1	32.4	17.2	15.1	35.0	1.0
New Zealand	364	7.8	68.5	15.9	1.5	7.6	6.4
DEVELOPING ADB MEMBER ECONOMIES[a]	**753,879**	**19.0**					
ALL ADB REGIONAL MEMBERS[a]	**760,818**	**18.4**					

... = data not available, – = magnitude equals zero; ADB = Asian Development Bank.

a Regional aggregates include reporting economies only.

Source: World Health Organization. 2018. Global Status Report on Road Safety 2018. Geneva.

Table 2.5.4: Rail Indicators—Total Route and Length per Land Area

ADB Regional Member	Rail Lines, Total Route (km)			Rail Network, Length per Land Area (km per km^2 '000)		
	2010	2015	2019	2010	2015	2019
Developing ADB Member Economies						
Central and West Asia						
Afghanistan	106.0 (2011)	106.0	123.0 (2017)	0.2 (2011)	0.2	0.2 (2017)
Armenia	871.1	823.6	793.4	30.6	28.9	27.9
Azerbaijan	2,792.0	2,446.0	2,490.0	33.8	29.6	30.1
Georgia	1,566.0	1,576.0	1,576.0	22.5	22.7	22.7
Kazakhstan	13,848.0	14,492.0	15,785.7 (2018)	5.1	5.4	5.8 (2018)
Kyrgyz Republic	...	...	...	...	...	...
Pakistan	7,791.0	7,791.0	7,791.0 (2017)	10.1	10.1	10.1 (2017)
Tajikistan	...	...	...	...	...	...
Turkmenistan	...	...	...	...	...	...
Uzbekistan	4,227.2	4,238.0	4,642.0 (2017)	9.9	10.0	10.9 (2017)
East Asia						
China, People's Republic of	91,200.0	121,000.0	139,900.0	9.7	12.9	14.9
Hong Kong, China	...	...	...	...	...	...
Korea, Republic of	...	...	...	...	...	...
Mongolia	...	1,810.0 (2016)	1,100.0	...	1.2 (2016)	0.7
Taipei,China	1,085.0	1,065.0	1,065.0	30.0	29.4	29.4
South Asia						
Bangladesh	2,460.0	2,877.0	2,956.0 (2018)	18.9	22.1	22.7 (2018)
Bhutan	...	...	...	...	...	...
India	64,460.0	66,252.0	67,415.0 (2018)	21.7	22.3	22.7 (2018)
Maldives	...	...	...	...	...	...
Nepal	...	...	...	...	...	...
Sri Lanka	1,263.0	1,568.0	...	20.1	25.0	...
Southeast Asia						
Brunei Darussalam	...	...	...	...	...	...
Cambodia	650.0	650.0	650.0 (2020)	3.7	3.7	3.7
Indonesia	4,816.4	5,286.0	6,221.7	2.7	2.9	3.4
Lao People's Democratic Republic	...	...	...	...	...	...
Malaysia	1,792.0	1,775.0	1,775.0 (2018)	5.5	5.4	5.4 (2018)
Myanmar	5,487.8	6,107.4	6,112.3	8.4	9.4	9.4
Philippines	452.0	452.0	452.0 (2020)	1.5	1.5	1.5
Singapore	...	...	...	...	...	...
Thailand	4,507.9	4,507.9	4,801.3 (2020)	8.8	8.8	8.8
Timor-Leste	...	...	...	...	...	...
Viet Nam	2,577.0	3,147.0	3,163.0 (2018)	8.3	10.1	10.2 (2018)
The Pacific						
Cook Islands	...	...	...	...	...	...
Fiji	...	590.0 (2014)	...	...	32.3 (2014)	...
Kiribati	...	...	...	...	...	...
Marshall Islands	...	...	...	...	...	...
Micronesia, Federated States of	...	...	...	...	...	...
Nauru	...	...	...	...	...	...
Niue	...	...	...	...	...	...
Palau	...	...	...	...	...	...
Papua New Guinea	...	...	...	...	...	...
Samoa	...	...	...	...	...	...
Solomon Islands	...	...	...	...	...	...
Tonga	...	...	...	...	...	...
Tuvalu	...	...	...	...	...	...
Vanuatu	...	...	...	...	...	...
Developed ADB Member Economies						
Australia	...	33,343.0	32,894.0	...	4.3	4.3
Japan	...	...	...	...	...	...
New Zealand	...	...	3,700.0	...	...	14.1

... = data not available; ADB = Asian Development Bank; km = kilometer; km^2 = square kilometer.

Sources: For Rail Lines: Asian Development Bank. Asian Transport Outlook Database. https://data.adb.org/dataset/asian-transport-outlook-database (accessed 23 March 2021). For Rail Network: Asian Development Bank estimates. For Land Area: World Bank. World Development Indicators. https://data.worldbank.org/indicator (accessed 2 June 2021)

Table 2.5.5: Rail Indicators—Passengers Carried and Goods Transported

ADB Regional Member	Passengers Carried[a] (p-km million)			Goods Transported[b] (t-km million)		
	2010	2015	2019	2010	2015	2019
Developing ADB Member Economies						
Central and West Asia						
Afghanistan	...	...	...	...	...	...
Armenia	125.6	104.3	145.4	743.2	640.3	863.8
Azerbaijan	2,747.0	2,945.0	3,156.0	8,331.0	6,269.0	5,211.0
Georgia	5,884.6	6,756.0	7,545.1	6,227.5	4,261.3	2,935.0
Kazakhstan	16,281.5	17,179.5	18,679.4 (2018)	213,200.0	267,362.0	283,345.2 (2018)
Kyrgyz Republic	98.7	40.8	37.1	737.7	917.8	870.4
Pakistan	...	...	...	1,757.3	4,773.5	8,080.4 (2017)
Tajikistan	...	...	1.7 (2017)	10,445.6	6,125.6	5,348.1 (2018)
Turkmenistan	1,685.0	...	...	9,715.0	...	...
Uzbekistan	3,500.0	4,180.5	4,983.3	22,300.0	22,934.9	23,444.6
East Asia						
China, People's Republic of	876,220.0	1,196,060.0	1,470,660.0	2,764,410.0	2,375,430.0	3,018,200.0
Hong Kong, China	...	...	...	...	...	...
Korea, Republic of	58,381.8	68,371.0	90,011.4 (2017)	9,452.4	9,479.3	7,357.0
Mongolia	1,220.0	996.7	1,111.5	10,286.7	11,462.6	17,384.1
Taipei,China	20,930.8	27,110.9	30,455.6	866.3	634.2	516.6
South Asia						
Bangladesh	8,253.0 (2012)	8,711.0	12,994.0 (2017)	693.0	694.0	1,237.0 (2017)
Bhutan	...	...	...	...	...	...
India	978,508.0	1,149,835.0 (2016)	1,157,174.0 (2018)	...	...	...
Maldives	...	...	...	...	...	...
Nepal	...	...	...	...	...	...
Sri Lanka	4,568.0	7,407.0	7,495.0 (2017)	162.8	127.4	145.0 (2017)
Southeast Asia						
Brunei Darussalam	...	...	...	...	...	...
Cambodia	...	...	...	...	...	...
Indonesia	20,340.0	22,296.0	29,066.0	6,559.0	10,057.0	15,573.0
Lao People's Democratic Republic	...	3.0	0.2	...	...	...
Malaysia	1,532.2	426.1	196.3 (2018)	1,482.8	1,474.5	1,233.2 (2018)
Myanmar	5,371.4	3,416.2	1,444.2	1,059.4	812.3	362.8
Philippines	...	...	...	...	...	...
Singapore	7,880.0	9,391.0 (2014)	...	...	...	...
Thailand	846.0	6,133.4	5,906.5 (2018)	...	2,545.3	2,769.1 (2018)
Timor-Leste	...	...	...	...	...	...
Viet Nam	4,377.9	4,149.6	3,170.5	3,960.9	4,035.5	3,763.2
The Pacific						
Cook Islands	...	...	...	...	...	...
Fiji	...	...	...	...	...	...
Kiribati	...	...	...	...	...	...
Marshall Islands	...	...	...	...	...	...
Micronesia, Federated States of	...	...	...	...	...	...
Nauru	...	...	...	...	...	...
Niue	...	...	...	...	...	...
Palau	...	...	...	...	...	...
Papua New Guinea	...	...	...	...	...	...
Samoa	...	...	...	...	...	...
Solomon Islands	...	...	...	...	...	...
Tonga	...	...	...	...	...	...
Tuvalu	...	...	...	...	...	...
Vanuatu	...	...	...	...	...	...
Developed ADB Member Economies						
Australia	14,990.0	16,020.0	17,590.0 (2018)	258,600.0	401,600.0	...
Japan	393,466.0	427,486.2	441,614.0 (2018)	20,398.0	21,519.0	19,992.5
New Zealand	...	...	...	4,768.0 (2012)	4,348.5	3,830.0

... = data not available; ADB = Asian Development Bank; p-km = passenger-kilometer; t-km = ton-kilometer.

a A passenger-kilometer, abbreviated as p-km, is a unit of measurement representing the transport of 1 passenger by a defined mode of transport over 1 kilometer.
b A ton-kilometer, abbreviated as t-km, is a unit of measurement representing the transport of 1 metric ton of goods (including packaging and tare weights of intermodal transport units) by a defined mode of transport over 1 kilometer. Only the distance on the national territory of the reporting economy is taken into account for national, international, and transit transport.

Source: Asian Development Bank. Asian Transport Outlook Database. https://data.adb.org/dataset/asian-transport-outlook-database (accessed 23 March 2021).

Table 2.5.6: Air Transport Indicators

ADB Regional Member	Aviation Passenger Transport[a] (p-km million)			Aviation Freight Transport[b] (t-km million)		
	2010	2015	2019	2010	2015	2019
Developing ADB Member Economies						
Central and West Asia						
Afghanistan	...	...	...	...	...	...
Armenia	1,278.6	27.4 (2016)	290.3	9.7	2.0 (2014)	0.3
Azerbaijan	1,613.0	3,338.0	4,750.0	139.0	582.0	947.0
Georgia	368.9	548.9	1,278.0	0.9	41.3	268.6
Kazakhstan	6,469.2	11,153.3	14,989.7 (2018)	90.1	42.7	57.6 (2018)
Kyrgyz Republic	814.2	1,966.1	1,707.0	64.4	57.4	8.5
Pakistan	...	...	...	206.7	181.4	159.4 (2017)
Tajikistan	...	...	193.4 (2017)	2.2	2.1	1.5 (2018)
Turkmenistan	2,712.0	...	...	29.0	...	...
Uzbekistan	5,800.0	6,786.0	10,998.1	168.0	131.1	119.0
East Asia						
China, People's Republic of	403,899.6	...	1,170,529.7	17,890.0	20,807.0	26,320.0
Hong Kong, China	...	...	...	...	...	...
Korea, Republic of	135,770.8	198,443.4	243,641.3 (2017)	145.0	112.0	...
Mongolia	907.2	1,993.5	3,109.4	4.2	7.7	13.9
Taipei,China	60,051.2	80,054.8	98,963.8	11,873.3	9,079.7	8,846.3
South Asia						
Bangladesh	5,027.0	6,645.0	7,072.0 (2018)	123.0	199.0	183.0 (2017)
Bhutan	...	...	...	...	...	...
India	103,171.0	145,787.0	...	...	...	...
Maldives	...	...	...	...	...	...
Nepal	...	...	...	62.8	69.4	...
Sri Lanka	9,399.6	12,737.3	...	1,472.7	1,146.4	...
Southeast Asia						
Brunei Darussalam	...	...	...	...	...	...
Cambodia	...	...	...	8.0 (2011)	...	...
Indonesia	75,805.2	88,464.9	124,612.7 (2018)	11,591.5	5,940.6	7,794.0 (2018)
Lao People's Democratic Republic	82.8	846.1	1,970.0	1.2	0.4	2.6
Malaysia	66,719.0	87,210.0	112,516.0 (2018)	...	...	...
Myanmar	566.1	1,452.2	1,639.9	1.3	5.0	5.1
Philippines	...	...	...	...	...	...
Singapore	...	...	...	...	...	...
Thailand	...	...	...	29,309.0	27,221.0	24,232.0
Timor-Leste	...	...	...	...	...	...
Viet Nam	21,162.0	42,068.4	77,183.9	426.8	599.5	1,169.1
The Pacific						
Cook Islands	...	...	...	...	...	...
Fiji	...	...	...	...	...	...
Kiribati	...	...	...	...	...	...
Marshall Islands	...	...	...	...	...	...
Micronesia, Federated States of	...	...	...	...	...	...
Nauru	...	...	...	...	...	...
Niue	...	...	...	...	...	...
Palau	...	...	...	...	...	...
Papua New Guinea	...	...	...	...	...	...
Samoa	...	...	...	...	...	...
Solomon Islands	...	...	...	...	...	...
Tonga	...	...	...	...	...	...
Tuvalu	...	...	...	...	...	...
Vanuatu	...	...	...	...	...	...
Developed ADB Member Economies						
Australia	60,220.0	70,130.0	73,480.0 (2018)	300.0	300.0	300.0 (2018)
Japan	133,649.0	172,984.0	199,012.0 (2018)	7,339.1	8,766.4	8,771.0 (2018)
New Zealand	...	...	...	...	...	...

... = data not available; ADB = Asian Development Bank; p-km = passenger-kilometer; t-km = ton-kilometer.

a A passenger-kilometer, abbreviated as p-km, is a unit of measurement representing the transport of 1 passenger by a defined mode of transport over 1 kilometer. For air transport, it includes both domestic and international flights.

b A ton-kilometer, abbreviated as t-km, is a unit of measurement representing the transport of 1 metric ton of goods (including packaging and tare weights of intermodal transport units) by a defined mode of transport over 1 kilometer. For air transport, it includes both domestic and international flights.

Source: Asian Development Bank. Asian Transport Outlook Database. https://data.adb.org/dataset/asian-transport-outlook-database (accessed 23 March 2021).

Table 2.5.7: Logistics

ADB Regional Member	Container Port Traffic (teu '000)			Liner Shipping Connectivity Index[a]			Logistics Performance Index[b]		
	2010	2015	2019	2010	2015	2019	2012	2016	2018
Developing ADB Member Economies									
Central and West Asia									
Afghanistan	...	...	...	...	...	...	2.3	2.1	1.9
Armenia	...	...	...	...	...	...	2.6	2.2	2.6
Azerbaijan	...	...	...	...	...	...	2.5	...	...
Georgia	210	222	277	5.3	5.7	6.8	...	2.4	2.4
Kazakhstan	...	...	...	...	...	...	2.7	2.8	2.8
Kyrgyz Republic	...	...	...	...	...	...	2.4	2.2	2.5
Pakistan	2,149	2,756	3,368	31.6	32.9	34.1	2.8	2.9	2.4
Tajikistan	...	...	...	...	...	...	2.3	2.1	2.3
Turkmenistan	...	...	...	...	...	...	...	2.2	2.4
Uzbekistan	...	...	...	...	...	...	2.5	2.4	2.6
East Asia									
China, People's Republic of	131,989	193,734	242,030	121.2	138.9	151.9	3.5	3.7	3.6
Hong Kong, China	23,600	20,114	18,360	91.0	94.2	89.5	4.1	4.1	3.9
Korea, Republic of	18,520	25,477	28,955	74.5	98.3	105.1	3.7	3.7	3.6
Mongolia	...	...	...	...	...	...	2.3	2.5	2.4
Taipei,China	12,497	14,492	15,298	...	...	...	...	...	...
South Asia									
Bangladesh	1,350	2,045	2,660	7.3	11.0	13.3	...	2.7	2.6
Bhutan	...	...	...	...	...	...	2.5	2.3	2.2
India	8,890	11,883	17,053	47.6	49.4	55.5	3.1	3.4	3.2
Maldives	50	84	108	6.2	3.1	7.4	2.5	2.5	2.7
Nepal	...	...	...	...	...	...	2.0	2.4	2.5
Sri Lanka	4,100	5,185	7,230	37.5	49.2	62.1	2.8	...	2.6
Southeast Asia									
Brunei Darussalam	93	128	282	5.1	4.9	7.7	...	2.9	2.7
Cambodia	286	474	779	6.1	7.6	8.0	2.6	2.8	2.6
Indonesia	9,010	12,032	14,764	33.0	35.7	44.4	2.9	3.0	3.2
Lao People's Democratic Republic	...	...	...	...	...	...	2.5	2.1	2.7
Malaysia	16,843	24,013	26,215	72.3	92.2	93.8	3.5	3.4	3.2
Myanmar	335	827	1,122	5.6	9.1	8.5	2.4	2.5	2.3
Philippines	5,589	7,210	8,984	21.2	22.4	30.6	3.0	2.9	2.9
Singapore	29,147	31,710	37,983	92.4	101.0	108.1	4.1	4.1	4.0
Thailand	6,819	9,463	10,756	40.5	42.5	52.9	3.2	3.3	3.4
Timor-Leste	37	49	53	1.6	5.8	2.9	...	...	...
Viet Nam	6,430	11,090	13,659	41.2	48.4	66.5	3.0	3.0	3.3
The Pacific									
Cook Islands	4	17	8	...	...	...	...	...	...
Fiji	257	255	146	12.8	12.7	11.2	2.4	2.3	2.4
Kiribati	30	35	52	...	...	...	...	...	...
Marshall Islands	20	42	31	3.8	5.7	4.9	...	...	...
Micronesia, Federated States of	7	10	25	...	...	...	...	...	...
Nauru	3 (2011)	9	5	1.3 (2011)	2.5	2.2	...	...	...
Niue	3 (2011)	4	4	...	...	...	...	...	...
Palau	24	24	16	3.9	3.9	3.4	...	...	...
Papua New Guinea	283	276	338	8.5	12.7	12.6	...	2.5	2.2
Samoa	22	28	27	...	...	...	...	...	...
Solomon Islands	63	196	128	6.3	11.2	10.7	...	2.4	2.6
Tonga	48	50	77	5.6	5.7	7.6	...	...	...
Tuvalu	2	14	5	1.0	3.0	2.0	...	...	...
Vanuatu	18	120	77	3.4	8.8	7.9	...	...	...
Developed ADB Member Economies									
Australia	6,372	7,621	8,282	30.8	32.5	34.3	3.7	...	3.8
Japan	18,966	20,138	21,709	72.4	74.8	71.2	3.9	4.0	4.0
New Zealand	2,331	3,119	3,444	21.3	23.4	31.9	3.4	3.4	3.9

... = data not available, ADB = Asian Development Bank, teu = twenty-foot equivalent unit.

a The Liner Shipping Connectivity Index captures how well economies are connected to global shipping networks. It is based on five components of the maritime transport sector: number of ships, their container-carrying capacity, maximum vessel size, number of services, and number of companies that deploy container ships in an economy's ports. The index generates a value of 100 for the economy with the highest average index in 2004.

b The index ranges from 1 to 5, with higher scores representing better performance.

Source: Asian Development Bank. Asian Transport Outlook Database. https://data.adb.org/dataset/asian-transport-outlook-database (accessed 23 March 2021).

Table 2.5.8: Access to Fixed Telephones, Mobile Phones, and Internet—Total Subscriptions
('000)

ADB Regional Member	Fixed Telephone Subscribers 2010	Fixed Telephone Subscribers 2019	Mobile Phone Subscribers 2010	Mobile Phone Subscribers 2019	Fixed Broadband Subscribers 2010	Fixed Broadband Subscribers 2019
Developing ADB Member Economies						
Central and West Asia[a]	**16,633.0**	**15,422.6**	**13,325.6**	**181,113.9**	**237,324.1**	**294,740.7**
Afghanistan	16.6	110.0	134.6	10,215.8	19,709.0	22,580.1
Armenia	592.3	551.4	451.6	3,865.4	3,464.5	3,618.7
Azerbaijan	1,506.6	1,796.0	1,673.2	9,100.1	10,697.1	10,750.3
Georgia	1,111.9	950.2	518.6	3,978.2	5,550.7	5,384.5
Kazakhstan	4,057.6	4,147.8	3,072.5	19,402.6	26,309.3	25,717.7
Kyrgyz Republic	489.1	408.0	298.9	5,275.5	7,579.4	8,622.6
Pakistan	6,079.1	3,537.6	2,461.9	99,185.8	125,899.6	165,405.8
Tajikistan	367.7	457.0	479.0 (2017)	5,940.8	8,489.0	9,904.0 (2017)
Turkmenistan	520.0	648.0	682.0 (2017)	3,197.6	7,842.0	9,377.0 (2017)
Uzbekistan	1,892.2	2,816.6	3,553.3	20,952.0	21,783.3	33,380.0
East Asia	**343,914.6**	**278,382.5**	**233,113.3**	**953,914.0**	**1,400,393.4**	**1,870,296.7**
China, People's Republic of	294,383.0	230,996.0	191,033.0	859,003.0	1,291,984.2	1,746,238.0
Hong Kong, China	4,361.7	4,331.7	4,029.6	13,793.7	16,724.4	21,455.7
Korea, Republic of	28,543.2	28,882.8	24,727.4	50,767.2	58,935.1	68,892.5
Mongolia	193.2	255.6	351.4	2,510.5	3,068.2	4,418.9
Taipei,China	16,433.5	13,916.3	12,971.9	27,839.5	29,681.5	29,291.5
South Asia[a]	**40,845.6**	**30,562.6**	**25,583.3**	**847,557.4**	**1,185,263.0**	**1,388,566.7**
Bangladesh	1,280.8	864.3	1,449.6	67,923.9	131,375.7	165,572.0
Bhutan	26.3	21.8	21.6	394.3	675.7	729.2
India	35,090.0	25,520.0	21,004.5	752,190.0	1,001,056.0	1,151,480.4
Maldives	28.4	21.9	16.7	494.4	739.8	828.0
Nepal	841.7	846.9	799.4 (2018)	9,195.6	27,516.1	39,178.5 (2018)
Sri Lanka	3,578.5	3,287.7	2,291.5	17,359.3	23,899.6	30,778.6
Southeast Asia[a]	**73,120.0**	**34,553.9**	**34,505.3**	**532,636.5**	**799,801.0**	**917,004.3**
Brunei Darussalam	79.9	76.0	86.6	435.1	463.4	574.8
Cambodia	358.9	256.4	56.4	8,150.8	20,850.5	21,418.7
Indonesia	40,931.1	10,378.0	9,662.1	211,290.2	338,948.3	341,277.5
Lao People's Democratic Republic	103.1	962.5	1,490.8	4,003.4	3,727.2	4,362.2
Malaysia	4,609.8	4,489.5	7,446.3	33,858.7	44,104.0	44,600.7
Myanmar	493.3	514.9	520.9 (2018)	594.0	40,993.7	61,144.0 (2018)
Philippines	3,335.4	3,223.8	4,255.8	83,150.1	117,838.1	167,322.4
Singapore	1,996.1	2,016.1	1,911.2	7,384.6	8,233.1	9,034.3
Thailand	6,835.1	5,309.0	5,415.0	71,726.3	102,942.0	129,614.0
Timor-Leste	2.9	2.7	2.1	473.0	1,376.7	1,425.3
Viet Nam	14,374.4	7,324.9	3,658.0	111,570.2	120,324.1	136,230.4
The Pacific[a]	**340.7**	**278.0**	**276.8**	**3,105.0**	**5,438.2**	**6,107.9**
Cook Islands	7.2	6.5 (2016)	6.6 (2017)	7.8	13.9 (2016)	14.5 (2017)
Fiji	129.8	72.6	76.5 (2018)	697.9	966.0	1,033.9 (2017)
Kiribati	8.4	1.5	0.8 (2017)	10.6	41.0	54.7
Marshall Islands	...	2.4 (2014)	...	...	15.5	16.0 (2017)
Micronesia, Federated States of	8.5	6.8	6.9 (2017)	27.5	22.5	23.1 (2017)
Nauru	...	...	...	6.2	9.4	10.0 (2017)
Niue	1.0	1.0	...	...	...	...
Palau	7.0	7.2	...	14.5	23.7	...
Papua New Guinea	121.2	150.0	158.0 (2017)	1,909.1	3,560.0	4,018.0 (2017)
Samoa	8.0	11.5	8.5 (2017)	90.0	120.5	124.2 (2017)
Solomon Islands	8.4	7.4	7.1	115.5	424.7	478.1
Tonga	31.0	13.2	6.6	54.3	73.5	62.1
Tuvalu	1.2	2.0	2.0 (2017)	1.6	6.6	8.0 (2017)
Vanuatu	7.1	4.8	3.8	169.9	174.8	265.2
Developed ADB Member Economies[a]	**78,123.7**	**74,055.6**	**72,323.2**	**150,497.1**	**191,929.7**	**220,794.1**
Australia	10,625.0	8,500.0	7,820.0	22,500.0	25,770.0	27,880.0
Japan	65,618.7	63,705.6	62,743.2	123,287.1	160,559.7	186,514.1
New Zealand	1,880.0	1,850.0	1,760.0 (2018)	4,710.0	5,600.0	6,400.0 (2018)
DEVELOPING ADB MEMBER ECONOMIES[a]	**474,856.2**	**359,210.3**	**306,816.7**	**2,518,342.9**	**3,628,234.2**	**4,476,740.6**
ALL ADB REGIONAL MEMBERS[a]	**552,980.0**	**433,265.9**	**379,139.9**	**2,668,840.0**	**3,820,163.9**	**4,697,534.7**

... = data not available, 0.0 = magnitude is less than half of unit employed, – = magnitude equals zero, ADB = Asian Development Bank.

a Regional aggregates are calculated as the sum of the reporting economies. Imputation was done for economies with missing data by substituting available data from the closest years.

Source: International Telecommunication Union. World Telecommunication/ICT Indicators Database. http://www.itu.int/en/ITU-D/Statistics/Pages/stat/default.aspx (accessed 20 May 2021).

Communications

Table 2.5.9: Access to Fixed Telephones, Mobile Phones, and Internet—Subscriptions per 100 People

ADB Regional Member	Fixed Telephone			Mobile Cellular			Fixed Broadband			Internet Users		
	2010	2015	2019	2010	2015	2019	2010	2015	2019	2010	2015	2019
Developing ADB Member Economies												
Central and West Asia[a]	**5.8**	**4.8**	**3.7**	**63.0**	**74.4**	**83.6**	**0.9**	**2.8**	**3.8**			
Afghanistan	0.1	0.3	0.4	35.0	57.3	59.4	0.0	0.0	0.1	4.0	8.3	11.4(2017)
Armenia	20.6	18.8	15.3	134.3	118.4	122.3	3.3	9.8	13.0	25.0	59.1	66.5
Azerbaijan	16.7	18.7	16.7	100.7	111.2	107.0	5.3	19.7	19.3	46.0	77.0	81.1
Georgia	27.1	23.6	13.0	97.1	137.9	134.7	4.5	15.8	23.6	26.9	47.6	68.8
Kazakhstan	25.0	23.6	16.6	119.4	149.7	138.6	5.4	13.1	13.5	31.6	70.8	81.9
Kyrgyz Republic	9.0	6.8	4.7	97.3	127.2	134.4	0.4	3.5	4.2	16.3	30.2	38.2(2017)
Pakistan	3.4	1.8	1.1	55.3	63.1	76.4	0.4	0.9	0.8	8.0	14.0	17.1
Tajikistan	4.9	5.4	5.4(2017)	78.9	100.4	111.5(2017)	0.1	0.1	0.1(2017)	11.6	19.0	22.0(2017)
Turkmenistan	10.2	11.6	11.8(2017)	62.9	140.9	162.9(2017)	0.0	0.1	0.1(2017)	3.0	15.0	21.3(2017)
Uzbekistan	6.6	9.1	10.8	73.5	70.4	101.2	0.4	5.8	13.9	15.9	42.8	55.2(2018)
East Asia[a]	**23.7**	**18.7**	**15.3**	**65.7**	**93.9**	**123.1**	**10.4**	**20.5**	**31.6**			
China, People's Republic of	21.5	16.4	13.3	62.8	91.8	121.8	9.2	19.7	31.3	34.3	50.3	64.6(2020)
Hong Kong, China	62.6	60.3	54.2	198.0	232.7	288.5	31.1	32.7	37.7	72.0	84.9	91.7
Korea, Republic of	57.6	56.8	48.3	102.5	116.0	134.5	34.7	39.4	42.8	83.7	89.9	96.2
Mongolia	7.1	8.5	10.9	92.3	102.3	137.0	2.8	6.9	9.8	10.2	22.5	51.1
Taipei,China	70.9	59.1	54.6	120.1	126.0	123.2	22.9	24.0	24.5	71.5	78.0	88.8
South Asia[a]	**2.9**	**2.0**	**1.6**	**59.3**	**78.2**	**86.9**	**0.8**	**1.5**	**1.9**			
Bangladesh	0.9	0.6	0.9	46.0	84.1	101.5	0.3	3.1	5.0	3.7	14.4	12.9
Bhutan	3.8	3.0	2.8	57.5	92.8	95.6	1.3	3.8	1.1	13.6	39.8	...
India	2.8	1.9	1.5	60.9	76.4	84.3	0.9	1.3	1.4	7.5	17.0	20.1(2018)
Maldives	7.8	4.8	3.1	135.2	162.6	156.0	4.3	5.1	10.0	26.5	54.5	63.2(2017)
Nepal	3.1	3.1	2.8(2018)	34.0	101.9	139.4(2018)	0.2	1.1	2.8(2018)	7.9	17.6	21.4(2017)
Sri Lanka	17.7	15.7	10.7	85.7	114.3	144.3	1.1	3.0	7.8	12.0	12.1	34.1(2017)
Southeast Asia[a]	**12.3**	**5.5**	**5.6**	**89.2**	**126.1**	**140.8**	**2.5**	**4.0**	**7.6**			
Brunei Darussalam	20.6	18.3	20.0	112.0	111.7	132.7	5.6	8.3	12.5	53.0	71.2	95.0
Cambodia	2.5	1.7	0.3	56.9	134.3	129.9	0.2	0.5	1.1	1.3	6.4	40.5(2018)
Indonesia	16.9	4.0	3.6	87.4	131.2	126.1	0.9	1.5	3.8	10.9	22.1	47.7
Lao People's Democratic Republic	1.6	14.3	20.8	64.1	55.3	60.8	0.1	0.2	1.1	7.0	18.2	25.5(2017)
Malaysia	16.3	14.8	23.3	120.0	145.7	139.6	7.4	10.1	9.3	56.3	71.1	84.2
Myanmar	1.0	1.0	1.0(2018)	1.2	77.8	113.8(2018)	0.0	0.1	0.2(2018)	0.3	21.7	23.6(2017)
Philippines[b]	3.5	3.2	3.9	88.5	115.4	154.8	1.9(2011)	2.8	5.5	25.0	36.0	43.0
Singapore	38.9	36.1	32.9	143.9	147.2	155.6	26.1	26.6	25.9	71.0	79.0	88.9
Thailand	10.2	7.7	7.8	106.7	149.8	186.2	4.8	9.1	14.5	22.4	39.3	66.7
Timor-Leste	0.3	0.2	0.2	43.3	115.1	110.2	0.0	0.1	0.0	3.0	23.0	27.5(2017)
Viet Nam	16.3	7.9	3.8	126.8	129.8	141.2	4.2	8.3	15.3	30.7	45.0	68.7
The Pacific[a,c]	**3.4**	**2.6**	**2.6(2017)**	**31.4**	**50.0**	**54.0(2017)**	**0.4**	**0.4**	**0.4(2017)**			
Cook Islands[d]	39.3	37.1(2016)	37.6(2017)	42.4	79.0(2016)	83.0(2017)	9.1	15.1(2013)	...	35.7	51.0	...
Fiji	15.1	8.4	8.7(2018)	81.2	111.2	117.8(2017)	2.7	1.5	1.5(2018)	20.0	42.5	50.0(2017)
Kiribati	8.2	1.3	0.7(2017)	10.3	37.0	46.5	0.8	0.1	0.1	9.1	13.0	14.6(2017)
Marshall Islands[e]	...	4.1(2014)	...	...	27.0	27.6(2017)	...	1.7	1.7(2017)	7.0	19.3	38.7(2017)
Micronesia, Federated States of	8.2	6.3	6.2(2017)	26.7	20.7	20.7(2017)	1.0	3.0	3.4(2017)	20.0	31.5	35.3(2017)
Nauru[f]	19.1(2009)	...	...	62.0	90.5	94.6(2017)	9.5	...	...	54.0(2011)	62.4(2017)	62.4(2017)
Niue	61.8	61.8	...	...	...	...	...	...	...	77.0	...	...
Palau	38.9	40.8	...	80.8	134.4	...	1.3	6.9	...	...	...	...
Papua New Guinea	1.7	1.9	1.9(2017)	26.1	43.9	47.6(2017)	0.1	0.2	0.2(2017)	1.3	7.9	11.2(2017)
Samoa	4.3	5.9	4.3(2017)	48.4	62.3	63.6(2017)	0.1	1.1	0.9(2017)	7.0	25.4	33.6(2017)
Solomon Islands	1.6	1.2	1.1	21.9	70.4	71.4	0.5	0.2	0.2	5.0	10.0	11.9(2017)
Tonga	29.8	13.1	6.4	52.2	72.9	59.4	1.1	2.4	3.5	16.0	38.7	41.2(2017)
Tuvalu	11.4	18.0	17.6(2017)	15.2	59.5	70.4(2017)	2.3	4.1	4.0(2017)	25.0	42.7	49.3(2017)
Vanuatu	3.0	1.8	1.3	71.9	64.5	88.4	0.2	1.6	2.6	8.0	22.4	25.7(2017)
Developed ADB Member Economies[a]	**50.4**	**47.3**	**46.4**	**97.1**	**122.6**	**141.0**	**26.3**	**30.1**	**33.7**			
Australia	48.0	35.5	31.0	101.6	107.7	110.6	24.9	28.5	34.7	76.0	84.6	86.5(2017)
Japan	51.0	49.8	49.5	95.9	125.5	147.0	26.5	30.4	33.5	78.2	91.1	92.7
New Zealand	43.0	40.1	37.1(2018)	107.8	121.4	134.9(2018)	25.0	31.4	34.7(2018)	80.5	88.2	90.8(2017)
DEVELOPING ADB MEMBER ECONOMIES[a]	**12.6**	**9.1**	**7.6**	**66.7**	**91.4**	**108.5**	**4.8**	**9.1**	**14.2**			
ALL ADB REGIONAL MEMBERS[a]	**14.7**	**10.9**	**9.3**	**70.7**	**96.2**	**113.9**	**5.9**	**10.3**	**15.4**			

... = data not available, 0.0 = magnitude is less than half of unit employed, ADB = Asian Development Bank.

a Regional aggregates are derived from Table 2.5.8 regional aggregate levels and population data from World Population Prospects 2019.
b For fixed broadband, the figure for 2010 refers to 2011.
c All aggregates for the Pacific region for 2019 refer to 2017.
d For fixed telephone and mobile cellular, the figures for 2015 refer to 2016. For fixed broadband, the figure for 2015 refers to 2013.
e For fixed telephone, the figure for 2015 refer to 2014.
f For fixed telephone, the figure for 2010 refers to 2009. For internet users, the figure for 2010 refers to 2011 and the figure for 2015 refers to 2017.

Source: International Telecommunication Union. World Telecommunication/ICT Indicators Database. http://www.itu.int/en/ITU-D/Statistics/Pages/stat/default.aspx (accessed 20 May 2021). United Nations. World Population Prospects 2019. https://population.un.org/wpp/Download/Standard/Population/ (accessed 20 May 2021).

Data Issues and Comparability

Issues with data organization, collection, compilation, and dissemination affect the availability, quality, and timeliness of road statistics. Some regions, especially the Pacific, have incomplete or no data.

Most data on telephone and internet subscriptions came from questionnaires sent by the International Telecommunication Union to participating economies. Other information and reports were sourced from national ministries in charge of telecommunications and from staff estimates.

Table 2.6.1: Electricity Production and Sources

ADB Regional Member	Total Electricity Production (kWh billion)		Sources of Electricity (% of total): Combustible Fuels[a]		Hydropower		Solar		Others[b]	
	2010	2018	2010	2018	2010	2018	2010	2018	2010	2018
Developing ADB Member Economies										
Central and West Asia[c]	**310.1**	**408.9**	**67.7**	**73.5**	**30.4**	**22.4**	**-**	**0.2**	**1.9**	**3.8**
Afghanistan	0.9	1.6(2019)	14.0	11.5(2019)	86.0	87.2(2019)	–	1.3(2019)	–	–(2019)
Armenia	6.5	7.8	22.2	43.3	39.4	29.8	–	0.2	38.5	26.7
Azerbaijan	18.7	25.2	81.6	92.5	18.4	7.0	–	0.2	–	0.3
Georgia	10.1	11.9(2019)	6.8	24.0(2019)	93.2	75.3(2019)	–	–(2019)	–	0.7(2019)
Kazakhstan	82.6	107.1	90.3	89.8	9.7	9.6	–	0.1	–	0.4
Kyrgyz Republic	12.1	15.1(2019)	8.2	8.0(2019)	91.8	92.0(2019)	–	–(2019)	–	–(2019)
Pakistan	94.4	136.7(2019)	62.7	65.6(2019)	33.7	24.2(2019)	–	0.5(2019)	3.6	9.8(2019)
Tajikistan	16.4	19.7	0.2	6.8	99.8	93.2	–	–	–	–
Turkmenistan	16.7	22.5	100.0	100.0	–	–	–	–	–	–
Uzbekistan	51.7	63.0(2019)	79.0	89.7(2019)	21.0	10.3(2019)	–	0.0(2019)	–	0.0(2019)
East Asia[c]	**4,996.3**	**8,074.9**	**78.3**	**71.5**	**15.3**	**15.9**	**0.0**	**2.4**	**6.4**	**10.2**
China, People's Republic of	4,207.2	7,166.1	79.2	71.1	17.2	17.2	–	2.5	3.6	9.2
Hong Kong, China	38.3	36.6	100.0	100.0	–	–	–	–	–	–
Korea, Republic of	499.5	590.1	68.6	73.8	1.3	1.2	0.2	1.6	30.0	23.4
Mongolia	4.3	6.5	100.0	100.0	–	–	–	–	–	–
Taipei,China	247.1	274.1(2019)	...	...	...	...	...	...	...	...
South Asia[c]	**1,017.1**	**1,629.0**	**82.6**	**81.8**	**12.9**	**9.5**	**0.0**	**2.5**	**4.4**	**6.3**
Bangladesh	40.8	78.6	98.1	98.2	1.9	1.4	–	0.4	–	0.0
Bhutan	7.3	8.9(2019)	0.0	0.0(2019)	100.0	99.9(2019)	0.0	0.1(2019)	–	0.0(2019)
India	954.5	1,521.8	83.3	81.8	12.0	8.9	–	2.6	4.7	6.7
Maldives	0.4	0.8	99.2	97.9	–	–	0.2	1.8	0.5	0.3
Nepal	3.2	4.9	0.1	0.0	99.9	99.7	–	0.0	–	0.3
Sri Lanka	10.8	16.0	47.2	56.8	52.3	40.0	0.1	1.2	0.5	2.0
Southeast Asia[c]	**676.5**	**1,086.4**	**85.3**	**79.6**	**11.8**	**17.4**	**0.0**	**0.6**	**2.9**	**2.5**
Brunei Darussalam	3.8	4.3	100.0	100.0	–	–	–	0.0	–	–
Cambodia	1.0	8.2	96.5	41.8	3.2	58.0	0.3	0.2	–	–
Indonesia	169.6	293.2	84.2	88.7	10.3	6.7	0.0	0.0	5.5	4.5
Lao People's Democratic Republic	8.4	34.4	–	36.5	100.0	63.5	–	0.0	–	–
Malaysia	116.8	170.6	94.6	84.2	5.4	15.4	0.0	0.4	–	–
Myanmar	8.6	26.7	28.2	44.5	71.8	55.5	–	0.0	–	–
Philippines	67.8	106.4(2019)	73.7	80.2(2019)	11.5	7.6(2019)	0.0	1.2(2019)	14.7	11.0(2019)
Singapore	45.4	53.1	100.0	99.7	–	–	0.0	0.3	–	–
Thailand	159.5	182.3	96.5	92.5	3.5	4.1	0.0	2.5	0.0	0.9
Timor-Leste	0.1	0.5(2019)	98.9	99.5(2019)	1.1	0.3(2019)	–	0.2(2019)	–	–(2019)
Viet Nam	95.4	213.1	70.5	60.3	29.4	39.5	–	0.0	0.1	0.1
The Pacific[c]	**5.1**	**6.3**	**63.9**	**68.4**	**27.7**	**23.7**	**0.0**	**1.1**	**8.4**	**6.9**
Cook Islands	0.0	0.0(2019)	100.0	74.4(2019)	–	–(2019)	–	25.6(2019)	–	–(2019)
Fiji	0.8	1.1(2019)	49.7	46.6(2019)	49.5	52.2(2019)	–	0.9(2019)	0.8	0.3(2019)
Kiribati	0.0	0.0(2019)	97.1	84.0(2019)	–	–(2019)	2.9	16.0(2019)	–	–(2019)
Marshall Islands	0.1	0.1(2019)	100.0	97.8(2019)	–	–(2019)	–	2.2(2019)	–	–(2019)
Micronesia, Federated States of	0.1	0.1(2019)	98.8	94.3(2019)	–	0.2(2019)	1.2	3.9(2019)	–	1.6(2019)
Nauru	0.0	0.0(2019)	99.6	96.8(2019)	–	–(2019)	0.4	3.2(2019)	–	–(2019)
Niue	0.0	0.0	97.9	87.9	–	–	2.1	12.1	–	–
Palau	0.1	0.1(2019)	100.0	99.7(2019)	–	–(2019)	–	0.3(2019)	–	–(2019)
Papua New Guinea	3.6	4.5	62.0	70.9	26.4	19.5	0.0	0.0	11.6	9.5
Samoa	0.1	0.2(2019)	64.1	60.8(2019)	35.9	25.6(2019)	0.0	13.5(2019)	–	0.1(2019)
Solomon Islands	0.1	0.1(2019)	99.4	96.5(2019)	0.6	0.8(2019)	–	2.7(2019)	–	–(2019)
Tonga	0.1	0.1(2019)	100.0	90.9(2019)	–	–(2019)	–	9.1(2019)	–	0.0(2019)
Tuvalu	0.0	0.0(2019)	100.0	75.7(2019)	–	–(2019)	–	24.3(2019)	–	–(2019)
Vanuatu	0.1	0.1(2019)	80.9	77.2(2019)	11.6	9.7(2019)	–	6.8(2019)	7.5	6.3(2019)
Developed ADB Member Economies	**1,468.4**	**1,363.1**	**68.6**	**76.3**	**8.8**	**9.6**	**0.3**	**5.3**	**22.4**	**8.7**
Australia	252.7	261.0	92.5	84.2	5.4	6.1	0.2	3.8	2.0	5.8
Japan	1,170.9	1,057.8	65.0	76.8	7.7	8.4	0.3	5.9	27.0	8.9
New Zealand	44.9	44.4	28.0	17.8	55.1	59.2	0.0	0.2	16.9	22.7
DEVELOPING ADB MEMBER ECONOMIES[c]	**7,005.1**	**11,205.6**	**79.1**	**73.9**	**15.3**	**15.3**	**0.0**	**2.1**	**5.5**	**8.6**
ALL ADB REGIONAL MEMBERS[c]	**8,473.5**	**12,568.7**	**77.3**	**74.2**	**14.2**	**14.7**	**0.1**	**2.5**	**8.5**	**8.7**

... = data not available, 0.0 = magnitude is less than half of unit employed, – = magnitude equals zero, ADB = Asian Development Bank.

a Electricity from combustible fuels refers to the production of electricity from the combustion of fuels that are capable of igniting or burning, which would include coal, natural gas, oil, and other combustible fuels.

b Includes chemical heat, geothermal, nuclear, tide, other marine electricity, wind, wave, and other sources of energy.

c Includes only reporting economies with data corresponding to the year heading.

Source: United Nations. Energy Statistics Database. http://data.un.org/Data.aspx?d=EDATA&f=cmID%3aEL (accessed 31 May 2021). For Taipei,China: Government of Taipei,China; Directorate-General of Budget, Accounting and Statistics; Official communication, 22 March 2021.

Table 2.6.2: Electric Power Consumption
(kWh per capita)

ADB Regional Member	2010	2015	2016	2017	2018
Developing ADB Member Economies					
Central and West Asia[a]	**851.3**	**915.2**	**919.3**	**947.0**	**985.3**
Afghanistan	82.2	113.0	124.0	124.4	127.5 (2019)
Armenia	1,622.0	1,836.2	1,816.7	1,909.5	1,830.3
Azerbaijan	1,485.6	2,138.0	2,122.0	2,030.1	2,091.0
Georgia	1,869.7	2,465.3	2,615.1	2,799.8	2,985.3
Kazakhstan	3,877.4	4,348.2	4,265.8	4,398.9	4,864.4
Kyrgyz Republic	1,313.3	1,789.4	1,716.7	1,807.8	1,898.0
Pakistan	429.7	453.4	469.1	496.7	505.4
Tajikistan	1,881.1	1,479.9	1,498.9	1,558.7	1,526.2
Turkmenistan	2,134.6	2,647.7	2,602.3	2,559.2	2,518.4
Uzbekistan	1,552.8	1,530.9	1,542.6	1,575.4	1,642.6 (2019)
East Asia[a]	**3,015.0**	**3,937.6**	**4,120.0**	**4,323.0**	**4,714.8**
China, People's Republic of	2,648.1	3,595.7	3,770.7	3,978.0	4,386.3
Hong Kong, China	6,009.3	6,110.8	6,078.2	5,999.2	6,010.1
Korea, Republic of	9,253.5	9,968.8	10,398.3	10,536.7	10,659.9
Mongolia	1,241.1	1,762.1	1,781.8	1,910.4	2,034.5
Taipei,China	10,654.8	10,958.0	11,182.4	11,415.5	11,527.7 (2019)
South Asia[a]	**519.6**	**728.7**	**751.1**	**790.0**	**804.0**
Bangladesh	233.9	331.2	374.6	412.4	436.3
Bhutan	2,814.9	2,826.2	2,726.9	2,931.7	3,210.2 (2019)
India	562.6	789.5	808.8	848.1	860.5
Maldives	926.9	1,279.4	1,327.0	1,377.9	1,415.5
Nepal	101.4	143.1	180.7	206.6	231.5
Sri Lanka	454.5	561.5	604.9	638.4	665.1
Southeast Asia[a]	**1,013.2**	**1,268.5**	**1,336.6**	**1,405.4**	**1,456.1**
Brunei Darussalam	8,401.2	9,006.7	8,690.0	8,334.9	8,585.9
Cambodia	142.4	321.1	383.9	423.1	505.5
Indonesia	609.1	823.5	825.0	924.4	940.7
Lao People's Democratic Republic	390.6	628.8	680.7	723.5	728.2
Malaysia	3,929.8	4,367.2	4,693.7	4,710.5	4,848.6
Myanmar	124.7	254.3	289.5	320.6	345.3
Philippines	588.1	664.0	715.3	739.7	802.6 (2019)
Singapore	8,234.3	8,496.5	8,600.9	8,685.7	8,762.3
Thailand	2,222.2	2,533.0	2,681.7	2,678.4	2,708.5
Timor-Leste	93.1	212.6	256.4	258.3	297.1 (2019)
Viet Nam	973.9	1,550.4	1,706.4	1,846.2	2,016.8
The Pacific[a]	**476.5**	**504.6**	**511.2**	**509.6**	**497.8**
Cook Islands	1,832.3	1,860.0	1,951.9	2,096.5	2,205.5 (2019)
Fiji	888.9	950.9	965.0	1,028.3	1,036.0 (2019)
Kiribati	192.4	203.7	219.5	219.0	207.5 (2019)
Marshall Islands	1,437.2	1,309.1	1,320.1	1,336.7	1,330.1 (2019)
Micronesia, Federated States of	510.9	423.4	418.0	409.1	404.3 (2019)
Nauru	2,038.2	1,868.1	2,005.0	2,430.7	2,723.9 (2019)
Niue	1,712.7	1,858.4	1,899.4	1,898.3	2,049.7
Palau	4,021.4	3,792.8	4,001.6	4,160.8	4,083.1 (2019)
Papua New Guinea	441.0	478.8	482.5	473.8	459.1
Samoa	500.2	596.6	668.7	688.0	692.6 (2019)
Solomon Islands	142.1	137.1	144.6	141.8	142.8 (2019)
Tonga	410.0	487.9	527.4	539.2	601.0 (2019)
Tuvalu	512.3	509.4	598.1	585.0	617.0 (2019)
Vanuatu	258.5	226.2	248.1	238.4	263.4 (2019)
Developed ADB Member Economies	**8,458.7**	**7,854.0**	**7,851.7**	**7,964.3**	**7,861.3**
Australia	9,968.5	9,414.7	9,330.5	9,350.3	9,380.3
Japan	8,169.5	7,529.5	7,545.8	7,679.7	7,546.2
New Zealand	9,311.1	8,759.7	8,538.0	8,435.5	8,337.3
DEVELOPING ADB MEMBER ECONOMIES[a]	**1,582.0**	**2,034.6**	**2,117.6**	**2,216.1**	**2,372.3**
ALL ADB REGIONAL MEMBERS[a]	**1,853.3**	**2,255.3**	**2,333.3**	**2,430.5**	**2,575.4**

... = data not available, ADB = Asian Development Bank, kWh = kilowatt-hour.

a Includes only reporting economies with data corresponding to the year heading.

Sources: For Electric Power Consumption: United Nations. Energy Statistics Database. http://data.un.org/Explorer.aspx?d=EDATA (accessed 31 May 2021). For per capita calculations: United Nations. World Population Prospects 2019. https://population.un.org/wpp/Download/Standard/Population/ (accessed 31 May 2021). For Taipei,China: Asian Development Bank estimates using economy's official sources.

Table 2.6.3: Use of Energy

ADB Regional Member	Energy Use (PJ)			GDP per Unit Use of Energy (constant 2017 $ million PPP per PJ)		
	2010	2015	2018	2010	2015	2018
Developing ADB Member Economies						
Central and West Asia	**10,127.9**	**10,549.4**	**12,227.9**	**148.7**	**179.1**	**176.0**
Afghanistan	136.2	136.4	142.4	419.4	521.8	531.0
Armenia	106.2	134.8	131.3	251.7	245.8	285.8
Azerbaijan	485.9	605.0	606.9	266.7	236.9	232.7
Georgia	139.8	197.8	204.1	263.8	237.4	260.2
Kazakhstan	3,363.4	3,018.1	3,103.4	100.7	141.2	150.4
Kyrgyz Republic	115.5	167.2	191.8	195.3	171.2	169.2
Pakistan	2,880.3	3,229.1	4,545.0	243.4	264.2	221.3
Tajikistan	143.4	166.6	198.6	118.6	143.2	148.2
Turkmenistan	951.4	1,159.8	1,160.3	46.1	62.3	74.9
Uzbekistan	1,805.9	1,734.5	1,944.1	73.6	109.8	114.5
East Asia[a]	**112,824.1**	**132,146.0**	**142,608.0**	**123.8**	**150.1**	**167.5**
China, People's Republic of	101,618.2	119,869.6	129,651.0	117.0	145.2	163.7
Hong Kong, China	544.0	575.9	589.3	663.2	724.3	772.1
Korea, Republic of	10,497.6	11,428.3	11,826.3	162.4	173.3	183.1
Mongolia	164.4	272.1	541.4	123.8	121.5	69.8
Taipei,China	...	...	...	...	...	...
South Asia	**31,562.4**	**38,883.8**	**42,280.8**	**187.0**	**207.5**	**234.0**
Bangladesh	1,493.3	1,803.3	1,963.5	285.0	320.6	365.0
Bhutan	56.8	63.8	70.9	98.9	115.0	120.8
India	29,193.2	36,065.5	39,184.3	178.7	198.1	224.3
Maldives	13.4	18.8	24.8	444.9	417.5	391.4
Nepal	445.6	499.4	592.9	142.8	157.5	154.1
Sri Lanka	360.1	432.9	444.5	513.5	576.0	627.2
Southeast Asia	**22,139.5**	**25,570.5**	**28,099.5**	**235.3**	**261.4**	**276.6**
Brunei Darussalam	135.7	113.8	156.0	194.1	230.2	166.1
Cambodia	223.3	294.9	343.7	174.1	186.5	196.6
Indonesia	8,074.5	8,747.4	10,414.5	248.2	299.8	292.3
Lao People's Democratic Republic	100.3	168.8	239.0	302.2	261.4	224.4
Malaysia	2,965.0	3,423.8	3,832.2	195.4	219.2	226.7
Myanmar	661.8	847.7	991.2	239.3	265.3	272.5
Philippines	1,631.1	2,049.7	2,392.6	341.0	363.7	379.6
Singapore	1,079.0	1,236.1	1,069.6	367.7	400.2	515.3
Thailand	4,930.8	5,694.9	5,677.8	196.4	196.7	221.2
Timor-Leste	4.4	8.0	7.9	722.3	495.2	487.9
Viet Nam	2,333.6	2,985.5	2,975.0	191.9	199.9	243.6
The Pacific[a]	**188.2**	**218.6**	**220.6**	**207.4**	**227.5**	**247.5**
Cook Islands	0.8	0.9	1.1	...	...	...
Fiji	21.5	24.8	25.0	422.3	440.3	489.1
Kiribati	1.3	1.4	1.6	148.1	174.0	166.1
Marshall Islands	2.0	2.0	2.0	102.8	104.0	113.6
Micronesia, Federated States of	1.5	2.1	2.2	244.0	177.0	179.7
Nauru	0.6	0.8	0.7	114.7	186.5	194.3
Niue	0.1	0.1	0.1	...	...	...
Palau	2.9	2.8	3.0	93.8	115.0	111.5
Papua New Guinea	140.9	166.4	166.6	176.9	199.1	216.6
Samoa	4.2	5.0	5.2	266.8	232.4	236.5
Solomon Islands	8.0	7.6	7.5	161.7	200.3	233.9
Tonga	1.7	1.7	1.9	322.4	358.7	341.7
Tuvalu	0.1	0.1	0.1	255.5	374.0	335.1
Vanuatu	2.7	2.9	3.5	283.7	286.1	264.8
Developed ADB Member Economies	**27,230.4**	**24,367.9**	**24,197.4**	**219.2**	**261.9**	**274.7**
Australia	5,396.3	5,330.1	5,393.1	183.7	212.8	227.7
Japan	20,995.3	18,086.1	17,859.3	229.3	279.6	291.8
New Zealand	838.8	951.7	945.0	195.3	198.5	220.4
DEVELOPING ADB MEMBER ECONOMIES[a]	**176,842.1**	**207,368.2**	**225,436.8**	**150.6**	**176.1**	**194.1**
ALL ADB REGIONAL MEMBERS[a]	**204,072.5**	**231,736.1**	**249,634.2**	**159.7**	**185.1**	**201.9**
WORLD[a]	**512,875.3**	**544,461.6**	**571,945.0**	**178.8**	**200.4**	**211.5**

... = data not available, – = magnitude equals zero, $ = United States dollars, ADB = Asian Development Bank, GDP = gross domestic product, PJ = petajoule, PPP = purchasing power parity.

a Aggregates include only reporting economies with data corresponding to the year heading.

Sources: For Energy Use: United Nations. Energy Statistics Database. https://data.un.org/SdmxBrowser/start (accessed 31 May 2021). For GDP per Unit Use of Energy: Asian Development Bank estimates.

Table 2.6.4: Energy Production and Imports

ADB Regional Member	Energy Production (PJ)			Energy Imports, Net (% of total energy use)		
	2010	2015	2018	2010	2015	2018
Developing ADB Member Economies						
Central and West Asia	**16,164.6**	**17,113.6**	**18,042.6**	**-59.6**	**-62.2**	**-47.6**
Afghanistan	41.4	61.0	89.3	69.6	55.3	37.3
Armenia	38.9	44.6	36.9	63.4	66.9	71.9
Azerbaijan	2,758.9	2,473.7	2,348.9	-467.8	-308.8	-287.0
Georgia	57.5	55.1	52.3	58.8	72.1	74.4
Kazakhstan	6,769.9	6,649.9	7,377.9	-101.3	-120.3	-137.7
Kyrgyz Republic	53.1	75.3	97.4	54.1	55.0	49.2
Pakistan	2,039.6	2,157.9	2,234.2	29.2	33.2	50.8
Tajikistan	114.7	131.3	164.6	20.0	21.2	17.1
Turkmenistan	1,981.9	3,407.3	3,331.4	-108.3	-193.8	-187.1
Uzbekistan	2,308.6	2,057.7	2,309.7	-27.8	-18.6	-18.8
East Asia[a]	**91,160.0**	**103,586.8**	**107,151.9**	**18.8**	**21.3**	**24.6**
China, People's Republic of	88,642.0	100,807.7	103,892.6	12.8	15.9	19.9
Hong Kong, China	...	...	...	...	...	...
Korea, Republic of	1,863.1	2,124.8	1,865.5	82.3	81.4	84.2
Mongolia	654.8	654.3	1,393.8	-298.4	-140.4	-157.4
Taipei,China	...	...	...	...	...	...
South Asia	**24,833.8**	**25,008.7**	**26,147.2**	**21.3**	**35.7**	**38.2**
Bangladesh	1,304.1	1,509.6	1,601.7	12.7	16.3	18.4
Bhutan	72.9	76.8	76.7	-28.4	-20.3	-8.2
India	22,888.0	22,817.7	23,846.8	21.6	36.7	39.1
Maldives	0.2	0.2	0.2	98.9	99.1	99.2
Nepal	384.4	423.6	446.3	13.7	15.2	24.7
Sri Lanka	184.3	180.8	175.5	48.8	58.2	60.5
Southeast Asia	**29,094.3**	**30,940.6**	**33,893.5**	**-31.4**	**-21.0**	**-20.6**
Brunei Darussalam	775.2	672.8	639.2	-471.3	-491.2	-309.9
Cambodia	151.7	183.9	210.8	32.1	37.6	38.7
Indonesia	16,606.8	17,376.8	20,571.5	-105.7	-98.7	-97.5
Lao People's Democratic Republic	97.7	162.1	291.4	2.6	4.0	-22.0
Malaysia	3,450.0	3,748.0	3,952.4	-16.4	-9.5	-3.1
Myanmar	968.5	1,175.8	1,214.8	-46.3	-38.7	-22.6
Philippines	923.7	998.6	1,117.9	43.4	51.3	53.3
Singapore	24.9	28.4	25.7	97.7	97.7	97.6
Thailand	2,951.7	3,157.3	3,051.5	40.1	44.6	46.3
Timor-Leste	397.1	402.2	265.1	-8,851.5	-4,948.2	-3,242.5
Viet Nam	2,747.2	3,034.7	2,553.2	-17.7	-1.6	14.2
The Pacific[a]	**106.8**	**242.1**	**247.0**	**41.5**	**-13.3**	**-13.0**
Cook Islands	...	0.0	0.0	...	98.7	96.5
Fiji	5.2	7.4	6.5	75.9	70.0	74.2
Kiribati	0.5	0.5	0.6	62.3	60.8	64.4
Marshall Islands	–	–	–	100.0	100.0	100.0
Micronesia, Federated States of	0.0	0.0	0.0	98.4	98.7	98.2
Nauru	0.0	0.0	0.0	99.9	99.9	99.4
Niue	0.0	0.0	0.0	80.3	83.7	82.4
Palau	...	0.0 (2016)	0.0	...	100.0 (2016)	100.0
Papua New Guinea	95.4	228.2	233.9	32.3	-37.1	-40.4
Samoa	1.5	1.6	1.7	63.3	67.6	67.6
Solomon Islands	3.2	3.3	3.3	59.6	56.4	56.0
Tonga	0.0	0.0	0.0	98.8	98.1	98.2
Tuvalu	0.0 (2012)	0.0	0.0	99.8 (2012)	97.4	94.6
Vanuatu	0.9	0.9	0.9	67.2	67.3	73.4
Developed ADB Member Economies	**18,645.2**	**18,154.4**	**20,065.5**	**31.5**	**25.5**	**17.1**
Australia	13,646.0	16,032.9	17,230.8	-152.9	-200.8	-219.5
Japan	4,224.1	1,341.5	2,100.0	79.9	92.6	88.2
New Zealand	775.2	779.9	734.7	7.6	18.0	22.3
DEVELOPING ADB MEMBER ECONOMIES[a]	**161,359.4**	**176,891.9**	**185,482.2**	**8.5**	**14.5**	**17.5**
ALL ADB REGIONAL MEMBERS[a]	**180,004.6**	**195,046.3**	**205,547.7**	**11.6**	**15.6**	**17.5**
WORLD[a]	**529,503.8**	**569,903.5**	**599,525.2**	**-3.4**	**-4.8**	**-7.5**

... = data not available, – = magnitude equals zero, ADB = Asian Development Bank, PJ = petajoule.

a The aggregates for energy production include only economies with available data corresponding to the year heading. The aggregates for net energy imports include only economies with available data corresponding to the year heading for both energy use and energy production. Net energy imports are calculated as the difference between total energy use and total energy production divided by total energy use.

Sources: For Energy Production: United Nations. Energy Statistics Database. https://data.un.org/SdmxBrowser/start (accessed 31 May 2021). For Net Energy Imports: Asian Development Bank estimates.

Table 2.6.5: Retail Prices of Fuel Energy
($/L)

ADB Regional Member	Gasoline (Premium)			Diesel		
	2010	2015	2020	2010	2015	2020
Developing ADB Member Economies						
Central and West Asia						
Afghanistan	...	...	...	...	...	...
Armenia	1.01	0.90	0.70	0.92	0.89	0.71
Azerbaijan	...	...	...	...	...	...
Georgia	1.03	0.82	0.70	1.00	0.82	0.72
Kazakhstan	0.58	0.56	0.38 (2019)	0.53	0.44	0.50 (2019)
Kyrgyz Republic	...	...	...	...	...	...
Pakistan	0.80	0.68	0.71 (2019)	0.83	0.78	0.81 (2019)
Tajikistan	...	...	...	...	...	...
Turkmenistan	...	...	...	...	...	...
Uzbekistan	...	...	...	...	...	...
East Asia						
China, People's Republic of	...	...	...	...	...	...
Hong Kong, China	1.75	1.77	2.01	1.25	1.41	1.83
Korea, Republic of	1.48	1.34	1.17	1.30	1.15	1.01
Mongolia	1.01	0.79	0.52	0.96	0.91	0.76
Taipei,China	0.94	0.75	0.75	0.82	0.68	0.66
South Asia						
Bangladesh	...	...	...	...	...	...
Bhutan	...	...	...	...	...	...
India	1.05	1.18 (2014)	...	0.83	0.91 (2014)	...
Maldives	...	...	...	...	...	...
Nepal	1.22	1.22	0.91	0.95	0.97	0.80
Sri Lanka	1.02	0.86	0.74	0.65	0.70	0.56
Southeast Asia						
Brunei Darussalam	...	...	...	...	...	...
Cambodia	...	...	...	...	...	...
Indonesia	0.50	0.66	0.69 (2019)	0.50	0.64	0.55 (2019)
Lao People's Democratic Republic	...	...	...	...	...	...
Malaysia	0.67	0.63	0.47	0.57	0.49	0.43
Myanmar	1.69 (2012)	0.76	0.59 (2019)	1.54 (2012)	0.80	0.65 (2019)
Philippines	0.96	0.90	0.95	0.76	0.60	0.71
Singapore	1.35	1.59	1.71	0.89	0.85	1.14
Thailand	1.02	0.81	0.70	0.91	0.72	0.72
Timor-Leste	...	...	...	...	...	...
Viet Nam	0.99 (2011)	0.85	...	0.93 (2011)	0.68	...
The Pacific						
Cook Islands	...	...	...	...	...	...
Fiji	...	...	...	...	...	...
Kiribati	...	...	...	...	...	...
Marshall Islands	...	...	...	...	...	...
Micronesia, Federated States of	...	...	...	...	...	...
Nauru	...	...	...	...	...	...
Niue	...	...	...	...	...	...
Palau	...	...	...	...	...	...
Papua New Guinea	...	...	...	...	...	...
Samoa	...	...	...	...	...	...
Solomon Islands	1.14	1.11	0.90	1.15	1.07	0.93
Tonga	...	...	...	...	...	...
Tuvalu	...	...	...	...	...	...
Vanuatu	1.50	1.84 (2013)	...	...	...	...
Developed ADB Member Economies						
Australia	1.09	0.89	0.73	1.09	0.87	0.75
Japan	1.64	1.23	1.38	1.28	0.97	1.10
New Zealand	1.34	1.41	1.37	0.85	0.80	0.78

... = data not available, $ = United States dollars, ADB = Asian Development Bank, L = liter.

Source: Economy's official sources.

Data Issues and Comparability

Energy data are compiled by the United Nations Statistics Division (UNSD) using standard procedures that follow the definitions of the United Nations International Recommendations for Energy Statistics.[3] The UNSD Annual Questionnaire on Energy Statistics to the UN member economies is the primary source of information for the UNSD energy database. Additional sources of information include national, regional, and international statistical publications. These include, but are not limited to, publications from the International Energy Agency, the Statistical Office of the European Communities (Eurostat), the International Atomic Energy Agency, the Organization of the Petroleum Exporting Countries, and the Organización Latinoamericana de Energía. The UNSD sometimes prepares estimates where official data are incomplete or inconsistent. For the indicator on GDP per unit use of energy, the energy statistics adopt the territory principle, while national accounts are being compiled on the residency principle, which could be a potential source of inconsistency, although in practice differences are not huge (UN 2016).

For data on access to electricity, the Sustainable Energy for All (SE4ALL) database from the SE4ALL Global Tracking Framework—led jointly by the Energy Sector Management Assistance Program, the International Energy Agency, and the World Bank—provides recent updates on the proportion of access for an entire economy, as well as in rural and urban areas. The data for this indicator are a combination of economy-reported data and modeled estimates by the World Bank.

Data for the household electrification indicator are lacking. Data are posted over a varied range of years (i.e., different starting and ending years) depending on data availability. Moreover, economies have different frequencies in collecting and reporting nationwide data on energy and electricity. These data may therefore not be comparable, limiting possibilities for analysis.

3 The full definitions can be found at https://unstats.un.org/UNSD/energy/ires/.

Land

Table 2.7.1: Agriculture Land Use
(% of total land area)

ADB Regional Member	Agricultural Land			Arable Land			Permanent Cropland		
	2010	2015	2018	2010	2015	2018	2010	2015	2018
Developing ADB Member Economies									
Central and West Asia[a]	**67.7**	**67.4**	**67.4**	**13.9**	**14.2**	**14.2**	**0.4**	**0.4**	**0.4**
Afghanistan	58.1	58.1	58.1	11.9	11.9	11.8	0.2	0.2	0.3
Armenia	60.9	58.9	58.9	15.8	15.7	15.7	1.9	2.0	2.1
Azerbaijan	57.7	57.7	57.8	22.8	23.4	25.4	2.8	2.9	3.1
Georgia	35.4	34.8	34.1	5.7	5.3	4.5	1.8	1.6	1.7
Kazakhstan	80.4	80.1	80.0	10.6	11.0	11.0	0.0	0.0	0.0
Kyrgyz Republic	55.3	55.0	55.0	6.7	6.7	6.7	0.4	0.4	0.4
Pakistan	45.7	47.0	47.1	38.1	39.4	39.6	1.1	1.0	1.0
Tajikistan	34.0	34.1	34.1	5.3	5.2	5.1	1.0	1.0	1.1
Turkmenistan	72.4	72.0	72.0	4.1	4.1	4.1	0.1	0.1	0.1
Uzbekistan	60.2	58.1	58.1	9.8	9.3	9.2	0.8	0.9	0.9
East Asia[a]	**58.1**	**58.0**	**58.0**	**11.2**	**11.1**	**11.0**	**1.4**	**1.5**	**1.5**
China, People's Republic of	56.1	56.1	56.1	12.9	12.7	12.7	1.6	1.7	1.7
Hong Kong, China	5.2	4.9	4.8	3.3	3.0	2.9	1.0	1.0	1.0
Korea, Republic of	18.2	17.8	16.9	15.5	15.0	14.1	2.1	2.2	2.3
Mongolia	73.5	73.0	72.8	0.8	0.9	0.9	0.0	0.0	0.0
Taipei,China	23.0	22.5	22.3	16.9	16.7	16.5	6.1	5.8	5.8
South Asia[a]	**58.6**	**58.6**	**58.7**	**50.3**	**50.1**	**50.1**	**4.2**	**4.5**	**4.5**
Bangladesh	71.0	70.4	70.7	59.9	59.4	59.7	6.5	6.4	6.4
Bhutan	13.6	13.8	13.5	2.6	2.6	2.5	0.3	0.3	0.2
India	60.4	60.4	60.4	52.8	52.6	52.6	4.1	4.4	4.4
Maldives	26.3	26.3	26.3	13.0	13.0	13.0	10.0	10.0	10.0
Nepal	28.8	28.7	28.7	15.2	14.7	14.7	1.1	1.5	1.5
Sri Lanka	41.8	44.3	45.4	19.1	21.0	22.2	15.6	16.2	16.2
Southeast Asia[a]	**29.4**	**30.8**	**31.5**	**15.7**	**16.3**	**16.6**	**9.8**	**10.7**	**11.1**
Brunei Darussalam	2.5	2.7	2.7	0.8	0.9	0.9	1.1	1.1	1.1
Cambodia	30.9	31.5	31.5	21.5	22.2	22.2	0.9	0.9	0.9
Indonesia	30.7	31.6	33.2	13.0	13.1	14.0	11.6	12.4	13.3
Lao People's Democratic Republic	9.6	10.8	10.4	6.1	7.1	6.7	0.6	0.7	0.7
Malaysia	22.5	26.1	26.1	2.6	2.5	2.5	19.0	22.7	22.7
Myanmar	19.2	19.5	19.7	16.5	16.7	17.0	2.2	2.3	2.3
Philippines	40.6	41.7	41.7	17.8	18.7	18.7	17.8	17.9	17.9
Singapore	1.1	0.9	0.9	0.9	0.8	0.8	0.1	0.1	0.1
Thailand	41.2	43.3	43.3	30.8	32.9	32.9	8.8	8.8	8.8
Timor-Leste	25.0	25.6	25.6	10.1	10.4	10.4	4.8	5.0	5.0
Viet Nam	34.7	39.2	39.2	20.8	22.6	22.5	11.9	14.5	14.6
The Pacific[a]	**4.0**	**4.1**	**4.1**	**1.0**	**1.1**	**1.1**	**2.1**	**2.1**	**2.1**
Cook Islands	5.6	6.3	6.3	2.9	4.2	4.2	2.7	2.1	2.1
Fiji	23.3	23.3	23.3	9.0	9.0	9.0	4.7	4.7	4.7
Kiribati	42.0	42.0	42.0	2.5	2.5	2.5	39.5	39.5	39.5
Marshall Islands	72.2	47.8	47.8	11.1	11.1	11.1	44.4	36.1	36.1
Micronesia, Federated States of	31.4	31.4	31.4	2.9	2.9	2.9	24.3	24.3	24.3
Nauru	20.0	20.0	20.0	–	–	–	20.0	20.0	20.0
Niue	19.2	19.2	19.2	3.8	3.8	3.8	11.5	11.5	11.5
Palau	9.3	9.3	9.3	0.7	0.7	0.7	4.3	4.3	4.3
Papua New Guinea	2.6	2.6	2.6	0.7	0.7	0.7	1.5	1.5	1.5
Samoa	14.7	26.7	26.7	4.2	11.5	11.5	8.3	11.0	11.0
Solomon Islands	3.8	4.0	4.2	0.7	0.7	0.7	2.9	3.0	3.2
Tonga	44.4	48.6	48.6	23.6	27.8	27.8	15.3	15.3	15.3
Tuvalu	60.0	60.0	60.0	–	–	–	60.0	60.0	60.0
Vanuatu	15.3	15.3	15.3	1.6	1.6	1.6	10.3	10.3	10.3
Developed ADB Member Economies[a]	**47.2**	**43.7**	**44.9**	**3.6**	**4.3**	**4.3**	**0.1**	**0.1**	**0.1**
Australia	49.0	45.3	46.7	3.3	4.0	4.0	0.1	0.0	0.0
Japan	12.6	12.3	12.1	11.7	11.5	11.4	0.9	0.8	0.8
New Zealand	43.3	40.7	39.8	1.9	1.8	1.9	0.3	0.3	0.3
DEVELOPING ADB MEMBER ECONOMIES[a]	**54.2**	**54.3**	**54.4**	**17.6**	**17.7**	**17.8**	**3.0**	**3.3**	**3.4**
ALL ADB REGIONAL MEMBERS[a]	**52.4**	**51.7**	**52.0**	**14.1**	**14.4**	**14.4**	**2.3**	**2.5**	**2.5**
WORLD[a]	**37.1**	**36.7**	**36.9**	**10.5**	**10.6**	**10.7**	**1.2**	**1.3**	**1.3**

– = magnitude equals zero, 0.0 = magnitude is less than half of unit employed, ADB = Asian Development Bank.

a Aggregates are weighted averages estimated using total land area for the respective year headings.

Source: Food and Agriculture Organization of the United Nations. FAOSTAT Database. http://www.fao.org/faostat/en/#data/RL (accessed 14 April 2021).

Table 2.7.2: Deforestation and Pollution

ADB Regional Member	Deforestation Rate[a,b] (average % change)			Carbon Dioxide Emissions[c] (t '000)			Nitrous Oxide Emissions (t '000 CO_2 equivalent)		
	2010	2015	2018	2010	2015	2018	2010	2015	2018
Developing ADB Member Economies									
Central and West Asia	**-0.02**	**-0.31**	**-0.20**	**595,360**	**613,570**	**685,440**	**94,140**	**105,490**	**111,950**
Afghanistan	–	–	–	8,670	7,990	7,440	5,990	8,590	8,960
Armenia	0.06	0.06	0.06	4,340	5,340	5,550	790	1,090	1,170
Azerbaijan	-0.44	-0.85	-1.05	24,150	32,170	32,020	3,290	4,010	4,160
Georgia	-0.22	–	–	5,320	9,200	9,460	1,780	2,190	2,090
Kazakhstan	0.24	-1.39	-0.87	223,570	206,640	220,450	11,000	10,990	10,980
Kyrgyz Republic	-0.40	-0.35	-1.45	6,350	10,270	11,000	1,660	1,810	1,990
Pakistan	1.01	0.81	1.07	140,620	163,590	208,370	51,840	56,300	60,950
Tajikistan	–	-0.56	–	2,420	4,760	7,330	1,580	1,940	1,980
Turkmenistan	–	–	–	57,360	72,080	71,730	3,430	3,460	3,430
Uzbekistan	-1.17	-1.14	-0.72	122,560	101,530	112,090	12,780	15,110	16,240
East Asia	**-1.07**	**-0.84**	**-0.80**	**9,327,576**	**10,730,065**	**11,250,453**	**508,910**	**570,038**	**567,642**
China, People's Republic of[e]	-1.19	-0.93	-0.88	8,470,570	9,830,430	10,313,460	486,770	542,900	538,790
Hong Kong, China[e]	...	...	...	...	...	...	...	...	...
Korea, Republic of	0.14	0.16	0.16	574,260	606,510	630,870	8,620	10,390	10,770
Mongolia	0.06	0.01	0.01	14,310	17,300	21,320	8,610	12,260	13,190
Taipei,China[e]	...	...	...	268,436	275,825	284,803 (2017)	4,910	4,488	4,892 (2017)
South Asia	**-0.26**	**-0.33**	**-0.32**	**1,735,030**	**2,251,040**	**2,554,230**	**272,660**	**285,320**	**293,820**
Bangladesh	0.17	0.05	–	50,580	71,690	82,760	26,060	28,210	29,240
Bhutan	-0.37	-0.07	-0.07	470	960	1,380	180	180	190
India	-0.27	-0.38	-0.37	1,665,310	2,150,220	2,434,520	237,170	246,030	253,790
Maldives	–	–	–	960	1,350	1,910	20	30	30
Nepal	-0.30	–	–	4,640	6,460	12,030	6,500	7,730	8,330
Sri Lanka	0.30	-0.24	0.15	13,070	20,360	21,630	2,730	3,140	2,240
Southeast Asia	**0.20**	**0.62**	**0.50**	**1,150,170**	**1,397,680**	**1,598,300**	**180,400**	**193,160**	**203,840**
Brunei Darussalam	0.45	–	–	6,860	5,980	7,140	140	150	150
Cambodia	0.18	3.79	1.82	4,920	8,580	11,160	4,510	4,970	5,160
Indonesia	0.16	0.97	0.64	416,940	490,840	583,110	81,450	89,070	95,690
Lao People's Democratic Republic	0.29	0.21	0.21	2,880	8,660	18,790	2,510	2,710	2,740
Malaysia	0.39	-0.53	0.26	199,110	232,550	239,620	11,910	11,760	11,120
Myanmar	1.08	0.96	0.98	8,280	19,010	32,520	17,250	20,010	21,340
Philippines	0.68	-0.50	-0.49	83,570	113,670	142,240	12,840	12,640	13,640
Singapore	-0.41	1.52	1.12	42,410	45,500	47,360	6,860	8,520	9,710
Thailand	-0.54	0.01	0.18	235,520	263,080	257,860	21,720	18,640	19,950
Timor-Leste	0.15	0.15	0.18	240	610	640	220	270	260
Viet Nam	-1.21	-0.97	-0.53	149,440	209,200	257,860	20,990	24,420	24,080
The Pacific	**0.01**	**0.06**	**0.07**	**7,520**	**9,380**	**11,240**	**4,350**	**4,420**	**4,460**
Cook Islands	-0.01	–	–	...	...	...	...	...	...
Fiji	-0.63	-0.61	-0.60	1,160	1,510	1,900	340	180	170
Kiribati	–	–	–	50	60	80	–	–	10
Marshall Islands	–	–	–	140	150	190	–	–	–
Micronesia, Federated States of	-0.04	-0.04	-0.05	110	150	180	20	30	30
Nauru	...	...	...	40	50	70	–	–	–
Niue	0.03	-0.05	-0.05	...	...	...	...	...	...
Palau	-0.24	-0.21	-0.22	210	220	290	– (2011)	–	–
Papua New Guinea	0.03	0.09	0.09	5,020	6,430	7,460	3,710	3,890	3,930
Samoa	0.29	0.29	0.29	190	240	320	50	60	60
Solomon Islands	0.03	0.03	0.03	340	310	370	30	30	30
Tonga	–	–	–	120	110	190	50	50	50
Tuvalu	–	–	–	10	10	10	–	–	–
Vanuatu	–	–	–	130	140	180	150	180	180
Developed ADB Member Economies	**0.13**	**-0.42**	**0.00**	**1,574,560**	**1,589,660**	**1,524,980**	**88,530**	**105,240**	**109,810**
Australia	0.17	-0.54	0.01	387,350	375,970	386,620	54,650	71,960	76,760
Japan	-0.04	0.02	–	1,156,080	1,181,500	1,106,150	19,600	18,220	18,010
New Zealand	0.00	0.00	-0.04	31,130	32,190	32,210	14,280	15,060	15,040
DEVELOPING ADB MEMBER ECONOMIES	**-0.73**	**-0.15**	**-0.18**	**12,815,656**	**15,001,735**	**16,099,663**	**1,060,460**	**1,158,428**	**1,181,712**
ALL ADB REGIONAL MEMBERS	**-0.54**	**-0.21**	**-0.14**	**14,390,216**	**16,591,395**	**17,624,643**	**1,148,990**	**1,263,668**	**1,291,522**

continued on next page

Table 2.7.2: Deforestation and Pollution *(continued)*

ADB Regional Member	Methane Emissions (t '000 CO_2 equivalent)			Other Greenhouse Gases[d] (t '000 CO_2 equivalent)		
	2010	2015	2018	2010	2015	2016
Developing ADB Member Economies						
Central and West Asia	**391,490**	**475,510**	**491,150**	**-12,708**	**-21,786**	**-2,334**
Afghanistan	30,010	76,590	81,510	2,582	-691	-1,800
Armenia	2,370	2,560	2,430	469	1,149	722
Azerbaijan	51,220	45,430	43,600	-54	-1,163	-514
Georgia	5,710	5,410	5,210	-248	1,005	1,190
Kazakhstan	41,490	40,440	41,360	-20,146	-20,260	-7,610
Kyrgyz Republic	4,150	4,710	4,990	1,569	3,669	2,918
Pakistan	119,250	139,810	151,020	-8,720	6,550	10,236
Tajikistan	4,340	5,240	5,520	-759	-753	260
Turkmenistan	30,880	50,200	49,580	-3,962	-6,292	-6,869
Uzbekistan	102,070	105,120	105,930	16,562	-4,999	-867
East Asia	**1,106,780**	**1,285,127**	**1,287,549**	**-262,353**	**-329,874**	**-305,156**
China, People's Republic of[e]	1,063,830	1,237,520	1,238,630	-285,418	-382,872	-364,711
Hong Kong, China[e]	...	...	...	..	..	..
Korea, Republic of	26,780	25,960	25,530	17,515	48,128	56,606
Mongolia	9,050	16,010	17,860	1,320	1,711	-224
Taipei,China[e]	7,120	5,637	5,529 (2017)	4,230	3,160	3,043 (2017)
South Asia	**765,090**	**772,970**	**792,120**	**-176,304**	**-248,524**	**-325,548**
Bangladesh	78,460	80,900	83,790	-8,226	2,224	1,514
Bhutan	900	870	860	-676	-595	-422
India	650,140	652,000	666,510	-166,579	-254,017	-333,368
Maldives	90	120	130	213	360	737
Nepal	26,050	29,430	30,800	-124	-605	1,576
Sri Lanka	9,450	9,650	10,030	-911	4,110	4,415
Southeast Asia	**654,190**	**664,090**	**685,600**	**-1,686**	**37,794**	**15,648**
Brunei Darussalam	10,090	9,480	8,830	-301	-1,160	-902
Cambodia	19,440	19,710	20,310	963	3,006	3,983
Indonesia	261,610	269,470	287,500	-4,542	-4,638	-32,216
Lao People's Democratic Republic	6,930	7,580	7,610	88	4,531	10,919
Malaysia	42,720	46,060	46,580	-1,220	-9,767	-29,432
Myanmar	64,630	65,940	65,790	-123	3,206	5,188
Philippines	62,450	65,410	67,660	191	5,719	4,267
Singapore	3,140	3,840	4,150	411	3,025	2,728
Thailand	90,550	80,780	84,140	5,664	26,494	28,220
Timor-Leste	6,580	6,000	5,280	-28	146	204
Viet Nam	86,050	89,820	87,750	-2,789	7,232	22,688
The Pacific	**8,720**	**13,240**	**13,440**			
Cook Islands	...	...	...	...	...	...
Fiji	820	620	670	36	-18	107
Kiribati	20	20	20	25	21	17
Marshall Islands	30	30	30	...	...	...
Micronesia, Federated States of	50	50	60	...	...	...
Nauru	-	-	-	49	...	...
Niue	...	...	...	...	...	...
Palau	20	20	20	..	191	228
Papua New Guinea	6,590	11,200	11,310	-1,062	-1,905	-1,267
Samoa	280	310	300	75	91	130
Solomon Islands	350	390	410	143	61	108
Tonga	90	100	100	-66	-115	-91
Tuvalu	10	10	10	9	...	...
Vanuatu	460	490	510	40	12	52
Developed ADB Member Economies	**177,600**	**188,140**	**192,710**	**-62,498**	**-59,251**	**-39,327**
Australia	119,320	133,430	139,070	-21,765	-29,898	-17,269
Japan	24,930	21,900	21,110	-39,416	-29,850	-21,412
New Zealand	33,350	32,810	32,530	-1,317	497	-646
DEVELOPING ADB MEMBER ECONOMIES	**2,926,270**	**3,210,937**	**3,269,859**	**-453,802**	**-564,051**	**-618,105**
ALL ADB REGIONAL MEMBERS	**3,103,870**	**3,399,077**	**3,462,569**	**-516,300**	**-623,301**	**-657,432**

... = data not available, - = magnitude equals zero, 0.00 = magnitude is less than half of unit employed, ADB = Asian Development Bank, CO_2 = carbon dioxide, t = metric ton.

a Rate refers to percentage change over previous year. A negative value indicates that the deforestation rate is decreasing (i.e., reforestation).
b Aggregates are calculated as the percentage change of the sum of forest land area of the reporting economies.
c Data from the World Bank are expressed in kiloton (kt), while data provided in the table are expressed in thousands of metric tons (t), using a conversion factor of 1 kt = 1000 metric tons.
d Other greenhouse gas emissions refer to hydrofluorocarbons, perfluorocarbons, and sulphur hexafluoride.
e For estimates for Hong Kong, China; the People's Republic of China; and Taipei,China, please directly refer to the FAOSTAT notes.

Sources: Food and Agriculture Organization of the United Nations. FAOSTAT Database. http://www.fao.org/faostat/en/#data/RL (accessed 1 June 2021); and World Bank. World Development Indicators Online. http://data.worldbank.org/indicator (accessed 9 July 2021). For Taipei,China: Directorate General of Budget, Accounting and Statistics. Statistical Yearbook 2019. https://eng.dgbas.gov.tw/ct.asp?xitem=41875&ctNode=2351&mp=2 (accessed 19 April 2021).

Table 2.7.3: Freshwater Resources

ADB Regional Member	Internal Renewable Freshwater Resources (m³ billion per year)	(m³ per inhabitant per year)	Annual Freshwater Withdrawals (m³ billion)	Water Productivity[a] (constant 2010 $ per m³)
	2017[b]	2017[c]	2017	2017
Developing ADB Member Economies				
Central and West Asia	**370**	**1,114**		
Afghanistan	47	1,299	20	1.0
Armenia	7	2,329	3	4.3
Azerbaijan	8	824	13	4.4
Georgia	58	14,501	2	9.2
Kazakhstan	64	3,559	22	8.7
Kyrgyz Republic	49	7,905	8	0.9
Pakistan	55	265	200	1.2
Tajikistan	63	7,146	10	0.9
Turkmenistan	1	244	28	1.5
Uzbekistan	16	511	59	1.3
East Asia[d]	**2,913**	**1,933**		
China, People's Republic of	2,813	1,936	592	17.2
Hong Kong, China	...	...	...	...
Korea, Republic of	65	1,269	29	48.4
Mongolia	35	11,176	0	26.9
Taipei,China	...	...	...	...
South Asia[d]	**1,880**	**1,214**		
Bangladesh	105	658	36	5.0
Bhutan	78	104,619	0	6.8
India	1,446	1,080	648	4.1
Maldives	0	60	0	827.8
Nepal	198	7,173	9	2.3
Sri Lanka	53	2,499	13	6.4
Southeast Asia[d]	**4,993**	**7,699**		
Brunei Darussalam	9	20,025	0	146.5
Cambodia	121	7,533	2	8.3
Indonesia	2,019	7,628	223	4.9
Lao People's Democratic Republic	190	27,384	7	1.6
Malaysia	580	18,647	7	54.4
Myanmar	1,003	18,785	33	2.4
Philippines	479	4,554	93	3.5
Singapore	1	105	0	654.4
Thailand	225	3,244	57	7.4
Timor-Leste	8	6,608	1	0.9
Viet Nam	359	3,799	82	2.1
The Pacific[d]				
Cook Islands	...	...	...	...
Fiji	29	32,537	0	48.1
Kiribati	...	...	...	...
Marshall Islands	...	...	...	...
Micronesia, Federated States of	...	...	...	...
Nauru	0	946	...	...
Niue	...	...	...	...
Palau	...	...	...	...
Papua New Guinea	801	94,927	0	52.8
Samoa	...	...	...	...
Solomon Islands	45	70,279	...	...
Tonga	...	...	...	...
Tuvalu	...	...	...	...
Vanuatu	10	35,025	...	...
Developed ADB Member Economies	**1,249**	**7,966**		
Australia	492	20,013	16	86.5
Japan	430	3,372	81	75.7
New Zealand	327	69,544	10	18.3
DEVELOPING ADB MEMBER ECONOMIES[d]	**11,039**	**2,729**		
ALL ADB REGIONAL MEMBERS[d]	**12,288**	**2,924**		

... = data not available, 0 = magnitude is less than half of unit employed, $ = United States dollars, ADB = Asian Development Bank, m³ = cubic meter.

a Gross domestic product in 2010 United States dollars per cubic meter of total freshwater withdrawal.
b Regional aggregates are calculated as the sum of the economies.
c Regional aggregates are weighted averages estimated using population.
d For reporting economies only.

Sources: Food and Agriculture Organization of the United Nations. AQUASTAT Database. http://www.fao.org/nr/water/aquastat/data/query/index.html (accessed 26 May 2021); and World Bank. World Development Indicators. http://data.worldbank.org/indicator (accessed 28 May 2021).

Data Issues and Comparability

Data on greenhouse gases (GHGs) have been compiled from the Emissions Database for Global Atmospheric Research, a joint project of the European Commission Joint Research Centre and the Netherlands Environmental Assessment Agency. This database applies a technology-based emissions factor approach consistently for all economies. It utilizes a consistent set of activity data for calculating various substances, GHGs, and air pollutants; and relies on the spatial allocation of emissions on a 0.1-degree by 0.1-degree grid.

There may be substantial uncertainty in economy-level data—especially for methane, nitrous oxide, and other GHGs—due to the limited accuracy of international activity data and the emission factors selected for calculating emissions on an economy level. However, since Intergovernmental Panel on Climate Change methodologies are consistently used, and data are based on international information sources, there is sound basis for comparability.[4]

The Food and Agricultural Organization of the United Nations monitors land use and forestry data using its own expert sources, country or economy reports, satellite imagery, and official data reported on through questionnaires conducted by the organization.

4 For more information on the methodologies of the Emissions Database for Global Atmospheric Research, go to https://edgar.jrc.ec.europa.eu/methodology.

Table 2.8.1: Government Net Lending/Net Borrowing
(% of GDP)

ADB Regional Member	2010	2015	2016	2017	2018	2019	2020
Developing ADB Member Economies							
Central and West Asia							
Afghanistan[a]	2.4	-1.4	0.2	-0.4	0.8	-1.7	-4.4
Armenia	-5.0	-4.8	-5.5	-4.8	-1.6	-0.8	-5.1*
Azerbaijan	15.4	-2.8	2.4	1.9	9.5	6.2	...
Georgia	-4.3	-1.0	-1.2	-0.1	-0.8	-1.6	-9.0
Kazakhstan	5.0	-2.2	-2.8	-3.0	1.4	-0.5	...
Kyrgyz Republic	-4.9	-1.4	-4.4	-3.1	-1.1	-0.1	3.3
Pakistan[b]	-6.0	-5.2	-4.5	-5.8	-6.5	-8.8	8.0
Tajikistan[c]	-9.2	-7.4	-10.1	-11.8	-10.6	-7.8	-0.1*
Turkmenistan	2.0	-0.7	-2.4	-2.8	-0.2	-0.3	...
Uzbekistan	...	3.3	4.0	1.5	3.2	0.5	-1.5
East Asia							
China, People's Republic of	-1.6	-3.4	-3.8	-3.7	-4.1	-4.9	-6.2
Hong Kong, China[d]	4.1	1.4	4.7	6.3	3.5	...	...
Korea, Republic of	1.1 (2012)	1.2	2.5	2.6	3.1	0.8	...
Mongolia	-3.2	-10.9	-23.0	-11.1	-4.1	-9.0	-20.4
Taipei,China	-2.6	0.2	-0.3	-0.1	0.1	0.5	...
South Asia							
Bangladesh[b]	-1.7	-2.2	-2.7	-3.0	-1.9	-4.6	-4.3
Bhutan[b]	1.5	1.5	-1.1	-3.5	-0.3	-0.8	...
India[d]	-4.9	-3.9	-3.5	-3.5	-3.4	-4.6	-9.4*
Maldives[e]	-12.9	-6.5	-10.0	-3.1	-5.2	-6.6	-27.5*
Nepal[f]	-1.4	1.1	1.4	-3.4	-5.4	-5.3	...
Sri Lanka	-6.3	-7.6	-5.3	-5.5	-5.4	-6.8	-13.4
Southeast Asia							
Brunei Darussalam[g]	15.1	-14.8	-16.7	-13.2	0.2	-5.6	-19.3
Cambodia	-4.5	-0.9	-0.4	-0.8	0.4	2.2	-4.0*
Indonesia	-0.6	-3.0	-1.9	-2.0	-1.7	-2.1	-6.1
Lao People's Democratic Republic[h]	-0.9	-3.7	-4.9	-5.2	-4.2	-2.7	...
Malaysia	-5.0	-3.1	-3.0	-2.9	-3.6	-3.4	...
Myanmar[i]	-4.4 (2012)	-4.4	-3.3	-3.7	-5.9 |	-4.0	...
Philippines	-3.3	-1.3	-2.2	-2.1	-3.1	-3.3	-7.5
Singapore[d]	7.5	4.2	5.0	7.6	4.8	7.5	...
Thailand[h]	-0.7	0.2	0.4	-0.4	0.1	0.4	-4.7
Timor-Leste	...	7.3	-10.4	8.5	5.1	-4.0	...
Viet Nam	-2.1	-4.3	3.6	2.7	2.8	3.4*	4.0*
The Pacific							
Cook Islands[b]	2.9	-7.8	1.4	8.7*	5.2*	5.4*	...
Fiji[j]	-2.6	-2.2	-0.8	-0.9	-4.6	...	...
Kiribati[b]	-6.9 (2011)	56.1	21.6	16.8	51.9*	19.0*	...
Marshall Islands[h]	3.5	2.8	3.9	4.4	2.5	-1.8	5.0*
Micronesia, Federated States of[h]	0.5	10.4	7.3	14.6	24.2	...	...
Nauru[b]	0.1	10.5	21.4	21.4	32.5*	16.1*	16.3*
Niue	...	...	...	...	...	...	...
Palau[h]	-1.0	5.2	3.6	4.8	6.2	0.3*	...
Papua New Guinea	...	...	...	-2.4	-2.6	-5.0*	-8.1*
Samoa[b]	-8.1 (2012)	-3.7	0.7	-0.6	1.3	4.6	...
Solomon Islands	5.6	0.8	-3.1	-0.9	1.5	-1.5	-2.4
Tonga[b]	...	...	1.5	3.6	2.9	3.1	...
Tuvalu	11.5 (2012)	40.0	4.8	...	...	...	...
Vanuatu	-1.6 (2012)	6.9	-0.3	2.2	8.4	...	...
Developed ADB Member Economies							
Australia[b]	-5.5	-2.9	-2.6	-2.2	-1.3	-1.2	-7.6
Japan[d]	-8.8	-3.6	-3.5	-2.9	-2.4	-3.0	...
New Zealand[b]	-3.4	-0.1	0.7	1.3	1.2	1.1	-5.6

... = data not available, | = marks break in series, * = preliminary, provisional, estimate, ADB = Asian Development Bank, GDP = gross domestic product.

Note: In general, economies follow the guidelines of the International Monetary Fund on Government Finance Statistics (GFS). Some economies still use the 1986 version of the GFS guidelines, while others have switched to the 2001 or 2014 guidelines. The comparability of the data in this table is limited by variations in the concepts and definitions used in different versions of the GFS framework. Data refer to government net lending/net borrowing as classified in the GFS 2001 or GFS 2014 framework, except for Bhutan; Brunei Darussalam; India, the Kyrgyz Republic, Maldives; Nauru; Pakistan; the People's Republic of China; Taipei,China; Tajikistan; Turkmenistan; and Viet Nam, where data refer to overall budgetary surplus/deficit as classified in the GFS 1986 framework. Data refer to general government, except for Bangladesh; Bhutan; Brunei Darussalam; Cambodia; the Federated States of Micronesia; Fiji; India; the Lao People's Democratic Republic; Malaysia; Maldives; the Marshall Islands; Nauru; Nepal; Palau; the Philippines; Solomon Islands; Sri Lanka; Taipei,China; Timor-Leste; Tonga; Tuvalu; Vanuatu; and Viet Nam, where data refer to central government. For Azerbaijan: Data for 2000–2007 (featured in the Key Indicators Database) are based on the state budget. For Cambodia: Data refer to central government excluding extra budgetary central government. For Pakistan: Data refer to the consolidated federal and provincial governments. For the People's Republic of China: Data refer to consolidated central and local governments. For Turkmenistan: Data prior to 2011 refer to central government.

a The longer time series featured in the Key Indicators Database refers to GFS data for 2005–2011 based on fiscal year beginning 21 March. For 2012, GFS data cover 9 months from 21 March to 20 December. For 2013 onward, GFS data are based on fiscal year ending 20 December. For 2005–2015, national accounts data are based on fiscal year beginning 21 March. For 2016 onward, national accounts data are based on fiscal year ending 20 December.
b Data are based on fiscal year ending 30 June.
c National accounts data prior to 2015 are based on the 1993 System of National Accounts while figures for 2015 onward are based on the 2008 System of National Accounts.
d Data are based on fiscal year beginning 1 April.
e For 2013 onward, data are calculated excluding net lending.
f Data are based on fiscal year ending 15 July.
g The longer time series featured in the Key Indicators Database refers to data for 2003 onward based on fiscal year beginning 1 April. Data are derived as excess of revenue over expenditure (ordinary plus charged) less the sum of contribution to a development fund, contribution to a government trust fund, and capital and currency adjustments.
h Data are based on fiscal year ending 30 September.
i The longer time series featured in the Key Indicators Database refers to GFS data for 2012–2018 based on fiscal year beginning 1 April. For 2019, GFS data are based on fiscal year beginning 1 October. For 2012–2015, national accounts data are based on fiscal year beginning 1 April. For 2016 onward, national accounts data are based on fiscal year beginning 1 October.
j The longer time series featured in the Key Indicators Database refers to GFS data for 2000–2014 based on fiscal year ending 31 December. For 2015 onward, GFS data are based on fiscal year ending 31 July. National accounts data are based on calendar year.

Sources: Economy's official sources. For Hong Kong, China; Kiribati (2011–2013); Nepal; and Timor-Leste: International Monetary Fund. Government Finance Statistics. https://data.imf.org/ (accessed April–July 2021). For Nauru (2012–2020): International Monetary Fund. Staff Country Reports. Republic of Nauru: 2019 Article IV. https://www.imf.org/en/Publications/CR/Issues/2020/01/29/Republic-of-Nauru-2019-Article-IV-Consultation-Press-Release-Staff-Report-and-Statement-by-49001 (accessed 9 May 2021).

Table 2.8.2: Government Taxes
(% of GDP)

ADB Regional Member	2010	2015	2016	2017	2018	2019	2020
Developing ADB Member Economies							
Central and West Asia							
Afghanistan[a]	8.8	7.1	8.2	8.7	9.5	8.4	7.5
Armenia	17.7	21.3	21.5	21.0	21.1	22.6	22.5*
Azerbaijan	12.3	15.7	14.7	13.3	13.1	14.3	...
Georgia	22.3	23.6	24.5	24.3	23.4	24.1	22.2
Kazakhstan	19.6	13.6	12.4	13.8	15.1	15.1	...
Kyrgyz Republic	17.9	19.7	19.7	19.5	20.5	19.6	17.9
Pakistan[b]	10.0	11.0	12.4	12.5	13.0	11.6	11.4*
Tajikistan[c]	18.0 |	20.8	20.4	20.3	20.5	20.4	18.6*
Turkmenistan	17.5 (2011)	15.6	...	...	...	...	...
Uzbekistan	...	20.3	20.0	17.3	19.8	19.4	19.6
East Asia							
China, People's Republic of	17.8	18.1	17.5	17.4	17.0	16.0	15.2
Hong Kong, China[d]	13.5	14.4	13.6	14.3	13.8	...	...
Korea, Republic of	18.0 (2012)	17.6	18.4	19.0	20.1	20.0	...
Mongolia	24.2	17.7	16.0	17.9	20.3	20.9	18.7
Taipei,China	7.7	8.6	8.7	8.6	8.9	9.0	...
South Asia							
Bangladesh[b]	10.2	8.9	8.8	9.1	7.4	8.9	7.7
Bhutan[b]	13.3	15.0	14.5	14.2	16.6	15.4	...
India[d]	7.5	6.9	7.2	7.3	7.0	6.7	6.8*
Maldives	8.8	19.4	19.8	20.2	19.3	19.0	17.5*
Nepal[e]	13.4	16.7	18.7	20.0	21.8	22.1	...
Sri Lanka	11.3	12.4	12.2	12.5	12.0	11.6	8.1
Southeast Asia							
Brunei Darussalam[f]	...	...	...	...	...	...	...
Cambodia	7.3	14.6	14.8	15.8	17.1	19.7	18.2*
Indonesia	12.1	12.0	11.6	11.2	11.5	11.1	9.5
Lao People's Democratic Republic[g]	13.8	13.5	12.9	12.2	11.7	11.4	...
Malaysia	13.3	14.1	13.6	12.9	12.0	12.0	...
Myanmar[h]	6.6 (2012)	7.5	8.4	7.9	7.4 |	7.0	...
Philippines	11.6	13.0	13.1	13.6	14.0	14.5	14.0
Singapore[d]	12.8	13.1	13.3	14.0	13.0	13.2	...
Thailand[g]	16.1	17.6	16.8	16.3	16.5	16.1	15.8
Timor-Leste	...	7.8	9.5	8.7	8.5	6.3	...
Viet Nam[i]	22.4	18.0	17.9	18.3	18.4	18.6*	16.9*
The Pacific							
Cook Islands[b]	27.0	23.5	26.3	26.0*	27.0*	27.8*	...
Fiji	...	...	...	...	...	...	...
Kiribati[b]	18.3 (2011)	22.7	25.5	22.6	21.7*	24.9*	...
Marshall Islands[g]	15.8	14.0	14.4	14.3	14.5	14.6	13.9*
Micronesia, Federated States of[g]	12.0	12.4	13.0	18.2	37.3	...	...
Nauru[b]	8.1 (2012)	21.7	23.0	21.2	29.6*	32.4*	42.4*
Niue	...	...	...	...	...	...	...
Palau[g]	17.0	20.3	19.9	19.8	21.2	20.0*	...
Papua New Guinea	...	...	...	12.3	13.2	13.0*	11.8*
Samoa[b]	20.9 (2012)	23.6	24.3	25.0	25.5	26.2	...
Solomon Islands	21.9	25.8	23.7	25.0	25.7	22.2	21.2
Tonga[b]	...	...	19.8	21.0	21.9	20.9	...
Tuvalu	28.5 (2012)	33.1	28.0	...	...	...	...
Vanuatu	16.5 (2012)	16.3	15.3	17.1	17.8	...	...
Developed ADB Member Economies							
Australia[b]	25.6	27.3	27.9	27.6	28.6	28.7	27.8
Japan[d]	15.6	18.6	18.3	18.7	19.1	18.7	...
New Zealand[b]	29.2	30.7	30.8	31.0	30.6	31.7	30.7

... = data not available, | = marks break in series, * = preliminary, provisional, estimate, ADB = Asian Development Bank, GDP = gross domestic product.

Note: In general, economies follow the guidelines of the International Monetary Fund on Government Finance Statistics (GFS). Some economies still use the 1986 version of the GFS guidelines, while others have switched to the 2001 or 2014 guidelines. The comparability of the data in this table is limited by variations in the concepts and definitions used in different versions of the GFS framework. Data refer to government taxes as classified in the GFS 2001 or GFS 2014 framework, except for Bhutan; Brunei Darussalam; India; the Kyrgyz Republic; Maldives; Nauru; Pakistan; the People's Republic of China; Taipei,China; Tajikistan; Turkmenistan; and Viet Nam, where data refer to tax revenue as classified in the GFS 1986 framework. Data refer to general government, except for Bangladesh; Bhutan; Brunei Darussalam; Cambodia; the Federated States of Micronesia; Fiji; India; the Lao People's Democratic Republic; Malaysia; Maldives; the Marshall Islands; Nauru; Nepal; Palau; the Philippines; Solomon Islands; Sri Lanka; Taipei,China; Timor-Leste; Tonga; Tuvalu; Vanuatu; and Viet Nam, where data refer to central government. For Armenia: Data prior to 2010 (featured in the Key Indicators Database) refer to central government. For Azerbaijan: Data for 2000–2007 (featured in the Key Indicators Database) are based on the state budget. For Cambodia: Data refer to central government excluding extra budgetary central government. For Pakistan: Data refer to the consolidated federal and provincial governments. For the People's Republic of China: Data refer to consolidated central and local governments. For Turkmenistan: Data prior to 2011 refer to central government.

a The longer time series featured in the Key Indicators Database refers to GFS data for 2005–2011 based on fiscal year beginning 21 March. For 2012, GFS data cover 9 months from 21 March to 20 December. For 2013 onward, GFS data are based on fiscal year ending 20 December. For 2005–2015, national accounts data are based on fiscal year beginning 21 March. For 2016 onward, national accounts data are based on fiscal year ending 20 December.

b Data are based on fiscal year ending 30 June.

c National accounts data prior to 2015 are based on the 1993 System of National Accounts while figures for 2015 onward are based on the 2008 System of National Accounts.

d Data are based on fiscal year beginning 1 April.

e Data are based on fiscal year ending 15 July.

f The longer time series featured in the Key Indicators Database refers to data for 2003 onward based on fiscal year beginning 1 April.

g Data are based on fiscal year ending 30 September.

h For 2012–2018, GFS data are based on fiscal year beginning 1 April. For 2019, GFS data are based on fiscal year beginning 1 October. For 2012–2015, national accounts data are based on fiscal year beginning 1 April. For 2016 onward, national accounts data are based on fiscal year beginning 1 October.

i Taxes include local government taxes.

Sources: Economy's official sources. For Hong Kong, China; Kiribati (2011–2013); Nepal; and Timor-Leste: International Monetary Fund. Government Finance Statistics. https://data.imf.org/ (accessed April–July 2021). For Nauru (2012–2020): International Monetary Fund. Staff Country Reports. Republic of Nauru: 2019 Article IV. https://www.imf.org/en/Publications/CR/Issues/2020/01/29/Republic-of-Nauru-2019-Article-IV-Consultation-Press-Release-Staff-Report-and-Statement-by-49001 (accessed 9 May 2021).

Table 2.8.3: Government Revenue
(% of GDP)

ADB Regional Member	2010	2015	2016	2017	2018	2019	2020
Developing ADB Member Economies							
Central and West Asia							
Afghanistan[a]	23.0	23.9	29.2	27.3	29.8	26.9	24.1
Armenia	23.2	23.8	23.8	22.9	23.0	24.7	26.0*
Azerbaijan	47.0	34.4	35.3	35.3	39.7	43.0	...
Georgia	26.9	30.4	31.1	31.0	28.6	29.2	27.2
Kazakhstan	25.5	17.6	17.6	19.9	19.6	19.1	...
Kyrgyz Republic	23.1	27.7	25.3	25.2	25.0	24.9	23.5
Pakistan[b]	14.2	14.4	15.0	15.5	15.2	12.7	15.9*
Tajikistan[c]	19.3 |	23.7	23.3	22.5	23.3	23.0	20.9*
Turkmenistan	15.8	16.6	11.7	14.9	13.5	13.0*	...
Uzbekistan	...	27.6	27.5	24.3	27.9	27.9	27.1
East Asia							
China, People's Republic of	20.2	22.1	21.4	20.7	19.9	19.3	18.0
Hong Kong, China[d]	22.3	21.7	24.6	25.8	23.8	...	...
Korea, Republic of	33.3 (2012)	32.2	32.6	33.2	33.4	34.1	...
Mongolia	32.0	25.8	24.4	26.1	28.5	29.3	25.5
Taipei,China	10.7	11.4	10.8	10.8	11.1	11.1	...
South Asia							
Bangladesh[b]	13.0	10.6	10.2	10.5	8.3	10.4	9.6
Bhutan[b]	27.4	21.4	19.8	19.5	22.8	17.9	...
India[d]	10.8	9.1	9.4	9.1	8.8	8.6	8.1*
Maldives	19.3	26.4	27.2	27.3	26.1	25.4	21.7*
Nepal[e]	18.1	21.1	23.3	23.8	26.5	25.8	...
Sri Lanka	13.0	13.3	14.1	13.8	13.5	12.6	9.2
Southeast Asia							
Brunei Darussalam[f]	49.0	20.9	23.0	23.1	32.9	26.4 |	12.2
Cambodia	13.8	18.5	19.8	20.4	22.1	24.8	22.1*
Indonesia	16.6	15.1	14.4	14.1	14.8	14.3	12.3
Lao People's Democratic Republic[g]	21.7	20.3	16.2	16.1	16.2	15.6	...
Malaysia	19.4	18.6	17.0	16.1	16.1	17.5	...
Myanmar[h]	9.8 (2012)	11.8	12.5	11.8	10.9 |	10.2	...
Philippines	12.9	14.7	14.5	14.9	15.5	16.1	15.9
Singapore[d]	16.8	18.0	18.5	20.2	18.2	21.0	...
Thailand[g]	20.6	22.2	21.4	20.8	21.2	20.9	20.7
Timor-Leste	...	91.1	88.1	81.4	86.3	65.4	...
Viet Nam[i]	26.7	23.5	24.4	25.7	25.6	25.6*	23.9*
The Pacific							
Cook Islands[b]	38.3	39.7	39.2	38.8	42.3*	39.2*	...
Fiji[j]	25.5	28.5	28.8	26.4	28.5	26.8	25.6
Kiribati[b]	64.4 (2011)	127.8	99.9	103.4	131.0*	121.3*	...
Marshall Islands[g]	62.3	58.8	61.0	68.3	62.6	61.9	70.1*
Micronesia, Federated States of[g]	67.7	66.2	69.0	80.2	90.5	79.8*	79.3*
Nauru[b]	39.2	74.5	91.6	100.6	108.5*	126.6*	116.9*
Niue	...	...	...	...	...	...	...
Palau[g]	46.7	41.2	42.0	40.0	44.4	43.5*	...
Papua New Guinea	...	...	...	15.5	17.7	16.3*	13.9*
Samoa[b]	30.2 (2012)	32.0	32.6	34.0	36.0	37.7	...
Solomon Islands	28.1	35.2	30.4	32.0	31.9	27.5	30.3
Tonga[b]	...	...	38.7	43.2	42.6	41.7	...
Tuvalu	105.3 (2012)	184.0	161.5	...	...	...	...
Vanuatu	21.8 (2012)	31.1	24.8	31.3	38.6	...	...
Developed ADB Member Economies							
Australia[b]	32.3	34.2	34.8	34.6	35.6	35.7	34.5
Japan[d]	29.9	35.0	34.7	34.9	35.5	35.2	...
New Zealand[b]	36.9	37.5	37.5	37.4	36.6	37.9	36.5

... = data not available, | = marks break in series, * = preliminary, provisional, estimate, ADB = Asian Development Bank, GDP = gross domestic product.

Note: In general, economies follow the guidelines of the International Monetary Fund on Government Finance Statistics (GFS). Some economies still use the 1986 version of the GFS guidelines, while others have switched to the 2001 or 2014 guidelines. The comparability of the data in this table is limited by variations in the concepts and definitions used in different versions of the GFS framework. Data refer to government revenue as classified in the GFS 2001 or GFS 2014 framework, except for Bhutan; Brunei Darussalam; India; the Kyrgyz Republic; Maldives; Nauru; Pakistan; the People's Republic of China; Taipei,China; Tajikistan; Turkmenistan; and Viet Nam, where data refer to total government revenue as classified in the GFS 1986 framework. Data refer to general government, except for Bangladesh; Bhutan; Brunei Darussalam; Cambodia; the Federated States of Micronesia; Fiji; India; the Lao People's Democratic Republic; Malaysia; Maldives; the Marshall Islands; Nauru; Nepal; Palau; the Philippines; Solomon Islands; Sri Lanka; Taipei,China; Timor-Leste; Tonga; Tuvalu; Vanuatu; and Viet Nam, where data refer to central government. For Cambodia: Data refer to central government excluding extra budgetary central government. For Pakistan: Data refer to the consolidated federal and provincial governments. For the People's Republic of China: Data refer to consolidated central and local governments. For Turkmenistan: Data prior to 2011 refer to central government.

a The longer time series featured in the Key Indicators Database refers to GFS data for 2005–2011 based on fiscal year beginning 21 March. For 2012, GFS data cover 9 months from 21 March to 20 December. For 2013 onward, GFS data are based on fiscal year ending 20 December. For 2005–2015, national accounts data are based on fiscal year beginning 21 March. For 2016 onward, national accounts data are based on fiscal year ending 20 December.

b Data are based on fiscal year ending 30 June.

c National accounts data prior to 2015 are based on the 1993 System of National Accounts while figures for 2015 onward are based on the 2008 System of National Accounts.

d Data are based on fiscal year beginning 1 April.

e Data are based on fiscal year ending 15 July.

f The longer time series featured in the Key Indicators Database refers to data for 2003 onward based on fiscal year beginning 1 April.

g Data are based on fiscal year ending 30 September.

h For 2012–2018, GFS data are based on fiscal year beginning 1 April. For 2019, GFS data are based on fiscal year beginning 1 October. For 2012–2015, national accounts data are based on fiscal year beginning 1 April. For 2016 onward, national accounts data are based on fiscal year beginning 1 October.

i Taxes include local government taxes.

j The longer time series featured in the Key Indicators Database refers to GFS data for 2000–2014 based on fiscal year ending 31 December. For 2015 onward, GFS data are based on fiscal year ending 31 July. National accounts data are based on calendar year.

Sources: Economy's official sources. For Hong Kong, China; Kiribati (2011–2013); Nepal; and Timor-Leste: International Monetary Fund. Government Finance Statistics. https://data.imf.org/ (accessed April–July 2021). For Nauru (2012–2020): International Monetary Fund. Staff Country Reports. Republic of Nauru: 2019 Article IV. https://www.imf.org/en/Publications/CR/Issues/2020/01/29/Republic-of-Nauru-2019-Article-IV-Consultation-Press-Release-Staff-Report-and-Statement-by-49001 (accessed 9 May 2021).

Table 2.8.4: Government Expenditure
(% of GDP)

ADB Regional Member	2010	2015	2016	2017	2018	2019	2020
Developing ADB Member Economies							
Central and West Asia							
Afghanistan[a]	20.6	25.2	29.0	27.7	29.0	28.6	28.5
Armenia	28.2	28.6	29.3	27.7	24.6	25.5	31.1*
Azerbaijan	31.6	37.2	32.8	33.5	30.2	36.8	...
Georgia	31.2	31.4	32.3	31.2	29.4	30.9	36.2
Kazakhstan	20.4	19.8	20.5	22.9	18.2	17.2	...
Kyrgyz Republic	31.2	31.3	31.8	31.3	27.7	27.1	28.7
Pakistan[b]	20.4	20.2	20.3	21.6	21.6	21.5	23.2*
Tajikistan[c]	27.2	31.9	33.4	34.6	34.0	30.8	30.2*
Turkmenistan	13.8	17.3	14.1	17.7	13.7	13.7*	...
Uzbekistan	...	24.3	23.6	22.8	24.7	27.4	28.5
East Asia							
China, People's Republic of	21.8	25.5	25.2	24.4	24.0	24.2	24.2
Hong Kong, China[d]	18.1	20.3	19.9	19.5	20.3	...	...
Korea, Republic of	...	31.1	30.2	30.7	30.3	33.2	...
Mongolia	35.2	36.8	47.3	37.1	32.6	38.3	45.9
Taipei,China	13.4	11.2	11.2	10.9	11.1	10.6	...
South Asia							
Bangladesh[b]	14.8	12.7	12.9	13.4	10.2	15.0	13.9
Bhutan[b]	35.6	29.8	32.6	32.8	34.5	25.0	...
India[d]	15.7	13.0	12.8	12.5	12.3	13.2	17.5*
Maldives	33.2	34.0	37.6	30.9	32.3	33.4	52.9*
Nepal[e]	19.5	20.1	21.9	27.2	31.9	31.1	...
Sri Lanka	19.3	20.9	19.5	19.3	18.9	19.5	22.6
Southeast Asia							
Brunei Darussalam[f]	34.0	35.7	39.7	36.3	32.8	32.0	31.5
Cambodia	18.3	19.4	20.2	21.2	21.7	22.6	26.1*
Indonesia	17.2	17.8	16.9	16.5	16.5	16.4	18.5
Lao People's Democratic Republic[g]	22.7	24.1	21.1	21.3	20.4	18.3	...
Malaysia	24.4	21.7	20.0	18.9	19.7	20.9	...
Myanmar[h]	...	16.2	15.8	15.5	16.8 |	14.2	...
Philippines	16.2	16.0	16.7	17.0	18.6	19.4	23.4
Singapore[d]	9.3	13.8	13.4	12.6	13.4	13.6	...
Thailand[g]	21.3	22.0	21.0	21.2	21.1	20.5	25.5
Timor-Leste	...	83.7	98.6	72.9	81.2	69.4	...
Viet Nam[i]	27.2	28.2	26.8	27.1	29.2*	29.1*	...
The Pacific							
Cook Islands[b]	35.5	47.5	37.8	30.1	37.1	35.1	...
Fiji[j]	30.7	34.4	33.4	27.9	34.1	30.8	29.2
Kiribati[b]	...	71.7	78.3	86.6	79.2*	102.3*	...
Marshall Islands[g]	58.8	56.0	57.1	64.0	60.1	63.7	65.1*
Micronesia, Federated States of[g]	67.2	55.9	61.8	64.5	55.5	...	...
Nauru[b]	83.6	83.1	93.4	100.5	96.8*	125.6*	118.4*
Niue	...	...	...	...	...	...	...
Palau[g]	25.8	26.4	27.1	29.3	33.5	34.3*	...
Papua New Guinea	...	...	...	17.9	20.3	21.2*	22.0*
Samoa[b]	...	35.7	31.9	34.7	34.7	33.1	...
Solomon Islands	22.1	26.7	25.7	25.5	25.2	25.4	27.8
Tonga[b]	...	...	37.2	39.6	39.7	38.6	...
Tuvalu	...	144.0	156.7	...	...	...	...
Vanuatu	...	24.2	25.2	29.1	30.2	...	...
Developed ADB Member Economies							
Australia[b]	37.8	37.1	37.4	36.8	36.8	36.9	42.1
Japan[d]	38.7	38.6	38.2	37.9	37.9	38.2	...
New Zealand[b]	40.3	37.6	36.8	36.0	35.4	36.8	42.1

... = data not available, | = marks break in series, * = preliminary, provisional, estimate, ADB = Asian Development Bank, GDP = gross domestic product.

Note: In general, economies follow the guidelines of the International Monetary Fund on Government Finance Statistics (GFS). Some economies still use the 1986 version of the GFS guidelines, while others have switched to the 2001 or 2014 guidelines. The comparability of the data in this table is limited by variations in the concepts and definitions used in different versions of the GFS framework. Data refer to government expenditure as classified in the GFS 2001 or GFS 2014 framework, except for Bhutan; Brunei Darussalam; India; the Kyrgyz Republic; Maldives; Nauru; Pakistan; the People's Republic of China; Taipei,China; Tajikistan; Turkmenistan; and Viet Nam, where data refer to total government expenditure as classified in the GFS 1986 framework. Data refer to general government, except for Bangladesh; Bhutan; Brunei Darussalam; Cambodia; the Federated States of Micronesia; Fiji; India; the Lao People's Democratic Republic; Malaysia; Maldives; the Marshall Islands; Nauru; Nepal; Palau; the Philippines; Solomon Islands; Sri Lanka; Taipei,China; Timor-Leste; Tonga; Tuvalu; Vanuatu; and Viet Nam, where data refer to central government. For Cambodia: Data refer to central government excluding extra budgetary central government. For Pakistan: Data refer to the consolidated federal and provincial governments. For the People's Republic of China: Data refer to consolidated central and local governments. For Turkmenistan: Data prior to 2011 refer to central government.

a The longer time series featured in the Key Indicators Database refers to GFS data for 2005–2011 based on fiscal year beginning 21 March. For 2012, GFS data cover 9 months from 21 March to 20 December. For 2013 onward, GFS data are based on fiscal year ending 20 December. For 2005–2015, national accounts data are based on fiscal year beginning 21 March. For 2016 onward, national accounts data are based on fiscal year ending 20 December.
b Data are based on fiscal year ending 30 June.
c National accounts data prior to 2015 are based on the 1993 System of National Accounts while data for 2015 onward are based on the 2008 System of National Accounts.
d Data are based on fiscal year beginning 1 April.
e Data are based on fiscal year ending 15 July.
f For 2003 onward, data are based on fiscal year beginning 1 April.
g Data are based on fiscal year ending 30 September.
h For 2012–2018, GFS data are based on fiscal year beginning 1 April. For 2019, data are based on fiscal year beginning 1 October. For 2012–2015, national accounts data are based on fiscal year beginning 1 April. For 2016 onward, national accounts data are based on fiscal year beginning 1 October.
i Includes local government expenditure.
j The longer time series featured in the Key Indicators Database refers to GFS data for 2000–2014 based on fiscal year ending 31 December. For 2015 onward, GFS data are based on fiscal year ending 31 July. National accounts data for are based on calendar year.

Sources: Economy's official sources. For Hong Kong, China; Kiribati (2011–2013); Nepal; and Timor-Leste: International Monetary Fund. Government Finance Statistics. https://data.imf.org/ (accessed April–July 2021). For Nauru (2012–2020): International Monetary Fund. Staff Country Reports. Republic of Nauru: 2019 Article IV. https://www.imf.org/en/Publications/CR/Issues/2020/01/29/Republic-of-Nauru-2019-Article-IV-Consultation-Press-Release-Staff-Report-and-Statement-by-49001 (accessed 9 May 2021).

Table 2.8.5: Government Expenditure by Economic Activity
(% of GDP)

ADB Regional Member	Health				Education				Social Protection			
	2010	2015	2019	2020	2010	2015	2019	2020	2010	2015	2019	2020
Developing ADB Member Economies												
Central and West Asia												
Afghanistan[a]	0.9	1.2	1.4	1.8	3.6	3.6	3.2	2.1	0.5	1.4	1.2	1.1
Armenia	1.6	1.7	1.5	2.4*	3.2	2.9	2.4	2.8*	7.1	7.7	7.0	8.9*
Azerbaijan	1.0	1.3	1.1	...	2.9	3.1	2.8	...	6.8	6.8	6.4	...
Georgia	2.1	2.7	2.7	3.7	2.8	4.4	4.4	4.4	6.5	7.3	6.8	9.5
Kazakhstan	2.5	2.1	2.0	...	3.5	3.3	3.7	...	4.5	4.5	5.9	...
Kyrgyz Republic	2.9	3.0	2.3	2.9	5.4	5.9	5.8	6.7	5.0	5.8	5.3	5.7
Pakistan[b]	...	...	...	...	...	...	...	...	...	...	...	...
Tajikistan[c]	1.4 |	2.0	2.3	2.6*	4.0 |	5.0	5.7	5.4*	3.5 |	5.2	4.5	3.5*
Turkmenistan	...	...	...	...	...	...	...	...	...	...	...	...
Uzbekistan	...	2.5	2.5	3.3	...	6.0	7.0	6.3	...	7.4	6.5	9.3
East Asia												
China, People's Republic of	1.2	1.7	1.7	1.9	3.0	3.8	3.5	3.6	2.2	2.8	3.0	3.2
Hong Kong, China[d]	2.4	3.2	3.0 (2018)	...	3.5	3.4	4.0 (2018)	...	2.4	2.9	3.4 (2018)	...
Korea, Republic of	0.2	0.3	0.2	...	2.8	3.0	3.7	...	4.3	5.3	6.8	...
Mongolia	2.5	2.5	2.4	...	5.1	3.0	3.7	...	11.1	7.6	7.5	...
Taipei,China	0.2	0.1	0.1	...	1.7	1.4	1.5	...	3.1	3.3	3.2	...
South Asia												
Bangladesh[b]	0.8	0.7	0.7	0.6	2.0	2.0	2.5	2.3	0.9	0.7	1.4	1.2
Bhutan[b]	3.0	2.8	2.8	...	6.7	6.0	5.4	...	3.1	3.2	2.4	...
India[d]	1.0 (2011)	1.2	1.3	...	4.4 (2011)	4.4	4.7	...	1.4 (2011)	1.8	2.0	...
Maldives	2.9	4.0	3.9	9.1*	5.3	4.6	4.2	5.8*	1.7	5.1	5.1	7.4*
Nepal[e]	1.5	1.4	1.0	...	3.9	3.7	1.0	...	0.8	0.7	1.2	...
Sri Lanka	1.2	1.6	1.6	...	1.6	2.1	1.9	...	1.7	5.0	...	...
Southeast Asia												
Brunei Darussalam[d]	1.8	2.3	2.0	...	3.6	4.1	3.6	...	0.8	0.8	0.7	...
Cambodia	1.3	1.3	1.4	1.5*	1.6	2.0	2.7	2.8*	0.5	0.8	0.9	1.1*
Indonesia	1.0	1.1	1.5	1.7	3.4	3.3	2.8	3.0	0.1	0.3	1.3	2.0
Lao People's Democratic Republic	...	...	...	...	...	...	...	...	...	...	...	...
Malaysia	2.0	2.0	2.0	...	6.1	4.8	4.2	...	...	...	...	...
Myanmar[f]	0.7 (2012)	1.0 |	0.8	...	1.5 (2012)	2.1 |	2.0	...	0.4 (2012)	0.8 |	0.9	...
Philippines[g]	0.3	0.8	0.9	1.1	2.4	2.8	3.4	3.9	1.6	1.3	1.5	3.0
Singapore[d]	1.2	2.1	2.2	...	3.0	2.9	2.6	...	1.1	1.8	0.9	...
Thailand[h]	...	1.1	1.3	1.4	...	3.8	3.0	3.1	...	2.5	3.1	5.6
Timor-Leste	4.0	3.7	3.4 (2018)	...	7.8	6.5	4.8 (2018)	...	16.3	11.7	8.7 (2018)	...
Viet Nam	...	...	...	...	...	...	...	...	...	...	...	...
The Pacific												
Cook Islands[b]	3.9	3.0	2.8*	...	4.0	3.5	3.2*	...	3.9	4.2	3.8*	...
Fiji	...	...	...	...	...	...	...	...	...	...	...	...
Kiribati[b]	...	9.9	12.0*	...	...	9.9	12.2*	...	...	1.4	2.2*	...
Marshall Islands[h]	8.1	7.5	...	...	20.4	16.4	...	...	–	–	...	...
Micronesia, Federated States of	...	...	...	...	...	...	...	...	...	...	...	...
Nauru	...	...	...	...	...	...	...	...	...	...	...	...
Niue	...	...	...	...	...	...	...	...	...	...	...	...
Palau	...	...	...	...	...	...	...	...	...	...	...	...
Papua New Guinea	...	...	...	...	...	...	...	...	...	...	...	...
Samoa[b]	3.6	5.4	5.0	5.3	5.8	4.5	4.5	4.9	1.1	2.1	1.2	1.3
Solomon Islands	...	...	...	...	...	...	...	...	...	...	...	...
Tonga	...	...	...	...	...	...	...	...	...	...	...	...
Tuvalu	8.5 (2012)	9.4	...	...	16.0 (2012)	23.2	...	...	6.1 (2012)	18.3	...	...
Vanuatu	2.9 (2011)	2.4	2.7 (2018)	...	6.2 (2011)	5.4	6.7 (2018)	...	0.0 (2011)	0.1	...	...
Developed ADB Member Economies												
Australia[b]	6.7	6.8	7.1	7.4	5.9	5.4	5.4	5.7	9.9	10.4	9.7	11.0
Japan[d]	6.8	7.3	7.4	...	2.8	2.6	2.5	...	2.1	2.5	2.6	...
New Zealand[b]	7.0	6.8	6.7	7.1	6.8	6.2	5.8	6.1	12.5	11.5	10.6	11.3

... = data not available, | = marks break in series, 0.0 = magnitude is less than half of unit employed, * = preliminary, provisional, estimate, ADB = Asian Development Bank, GDP = gross domestic product.

Note: In general, economies follow the guidelines of the International Monetary Fund on Government Finance Statistics (GFS). Some economies still use the 1986 version of the GFS guidelines, while others have switched to the 2001 or 2014 guidelines. The comparability of the data in this table is limited by variations in the concepts and definitions used in different versions of the GFS framework. The table refers to government expenditure by economic activity as classified in the GFS 2001 or GFS 2014 framework, except for Bhutan; Brunei Darussalam; India; the Kyrgyz Republic; Maldives; the People's Republic of China; and Taipei,China, where data refer to health, education, and social security and welfare, as classified in the GFS 1986 framework. Data refer to general government, except for Bangladesh; Bhutan; Brunei Darussalam; Cambodia; India; Malaysia; Maldives; the Marshall Islands; Nepal; the Philippines; Samoa; Sri Lanka; Taipei,China; Timor-Leste; Tuvalu; and Vanuatu, where data refer to central government. For Cambodia: Data refer to central government excluding extra budgetary central government. For the People's Republic of China: Data refer to consolidated central and local governments.

a The longer time series featured in the Key Indicators Database refers to GFS data for 2005–2011 based on fiscal year beginning 21 March. For 2012, GFS data cover 9 months from 21 March to 20 December. For 2013 onward, GFS data are based on fiscal year ending 20 December. For 2005–2015, national accounts data are based on fiscal year beginning 21 March. For 2016 onward, national accounts data are based on fiscal year ending 20 December.
b Data are based on fiscal year ending 30 June.
c National accounts data prior to 2015 are based on the 1993 System of National Accounts while data for 2015 onward are based on the 2008 System of National Accounts.
d Data are based on fiscal year beginning 1 April.
e Data are based on fiscal year ending 15 July.
f For 2012–2018, GFS data are based on fiscal year beginning 1 April. For 2019, GFS data are based on fiscal year beginning 1 October. For 2012–2015, national accounts data are based on fiscal year beginning 1 April. For 2016 onward, national accounts data are based on fiscal year beginning 1 October.
g For 2000–2013, data on education include expenditure on recreation, culture, and religion.
h Data are based on fiscal year ending 30 September.

Sources: Economy's official sources. For Hong Kong, China; Kiribati (2011–2013); Nepal; and Timor-Leste: International Monetary Fund. Government Finance Statistics. https://data.imf.org/ (accessed April–July 2021). For Nauru (2012–2020): International Monetary Fund. Staff Country Reports. Republic of Nauru: 2019 Article IV. https://www.imf.org/en/Publications/CR/Issues/2020/01/29/Republic-of-Nauru-2019-Article-IV-Consultation-Press-Release-Staff-Report-and-Statement-by-49001 (accessed 9 May 2021).

Table 2.8.6: Indicators for Business Startups

ADB Regional Member	Time Required to Start a Business (days)					Score (Starting a Business)[a]					Rank[b]
	2010	2015	2018	2019	2020	2010	2015	2018	2019	2020	2020
Developing ADB Member Economies											
Central and West Asia											
Afghanistan	9.5	8.5	8.5	8.5	8.5	87.3	91.0	82.6	92.0	92.0	52
Armenia	14.0	5.0	5.0	4.0	4.0	88.9	94.3	94.3	96.1	96.1	10
Azerbaijan	10.0	5.5	3.5	3.5	3.5	89.9	93.9	96.1	96.1	96.2	9
Georgia	3.0	2.0	2.0	2.0	1.0	96.0	97.7	97.8	99.3	99.6	2
Kazakhstan	26.0	16.0	9.0	5.0	5.0	81.8	87.2	91.9	93.0	94.4	22
Kyrgyz Republic	15.0	10.0	10.0	10.0	10.0	89.8	92.9	92.9	93.0	93.0	42
Pakistan	...	20.0	16.5	16.5	16.5	...	75.6	76.6	81.9	89.3	72
Tajikistan	42.0	28.0	10.0	10.0	7.0	69.7	85.8	90.8	91.0	93.2	36
Turkmenistan	...	...	...	...	...	...	...	...	...	...	...
Uzbekistan	14.0	7.5	5.0	3.0	3.0	82.7	90.5	95.5	96.0	96.2	8
East Asia											
China, People's Republic of	...	29.4	22.9	8.6	8.6	...	80.9	85.4	93.4	94.1	27
Hong Kong, China	6.0	2.5	1.5	1.5	1.5	95.5	96.4	98.1	98.1	98.2	5
Korea, Republic of	14.0	8.0	8.0	8.0	8.0	84.5	91.9	93.4	93.4	93.4	33
Mongolia	17.0	16.0	12.0	12.0	12.0	82.4	87.1	86.6	86.7	86.7	100
Taipei,China	22.0	10.0	10.0	10.0	10.0	86.8	94.4	94.4	94.4	94.4	21
South Asia											
Bangladesh	...	19.5	19.5	19.5	19.5	...	81.4	80.6	80.8	82.4	131
Bhutan	46.0	15.0	12.0	12.0	12.0	77.4	85.5	86.3	86.4	86.4	103
India	...	35.0	29.8	16.5	17.5	...	61.8	73.9	81.0	81.6	136
Maldives	12.0	12.0	12.0	12.0	12.0	88.3	88.8	89.1	89.2	89.2	74
Nepal	31.0	17.0	18.5	18.5	22.5	76.8	83.0	81.8	82.1	81.7	135
Sri Lanka	44.0	11.0	9.0	9.0	8.0	72.1	83.0	87.7	87.9	88.2	85
Southeast Asia											
Brunei Darussalam	121.5	104.5	12.5	5.5	5.5	48.8	48.7	90.2	94.9	94.9	16
Cambodia	102.0	101.0	99.0	99.0	99.0	34.0	37.3	51.9	52.8	52.4	187
Indonesia	...	53.9	24.5	21.0	12.6	...	64.1	76.1	79.4	81.2	140
Lao People's Democratic Republic	86.0	88.0	174.0	174.0	173.0	62.0	64.9	60.9	60.9	62.7	181
Malaysia	18.5	7.5	23.5	13.5	17.5	79.6	89.3	80.1	82.8	83.3	126
Myanmar	...	77.0	14.0	14.0	7.0	...	17.7	75.4	77.3	89.3	70
Philippines	34.0	26.0	39.0	34.0	33.0	62.6	67.2	64.2	69.3	71.3	171
Singapore	2.5	2.5	2.5	1.5	1.5	96.5	96.5	96.5	98.2	98.2	4
Thailand	34.0	31.0	6.0	6.0	6.0	77.7	82.7	92.0	92.3	92.4	47
Timor-Leste	157.0	15.0	13.0	13.0	13.0	41.9	81.0	72.6	89.4	89.4	68
Viet Nam	37.0	34.0	22.0	17.0	16.0	75.9	79.2	82.0	84.8	85.1	115
The Pacific											
Cook Islands	...	...	...	...	...	...	...	...	...	...	...
Fiji	44.0	58.0	40.0	40.0	40.0	75.6	68.0	73.3	73.4	73.6	163
Kiribati	31.0	31.0	31.0	31.0	31.0	76.5	76.7	77.5	78.2	78.4	149
Marshall Islands	17.0	17.0	17.0	17.0	17.0	87.9	88.4	88.5	88.4	88.4	83
Micronesia, Federated States of	16.0	16.0	16.0	16.0	16.0	70.3	69.6	69.6	69.6	69.6	174
Nauru	...	...	...	...	...	...	...	...	...	...	...
Niue	...	...	...	...	...	...	...	...	...	...	...
Palau	28.0	28.0	28.0	28.0	28.0	81.6	81.8	82.0	81.9	82.1	132
Papua New Guinea	52.0	53.0	41.0	41.0	41.0	77.3	77.0	79.9	79.9	80.1	142
Samoa	9.0	9.0	9.0	9.0	9.0	92.2	92.3	92.5	92.6	92.6	46
Solomon Islands	55.0	9.0	9.0	9.0	9.0	68.7	84.6	85.4	85.5	85.6	110
Tonga	25.0	16.0	16.0	16.0	16.0	88.4	90.8	90.8	90.9	90.9	62
Tuvalu	...	...	...	...	...	...	...	...	...	...	...
Vanuatu	47.0	35.0	18.0	18.0	18.0	71.3	75.3	81.2	81.5	81.5	137
Developed ADB Member Economies											
Australia	2.5	2.5	2.5	2.5	2.0	96.5	96.5	96.5	96.5	96.6	7
Japan	...	11.2	11.2	11.2	11.2	...	86.1	86.1	86.1	86.1	106
New Zealand	0.5	0.5	0.5	0.5	0.5	99.9	100.0	100.0	100.0	100.0	1
DEVELOPING ADB MEMBER ECONOMIES[c]	**35.5**	**26.6**	**21.5**	**19.8**	**19.5**						
ALL ADB REGIONAL MEMBERS[c]	**33.6**	**25.1**	**20.3**	**18.8**	**18.5**						
WORLD[c]	**37.7**	**24.4**	**21.5**	**20.4**	**19.5**						

... = data not available, ADB = Asian Development Bank

a The score for ease of starting a business is the simple average of the scores for four component indicators: procedures, time, and cost for an entrepreneur to start and formally operate a business, and the paid-in minimum capital requirement. The score is reflected on a scale from 0 to 100, where 0 represents the lowest and 100 represents the best performance.

b Rank among the 190 economies as presented in the World Bank's Doing Business 2020. The rank is determined by each economy's score for starting a business.

c Aggregates are ADB estimates using data from Doing Business 2020. Estimates were calculated as the arithmetic average for reporting economies with data corresponding to the year heading.

Source: World Bank. Doing Business. https://www.doingbusiness.org/ (accessed 4 June 2021).

Table 2.8.7: Corruption Perceptions Index

ADB Regional Member	2010	2015	2016	2017	2018	2019	2020	Rank in 2019[a]	Rank in 2020[a]
Developing ADB Member Economies									
Central and West Asia									
Afghanistan	1.4 |	11.0	15.0	15.0	16.0	16.0	19.0	173	165
Armenia	2.6 |	35.0	33.0	35.0	35.0	42.0	49.0	77	60
Azerbaijan	2.4 |	29.0	30.0	31.0	25.0	30.0	30.0	126	129
Georgia	3.8 |	52.0	57.0	56.0	58.0	56.0	56.0	44	45
Kazakhstan	2.9 |	28.0	29.0	31.0	31.0	34.0	38.0	113	94
Kyrgyz Republic	2.0 |	28.0	28.0	29.0	29.0	30.0	31.0	126	124
Pakistan	2.3 |	30.0	32.0	32.0	33.0	32.0	31.0	120	124
Tajikistan	2.1 |	26.0	25.0	21.0	25.0	25.0	25.0	153	149
Turkmenistan	1.6 |	18.0	22.0	19.0	20.0	19.0	19.0	165	165
Uzbekistan	1.6 |	19.0	21.0	22.0	23.0	25.0	26.0	153	146
East Asia									
China, People's Republic of	3.5 |	37.0	40.0	41.0	39.0	41.0	42.0	80	78
Hong Kong, China	8.4 |	75.0	77.0	77.0	76.0	76.0	77.0	16	11
Korea, Republic of	5.4 |	54.0	53.0	54.0	57.0	59.0	61.0	39	33
Mongolia	2.7 |	39.0	38.0	36.0	37.0	35.0	35.0	106	111
Taipei,China	5.8 |	62.0	61.0	63.0	63.0	65.0	65.0	28	28
South Asia									
Bangladesh	2.4 |	25.0	26.0	28.0	26.0	26.0	26.0	146	146
Bhutan	5.7 |	65.0	65.0	67.0	68.0	68.0	68.0	25	24
India	3.3 |	38.0	40.0	40.0	41.0	41.0	40.0	80	86
Maldives	2.3 |	...	36.0	33.0	31.0	29.0	43.0	130	75
Nepal	2.2 |	27.0	29.0	31.0	31.0	34.0	33.0	113	117
Sri Lanka	3.2 |	37.0	36.0	38.0	38.0	38.0	38.0	93	94
Southeast Asia									
Brunei Darussalam	5.5 |	...	58.0	62.0	63.0	60.0	60.0	35	35
Cambodia	2.1 |	21.0	21.0	21.0	20.0	20.0	21.0	162	160
Indonesia	2.8 |	36.0	37.0	37.0	38.0	40.0	37.0	85	102
Lao People's Democratic Republic	2.1 |	25.0	30.0	29.0	29.0	29.0	29.0	130	134
Malaysia	4.4 |	50.0	49.0	47.0	47.0	53.0	51.0	51	57
Myanmar	1.4 |	22.0	28.0	30.0	29.0	29.0	28.0	130	137
Philippines	2.4 |	35.0	35.0	34.0	36.0	34.0	34.0	113	115
Singapore	9.3 |	85.0	84.0	84.0	85.0	85.0	85.0	4	3
Thailand	3.5 |	38.0	35.0	37.0	36.0	36.0	36.0	101	104
Timor-Leste	2.5 |	28.0	35.0	38.0	35.0	38.0	40.0	93	86
Viet Nam	2.7 |	31.0	33.0	35.0	33.0	37.0	36.0	96	104
The Pacific									
Cook Islands	...	...	...	...	...	...	...	...	...
Fiji	...	...	...	...	...	...	...	...	...
Kiribati	3.2 |	...	...	...	...	...	...	...	...
Marshall Islands	...	...	...	...	...	...	...	...	...
Micronesia, Federated States of	...	...	...	...	...	...	...	...	...
Nauru	...	...	...	...	...	...	...	...	...
Niue	...	...	...	...	...	...	...	...	...
Palau	...	...	...	...	...	...	...	...	...
Papua New Guinea	2.1 |	25.0	28.0	29.0	28.0	28.0	27.0	137	142
Samoa	4.1 |	...	...	...	...	...	...	...	...
Solomon Islands	2.8 |	...	42.0	39.0	44.0	42.0	42.0	77	78
Tonga	3.0 |	...	...	...	...	...	...	...	...
Tuvalu	...	...	...	...	...	...	...	...	...
Vanuatu	3.6 |	...	...	43.0	46.0	46.0	43.0	64	75
Developed ADB Member Economies									
Australia	8.7 |	79.0	79.0	77.0	77.0	77.0	77.0	12	11
Japan	7.8 |	75.0	72.0	73.0	73.0	73.0	74.0	20	19
New Zealand	9.3 |	88.0	90.0	89.0	87.0	87.0	88.0	1	1

... = data not available, | = marks break in the series, ADB = Asian Development Bank.

Note: The Key Indicators Database features a longer time series of scores on the Corruption Perceptions Index. This includes scores for 2000–2011, which refer to perceptions of the degree of corruption as seen by business people and analysts, and are not comparable over time. Those scores range from 0 (highly corrupt) to 10 (very clean). From 2012 onward, an updated methodology was used to calculate scores, and these are presented on a scale from 0 (highly corrupt) to 100 (very clean). Due to the differences in methodology, scores prior to 2012 should not be compared with scores from 2012 onward.

a Based on Transparency International's methodology, an economy's rank indicates its position relative to the Corruption Perceptions Index of other economies of the world; 2019 and 2020 rankings compare 180 economies.

Source: Transparency International. Corruption Perceptions Index. https://www.transparency.org/ (accessed 3 June 2021).

Data Issues and Comparability

Most economies generally follow the IMF's Government Finance Statistics (GFS) guidelines: some still use the 1986 version, while others have switched to the 2001 or 2014 versions. The comparability of the data is limited by variations in the concepts and definitions used in different versions of the GFS framework. Furthermore, there is no single framework for an extended time series available in most economies that are using the 2014 guidelines, with most economies recording their transactions on a cash basis (and a few on an accrual basis).

Data on government expenditures and revenue are derived from economy's official sources and are therefore not standard throughout Asia and the Pacific. Data refer to general government for some economies, and central government for other economies.

Statistics on the time, score, and rank for registering new businesses, and on perceived corruption, are taken from nonofficial sources. Common procedures are used in all economies and the researchers producing these data have refined their procedures over several surveys. However, because of the subjective nature of many of the data, they can only be used to give a broad idea of trends, levels, and rankings, so small changes from one year to the next should be interpreted with caution.

PART III

Global Value Chains

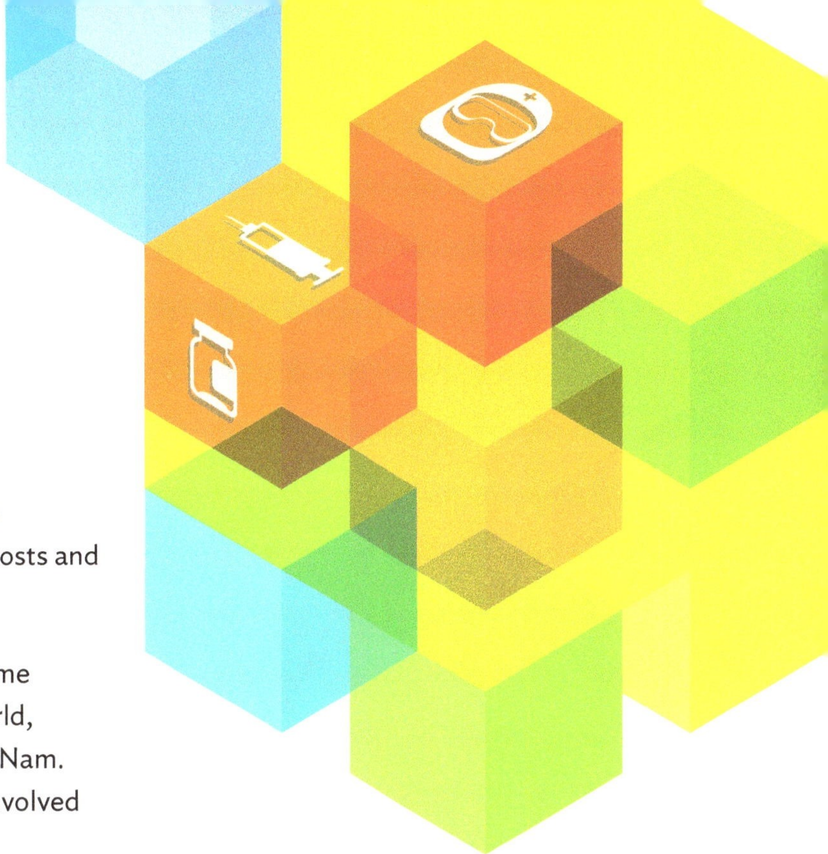

The COVID-19 Shock and the Two Faces of Global Value Chains

Snapshot

- The coronavirus disease 2019 (COVID-19) pandemic has sharpened debates over the costs and benefits of global value chains (GVCs).
- Asia and the Pacific continues to feature some of the most integrated economies in the world, including Singapore; Taipei,China; and Viet Nam. In 2020, some 39% of the region's exports involved indirect trading.
- Examining pandemic-induced demand shocks under varying hypothetical states of openness point to the amplifying effect of GVCs, as well as to the diverse experience of economies.
- Participation in GVCs and the size of the pandemic-related shock to gross domestic product (GDP) appear to have a U-shaped relationship. Greater participation is associated with a larger negative shock in 2020, but the relationship reverses beyond a certain point.

While debates over the risks of extended supply chains predate the COVID-19 pandemic, the unprecedented disruptions the coronavirus caused have escalated calls for some reshoring of economic activities and for greater economic self-sufficiency. What insights can a statistical analysis of the relationship between participation in GVCs and the economic impact from COVID-19 provide? Are economies that are more extensively embedded in international production networks more negatively affected by the pandemic, or less negatively affected?

In 2021, *Key Indicators for Asia and the Pacific (Key Indicators)* investigates this relationship between GVCs and economic performance during the pandemic. Using counterfactual exercises, it finds a wide range of outcomes for economies. However, on average, GVCs slightly amplified the effect of shocks via exposure to depressed foreign demand, compared to the counterfactual scenarios of autarky and bilateral-only trade. In a cross-economy analysis, it also finds a U-shaped relationship between GVC participation and the COVID-19 shock to growth, indicating again the heterogeneity of outcomes among economies. GVCs clearly have the power to both mitigate and amplify global disruptions.

In a continuing effort to sharpen analytical tools, this edition of *Key Indicators* also revisits the GVC framework the publication first presented in 2015, updating and streamlining it in a new exposition that can be found in Appendix 3.1. The analyses and tables in Part III all follow this revised framework. Because calculation of the indicators relies on the Asian Development Bank's Multiregional Input–Output (MRIO) Database, only 26 of the bank's 49 member economies from Asia and the Pacific can be included: 24 developing economies, plus Australia and Japan.[1]

The COVID-19 Shock Under Different Trading Scenarios

Shocks such as the COVID-19 pandemic highlight the trade-offs that come with global economic integration. While an economy that is highly reliant on foreign markets is dependent on other economies whose performance has been hit hard by lockdowns, diversification can provide a buffer against plunges in domestic demand.

Quantifying this trade-off can be done through a counterfactual exercise that models COVID-19 demand shocks through prevailing input-output structures under three scenarios: autarky, classical trading, and GVCs. Depending on the scenario, an economy's GDP is modeled to respond only to certain sources of demand. The first scenario of

1 The data presented in Part III are not official statistics. Production and trade data from various sources were integrated into the input–output economic framework and adjusted to conform with specific macroeconomic concepts. As such, data and statistics presented here could differ from relevant official statistics.

autarky assumes no cross-border trading, so the entirely self-reliant economy responds solely to shocks in domestic demand. The second scenario of classical trading allows cross-border trade, but assumes it to be entirely bilateral, with no re-exporting. GDP responds to domestic demand shocks and demand fluctuations of direct importers. Finally, the GVC scenario is the world as it is, with value-added crossing multiple borders before final consumption. GDP in this case responds to the demand of economies with which it is linked through the global supply chain. All channels of demand are open. Details of this methodology are given in Box 3.1.

Figure 3.1 presents the results of the counterfactual exercise described. Mongolia, Cambodia, and Singapore had the most to gain, respectively, from shifting from an autarkic scenario to one that allows trading. To take Mongolia as an example, estimates suggest that under real-world conditions, the COVID-19 shock resulted in a 17% contraction in its nominal GDP, relative to what it would have been without the pandemic. However, turning off indirect trading channels would have worsened this to a 17.9% contraction. Even this pales in comparison to the steep 20.9% contraction that would have resulted if Mongolia were forced to rely solely on domestic demand. As a developing economy with a small population, the country undoubtedly benefits from tapping into foreign markets, even during a global health crisis.

Box 3.1: Methodology to Assess the COVID-19 Shock under Different Scenarios

Input–output analysis allows one to distinguish the channels by which demand shocks impact the gross domestic product (GDP) of an economy. Different scenarios are identified by turning certain channels on and off. The present analysis identifies three:

Autarkic scenario. Only domestic channels are open. Foreign demand does not impact GDP at all.

Classical trading scenario. Trading occurs, but only directly, i.e., there is no re-exporting. This corresponds to the classical idea of trade commonly assumed in economics textbooks. Domestic demand and the demand of the bilateral partner impact GDP.

Global value chain scenario. Both direct and indirect trading occur. GDP is responsive to demand from all economies. This scenario corresponds to real-world conditions.

The COVID-19 shock is estimated by the difference in reported final demand for 2020 and forecasts for 2020 made by the World Bank at the start of the year (World Bank 2020), a methodology similar in spirit to Giglioli et al. (2021). The World Bank has the widest set of final demand forecasts, so its dataset is used here. All other data are derived from the Asian Development Bank's 2020 Multiregional Input–Output Database. Values are in current prices.

Under scenario R, the impact of the COVID-19 shock to the GDP of economy s is given by

$$\text{Shock}_s^R = \frac{\text{GDP}_s^R(\mathbf{Y}^{\text{actual}}) - \text{GDP}_s^R(\mathbf{Y}^{\text{forecast}})}{\text{GDP}_s^R(\mathbf{Y}^{\text{forecast}})}$$

A comparison of $\text{Shock}_s^{\text{Autarky}}$, $\text{Shock}_s^{\text{Classical}}$, and $\text{Shock}_s^{\text{GVC}}$ provides a heuristic explanation of how the presence of global value chains dampens or intensifies global demand shocks.

Sources

S. Giglioli, G. Giovannetti, E. Marvasi, and A. Vivoli. 2021. The Resilience of Global Value Chains During the Covid-19 Pandemic: The Case of Italy. *UniFI DISEI Working Paper No. 07/2021*. Florence, Italy: Università degli Studi Firenze Dipartimento di Scienze per L'Economia e L'Impresa.

World Bank. 2020. *Global Economic Prospects: Slow Growth, Policy Challenges (January 2020)*. Washington, DC: World Bank.

Figure 3.1: The COVID-19 Shock under Different Trading Scenarios

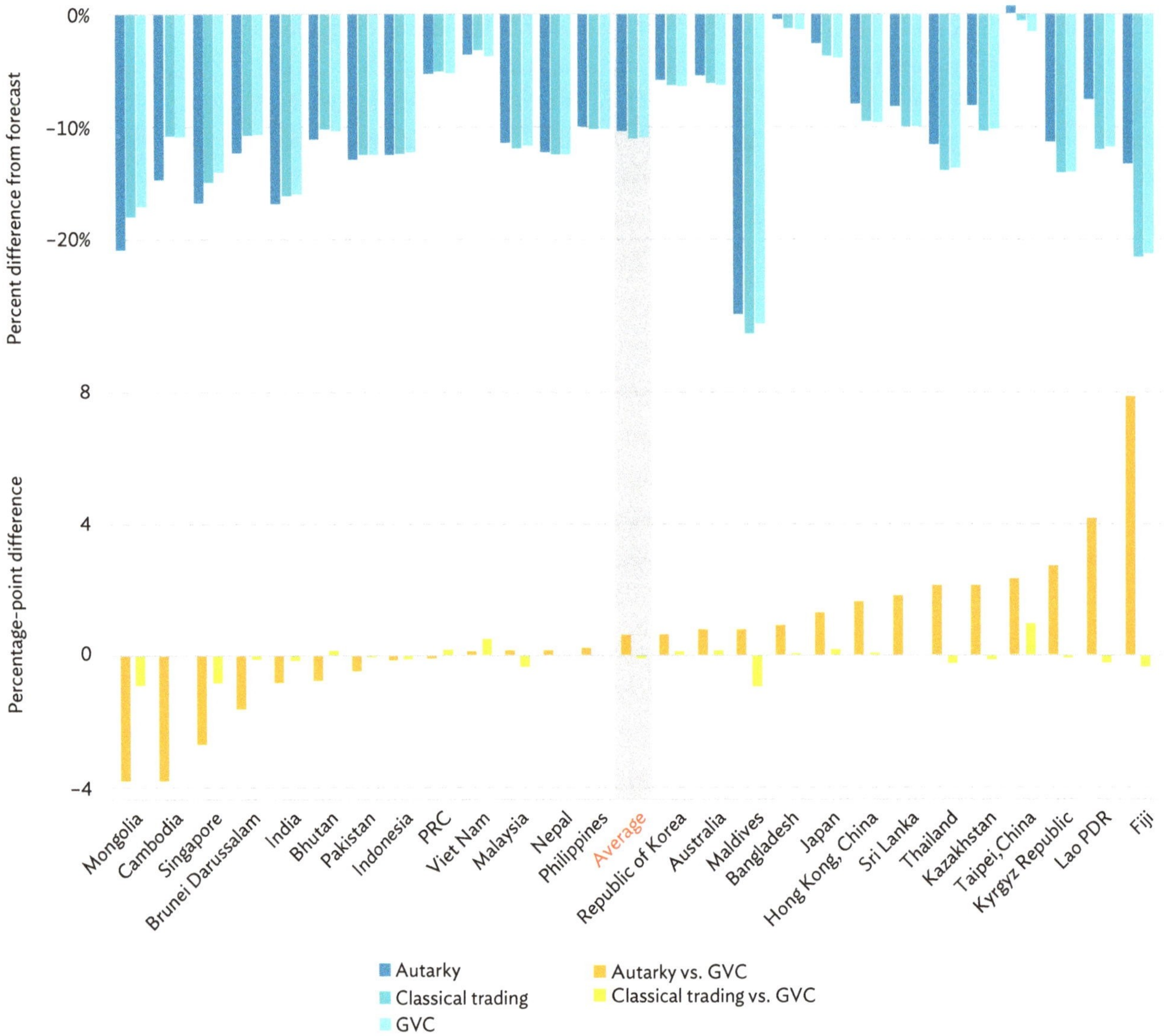

GVC = global value chain, Lao PDR = Lao People's Democratic Republic, PRC = People's Republic of China.
Note: Average is unweighted.
Sources: Asian Development Bank estimates; and Asian Development Bank Multiregional Input–Output Database, 2021.

On the other end is Fiji, a tourism-oriented economy. Under the GVC scenario, the COVID-19 shock contracted the country's nominal GDP by 21.2% relative to a pandemic-free 2020, comparable to the 21.5% contraction under the classical trading scenario. However, excluding all external demand channels brings the contraction down to 13.3%. Fiji's high exposure to foreign demand has clearly amplified the shock of COVID-19. Indeed, it is notable that the only other economy that experienced a worse shock was Maldives, another small, tourism-reliant island economy.

On average, GVCs have tended to amplify rather than dampen the COVID-19 shock for the 26 economies studied, with the shock being 0.6 points smaller under autarky compared with a GVC world. Note, however, that the difference is relatively small when compared with the realized shock of –10.9%. The average may also be skewed by the overrepresentation of trade-oriented developing economies in the sample. Indeed, a more sophisticated exercise performed by the Organisation for Economic Co-operation and Development (OECD) using a computable general equilibrium trade model finds that, in the presence of shocks, a "localized" regime tends to feature *lower* levels of GDP and *increased* instability relative to an "interconnected" regime (OECD 2021).

Global Value Chain Participation and COVID-19 Outcomes

For a clearer idea of how integration correlates with COVID-19 outcomes, a measure for GVC participation is necessary. This is obtained by categorizing the value of gross exports into those that stem from direct trading and those that stem from indirect trading. The latter consists of re-exports, imported inputs, and the purely double-counted quantities that arise when value-added crosses the same border twice or more. Details for decomposing exports are given in Box 3.2 and Appendix 3.1.

Box 3.2: Methodology to Assess Relationship Between Global Value Chain Participation and the COVID-19 Shock

Gross exports mask several distinct quantities that each provide information on the exporting economy's global value chain (GVC) engagement. Disentangling these is the purpose of a value-added trade accounting framework, discussed more thoroughly in Appendix 3.1. To summarize, gross exports may be divided into five main categories:

DAVAX. Domestic value-added (DVA) exported to, and directly absorbed by, the importer.

REX. DVA exported to and re-exported by the importer, to eventually be absorbed abroad.

REF. DVA exported to and re-exported by the importer, to eventually be absorbed back home.

FVA. Foreign value-added. Imported inputs of goods and services in the overall exports of an economy.

PDC. Pure double-counting. In a GVC, some goods or services may cross the same border on two or more occasions.

DAVAX is direct trading, where value-added solely from the exporter is sent to, and absorbed solely by, the importer. The rest involve multiple border crossings before final consumption. Such indirect trading is what is understood in this analysis as GVC participation. The share of indirect trading in gross exports is the trade-based GVC participation rate.

As in Box 3.1, the COVID-19 shock is the difference between forecasted and actual growth rates for 2020. This time, the variable of interest is gross domestic product. Forecasts are from the October 2019 edition of the International Monetary Fund's *World Economic Outlook* (IMF 2019), while actual growth rates are from the IMF's April 2021 edition (IMF 2021). The IMF has the most complete set of gross domestic product forecasts for the Asian Development Bank Multiregional Input-Output economies.

In correlating GVC participation rates and the COVID-19 shock, participation rates for 2019 are used since rates for 2020 would have adjusted in some way to the pandemic, muddling the direction of causality.

Sources

International Monetary Fund (IMF). 2019. *World Economic Outlook: Global Manufacturing Downturn, Rising Trade Barriers.* Washington, DC: International Monetary Fund.

IMF. 2021. *World Economic Outlook: Managing Divergent Recoveries.* Washington, DC: International Monetary Fund.

Looking at Asia and the Pacific's exports in Figure 3.2 gives a notion of how integrated each economy is to GVCs. The green and red regions represent the import content of exports and thus gauge integration in a backward sense. The leaders here are the financial hub of Singapore and the manufacturing hubs of Viet Nam and Cambodia, all of whom had import contents of over 40%. These three take in substantial foreign value-added for processing, after which they pass this value-added along the chain. On the other end are economies such as Australia and Kazakhstan, whose commodity-rich exports naturally comprise mostly domestic content. Size is also a factor as large economies such as Indonesia, Japan, and the People's Republic of China are able to source much of their inputs domestically.

Figure 3.2: Value-Added Categories in Asia and the Pacific's Exports, 2020

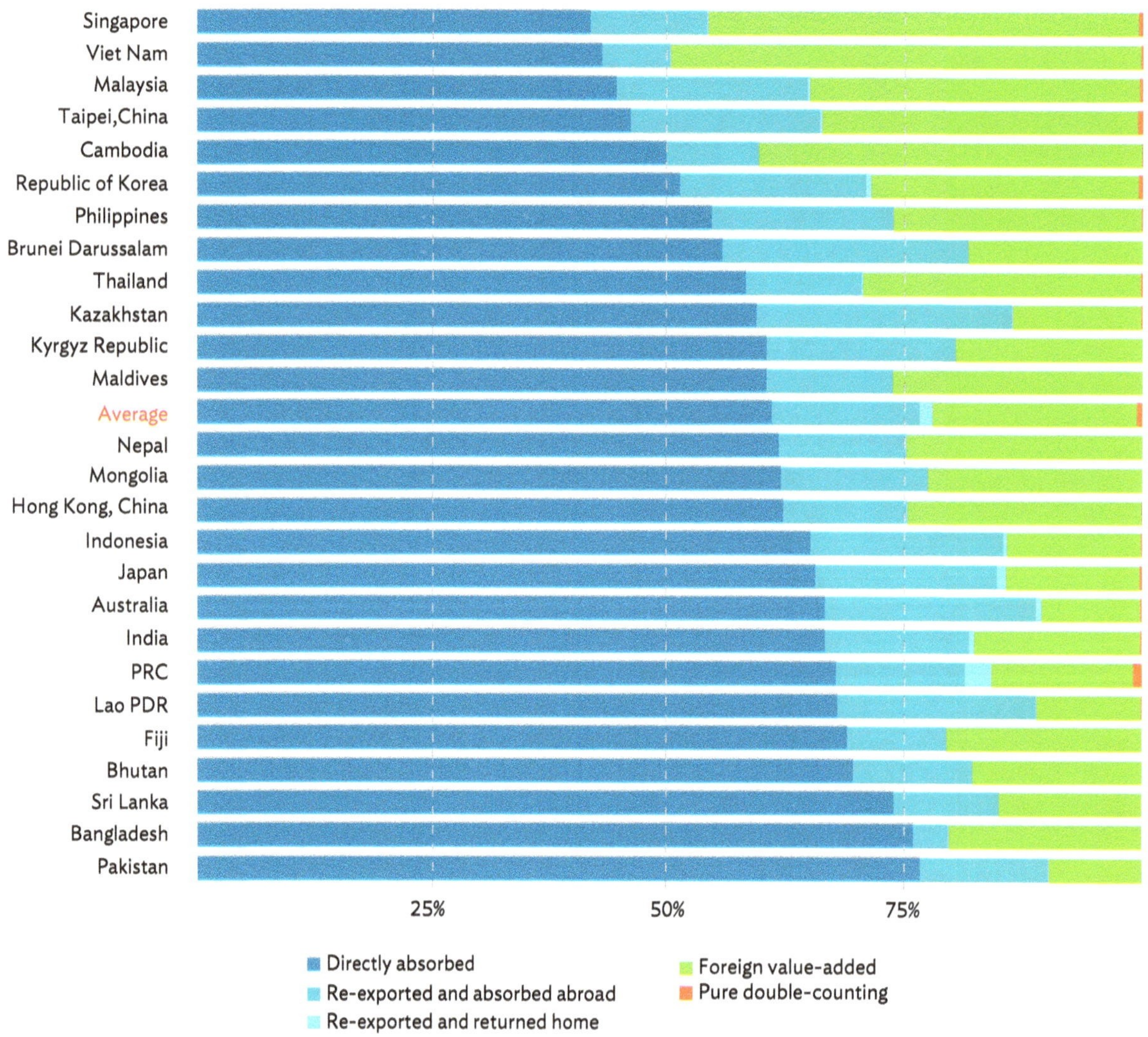

Lao PDR = Lao People's Democratic Republic, PRC = People's Republic of China

Note: Average is weighted by gross exports.

Sources: Asian Development Bank estimates based on Koopman, Wang, and Wei (2014) and Borin and Mancini (2019); and Asian Development Bank Multiregional Input–Output Database, 2021.

Integration in the forward sense is measured by the medium and light blue regions, which represent how much of exports go on to be re-exported. The commodity-rich economies dominate this time, with Brunei Darussalam and Kazakhstan having over 25% of what they export passed further along the chain. The landlocked Lao People's Democratic Republic also exhibited high forward integration, with re-exports occurring on 21% of its exports, possibly due to its reliance on ports in Viet Nam and Thailand for shipping its goods elsewhere. The fact that the backward-integrated economies of Cambodia and Viet Nam registered fairly low forward integration implies that they tend to serve final markets. A special type of forward integration, measured by the light blue regions, involves an economy's exports eventually making their way back to its own domestic consumers. This suggests an economy that is positioned in the more upstream end of value chains. Of the economies sampled, only the People's Republic of China had substantial exports of this kind.

The sum of backward and forward integration is equivalent to the share of indirect trading, what this analysis calls the GVC participation rate. The economies in Figure 3.2 are arranged in descending order of integration. The most integrated economies—Singapore; Viet Nam; Malaysia; Taipei,China; and Cambodia—are all in East Asia or Southeast Asia, and all registered GVC participation rates of 50% and above. The least integrated region was South Asia, with Bangladesh, Bhutan, India, Nepal, Pakistan, and Sri Lanka appearing in the bottom half of the chart. For Bangladesh and Pakistan in particular, over 75% of their trading was of the direct kind. Bucking the trend for the region is Maldives, whose substantial import content placed it among those with above-average integration.

The variation in rates of GVC participation across these 26 economies provides an opportunity for examining how integration correlates with the size of the COVID-19 shock, again measured by the difference between forecasted and actual growth (Box 3.2). Results are plotted in Figure 3.3, which has GVC participation rates on the horizontal axis and the COVID-19 shock in log scale on the vertical axis. Point sizes reflect nominal GDP. A quadratic curve is fitted to reveal the estimated relationship, with the shaded band representing the 95% confidence interval.

Despite the limited sample size, a distinct U-shaped curve is detected between trade integration and the size of the COVID-19 shock. It appears that higher GVC participation is associated with larger negative shocks until a rate of about 45%, after which it becomes associated with smaller negative shocks. Contrast the experience of Pakistan, whose participation rate was 25% and whose 2020 growth was just 2.8 percentage points below the forecast, with that of Thailand, whose participation rate was 43% and whose growth was 9.1 points lower than the forecast. Then compare this with Viet Nam, whose participation rate was 59% and whose growth was just 3.6 points below the forecast.

It must be noted, however, that the estimated relationship has significant noise, especially at the highest rates of participation, largely because of the scarcity of data points. Indeed, the COVID-19 shock varied greatly for the three most integrated economies in the sample. Whereas Taipei,China actually exceeded its forecast in 2020, the negative shock for Singapore was quite large at 6.4 percentage points. Viet Nam, meanwhile, adhered closely to the fitted curve.

One explanation for the overall U-shaped relationship is the temporal heterogeneity in realized shocks uncovered by Giglioli et al. (2021). These researchers found that higher GVC participation was associated with larger shocks during the first wave of the pandemic (October 2019 to April 2020), but with smaller shocks in the second wave (April to October 2020). By looking at 2020 as a whole, Figure 3.3 may be conflating the two results.

Figure 3.3: Relationship Between Global Value Chain Participation and the COVID-19 Shock

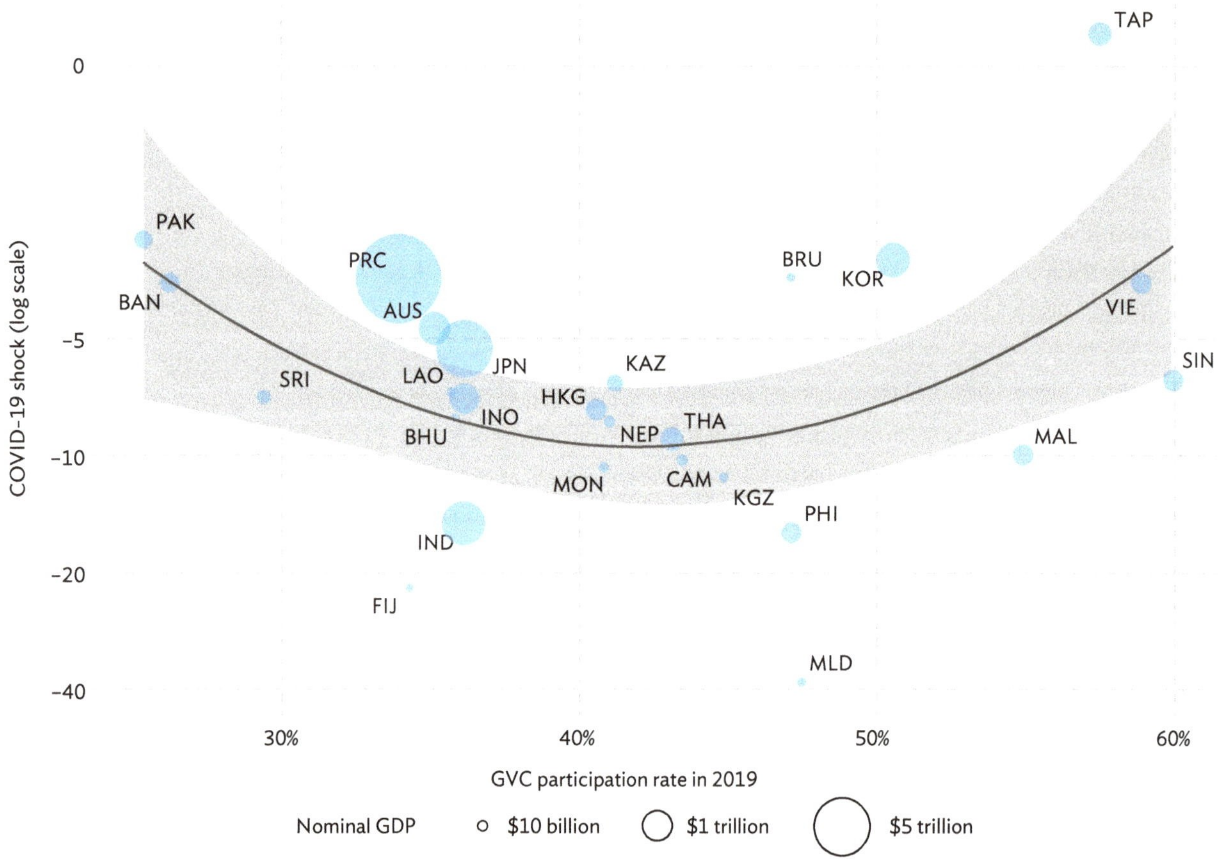

BAN = Bangladesh; BRU = Brunei Darussalam; BHU = Bhutan; FIJ = Fiji; GDP = gross domestic product; GVC = global value chain; HKG = Hong Kong, China; INO = Indonesia; IND = India; JPN = Japan; KAZ = Kazakhstan; KGZ = Kyrgyz Republic; CAM = Cambodia; KOR = Republic of Korea; LAO = Lao People's Democratic Republic; MAL = Malaysia; MLD = Maldives; MON = Mongolia; NEP = Nepal; PAK = Pakistan; PHI = Philippines, PRC = People's Republic of China; SIN = Singapore; SRI = Sri Lanka; THA = Thailand; TAP = Taipei,China; VIE = Viet Nam.

Notes: COVID-19 shock is difference between forecasted and actual growth rates for 2020. GVC participation is trade-based, computed based on the methodology of Koopman, Wang, and Wei (2014) and Borin and Mancini (2019). Shaded area is the 95% confidence interval of the fitted quadratic polynomial.

Sources: Asian Development Bank Multiregional Input–Output Database, 2021; forecasted growth rates from the International Monetary Fund's *World Economic Outlook* (October 2019); and actual growth rates from the International Monetary Fund's *World Economic Outlook* (April 2021).

On a final note, it must be emphasized that Figure 3.3 is specific to the COVID-19 pandemic and, given a different shock, these results may not necessarily hold. As such, no prescriptive conclusions regarding an "optimal" GVC participation rate should be taken from these outcomes.

Conclusion

The COVID-19 pandemic has revealed quite dramatically the two faces of GVCs. On the one hand, by connecting producers and consumers in long and complex supply chains, GVCs allow for the diversification of economic activity, and this can lower risk. On the other hand, a system-wide crisis like the 2020 pandemic turns these connections into channels for the amplification of shocks, thereby heightening risk. As the fates of economies become more entangled with one another, underperformance anywhere becomes a concern everywhere.

Nevertheless, just as success rates in managing the coronavirus stem largely from good policymaking, so too will the consequences of global integration. It is this that will ultimately determine which of the two faces of GVCs becomes ascendant for each economy in a post-pandemic world.

Appendix 3.1: An Analytical Framework for Studying Global Value Chains

Introduction

A host of competing frameworks for studying global value chains (GVCs) has proliferated in recent years.[2] Not only are the same quantities known under different terms, the same terms may also be measured by different quantities. The aim of this appendix is to describe the particular framework used in *Key Indicators for Asia and the Pacific 2021* (2021) and other GVC-related publications of the Asian Development Bank (ADB). It also serves to update the framework presented in KI2015, incorporating developments in the literature and streamlining where necessary.

As in KI2015, the present framework adopts an input–output approach to studying GVCs. This analyzes inter-sectoral linkages within and across economies by keeping track of three variables: value-added, final consumption, and intermediate input use. Input–output modeling is the foundation by which the key concepts of this framework are defined, foremost among which is the phenomenon of indirect trading. Whereas direct trading involves value-added crossing one border to be consumed, indirect trading sees value-added hopping across several borders before final consumption, a result of importing inputs on the one hand and re-exporting inputs on the other. Thus, trade between Japan and India becomes a conduit by which Viet Nam value-added makes its way to Kazakhstan: such is the mark of GVCs.

This appendix first goes through the foundations of input–output analysis and what are called "VB" decompositions before deriving the value-added trade accounting framework, under which indirect trading and its different forms may be defined. Some knowledge of linear algebra is assumed, though concepts are also described in plain language. The appendix ends with a discussion of data issues.

The Input–Output Framework

The approach to GVCs adopted by this framework is mathematically rooted in input–output analysis.[3] Let there be *G* economies in the world, indexed by $r, s, t, u = 1, ..., G$. Production in each economy is divided into *N* sectors, indexed by $i, j = 1, ..., N$. Production is assumed to be done in fixed proportions, also called Leontief production, so that the output of an economy–sector (r, i), denoted $x_{(r,i)}$, is given by

$$x_{(r,i)} = z_{(1,1),(r,i)} + z_{(1,2),(r,i)} + ... + z_{(s,j),(r,i)} + ... + z_{(G,N),(r,i)} + va_{(r,i)}, \quad (1)$$

2 For a sense of this diversity, see Satoshi Inomata's (2017) survey.

3 See Miller and Blair (2009) for a textbook treatment.

where $z_{(s,j),(r,i)}$ are inputs purchased by (r,i) from (s,j) and $va_{(r,i)}$ is (r,i) value-added. One may also call z "intermediate inputs" and va "primary inputs". Note that variable subscripts denote flows from left to right, so that $z_{(s,j),(r,i)}$ means inputs are flowing from (s,j) to (r,i). An asterisk means all entities, as in $z_{(s,j),*}$ or $z_{*,(r,i)}$.

Output of (r,i) is either consumed or used as inputs:

$$x_{(r,i)} = z_{(r,i),(1,1)} + z_{(r,i),(1,2)} + \dots + z_{(r,i),(u,i)} + \dots + z_{(r,i),(G,N)} + \\ y_{(r,i),1} + \dots + y_{(r,i),u} + \dots + y_{(r,i),G}, \tag{2}$$

where $y_{(r,i),u}$ are (r,i) output consumed in economy u. Market clearing is assumed to always hold, so equations (1) and (2) are equal.

These relationships are more neatly presented in a table. For the case of three economies $\{C, J, U\}$ and two sectors {1, 2}, the full table is as follows:

			Buying economies									Total sales
			Intermediate sales						Final sales			
			C		J		U		C	J	U	
			1	2	1	2	1	2				
Selling economies	C	1	$z_{C1,C1}$	$z_{C1,C2}$	$z_{C1,J1}$	$z_{C1,J2}$	$z_{C1,U1}$	$z_{C1,U2}$	$y_{C1,C}$	$y_{C1,J}$	$y_{C1,U}$	x_{C1}
		2	$z_{C2,C1}$	$z_{C2,C2}$	$z_{C2,J1}$	$z_{C2,J2}$	$z_{C2,U1}$	$z_{C2,U2}$	$y_{C2,C}$	$y_{C2,J}$	$y_{C2,U}$	x_{C2}
	J	1	$z_{J1,C1}$	$z_{J1,C2}$	$z_{J1,J1}$	$z_{J1,J2}$	$z_{J1,U1}$	$z_{J1,U2}$	$y_{J1,C}$	$y_{J1,J}$	$y_{J1,U}$	x_{J1}
		2	$z_{J2,C1}$	$z_{J2,C2}$	$z_{J2,J1}$	$z_{J2,J2}$	$z_{J2,U1}$	$z_{J2,U2}$	$y_{J2,C}$	$y_{J2,J}$	$y_{J2,U}$	x_{J2}
	U	1	$z_{U1,C1}$	$z_{U1,C2}$	$z_{U1,J1}$	$z_{U1,J2}$	$z_{U1,U1}$	$z_{U1,U2}$	$y_{U1,C}$	$y_{U1,J}$	$y_{U1,U}$	x_{U1}
		2	$z_{U2,C1}$	$z_{U2,C2}$	$z_{U2,J1}$	$z_{U2,J2}$	$z_{U2,U1}$	$z_{U2,U2}$	$y_{U2,C}$	$y_{U2,J}$	$y_{U2,U}$	x_{U2}
Value-added			va_{C1}	va_{C2}	va_{J1}	va_{J2}	va_{U1}	va_{U2}				
Total outlays			x_{C1}	x_{C2}	x_{J1}	x_{J2}	x_{U1}	x_{U2}				

The *GN* equations of (1) are arranged in columns while the *GN* equations of (2) are arranged in rows. It is clear that for larger *G* and *N* , representation in table form becomes unwieldy. One fix would be to collect economy-specific terms into matrices and vectors:

		Buying economies						Total sales
		Intermediate sales			Final sales			
		C	J	U	C	J	U	
Selling economies	C	$\mathbf{Z}_{CC}$	$\mathbf{Z}_{CJ}$	$\mathbf{Z}_{CU}$	$\mathbf{y}_{CC}$	$\mathbf{y}_{CJ}$	$\mathbf{y}_{CU}$	$\mathbf{x}_C$
	J	$\mathbf{Z}_{JC}$	$\mathbf{Z}_{JJ}$	$\mathbf{Z}_{JU}$	$\mathbf{y}_{JC}$	$\mathbf{y}_{JJ}$	$\mathbf{y}_{JU}$	$\mathbf{x}_J$
	U	$\mathbf{Z}_{UC}$	$\mathbf{Z}_{UJ}$	$\mathbf{Z}_{UU}$	$\mathbf{y}_{UC}$	$\mathbf{y}_{UJ}$	$\mathbf{y}_{UU}$	$\mathbf{x}_U$
Value-added		$\mathbf{va}_C$	$\mathbf{va}_J$	$\mathbf{va}_U$				
Total outlays		$\mathbf{x}'_C$	$\mathbf{x}'_J$	$\mathbf{x}'_U$				

Uppercase letters in bold denote matrices while lowercase letters in bold denote vectors. These may further be collected into larger matrices and vectors: all $\mathbf{Z}_{sr}$'s into the $GN \times GN$ matrix $\mathbf{Z}$, all $\mathbf{y}_{sr}$'s into the $GN \times G$ matrix $\mathbf{Y}$, all $\mathbf{va}_s$'s into the $1 \times GN$ vector $\mathbf{va}$, and all $\mathbf{x}_s$'s into the $GN \times 1$ vector $\mathbf{x}$. Equation (2) may be rewritten as

$$\mathbf{x} = \mathbf{Z} \cdot \mathbf{i}_{GN} + \mathbf{Y} \cdot \mathbf{i}_G,$$

where $\mathbf{i}_M = [1, 1, ..., 1]'$ is a vector of 1's with length M that serves to sum up $\mathbf{Z}$ and $\mathbf{Y}$ by rows. It will be useful to separately denote the vector $\mathbf{Y} \cdot \mathbf{i}_G$ as $\mathbf{y}$, so the above can be written more simply as

$$\mathbf{x} = \mathbf{Zi} + \mathbf{y}. \tag{3}$$

Gross exports are the total sales of an economy–sector to another economy. To get an expression for this, the $\mathbf{Z}$ and $\mathbf{Y}$ matrices must be split between domestic and foreign sales:

$$\mathbf{Z} = \mathbf{Z}^d + \mathbf{Z}^f \tag{4}$$

$$\mathbf{Y} = \mathbf{Y}^d + \mathbf{Y}^f \tag{5}$$

Visualizing this using the three-economy, two-sector example,

$$\begin{bmatrix} \mathbf{Z}_{CC} & \mathbf{Z}_{CJ} & \mathbf{Z}_{CU} \\ \mathbf{Z}_{JC} & \mathbf{Z}_{JJ} & \mathbf{Z}_{JU} \\ \mathbf{Z}_{UC} & \mathbf{Z}_{UJ} & \mathbf{Z}_{UU} \end{bmatrix} = \begin{bmatrix} \mathbf{Z}_{CC} & \mathbf{0} & \mathbf{0} \\ \mathbf{0} & \mathbf{Z}_{JJ} & \mathbf{0} \\ \mathbf{0} & \mathbf{0} & \mathbf{Z}_{UU} \end{bmatrix} + \begin{bmatrix} \mathbf{0} & \mathbf{Z}_{CJ} & \mathbf{Z}_{CU} \\ \mathbf{Z}_{JC} & \mathbf{0} & \mathbf{Z}_{JU} \\ \mathbf{Z}_{UC} & \mathbf{Z}_{UJ} & \mathbf{0} \end{bmatrix}$$

$$\begin{bmatrix} \mathbf{y}_{CC} & \mathbf{y}_{CJ} & \mathbf{y}_{CU} \\ \mathbf{y}_{JC} & \mathbf{y}_{JJ} & \mathbf{y}_{JU} \\ \mathbf{y}_{UC} & \mathbf{y}_{UJ} & \mathbf{y}_{UU} \end{bmatrix} = \begin{bmatrix} \mathbf{y}_{CC} & \mathbf{0} & \mathbf{0} \\ \mathbf{0} & \mathbf{y}_{JJ} & \mathbf{0} \\ \mathbf{0} & \mathbf{0} & \mathbf{y}_{UU} \end{bmatrix} + \begin{bmatrix} \mathbf{0} & \mathbf{y}_{CJ} & \mathbf{y}_{CU} \\ \mathbf{y}_{JC} & \mathbf{0} & \mathbf{y}_{JU} \\ \mathbf{y}_{UC} & \mathbf{y}_{UJ} & \mathbf{0} \end{bmatrix}$$

The exports vector is defined as

$$\mathbf{e} \equiv \mathbf{Z}^f \cdot \mathbf{i}_{GN} + \mathbf{Y}^f \cdot \mathbf{i}_G = \mathbf{Z}^f \mathbf{i} + \mathbf{y}^f. \tag{6}$$

It is also useful to construct an exports matrix $\mathbf{E}$ that identifies the destinations of each economy–sector's exports. This is done by post-multiplying an aggregator matrix to the $GN \times GN$ matrix $\mathbf{Z}^f$ to turn it into a $GN \times G$ matrix. Thus,

$$\mathbf{E} \equiv \mathbf{Z}^f \cdot (\mathbf{I}_G \otimes \mathbf{i}_N) + \mathbf{Y}^f, \tag{7}$$

where $\otimes$ denote a Kronecker product. Written out,

$$\mathbf{E} \equiv \begin{bmatrix} 0 & z_{C1,J1} + z_{C1,J2} & z_{C1,U1} + z_{C1,U2} \\ 0 & z_{C2,J1} + z_{C2,J2} & z_{C2,U1} + z_{C2,U2} \\ z_{J1,C1} + z_{J1,C2} & 0 & z_{J1,U1} + z_{J1,U2} \\ z_{J2,C1} + z_{J2,C2} & 0 & z_{J2,U1} + z_{J2,U2} \\ z_{U1,C1} + z_{U1,C2} & z_{U1,J1} + z_{U1,J2} & 0 \\ z_{U2,C1} + z_{U2,C2} & z_{U2,J1} + z_{U2,J2} & 0 \end{bmatrix} + \begin{bmatrix} 0 & y_{C1,J} & y_{C1,U} \\ 0 & y_{C2,J} & y_{C2,U} \\ y_{J1,C} & 0 & y_{J1,U} \\ y_{J2,C} & 0 & y_{J2,U} \\ y_{U1,C} & y_{U1,J} & 0 \\ y_{U2,C} & y_{U2,J} & 0 \end{bmatrix}$$

$$= \begin{bmatrix} 0 & e_{C1,J} & e_{C1,U} \\ 0 & e_{C2,J} & e_{C2,U} \\ e_{J1,C} & 0 & e_{J1,U} \\ e_{J2,C} & 0 & e_{J2,U} \\ e_{U1,C} & e_{U1,J} & 0 \\ e_{U2,C} & e_{U2,J} & 0 \end{bmatrix} = \begin{bmatrix} \mathbf{0} & \mathbf{e}_{CJ} & \mathbf{e}_{CU} \\ \mathbf{e}_{JC} & \mathbf{0} & \mathbf{e}_{JU} \\ \mathbf{e}_{UC} & \mathbf{e}_{UJ} & \mathbf{0} \end{bmatrix}$$

The technical coefficient $a_{(s,j),(r,i)}$ is the share of inputs from (s,j) in the output of (r,i): $a_{(s,j),(r,i)} \equiv z_{(s,j),(r,i)}/x_{(r,i)}$. Collect all these into the $GN \times GN$ matrix of technical coefficients $\mathbf{A}$. This may be used to rewrite (3) as

$$\mathbf{x} = \mathbf{A}\mathbf{x} + \mathbf{y}. \tag{8}$$

Solving for $\mathbf{x}$ gives

$$\mathbf{x} = (\mathbf{I} - \mathbf{A})^{-1}\mathbf{y} = \mathbf{B}\mathbf{y}, \tag{9}$$

where the $GN \times GN$ matrix $\mathbf{B}$ is called the global Leontief inverse matrix.

VB Decomposition

Equation (9) is central to analyzing cross-economy and cross-sectoral linkages. It is clearer to see this if (8) and (9) are rewritten to isolate a single economy s:

$$\mathbf{x}_s = \sum_r^G \mathbf{A}_{sr}\mathbf{x}_r + \sum_r^G \mathbf{y}_{sr} \tag{10}$$

$$= \sum_r^G \sum_u^G \mathbf{B}_{sr}\mathbf{y}_{ru} \tag{11}$$

Equation (10) says that s's output $\mathbf{x}_s$ is used as intermediates in r's output or sold as final goods to r (for all $r = 1, ..., G$). The output of each r can in turn be used as intermediates by other economies, whose outputs are then used by further economies, and so on in a potentially infinite series of production stages. Equation (11) summarizes these to identify the final landing stage of s's output. The product $\mathbf{B}_{sr}\mathbf{y}_{ru}$ is s output that is "completed" into a final good by r, which then sends it to u for final absorption.

In most analyses, value-added rather than output is the preferred metric. Define the vector $\mathbf{v}$ with (s,i)th element $v_{(s,i)} \equiv va_{(s,i)}/x_{(s,i)}$. This gives the value-added-to-output ratio for each economy–sector. It follows that $\sum_{(s,j)} a_{(s,j),(r,i)} + v_{(r,i)} = 1$. Premultiplying this to (11) converts everything to value-added terms:

$$\mathbf{v}_s\mathbf{x}_s \equiv va_s = \mathbf{v}_s \sum_r^G \sum_u^G \mathbf{B}_{sr}\mathbf{y}_{ru}. \tag{12}$$

Note that this ends up summing sector-level quantities into the aggregate level. To prevent this, see the section on sector breakdowns.

This expression gives the value-added generated in economy s that is eventually consumed in economy u. It can be tweaked to measure other flows. For example, $\mathbf{v}_s\mathbf{B}_{sr}\mathbf{y}_{ru}$ considers s value-added embodied in final goods completed in r that are sold to u. To measure s value-added embodied in r's total exports, one may instead write $\mathbf{v}_s\mathbf{B}_{sr}\mathbf{e}_{r*}$. These expressions are called VB decompositions and they serve to identify the value-added origins of certain quantities.

Even more specific flows may be derived by defining input use structures for domestic intermediates $\mathbf{Z}^d$ and foreign intermediates $\mathbf{Z}^f$ separately, yielding $\mathbf{A}^d$ and $\mathbf{A}^f$ where $\mathbf{A} = \mathbf{A}^d + \mathbf{A}^f$. Equation (8) can be rewritten as

$$\mathbf{x} = (\mathbf{A}^d\mathbf{x} + \mathbf{y}^d) + (\mathbf{A}^f\mathbf{x} + \mathbf{y}^f). \tag{13}$$

Moreover, since $\mathbf{Z}^f\mathbf{i} = \mathbf{A}^f\mathbf{x}$, the exports vector (6) can also be rewritten as

$$\mathbf{e} = \mathbf{A}^f\mathbf{x} + \mathbf{y}^f. \tag{14}$$

Plugging this into (13) and solving for $\mathbf{x}$,

$$\begin{aligned}\mathbf{x} &= (\mathbf{A}^d\mathbf{x} + \mathbf{y}^d) + \mathbf{e}\\ &= (\mathbf{I} - \mathbf{A}^d)^{-1}(\mathbf{y}^d + \mathbf{e})\\ &= \mathbf{B}^d(\mathbf{y}^d + \mathbf{e}).\end{aligned} \tag{15}$$

The matrix $\mathbf{B}^d$ is called the local Leontief inverse matrix. Its interpretation is the same as the $\mathbf{B}$ matrix, except it assumes an input structure that precludes buying and selling inputs abroad. As such, only the block diagonal elements are non-zero. This isolates the purely domestic portion of production. Compare $\mathbf{v}_s\mathbf{B}_{ss}\mathbf{y}_{ss}$ and $\mathbf{v}_s\mathbf{B}^d_{ss}\mathbf{y}_{ss}$. While they both measure s value-added in its own final consumption, the first expression allows for some processing abroad while the second restricts it to purely domestic linkages. This will be crucial in disentangling direct and indirect trading.

Decomposing Exports into Value-Added Categories

Gross exports mask several distinct forms of trading. A substantial portion for most economies is direct trading, where value-added crosses one border before being consumed. The rest involves indirect trading, which itself can take three forms. It can arise from the use of imported inputs, so that one economy's exports contain value-added from another economy. It can arise from re-exports, so that one economy's value-added gets absorbed somewhere other than its direct importer. Finally, it can arise from what is called "pure" double-counting, when value-added crosses the same border twice or more and ends up leaving duplicate footprints in trade statistics.

Figure A3.1 presents the full breakdown of exports. With some revisions, this follows the KI2015 breakdown,[4] which itself was based on Koopman, Wang, and Wei (2014)

[4] See Figure 4.7 on p. 393 of that publication.

and Wang, Wei, and Zhu (2013, revised 2018). At the first level, exports from s to r are divided into domestic value-added (DVA), foreign value-added (FVA), and pure double-counting (PDC). Next, exports of domestic value-added are divided into those that are directly absorbed by the importer and those that the importer re-exports. The latter are further divided by the place of ultimate absorption: in r, in s, or in some third economy. Note that any of these categories can be broken down even further—the economy origin of foreign value-added, for example, or the identity of any third economies absorbing re-exports. The breakdown given here attempts a balance between exhaustiveness and parsimony.

Figure A3.1: The Value-Added Trade Accounting Framework

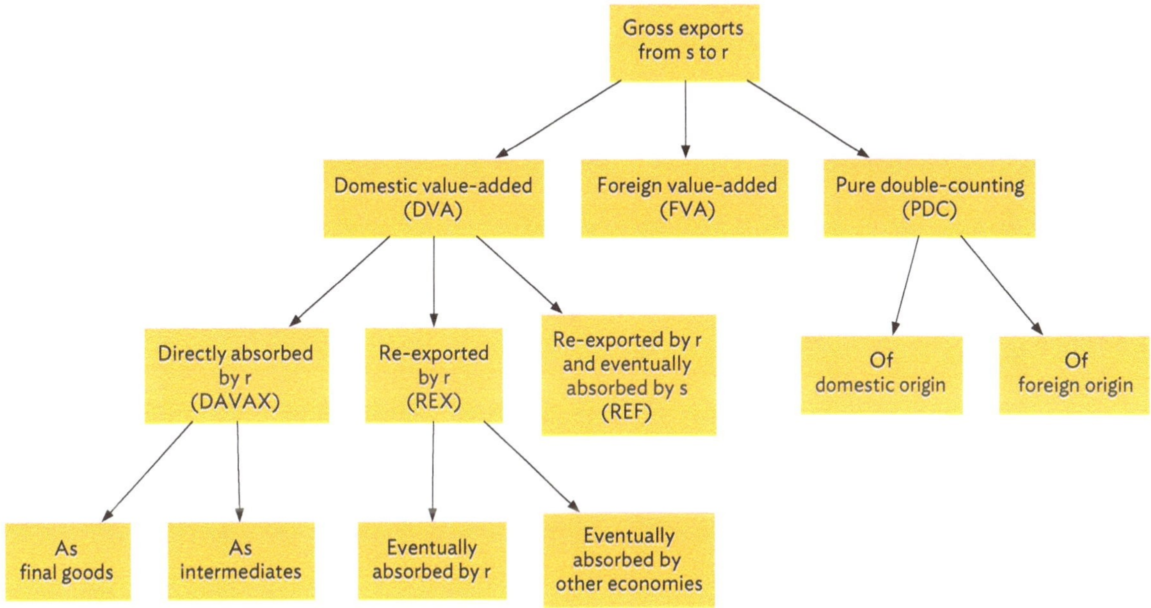

Source: Authors' drawing based on Koopman, Wang, and Wei (2014) and Borin and Mancini (2019).

To derive all these mathematically, begin with the VB decomposition of gross exports:

$$E_{sr} = \sum_t \mathbf{v}_t \mathbf{B}_{ts} \mathbf{e}_{sr}. \tag{16}$$

This distinguishes the value-added origins of s exports to r, denoted E_{sr}, between domestic (s) and foreign ($t \neq s$) sources. To extract pure double-counting, Borin and Mancini (2019) proposed the following methodology. Define $\mathbf{A}^{\not{s}}$ as the matrix $\mathbf{A}$ with all $\mathbf{A}_{su}$, $s \neq u$, set to zero. This depicts the pattern of global input use if economy s did not export any intermediates. Using the three-economy, two-sector example with $s = C$,

$$\mathbf{A}^{\not{C}} = \begin{bmatrix} \mathbf{A}_{CC} & 0 & 0 \\ \mathbf{A}_{JC} & \mathbf{A}_{JJ} & \mathbf{A}_{JU} \\ \mathbf{A}_{UC} & \mathbf{A}_{UJ} & \mathbf{A}_{UU} \end{bmatrix}$$

Moreover, define $\mathbf{A}^{s}$ as the complement of $\mathbf{A}^{\not s}$, so that

$$\mathbf{A}^{\not s} = \mathbf{A} - \mathbf{A}^{s}. \tag{17}$$

The matrix $\mathbf{B}^{\not s} \equiv (\mathbf{I} - \mathbf{A}^{\not s})^{-1}$ is, like $\mathbf{B}^{d}$, a modification of the global Leontief inverse under a particular input use structure. In this case, it assumes no economy besides s can use s intermediate inputs, though s can still use every other economy's inputs. This precludes s using imported inputs embedded with its own value-added to make its exports, thereby excluding double-counting. Plugging this into (16) will therefore give

$$E_{sr} = \sum_{t} \mathbf{v}_t \mathbf{B}^{\not s}_{ts} \mathbf{e}_{sr} + \text{Pure double-counting.}$$

To get an expression for the double-counting term, write

$$\mathbf{I} = \mathbf{B}^{\not s}(\mathbf{I} - \mathbf{A}^{\not s}),$$

which follows by definition of matrix inversion. Inserting (17) gives

$$\begin{aligned} \mathbf{I} &= \mathbf{B}^{\not s}(\mathbf{I} - \mathbf{A} + \mathbf{A}^{s}) \\ &= \mathbf{B}^{\not s}(\mathbf{I} - \mathbf{A}) + \mathbf{B}^{\not s}\mathbf{A}^{s}. \end{aligned}$$

Post-multiplying both sides by $\mathbf{B}$ gives

$$\mathbf{B} = \mathbf{B}^{\not s} + \mathbf{B}^{\not s}\mathbf{A}^{s}\mathbf{B},$$

for which the tth block matrix on the sth column is

$$\mathbf{B}_{ts} = \mathbf{B}^{\not s}_{ts} + \mathbf{B}^{\not s}_{ts} \sum_{s \neq u} \mathbf{A}_{su}\mathbf{B}_{us}. \tag{18}$$

Expression (18) may then be used on (16) to get

$$E_{sr} = \underbrace{\mathbf{v}_s \mathbf{B}^{\not s}_{ss} \mathbf{e}_{sr}}_{DVA_{sr}} + \underbrace{\sum_{t \neq s} \mathbf{v}_t \mathbf{B}^{\not s}_{ts} \mathbf{e}_{sr}}_{FVA_{sr}} + \underbrace{\sum_{t} \mathbf{v}_t \mathbf{B}^{\not s}_{ts} \sum_{s \neq u} \mathbf{A}_{su}\mathbf{B}_{us}\mathbf{e}_{sr}}_{PDC_{sr}}. \tag{19}$$

The use of (18) is the most significant innovation from the KI2015 framework. Discrepancies between the present framework and KI2015 are solely due to this.

DVA_{sr} is divided into those directly absorbed by r and those re-exported by r. Express (14) and (15) in bilateral terms and combine to get

$$\mathbf{e}_{sr} = \mathbf{y}_{sr} + \mathbf{A}_{sr}\mathbf{B}^{d}_{rr}\mathbf{y}_{rr} + \mathbf{A}_{sr}\mathbf{B}^{d}_{rr}\mathbf{e}_{r*}.$$

This simply states that all exports to r must either be final goods consumed by r or intermediates used by r. Output in the latter may in turn be absorbed by r or re-exported and absorbed elsewhere. Using this to expand DVA_{sr} gives

$$DVA_{sr} = \mathbf{v}_s\mathbf{B}^g_{ss}\left[\mathbf{y}_{sr} + \mathbf{A}_{sr}\mathbf{B}^d_{rr}\mathbf{y}_{rr} + \mathbf{A}_{sr}\mathbf{B}^d_{rr}\mathbf{e}_{r*}\right].$$

The first two terms comprise exports to r that are absorbed in r without passing through any other border. These are termed "directly absorbed value-added exports" or *DAVAX*. Economy r's re-exports, $\mathbf{A}_{sr}\mathbf{B}^d_{rr}\mathbf{e}_{r*}$, may be broken down into those that ultimately end up back in economy s, called "reflection" (*REF*) following Koopman, Wang, and Wei (2014), and those that end up elsewhere (*REX*). It is also helpful to extract from the latter those that are ultimately absorbed by the direct importer r.

$$\begin{aligned} DVA_{sr} = & \underbrace{\mathbf{v}_s\mathbf{B}^g_{ss}\left[\mathbf{y}_{sr} + \mathbf{A}_{sr}\mathbf{B}^d_{rr}\mathbf{y}_{rr}\right]}_{DAVAX_{sr}} \\ & + \underbrace{\mathbf{v}_s\mathbf{B}^g_{ss}\mathbf{A}_{sr}\mathbf{B}^d_{rr}\left[\sum_{u\neq r,s}\mathbf{y}_{ru} + \sum_{u\neq r}\mathbf{A}_{ru}\left(\sum_k\sum_{\ell\neq s,r}\mathbf{B}_{uk}\mathbf{y}_{k\ell} + \sum_k\mathbf{B}_{uk}\mathbf{y}_{kr}\right)\right]}_{REX_{sr}} \\ & + \underbrace{\mathbf{v}_s\mathbf{B}^g_{ss}\mathbf{A}_{sr}\mathbf{B}^d_{rr}\left[\mathbf{y}_{rs} + \sum_{u\neq r}\mathbf{A}_{ru}\sum_k\mathbf{B}_{uk}\mathbf{y}_{ks}\right]}_{REF_{sr}}. \end{aligned} \quad (20)$$

Each term has two or more sub-terms, referred to sequentially as *DAVAX*1, *DAVAX*2, and so on. This decomposition may also be done on *FVA* but is omitted here.

Equations (19) and (20) comprise the value-added trade accounting framework.[5]A full description of each term is given in Table A3.1, along with their counterparts, if any, to KI2015.[6] Overall, the present framework streamlines KI2015's 16 terms into 5 broad categories: *DAVAX*, *REX*, *REF*, *FVA*, and *PDC*. These may be elaborated into 10 finer categories.

Sector Breakdowns

Equations (19) and (20) yield aggregate, economy-wide figures, though oftentimes the analysis requires a more granular, sector-level perspective. Borin and Mancini (2019) gave three main approaches to breaking down aggregate figures by sector.[7]

5 In Borin and Mancini's (2019) taxonomy of trade accounting frameworks, this is a source-based approach from the exporter's perspective.

6 Note that this is only a conceptual correspondence, meaning they intend to measure the same thing. Most terms, however, cannot mathematically be reconciled with those in KI2015 due to the use of (18). Note also that REX1, REX2, and REX3 have no counterparts in KI2015, though their sum conceptually corresponds to the sum of terms 3, 4, and 5.

7 In KI2015, breakdown by export sectors is called "backward-linkage-based" while breakdown by origin sectors is called "forward-linkage-based". See pp. 393–95 of that publication.

Table A3.1: Description of Value-Added Categories			
Term	Formula	Description	KI2015
DAVAX1	$\mathbf{v}_s\mathbf{B}^{\not g}_{ss}\mathbf{y}_{sr}$	DVA completed in s and sent to r	1
DAVAX2	$\mathbf{v}_s\mathbf{B}^{\not g}_{ss}\mathbf{A}_{sr}\mathbf{B}^{d}_{rr}\mathbf{y}_{rr}$	DVA in intermediates sent to, completed by, and absorbed in r	2
REX1	$\mathbf{v}_s\mathbf{B}^{\not g}_{ss}\mathbf{A}_{sr}\mathbf{B}^{d}_{rr}\sum_{u\neq r,s}\mathbf{y}_{ru}$	DVA in intermediates sent to and completed by r then exported to third economy	n.a.
REX2	$\mathbf{v}_s\mathbf{B}^{\not g}_{ss}\mathbf{A}_{sr}\mathbf{B}^{d}_{rr}\sum_{u\neq r.s}\mathbf{A}_{ru}\sum_k\sum_{\ell\neq s.r}\mathbf{B}_{uk}\mathbf{y}_{k\ell}$	DVA in intermediates sent to and re-exported by r and eventually absorbed in third economy	n.a.
REX3	$\mathbf{v}_s\mathbf{B}^{\not g}_{ss}\mathbf{A}_{sr}\mathbf{B}^{d}_{rr}\sum_{u\neq r,s}\mathbf{A}_{ru}\sum_k\mathbf{B}_{uk}\mathbf{y}_{kr}$	DVA in intermediates sent to and re-exported by r and eventually absorbed in r	n.a.
REF1	$\mathbf{v}_s\mathbf{B}^{\not g}_{ss}\mathbf{A}_{sr}\mathbf{B}^{d}_{rr}\mathbf{y}_{rs}$	DVA in intermediates sent to and completed by r then exported to s	6
REF2	$\mathbf{v}_s\mathbf{B}^{\not g}_{ss}\mathbf{A}_{sr}\mathbf{B}^{d}_{rr}\sum_{u\neq r}\mathbf{A}_{ru}\sum_k\mathbf{B}_{uk}\mathbf{y}_{ks}$	DVA in intermediates sent to and re-exported by r and eventually absorbed in s	7-8
FVA	$\sum_{t\neq s}\mathbf{v}_t\mathbf{B}^{\not g}_{ts}\mathbf{e}_{sr}$	FVA in gross exports	11-14
PDC1	$\mathbf{v}_s\mathbf{B}^{\not g}_{ss}\sum_{s\neq u}\mathbf{A}_{su}\mathbf{B}_{us}\mathbf{e}_{sr}$	PDC of domestic origin	9-10
PDC2	$\sum_{t\neq s}\mathbf{v}_t\mathbf{B}^{\not g}_{ts}\sum_{s\neq u}\mathbf{A}_{su}\mathbf{B}_{us}\mathbf{e}_{sr}$	PDC of foreign origin	15-16

DVA = domestic value-added, FVA = foreign value-added, n.a. = not applicable, PDC = pure double-counting.
Source: Authors' calculations based on Borin and Mancini (2019).

1. *By export sectors.* Aggregate values are broken down by the sector that actually exports. This approach gives figures that may be directly compared with balance of payments data.

2. *By origin sectors.* Aggregate values are broken down by where value-added originated from. Services, for example, are often not directly exported but instead are embedded in merchandise exports. This approach highlights such phenomena.

3. *By destination sectors.* Aggregate values are broken down by the sector under which the value-added is ultimately absorbed.

These sector breakdowns are achieved by "diagonalizing" certain vectors, i.e. arranging their elements on the main diagonal of a matrix that is otherwise filled with zeroes. This is denoted by a "hat" over the vector, as in $\hat{\mathbf{v}}$. Demonstrating with the simplest VB expressions,

$$\widehat{\mathbf{v}_s\mathbf{B}_{sr}\mathbf{y}_{ru}} \quad \text{Export-sector breakdown} \tag{21}$$

$$\hat{\mathbf{v}}_s\mathbf{B}_{sr}\mathbf{y}_{ru} \quad \text{Origin-sector breakdown} \tag{22}$$

$$\mathbf{v}_s\mathbf{B}_{sr}\hat{\mathbf{y}}_{ru} \quad \text{Destination-sector breakdown} \tag{23}$$

Diagonalize either $\mathbf{v}$ or $\mathbf{vB}$ in (16) or $\mathbf{y}$ in (19)–(20) to get the desired breakdown.

Global Value Chain Participation

The GVC participation rate measures the extent to which an economy is participating in GVCs. Two approaches to calculating this may be found in the literature. The trade-based approach traces its roots to the vertical specialization measure of Hummels, Ishii, and Yi (2001), who defined GVCs as trade that crosses at least two borders before final consumption—what might be called indirect trade. Their paper only provides a backward measure of this in the form of the import content of exports. Calculation of the forward end—exports that are re-exported by the direct partner—would only come with the trade accounting framework of Koopman et al. (2014). In the terminology of Borin and Mancini (2019), vertical specialization becomes GVC exports (*GVCX*) and are defined as follows:

$$GVCXbackward_{sr} = FVA_{sr} + PDC_{sr}, \tag{24}$$

$$GVCXforward_{sr} = REX_{sr} + REF_{sr}. \tag{25}$$

Total GVC exports are the sum of the two. The trade-based GVC participation rate is obtained by dividing these with gross exports.

$$GVCP_{sr}^{\text{Trade}} = \frac{GVCXbackward_{sr}}{E_{sr}} + \frac{GVCXforward_{sr}}{E_{sr}}. \tag{26}$$

This may be split up to include only backward GVCs or only forward GVCs. It may also be summed across all trading partners r to get an overall rate. In breaking this rate down by sector, it is more intuitive to use the export-sector breakdown since the denominator is gross exports.

Alternatively, Wang, Wei, Yu, and Zhu (2017) propose a production-based measure of GVC participation, computed as follows:[8]

$$GVCP_{s}^{\text{Production}} = \frac{\sum_{r\neq s} DAVAX2_{sr} + REX_{sr} + REF_{sr}}{va_s}. \tag{27}$$

This is the share of domestic value-added sent abroad in an unfinished state. Note that this is defined only for the sum of s's trading partners. In breaking this rate down by sector, it is more intuitive to use the origin-sector breakdown since the denominator is domestic value-added.

Revealed Comparative Advantage

The revealed comparative advantage (RCA) index is a classic trade indicator first proposed by Béla Balassa (1965). It uses existing patterns of trade to identify where an economy's comparative advantage lies. Formally, the economy s's RCA index for sector i is given by

$$RCA_{(s,i)} = \frac{E_{(s,i)}/E_s}{\sum_r E_{(r,i)}/\sum_r E_r}, \tag{28}$$

8 This is called the forward GVC participation rate by Wang et al. (2017). Their backward GVC participation rate is not covered in this framework.

where $\sum_r E_{(r,i)}$ is the sum of sector i exports from all economies and $\sum_r E_r$ is the total exports of all economies. This compares the share of i in s's exports with the average share of i in all economies' exports. If $RCA_{(s,i)} > 1$, then economy s is said to have a revealed comparative advantage in sector i. For example, if textiles are 50% of Cambodia's exports while for the average economy textiles are only 40% of exports, then Cambodia's RCA index in textiles is 50/40 = 1.25, which implies that it is specializing in that sector.

The formula in (28) uses gross exports, but the various components that make it up may also be used to reveal other types of specialization. One that is particularly illuminating is the value-added exports (*VAX*) measure of Johnson and Noguera (2012), defined as all exports of domestic value-added absorbed abroad:[9]

$$VAX_{sr} = DAVAX_{sr} + REX_{sr}. \tag{29}$$

Breaking this down by sector (using any approach) allows for its use in the RCA formula, resulting in a value-added-adjusted version of the index:

$$RCA^{\text{VAX}}_{(s,i)} = \frac{VAX_{(s,i)}/VAX_s}{\sum_r VAX_{(r,i)}/\sum_r VAX_r}. \tag{30}$$

The RCA and RCA^{VAX} may give very different indices in the presence of substantial foreign value-added.

Data Sources

The tools developed above are implemented using the rich information found in an inter-country input–output (ICIO) table. This combines national accounts data, balance of payments data, gross trade statistics, benchmark input–output tables, and other relevant information from as many economies as possible to form one global input–output table. Several such datasets have been constructed since KI2015 was published, including the Organisation for Economic Co-operation and Development's ICIO Tables and the World Input-Output Database (WIOD).

Most ADB analyses rely on its own Multiregional Input–Output (MRIO) Database, an expansion of the WIOD (Timmer et al., 2015). The ADB MRIO project, begun in 2014, synthesized the WIOD with statistics from its partners in Asia and the Pacific to construct a database that currently covers 62 economies plus a residual "rest of the world" entity (see Table A3.2). Each one is divided into 35 sectors based on the International Standard Industrial Classification of All Economic Activities (ISIC) revision 3.1 (Table A3.3), with 15- and 5-sector level aggregations also available (Table A3.4). With a dedicated team updating it annually using the latest published statistics,

9 KI2015 calls this VAX_G or VAX_F depending on the sector breakdown. See pp. 392–95.

the ADB MRIO is generally the most up-to-date ICIO in existence and features the widest coverage of developing Asia.

Of course, ICIOs are not without their caveats. Not only can benchmark input–output tables be several years outdated, their very accuracy hinges upon the ability of national statistics agencies to measure economic activity—a challenge for even the most advanced economies. Not all comply with the latest statistical guidelines from the United Nations and the International Monetary Fund, raising issues of international comparability. Many cells in an ICIO are not so much data as they are educated guesses by the compiler.

Economy coverage can also distort calculations in the accounting framework, particularly re-exports. This is because for the relationship $C \rightarrow J \rightarrow U$ to be counted, at least two entities must be covered in the ICIO. If, say, J and U are not, then they would be aggregated into the "rest of the world", in which case the relationship becomes $C \rightarrow$ Rest of the world. What ought to have been a GVC ends up looking like direct trading.

Table A3.2: Economies in the ADB Multiregional Input–Output Database

	Code	Name		Code	Name		Code	Name
1	AUS	Australia	22	IND	India	43	USA	United States
2	AUT	Austria	23	IRE	Ireland	44	BAN	Bangladesh
3	BEL	Belgium	24	ITA	Italy	45	MAL	Malaysia
4	BGR	Bulgaria	25	JPN	Japan	46	PHI	Philippines
5	BRA	Brazil	26	KOR	Republic of Korea	47	THA	Thailand
6	CAN	Canada	27	LTU	Lithuania	48	VIE	Viet Nam
7	SWI	Switzerland	28	LUX	Luxembourg	49	KAZ	Kazakhstan
8	PRC	People's Republic of China	29	LVA	Latvia	50	MON	Mongolia
9	CYP	Cyprus	30	MEX	Mexico	51	SRI	Sri Lanka
10	CZE	Czech Republic	31	MLT	Malta	52	PAK	Pakistan
11	GER	Germany	32	NET	Netherlands	53	FIJ	Fiji
12	DEN	Denmark	33	NOR	Norway	54	LAO	Lao People's Democratic Republic
13	SPA	Spain	34	POL	Poland	55	BRU	Brunei Darussalam
14	EST	Estonia	35	POR	Portugal	56	BHU	Bhutan
15	FIN	Finland	36	ROU	Romania	57	KGZ	Kyrgyz Republic
16	FRA	France	37	RUS	Russia	58	CAM	Cambodia
17	UKG	United Kingdom	38	SVK	Slovak Republic	59	MLD	Maldives
18	GRC	Greece	39	SVN	Slovenia	60	NEP	Nepal
19	HRV	Croatia	40	SWE	Sweden	61	SIN	Singapore
20	HUN	Hungary	41	TUR	Turkey	62	HKG	Hong Kong, China
21	INO	Indonesia	42	TAP	Taipei,China	63	RoW	Rest of the world

ADB = Asian Development Bank.

Note: Three-letter codes are from the ADB *Handbook of Style and Usage* (2017 edition) where available. Otherwise, three-letter codes from the International Organization for Standardization (ISO) are used.

Source: Asian Development Bank Multiregional Input–Output Database, 2021.

In this regard, it must be noted that coverage in the current ADB MRIO is lacking for Africa, Latin America, and the Middle East. An expanded version of the MRIO is available that includes additional coverage for Latin American economies, albeit for the years 2007, 2011, and 2017 only.

Table A3.3: Sectors in the ADB Multiregional Input–Output Database

	Name	Short Name	ISIC 3.1
1	Agriculture, hunting, forestry, and fishing	Agriculture	A–B
2	Mining and quarrying	Mining	C
3	Food, beverages, and tobacco	Food & beverages	D15–16
4	Textiles and textile products	Textiles	D17–18
5	Leather, leather products, and footwear	Leather	D19
6	Wood and products of wood and cork	Wood	D20
7	Pulp, paper, printing, and publishing	Paper	D21–22
8	Coke, refined petroleum, and nuclear fuel	Refined fuels	D23
9	Chemicals and chemical products	Chemicals	D24
10	Rubber and plastics	Rubber	D25
11	Other non-metallic mineral	Other minerals	D26
12	Basic metals and fabricated metal	Metals	D27–28
13	Machinery, not elsewhere classified	Other machinery	D29
14	Electrical and optical equipment	Electricals	D30–33
15	Transport equipment	Transport equipment	D34–35
16	Manufacturing, not elsewhere classified; recycling	Other manufacturing	D36–37
17	Electricity, gas, and water supply	Utilities	E
18	Construction	Construction	F
19	Sale and repair of motor vehicles and motorcycles; retail sale of fuel	Sale of motor vehicles	G50
20	Wholesale trade, except of motor vehicles and motorcycles	Wholesale trade	G51
21	Retail trade and repair, except of motor vehicles and motorcycles	Retail trade & repair	G52
22	Hotels and restaurants	Hotels & restaurants	H
23	Inland transport	Inland transport	I60
24	Water transport	Water transport	I61
25	Air transport	Air transport	I62
26	Other supporting transport activities	Other transport services	I63
27	Post and telecommunications	Telecommunications	I64
28	Financial intermediation	Finance	J65–67
29	Real estate activities	Real estate	K70
30	Renting of machinery & equipment and other business activities	Other business services	K71–74
31	Public administration and defence; compulsory social security	Public administration	L
32	Education	Education	M
33	Health and social work	Social work	N
34	Other community, social, and personal services	Other personal services	O
35	Private households with employed persons	Private households	P

ADB = Asian Development Bank, ISIC = International Standard Industrial Classification of All Economic Activities.
Source: Asian Development Bank Multiregional Input–Output Database, 2021.

Table A3.4: Sectors Aggregations

15-Sector Aggregation	5-Sector Aggregation	Correspondence
Agriculture, hunting, forestry, and fishing	Primary	1
Mining and quarrying	Primary	2
Light manufacturing	Low-technology manufacturing	3–7, 10–11, 16
Heavy manufacturing	Medium- to high-technology manufacturing	8–9, 12–15
Utilities	Low-technology manufacturing	17
Construction	Low-technology manufacturing	18
Trade services	Business services	19–21
Hotels and restaurants	Business services	22
Transport services	Business services	23–26
Telecommunications	Business services	27
Financial intermediation	Business services	28
Real estate, renting, and business activities	Business services	29–30
Public administration and defense	Personal and public services	31
Education, health, and social work	Personal and public services	32–33
Other personal services	Personal and public services	34–35

Source: Asian Development Bank Multiregional Input–Output Database, 2021.

Summary

This appendix has covered the various conventions and approaches to GVC analysis used in the *Key Indicators for Asia and the Pacific* and various other ADB publications. Its major preoccupation is characterizing the different types of value-added trade masked by gross export statistics. To this end, exports are decomposed into five main categories: domestic value-added directly absorbed (DAVAX), domestic value-added re- exported and absorbed abroad (REX), domestic value-added re-exported and brought back home (REF), foreign value-added (FVA), and pure double-counting (PDC). These terms form the core of GVC analysis. Their relative shares, their individual trends, and their sector make-up all reveal something about the exporting economy's GVC engagement. They may also be used to calculate associated indicators, including the GVC participation rate and the value-added-adjusted revealed comparative advantage index.

On a final note, it should be emphasized that the inclusion or exclusion of certain approaches in this framework is not intended as an argument over their validity, usefulness, or importance. The objective is merely to provide a coherent framework that best suits the needs of this publication and its users. Indeed, the framework has been kept relatively sparse to allow for flexibility in incorporating other methodologies as the need arises.

References

Asian Development Bank (ADB). 2015. *Key Indicators for Asia and the Pacific 2015*. Manila, Philippines: Asian Development Bank.

B. Balassa. 1965. Trade Liberalisation and "Revealed" Comparative Advantage. *The Manchester School*. 33 (2). pp. 99–123.

A. Borin and M. Mancini. 2019. Measuring What Matters in Global Value Chains and Value-Added Trade. *Policy Research Working Paper No. 8804*. Washington, DC: World Bank.

S. Giglioli, G. Giovannetti, E. Marvasi, and A. Vivoli. 2021. The Resilience of Global Value Chains During the Covid-19 Pandemic: The Case of Italy. *UniFI DISEI Working Paper No. 07/2021*. Florence, Italy: Università degli Studi Firenze Dipartimento di Scienze per L'Economia e L'Impresa.

D. Hummels, J. Ishii, and K. M. Yi. 2001. The Nature and Growth of Vertical Specialization in World Trade. *Journal of International Economics*. 54. pp. 75–96.

S. Inomata. 2017. Analytical Frameworks for Global Value Chains: An Overview. In World Bank, *Global Value Chain Development Report 2017: Measuring and Analyzing the Impact of GVCs on Economic Development*. pp. 15–35. Washington, DC: World Bank.

International Monetary Fund (IMF). 2019. *World Economic Outlook: Global Manufacturing Downturn, Rising Trade Barriers*. Washington, DC: International Monetary Fund.

IMF. 2021. *World Economic Outlook: Managing Divergent Recoveries*. Washington, DC: International Monetary Fund.

R. C. Johnson and G. Noguera. 2012. Accounting for Intermediates: Production Sharing and Trade in Value Added. *Journal of International Economics*. 86. pp. 224–236.

R. Koopman, Z. Wang, and S. J. Wei. 2014. Tracing Value-Added and Double Counting in Gross Exports. *American Economic Review*. 104 (2). pp. 459–494.

R. E. Miller and P. D. Blair. 2009. *Input–Output Analysis: Foundations and Extensions* (2nd ed.). Cambridge, UK: Cambridge University Press.

Organisation for Economic Co-operation and Development (OECD). 2021. *Global Value Chains: Efficiency and Risks in the Context of COVID-19*. Paris, France: Organisation for Economic Co-operation and Development.

M. P. Timmer, E. Dietzenbacher, B. Los, R. Stehrer, and G. J. de Vries. 2015. An Illustrated User Guide to the World Input–Output Database: The Case of Global Automotive Production. *Review of International Economics*. 23 (3). pp. 575–605.

Z. Wang, S. J. Wei, X. Yu, and K. Zhu. 2017. Measures of Participation in Global Value Chains and Global Business Cycles. *NBER Working Paper No. 23222*. Cambridge, MA: National Bureau of Economic Research.

Z. Wang, S. J. Wei, and K. Zhu. 2018. Quantifying International Production Sharing at the Bilateral and Sector Levels. *NBER Working Paper No.* 19677. Cambridge, MA: National Bureau of Economic Research.

World Bank. 2020. *Global Economic Prospects: Slow Growth, Policy Challenges (January 2020)*. Washington, DC: World Bank.

Global Value Chain Tables for Economies of Asia and the Pacific

ADB Regional Member	Exports ($ million)	DAVAX	REX	REF	FVA	PDC
		(% share in exports)				
Australia						
2000	91,972.28	61.71	22.78	0.38	15.02	0.10
2010	274,868.26	60.75	25.73	0.67	12.69	0.16
2019	329,944.26	64.84	22.74	0.51	11.78	0.13
2020	301,596.63	66.54	22.38	0.51	10.45	0.12
Bangladesh						
2000	5,435.78	77.75	8.86	0.01	13.37	0.01
2010	18,348.86	74.40	11.63	0.03	13.93	0.01
2019	46,130.81	73.72	3.56	0.02	22.70	0.01
2020	44,090.49	75.96	3.69	0.02	20.32	0.01
Bhutan						
2000	73.51	72.81	18.13	0.00	9.05	0.00
2010	520.74	65.48	18.41	0.01	16.11	0.00
2019	860.58	64.15	13.88	0.00	21.96	0.00
2020	791.17	69.60	12.60	0.00	17.79	0.00
Brunei Darussalam						
2000	3,475.50	67.12	29.51	0.01	3.37	0.00
2010	8,999.89	62.67	29.62	0.01	7.71	0.00
2019	7,804.89	52.87	28.16	0.01	18.95	0.00
2020	6,886.06	55.82	25.92	0.02	18.23	0.00
Cambodia						
2000	1,257.80	62.83	8.86	0.01	28.30	0.00
2010	4,040.54	61.95	10.81	0.01	27.23	0.00
2019	16,549.26	56.58	7.48	0.02	35.92	0.01
2020	19,340.27	49.97	9.64	0.02	40.36	0.01
Fiji						
2000	639.98	72.41	11.53	0.02	16.04	0.00
2010	1,159.77	60.56	11.01	0.01	28.42	0.00
2019	2,645.44	65.69	10.67	0.00	23.63	0.00
2020	1,233.12	69.00	10.48	0.00	20.51	0.00
Hong Kong, China						
2000	86,577.91	62.38	12.85	0.21	24.40	0.17
2010	143,433.66	57.62	12.74	0.15	29.30	0.20
2019	142,327.74	59.47	13.76	0.08	26.64	0.05
2020	113,828.98	62.23	12.99	0.06	24.68	0.04
India						
2000	62,071.02	69.09	17.68	0.29	12.89	0.05
2010	315,327.88	61.41	18.88	0.67	18.88	0.15
2019	532,597.09	63.87	15.86	0.54	19.59	0.14
2020	477,804.32	66.56	15.30	0.50	17.51	0.13
Indonesia						
2000	70,239.44	62.88	18.43	0.25	18.32	0.12
2010	183,521.00	59.96	24.46	0.54	14.93	0.12
2019	206,430.97	63.84	20.22	0.39	15.47	0.08
2020	181,713.75	65.04	20.42	0.34	14.13	0.07

Table 3.1.1: Value-Added Decomposition of Exports

continued on next page

Table 3.1.1: continued

ADB Regional Member	Exports	DAVAX	REX	REF	FVA	PDC
	($ million)	(% share in exports)				
Japan						
2000	515,441.61	69.50	19.23	1.96	8.95	0.36
2010	835,356.24	62.88	20.20	1.22	15.30	0.40
2019	894,082.18	63.84	19.24	0.89	15.79	0.25
2020	781,053.86	65.61	19.17	0.90	14.11	0.21
Kazakhstan						
2000	9,064.78	49.55	32.17	0.24	17.92	0.11
2010	62,623.70	58.35	31.34	0.17	10.10	0.05
2019	66,197.68	58.83	27.03	0.15	13.95	0.05
2020	53,390.76	59.39	26.88	0.16	13.52	0.04
Kyrgyz Republic						
2000	509.36	56.00	25.82	0.02	18.16	0.00
2010	2,289.01	53.74	13.49	0.01	32.76	0.00
2019	3,125.63	55.15	19.27	0.03	25.54	0.01
2020	2,009.56	60.46	19.93	0.03	19.57	0.01
Lao People's Democratic Republic						
2000	451.94	63.62	20.95	0.02	15.40	0.00
2010	1,548.12	63.43	21.01	0.01	15.54	0.00
2019	6,985.18	64.24	19.43	0.05	16.27	0.01
2020	6,489.32	67.95	20.96	0.05	11.03	0.01
Malaysia						
2000	105,312.16	32.72	14.26	0.18	51.73	1.10
2010	219,918.13	39.23	19.09	0.30	40.39	1.00
2019	237,991.06	45.10	19.72	0.32	34.54	0.31
2020	207,126.43	44.67	20.04	0.29	34.70	0.30
Maldives						
2000	472.72	59.50	13.30	0.00	27.19	0.00
2010	1,790.11	54.63	14.56	0.00	30.81	0.00
2019	3,894.41	52.55	14.99	0.00	32.45	0.00
2020	2,112.80	60.48	13.26	0.00	26.26	0.00
Mongolia						
2000	440.70	55.52	16.02	0.00	28.45	0.00
2010	2,954.96	55.50	20.27	0.01	24.21	0.00
2019	8,412.58	59.20	14.85	0.01	25.94	0.00
2020	7,745.71	61.94	15.53	0.01	22.52	0.00
Nepal						
2000	983.64	71.35	11.52	0.02	17.11	0.00
2010	1,066.56	68.43	14.15	0.03	17.38	0.00
2019	2,666.05	58.99	13.65	0.07	27.29	0.01
2020	2,233.86	61.70	13.40	0.06	24.83	0.01
Pakistan						
2000	8,646.67	73.81	20.23	0.05	5.91	0.00
2010	21,098.76	71.42	20.30	0.06	8.22	0.00
2019	25,609.98	74.58	14.18	0.03	11.20	0.00
2020	24,694.44	76.69	13.54	0.03	9.74	0.00
People's Republic of China						
2000	262,017.65	69.21	13.87	0.89	15.75	0.28
2010	1,697,752.15	64.92	13.58	1.95	18.54	1.01
2019	2,664,102.84	66.07	14.31	2.48	16.35	0.79
2020	2,732,326.31	67.78	13.63	2.77	14.94	0.88

continued on next page

Table 3.1.1: continued

Table 3.1.1: Value-Added Decomposition of Exports

ADB Regional Member	Exports ($ million)	DAVAX	REX	REF (% share in exports)	FVA	PDC
Philippines						
2000	26,395.30	56.91	23.01	0.10	19.91	0.06
2010	52,542.26	57.56	21.24	0.13	20.99	0.09
2019	82,157.70	52.87	19.89	0.13	27.05	0.07
2020	69,912.73	54.64	19.10	0.11	26.09	0.06
Republic of Korea						
2000	191,712.52	54.25	16.11	0.36	28.99	0.30
2010	518,902.44	48.96	15.05	0.35	35.18	0.46
2019	657,824.28	49.44	19.22	0.51	30.45	0.38
2020	601,614.53	51.39	19.48	0.57	28.16	0.39
Singapore						
2000	112,950.26	33.24	12.56	0.19	52.86	1.15
2010	284,178.19	34.17	12.50	0.10	52.44	0.79
2019	452,607.13	40.07	11.53	0.10	47.80	0.50
2020	395,395.42	42.00	12.21	0.10	45.26	0.44
Sri Lanka						
2000	4,661.43	64.95	16.51	0.02	18.51	0.00
2010	10,245.45	65.61	13.73	0.02	20.64	0.01
2019	14,620.00	70.58	12.50	0.02	16.90	0.00
2020	10,068.97	73.83	11.17	0.01	14.99	0.00
Taipei,China						
2000	171,251.23	46.96	15.13	0.33	37.00	0.57
2010	315,573.89	38.54	17.63	0.22	43.02	0.59
2019	388,731.34	42.54	19.37	0.20	37.53	0.37
2020	391,353.42	46.19	19.79	0.28	33.23	0.50
Thailand						
2000	55,961.91	56.34	14.14	0.16	29.27	0.10
2010	152,231.46	51.27	14.96	0.20	33.40	0.16
2019	323,768.89	56.91	13.03	0.19	29.71	0.16
2020	258,073.19	58.27	12.13	0.19	29.28	0.14
Viet Nam						
2000	17,155.07	63.35	11.88	0.06	24.68	0.03
2010	83,473.61	45.51	9.77	0.07	44.55	0.10
2019	279,720.22	41.17	7.83	0.08	50.71	0.21
2020	274,570.72	43.30	7.01	0.09	49.40	0.20

0.00 = magnitude is less than half of unit employed, $ = United States dollars, ADB = Asian Development Bank, DAVAX = domestic value-added immediately absorbed by direct importer, FVA = foreign value-added, PDC = pure double-counted terms, REF = re-exported domestic value-added absorbed by home economy, REX = re-exported domestic value-added absorbed abroad.

Source: Asian Development Bank Multiregional Input-Output Database, 2021.

Table 3.2.1: Value-Added Decomposition of Exports—Primary Sector

ADB Regional Member	By Export Sectors				By Origin Sectors			
	Total	DAVAX	REX+REF	FVA+PDC	Total	DAVAX	REX+REF	FVA+PDC
	($ million)	(% share in total)			($ million)	(% share in total)		
Australia								
2000	26,725.77	61.30	28.11	10.59	25,770.63	60.80	26.11	13.09
2010	138,753.90	57.61	32.19	10.21	113,395.48	59.54	31.27	9.18
2019	182,596.22	64.49	26.36	9.15	144,448.94	66.78	27.24	5.97
2020	183,574.81	66.29	25.50	8.22	138,758.81	68.53	26.42	5.04
Bangladesh								
2000	121.37	79.20	16.63	4.17	862.28	75.66	8.15	16.19
2010	483.48	78.02	16.14	5.84	3,229.70	68.62	11.93	19.45
2019	382.14	64.38	25.85	9.77	6,175.23	57.23	3.12	39.65
2020	413.35	70.17	20.73	9.10	5,784.49	60.29	3.12	36.59
Bhutan								
2000	7.88	88.89	5.98	5.13	9.78	85.05	6.07	8.88
2010	72.77	80.72	13.01	6.27	86.63	72.49	11.59	15.92
2019	197.81	75.91	13.52	10.58	182.59	71.41	12.46	16.13
2020	197.59	81.02	11.50	7.48	199.60	78.80	10.63	10.57
Brunei Darussalam								
2000	2,169.39	63.92	33.75	2.33	2,102.92	65.73	33.65	0.61
2010	4,845.01	63.11	29.93	6.97	6,087.70	65.77	31.33	2.90
2019	6,821.88	53.57	29.51	16.92	5,720.14	60.73	33.33	5.94
2020	5,690.40	55.86	27.30	16.84	4,744.32	63.19	30.71	6.10
Cambodia								
2000	47.52	53.03	36.45	10.52	167.38	57.61	16.61	25.78
2010	221.32	58.25	31.83	9.92	722.07	55.25	16.27	28.48
2019	1,393.74	62.03	22.71	15.26	2,985.11	48.79	13.73	37.48
2020	6,022.26	58.71	20.69	20.60	6,354.17	54.24	19.06	26.70
Fiji								
2000	172.57	70.54	16.59	12.87	114.48	72.85	12.71	14.44
2010	85.34	63.70	8.86	27.44	202.74	43.04	6.40	50.56
2019	117.78	69.92	13.90	16.18	318.03	57.46	8.75	33.79
2020	92.06	75.09	12.70	12.21	176.53	66.49	9.90	23.62
Hong Kong, China								
2000	150.25	40.36	16.09	43.55	1,569.69	2.75	1.04	96.20
2010	87.98	36.85	12.44	50.71	2,971.36	0.87	0.29	98.84
2019	274.01	66.00	1.58	32.42	3,971.46	3.27	0.10	96.63
2020	261.83	69.75	3.35	26.90	3,376.46	3.66	0.20	96.15
India								
2000	4,856.34	79.02	17.38	3.60	10,617.19	71.37	14.67	13.96
2010	24,905.40	70.99	24.14	4.87	59,870.01	48.92	16.42	34.66
2019	19,195.93	71.90	22.80	5.30	83,810.36	47.26	12.09	40.65
2020	21,063.05	72.65	22.09	5.26	69,702.39	53.26	12.35	34.39
Indonesia								
2000	10,956.37	66.00	29.43	4.58	21,509.02	65.54	23.59	10.87
2010	48,635.33	54.07	39.31	6.62	70,637.24	58.18	32.83	8.99
2019	44,012.45	68.31	27.22	4.46	69,736.27	66.81	24.82	8.37
2020	42,009.11	68.78	27.37	3.85	64,442.18	68.23	24.85	6.91
Japan								
2000	1,031.73	71.19	17.63	11.18	12,409.58	24.69	7.40	67.92
2010	2,588.34	47.83	19.86	32.31	47,226.26	9.42	3.67	86.91
2019	2,858.23	71.10	12.03	16.86	45,571.11	11.27	3.07	85.67
2020	2,713.84	66.35	18.04	15.61	34,090.95	13.28	3.84	82.88

continued on next page

Table 3.2.1: continued

ADB Regional Member	Table 3.2.1: Value-Added Decomposition of Exports—Primary Sector							
	By Export Sectors				*By Origin Sectors*			
	Total	DAVAX	REX+REF	FVA+PDC	Total	DAVAX	REX+REF	FVA+PDC
	($ million)	(% share in total)			($ million)	(% share in total)		
Kazakhstan								
2000	2,093.67	50.07	29.99	19.94	2,012.08	50.89	30.50	18.61
2010	35,319.37	55.66	33.81	10.52	29,863.08	58.50	35.63	5.87
2019	39,735.23	56.03	29.42	14.56	27,304.07	62.32	32.38	5.29
2020	33,254.77	55.99	29.99	14.03	22,316.27	62.46	32.82	4.73
Kyrgyz Republic								
2000	110.71	73.86	18.76	7.37	190.16	65.03	24.12	10.85
2010	968.93	54.51	11.74	33.75	835.30	51.98	11.14	36.88
2019	581.71	55.46	15.04	29.50	413.62	57.63	13.02	29.35
2020	558.32	63.00	15.25	21.75	335.98	70.80	13.19	16.01
Lao People's Democratic Republic								
2000	114.70	70.56	24.74	4.70	155.23	68.39	22.26	9.34
2010	907.38	62.28	21.94	15.78	809.96	67.48	23.18	9.34
2019	2,248.19	66.55	23.62	9.83	2,511.65	64.71	22.70	12.60
2020	3,267.58	71.53	21.88	6.58	3,172.99	72.00	22.07	5.93
Malaysia								
2000	9,488.77	60.03	26.53	13.44	15,612.79	55.47	22.12	22.41
2010	21,085.70	39.49	49.40	11.11	53,328.29	41.49	27.35	31.16
2019	19,973.06	62.12	29.33	8.55	50,168.18	49.65	23.31	27.04
2020	18,434.66	61.67	30.06	8.27	40,497.05	49.83	23.47	26.70
Maldives								
2000	16.65	83.51	2.31	14.18	48.52	45.20	4.60	50.20
2010	19.57	47.18	7.76	45.05	176.15	41.17	10.56	48.28
2019	76.70	53.95	11.46	34.59	455.88	37.47	7.90	54.63
2020	81.83	56.22	16.98	26.80	278.15	53.17	8.62	38.21
Mongolia								
2000	186.64	58.61	18.51	22.88	175.39	69.79	20.73	9.47
2010	2,098.21	54.11	20.96	24.93	1,553.48	62.46	23.63	13.91
2019	6,424.56	61.29	15.21	23.49	3,923.93	75.28	18.52	6.21
2020	6,018.95	64.78	15.21	20.01	3,948.58	77.24	18.57	4.20
Nepal								
2000	115.86	84.48	6.86	8.67	211.27	80.15	7.12	12.73
2010	78.02	87.69	4.35	7.96	179.95	66.54	6.48	26.98
2019	31.74	84.39	6.95	8.66	514.75	50.05	9.34	40.61
2020	69.55	83.55	8.51	7.94	481.18	60.00	10.61	29.39
Pakistan								
2000	457.76	80.41	17.15	2.44	2,393.04	74.91	19.81	5.28
2010	1,533.92	78.83	17.83	3.34	7,852.68	71.72	20.26	8.02
2019	969.80	72.41	24.21	3.38	9,450.42	76.25	13.48	10.27
2020	1,005.84	74.80	22.32	2.89	9,498.67	78.59	12.92	8.49
People's Republic of China								
2000	10,027.21	67.30	26.19	6.51	37,969.27	70.31	15.89	13.81
2010	22,608.99	67.80	22.56	9.64	264,170.13	57.67	13.13	29.20
2019	25,965.70	77.05	16.50	6.44	330,548.30	57.43	14.32	28.26
2020	27,059.00	76.92	17.27	5.81	380,083.90	63.33	14.83	21.84
Philippines								
2000	680.90	78.83	14.11	7.06	2,627.36	55.86	10.86	33.28
2010	1,265.16	68.48	23.36	8.16	7,417.79	54.62	13.76	31.62
2019	3,381.88	72.57	17.00	10.43	9,086.81	42.72	9.95	47.33
2020	3,359.21	73.75	15.88	10.37	7,447.62	50.82	10.48	38.70

continued on next page

Table 3.2.1: continued

Table 3.2.1: Value-Added Decomposition of Exports—Primary Sector

ADB Regional Member	*By Export Sectors*				*By Origin Sectors*			
	Total	DAVAX	REX+REF	FVA+PDC	Total	DAVAX	REX+REF	FVA+PDC
	($ million)	(% share in total)			($ million)	(% share in total)		
Republic of Korea								
2000	532.02	84.28	5.33	10.39	15,611.89	16.84	3.58	79.57
2010	775.91	72.52	10.84	16.65	60,758.95	6.22	1.57	92.21
2019	2,443.94	67.77	15.11	17.12	56,802.10	8.91	2.21	88.88
2020	2,018.74	70.81	14.07	15.12	44,441.59	12.11	2.85	85.03
Singapore								
2000	117.35	49.11	16.68	34.21	7,263.86	0.62	0.21	99.17
2010	59.94	49.53	17.97	32.51	27,490.63	0.14	0.05	99.81
2019	77.97	36.15	33.32	30.53	23,510.61	0.20	0.09	99.70
2020	70.84	55.55	16.06	28.39	16,884.69	0.34	0.07	99.59
Sri Lanka								
2000	1,518.80	65.47	19.47	15.06	1,351.62	69.52	20.34	10.13
2010	378.54	67.24	21.06	11.70	1,433.07	47.72	10.45	41.83
2019	887.83	69.60	19.16	11.24	1,671.48	56.38	14.52	29.10
2020	800.59	74.19	16.18	9.63	1,275.53	63.35	13.78	22.87
Taipei,China								
2000	1,525.12	78.21	3.04	18.75	8,209.79	18.46	2.58	78.96
2010	1,651.57	64.55	9.87	25.58	33,393.75	4.47	1.11	94.42
2019	1,190.03	65.61	14.30	20.09	29,452.72	6.49	1.43	92.08
2020	1,502.82	60.28	12.81	26.91	25,200.40	6.68	1.59	91.73
Thailand								
2000	1,259.04	58.73	23.17	18.10	5,879.45	44.84	9.10	46.05
2010	4,913.82	63.41	23.45	13.14	20,241.12	39.20	10.21	50.58
2019	19,271.34	71.16	15.72	13.12	51,478.57	44.14	7.44	48.42
2020	29,259.83	75.18	12.94	11.88	46,210.46	53.15	8.43	38.43
Viet Nam								
2000	3,288.22	58.78	18.24	22.97	3,357.81	68.85	16.87	14.28
2010	13,065.86	49.38	14.65	35.97	20,486.08	47.53	10.53	41.94
2019	17,481.17	47.61	13.17	39.22	47,115.34	36.35	7.80	55.85
2020	17,909.45	50.00	11.99	38.01	44,088.95	38.91	7.08	54.01

0.00 = magnitude is less than half of unit employed, $ = United States dollars, ADB = Asian Development Bank, DAVAX = domestic value-added immediately absorbed by direct importer, FVA = foreign value-added, PDC = pure double-counted terms, REF = re-exported domestic value-added absorbed by home economy, REX = re-exported domestic value-added absorbed abroad.

Source: Asian Development Bank Multiregional Input-Output Database, 2021.

Table 3.2.2: Value-Added Decomposition of Exports—Low-Technology Manufacturing Sector

ADB Regional Member	By Export Sectors				By Origin Sectors			
	Total	DAVAX	REX+REF	FVA+PDC	Total	DAVAX	REX+REF	FVA+PDC
	($ million)	(% share in total)			($ million)	(% share in total)		
Australia								
2000	14,496.81	72.43	11.33	16.24	11,471.59	67.61	17.70	14.69
2010	25,502.55	76.44	10.16	13.40	26,035.47	66.26	19.57	14.17
2019	31,216.82	79.73	7.48	12.79	30,235.82	69.10	16.82	14.09
2020	29,591.88	80.92	7.23	11.85	28,542.14	71.02	16.43	12.54
Bangladesh								
2000	4,754.40	78.29	7.13	14.58	2,440.49	83.83	7.76	8.41
2010	15,825.13	72.99	11.53	15.48	7,116.85	78.92	12.33	8.76
2019	40,439.64	73.86	1.48	24.66	21,287.34	85.55	1.85	12.61
2020	37,151.07	75.76	1.61	22.63	19,653.27	86.35	2.01	11.64
Bhutan								
2000	35.62	68.80	24.67	6.52	35.81	69.53	24.79	5.68
2010	210.42	58.63	29.51	11.86	229.08	63.82	26.48	9.70
2019	178.58	58.14	17.08	24.78	238.15	64.18	15.98	19.84
2020	190.73	66.16	14.18	19.66	221.87	68.73	14.53	16.74
Brunei Darussalam								
2000	101.98	70.66	13.38	15.96	77.91	57.72	15.66	26.61
2010	28.32	46.56	14.48	38.96	130.84	26.34	11.29	62.37
2019	87.22	44.65	12.31	43.04	277.36	14.19	4.74	81.08
2020	73.80	46.68	12.85	40.47	261.49	16.70	5.40	77.90
Cambodia								
2000	702.61	60.72	3.07	36.21	487.76	71.10	3.77	25.13
2010	2,124.18	59.62	4.39	35.98	1,480.40	72.13	5.52	22.35
2019	9,845.47	54.86	1.22	43.92	5,489.03	66.91	1.95	31.14
2020	9,415.78	42.62	1.09	56.29	5,612.74	58.72	1.49	39.79
Fiji								
2000	257.41	80.07	5.95	13.98	165.39	81.56	6.95	11.49
2010	207.66	66.04	10.14	23.83	167.80	66.59	10.29	23.11
2019	848.71	72.64	5.71	21.66	530.87	80.26	6.83	12.91
2020	654.14	74.04	6.26	19.71	336.12	84.98	6.97	8.05
Hong Kong, China								
2000	11,772.32	54.11	9.95	35.94	9,807.04	53.44	10.54	36.02
2010	10,503.80	42.68	8.57	48.75	7,484.96	40.15	8.64	51.21
2019	14,611.49	44.19	9.79	46.02	9,838.40	35.87	7.36	56.78
2020	16,257.59	56.62	6.76	36.62	9,728.82	47.70	4.09	48.22
India								
2000	22,169.57	76.19	11.78	12.03	11,653.72	76.67	14.64	8.69
2010	50,210.11	68.54	12.88	18.57	30,081.17	65.01	16.20	18.79
2019	123,310.12	70.55	11.77	17.67	66,017.69	68.05	14.65	17.30
2020	104,822.64	72.58	11.38	16.04	57,391.15	69.38	14.09	16.54
Indonesia								
2000	27,080.91	66.42	12.65	20.93	14,315.21	72.09	14.46	13.45
2010	61,583.24	66.92	17.05	16.03	33,684.61	71.00	18.18	10.81
2019	74,137.69	65.23	13.87	20.90	43,196.58	72.30	15.63	12.08
2020	66,082.28	66.99	13.84	19.16	38,776.36	73.32	15.54	11.14
Japan								
2000	26,161.90	65.95	26.01	8.04	52,716.80	68.77	22.82	8.41
2010	48,927.35	59.56	27.21	13.23	80,240.63	62.47	24.30	13.23
2019	62,809.14	62.86	24.46	12.68	87,568.99	63.33	22.06	14.61
2020	52,198.83	64.42	23.91	11.67	75,136.17	64.71	21.72	13.57

continued on next page

Table 3.2.2: continued

Table 3.2.2: Value-Added Decomposition of Exports—Low-Technology Manufacturing Sector

ADB Regional Member	*By Export Sectors* Total ($ million)	DAVAX (% share in total)	REX+REF	FVA+PDC	*By Origin Sectors* Total ($ million)	DAVAX (% share in total)	REX+REF	FVA+PDC
Kazakhstan								
2000	156.80	62.30	18.64	19.05	416.80	39.21	19.51	41.27
2010	1,221.46	70.28	15.25	14.46	2,102.76	53.70	20.07	26.23
2019	1,810.99	70.03	12.29	17.69	3,117.53	50.88	14.82	34.30
2020	1,191.67	70.07	10.89	19.04	2,367.96	49.00	14.64	36.35
Kyrgyz Republic								
2000	107.88	64.00	13.74	22.26	65.52	61.98	20.88	17.13
2010	221.19	45.45	7.59	46.96	170.79	44.18	7.87	47.95
2019	377.69	65.79	4.95	29.25	335.85	60.70	7.67	31.63
2020	308.47	73.21	4.89	21.89	233.54	69.06	8.06	22.88
Lao People's Democratic Republic								
2000	198.05	64.19	19.79	16.02	129.68	70.58	23.52	5.89
2010	420.02	68.47	19.56	11.98	323.33	71.53	22.06	6.41
2019	3,381.40	61.56	24.49	13.95	2,293.66	67.58	26.28	6.14
2020	2,367.79	65.68	22.15	12.16	1,997.24	70.71	24.70	4.60
Malaysia								
2000	15,450.36	50.28	11.74	37.99	12,018.14	44.07	13.61	42.32
2010	47,247.04	55.04	11.19	33.77	23,164.01	48.36	13.64	38.01
2019	32,992.12	55.71	15.33	28.96	23,535.32	51.22	17.10	31.68
2020	28,778.47	55.58	15.48	28.94	22,014.81	51.22	17.63	31.15
Maldives								
2000	41.24	57.45	2.97	39.58	74.57	37.19	4.32	58.50
2010	30.89	46.84	9.47	43.69	163.05	39.09	9.77	51.14
2019	288.43	50.80	5.01	44.19	405.61	28.15	5.63	66.23
2020	226.97	61.17	2.42	36.41	222.88	42.89	6.07	51.04
Mongolia								
2000	73.14	60.23	13.16	26.61	51.81	49.06	11.50	39.44
2010	125.72	64.31	12.46	23.23	184.56	48.17	15.06	36.78
2019	440.45	55.78	5.86	38.36	788.10	52.88	10.33	36.79
2020	303.11	57.02	6.45	36.52	624.63	52.55	10.91	36.54
Nepal								
2000	320.59	73.57	6.76	19.67	177.38	77.68	9.73	12.60
2010	222.11	69.85	5.25	24.90	139.46	74.74	9.17	16.09
2019	864.25	61.16	12.50	26.34	427.87	63.49	13.54	22.97
2020	746.45	63.53	12.48	23.99	376.00	65.65	13.27	21.07
Pakistan								
2000	4,126.97	73.28	20.93	5.80	1,547.54	74.68	20.70	4.62
2010	13,347.57	70.54	21.26	8.20	4,644.71	73.50	21.47	5.03
2019	17,459.00	77.32	12.73	9.95	5,990.14	79.89	13.04	7.08
2020	17,166.67	79.19	12.01	8.80	5,854.49	81.54	12.22	6.24
People's Republic of China								
2000	89,008.78	77.32	8.30	14.38	62,252.69	78.53	11.08	10.39
2010	373,984.43	77.76	8.83	13.41	272,156.55	75.81	12.28	11.90
2019	756,002.25	77.43	11.62	10.94	556,322.86	77.04	14.46	8.50
2020	795,160.61	78.53	11.63	9.85	570,188.04	77.60	14.17	8.22
Philippines								
2000	5,470.18	75.29	8.28	16.43	4,865.64	75.55	12.00	12.45
2010	10,611.31	72.05	13.90	14.05	8,452.68	68.88	16.78	14.34
2019	7,314.44	68.78	11.03	20.19	9,430.65	61.98	15.00	23.02
2020	6,881.12	72.01	9.62	18.38	8,411.94	63.74	14.09	22.17

continued on next page

Table 3.2.2: continued

Table 3.2.2: Value-Added Decomposition of Exports—Low-Technology Manufacturing Sector

ADB Regional Member	*By Export Sectors*				*By Origin Sectors*			
	Total	DAVAX	REX+REF	FVA+PDC	Total	DAVAX	REX+REF	FVA+PDC
	($ million)	(% share in total)			($ million)	(% share in total)		
Republic of Korea								
2000	34,138.32	57.02	19.44	23.54	26,361.81	58.06	19.09	22.85
2010	36,177.69	52.19	19.21	28.60	47,343.65	46.34	16.00	37.66
2019	53,286.78	52.65	19.65	27.69	71,638.92	50.53	19.76	29.71
2020	47,350.17	55.46	18.81	25.73	67,477.93	52.52	19.58	27.91
Singapore								
2000	5,151.22	41.35	10.45	48.20	8,091.19	30.32	9.49	60.19
2010	8,485.95	40.51	9.73	49.76	16,702.72	27.00	8.54	64.46
2019	13,707.02	49.53	8.81	41.66	25,105.60	32.01	7.11	60.88
2020	12,548.95	52.42	7.55	40.03	22,822.73	34.27	7.20	58.53
Sri Lanka								
2000	570.61	63.77	9.42	26.81	426.78	52.52	8.69	38.79
2010	5,583.43	69.14	9.34	21.51	3,644.52	77.59	10.70	11.72
2019	6,719.73	76.16	7.00	16.84	4,784.88	83.20	8.18	8.63
2020	5,491.93	79.41	5.98	14.60	3,762.45	85.47	6.81	7.71
Taipei,China								
2000	23,825.38	50.18	17.22	32.60	20,583.19	51.27	17.35	31.38
2010	22,044.54	41.54	15.90	42.56	25,462.70	36.95	15.23	47.82
2019	28,104.02	48.26	17.71	34.02	33,609.75	42.49	17.64	39.88
2020	26,575.65	50.86	18.30	30.84	36,002.73	46.07	18.79	35.14
Thailand								
2000	18,211.69	61.92	11.08	27.00	11,280.17	69.97	14.54	15.49
2010	32,265.52	60.06	13.83	26.11	23,460.57	63.11	17.48	19.40
2019	82,905.77	64.30	10.59	25.11	49,623.02	65.91	14.12	19.97
2020	76,756.81	66.56	10.01	23.43	42,496.31	67.91	13.37	18.72
Viet Nam								
2000	8,972.60	65.22	8.82	25.96	5,781.43	75.37	10.63	14.00
2010	42,158.30	46.31	5.81	47.89	20,036.37	65.61	8.70	25.69
2019	127,084.77	47.51	5.11	47.38	66,864.20	61.03	7.22	31.75
2020	127,414.33	49.94	4.42	45.64	67,062.38	62.59	6.20	31.21

0.00 = magnitude is less than half of unit employed, $ = United States dollars, ADB = Asian Development Bank, DAVAX = domestic value-added immediately absorbed by direct importer, FVA = foreign value-added, PDC = pure double-counted terms, REF = re-exported domestic value-added absorbed by home economy, REX = re-exported domestic value-added absorbed abroad.

Source: Asian Development Bank Multiregional Input-Output Database, 2021.

Table 3.2.3: Value-Added Decomposition of Exports—Medium- and High-Technology Manufacturing Sector

ADB Regional Member	By Export Sectors				By Origin Sectors			
	Total	DAVAX	REX+REF	FVA+PDC	Total	DAVAX	REX+REF	FVA+PDC
	($ million)	(% share in total)			($ million)	(% share in total)		
Australia								
2000	25,527.67	50.58	25.99	23.43	15,838.67	52.46	24.79	22.76
2010	53,320.57	52.83	23.52	23.65	30,345.81	50.14	21.36	28.50
2019	52,493.99	50.21	25.01	24.78	29,070.23	47.26	19.76	32.99
2020	43,230.03	53.01	23.92	23.07	26,304.91	48.72	18.13	33.15
Bangladesh								
2000	117.09	77.85	10.44	11.72	302.91	48.41	5.41	46.18
2010	428.51	77.31	8.74	13.95	1,055.88	47.68	6.60	45.72
2019	738.17	68.93	15.82	15.25	3,253.77	39.43	3.22	57.35
2020	703.62	70.67	14.29	15.04	2,991.27	44.11	3.24	52.65
Bhutan								
2000	8.00	83.43	5.40	11.18	5.27	71.36	5.28	23.37
2010	103.79	75.02	3.79	21.19	52.37	63.52	4.64	31.83
2019	274.91	67.14	9.64	23.22	155.63	65.66	8.23	26.12
2020	212.42	69.98	10.36	19.67	108.49	64.26	8.26	27.48
Brunei Darussalam								
2000	750.34	74.40	22.83	2.76	759.04	72.13	23.85	4.02
2010	3,482.84	63.16	30.96	5.87	1,823.39	62.90	30.35	6.75
2019	350.51	54.54	24.66	20.80	807.60	41.20	20.64	38.17
2020	768.48	62.22	21.68	16.10	999.73	51.53	20.53	27.94
Cambodia								
2000	8.69	57.04	6.26	36.70	78.51	9.75	1.34	88.91
2010	26.33	53.93	9.90	36.16	225.10	10.82	2.06	87.12
2019	794.35	37.42	25.95	36.63	1,417.21	18.63	11.63	69.74
2020	741.94	41.75	22.98	35.27	1,640.32	16.44	8.30	75.26
Fiji								
2000	87.50	55.29	12.35	32.36	54.08	43.23	8.68	48.09
2010	24.77	54.45	7.98	37.57	97.19	18.32	2.81	78.87
2019	105.44	52.13	17.18	30.69	212.09	26.87	6.16	66.97
2020	67.07	53.30	18.86	27.85	104.56	33.41	8.83	57.75
Hong Kong, China								
2000	6,011.08	28.56	13.20	58.25	3,011.17	21.56	9.86	68.58
2010	11,308.48	15.11	5.86	79.03	4,647.94	8.24	3.33	88.44
2019	22,325.98	39.41	12.14	48.44	5,595.81	7.35	2.58	90.08
2020	20,515.07	44.11	12.77	43.12	4,722.52	8.57	3.02	88.41
India								
2000	13,684.72	54.86	22.88	22.26	10,005.58	58.64	21.15	20.21
2010	100,793.88	45.90	19.49	34.61	53,782.36	56.28	22.10	21.62
2019	180,559.84	48.73	19.96	31.31	108,321.35	59.32	22.63	18.05
2020	156,833.81	51.95	19.38	28.66	95,954.27	61.87	21.62	16.51
Indonesia								
2000	26,542.40	56.72	20.76	22.52	16,224.43	57.33	20.19	22.48
2010	58,384.31	54.68	23.23	22.09	37,828.88	55.59	22.88	21.53
2019	59,593.31	56.39	24.16	19.45	39,330.22	56.33	21.37	22.30
2020	59,373.62	59.65	23.14	17.21	36,717.43	59.28	21.13	19.60
Japan								
2000	386,892.57	69.50	20.44	10.06	242,077.00	72.33	21.10	6.57
2010	591,965.90	60.90	20.94	18.16	353,129.22	67.51	22.59	9.90
2019	635,385.75	61.39	19.32	19.29	382,743.83	68.88	21.74	9.38
2020	557,361.07	63.36	19.49	17.16	336,145.69	70.24	21.65	8.11

continued on next page

Table 3.2.3: continued

Table 3.2.3: Value-Added Decomposition of Exports—Medium- and High-Technology Manufacturing Sector								
ADB Regional Member	By Export Sectors				By Origin Sectors			
	Total ($ million)	DAVAX (% share in total)	REX+REF	FVA+PDC	Total ($ million)	DAVAX (% share in total)	REX+REF	FVA+PDC
Kazakhstan								
2000	5,818.86	47.74	34.70	17.57	4,427.96	52.19	37.78	10.03
2010	12,532.59	51.17	38.24	10.60	9,751.63	48.01	33.79	18.20
2019	16,951.68	60.04	28.46	11.50	13,588.96	54.38	25.68	19.94
2020	13,842.83	63.06	25.46	11.48	11,260.98	56.73	23.34	19.93
Kyrgyz Republic								
2000	260.91	44.60	34.63	20.77	154.67	45.69	32.66	21.65
2010	791.22	54.24	16.92	28.84	716.40	58.58	18.30	23.12
2019	1,012.96	44.65	35.24	20.11	1,082.92	41.92	32.34	25.73
2020	701.03	49.41	34.64	15.95	720.83	47.76	33.14	19.10
Lao People's Democratic Republic								
2000	5.00	38.51	25.61	35.88	30.51	17.10	6.98	75.91
2010	15.09	35.81	10.12	54.07	91.29	14.54	4.49	80.98
2019	356.51	39.30	24.38	36.33	501.73	27.89	15.46	56.64
2020	372.60	43.67	25.59	30.74	426.25	35.16	19.06	45.77
Malaysia								
2000	69,125.49	21.67	13.20	65.13	43,863.32	24.20	14.07	61.73
2010	119,327.97	28.14	16.77	55.09	66,965.61	33.57	19.68	46.75
2019	143,078.44	35.39	20.07	44.54	71,538.15	37.92	20.18	41.90
2020	138,134.95	37.90	19.52	42.58	66,975.30	39.07	19.25	41.69
Maldives								
2000	0.11	70.90	6.82	22.27	14.04	0.59	0.11	99.30
2010	0.78	49.03	12.24	38.74	62.25	4.34	1.10	94.56
2019	21.22	53.56	10.86	35.57	139.60	7.46	1.54	91.00
2020	16.70	60.69	6.96	32.35	71.19	11.98	1.46	86.56
Mongolia								
2000	29.52	42.62	10.80	46.59	25.92	32.82	8.54	58.64
2010	57.57	48.00	17.37	34.63	285.03	11.61	4.24	84.14
2019	349.11	36.98	27.34	35.68	757.95	21.67	11.63	66.70
2020	374.62	32.46	34.95	32.60	628.36	26.88	14.05	59.07
Nepal								
2000	122.74	54.76	9.09	36.16	108.26	44.99	7.27	47.73
2010	83.42	55.12	5.26	39.62	87.78	41.64	4.56	53.80
2019	110.29	41.76	5.44	52.80	231.11	19.89	2.98	77.13
2020	96.73	44.35	6.11	49.54	197.03	22.49	3.47	74.05
Pakistan								
2000	416.24	64.93	19.71	15.35	448.51	67.41	17.66	14.94
2010	1,352.34	63.15	15.26	21.59	1,282.12	57.36	14.51	28.13
2019	2,367.85	57.61	14.45	27.94	2,027.12	58.84	13.35	27.81
2020	2,364.37	61.50	15.73	22.77	1,964.23	61.51	14.16	24.34
People's Republic of China								
2000	111,726.30	63.14	15.97	20.88	77,876.32	65.22	15.31	19.47
2010	1,012,324.70	59.38	15.83	24.79	593,003.97	64.71	16.53	18.75
2019	1,658,576.35	60.90	17.85	21.26	811,263.01	63.30	17.58	19.12
2020	1,685,022.75	62.68	17.47	19.86	796,197.48	63.90	16.91	19.19
Philippines								
2000	16,346.53	46.12	30.66	23.22	11,797.38	50.58	31.89	17.53
2010	21,597.88	38.72	24.28	37.00	12,371.52	41.13	24.60	34.28
2019	33,222.98	35.18	16.72	48.11	19,934.23	39.06	17.50	43.43
2020	29,610.16	37.20	16.67	46.13	17,410.14	40.07	16.96	42.97

continued on next page

Table 3.2.3: continued

Table 3.2.3: Value-Added Decomposition of Exports—Medium- and High-Technology Manufacturing Sector

ADB Regional Member	By Export Sectors				By Origin Sectors			
	Total	DAVAX	REX+REF	FVA+PDC	Total	DAVAX	REX+REF	FVA+PDC
	($ million)	(% share in total)			($ million)	(% share in total)		
Republic of Korea								
2000	134,640.73	50.80	15.63	33.56	87,358.31	59.50	18.38	22.13
2010	427,862.23	47.19	14.50	38.31	246,488.91	59.43	18.42	22.15
2019	516,721.85	46.80	20.19	33.01	300,773.76	56.88	24.80	18.32
2020	480,794.35	48.91	20.55	30.55	281,139.30	57.68	24.52	17.81
Singapore								
2000	68,194.56	25.38	10.97	63.65	39,007.84	33.93	14.57	51.50
2010	139,236.37	24.26	10.19	65.55	76,495.21	35.32	14.59	50.09
2019	225,308.17	36.27	11.35	52.38	100,040.28	47.46	15.23	37.31
2020	196,386.36	37.48	12.61	49.90	90,425.66	49.04	16.81	34.15
Sri Lanka								
2000	40.62	45.61	11.26	43.13	245.46	7.50	1.90	90.60
2010	898.89	49.33	9.56	41.11	938.75	49.24	9.37	41.39
2019	1,051.63	46.53	11.77	41.69	1,307.16	46.82	11.14	42.04
2020	818.46	48.86	13.02	38.12	939.80	48.54	11.89	39.57
Taipei,China								
2000	119,181.53	41.81	14.01	44.18	81,390.00	48.45	16.40	35.16
2010	240,938.23	34.13	17.39	48.48	151,056.61	45.17	23.30	31.53
2019	310,111.41	39.68	20.04	40.28	197,017.66	48.06	24.30	27.64
2020	313,680.94	43.47	20.59	35.94	201,029.85	51.31	24.29	24.40
Thailand								
2000	20,839.73	44.29	16.34	39.37	13,864.17	48.46	16.89	34.65
2010	79,185.74	40.79	14.82	44.39	43,479.01	47.76	16.79	35.45
2019	123,830.13	42.76	13.04	44.20	69,554.26	51.88	14.20	33.92
2020	112,133.00	45.27	12.55	42.17	60,578.88	54.82	13.69	31.49
Viet Nam								
2000	2,188.72	54.57	15.80	29.63	3,115.76	46.88	11.36	41.76
2010	17,018.58	33.36	13.62	53.02	17,501.23	30.01	11.10	58.89
2019	111,142.03	29.76	9.38	60.86	78,828.86	30.15	9.16	60.69
2020	107,555.70	31.55	8.67	59.78	77,134.70	32.08	8.25	59.66

0.00 = magnitude is less than half of unit employed, $ = United States dollars, ADB = Asian Development Bank, DAVAX = domestic value-added immediately absorbed by direct importer, FVA = foreign value-added, PDC = pure double-counted terms, REF = re-exported domestic value-added absorbed by home economy, REX = re-exported domestic value-added absorbed abroad.

Source: Asian Development Bank Multiregional Input–Output Database, 2021.

ADB Regional Member	By Export Sectors				By Origin Sectors			
	Total	DAVAX	REX+REF	FVA+PDC	Total	DAVAX	REX+REF	FVA+PDC
	($ million)	(% share in total)			($ million)	(% share in total)		
Australia								
2000	21,285.45	66.52	22.19	11.29	33,898.04	63.71	22.17	14.12
2010	50,135.67	67.14	23.53	9.34	93,265.12	62.86	24.64	12.50
2019	53,969.08	69.31	22.07	8.62	115,010.64	65.10	21.37	13.53
2020	38,287.97	69.57	23.25	7.18	99,269.25	66.70	21.53	11.77
Bangladesh								
2000	376.20	69.23	27.21	3.57	1,497.04	73.56	11.50	14.93
2010	1,427.57	83.03	11.58	5.39	4,870.33	73.28	11.12	15.60
2019	4,406.37	73.96	18.35	7.69	13,554.95	70.15	6.47	23.38
2020	5,613.71	78.44	14.50	7.06	13,765.70	73.95	6.32	19.73
Bhutan								
2000	17.78	68.87	17.29	13.84	19.51	71.78	16.14	12.08
2010	123.96	59.38	15.58	25.05	141.03	63.98	15.25	20.77
2019	203.59	53.78	17.05	29.17	274.21	59.06	16.33	24.61
2020	184.39	60.38	14.57	25.06	250.35	65.84	14.36	19.81
Brunei Darussalam								
2000	442.57	69.08	24.47	6.45	522.24	66.63	23.73	9.64
2010	612.82	57.08	20.86	22.06	887.36	46.79	19.75	33.46
2019	502.01	42.72	16.52	40.76	932.03	26.98	11.21	61.81
2020	323.02	41.32	16.33	42.36	806.12	31.03	12.19	56.78
Cambodia								
2000	429.90	67.33	13.66	19.00	472.05	64.36	11.57	24.08
2010	1,597.60	65.72	16.09	18.19	1,525.56	62.72	14.38	22.90
2019	4,486.93	61.95	13.29	24.76	6,390.98	60.38	8.50	31.13
2020	3,133.54	57.07	11.09	31.84	5,502.31	47.34	7.81	44.85
Fiji								
2000	119.47	70.76	15.89	13.35	270.51	71.94	13.84	14.22
2010	824.07	58.88	11.41	29.71	662.28	70.55	13.76	15.70
2019	1,168.90	56.59	14.43	28.98	1,249.23	62.75	14.09	23.16
2020	329.68	57.28	17.15	25.57	518.22	64.17	13.49	22.33
Hong Kong, China								
2000	68,177.65	66.80	13.54	19.66	67,999.51	67.00	13.89	19.12
2010	120,938.90	61.51	13.61	24.88	123,002.96	62.01	13.83	24.16
2019	104,499.94	65.76	14.82	19.42	117,685.28	65.84	15.42	18.73
2020	76,205.59	68.12	14.54	17.34	92,090.03	68.67	15.00	16.32
India								
2000	18,750.86	65.57	23.98	10.45	26,304.38	67.21	20.93	11.86
2010	128,576.97	66.23	22.93	10.84	155,335.29	65.50	21.82	12.68
2019	193,972.89	70.89	16.18	12.93	250,867.28	69.28	16.22	14.50
2020	181,358.66	73.27	15.23	11.49	233,872.35	71.04	15.43	13.54
Indonesia								
2000	4,957.81	68.37	17.21	14.43	17,168.40	57.78	14.98	27.24
2010	12,909.05	69.99	18.89	11.12	38,017.38	57.54	19.38	23.07
2019	23,554.62	67.40	21.20	11.40	49,005.57	58.13	18.79	23.07
2020	11,586.88	65.63	24.53	9.84	38,351.45	57.20	19.06	23.74
Japan								
2000	99,395.41	70.06	23.14	6.80	195,495.78	69.08	21.83	9.09
2010	188,197.35	69.88	21.53	8.59	333,922.40	65.76	22.02	12.22
2019	177,441.39	70.96	22.56	6.47	344,725.30	64.69	20.54	14.78
2020	155,308.87	72.30	21.90	5.80	307,695.54	66.06	20.19	13.75

Table 3.2.4: Value-Added Decomposition of Exports—Business Services Sector

continued on next page

Table 3.2.4: continued

Table 3.2.4: Value-Added Decomposition of Exports—Business Services Sector

ADB Regional Member	By Export Sectors				By Origin Sectors			
	Total	DAVAX	REX+REF	FVA+PDC	Total	DAVAX	REX+REF	FVA+PDC
	($ million)	(% share in total)			($ million)	(% share in total)		
Kazakhstan								
2000	980.87	56.83	26.70	16.47	2,164.81	45.56	26.34	28.10
2010	13,190.45	70.59	21.16	8.25	20,571.55	63.61	26.06	10.32
2019	7,597.41	67.87	16.33	15.80	21,750.00	58.92	23.67	17.41
2020	5,029.97	69.09	15.98	14.93	17,096.54	59.23	24.00	16.78
Kyrgyz Republic								
2000	22.91	57.35	21.71	20.94	93.00	50.00	22.55	27.45
2010	239.78	54.88	13.57	31.55	511.46	52.14	12.02	35.85
2019	956.73	58.65	12.28	29.06	1,132.53	62.50	13.47	24.03
2020	362.94	63.72	13.63	22.65	633.23	64.30	13.90	21.80
Lao People's Democratic Republic								
2000	117.17	55.45	20.40	24.15	122.67	60.28	21.11	18.61
2010	192.38	59.35	21.37	19.28	310.56	59.07	19.65	21.28
2019	993.45	71.16	3.85	24.99	1,648.32	70.76	6.69	22.56
2020	480.33	73.49	5.91	20.60	875.49	64.13	10.12	25.75
Malaysia								
2000	10,818.36	52.73	16.06	31.21	32,096.27	29.85	12.19	57.96
2010	31,179.87	56.26	22.10	21.63	70,966.67	41.42	16.19	42.38
2019	39,762.62	61.27	19.69	19.04	87,155.21	47.20	19.41	33.38
2020	20,610.07	57.97	24.38	17.65	72,755.78	45.42	20.90	33.68
Maldives								
2000	408.42	58.39	14.93	26.68	326.40	69.15	17.39	13.46
2010	1,707.77	54.88	14.63	30.49	1,346.78	60.66	16.21	23.13
2019	3,472.73	52.60	15.87	31.54	2,703.06	60.36	17.87	21.76
2020	1,762.91	60.47	14.48	25.05	1,356.67	65.66	15.20	19.14
Mongolia								
2000	145.76	51.76	15.49	32.75	180.94	47.41	14.12	38.47
2010	667.77	58.67	20.01	21.32	884.70	59.02	20.82	20.17
2019	1,156.98	55.22	12.72	32.06	2,774.84	49.38	12.17	38.45
2020	1,009.92	57.06	13.25	29.69	2,401.71	49.44	12.49	38.07
Nepal								
2000	289.89	68.32	17.90	13.78	389.45	68.87	14.83	16.30
2010	354.90	63.49	19.43	17.08	430.20	67.46	17.74	14.80
2019	1,309.53	55.49	16.22	28.29	1,298.75	65.03	17.43	17.54
2020	1,046.26	57.91	15.97	26.12	1,015.17	65.71	16.83	17.46
Pakistan								
2000	3,163.92	72.67	21.39	5.94	3,740.71	72.00	21.75	6.25
2010	3,963.22	70.73	22.83	6.44	6,444.28	70.61	22.30	7.09
2019	2,618.76	71.19	20.83	7.98	6,396.84	70.54	16.80	12.66
2020	2,184.67	73.18	20.12	6.71	5,817.32	72.41	15.91	11.68
People's Republic of China								
2000	43,309.46	68.02	22.16	9.82	76,968.89	65.42	16.62	17.97
2010	276,698.17	67.07	23.07	9.87	534,089.96	63.33	17.33	19.34
2019	208,236.42	64.74	26.53	8.74	873,596.18	64.73	18.20	17.07
2020	207,926.89	66.98	25.17	7.85	885,967.74	66.54	17.73	15.72
Philippines								
2000	3,802.32	72.46	13.92	13.62	6,821.05	55.60	20.89	23.51
2010	18,372.71	70.00	22.24	7.75	23,259.95	63.01	23.88	13.11
2019	35,847.81	63.15	25.16	11.69	41,065.97	59.25	24.54	16.20
2020	28,102.82	65.42	24.61	9.98	34,478.87	60.19	23.43	16.37

continued on next page

Table 3.2.4: continued

Table 3.2.4: Value-Added Decomposition of Exports—Business Services Sector

ADB Regional Member	By Export Sectors				By Origin Sectors			
	Total	DAVAX	REX+REF	FVA+PDC	Total	DAVAX	REX+REF	FVA+PDC
	($ million)	(% share in total)			($ million)	(% share in total)		
Republic of Korea								
2000	21,951.07	69.88	17.27	12.85	58,358.15	54.85	16.00	29.15
2010	50,284.70	59.97	20.20	19.83	150,005.44	49.27	15.69	35.04
2019	72,438.39	60.32	18.50	21.18	207,657.59	48.38	17.70	33.92
2020	60,673.94	62.54	19.10	18.36	189,813.02	50.02	18.11	31.86
Singapore								
2000	39,108.58	45.50	16.19	38.32	55,615.30	37.63	13.75	48.62
2010	135,393.07	43.79	15.19	41.02	158,805.66	40.71	14.40	44.89
2019	211,675.54	43.23	12.14	44.63	295,011.12	41.89	11.92	46.19
2020	184,786.09	45.82	12.32	41.86	257,835.85	43.46	12.19	44.35
Sri Lanka								
2000	1,856.14	61.36	19.58	19.06	1,954.76	64.56	19.51	15.93
2010	3,182.17	63.58	22.07	14.35	4,048.68	65.16	18.69	16.15
2019	5,846.80	68.50	17.98	13.51	6,417.84	69.78	15.50	14.72
2020	2,925.22	70.16	19.06	10.78	3,823.08	72.04	14.40	13.56
Taipei,China								
2000	25,911.94	64.80	21.54	13.66	57,793.88	47.66	15.61	36.73
2010	49,626.00	56.71	21.54	21.75	98,814.21	40.16	16.16	43.68
2019	45,884.61	55.21	18.40	26.39	119,416.24	41.87	17.16	40.97
2020	46,063.73	59.13	18.52	22.35	119,569.21	45.62	17.67	36.71
Thailand								
2000	14,187.30	64.99	15.33	19.68	23,289.25	56.83	14.25	28.92
2010	31,849.89	63.61	16.76	19.63	60,392.31	52.44	15.06	32.50
2019	92,140.75	65.32	15.26	19.42	144,287.63	60.63	14.49	24.88
2020	37,558.58	66.03	15.67	18.30	103,438.00	58.92	12.85	28.23
Viet Nam								
2000	2,315.33	67.49	13.19	19.33	4,505.15	54.14	11.17	34.70
2010	10,830.04	55.92	13.99	30.09	24,297.05	39.12	9.58	51.30
2019	23,061.48	55.56	11.92	32.53	82,299.78	39.39	7.50	53.12
2020	20,638.59	56.77	10.63	32.59	81,619.20	41.50	6.84	51.65

0.00 = magnitude is less than half of unit employed, $ = United States dollars, ADB = Asian Development Bank, DAVAX = domestic value-added immediately absorbed by direct importer, FVA = foreign value-added, PDC = pure double-counted terms, REF = re-exported domestic value-added absorbed by home economy, REX = re-exported domestic value-added absorbed abroad.

Source: Asian Development Bank Multiregional Input-Output Database, 2021.

Table 3.2.5: Value-Added Decomposition of Exports—Personal and Public Services Sector								
ADB Regional Member	*By Export Sectors*				*By Origin Sectors*			
	Total	DAVAX	REX+REF	FVA+PDC	Total	DAVAX	REX+REF	FVA+PDC
	($ million)	(% share in total)			($ million)	(% share in total)		
Australia								
2000	3,936.58	71.27	20.09	8.64	4,993.33	68.70	22.06	9.24
2010	7,155.56	80.05	13.49	6.45	11,826.37	70.76	21.45	7.79
2019	9,668.15	77.91	12.37	9.72	11,178.63	71.42	17.36	11.23
2020	6,911.94	79.50	12.36	8.13	8,721.53	72.10	17.64	10.26
Bangladesh								
2000	66.73	84.25	13.19	2.56	333.07	84.15	10.23	5.62
2010	184.17	82.53	12.53	4.94	2,076.11	84.10	12.80	3.10
2019	164.49	74.77	17.79	7.45	1,859.51	79.07	4.51	16.42
2020	208.74	74.34	18.89	6.77	1,895.76	81.05	5.02	13.93
Bhutan								
2000	4.24	73.14	13.35	13.51	3.14	80.92	13.83	5.26
2010	9.81	75.30	11.16	13.54	11.64	72.74	10.69	16.58
2019	5.69	70.45	18.85	10.69	10.00	47.08	11.22	41.71
2020	6.04	72.79	18.33	8.88	10.86	58.46	12.59	28.94
Brunei Darussalam								
2000	11.22	89.53	2.18	8.28	13.39	74.18	6.07	19.75
2010	30.90	63.57	18.47	17.96	70.60	56.56	21.53	21.91
2019	43.26	62.80	14.20	23.00	67.78	42.84	12.56	44.60
2020	30.36	63.67	13.09	23.24	74.40	49.65	15.95	34.41
Cambodia								
2000	69.08	63.68	19.43	16.90	52.10	68.30	18.69	13.02
2010	71.12	60.85	19.33	19.82	87.40	62.89	16.04	21.07
2019	28.77	70.51	8.28	21.20	266.93	41.64	6.13	52.24
2020	26.75	64.94	7.46	27.60	230.72	20.33	3.67	76.00
Fiji								
2000	3.02	86.64	6.74	6.62	35.52	76.31	16.26	7.43
2010	17.93	67.82	17.78	14.40	29.75	61.77	12.39	25.84
2019	404.61	79.73	7.60	12.67	335.22	85.96	8.70	5.34
2020	90.17	80.79	8.32	10.88	97.70	82.27	9.47	8.26
Hong Kong, China								
2000	466.59	67.95	17.87	14.18	4,190.48	59.97	12.29	27.74
2010	594.50	69.05	17.07	13.88	5,326.43	55.63	12.36	32.01
2019	616.31	79.63	10.20	10.17	5,236.79	59.04	12.73	28.23
2020	588.90	83.11	8.97	7.92	3,911.15	62.11	12.70	25.18
India								
2000	2,609.53	90.28	2.75	6.97	3,490.13	81.04	7.76	11.20
2010	10,841.53	93.53	0.48	5.99	16,259.05	78.73	7.27	14.00
2019	15,558.31	89.07	6.41	4.51	23,580.41	74.51	9.75	15.74
2020	13,726.16	89.46	6.45	4.08	20,884.15	74.67	9.45	15.88
Indonesia								
2000	701.94	71.61	15.78	12.61	1,022.36	51.43	12.89	35.69
2010	2,009.07	78.39	12.04	9.57	3,352.89	63.14	15.83	21.04
2019	5,132.90	75.57	17.34	7.09	5,162.33	64.29	16.98	18.73
2020	2,661.86	75.40	18.60	6.00	3,426.34	60.91	17.87	21.23
Japan								
2000	1,959.98	87.47	9.29	3.25	12,742.35	68.89	19.87	11.24
2010	3,677.31	78.68	16.24	5.08	20,837.74	61.05	21.05	17.90
2019	15,587.68	85.13	9.36	5.51	33,472.94	70.24	15.76	14.00
2020	13,471.26	86.09	8.93	4.98	27,985.51	71.11	15.23	13.67

continued on next page

Table 3.2.5: continued

Table 3.2.5: Value-Added Decomposition of Exports—Personal and Public Services Sector								
ADB Regional Member	*By Export Sectors*				*By Origin Sectors*			
	Total ($ million)	DAVAX (% share in total)	REX+REF	FVA+PDC	Total ($ million)	DAVAX (% share in total)	REX+REF	FVA+PDC
Kazakhstan								
2000	14.59	75.07	4.99	19.94	43.14	16.63	2.00	81.37
2010	359.83	82.04	6.10	11.86	334.69	50.67	4.95	44.38
2019	102.38	75.25	11.03	13.73	437.12	30.70	10.61	58.68
2020	71.51	75.81	11.05	13.14	349.00	28.65	10.32	61.03
Kyrgyz Republic								
2000	6.96	70.99	9.77	19.24	6.01	63.14	9.39	27.47
2010	67.89	59.80	17.78	22.42	55.06	61.96	18.01	20.02
2019	196.54	70.88	11.52	17.60	160.71	74.55	13.00	12.45
2020	78.80	75.90	10.86	13.24	85.98	74.95	12.83	12.22
Lao People's Democratic Republic								
2000	17.03	73.92	11.94	14.14	13.86	77.10	12.22	10.69
2010	13.25	74.00	11.89	14.12	12.97	57.83	9.28	32.89
2019	5.63	83.59	5.89	10.52	29.83	18.48	1.16	80.36
2020	1.02	81.56	8.16	10.28	17.35	6.70	0.71	92.59
Malaysia								
2000	429.18	72.53	4.33	23.14	1,721.64	17.75	2.34	79.90
2010	1,077.55	76.06	2.01	21.93	5,493.55	19.40	3.94	76.66
2019	2,184.82	70.55	11.02	18.43	5,594.21	37.59	11.08	51.33
2020	1,168.27	72.95	10.63	16.42	4,883.48	37.94	12.82	49.24
Maldives								
2000	6.30	81.37	4.77	13.87	9.19	63.10	7.34	29.56
2010	31.09	53.62	19.82	26.55	41.87	52.72	16.82	30.46
2019	35.33	58.89	20.89	20.22	190.26	62.83	20.93	16.24
2020	24.38	68.82	18.44	12.74	183.91	73.42	19.28	7.29
Mongolia								
2000	5.64	56.85	12.28	30.87	6.65	38.53	8.35	53.13
2010	5.69	77.16	7.68	15.16	47.18	54.32	17.56	28.12
2019	41.48	68.79	9.65	21.55	167.76	44.63	9.57	45.80
2020	39.12	70.73	9.34	19.93	142.44	44.57	9.61	45.82
Nepal								
2000	134.57	76.40	15.48	8.11	97.27	79.94	16.01	4.05
2010	328.11	71.63	19.17	9.20	229.16	78.16	20.32	1.52
2019	350.22	69.83	10.59	19.58	193.57	78.97	13.62	7.41
2020	274.86	71.75	10.47	17.79	164.48	79.85	13.51	6.64
Pakistan								
2000	481.77	87.19	10.85	1.96	516.87	84.75	12.74	2.51
2010	901.72	87.26	8.15	4.59	874.97	84.16	9.69	6.15
2019	2,194.56	76.11	13.43	10.47	1,745.46	80.43	13.73	5.84
2020	1,972.90	77.98	12.85	9.17	1,559.73	81.99	13.08	4.93
People's Republic of China								
2000	7,945.89	72.56	15.08	12.36	6,950.44	66.42	14.57	19.01
2010	12,135.87	77.14	12.18	10.68	34,331.54	62.67	14.41	22.92
2019	15,322.12	64.73	25.48	9.78	92,372.49	68.00	19.39	12.61
2020	17,157.06	66.48	24.92	8.60	99,889.15	70.62	19.12	10.27
Philippines								
2000	95.37	76.55	12.46	10.99	283.87	42.02	16.23	41.76
2010	695.20	72.86	18.01	9.13	1,040.31	60.05	18.10	21.85
2019	2,390.59	68.12	20.52	11.36	2,640.05	60.29	21.13	18.58
2020	1,959.43	69.70	19.75	10.55	2,164.17	60.96	20.15	18.90

continued on next page

Table 3.2.5: continued

Table 3.2.5: Value-Added Decomposition of Exports—Personal and Public Services Sector								
	By Export Sectors				*By Origin Sectors*			
ADB Regional Member	Total	DAVAX	REX+REF	FVA+PDC	Total	DAVAX	REX+REF	FVA+PDC
	($ million)	(% share in total)			($ million)	(% share in total)		
Republic of Korea								
2000	450.37	76.71	13.52	9.77	4,022.33	51.69	14.47	33.84
2010	3,801.91	67.30	17.80	14.90	14,305.48	55.43	17.23	27.34
2019	12,933.32	76.93	9.94	13.13	20,951.90	59.15	14.68	26.17
2020	10,777.32	78.04	10.04	11.92	18,742.68	60.07	15.30	24.63
Singapore								
2000	378.55	69.07	7.83	23.10	2,972.07	30.04	9.61	60.35
2010	1,002.85	58.25	21.85	19.90	4,683.96	19.42	7.22	73.36
2019	1,838.44	71.87	8.19	19.94	8,939.52	24.79	4.90	70.31
2020	1,603.17	73.00	9.02	17.98	7,426.48	24.09	4.59	71.32
Sri Lanka								
2000	675.26	72.11	8.37	19.53	682.82	85.44	10.63	3.93
2010	202.41	73.90	16.27	9.83	180.43	61.10	13.39	25.52
2019	114.01	77.21	12.61	10.19	438.64	69.51	12.66	17.83
2020	32.77	80.00	11.51	8.49	268.11	74.43	11.75	13.83
Taipei,China								
2000	807.26	80.29	6.89	12.82	3,274.33	42.05	10.15	47.80
2010	1,313.56	77.75	6.55	15.70	6,846.63	41.08	13.43	45.49
2019	3,441.27	76.56	9.44	14.01	9,234.97	48.40	14.68	36.91
2020	3,530.27	77.62	10.89	11.49	9,551.23	50.18	15.06	34.76
Thailand								
2000	1,464.14	72.49	7.60	19.91	1,648.86	63.40	10.05	26.55
2010	4,016.49	74.79	9.65	15.56	4,658.44	61.80	10.98	27.22
2019	5,620.91	73.16	13.95	12.90	8,825.41	59.68	13.51	26.81
2020	2,364.99	73.13	15.00	11.87	5,349.54	52.55	11.72	35.73
Viet Nam								
2000	390.19	83.63	1.39	14.98	394.92	75.88	2.37	21.75
2010	400.82	70.80	4.42	24.78	1,152.87	30.37	3.77	65.86
2019	950.78	60.27	16.75	22.99	4,612.05	22.55	5.40	72.06
2020	1,052.66	61.45	16.68	21.87	4,665.50	24.12	5.41	70.47

0.00 = magnitude is less than half of unit employed, $ = United States dollars, ADB = Asian Development Bank, DAVAX = domestic value-added immediately absorbed by direct importer, FVA = foreign value-added, PDC = pure double-counted terms, REF = re-exported domestic value-added absorbed by home economy, REX = re-exported domestic value-added absorbed abroad.

Source: Asian Development Bank Multiregional Input-Output Database, 2021.

Table 3.3.1: Global Value Chain Participation Rates

ADB Regional Member	Trade-Based (export-sector breakdown) 2000	2010	2019	2020	Production-Based (origin-sector breakdown) 2000	2010	2019	2020
Australia								
Aggregate	38.29	39.25	35.16	33.46	15.44	16.56	18.47	17.66
Primary	38.70	42.39	35.51	33.71	55.75	63.34	74.68	76.06
Low-technology manufacturing	27.57	23.56	20.27	19.08	10.96	8.30	9.98	9.68
Medium- to high-technology manufacturing	49.42	47.17	49.79	46.99	33.53	30.35	33.47	28.16
Business services	33.48	32.86	30.69	30.43	10.96	10.91	11.57	10.56
Personal and public services	28.73	19.95	22.09	20.50	4.32	3.49	2.28	1.83
Bangladesh								
Aggregate	22.25	25.60	26.28	24.04	2.50	4.60	1.65	1.54
Primary	20.80	21.98	35.62	29.83	1.40	4.58	1.30	1.28
Low-technology manufacturing	21.71	27.01	26.14	24.24	4.48	9.24	1.73	1.63
Medium- to high-technology manufacturing	22.15	22.69	31.07	29.33	2.00	2.95	1.49	1.27
Business services	30.77	16.97	26.04	21.56	2.80	3.19	2.38	2.18
Personal and public services	15.75	17.47	25.23	25.66	1.32	3.17	0.45	0.48
Bhutan								
Aggregate	27.19	34.52	35.85	30.40	10.61	20.22	16.08	14.69
Primary	11.11	19.28	24.09	18.98	3.68	16.38	15.02	15.27
Low-technology manufacturing	31.20	41.37	41.86	33.84	21.33	31.81	17.70	16.62
Medium- to high-technology manufacturing	16.57	24.98	32.86	30.02	6.14	12.57	41.92	43.27
Business services	31.13	40.62	46.22	39.62	12.68	18.32	17.17	15.42
Personal and public services	26.86	24.70	29.55	27.21	2.32	2.05	0.93	1.13
Brunei Darussalam								
Aggregate	32.88	37.33	47.13	44.18	48.22	55.49	45.36	44.88
Primary	36.08	36.89	46.43	44.14	91.30	79.15	85.11	90.93
Low-technology manufacturing	29.34	53.44	55.35	53.32	15.29	9.67	6.81	7.32
Medium- to high-technology manufacturing	25.60	36.84	45.46	37.78	74.90	76.77	25.60	33.57
Business services	30.92	42.92	57.28	58.68	21.66	20.89	10.38	10.77
Personal and public services	10.47	36.43	37.20	36.33	0.23	2.01	0.97	1.56
Cambodia								
Aggregate	37.17	38.05	43.42	50.03	8.64	10.79	12.78	23.27
Primary	46.97	41.75	37.97	41.29	5.14	7.20	15.38	61.44
Low-technology manufacturing	39.28	40.38	45.14	57.38	5.58	9.09	3.84	3.50
Medium- to high-technology manufacturing	42.96	46.07	62.58	58.25	4.40	6.78	64.74	65.76
Business services	32.67	34.28	38.05	42.93	15.18	19.02	19.57	18.81
Personal and public services	36.32	39.15	29.49	35.06	9.65	3.71	2.14	1.27
Fiji								
Aggregate	27.59	39.44	34.31	31.00	18.05	16.64	21.77	12.71
Primary	29.46	36.30	30.08	24.91	22.66	14.59	13.77	14.46
Low-technology manufacturing	19.93	33.96	27.36	25.96	16.77	13.84	16.45	14.19
Medium- to high-technology manufacturing	44.71	45.55	47.87	46.70	36.62	13.88	31.51	30.33
Business services	29.24	41.12	43.41	42.72	20.45	22.07	27.27	13.42
Personal and public services	13.36	32.18	20.27	19.21	6.63	2.44	18.70	6.49
Hong Kong, China								
Aggregate	37.62	42.38	40.53	37.77	19.70	24.22	16.34	12.94
Primary	59.64	63.15	34.00	30.25	26.97	19.77	4.13	8.66
Low-technology manufacturing	45.89	57.32	55.81	43.38	14.85	12.78	9.03	5.14
Medium- to high-technology manufacturing	71.44	84.89	60.59	55.89	59.37	60.54	65.71	60.85
Business services	33.20	38.49	34.24	31.88	24.30	29.48	20.40	16.29
Personal and public services	32.05	30.95	20.37	16.89	4.62	4.77	2.98	2.35

continued on next page

Table 3.3.1: continued

Table 3.3.1: Global Value Chain Participation Rates

ADB Regional Member	Trade-Based (export-sector breakdown)				Production-Based (origin-sector breakdown)			
	2000	2010	2019	2020	2000	2010	2019	2020
India								
Aggregate	30.91	38.59	36.13	33.44	6.40	9.73	8.83	8.96
Primary	20.98	29.01	28.10	27.35	4.32	8.47	5.50	5.23
Low-technology manufacturing	23.81	31.46	29.45	27.42	6.07	5.06	6.21	6.31
Medium- to high-technology manufacturing	45.14	54.10	51.27	48.05	11.39	14.66	18.31	18.47
Business services	34.43	33.77	29.11	26.73	9.03	14.02	11.11	11.87
Personal and public services	9.72	6.47	10.93	10.54	0.88	1.24	1.85	1.79
Indonesia								
Aggregate	37.12	40.04	36.16	34.96	21.45	16.18	11.52	10.88
Primary	34.00	45.93	31.69	31.22	34.64	31.15	24.39	23.66
Low-technology manufacturing	33.58	33.08	34.77	33.01	18.00	11.51	8.32	7.66
Medium- to high-technology manufacturing	43.28	45.32	43.61	40.35	35.87	25.14	19.99	22.16
Business services	31.63	30.01	32.60	34.37	12.22	8.78	6.69	5.62
Personal and public services	28.39	21.61	24.43	24.60	2.84	2.35	2.42	1.51
Japan								
Aggregate	30.50	37.12	36.16	34.39	5.50	7.58	8.82	8.09
Primary	28.81	52.17	28.90	33.65	2.78	5.06	5.33	5.49
Low-technology manufacturing	34.05	40.44	37.14	35.58	3.63	5.91	6.76	5.92
Medium- to high-technology manufacturing	30.50	39.10	38.61	36.64	17.17	24.16	27.95	26.33
Business services	29.94	30.12	29.04	27.70	4.67	6.65	7.79	7.18
Personal and public services	12.53	21.32	14.87	13.91	0.69	0.84	1.44	1.22
Kazakhstan								
Aggregate	50.45	41.65	41.17	40.61	38.59	35.94	26.72	24.27
Primary	49.93	44.34	43.97	44.01	49.10	67.12	59.51	59.87
Low-technology manufacturing	37.70	29.72	29.97	29.93	10.30	6.81	7.45	5.51
Medium- to high-technology manufacturing	52.26	48.83	39.96	36.94	56.98	59.68	62.44	50.72
Business services	43.17	29.41	32.13	30.91	27.35	25.63	16.61	15.19
Personal and public services	24.93	17.96	24.75	24.19	0.37	0.70	0.65	0.52
Kyrgyz Republic								
Aggregate	44.00	46.26	44.85	39.54	24.42	19.29	18.23	13.91
Primary	26.14	45.49	44.54	37.00	26.02	29.06	11.82	10.67
Low-technology manufacturing	36.00	54.55	34.21	26.79	15.54	6.89	6.12	5.81
Medium- to high-technology manufacturing	55.40	45.76	55.35	50.59	60.29	49.12	65.67	46.71
Business services	42.65	45.12	41.35	36.28	18.61	12.55	15.59	11.15
Personal and public services	29.01	40.20	29.12	24.10	1.50	4.03	5.42	3.15
Lao People's Democratic Republic								
Aggregate	36.38	36.57	35.76	32.05	16.65	15.81	20.98	24.16
Primary	29.44	37.72	33.45	28.47	13.02	25.71	43.27	67.17
Low-technology manufacturing	35.81	31.53	38.44	34.32	31.14	18.78	29.79	22.93
Medium- to high-technology manufacturing	61.49	64.19	60.70	56.33	15.92	8.11	39.18	40.42
Business services	44.55	40.65	28.84	26.51	21.48	8.02	5.79	5.38
Personal and public services	26.08	26.00	16.41	18.44	2.67	0.57	0.04	0.02
Malaysia								
Aggregate	67.28	60.77	54.90	55.33	42.26	33.06	32.82	31.19
Primary	39.97	60.51	37.88	38.33	58.45	49.38	55.76	51.83
Low-technology manufacturing	49.72	44.96	44.29	44.42	33.05	24.64	22.80	23.10
Medium- to high-technology manufacturing	78.33	71.86	64.61	62.10	58.74	52.97	56.67	56.42
Business services	47.27	43.74	38.73	42.03	35.71	27.40	27.46	26.01
Personal and public services	27.47	23.94	29.45	27.05	1.67	1.84	3.56	3.61

continued on next page

Table 3.3.1: continued

Table 3.3.1: Global Value Chain Participation Rates

ADB Regional Member	Trade-Based (export-sector breakdown)				Production-Based (origin-sector breakdown)			
	2000	2010	2019	2020	2000	2010	2019	2020
Maldives								
Aggregate	40.50	45.37	47.45	39.52	34.50	30.23	30.91	24.64
Primary	16.49	52.82	46.05	43.78	20.99	36.38	31.43	23.54
Low-technology manufacturing	42.55	53.16	49.20	38.83	13.77	19.38	8.34	8.10
Medium- to high-technology manufacturing	29.10	50.97	46.44	39.31	7.63	16.54	49.90	22.80
Business services	41.61	45.12	47.40	39.53	46.13	39.27	40.96	35.13
Personal and public services	18.63	46.38	41.11	31.18	5.02	3.93	11.99	12.63
Mongolia								
Aggregate	44.48	44.50	40.80	38.06	25.08	28.91	34.12	37.76
Primary	41.39	45.89	38.71	35.22	31.23	47.46	54.48	66.20
Low-technology manufacturing	39.77	35.69	44.22	42.98	19.02	11.27	15.73	13.54
Medium- to high-technology manufacturing	57.38	52.00	63.02	67.54	46.74	32.45	44.24	43.74
Business services	48.24	41.33	44.78	42.94	25.93	24.03	28.92	30.22
Personal and public services	43.15	22.84	31.21	29.27	1.55	3.41	3.96	3.29
Nepal								
Aggregate	28.65	31.57	41.01	38.30	9.58	3.69	4.38	3.80
Primary	15.52	12.31	15.61	16.45	4.85	1.08	3.01	3.15
Low-technology manufacturing	26.43	30.15	38.84	36.47	8.49	2.51	5.75	5.51
Medium- to high-technology manufacturing	45.24	44.88	58.24	55.65	24.33	5.37	3.16	3.44
Business services	31.68	36.51	44.51	42.09	11.67	4.38	5.65	4.70
Personal and public services	23.60	28.37	30.17	28.25	14.75	9.14	2.02	1.51
Pakistan								
Aggregate	26.19	28.58	25.42	23.31	6.65	6.22	3.65	3.55
Primary	19.59	21.17	27.59	25.20	6.30	8.44	4.57	4.54
Low-technology manufacturing	26.72	29.46	22.68	20.81	6.19	9.95	5.13	5.08
Medium- to high-technology manufacturing	35.07	36.85	42.39	38.50	4.82	5.66	6.07	6.98
Business services	27.33	29.27	28.81	26.82	9.21	4.67	2.57	2.39
Personal and public services	12.81	12.74	23.89	22.02	2.51	2.20	2.90	2.38
People's Republic of China								
Aggregate	30.79	35.08	33.93	32.22	8.22	10.66	6.98	7.01
Primary	32.70	32.20	22.95	23.08	6.82	9.57	7.70	8.73
Low-technology manufacturing	22.68	22.24	22.57	21.47	6.74	7.59	6.78	6.92
Medium- to high-technology manufacturing	36.86	40.62	39.10	37.32	12.56	16.15	12.85	12.39
Business services	31.98	32.93	35.26	33.02	9.68	11.90	6.64	6.59
Personal and public services	27.44	22.86	35.27	33.52	2.18	2.05	1.62	1.73
Philippines								
Aggregate	43.09	42.44	47.13	45.36	14.53	14.17	11.43	10.23
Primary	21.17	31.52	27.43	26.25	7.43	10.58	7.97	7.19
Low-technology manufacturing	24.71	27.95	31.22	27.99	8.53	8.67	4.66	4.54
Medium- to high-technology manufacturing	53.88	61.28	64.82	62.80	44.43	32.94	27.89	29.83
Business services	27.54	30.00	36.85	34.58	10.37	17.53	14.81	12.71
Personal and public services	23.45	27.14	31.88	30.30	1.03	2.69	3.66	3.09
Republic of Korea								
Aggregate	45.75	51.04	50.56	48.61	14.73	17.66	20.03	19.02
Primary	15.72	27.48	32.23	29.19	6.87	9.47	12.52	11.73
Low-technology manufacturing	42.98	47.81	47.35	44.54	14.29	13.84	15.45	14.27
Medium- to high-technology manufacturing	49.20	52.81	53.20	51.09	30.86	35.71	46.25	44.90
Business services	30.12	40.03	39.68	37.46	12.17	14.65	15.25	14.58
Personal and public services	23.29	32.70	23.07	21.96	1.67	2.82	3.10	2.83

continued on next page

Table 3.3.1: continued

Table 3.3.1: Global Value Chain Participation Rates

ADB Regional Member	Trade-Based (export-sector breakdown)				Production-Based (origin-sector breakdown)			
	2000	2010	2019	2020	2000	2010	2019	2020
Singapore								
Aggregate	66.76	65.83	59.93	58.00	40.04	44.07	41.39	42.19
Primary	50.89	50.47	63.85	44.45	46.10	40.85	36.45	35.77
Low-technology manufacturing	58.65	59.49	50.47	47.58	18.61	19.60	19.93	24.07
Medium- to high-technology manufacturing	74.62	75.74	63.73	62.52	58.41	54.93	52.73	56.23
Business services	54.50	56.21	56.77	54.18	44.00	50.93	47.42	46.55
Personal and public services	30.93	41.75	28.13	27.00	6.67	4.01	3.52	3.27
Sri Lanka								
Aggregate	35.05	34.39	29.42	26.17	16.71	7.24	6.72	4.41
Primary	34.53	32.76	30.40	25.81	21.30	6.66	7.26	5.58
Low-technology manufacturing	36.23	30.86	23.84	20.59	3.57	8.02	5.69	4.30
Medium- to high-technology manufacturing	54.39	50.67	53.47	51.14	20.99	9.36	11.54	10.34
Business services	38.64	36.42	31.50	29.84	23.87	10.37	9.84	5.75
Personal and public services	27.89	26.10	22.79	20.00	12.65	0.63	0.97	0.59
Taipei,China								
Aggregate	53.04	61.46	57.46	53.81	19.99	28.43	30.33	29.69
Primary	21.79	35.45	34.39	39.72	8.55	11.97	11.53	10.29
Low-technology manufacturing	49.82	58.46	51.74	49.14	22.98	24.19	27.25	25.73
Medium- to high-technology manufacturing	58.19	65.87	60.32	56.53	44.28	59.89	66.62	64.05
Business services	35.20	43.29	44.79	40.87	15.68	20.94	19.45	19.50
Personal and public services	19.71	22.25	23.44	22.38	1.47	2.74	3.67	3.70
Thailand								
Aggregate	43.66	48.73	43.09	41.73	19.71	20.09	22.52	19.76
Primary	41.27	36.59	28.84	24.82	18.35	18.28	31.71	38.50
Low-technology manufacturing	38.08	39.94	35.70	33.44	20.06	19.23	26.57	24.57
Medium- to high-technology manufacturing	55.71	59.21	57.24	54.73	34.78	33.11	32.10	31.19
Business services	35.01	36.39	34.68	33.97	19.75	20.71	22.21	17.21
Personal and public services	27.51	25.21	26.84	26.87	3.53	4.34	4.88	2.49
Viet Nam								
Aggregate	36.65	54.49	58.83	56.70	19.56	21.75	24.79	22.48
Primary	41.22	50.62	52.39	50.00	26.83	33.56	31.81	28.89
Low-technology manufacturing	34.78	53.69	52.49	50.06	17.86	15.29	17.70	15.92
Medium- to high-technology manufacturing	45.43	66.64	70.24	68.45	20.55	33.05	50.42	45.47
Business services	32.51	44.08	44.44	43.23	21.39	20.89	25.47	23.71
Personal and public services	16.37	29.20	39.73	38.55	1.33	1.55	2.43	2.39

ADB = Asian Development Bank.
Source: Asian Development Bank Multiregional Input–Output Database, 2021.

ADB Regional Member	Gross		Value-Added			
			By Export Sectors		By Origin Sectors	
	Exports	RCA	VAX	RCA	VAX	RCA
	($ million)	(ratio)	($ million)	(ratio)	($ million)	(ratio)
Australia						
2000	26,725.77	3.55	23,782.71	3.25	22,292.23	2.67
2010	138,753.90	4.72	123,469.06	4.18	102,072.84	2.77
2019	182,596.22	5.75	164,724.32	5.05	134,882.84	3.49
2020	183,574.81	6.34	167,359.74	5.65	130,882.53	3.80
Bangladesh						
2000	121.37	0.27	116.26	0.26	722.57	1.43
2010	483.48	0.25	455.01	0.23	2,600.60	1.06
2019	382.14	0.09	344.38	0.09	3,725.71	0.78
2020	413.35	0.10	375.31	0.10	3,667.23	0.81
Bhutan						
2000	7.88	1.31	7.47	1.19	8.91	1.24
2010	72.77	1.31	68.19	1.25	72.82	1.08
2019	197.81	2.39	176.87	2.34	153.13	1.70
2020	197.59	2.60	182.80	2.54	178.50	2.14
Brunei Darussalam						
2000	2,169.39	7.63	2,118.64	6.70	2,089.91	5.80
2010	4,845.01	5.04	4,507.13	4.36	5,910.52	4.59
2019	6,821.88	9.08	5,666.79	7.95	5,379.43	6.35
2020	5,690.40	8.61	4,731.04	7.61	4,453.91	6.16
Cambodia						
2000	47.52	0.46	42.46	0.50	124.17	1.28
2010	221.32	0.51	198.95	0.54	516.01	1.13
2019	1,393.74	0.87	1,179.73	0.99	1,864.90	1.31
2020	6,022.26	3.24	4,778.98	3.75	4,654.98	3.14
Fiji						
2000	172.57	3.29	150.32	2.97	97.93	1.70
2010	85.34	0.69	61.91	0.60	100.22	0.78
2019	117.78	0.46	98.71	0.43	210.54	0.78
2020	92.06	0.78	80.81	0.75	134.83	1.07
Hong Kong, China						
2000	150.25	0.02	84.02	0.01	59.08	0.01
2010	87.98	0.01	43.26	0.00	34.46	0.00
2019	274.01	0.02	185.13	0.02	133.89	0.01
2020	261.83	0.02	191.30	0.02	129.99	0.01
India						
2000	4,856.34	0.96	4,665.71	0.92	9,109.74	1.58
2010	24,905.40	0.74	23,505.40	0.75	38,826.75	0.99
2019	19,195.93	0.37	18,028.68	0.38	49,413.42	0.87
2020	21,063.05	0.46	19,814.70	0.46	45,479.81	0.90
Indonesia						
2000	10,956.37	1.91	10,384.20	1.93	19,078.74	3.11
2010	48,635.33	2.48	44,875.04	2.33	63,703.78	2.65
2019	44,012.45	2.21	41,763.72	2.13	63,535.73	2.73
2020	42,009.11	2.41	40,171.70	2.34	59,710.39	2.99

continued on next page

Table 3.4.1: continued

Table 3.4.1: Revealed Comparative Advantage Indices—Primary Sector

ADB Regional Member	*Gross*		*Value-Added*			
	Exports	RCA	*By Export Sectors* VAX	*By Export Sectors* RCA	*By Origin Sectors* VAX	*By Origin Sectors* RCA
	($ million)	(ratio)	($ million)	(ratio)	($ million)	(ratio)
Japan						
2000	1,031.73	0.02	890.50	0.02	3,887.29	0.08
2010	2,588.34	0.03	1,711.11	0.02	6,074.02	0.06
2019	2,858.23	0.03	2,355.16	0.03	6,460.95	0.06
2020	2,713.84	0.04	2,260.21	0.03	5,770.12	0.07
Kazakhstan						
2000	2,093.67	2.82	1,674.19	2.40	1,634.39	2.06
2010	35,319.37	5.28	31,564.94	4.52	28,072.06	3.22
2019	39,735.23	6.24	33,917.27	5.29	25,830.18	3.39
2020	33,254.77	6.49	28,556.65	5.61	21,234.06	3.59
Kyrgyz Republic						
2000	110.71	2.66	102.52	2.61	169.49	3.79
2010	968.93	3.96	641.80	3.35	527.15	2.21
2019	581.71	1.93	409.72	1.56	291.99	0.94
2020	558.32	2.89	436.57	2.45	282.04	1.36
Lao People's Democratic Republic						
2000	114.70	3.10	109.27	3.04	140.69	3.43
2010	907.38	5.48	764.07	4.70	734.23	3.62
2019	2,248.19	3.34	2,026.34	3.07	2,194.22	2.80
2020	3,267.58	5.24	3,051.26	4.79	2,983.53	4.02
Malaysia						
2000	9,488.77	1.10	8,189.24	1.76	12,078.59	2.27
2010	21,085.70	0.90	18,483.82	1.16	36,412.68	1.83
2019	19,973.06	0.87	18,160.07	1.04	36,368.80	1.76
2020	18,434.66	0.93	16,808.10	1.14	29,514.76	1.71
Maldives						
2000	16.65	0.43	14.29	0.44	24.16	0.65
2010	19.57	0.10	10.75	0.07	91.11	0.47
2019	76.70	0.20	50.16	0.17	206.81	0.59
2020	81.83	0.40	59.90	0.35	171.88	0.86
Mongolia						
2000	186.64	5.17	143.93	4.85	158.76	4.69
2010	2,098.21	6.64	1,574.82	5.65	1,337.17	3.85
2019	6,424.56	7.93	4,914.55	7.00	3,679.88	4.41
2020	6,018.95	8.09	4,814.09	7.26	3,782.32	4.91
Nepal						
2000	115.86	1.44	105.79	1.38	184.33	2.11
2010	78.02	0.68	71.77	0.65	131.34	0.96
2019	31.74	0.12	28.98	0.13	305.33	1.18
2020	69.55	0.32	63.97	0.35	339.38	1.57
Pakistan						
2000	457.76	0.65	446.36	0.58	2,265.74	2.60
2010	1,533.92	0.68	1,481.48	0.62	7,218.31	2.41
2019	969.80	0.39	936.13	0.37	8,477.17	2.78
2020	1,005.84	0.42	975.85	0.40	8,689.81	3.03

continued on next page

Table 3.4.1: continued

Table 3.4.1: Revealed Comparative Advantage Indices—Primary Sector

ADB Regional Member	*Gross*		*Value-Added*			
			By Export Sectors		*By Origin Sectors*	
	Exports	RCA	VAX	RCA	VAX	RCA
	($ million)	(ratio)	($ million)	(ratio)	($ million)	(ratio)
People's Republic of China						
2000	10,027.21	0.47	9,206.17	0.45	32,363.64	1.39
2010	22,608.99	0.12	19,908.83	0.12	182,932.06	0.89
2019	25,965.70	0.10	23,724.84	0.10	230,431.48	0.80
2020	27,059.00	0.10	24,694.18	0.10	288,004.99	1.01
Philippines						
2000	680.90	0.32	631.98	0.32	1,751.05	0.77
2010	1,265.16	0.23	1,159.19	0.23	5,065.89	0.79
2019	3,381.88	0.43	3,021.41	0.45	4,776.47	0.60
2020	3,359.21	0.50	3,005.17	0.53	4,558.48	0.69
Republic of Korea						
2000	532.02	0.03	476.08	0.04	3,177.46	0.22
2010	775.91	0.01	644.49	0.02	4,710.59	0.09
2019	2,443.94	0.04	2,013.45	0.04	6,278.68	0.10
2020	2,018.74	0.03	1,704.18	0.04	6,613.99	0.12
Singapore						
2000	117.35	0.01	76.97	0.02	59.96	0.01
2010	59.94	0.00	40.38	0.00	51.85	0.00
2019	77.97	0.00	54.07	0.00	69.73	0.00
2020	70.84	0.00	50.67	0.00	69.00	0.00
Sri Lanka						
2000	1,518.80	3.98	1,289.60	3.61	1,214.27	2.98
2010	378.54	0.35	334.09	0.33	833.40	0.66
2019	887.83	0.63	787.87	0.58	1,184.76	0.73
2020	800.59	0.83	723.29	0.77	983.58	0.89
Taipei,China						
2000	1,525.12	0.11	1,238.11	0.12	1,723.69	0.15
2010	1,651.57	0.05	1,227.34	0.06	1,858.65	0.07
2019	1,190.03	0.03	948.60	0.03	2,328.91	0.07
2020	1,502.82	0.04	1,094.80	0.04	2,077.76	0.06
Thailand						
2000	1,259.04	0.27	1,025.74	0.28	3,164.86	0.75
2010	4,913.82	0.30	4,256.10	0.34	9,979.24	0.64
2019	19,271.34	0.62	16,697.37	0.65	26,496.22	0.87
2020	29,259.83	1.18	25,733.42	1.28	28,398.67	1.22
Viet Nam						
2000	3,288.22	2.34	2,528.70	2.08	2,874.93	2.08
2010	13,065.86	1.46	8,342.36	1.45	11,871.13	1.66
2019	17,481.17	0.65	10,593.48	0.69	20,750.06	1.13
2020	17,909.45	0.68	11,069.55	0.73	20,226.25	1.14

0.00 = magnitude is less than half of unit employed, $ = United States dollars, ADB = Asian Development Bank, RCA = revealed comparative advantage, VAX = value-added exports.

Source: Asian Development Bank Multiregional Input-Output Database, 2021.

Table 3.4.2: Revealed Comparative Advantage Indices—Low-Technology Manufacturing Sector

ADB Regional Member	*Gross*		*Value-Added*			
			By Export Sectors		*By Origin Sectors*	
	Exports	RCA	VAX	RCA	VAX	RCA
	($ million)	(ratio)	($ million)	(ratio)	($ million)	(ratio)
Australia						
2000	14,496.81	0.87	12,111.86	0.85	9,750.75	0.84
2010	25,502.55	0.60	22,019.44	0.59	22,217.75	0.73
2019	31,216.82	0.55	27,178.70	0.54	25,868.85	0.64
2020	29,591.88	0.54	26,041.26	0.52	24,859.21	0.63
Bangladesh						
2000	4,754.40	4.82	4,060.88	4.73	2,234.99	3.16
2010	15,825.13	5.59	13,370.76	5.40	6,491.51	3.20
2019	40,439.64	5.14	30,465.21	4.89	18,602.15	3.73
2020	37,151.07	4.66	28,742.70	4.37	17,363.57	3.37
Bhutan						
2000	35.62	2.67	33.30	2.73	33.77	3.37
2010	210.42	2.62	185.46	2.70	206.85	3.68
2019	178.58	1.22	134.33	1.14	190.90	2.03
2020	190.73	1.33	153.24	1.26	184.72	1.94
Brunei Darussalam						
2000	101.98	0.16	85.69	0.14	57.17	0.11
2010	28.32	0.02	17.29	0.01	49.23	0.05
2019	87.22	0.07	49.67	0.04	52.48	0.06
2020	73.80	0.06	43.93	0.04	57.79	0.07
Cambodia						
2000	702.61	3.08	448.19	2.72	365.19	2.70
2010	2,124.18	3.41	1,359.81	2.94	1,149.50	3.04
2019	9,845.47	3.49	5,520.82	2.98	3,779.55	2.55
2020	9,415.78	2.69	4,115.25	1.91	3,379.15	2.00
Fiji						
2000	257.41	2.22	221.42	2.26	146.38	1.82
2010	207.66	1.16	158.17	1.21	129.01	1.21
2019	848.71	1.88	664.89	1.88	462.32	1.63
2020	654.14	2.93	525.23	2.86	309.06	2.15
Hong Kong, China						
2000	11,772.32	0.75	7,514.49	0.63	6,253.03	0.64
2010	10,503.80	0.47	5,374.88	0.35	3,645.26	0.28
2019	14,611.49	0.60	7,881.98	0.43	4,249.59	0.29
2020	16,257.59	0.79	10,300.66	0.64	5,036.45	0.40
India						
2000	22,169.57	1.97	19,474.14	1.98	10,619.38	1.31
2010	50,210.11	1.03	40,690.03	1.02	24,269.49	0.75
2019	123,310.12	1.36	101,147.69	1.36	54,324.04	0.91
2020	104,822.64	1.21	87,729.37	1.20	47,684.96	0.83
Indonesia						
2000	27,080.91	2.13	21,383.75	2.05	12,372.26	1.44
2010	61,583.24	2.18	51,554.52	2.11	29,945.12	1.50
2019	74,137.69	2.11	58,494.28	1.93	37,877.97	1.56
2020	66,082.28	2.01	53,305.70	1.83	34,378.77	1.51

continued on next page

Table 3.4.2: continued

Table 3.4.2: Revealed Comparative Advantage Indices—Low-Technology Manufacturing Sector

ADB Regional Member	*Gross*		*Value-Added*			
			By Export Sectors		*By Origin Sectors*	
	Exports	RCA	VAX	RCA	VAX	RCA
	($ million)	(ratio)	($ million)	(ratio)	($ million)	(ratio)
Japan						
2000	26,161.90	0.28	23,385.04	0.28	47,154.78	0.69
2010	48,927.35	0.38	41,668.15	0.38	68,496.57	0.77
2019	62,809.14	0.41	54,040.25	0.42	73,843.13	0.71
2020	52,198.83	0.37	45,462.71	0.37	64,158.63	0.66
Kazakhstan						
2000	156.80	0.10	126.52	0.09	244.04	0.22
2010	1,221.46	0.13	1,042.43	0.12	1,547.93	0.21
2019	1,810.99	0.16	1,483.72	0.15	2,041.65	0.26
2020	1,191.67	0.12	958.54	0.11	1,501.37	0.22
Kyrgyz Republic						
2000	107.88	1.17	83.83	1.10	54.27	0.87
2010	221.19	0.63	117.29	0.48	88.86	0.45
2019	377.69	0.71	267.10	0.66	229.49	0.70
2020	308.47	0.85	240.86	0.80	180.05	0.76
Lao People's Democratic Republic						
2000	198.05	2.42	166.31	2.38	122.03	2.13
2010	420.02	1.76	369.69	1.80	302.58	1.80
2019	3,381.40	2.84	2,907.29	2.81	2,150.99	2.63
2020	2,367.79	2.02	2,078.08	1.93	1,903.71	2.25
Malaysia						
2000	15,450.36	0.81	9,563.10	1.06	6,912.77	0.93
2010	47,247.04	1.39	31,210.45	1.55	14,310.78	0.87
2019	32,992.12	0.81	23,375.85	0.87	16,023.34	0.74
2020	28,778.47	0.77	20,403.13	0.81	15,110.78	0.77
Maldives						
2000	41.24	0.48	24.92	0.40	30.95	0.60
2010	30.89	0.11	17.39	0.09	79.67	0.50
2019	288.43	0.43	160.98	0.35	136.99	0.37
2020	226.97	0.59	144.33	0.50	109.12	0.48
Mongolia						
2000	73.14	0.92	53.68	0.93	31.37	0.66
2010	125.72	0.28	96.51	0.27	116.67	0.41
2019	440.45	0.31	271.45	0.25	498.11	0.57
2020	303.11	0.22	192.39	0.17	396.36	0.45
Nepal						
2000	320.59	1.80	257.48	1.73	155.02	1.27
2010	222.11	1.35	166.76	1.20	116.99	1.03
2019	864.25	1.90	635.70	1.88	329.21	1.21
2020	746.45	1.85	566.63	1.81	296.45	1.21
Pakistan						
2000	4,126.97	2.63	3,886.11	2.62	1,475.34	1.21
2010	13,347.57	4.10	12,245.15	4.02	4,408.53	1.77
2019	17,459.00	4.00	15,719.06	3.95	5,565.15	1.75
2020	17,166.67	3.84	15,652.53	3.76	5,488.11	1.68

continued on next page

Table 3.4.2: continued

Table 3.4.2: Revealed Comparative Advantage Indices—Low-Technology Manufacturing Sector

ADB Regional Member	*Gross*		*Value-Added*			
	Exports	RCA	*By Export Sectors*		*By Origin Sectors*	
			VAX	RCA	VAX	RCA
	($ million)	(ratio)	($ million)	(ratio)	($ million)	(ratio)
People's Republic of China						
2000	89,008.78	1.87	75,841.51	1.91	55,405.36	1.70
2010	373,984.43	1.43	321,025.77	1.53	236,076.68	1.38
2019	756,002.25	1.66	663,082.18	1.77	497,976.29	1.66
2020	795,160.61	1.61	704,897.93	1.69	510,666.58	1.57
Philippines						
2000	5,470.18	1.14	4,569.30	1.19	4,256.83	1.34
2010	10,611.31	1.31	9,113.48	1.40	7,232.81	1.36
2019	7,314.44	0.52	5,832.38	0.56	7,250.76	0.87
2020	6,881.12	0.54	5,613.12	0.58	6,540.33	0.87
Republic of Korea						
2000	34,138.32	0.98	26,011.16	1.06	20,256.50	1.00
2010	36,177.69	0.45	25,680.80	0.49	29,344.92	0.69
2019	53,286.78	0.47	38,185.68	0.48	49,950.08	0.79
2020	47,350.17	0.43	34,865.67	0.44	48,244.33	0.77
Singapore						
2000	5,151.22	0.25	2,658.69	0.28	3,207.41	0.41
2010	8,485.95	0.19	4,256.02	0.20	5,924.00	0.35
2019	13,707.02	0.18	7,982.77	0.20	9,803.27	0.30
2020	12,548.95	0.18	7,514.64	0.19	9,449.63	0.30
Sri Lanka						
2000	570.61	0.68	417.44	0.61	261.14	0.46
2010	5,583.43	3.53	4,381.50	3.41	3,217.02	3.08
2019	6,719.73	2.70	5,587.29	2.63	4,371.53	2.57
2020	5,491.93	3.01	4,689.42	2.93	3,471.80	2.77
Taipei,China						
2000	23,825.38	0.77	16,001.76	0.82	14,066.63	0.88
2010	22,044.54	0.45	12,630.83	0.45	13,246.06	0.58
2019	28,104.02	0.42	18,493.17	0.44	20,148.10	0.60
2020	26,575.65	0.38	18,323.63	0.38	23,263.58	0.61
Thailand						
2000	18,211.69	1.79	13,279.33	1.84	9,518.81	1.61
2010	32,265.52	1.37	23,795.87	1.50	18,862.91	1.46
2019	82,905.77	1.50	61,981.79	1.56	39,623.64	1.25
2020	76,756.81	1.64	58,680.19	1.73	34,469.09	1.29
Viet Nam						
2000	8,972.60	2.88	6,640.38	2.82	4,969.67	2.57
2010	42,158.30	3.27	21,958.12	3.02	14,880.97	2.51
2019	127,084.77	2.66	66,818.94	2.79	45,594.52	2.38
2020	127,414.33	2.56	69,212.99	2.68	46,093.17	2.28

0.00 = magnitude is less than half of unit employed, $ = United States dollars, ADB = Asian Development Bank, RCA = revealed comparative advantage, VAX = value-added exports.

Source: Asian Development Bank Multiregional Input–Output Database, 2021.

Table 3.4.3: Revealed Comparative Advantage Indices—Medium- and High-Technology Manufacturing Sector

ADB Regional Member	*Gross*		*Value-Added*			
			By Export Sectors		*By Origin Sectors*	
	Exports	RCA	VAX	RCA	VAX	RCA
	($ million)	(ratio)	($ million)	(ratio)	($ million)	(ratio)
Australia						
2000	25,527.67	0.57	19,423.42	0.57	12,163.19	0.52
2010	53,320.57	0.41	40,345.94	0.41	21,517.14	0.33
2019	52,493.99	0.33	39,240.21	0.32	19,370.10	0.25
2020	43,230.03	0.29	33,044.16	0.28	17,485.68	0.24
Bangladesh						
2000	117.09	0.04	103.32	0.05	162.97	0.12
2010	428.51	0.05	368.54	0.06	572.94	0.13
2019	738.17	0.03	624.88	0.04	1,387.11	0.15
2020	703.62	0.03	597.13	0.04	1,415.75	0.15
Bhutan						
2000	8.00	0.22	7.10	0.24	4.04	0.20
2010	103.79	0.42	81.78	0.45	35.69	0.30
2019	274.91	0.67	211.06	0.73	114.97	0.65
2020	212.42	0.55	170.63	0.59	78.67	0.45
Brunei Darussalam						
2000	750.34	0.45	729.58	0.49	728.51	0.73
2010	3,482.84	0.82	3,278.03	0.95	1,700.14	0.75
2019	350.51	0.09	277.53	0.10	499.27	0.30
2020	768.48	0.23	644.61	0.26	720.21	0.48
Cambodia						
2000	8.69	0.01	5.50	0.01	8.70	0.03
2010	26.33	0.01	16.80	0.01	28.98	0.04
2019	794.35	0.10	502.53	0.11	428.14	0.15
2020	741.94	0.08	479.11	0.09	404.87	0.13
Fiji						
2000	87.50	0.28	59.15	0.25	28.05	0.17
2010	24.77	0.05	15.46	0.05	20.53	0.09
2019	105.44	0.08	73.07	0.08	70.04	0.13
2020	67.07	0.11	48.38	0.11	44.16	0.17
Hong Kong, China						
2000	6,011.08	0.14	2,501.37	0.09	942.91	0.05
2010	11,308.48	0.17	2,368.63	0.06	536.56	0.02
2019	22,325.98	0.33	11,503.35	0.26	554.95	0.02
2020	20,515.07	0.37	11,661.58	0.31	546.91	0.02
India						
2000	13,684.72	0.46	10,593.81	0.45	7,952.09	0.49
2010	100,793.88	0.68	65,336.73	0.62	41,795.94	0.61
2019	180,559.84	0.71	122,907.61	0.68	88,014.73	0.78
2020	156,833.81	0.67	111,017.61	0.64	79,522.41	0.76
Indonesia						
2000	26,542.40	0.78	20,496.10	0.82	12,536.25	0.73
2010	58,384.31	0.68	45,240.57	0.71	29,524.95	0.70
2019	59,593.31	0.60	47,727.12	0.64	30,396.53	0.66
2020	59,373.62	0.67	48,926.97	0.71	29,391.31	0.71

continued on next page

Table 3.4.3: continued

Table 3.4.3: Revealed Comparative Advantage Indices—Medium- and High-Technology Manufacturing Sector

ADB Regional Member	*Gross*		*Value-Added*			
			By Export Sectors		*By Origin Sectors*	
	Exports	RCA	VAX	RCA	VAX	RCA
	($ million)	(ratio)	($ million)	(ratio)	($ million)	(ratio)
Japan						
2000	386,892.57	1.55	340,807.42	1.69	221,543.92	1.62
2010	591,965.90	1.51	477,483.51	1.66	313,702.15	1.66
2019	635,385.75	1.49	507,558.51	1.60	343,261.10	1.75
2020	557,361.07	1.46	457,081.30	1.56	305,760.13	1.72
Kazakhstan						
2000	5,818.86	1.33	4,780.92	1.47	3,971.48	1.79
2010	12,532.59	0.43	11,180.24	0.48	7,960.73	0.52
2019	16,951.68	0.54	14,960.43	0.61	10,850.53	0.72
2020	13,842.83	0.53	12,215.25	0.60	8,989.69	0.73
Kyrgyz Republic						
2000	260.91	1.06	206.67	1.13	121.17	0.97
2010	791.22	0.74	562.96	0.88	550.72	1.31
2019	1,012.96	0.68	808.98	0.81	804.02	1.31
2020	701.03	0.71	589.07	0.82	583.02	1.35
Lao People's Democratic Republic						
2000	5.00	0.02	3.20	0.02	7.35	0.06
2010	15.09	0.02	6.93	0.01	17.36	0.05
2019	356.51	0.11	226.48	0.09	217.09	0.14
2020	372.60	0.12	257.52	0.10	230.68	0.15
Malaysia						
2000	69,125.49	1.36	23,976.75	1.10	16,699.51	1.13
2010	119,327.97	1.15	53,350.69	1.01	35,498.82	1.02
2019	143,078.44	1.26	78,899.57	1.19	41,365.35	1.02
2020	138,134.95	1.37	78,951.73	1.33	38,892.57	1.08
Maldives						
2000	0.11	0.00	0.09	0.00	0.10	0.00
2010	0.78	0.00	0.48	0.00	3.39	0.01
2019	21.22	0.01	13.67	0.01	12.56	0.02
2020	16.70	0.02	11.30	0.02	9.57	0.02
Mongolia						
2000	29.52	0.14	15.77	0.11	10.72	0.11
2010	57.57	0.04	37.62	0.04	45.19	0.07
2019	349.11	0.09	224.52	0.08	252.38	0.15
2020	374.62	0.10	252.47	0.09	257.16	0.16
Nepal						
2000	122.74	0.26	78.29	0.22	56.54	0.23
2010	83.42	0.17	50.31	0.14	40.51	0.17
2019	110.29	0.09	51.94	0.06	52.75	0.10
2020	96.73	0.09	48.73	0.07	51.07	0.11
Pakistan						
2000	416.24	0.10	351.95	0.10	381.24	0.16
2010	1,352.34	0.14	1,059.36	0.13	920.66	0.17
2019	2,367.85	0.19	1,704.98	0.18	1,462.54	0.24
2020	2,364.37	0.20	1,824.84	0.18	1,485.35	0.25

continued on next page

Table 3.4.3: continued

Table 3.4.3: Revealed Comparative Advantage Indices—Medium- and High-Technology Manufacturing Sector

ADB Regional Member	*Gross*		*Value-Added*			
			By Export Sectors		*By Origin Sectors*	
	Exports	RCA	VAX	RCA	VAX	RCA
	($ million)	(ratio)	($ million)	(ratio)	($ million)	(ratio)
People's Republic of China						
2000	111,726.30	0.88	87,248.26	0.91	61,969.84	0.95
2010	1,012,324.70	1.27	739,119.52	1.34	468,584.55	1.29
2019	1,658,576.35	1.30	1,258,527.89	1.37	633,670.18	1.12
2020	1,685,022.75	1.26	1,295,618.77	1.31	618,825.59	1.04
Philippines						
2000	16,346.53	1.28	12,529.50	1.35	9,713.08	1.54
2010	21,597.88	0.87	13,567.24	0.79	8,108.81	0.72
2019	33,222.98	0.85	17,203.51	0.67	11,253.21	0.71
2020	29,610.16	0.87	15,921.42	0.70	9,911.98	0.72
Republic of Korea						
2000	134,640.73	1.45	88,943.42	1.50	67,652.55	1.68
2010	427,862.23	1.75	262,523.37	1.91	190,845.39	2.11
2019	516,721.85	1.64	343,452.69	1.78	243,748.34	2.04
2020	480,794.35	1.64	331,070.76	1.75	229,074.25	2.00
Singapore						
2000	68,194.56	1.25	24,660.43	1.08	18,820.50	1.22
2010	139,236.37	1.04	47,834.82	0.87	38,073.96	1.05
2019	225,308.17	1.04	107,066.03	1.07	62,587.47	1.01
2020	196,386.36	1.02	98,202.51	1.03	59,435.53	1.03
Sri Lanka						
2000	40.62	0.02	23.08	0.01	23.07	0.02
2010	898.89	0.19	529.18	0.16	550.02	0.25
2019	1,051.63	0.15	612.99	0.12	757.38	0.24
2020	818.46	0.17	506.30	0.13	567.75	0.25
Taipei,China						
2000	119,181.53	1.44	66,154.66	1.41	52,477.02	1.65
2010	240,938.23	1.62	123,613.98	1.68	102,999.65	2.13
2019	310,111.41	1.67	184,569.14	1.79	142,086.95	2.24
2020	313,680.94	1.64	200,013.12	1.75	151,272.60	2.18
Thailand						
2000	20,839.73	0.77	12,589.18	0.73	9,028.36	0.77
2010	79,185.74	1.11	43,859.76	1.05	27,957.42	1.02
2019	123,830.13	0.80	68,825.75	0.71	45,790.99	0.77
2020	112,133.00	0.89	64,616.22	0.80	41,361.21	0.85
Viet Nam						
2000	2,188.72	0.26	1,538.72	0.27	1,812.90	0.47
2010	17,018.58	0.43	7,980.42	0.42	7,182.36	0.57
2019	111,142.03	0.83	43,378.81	0.74	30,905.20	0.85
2020	107,555.70	0.80	43,121.88	0.70	31,025.65	0.84

0.00 = magnitude is less than half of unit employed, $ = United States dollars, ADB = Asian Development Bank, RCA = revealed comparative advantage, VAX = value-added exports.

Source: Asian Development Bank Multiregional Input-Output Database, 2021.

Table 3.4.4: Revealed Comparative Advantage Indices—Business Services Sector

ADB Regional Member	Gross		Value-Added			
			By Export Sectors		By Origin Sectors	
	Exports	RCA	VAX	RCA	VAX	RCA
	($ million)	(ratio)	($ million)	(ratio)	($ million)	(ratio)
Australia						
2000	21,285.45	1.00	18,808.49	0.94	28,990.34	0.92
2010	50,135.67	0.73	45,190.49	0.68	81,047.00	0.84
2019	53,969.08	0.71	49,117.29	0.67	98,962.53	0.81
2020	38,287.97	0.60	35,389.79	0.57	87,147.65	0.78
Bangladesh						
2000	376.20	0.30	362.64	0.30	1,273.29	0.67
2010	1,427.57	0.31	1,350.34	0.31	4,109.44	0.64
2019	4,406.37	0.41	4,063.29	0.45	10,381.09	0.69
2020	5,613.71	0.60	5,211.25	0.64	11,043.16	0.75
Bhutan						
2000	17.78	1.05	15.32	0.89	17.15	0.63
2010	123.96	0.95	92.91	0.76	111.74	0.63
2019	203.59	1.02	144.19	0.84	206.72	0.73
2020	184.39	1.09	138.19	0.91	200.75	0.74
Brunei Darussalam						
2000	442.57	0.55	413.99	0.48	471.86	0.35
2010	612.82	0.27	477.62	0.20	590.42	0.17
2019	502.01	0.28	297.33	0.18	355.91	0.13
2020	323.02	0.22	186.13	0.14	348.31	0.15
Cambodia						
2000	429.90	1.48	348.18	1.49	358.36	0.98
2010	1,597.60	1.58	1,306.95	1.58	1,176.05	0.98
2019	4,486.93	1.17	3,375.39	1.25	4,401.07	0.99
2020	3,133.54	0.76	2,135.29	0.79	3,033.63	0.63
Fiji						
2000	119.47	0.81	103.49	0.74	231.97	1.06
2010	824.07	2.85	579.20	2.48	558.28	1.65
2019	1,168.90	1.91	830.10	1.61	959.86	1.13
2020	329.68	1.26	245.34	1.07	402.45	0.98
Hong Kong, China						
2000	68,177.65	3.41	54,630.58	3.24	54,854.90	2.08
2010	120,938.90	3.38	90,648.77	3.26	93,083.50	2.27
2019	104,499.94	3.17	84,099.94	3.16	95,530.60	2.18
2020	76,205.59	3.14	62,929.35	3.15	76,987.86	2.16
India						
2000	18,750.86	1.31	16,702.97	1.20	23,086.61	1.06
2010	128,576.97	1.63	113,471.83	1.59	134,359.57	1.30
2019	193,972.89	1.57	167,705.66	1.55	213,065.85	1.19
2020	181,358.66	1.78	159,426.74	1.75	200,933.33	1.23
Indonesia						
2000	4,957.81	0.31	4,231.94	0.29	12,464.98	0.54
2010	12,909.05	0.28	11,437.62	0.26	29,108.94	0.46
2019	23,554.62	0.49	20,783.75	0.47	37,532.67	0.51
2020	11,586.88	0.30	10,391.38	0.29	29,120.88	0.45

continued on next page

Table 3.4.4: continued

Table 3.4.4: Revealed Comparative Advantage Indices—Business Services Sector

ADB Regional Member	*Gross*		*Value-Added*			
			By Export Sectors		*By Origin Sectors*	
	Exports	RCA	VAX	RCA	VAX	RCA
	($ million)	(ratio)	($ million)	(ratio)	($ million)	(ratio)
Japan						
2000	99,395.41	0.84	90,393.05	0.76	173,693.80	0.94
2010	188,197.35	0.90	169,702.93	0.87	288,896.38	1.02
2019	177,441.39	0.86	164,145.62	0.86	290,641.83	0.93
2020	155,308.87	0.93	144,621.99	0.94	262,513.63	0.95
Kazakhstan						
2000	980.87	0.47	815.21	0.43	1,550.58	0.52
2010	13,190.45	0.84	12,062.00	0.76	18,399.88	0.80
2019	7,597.41	0.50	6,382.92	0.44	17,929.86	0.75
2020	5,029.97	0.44	4,268.80	0.40	14,200.37	0.74
Kyrgyz Republic						
2000	22.91	0.19	18.10	0.17	67.45	0.40
2010	239.78	0.42	164.10	0.38	328.06	0.52
2019	956.73	1.32	678.56	1.14	860.11	0.88
2020	362.94	0.85	280.68	0.75	494.99	0.73
Lao People's Democratic Republic						
2000	117.17	1.12	88.85	0.90	99.82	0.64
2010	192.38	0.61	155.27	0.42	244.46	0.46
2019	993.45	0.99	745.21	0.49	1,276.40	0.52
2020	480.33	0.35	381.33	0.28	649.90	0.27
Malaysia						
2000	10,818.36	0.44	7,423.89	0.58	13,446.26	0.67
2010	31,179.87	0.57	24,363.91	0.68	40,748.04	0.78
2019	39,762.62	0.72	32,057.84	0.81	57,800.42	0.89
2020	20,610.07	0.47	16,889.29	0.54	48,037.75	0.86
Maldives						
2000	408.42	3.74	299.43	3.36	282.47	2.02
2010	1,707.77	3.82	1,187.02	3.41	1,035.21	2.05
2019	3,472.73	3.86	2,377.37	3.54	2,114.65	1.91
2020	1,762.91	3.92	1,321.18	3.64	1,096.92	1.69
Mongolia						
2000	145.76	1.43	98.02	1.20	111.32	0.87
2010	667.77	0.91	525.31	0.83	706.16	0.77
2019	1,156.98	0.59	785.93	0.49	1,707.71	0.65
2020	1,009.92	0.61	709.97	0.51	1,487.23	0.59
Nepal						
2000	289.89	1.28	249.90	1.19	325.89	0.99
2010	354.90	1.33	294.21	1.19	366.41	1.02
2019	1,309.53	2.12	938.33	1.90	1,070.09	1.31
2020	1,046.26	2.20	772.45	1.98	837.29	1.20
Pakistan						
2000	3,163.92	1.58	2,974.51	1.41	3,505.08	1.06
2010	3,963.22	0.75	3,705.26	0.68	5,982.96	0.76
2019	2,618.76	0.44	2,408.26	0.41	5,584.80	0.58
2020	2,184.67	0.42	2,036.93	0.39	5,135.98	0.55

continued on next page

Table 3.4.4: continued

Table 3.4.4: Revealed Comparative Advantage Indices—Business Services Sector

ADB Regional Member	*Gross*		*Value-Added*			
			By Export Sectors		*By Origin Sectors*	
	Exports	RCA	VAX	RCA	VAX	RCA
	($ million)	(ratio)	($ million)	(ratio)	($ million)	(ratio)
People's Republic of China						
2000	43,309.46	0.72	38,454.10	0.68	62,355.23	0.71
2010	276,698.17	0.65	241,959.15	0.65	419,270.99	0.77
2019	208,236.42	0.34	182,631.75	0.33	701,193.25	0.78
2020	207,926.89	0.36	184,015.19	0.36	720,456.54	0.78
Philippines						
2000	3,802.32	0.62	3,281.15	0.60	5,210.67	0.61
2010	18,372.71	1.40	16,929.62	1.45	20,181.00	1.20
2019	35,847.81	1.89	31,604.89	2.07	34,351.57	1.36
2020	28,102.82	1.89	25,261.56	2.10	28,788.21	1.34
Republic of Korea						
2000	21,951.07	0.50	19,041.80	0.55	41,142.65	0.75
2010	50,284.70	0.39	40,075.75	0.43	96,904.56	0.72
2019	72,438.39	0.48	56,804.17	0.49	136,291.55	0.72
2020	60,673.94	0.47	49,274.68	0.50	128,401.45	0.72
Singapore						
2000	39,108.58	1.50	24,049.64	1.80	28,474.43	1.36
2010	135,393.07	1.91	79,715.69	2.14	87,353.49	1.62
2019	211,675.54	2.02	116,957.42	1.96	158,420.67	1.61
2020	184,786.09	2.19	107,242.22	2.15	143,242.52	1.60
Sri Lanka						
2000	1,856.14	1.72	1,501.95	1.53	1,642.92	1.07
2010	3,182.17	1.24	2,724.77	1.19	3,393.87	1.03
2019	5,846.80	1.73	5,055.48	1.63	5,471.97	1.07
2020	2,925.22	1.36	2,609.24	1.31	3,304.10	0.93
Taipei,China						
2000	25,911.94	0.66	22,242.32	0.81	36,370.17	0.84
2010	49,626.00	0.63	38,689.72	0.78	55,443.05	0.77
2019	45,884.61	0.51	33,682.34	0.55	70,273.37	0.69
2020	46,063.73	0.55	35,663.58	0.59	75,388.77	0.70
Thailand						
2000	14,187.30	1.10	11,375.75	1.12	16,520.15	1.03
2010	31,849.89	0.84	25,533.65	0.90	40,648.61	0.99
2019	92,140.75	1.23	74,056.53	1.28	108,093.68	1.13
2020	37,558.58	0.68	30,580.31	0.72	74,031.78	0.98
Viet Nam						
2000	2,315.33	0.58	1,866.70	0.56	2,939.73	0.56
2010	10,830.04	0.52	7,564.69	0.58	11,819.22	0.63
2019	23,061.48	0.36	15,540.36	0.44	38,526.25	0.67
2020	20,638.59	0.35	13,894.55	0.43	39,400.00	0.68

0.00 = magnitude is less than half of unit employed, $ = United States dollars, ADB = Asian Development Bank, RCA = revealed comparative advantage, VAX = value-added exports.

Source: Asian Development Bank Multiregional Input-Output Database, 2021.

Table 3.4.5: Revealed Comparative Advantage Indices—Personal and Public Services Sector

ADB Regional Member	*Gross*		*Value-Added*			
			By Export Sectors		*By Origin Sectors*	
	Exports	RCA	VAX	RCA	VAX	RCA
	($ million)	(ratio)	($ million)	(ratio)	($ million)	(ratio)
Australia						
2000	3,936.58	1.96	3,584.89	1.85	4,514.84	1.52
2010	7,155.56	1.36	6,675.31	1.22	10,845.51	1.24
2019	9,668.15	1.21	8,710.38	1.05	9,886.58	0.83
2020	6,911.94	1.04	6,337.10	0.91	7,796.97	0.73
Bangladesh						
2000	66.73	0.56	65.01	0.55	314.29	1.74
2010	184.17	0.52	175.01	0.48	2,011.01	3.47
2019	164.49	0.15	152.13	0.15	1,553.83	1.06
2020	208.74	0.21	194.42	0.21	1,631.10	1.17
Bhutan						
2000	4.24	2.64	3.66	2.20	2.98	1.16
2010	9.81	0.98	8.48	0.84	9.71	0.61
2019	5.69	0.27	5.08	0.26	5.83	0.21
2020	6.04	0.35	5.50	0.32	7.72	0.30
Brunei Darussalam						
2000	11.22	0.15	10.29	0.12	10.74	0.08
2010	30.90	0.18	25.35	0.13	55.12	0.18
2019	43.26	0.23	33.31	0.18	37.55	0.14
2020	30.36	0.20	23.30	0.16	48.79	0.22
Cambodia						
2000	69.08	2.52	57.40	2.56	45.31	1.31
2010	71.12	0.92	57.02	0.84	68.98	0.64
2019	28.77	0.07	22.67	0.07	127.48	0.29
2020	26.75	0.06	19.37	0.06	55.36	0.12
Fiji						
2000	3.02	0.22	2.82	0.21	32.87	1.60
2010	17.93	0.81	15.35	0.80	22.06	0.72
2019	404.61	6.31	353.33	6.09	317.33	3.83
2020	90.17	3.31	80.36	3.15	89.63	2.31
Hong Kong, China						
2000	466.59	0.25	399.72	0.25	3,020.26	1.21
2010	594.50	0.22	511.16	0.22	3,614.63	0.98
2019	616.31	0.18	553.19	0.18	3,754.55	0.88
2020	588.90	0.23	541.92	0.24	2,923.61	0.86
India						
2000	2,609.53	1.93	2,427.05	1.81	3,095.85	1.50
2010	10,841.53	1.79	10,191.74	1.75	13,943.98	1.50
2019	15,558.31	1.21	14,824.19	1.21	19,795.78	1.14
2020	13,726.16	1.30	13,139.26	1.29	17,507.16	1.13
Indonesia						
2000	701.94	0.46	612.49	0.43	656.25	0.30
2010	2,009.07	0.57	1,813.15	0.51	2,638.12	0.46
2019	5,132.90	1.03	4,754.93	0.95	4,180.91	0.59
2020	2,661.86	0.66	2,495.24	0.62	2,689.65	0.44

continued on next page

Table 3.4.5: continued

Table 3.4.5: Revealed Comparative Advantage Indices—Personal and Public Services Sector						
ADB Regional Member	*Gross*		*Value-Added*			
			By Export Sectors		*By Origin Sectors*	
	Exports	RCA	VAX	RCA	VAX	RCA
	($ million)	(ratio)	($ million)	(ratio)	($ million)	(ratio)
Japan						
2000	1,959.98	0.17	1,877.49	0.16	11,073.71	0.63
2010	3,677.31	0.23	3,466.75	0.22	16,863.33	0.66
2019	15,587.68	0.72	14,662.95	0.69	28,555.49	0.94
2020	13,471.26	0.78	12,743.85	0.74	23,967.54	0.91
Kazakhstan						
2000	14.59	0.07	11.68	0.06	8.03	0.03
2010	359.83	0.30	317.07	0.25	186.08	0.09
2019	102.38	0.06	88.28	0.05	180.41	0.08
2020	71.51	0.06	62.08	0.05	135.84	0.07
Kyrgyz Republic						
2000	6.96	0.63	5.62	0.54	4.36	0.27
2010	67.89	1.55	52.66	1.49	44.03	0.78
2019	196.54	2.60	161.95	2.42	140.69	1.47
2020	78.80	1.77	68.36	1.62	75.46	1.18
Lao People's Democratic Republic						
2000	17.03	1.73	14.62	1.54	12.38	0.85
2010	13.25	0.45	11.38	0.38	8.71	0.18
2019	5.63	0.03	5.04	0.03	5.86	0.02
2020	1.02	0.01	0.92	0.01	1.29	0.01
Malaysia						
2000	429.18	0.19	329.67	0.27	345.51	0.18
2010	1,077.55	0.26	841.16	0.29	1,279.71	0.27
2019	2,184.82	0.38	1,779.24	0.40	2,714.65	0.43
2020	1,168.27	0.26	974.80	0.28	2,471.19	0.47
Maldives						
2000	6.30	0.61	5.43	0.63	6.47	0.49
2010	31.09	0.91	22.84	0.80	29.11	0.64
2019	35.33	0.37	28.19	0.37	159.35	1.48
2020	24.38	0.52	21.28	0.52	170.49	2.76
Mongolia						
2000	5.64	0.59	3.90	0.50	3.12	0.26
2010	5.69	0.10	4.82	0.09	33.91	0.41
2019	41.48	0.20	32.54	0.18	90.92	0.36
2020	39.12	0.23	31.32	0.20	77.17	0.32
Nepal						
2000	134.57	6.28	123.63	6.09	93.31	2.99
2010	328.11	16.04	297.80	14.69	225.59	6.98
2019	350.22	5.42	281.61	5.06	179.19	2.26
2020	274.86	5.57	225.94	5.17	153.52	2.31
Pakistan						
2000	481.77	2.56	472.21	2.33	503.74	1.62
2010	901.72	2.23	860.10	1.93	820.90	1.16
2019	2,194.56	3.54	1,964.22	3.01	1,642.99	1.76
2020	1,972.90	3.62	1,791.49	3.09	1,482.39	1.68

continued on next page

Table 3.4.5: continued

Table 3.4.5: Revealed Comparative Advantage Indices—Personal and Public Services Sector

ADB Regional Member	*Gross*		*Value-Added*			
			By Export Sectors		*By Origin Sectors*	
	Exports	RCA	VAX	RCA	VAX	RCA
	($ million)	(ratio)	($ million)	(ratio)	($ million)	(ratio)
People's Republic of China						
2000	7,945.89	1.39	6,926.55	1.28	5,582.52	0.67
2010	12,135.87	0.37	10,730.08	0.35	25,879.07	0.53
2019	15,322.12	0.24	13,484.30	0.22	78,179.74	0.89
2020	17,157.06	0.28	15,260.81	0.26	86,533.18	0.98
Philippines						
2000	95.37	0.17	84.81	0.16	165.11	0.20
2010	695.20	0.69	631.27	0.66	812.29	0.53
2019	2,390.59	1.20	2,116.61	1.23	2,146.78	0.88
2020	1,959.43	1.27	1,750.49	1.30	1,752.75	0.86
Republic of Korea						
2000	450.37	0.11	405.30	0.12	2,648.62	0.51
2010	3,801.91	0.38	3,216.42	0.42	10,335.36	0.85
2019	12,933.32	0.81	11,204.09	0.86	15,391.44	0.83
2020	10,777.32	0.81	9,467.81	0.85	14,049.08	0.83
Singapore						
2000	378.55	0.15	290.94	0.23	1,174.38	0.59
2010	1,002.85	0.18	801.93	0.26	1,245.55	0.26
2019	1,838.44	0.17	1,470.24	0.22	2,649.41	0.28
2020	1,603.17	0.18	1,313.80	0.24	2,127.16	0.25
Sri Lanka						
2000	675.26	6.65	543.35	5.78	655.94	4.51
2010	202.41	1.03	183.09	0.98	134.36	0.45
2019	114.01	0.32	102.38	0.29	360.37	0.72
2020	32.77	0.15	29.99	0.13	231.01	0.68
Taipei,China						
2000	807.26	0.22	703.00	0.27	1,702.33	0.42
2010	1,313.56	0.22	1,106.15	0.27	3,720.60	0.57
2019	3,441.27	0.37	2,956.11	0.43	5,812.03	0.59
2020	3,530.27	0.41	3,120.51	0.46	6,212.92	0.61
Thailand						
2000	1,464.14	1.20	1,171.61	1.19	1,209.43	0.80
2010	4,016.49	1.38	3,387.04	1.46	3,384.24	0.91
2019	5,620.91	0.72	4,887.96	0.75	6,444.87	0.69
2020	2,364.99	0.41	2,080.86	0.44	3,430.24	0.48
Viet Nam						
2000	390.19	1.04	331.71	1.03	308.98	0.63
2010	400.82	0.25	301.41	0.28	393.33	0.23
2019	950.78	0.14	731.20	0.19	1,286.76	0.23
2020	1,052.66	0.17	821.24	0.23	1,375.13	0.25

0.00 = magnitude is less than half of unit employed, $ = United States dollars, ADB = Asian Development Bank, RCA = revealed comparative advantage, VAX = value-added exports.

Source: Asian Development Bank Multiregional Input–Output Database, 2021.

PART IV

Stories Behind the Data: Initiatives of National Statistical Systems to Provide Actionable Insights Through Timely Data

Overview

The provision of timely and reliable data is crucial in making informed policy decisions. Development planners turn to data as they design programs and policies to help improve the lives of the poor and promote inclusive and sustainable growth. By showing which policies and programs work, as well as highlighting those that do not, knowledge gained from data also helps improve service delivery. Thus, the importance of data in both formulating plans and tracking progress towards the 2030 Agenda for Sustainable Development cannot be overstated.

The 2019 High Level Political Forum on Sustainable Development highlighted the challenges in generating the data and statistics needed for tracking progress towards the Sustainable Development Goals (SDGs) and associated targets (ECOSOC 2019). For example, the United Nations Economic and Social Commission for Asia and the Pacific (UNESCAP) has reported that, for 2020, only about 49% of the indicators have sufficient data for tracking progress (UNESCAP 2021). This raises an important question: How can the SDGs be achieved when high-quality data are lacking in guiding policy decisions?

In addition to accuracy, reliability, and granularity, the Fundamental Principles of Official Statistics cites timeliness as an important attribute of data (UNSD 2014). Uneven progress in SDG and other development targets underscores the need for timely data to make real-time decisions on critical policies and programs to achieve global and regional development goals by 2030. Thus, there is an urgent need to advance efforts to provide high-quality and timely data for policymaking.

The COVID-19 pandemic has brought into sharp focus the importance of high-quality and timely data in daily life. Infection rates, the number of deaths, and vaccination rates now influence the decisions of governments to constrain or allow freedom of movement and economic activity. In a dynamic environment where scenarios change rapidly, appropriate data are also crucial to promptly assess the impacts of restrictions on peoples' lives and livelihoods, and to develop suitable responses to the health crisis.

Ironically, however, lockdowns and other pandemic restrictions have seriously impeded the traditional methods of data collection used by national statistical systems (NSSs), hindering statistical capacity worldwide and curbing the ability to produce high-quality data and statistics in a timely manner. This has spurred NSSs to embrace and accelerate alternative data collection strategies such as the use of digital technology, which provides new options for faster collection, processing, and dissemination of data.

In line with this trend, the Economic Research and Regional Cooperation Department's Statistics and Data Innovation Unit (EROD-SDI) of the Asian Development Bank (ADB) conducted a survey on initiatives that national statistics offices (NSOs) have undertaken over the years to provide more timely data. This request for information generated detailed responses from 28 of the bank's regional member economies[1]. The survey shows that, even before the COVID-19 pandemic, NSOs had already begun using new tools, such as big data and innovative data capture, to access more timely information. The EROD-SDI was then able to assess whether existing NSO initiatives were accelerated because of the pandemic, and to identify further efforts to promote agile and resilient statistics systems amid a period of uncertainty.

Why Do We Need Timely Data?

Timely data are important both in designing policies aligned with specific objectives and goals, and in monitoring and evaluating those policies for appropriate calibration when needed. This was clearly illustrated when the COVID-19 pandemic struck, as governments needed timely data to react quickly to evolving scenarios and to strike a balance between reducing the spread of the virus and minimizing the impacts on the economy and human well-being.

In developing economies, national data and statistics systems often work with limited capacity and resources, affecting their ability to provide timely data in rapidly evolving situations. To address these data gaps, NSSs used forecasts and simulations to assess the socioeconomic impacts of the COVID-19 pandemic, and these data proved essential in developing preliminary intervention programs and plans for recovery. However, later comparisons between the initial forecasts and latest statistics released by NSSs and other relevant government ministries revealed that, in some instances, there were significant differences between the two. It is therefore important to continuously fine-tune methods of data compilation, estimation, and forecasting in order to ensure that the timely release of accurate data and statistics is not compromised, ensuring actionable insights for policymaking.

1 The EROD-SDI survey garnered responses from the following economies: Afghanistan; Armenia; Azerbaijan; Bhutan; Brunei Darussalam; the Cook Islands; the Federated States of Micronesia; Fiji; Georgia; Hong Kong, China; Indonesia; Kazakhstan; Malaysia; Mongolia; Nepal; Pakistan; the Philippines; the People's Republic of China; the Marshall Islands; the Republic of Korea; Singapore; Solomon Islands; Sri Lanka; Taipei,China; Thailand; Uzbekistan; Vanuatu; and Viet Nam.

Background on Data Collection Capacity in Asia and the Pacific

Box 4.1 summarizes the datasets commonly compiled by NSSs, while Figure 4.1 shows how frequently these data are collected in the economies surveyed by the EROD-SDI. In general, collecting comprehensive data requires significant resources. One estimate suggests that the cost of conducting a household income and expenditure survey, for instance, is approximately $1.7 million (UNSDSN 2015). For many developing economies of Asia and the Pacific, these high costs create a barrier to conducting comprehensive data collection as frequently as needed.

Figure 4.1: Frequency of Surveys and Censuses in Developing Economies

A significant proportion of developing economies in Asia and the Pacific conducted surveys and censuses too infrequently or not at all.

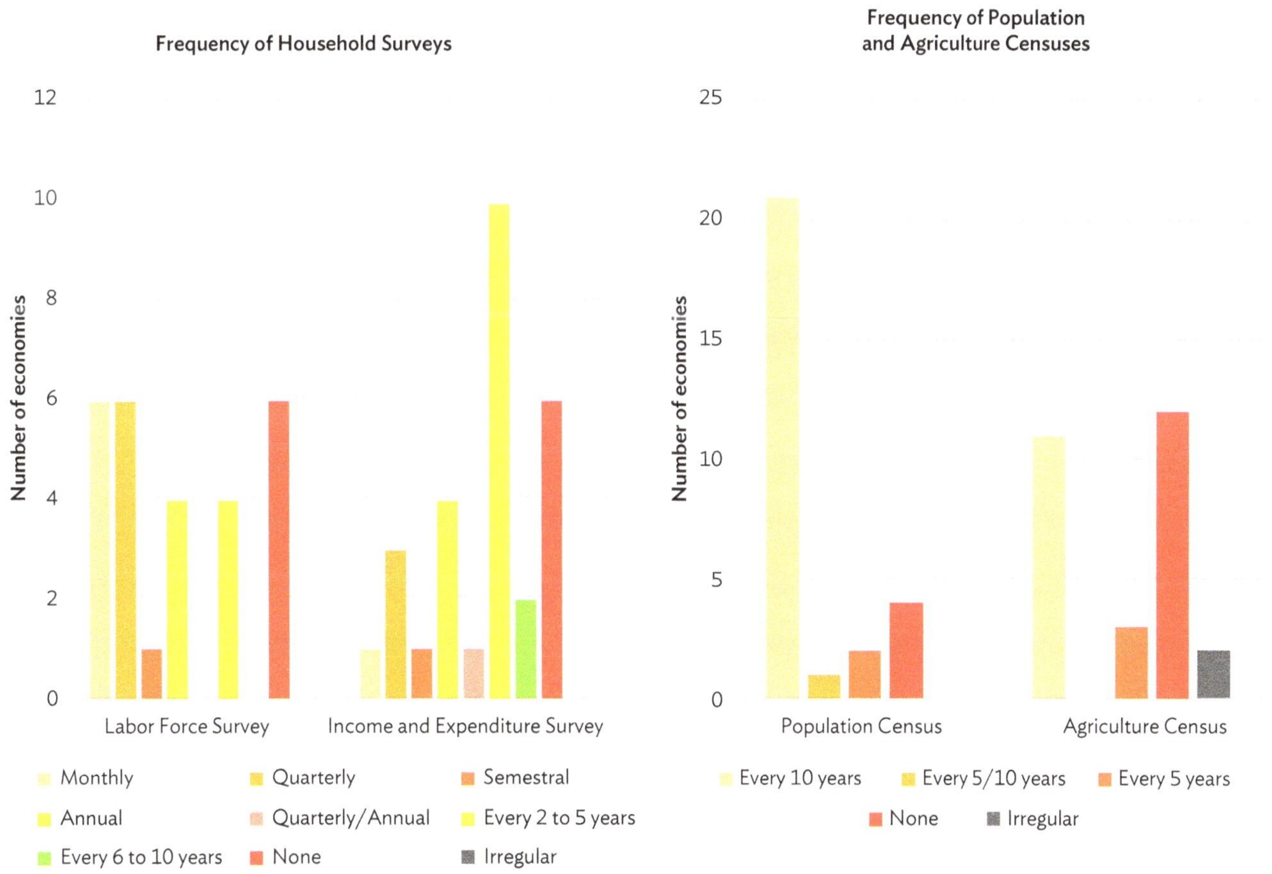

Note: The analysis uses results from 28 regional member economies of the Asian Development Bank.
Source: Asian Development Bank estimates using data from the Survey on National Statistics Offices' Initiatives to Enhance Timeliness of Data and Statistics.

Box 4.1: Conventional Data Collection Initiatives by National Statistical Systems

Censuses, surveys, and administrative data are three sources of data conventionally used by national statistical systems (NSSs) to provide socioeconomic data. Sample surveys, such as those conducted on households and enterprises, constitute a major data source for Sustainable Development Goal (SDG) targets and other development indicators (DHS Program 2017). Examples of household surveys include household income and expenditure surveys, demographic and health surveys, and labor force surveys.

Each data source has its advantages and limitations. Since a census gathers information from a complete set of all units of a target population, it is accurately representative and can be used for more granular disaggregation. However, while a census serves as a fundamental source of baseline information on the structure and key characteristics of the population over time, collecting data from a larger population is resource-intensive and involves lengthy analysis and a longer time frame for publication. Meanwhile, a sample survey collects information from a subset of a target population and often relies on census data in setting sample weight. Hence, compared to a census, it generally takes less time and expense to conduct a sample survey and publish the data. Surveys also collect more detailed information than do censuses.

Sample surveys are, by definition, subject to sampling errors. Response rates greatly affect the survey results and the quality of responses. Interviewees may have difficulty recalling correct answers, or may not be totally honest, and this affects the quality of their responses. Periodic reviews of a survey's sampling design are also needed so that samples and weights correctly represent the population. As with censuses, comparability over time is also a challenge, given how estimates of key variables may require similar designs and methods that are highly unlikely to be perfectly replicated. Furthermore, adequately trained personnel are necessary to administer the survey with the least deviation from the standard.

In addition to censuses and sample surveys, NSSs are using administrative data as a main or supplementary source of information for several SDG indicators. Using administrative data has several advantages. First, administrative data usually contains a complete count of units, which can derive disaggregated data from smaller areas of interests. Second, making use of existing data costs less than designing a new data collection initiative to serve specific data needs. Third, readily available data through administrative registers have proved their significance during crises. For example, the COVID-19 pandemic highlighted the importance of timely data in order to prepare well-informed interventions to support the people affected by the crisis. However, the use of administrative data is sometimes limited to a specific administrative purpose and might not be suitable for another statistical purpose due to its comparability and confidentiality. NSSs therefore need to carefully select different data sources to complement censuses, using only applicable sample surveys and administrative data.

Reference: Demographic and Health Survey (DHS) Program. 2017. *Measuring the SDGs: The Role of Household Surveys.* 11 January. https://blog.dhsprogram.com/measuring-sdgs/.

Asia and the Pacific has made some progress on conducting regular and timely data collection.

The Statistical Capacity Indicator (SCI) compiled by the World Bank provides additional insights on the capacity of the region's NSSs to provide timely data. In general, the SCI measures the capacity to collect, analyze, and disseminate high-quality data. Scores are based on three important dimensions: (i) statistical methodology, which measures an NSS's ability to adhere to international statistical standards and methods; (ii) source data, which reflects capacity to collect data in line with internationally recommended frequency and whether administrative data can be used for purposes of statistical estimation; and (iii) periodicity and timeliness, which scores an NSS on the basis of availability and periodicity of key socioeconomic indicators (World Bank 2021a). Recently, the World Bank developed an updated set of measurements, the Statistical Performance Indicator (SPI), which considers five pillars: data use, data services, data products, data sources, and data infrastructure. The SPI is set to be more comprehensive and forward-looking than the SCI (World Bank 2021b). However, the SCI, which has time series data, is still being used to show the trend of how statistical capacity is evolving in the subregions of Asia and the Pacific over time (Figure 4.2).

Figure 4.2: Statistical Capacity Indicator in Asia and the Pacific, by Subregion

Some aspects of Asia and the Pacific's statistical capacity have improved over time.

Note: The analysis uses data from ADB regional member economies for which estimates of the Statistical Capacity Indicator are available.

Source: Asian Development Bank estimates using data from World Bank. Statistical Capacity Indicator. https://datatopics.worldbank.org/statisticalcapacity/SCIdashboard.aspx (accessed 22 December 2020).

Figure 4.2 summarizes how Asia and the Pacific's statistical capacity has evolved since 2005. Data show that overall statistical capacity in the region has improved steadily over time, although variations across individual economies exist.

Assessing the three SCI dimensions, Asia and the Pacific scored highest on periodicity and timeliness, with signs of improvement over time. However, the most significant improvement for the region as a whole was observed in statistical methodology. Meanwhile, the region's scores on source data went down marginally from 2005 to 2020. By subregion, East Asia posted strong improvement in methodology and the most significant improvement in overall score, while the Pacific posted an improvement in source data, albeit from a lower base than other subregions. Southeast Asia maintained the highest score for periodicity and timeliness.

Impacts of the COVID-19 pandemic on statistical activities in three economies

Well before 2020, the statistics community of Asia and the Pacific had increasingly recognized that a lot of the data needed for effective policymaking and evaluation were not readily available. For a number of years, NSSs in the region have been working on initiatives to exploit alternative data sources and digital methods of collection. The many and varied disruptions caused by the COVID-19 pandemic have prompted NSOs to speed up some of their initiatives in these areas, as has been observed in Malaysia, the Philippines, and Thailand.

Malaysia

Even before the pandemic, the Department of Statistics Malaysia (DOSM) was exploring mixed-mode approaches to providing timely data. In implementing its surveys, the DOSM has gradually been moving away from traditional data collection to computer-assisted personal interviewing (CAPI), drop off and pick up of self-administered questionnaires, and email communication. These strategies have reduced field work costs and enhanced the department's ability to analyze and disseminate data quickly.

When the pandemic began, the DOSM recognized its role in helping craft policies responsive to an environment with many uncertainties. It produced quick surveys, such as those gauging households' ability to survive during lockdowns, without jobs and sources of income. Similarly, it conducted surveys among businesses and enterprises to assess their pandemic needs. The DOSM also came up with weekly and daily statistics to keep policymakers informed on various indicators, e.g., the number of visitors at recreational or theme parks, business outlets opened in certain areas, weekend occupancy rates in budget hotels, and the number of people on particular streets.

To leverage existing administrative data, the DOSM integrated information from the employees' provident fund and the inland revenue board, which covers 70% to 80% of Malaysia's population. This provided policymakers with immediate snapshots of how the pandemic was affecting the labor market. The DOSM has also started to explore nontraditional data sources such as gathering data from media outlets and web-scraping for its price surveys. More granular export and import data at the local level, specifically by province, are now available due to big data initiatives.

Other initiatives by the DOSM include: (i) data usually released quarterly (e.g., agriculture administrative data) are now available on a monthly basis; (ii) quarterly gross domestic product (GDP) broken down into monthly estimates to better assess the impacts of different pandemic response policies; (ii) additional indicators of underutilization in the labor market, i.e., time-related underemployment and skill-related underemployment; (iv) a quarterly labor market review; and (v) labor force statistics by state on a quarterly basis and district-level statistics on annual basis.

The DOSM faced enormous challenges in conducting the 2020 Population and Housing Census (MyCensus 2020), commenced on 7 July 2020. However, adopting technology in the pre-pandemic planning of the census—principally by developing the Malaysia Integrated Population Census System—created opportunities to use technology-based data collection. MyCensus 2020 is now in the final stage of online data collection and the DOSM is leveraging administrative data to complement and cross-check census data.

The DOSM continues to play a prominent role in steering policy direction through its membership in the Higher Level Task Force of the National Employment Council, which was set up in October 2020 to address labor market issues across Malaysia. The DOSM provides the most recent data to inform the work of the council in shaping policy and monitoring government initiatives. Along this line, the DOSM is also involved in providing vital information to the members of the Economic Action Council, especially with respect to unemployment and underemployment.

Malaysia is also in the process of forming a statistics council, headed by the Prime Minister, to assist evidence-based policymaking.

The Philippines

The Philippine Statistics Authority (PSA) has long been undertaking initiatives to capitalize on technology-based solutions for data collection and dissemination. Through its adoption of CAPI and computer-assisted telephone interviewing (CATI) processes, the time lag between conducting the labor force survey and releasing the statistics was shortened from 40 days to 35 days; the time lag on the survey of information communication and technology declined from 2 years to 1 year; and the difference between data collection and release of statistics from the annual survey of business and industry fell from 1 year (or longer) to 8 months.

Since the onset of the pandemic, innovative initiatives have helped the PSA deliver its data publications without delay. For example, initiatives to train enumerators in using customized CAPI methods have ensured that data are released on time. Moreover, the authority experimented with web-scraping in the capital region for its price survey. As the pandemic prevented enumerators from reaching store outlets, due to lockdowns and fear of face-to-face interviews, this kind of initiative to access online prices is expected to aid in validating more than half of the commodity prices the PSA surveys monthly.

There have, however, been some limitations in areas where there is still low internet activity or where computer literacy of households and respondents is less advanced. Moreover, the PSA's agricultural survey was postponed due to difficulty in hiring statistical researchers and unavailability of transportation to some areas due to geographical lockdowns.

To address repercussions of community quarantines on the labor market, the PSA started to produce more frequent labor force surveys—from quarterly to monthly.

To improve targeting and prioritization of social assistance, the authority, together with local government units (LGUs), is also preparing for the roll-out of a community-based monitoring system by 2022. The PSA is leveraging its expertise in conducting censuses to help the LGUs shepherd this initiative. However, the authority recognizes that some LGUs might have difficulties in operating the system and is encouraging development partners to collaborate with these government units.

Thailand

The efforts of the National Statistical Office of Thailand (NSO) to improve timeliness of data began with a shift to CAPI from traditional pen-and-paper methods before pandemic. Around this time, the NSO also started shifting to CATI and computer-assisted web interviewing (CAWI). Additionally, the office cross-referenced its surveys or censuses and, where possible, merged questions to streamline data collection processes.

Initially scheduled in April 2020, Thailand's Census of Population and Housing was seen as an excellent opportunity to employ various digital initiatives and benefit from associated time and cost efficiencies. One of the proposals was to use tablets for faster data consistency checks, reduction of response processing times, and immediate uploading of survey information to the cloud. However, the census was subsequently postponed due to pandemic restrictions and business closures. In response, the NSO allocated B10 million to study the implementation of a register-based census to become more resilient to disruptions in field operations. Research on the feasibility of using big data for forecasting population numbers is also underway.

The NSO has helped pioneer the use of satellite population maps to provide detailed population data, which is especially useful in times when face-to-face data gathering is not feasible. The technique, which has been researched in partnership with the Asian Development Bank, can deliver more reliable and geographically granular population density maps than conventional methods (Tatem et al. 2007).

In particular, the study applied the method proposed by Stevens et al. (2015) to compile granular population data for 2020. It attempted to forecast gridded population distribution in the Thai provinces of Udon Thani, Uthai Thani, and Samut Songkhram (Figure 4.3).

The methodology entailed combining census data with publicly available spatial data such as land cover classes, elevation, slope, and nighttime lights, then estimating a random forest model to obtain population density estimates at the 100 meter by 100 meter grid-level. Using the information on average annual population growth in Thailand from

Figure 4.3: Forecasts of Population Density in Three Thai Provinces, 2020

Population density estimates derived from satellite imagery of *Udon Thani, Uthai Thani,* and *Samut Songkhram* provinces.

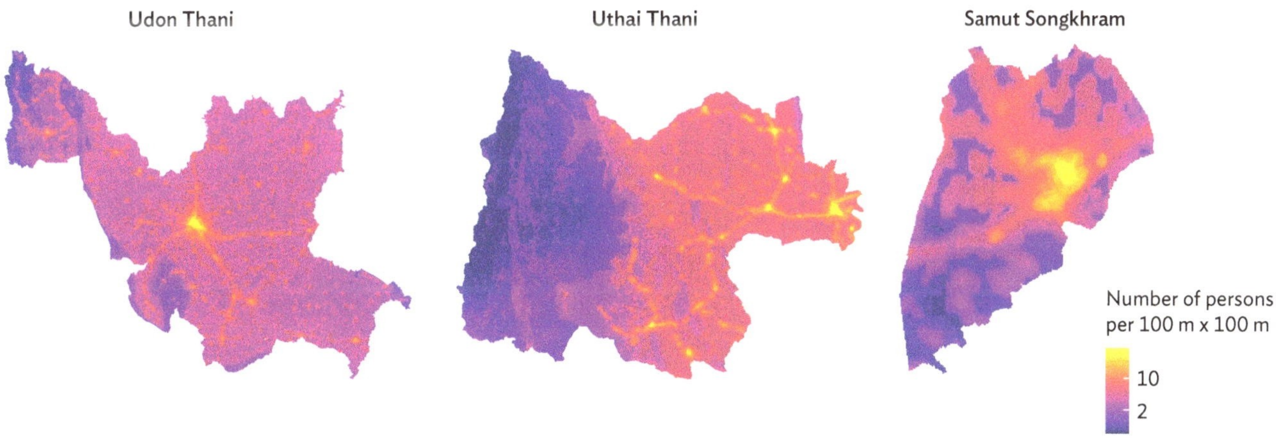

m = meter.

Source: T. Mitterling, K. Fenz, A. Martinez, J. Bulan, M. Addawe, R. Durante, and M. Martillan. Forthcoming. *Compiling Granular Population Data Using Geospatial Information.*

2013 to 2017, another model was trained to predict population growth beyond 2017. After applying these predicted growth rates to grid-level population data from 2017, granular forecasts of population density for 2020 were obtained. Nevertheless, further research is needed to assess the accuracy of such forecasts once official population numbers are available.

In response to the pandemic, the NSO also had to recalibrate arrangements for its other data collection activities. For instance, instead of collecting price data directly from stores, current prices were obtained through telephone interviews or from relevant websites. Similarly, enterprise surveys used telephone interviewing, questionnaires by post or e-mail, and data from business registers. Imputation techniques were applied to supplement missing survey samples.

Together with exploring strategies on how to provide timely data and statistics amid the COVID-19 pandemic, examining the impact of those strategies on data quality is equally important. For example, given that census results are used as population frames for other surveys, it is important to ensure that new ways of collecting census data still deliver high-quality results. Additionally, given that administrative data systems are playing a more important role in producing data and statistics for development, the NSO recognizes the need to develop the skills of other government ministries that manage such administrative databases, to ensure they follow the same scientific rigor required when collecting, processing, and analyzing other types of data commonly handled by the NSO. For instance, administrative data sets and registration records produced by various ministries require skills in eliminating duplication and error. The NSO acknowledges the need to develop the skills of ministries' information technology officers in dealing with administrative data.

How the Pandemic Influenced Data Capture More Broadly

Only with accurate, trustworthy, and timely data can governments and institutions fight the COVID-19 pandemic and mitigate the short- and long-term socioeconomic effects of containment measures.

Figure 4.4 illustrates the relationship between statistical performance (using the SPI) and the proportion of scheduled activities that were fully implemented or encountered just minimal delays in 2020 (using data from the EROD-SDI survey).[2] The results suggest that, although there is a positive association between the two measures, the value of the SPI is not a strong predictor of whether or not scheduled data collection activities were completed. In fact, a majority of the surveyed economies —including Indonesia, Fiji, Kazakhstan, Malaysia, the Philippines, Singapore, and others—were able to push through with more than half of their scheduled data collection activities.

2 Surveyed economies that did not have SPI values for the reference period were: Brunei Darussalam; the Cook Islands; Hong Kong, China; Palau; and Taipei,China.

Figure 4.4: Association between the Statistical Performance Indicator and Scheduled Data Collection Activities

Many national statistical offices pushed through with data collection activities scheduled for 2020.

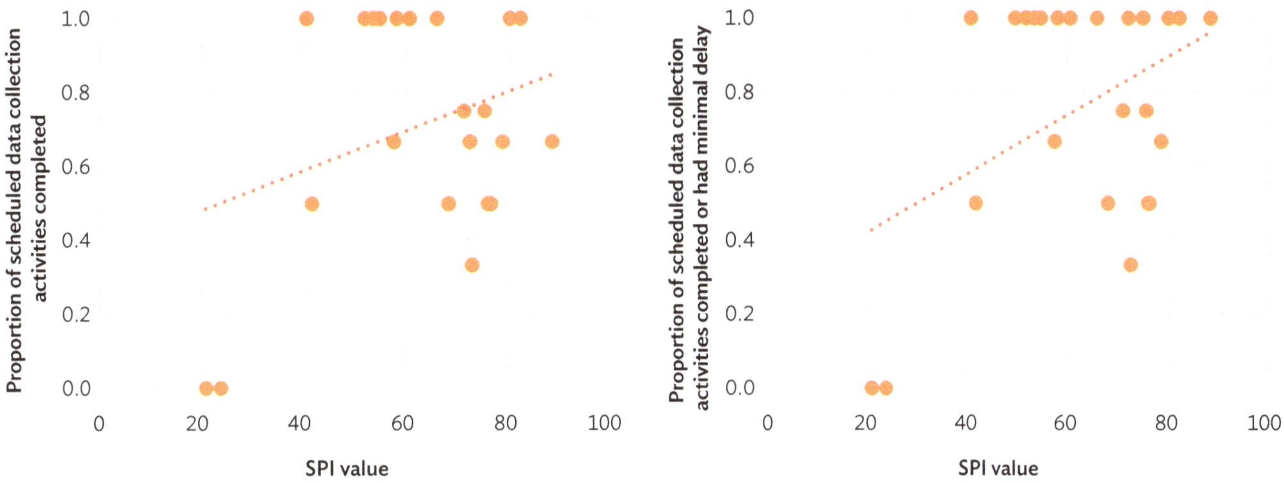

SPI = Statistical Performance Indicator.

Sources: Asian Development Bank estimates using data from the Survey on National Statistics Offices' Initiatives to Enhance Timeliness of Data and Statistics; and World Bank. Statistical Performance Indicators. https://databank.worldbank.org/source/statistical-performance-indicators-(spi) (accessed 27 July 2021).

Initiatives such as the shift to technology-assisted data collection enhanced the capacity to generate timely data, in spite of lockdowns, work-from-home arrangements, and concerns of field staff about face-to-face interviews.

NSOs undertook new initiatives to calibrate data collection, compilation, and dissemination of activities to adapt to the pandemic situation. This was to ensure continuity of critical data series such as economic output, employment, prices, household income and/or consumption, and poverty. These strategies provided important lessons in building more resilient statistical systems.

Population and housing censuses were severely impacted by the pandemic.

As a census entails a complete enumeration of the population in a specific economy or area, it is considered one of the most complex and massive data collection activities, requiring rigorous planning. In many economies, a census of population and housing is conducted only once every 10 years due to the time and resources needed for planning and implementation. Despite this long lead-in, many NSOs in developing economies of Asia and the Pacific still encounter challenges when conducting a census. For instance, high staff turnover often prompts NSOs to largely focus on training their staff on collection and processing of data, and less time is provided on strengthening their capacity to do in-depth analysis of census data. Such limited capacity contributes to delays in releasing census results (UNFPA 2017).

Nevertheless, improvements have been made in how economies conduct census operations. As observed in the 2010 round of the World Population Housing Census Programme—one of the longest-standing global statistical initiatives of the United Nations—technology solutions were already being applied in census preparations and data capture. Several economies were using geographic information system (GIS) mapping technologies to digitize maps of census enumeration areas. Some NSOs had started using scanners for data entry, while others adopted electronic questionnaires through tablets.

As economies prepared for the 2020 round of the World Population and Housing Census Programme, adoption of technological solutions increased severalfold, and this paved the way for census data being released earlier than usual. For instance, based on the EROD-SDI survey, the gap between field operations and dissemination of key results shortened by up to a year for a number of economies, mostly because of the advanced methods of data capture.

Globally, 120 countries and economies were scheduled to conduct their respective population censuses in 2020, but these activities were either interrupted, delayed, postponed, or cancelled (UNCTAD 2021). NSOs worldwide were forced to adjust and look for workarounds to push through with their census activities. Some rescheduled their census activities by a few weeks or months, while some changed their mode of data collection. In Asia and the Pacific, the EROD-SDI survey showed that among 10 economies that had scheduled their censuses in 2020, six were forced to reschedule field operations for either later in 2020 or into 2021.

Economies that were able to push through with the 2020 census had to adopt mixed data collection approaches. Some transitioned to telephone interviews and web-based data collection, while others utilized postal services to drop off and pick up questionnaires when needed. Some Asian economies moved towards an approach where the initial data source will come largely from existing administrative data and be further enhanced by results from field enumeration, which has included a shift from full pen-and-paper interviewing to CAPI and CAWI. This initiative is seen to be the first step towards a register-based census. By previously investing in a resident registry with biometric verification technology, some economies were able to leverage their administrative data to produce a cheaper and timelier census without compromising data quality.

Despite the strides NSOs have taken to improve and hasten the conduct and release of census results, many statistics offices still recognize that there are obstacles in data collection. These include inconsistencies in administrative data, lack of internet availability in some areas, insufficiency of server performance and memory of tablet devices, and lack of preparedness of enumerators and respondents in transitioning to technology-based interview methods. To address these issues, some economies have continued to pursue capacity-building initiatives, especially in the use of new methods to facilitate timely census data compilation.

Use of nontraditional datasets to provide richer insights into economic activities has accelerated.

Compiling a set of economic indicators is a crucial first step to understanding the economy. This requires the collection of multiple types of data. For instance, agricultural surveys and censuses provide information on areas cultivated with different types of crops, animal production, expenditure, and number of agricultural workers; while enterprise surveys and censuses produce specific information on nonagricultural establishments, sales and revenue, expenditure, and size of nonagricultural employment. Furthermore, administrative data sources, such as the financial statements of businesses, also provide vital information when compiling economic indicators.

Economic indicators help policymakers and planners weigh the benefits and potential downsides of alternative investments, make business decisions, design economic policies, and monitor national progress. To ensure data harmonization, the System of National Accounts (SNA), an internationally agreed set of recommendations on how to measure economic activity, provides a conceptual framework that economies can follow in compiling statistical sources. The latest version is the 2008 SNA (UNSD 2008).[3]

The results of the EROD-SDI survey reflect the challenges faced by NSOs in collating timely economic statistics during the pandemic. A number of NSOs (e.g., the Republic of Korea, Singapore, and Thailand) adapted imputation techniques, while others (e.g., Sri Lanka and Hong Kong, China) turned to alternative data sources such as firms' annual reports to complement missing data.

In particular, NSOs have faced several challenges in compiling official GDP estimates, which are usually released with a certain time lag, since statistics agencies need time to compile national accounts estimates using available data from regular surveys, administrative data, and other sources of information. The estimates have therefore traditionally been released quarterly, semi annually, and/or annually.

Faced with challenges in data collection because of pandemic restrictions, as well as an escalating requirement to produce and release reliable and timely GDP numbers more frequently, NSOs have explored alternative collection methods and new data sources.

---

3 Given the important role of economic indicators in supporting policies promoting economic growth, international development institutions usually support initiatives that strengthen the capacity of national statistics systems in compiling such data. For instance, the National Accounts Section of the United Nations Statistics Division contributes to the international coordinated development and updating of the SNA. The section also undertakes methodological research to address some of the issues outlined in the SNA's research agenda (UNSD 2008). Other development and multilateral institutions such as the International Monetary Fund, PARIS21, the World Bank, etc., also contribute to similar initiatives. In Asia and the Pacific, ADB's EROD-SDI provides technical assistance to a number of developing economies in compiling supply and use tables and input-output tables used as the basis for compiling a wide range of economic accounts. This year's special supplement of *Key Indicators for the Asia and the Pacific* also presents ADB's recent work on measuring the digital economy, which broadly aligns with the SNA research agenda since, currently, digital transformation is largely invisible in the core economic accounts.

One alternative method employed to produce early GDP estimates is the use of big data for macroeconomic "nowcasting".

Big data—including information on financial markets, electronic payments, mobile phone usage, satellite images, online prices, online searches, and social media postings—may be used to complement existing data from surveys and administrative data sources (Buono et al. 2018). In nowcasting GDP growth, initial estimates are calculated at the start of the reference period and then continually updated as new information becomes available, using statistical models such as time-series autoregressive models or mixed data sampling regressions.

The Organisation for Economic Co-operation and Development has been publishing a weekly tracker of GDP growth to provide real time high-frequency indicators of economic activity. It applies a machine learning model to a panel of Google Trends data for 46 economies, including India, Indonesia, and the People's Republic of China, then aggregates information about search behavior related to consumption, labor markets, housing, trade, industrial activity, and economic uncertainty (OECD 2021).

In addition to the use of big data, there have also been efforts to enhance the use of conventional data sources such as establishment surveys and/or censuses. For example, the Reserve Bank of India used real-time tracking of high-frequency activity indicators to provide timely information on the state of the economy and give directional movements in quarterly GDP growth ahead of official releases, which generally happen 7–8 weeks after the end of the reference quarter (RBI 2020). This nowcasting of GDP growth is based on an economic activity index estimated from 27 monthly indicators using a dynamic factor model.

Studies have also explored the use of satellite images and spatial data to complement conventional GDP estimation, specifically the presence of night-lights as a proxy indicator of economic growth. Within the satellite imagery, increases in nighttime luminosity over time depict the transition of countries or regions into more economically developed areas (Hu and Yao 2019). For instance, in a study by the Reserve Bank of India, a statistically significant relationship between night lights and value-added in agriculture and private consumption expenditure was found, together with a strong correlation between night-lights and the gross state domestic product (Prakash et al. 2019).

Technology-based collection of labor and employment data has supplemented traditional methods.

Among NSOs from Asia and the Pacific that responded to the EROD-SDI survey, some indicated postponement or temporary suspensions in conducting their labor force surveys (LFS). In most developing economies of the region, face-to-face interviews remain the primary mode of labor survey data collection, either through pen-and-

Figure 4.5: Association between the Statistical Performance Indicator and Use of Computer-Assisted Data Collection

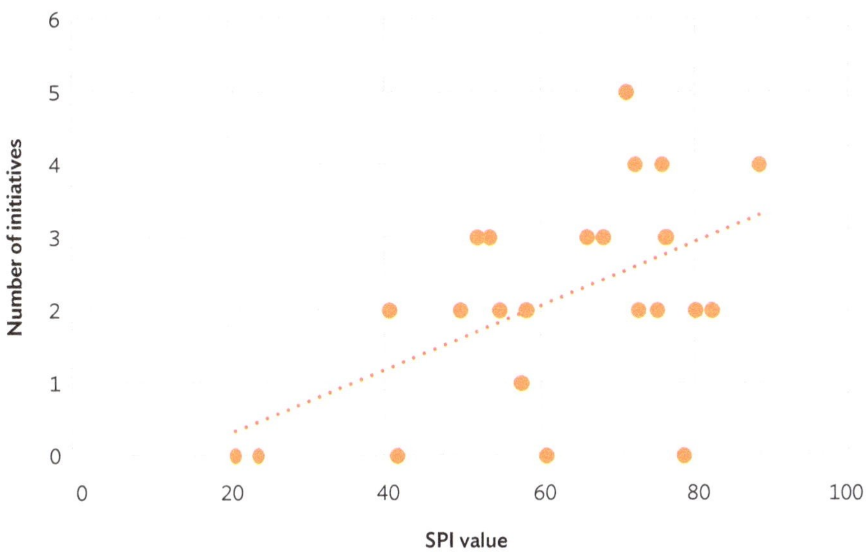

SPI = Statistical Performance Indicator.
Sources: Asian Development Bank estimates using data from the Survey on National Statistics Offices' Initiatives to Enhance Timeliness of Data and Statistics; and World Bank. Statistical Performance Indicators. https://databank.worldbank.org/source/statistical-performance-indicators-(spi) (accessed 27 July 2021)..

paper interviewing or CAPI. These modes of data collection have been greatly affected by restrictions imposed to curb the spread of COVID-19. In response, economies that already had existing systems for telephone or web-based interviewing shifted to alternative data collection methods such as CATI and CAWI, sometimes in combination with face-to-face interviews.

Some economies applied different data collection methods where different pandemic restrictions were in place. For example, in COVID-19 red zones, Indonesia used drop off and pick up of self-enumerated questionnaires or CATI, while continuing face-to-face interviews in COVID-19 green zones. In Sri Lanka, field data collection scheduled for March and April was postponed until May, with data collection in lockdown areas performed using CATI (a first for Sri Lanka's LFS). Meanwhile, some economies implemented certain adjustments for sampling errors (e.g., Armenia used re weighting procedures).

In higher-income economies, where use of CATI and CAWI was already part of regular operations, the pandemic had less impact on data collection processes. For example, Singapore and Hong Kong, China simply used a higher proportion of online participation and phone interviews and completed their LFS on schedule.

The challenges and limitations in conducting field survey operations during the pandemic highlight the need for NSOs to improve their systems in terms of data collection and to explore other estimation methodologies that utilize big data to complement data from standard LFS or administrative reports.[4]

Figure 4.5 shows the relationship between the World Bank's SPI and number of data collection activities (LFS and non-LFS) that employed computer-assisted interview methods in economies surveyed by EROD-SDI.

Data integration methods are enhancing compilation of household income, poverty, and other socioeconomic development statistics.

Data on household income, consumption expenditure, and poverty comprise an integral part of designing, monitoring, targeting, and evaluating poverty alleviation programs.

However, considering the costs and length of time it takes to collect and process household income and expenditure surveys or living standards surveys using conventional techniques, NSOs have continuously explored using data integration methods to provide data in more timely and cost-effective ways. For instance, efforts to complement household survey data with big data for poverty estimation have been increasing, with such initiatives being especially useful and relevant during times of pandemic and other crises.

Based on a 2017 survey conducted by ADB and UNESCAP, the use of big data (such as geospatial and social media data) helps improve the granularity, accuracy, and timeliness of statistics on poverty and welfare (Albert et al. 2019).

The use of data from satellite images and the application of machine-learning technologies have also been studied as applications for estimating poverty. For example, an ADB study in 2016 assessed the use of satellite imagery to analyze the correlation between nighttime lights and socioeconomic indicators, including headcount poverty rates. Empirical data on the official headcount poverty rates, along with other socioeconomic indicators from the Philippines, and data from satellite images were used in the analysis. Results showed that, over time, average luminosity had increased and the areas covered by lights had expanded, which may indicate economic growth and improvements in living standards (Martinez 2016).

---

4 In addition to technology solutions in collecting data on work and employment, studies have explored nowcasting methods that use big data, such as social media postings as reference indicators of unemployment. These alternative methodologies could provide timelier data on labor market indicators, owing to the real-time availability and frequency of the information. For example, in estimating the number of hours worked, the International Labour Organization (ILO 2020) applied principal component analysis using the latest available data from labor force surveys; administrative labor market data (e.g., registered unemployment); up-to-date mobile phone data from Google Community Mobility Reports; the most recent Google Trends data; and COVID-19 Government Response Stringency Index, including data on COVID-19 incidence. Use of social media data, such as Twitter posts and Google searches, as well as smartphone global positioning system (GPS) data, were also explored to track and predict unemployment rates (ILO 2020). The use of massive location data from smartphones (GPS log data) was found to be useful in nowcasting unemployment rates and predicting the status of labor markets in Japan (Moriwaki 2019).

The initiative was further expanded by including information from daytime satellite imagery. Machine-learning algorithms were combined with data from satellite imagery to try to predict official poverty estimates. The approach was tested using official poverty statistics and satellite data for the Philippines and Thailand (ADB 2020; ADB 2021).

While the focus of such study is to produce poverty statistics that are more granular than what can be derived from using household surveys alone, in principle, similar techniques can be explored to enhance poverty data, since satellite images are available more frequently than household surveys can feasibly be conducted. In other economies, there are attempts to integrate different types of data (including telecommunications data) to provide more dynamic poverty maps (Jean et al. 2016; Engstrom et al. 2017; Newhouse 2016).

In addition to big data-related research on enhancing the quality of poverty statistics, including timeliness, the EROD-SDI survey also highlighted initiatives undertaken by some economies to enhance survey-based estimation of poverty. Many economies in the EROD-SDI survey have been utilizing technology in enhancing their data collection methodologies. Economies that were initially using paper-based survey forms and face-to-face interviews have moved to using telephone and web interviews (CATI and CAWI), while others have taken the additional step of ensuring that surveys are self-administered and can be accessed online. For example, Taipei,China has started linking its household survey to other available databases to facilitate timely release of data.

When the COVID-19 pandemic struck, some economies transitioned to digital technologies for data collection, given mobility restrictions and reluctance to conduct face-to-face interviews. For example, in Armenia; Bhutan; Georgia; Hong Kong, China; and Mongolia, lockdowns halted several field operations, hence, NSOs moved towards conducting phone interviews. Challenges were not just in data collection; NSO employees also had to adapt to changes brought by the pandemic. In Indonesia, for example, NSO enumerators had to go through various instructor and enumerator trainings. Moreover, work-from-home arrangements were a challenge for NSO employees in Indonesia and Sri Lanka as they had to do data cleaning and verifying of survey results from their homes.

Development institutions have played a key role in helping statistics offices bridge gaps in consumer price data.

The COVID-19 pandemic caused changes in individual and household consumption and spending patterns, and these changes could affect specific items in the fixed consumer price index (CPI) basket. For example, due to lockdowns and travel restrictions, spending on transportation and accommodation was significantly reduced. Meanwhile, as people shifted to work-from-home arrangements, spending on food for home consumption increased and spending at restaurants fell. Hence, the question arises of whether CPI weights should be adjusted to capture these changes in household or personal expenditure patterns.

To address the potential measurement bias of consumer price inflation brought by possible changes in CPI weights, some studies—including one by the International Monetary Fund (IMF)—recommended that, in estimating inflation during the COVID-19 pandemic, adjustments to CPI weights can be applied only if there are data to support them, since there is still incomplete information related to pandemic expenditure patterns (Reinsdorf et al. 2020).

In economies such as Australia and New Zealand, CPI weights were adjusted only for specific expenditure items, following advice from international bodies that CPI weights should not be adjusted for short-term fluctuations and that adjustments should only be made if there are enough data to support the adjustment. In the case of New Zealand, CPI weights were adjusted for international airfares and overseas accommodation, which generally had high weights in the country's CPI. However, due to border closures, there was significant reduction in spending on these items (Stats NZ 2020). Similarly, in Australia, adjustments were made only for specific categories, including international holiday travel and accommodation, child care, restaurant meals, and grocery items, to capture the price changes during the pandemic (ABS 2020).

Restrictions in face-to-face data collection also meant challenges in terms of collecting price data to estimate CPI in economies of Asia and the Pacific.

One alternative method in gathering price data for CPI estimation, already implemented in higher-income economies, is the use of live scanners, specifically for fast-moving consumer goods such as grocery products. Scanners can be used to estimate price indices in real time, providing up-to-date information on inflation risks, especially during economic crises. Furthermore, because data can be collected in real time, this facilitates timely tracking of variations in spending patterns to help in monitoring inflation risks (Jaravel and O'Connell 2020).

In 2020, Japan started to use web-scraping and expanded the use of scanner data to estimate its CPI. However, one drawback has been that the range of goods or services for which scanner data are available is limited and the adjustment of product quality is necessary (Watanabe and Watanabe 2014).

In addition, another IMF study recommended imputing for missing price data as a result of temporary business closures caused by the pandemic, by using the short-term relative change in available collected prices of similar varieties within the elementary aggregate. If an entire index is missing, either the next level up in aggregation or the "All Items" index is used to impute for the missing index. The All Items index is then compiled using the imputed and collected subcomponent indices (IMF 2020).

The EROD-SDI survey shows that many economies in Asia and the Pacific (e.g., Armenia; Bhutan; Georgia; Hong Kong, China; Indonesia; the Philippines; and Singapore) applied the imputation technique for locked-down outlets or carried forward when prices were not available. These adjustments made use of alternative data sources and exploited available data (Ducharme et al. 2020). In Bhutan, for example, the inability to physically go to stores and collect prices was augmented by using online prices. The IMF recommendations were also applied to ensure the continuity of price data (e.g., in Uzbekistan), where some price data were not collected. Economies often verified the imputed price with suppliers of goods and services and with other experts.[5]

Addressing the Sustainable Development Agenda Beyond the COVID-19 Pandemic

In 2019, the United Nations launched Data For Now (Data4Now), a global initiative to increase the use of robust methods and tools that can improve the timeliness, coverage, and quality of data for development. The initiative works through collaboration and partnership, technical and capacity support, and information sharing. Developing Asian economies participating in this project include Bangladesh, Mongolia, and Nepal.

In Bangladesh, two important development indicators have been prioritized: the first is the ability to estimate annual poverty indicators at the local level; the second is to generate data to support climate action initiatives. In pursuing the advancement of these indicators, innovative solutions to maximize use of traditional and nontraditional data have been utilized (UNSD 2020). Mongolia, on the other hand, identified the need for more timely data in terms of land use and crop yields. Meanwhile, Nepal concentrated on its need to produce more robust data on domestic tourism and urban–rural migration (GPSDD 2019). Data4Now is planning to expand its collaboration with at least 10 additional economies by 2023.

ADB is also contributing to strengthening the capacity of NSOs to provide up-to-date and timely data that can be used to monitor the development targets. These initiatives relate to the use of CAPI and other technologies for data collection, enhanced data compilation under the International Comparison Program (ICP), and adopting international standards of sharing data to ensure better flow of information (Box 4.2).

5 Other steps were undertaken during the pandemic to address the disruptions in price data collection activities, although a number of such initiatives may be considered extensions of earlier initiatives. Prior to the pandemic, a number of economies (e.g., Armenia; Hong Kong, China; and the Philippines) advanced the shift from pen-and-paper interviewing to CAPI. The shift from face-to-face interviewing to telephone or internet-based surveys was also implemented (e.g., in Malaysia and Viet Nam). In particular, the pandemic accelerated economies' adoption of survey methods that do not require personal interviews (e.g., in Indonesia and Malaysia). To ensure that respondents participated in the various censuses and surveys conducted, some NSOs resorted to sending reminders via SMS or letters. Some economies also used live scanner data in addition to survey data. For example, Azerbaijan and Taipei,China used scanner data from the database of trade network and web-scraping data, respectively. Despite hurdles faced by NSOs during the pandemic, some economies continued to pursue capacity-building initiatives, especially in the use of new data collection methods. This will prove advantageous to NSOs in developing Asia.

Box 4.2: How ADB's Statistical Initiatives Support Compilation of Timely Data

Computer-Assisted Personal Interviewing and Other Technology Solutions

Information technology has transformed field data collection methods by using computer-assisted techniques in personal, telephone, and web interviewing (known as CAPI, CATI, and CAWI, respectively). These techniques are invaluable during health crises as they allow for contactless data collection. Furthermore, with built-in data checks, navigation tools, easy data transfer options, and the ability to capture information (such as global positioning system coordinates and photos), CAPI, CATI, and CAWI not only reduce the overall time to produce a clean dataset, but are also expected to improve data quality.

A study by the Asian Development Bank (ADB) in Sri Lanka and Viet Nam to quantify the benefits of these techniques, particularly CAPI, showed that there was a reduction in the number of errors by 6.2 per interview in Sri Lanka, and 0.8 per interview in Viet Nam (ADB 2019). Both economies have also adopted CAPI in their recent surveys and censuses. ADB is looking at replicating and extending the work on CAPI, CATI, and CAWI in the Pacific's household income and expenditure surveys conducted across Nauru, Samoa, and Tuvalu. Meanwhile, ADB has conducted three iterations of massive open online courses on CAPI. The latest iteration in 2021 saw a total of 1,692 registrants from 112 different economies. From these, a completion of 30%, or over 500 individuals, was achieved. A fourth iteration is planned for 2022, and will feature more information on CATI and CAWI.

International Comparison Program

ADB is the regional agency coordinating implementation of the International Comparison Program (ICP) in 22 economies of Asia and the Pacific. The region covers over half of the world's population and about one-third of global gross domestic product in purchasing power parity terms.[a] The ICP requires collection of prices of more than 1,300 well-defined goods and services, representing household consumption, government consumption, construction, and machinery and equipment, across all participating economies. Purchasing power parities (PPPs) from the ICP are meaningful and useful only if they are estimated using reliable and accurate price data to ensure "like with like" comparisons. This requires rigorous statistical validation and verifications of prices within and across all economies.

Recognizing the data quality and timeliness requirements of ICP operations in economies with varying statistical capacities, ADB has been providing technological support to national implementing agencies through a data management tool: the ICP Asia Pacific Software Suite (ICP-APSS). The ICP-APSS facilitates multiple data management functions such as timely data quality checks, verifications at various levels, minimization of nonsampling errors, and efficient data preparation allowing more time for validation and analysis.

For the ongoing 2021 ICP cycle, the ICP-APSS has been developed into a web-based application, incorporating several new features and modules for all ICP surveys. As the national implementing agencies continue to implement price surveys for the 2021 cycle, amid the constraints of the COVID-19 pandemic, the ICP-APSS provides operational resilience and acts as a valuable tool for data management and submission of high-quality and timely price data to ADB.

Statistical Data and Metadata Exchange

ADB is assisting in the implementation of the Statistical Data and Metadata Exchange (SDMX), an international initiative aimed at standardizing the mechanisms and processes for the exchange of statistical data and metadata.

The SDMX will promote efficient sharing of data, both within and across national statistics systems, and with external partners and/or organizations. Establishing and adhering to a set of internationally recognized standards for access to data and metadata will ensure that such exchanges are timely, easily understandable, reliable, and user-friendly.

ADB is coordinating with SDMX sponsor organizations and development partners in the region to support the bank's developing member economies in implementing the SDMX.

Reference: Asian Development Bank. 2019. *The CAPI Effect: Boosting Survey Data Through Mobile Technology: A Special Supplement of the Key Indicators for Asia and the Pacific 2019*. Manila: ADB. DOI: https://dx.doi.org/10.22617/FLS190429-3.

---

[a] The ICP is the largest global collaborative statistical undertaking, with 176 economies participating in its 2017 cycle. The ICP follows an integrated work program at the national, regional, and global levels to facilitate the compilation of PPPs and PPP-based expenditure estimates for gross domestic product and its expenditure.

novative data sourcing and collection. Data integration and digital chnologies can help provide more timely data needed to facilitate idence-based policymaking (Photo by Kevin Ku).

Summary and Conclusion

Even before the COVID-19 pandemic, Asia and the Pacific's national statistics offices were exploring innovative methods for providing timely data.

The 2030 Agenda for Sustainable Development was laid out to *"end poverty, protect the planet, and improve the lives and prospects of everyone, everywhere."* In monitoring progress toward the agenda's goals and targets, the provision of quality, accessible, timely, and reliable disaggregated data is critical.

As such, part of the agenda aims to strengthen the capacity of NSOs and other organizational bodies responsible for compiling development indicators to ensure high-quality data. However, for several of the Sustainable Development Goals, many developing economies do not have internationally comparable data or, when they do, these are produced infrequently and with substantial time lags.

Prior to the COVID-19 pandemic, efforts were already being made to modernize and expedite the process of collecting and encoding data in a number of economies that responded to the EROD-SDI survey. As a result, traditional pen-and-paper surveys were shifting to the CAPI, CATI, or CAWI techniques.

In addition to adopting more modern data collection methods, there were initiatives to use nontraditional data sources. For instance, in estimating economic and poverty statistics, an increasing number of NSOs were planning to use, or had already started using, satellite imagery and other types of big data.

However, providing timely data should not come at the cost of data quality. In the EROD-SDI survey, it was evident that NSOs, with assistance from development institutions, had made efforts to improve both timeliness and data quality prior to the pandemic. As a result, the time from conduct of censuses and surveys to release of information shortened in many economies. Specific initiatives in data collection, processing, and dissemination also improved the quality of data being produced.

At the height of the pandemic, national statistics offices in the region stepped up to deliver timely data.

When the COVID-19 pandemic pushed economies into lockdown in the first quarter of 2020, data collection and statistical operations in national statistical systems were obviously affected.

To ensure continuity of key data collection activities, NSOs acted immediately by adopting innovative solutions such as (i) hastening the shift from traditional face-to-face interviewing to virtual data collection methods such as CATI, CAWI, and web-based self-reporting; (ii) employing statistical techniques to facilitate representativeness of incomplete data; (iii) designing secure data access and exchange architectures; and (iv) accelerating efforts in collecting and/or integrating information from nontraditional data sources such as big data.

National statistical systems provided vital data assessing the impact of the pandemic on various sectors of the economy as well as socioeconomic data to identify the most vulnerable segments of the population. This information provided a basis for designing targeted policies and support measures. Moreover, the solutions implemented by some NSOs have provided important lessons for other economies in the region.

Moving forward, data integration and digital technologies can provide impetus for statistical innovation.

As technology continues to advance and become more ubiquitous, and while the world's key development issues remain unresolved, the role of data becomes more vital in designing policies, monitoring programs, and ensuring good governance.

The COVID-19 pandemic has shed light on the importance of timely statistics and the need to invest in the agility and resilience of information systems. While Asia and the Pacific's national data and statistics systems had already started to adopt innovative digital technologies to provide timely data, the pandemic provided an opportunity to accelerate more innovative solutions such as the integration of big data.

As the world begins to recover from the COVID-19 pandemic, NSOs need to constantly evaluate their resources and technical capacities so that they can continue to make investments in innovative solutions that can provide timely yet high-quality data. Such solutions may draw on a combination of traditional and modern data sources and techniques to deliver accurate data for effective policymaking. Furthermore, the use of innovative data sources and disruptive digital technologies may require navigation of issues such as need for new business models, public-private partnerships, and data confidentiality concerns.

References

J. Albert, A. Martinez, K. Miradora, J. Lapuz, M. Martillan, C. De Dios, and I. Sebastian. 2019. *Readiness of National Statistical Systems in Asia and the Pacific for Leveraging Big Data to Monitor the SDGs*. ADB Brief No. 106.

D. Anderson and P. Anderson. 1973. Population Estimates by Humans and Machines. *Photogrammetric Engineering*. 39. pp. 147–154.

Asian Development Bank (ADB). 2020. *Mapping Poverty Through Data Integration and Artificial Intelligence: A Special Supplement to the Key Indicators for Asia and The Pacific 2020*. Manila: ADB.

Australia Bureau of Statistics (ABS). 2020. Consumer Price Index, Australia: March 2020. https://www.abs.gov.au/statistics/economy/price-indexes-and-inflation/consumer-price-index-australia/mar-2020#note-on-the-impact-of-covid-19-on-the-consumer-price-index.

B. Bhaduri, E. Bright, P. Coleman, and M. L. Urban. 2007. LandScan USA: A High-Resolution Geospatial and Modeling Approach for Population Distribution and Dynamics. *Geojournal*. 69. pp. 103–117.

D. Buono, G. Kapetanios, M. Marcellino, G.L. Mazzi, and F. Papailias. 2018. *Evaluation of Nowcasting/ Flash Estimation Based on a Big Set of Indicators*. Paper presented for the 16th Conference of the International Association of Statisticians (IAOS). OECD Headquarters. Paris, France. 19–21 September 2018.

L. Castro. 2008. *Improving Social Statistics in the Philippines through Effective Coordination*. United Nations Expert Group Meeting on the Scope and Content of Social Statistics. United Nations, New York. 9–12 September 2008. https://unstats.un.org/unsd/demographic/meetings/egm/NewYork_8-12Sep.2008/EGM%20Papers/Philippines%20-%20Coordination.pdf.

L. M. Ducharme, J. Tebrake, and Z. Zhan. 2020. Keeping Economic Data Flowing during COVID-19. *International Monetary Fund Blog*. 26 May. https://blogs.imf.org/2020/05/26/keeping-economic-data-flowing-during-covid-19/.

R. Engstrom, J. Hersh, and D. Newhouse. 2017. Poverty from Space: Using High-Resolution Satellite Imagery for Estimating Economic Well-Being. *Policy Research Working Paper No. 8284*. Washington, DC: World Bank.

Global Partnership for Sustainable Development Data (GPSDD). 2019. Data for the Goals Data4Now. https://www.data4sdgs.org/sites/default/files/2019-09/Data%20for%20Now%20Two-Pager.pdf (accessed April 21, 2020).

GPSDD. 2019. Inception Workshop Summary. https://www.data4sdgs.org/sites/default/files/services_files/Data%20for%20Now_Inception%20workshop_Summary%20report.pdf.

Y. Hu and J. Yao. 2019. Illuminating Economic Growth. *IMF Working Paper Series No. 19/77*. Washington, DC: International Monetary Fund.

International Labour Organization (ILO). 2020. *ILO Monitor: COVID-19 and the World of Work. Fifth Edition*. Geneva: ILO.

International Monetary Fund (IMF). 2017. *Quarterly Accounts Manual- 2017 Edition*. Washington, DC: IMF.

IMF. 2020. Consumer Price Index. Special Series on Statistical Issues in Response to COVID-19. Washington: IMF. https://www.imf.org/en/Publications/SPROLLs/covid19-special-notes#stats.

X. Jaravel and M. O'Connell. 2020. Real-time Inflation Measurement During COVID-19. *VoxEU: Center for Economic Policy Research*. 26 July. https://voxeu.org/article/real-time-inflation-measurement-during-covid-19.

N. Jean, M. Burke, M. Xie, W.M. Davis, D. Lobell, and S. Ermon. 2016. *Science*. 353 (6301). pp. 790-794.

C. Linard, M. Gilbert, and A. Tatem. 2011. Assessing the Use of Global Land Cover Data for Guiding Large Area Population Distribution Modelling. *GeoJournal*. 76. pp. 525–53.

C. Linard, M. Gilbert, R. Snow, A. Noor, and A. Tatem. 2012. Population Distribution, Settlement Patterns and Accessibility across Africa in 2010. *PLoS ONE*. 7 (2). e31743. https://doi.org/10.1371/journal.pone.0031743.

A. Martinez. 2016. How Nighttime Lights Help Us Study Development Indicators. *Asian Development Blog*. 22 December. https://blogs.adb.org/blog/how-nighttime-lights-help-us-study-development-indicators.

A. Martinez, and J.A. Albert. 2018. Big Data Can Transform SDG Performance. Here's How. *Asian Development Blog*. 21 June. https://blogs.adb.org/blog/big-data-can-transform-sdg-performance-here-s-how.

T. Mitterling, K. Fenz, A. Martinez, J. Bulan, M. Addawe, R. Durante, and M. Martillan. Forthcoming. *Compiling Granular Population Data Using Geospatial Information*.

D. Moriwaki. 2019. *Nowcasting Unemployment Rates with Smartphone GPS Data*. http://www.master-project-h2020.eu/wp-content/uploads/2019/07/MASTER2019_paper_4.pdf.

D. Newhouse. 2016. Mapping Poverty by Satellite, In *Big Data Innovation Challenge: Pioneering Approaches to Data-Driven Development*. Washington, DC: World Bank.

Organisation for Economic Co-operation and Development (OECD). 2021. The OECD Weekly Tracker of Economic Activity. https://www.oecd.org/economy/weekly-tracker-of-gdp-growth/.

A. Prakash, A.K. Shukla, C. Bhowmick, and R.C.M. Beyer. 2019. Night-Time Luminosity: Does it Brighten Understanding of Economic Activity in India? *Reserve Bank of India Occasional Papers*. 40 (1).

M. Reinsdorf, J. Tebrake, N. O'Hanlon, and B. Graf. 2020. CPI Weights and COVID-19 Expenditure Patterns. *Special Series Note on COVID-19*. Washington, DC: IMF.

Reserve Bank of India (RBI). 2020. RBI Bulletin: November 2020. https://www.rbi.org.in/Scripts/BS_PressReleaseDisplay.aspx?prid=50650.

Stats New Zealand (NZ). 2020. Impacts of COVID-19 on the 2020 CPI Re-Weight. 11 September. https://www.stats.govt.nz/methods/impacts-of-covid-19-on-the-2020-cpi-re-weight.

F. Stevens, A. Gaughan, C. Linard, and A. Tatem. 2015. Disaggregating Census Data for Population Mapping Using Random Forests with Remotely-Sensed and Ancillary Data. *PLoS ONE*. 10 (2). e0107042. https://doi.org/10.1371/journal.pone.0107042.

P.C. Sutton, D. Roberts, C. Elvidge, and K. Baugh. 2001. Census from Heaven: An Estimate of the Global Population Using Nighttime Satellite Imagery, *International Journal of Remote Sensing.* 22 (16). pp. 3061–3076.

A. Tatem, A. Noor, C. von Hagen, A. Di Gregorio, and S. Hay. 2007. High Resolution Population Maps for Low Income Nations: Combining Land Cover and Census in East Africa. *PLoS ONE.* 2 (12). e1298. https://doi.org/10.1371/journal.pone.0001298.

United Nations Conference on Trade and Development (UNCTAD). 2021. COVID-19: Measurement Issues and Assessments. *SDG Pulse.* July 2. https://sdgpulse.unctad.org/covid-19/.

United Nations Economic and Social Commission for Asia and the Pacific (UNESCAP). 2021. *Asia and the Pacific SDG Progress Report 2021.* https://www.unescap.org/sites/default/d8files/knowledge-products/ESCAP_Asia_and_the_Pacific_SDG_Progress_Report_2021.pdf.

UNESCAP, ADB, and United Nations Development Programme (UNDP). 2021. *Responding to the COVID-19 Pandemic: Leaving No One Behind.* Bangkok.

United Nations Economic and Social Council (ECOSOC). 2019. Special Edition: Progress Towards the Sustainable Development Goals. Report of the Secretary-General. In *High-level Political Forum on Sustainable Development*, convened under the auspices of the Economic and Social Council. 2019 Session. 26 July 2018 to 24 July 2019. Agenda Items 5(a) and 6. https://undocs.org/E/2019/68.

United Nations Population Fund (UNFPA). 2017. *UNFPA Strategy for the 2020 Round of Population and Housing Censuses (2015–2024).* UNFPA Inter-Divisional Working Group on Census.

United Nations Statistics Division (UNSD). 2008. The System of National Accounts. https://unstats.un.org/unsd/nationalaccount/sna.asp.

UNSD. 2014. Fundamental Principles of Official Statistics. https://unstats.un.org/unsd/dnss/gp/fundprinciples.aspx.

UNSD. 2019. Data For Now. https://unstats.un.org/capacity-development/data-for-now (accessed 21 April 2020).

UNSD. 2020. Data For Now in Bangladesh. https://unstats.un.org/capacity-development/data-for-now/data-for-now-in-Bangladesh/ (accessed 21 April 2021).

United Nations Sustainable Development Solutions Network (UNSDSN). 2015. *Data for Development: A Needs Assessment for SDG Monitoring and Statistical Capacity Development.* https://sustainabledevelopment.un.org/content/documents/2017Data-for-Development-Full-Report.pdf.

K. Watanabe and T. Watanabe. 2014. Estimating Daily Inflation Using Scanner Data: A Progress Report. *UTokyo Price Project Working Paper Series 020.* University of Tokyo, Graduate School of Economics.

World Bank. Undated. *Notes on the Statistical Capacity Indicator.* https://datatopics.worldbank.org/statisticalcapacity/files/Note.pdf.

World Bank. 2021a. *Statistical Capacity Indicators Databank.* https://databank.worldbank.org/reports.aspx?source=Statistical-capacity-indicators.

World Bank. 2021b. *Measuring the Statistical Performance of Countries: An Overview of Updates to the World Bank Statistical Capacity Index.* https://documents1.worldbank.org/curated/en/815721616086786412/pdf/Measuring-the-Statistical-Performance-of-Countries-An-Overview-of-Updates-to-the-World-Bank-Statistical-Capacity-Index.pdf.

Definitions

Regional Trends and Tables

Indicator	Definition
PEOPLE	
Population	
Midyear Population	Estimates of the midyear de facto population. De facto population includes all persons physically present in the country or economy during the census day, including foreign, military, and diplomatic personnel and their accompanying household members; and transient foreign visitors in the economy or in harbors. Note: Some economies have population data referenced to different period end points (e.g., 1 January for the Kyrgyz Republic, 31 December for the People's Republic of China, and 1 October for India).
Growth Rates in Population	Number of people added to (or subtracted from) a population over a given period of time because of natural increase and net migration, expressed as a percentage of the population at the given period of time.
Net International Migration Rate	Number of immigrants minus the number of emigrants over a period, divided by the person-years lived by the population of the receiving country or economy over that period. It is expressed as net number of migrants per 1,000 population.
Urban Population (as % of total population)	Population living in urban areas, defined in accordance with the national definition or as used in the most recent population census. Because of national differences in the characteristics that distinguish urban from rural areas, the distinction between urban and rural populations is not amenable to a single definition that would be applicable to all countries or economies. National definitions are most commonly based on size of locality. Population that is not urban is considered rural. The estimated population living in urban areas at midyear as a percentage of the total midyear population in an economy.
Age Dependency Ratio	Ratio of the nonworking-age population to the working-age population. Since economies define working age differently, a straightforward application of the definition will lead to noncomparable data. The Asian Development Bank therefore uses the following United Nations definition that can be calculated directly from an age distribution: $\frac{\text{Population aged (0–14) + (65 and over) years}}{\text{Population aged (15–64) years}} \times 100$
Labor Force and Employment	
Labor Force Participation Rate	Percentage of the labor force to the working-age population. The labor force is the sum of those employed and unemployed but seeking work. The labor force participation rate measures the extent of the economically active working-age population in an economy. It provides an indication of the relative size of the supply of labor available for the production of goods and services in the economy. It must be noted that the definition of working-age population varies across economies. Note: Recommendations from the 19th International Conference of Labour Statisticians have been adopted by some economies, and hence these economies may not have comparable data across years. The conference provides the statistical concept of work for reference purposes; and the operational concepts, definitions, and guidelines for (i) three distinct subsets of work activities, referred to as forms of work, which include own-use production work, employment work, and volunteer work; (ii) related classifications of the population according to their labor force status and main work status; and (iii) measures of labor underutilization. The concept of employment has also been refined to refer to work for pay or profit.
Employment in Agriculture	Employment in agriculture, including forestry and fishing, that corresponds to division 1 (International Standard of Industrial Classification [ISIC] revision 2), tabulation categories A and B (ISIC revision 3), and category A of ISIC revision 4.

(continued on next page)

Indicator	Definition
Employment in Industry	Employment in industry includes mining and quarrying; manufacturing; electricity, gas, steam, and air-conditioning supply; water supply; sewage, waste management, and remediation activities; and construction.
Employment in Mining and Quarrying	Employment in mining and quarrying that corresponds to division 2 (ISIC revision 2), tabulation category C (ISIC revision 3), and category B of ISIC revision 4.
Employment in Manufacturing	Employment in manufacturing that corresponds to division 3 (ISIC revision 2), tabulation category D (ISIC revision 3), and category C of ISIC revision 4.
Employment in Electricity, Gas, Steam, and Air-Conditioning Supply; Water Supply; Sewerage, Waste Management and Remediation Activities	Employment in electricity, gas, steam, and air-conditioning supply; water supply; sewerage, waste management, and remediation activities that corresponds to division 4 (ISIC revision 2), tabulation category E (ISIC revision 3), and categories D and E of ISIC revision 4.
Employment in Construction	Employment in construction that corresponds to division 5 (ISIC revision 2), tabulation category F (ISIC revisions 3), and category F of ISIC revision 4.
Employment in Service	Employment in service includes wholesale and retail trade; repair of motor vehicles and motorcycles; accommodation and food service activities; transportation and storage; information and communication; financial and insurance activities; real estate activities; and other services.
Employment in Wholesale and Retail Trade; Repair of Motor Vehicles and Motorcycles	Employment in wholesale and retail trade; repair of motor vehicles and motorcycles that corresponds to division 6 (subdivisions 61 and 62, ISIC revision 2); tabulation category G (ISIC revision 3); and category G of ISIC revision 4.
Employment in Transportation and Storage	Employment in transport and storage that corresponds to division 7 (subdivision 71, ISIC revision 2); tabulation category I (subcategories 60–63, ISIC revision 3); and category H of ISIC revision 4.
Employment in Accommodation and Food Service Activities	Employment in accommodation and food service activities that corresponds to division 6 (subdivision 63, ISIC revision 2); tabulation category H (ISIC revision 3); and category I of ISIC revision 4.
Employment in Information and Communication	Employment in information and communication that corresponds to division 7 (subdivision 72, ISIC revision 2); tabulation category I (subcategory 64, ISIC revision 3); and category J of ISIC revision 4.
Employment in Financial and Insurance Activities	Employment in financial and insurance activities that corresponds to division 8 (subdivisions 81–82, ISIC revision 2), tabulation category J (ISIC revision 3), and category K of ISIC revision 4.
Employment in Real Estate Activities	Employment in real estate activities that corresponds to division 8 (subdivision 83, ISIC revision 2); tabulation category K (subcategory 70, ISIC revision 3); and category L of ISIC revision 4.
Employment in Other Services	Employment in other services that corresponds to divisions 9 and 0 (ISIC revision 2), tabulation categories L to Q (ISIC revision 3), and categories M to U of ISIC revision 4.
Underemployment	Persons in time-related underemployment comprise all persons in employment who satisfy the following three criteria during the reference period: a) are willing to work additional hours; b) are available to work additional hours i.e., are ready, within a specified subsequent period, to work additional hours given opportunities for additional work; and c) worked less than a threshold relating to working time (i.e., persons whose hours actually worked in all jobs during the reference period were below a threshold, to be chosen according to national circumstances). The time-related underemployment (TRU) rate is calculated as follows: $\text{TRU (\%)} = \frac{\text{Persons in time-related underemployment}}{\text{Persons employed}} \times 100$
Poverty Indicators	
Proportion of Population below $1.90 a Day (2011 PPP)	Percentage of the population living on less than $1.90 a day at 2011 purchasing power parity (PPP).
Proportion of Population below $3.20 a Day (2011 PPP)	Percentage of the population living on less than $3.20 a day at 2011 PPP.

(continued on next page)

Indicator	Definition
Income Ratio of Highest 20% to Lowest 20%	Income or consumption share that accrues to the richest 20% of the population, divided by the income or consumption share of the lowest 20% of the population.
Gini Coefficient or Index	Measure of the degree to which an economy's income distribution diverges from perfect equal distribution. A value of zero (0) implies perfect equality while a value of one (1) implies perfect inequality.
Human Development Index	Composite index of long and healthy life (measured by life expectancy at birth), knowledge (measured by expected years of schooling and mean years of schooling), and decent standard of living (measured by gross national income per capita in United States [US] PPP dollars).
Social Indicators	
Life Expectancy at Birth	Number of years that a newborn is expected to live if prevailing patterns of mortality at the time of his or her birth are to stay the same throughout his or her life.
Crude Birth Rate	Ratio of the total number of live births in a given period to the midyear total population of the same period, expressed per 1,000 people.
Crude Death Rate	Ratio of the number of deaths occurring within a given period to the midyear total population of the same period, expressed per 1,000 people.
Total Fertility Rate	Number of children that would be born to a woman if she were to live to the end of her childbearing years and bear children in accordance with current age-specific fertility rates.
Primary Education Completion Rate	Total number of new entrants in the last grade of primary education, regardless of age, expressed as a percentage of the total population at the theoretical entrance age to the last grade of primary education. This indicator is also known as "gross intake ratio to the last grade of primary." The ratio can exceed 100% due to overaged and underaged children who enter primary school late, early, and/or repeat grades.
Adult Literacy Rate	The percentage of the population aged 15 years and older who can both read and write (with understanding) a short simple statement on his or her everyday life. Generally, literacy also encompasses numeracy, i.e., the ability to make simple arithmetic calculations.
Expected years of schooling, primary to tertiary	Number of years a person of school entrance age can expect to spend within the specified level of education (from primary to tertiary level).
Mean years of schooling	Average number of completed years of education of an economy's population aged 25 years and older, excluding years spent repeating individual grades.
Pupil to qualified teacher ratio	The total number of pupils and students in the relevant level in a given academic year expressed as a percentage of the number of qualified teachers in the same level in that academic year. A qualified teacher has the minimum academic qualifications necessary to teach at a specific level of education in a given economy. This is usually related to the subject(s) they teach. The higher the pupil to qualified teacher ratio, the lower the relative access of pupils to qualified teachers.
Pupil to trained teacher ratio	The total number of pupils and students in the relevant level in a given academic year expressed as a percentage of the number of trained teachers in the same level in that academic year. A trained teacher has fulfilled at least the minimum organized teacher-training requirements (pre-service or in-service) to teach a specific level of education according to the relevant national policy or law. These requirements usually include pedagogical knowledge (broad principles and strategies of classroom management and organization that transcend the subject matter being taught—typically approaches, methods, and techniques of teaching) and professional knowledge (knowledge of statutory instruments and other legal frameworks that govern the teaching profession). The higher the pupil to trained teacher ratio, the lower the relative access of pupils to trained teachers. Results can be compared with established national norms on the number of pupils per trained teacher for each level of education.
Physicians	Physicians, including general and specialist medical practitioners, expressed in terms of the number per 1,000 people.

(continued on next page)

Indicator	Definition
Hospital Beds	In-patient beds for both acute and chronic care available in public, private, general, and specialized hospitals and rehabilitation centers expressed in terms of the number per 1,000 people.
Number of Adults Living with HIV	All adults, defined as men and women aged 15 years and older, with HIV infection, whether or not they have developed symptoms of AIDS, estimated to be alive at the end of a specific year.
ECONOMY AND OUTPUT	
National Accounts	
Gross Domestic Product	Unduplicated market value of the total production activity of all resident producer units within the area's economic territory during a given period. It is calculated without making deductions for depreciation of fabricated assets or for depletion and degradation of natural resources. Transfer payments are excluded from the calculation of gross domestic product (GDP). GDP can be calculated using the production, expenditure, and income approaches. Production-based GDP is the sum of the gross value added by all resident producers in the economy, plus any taxes and minus any subsidies not included in the value of the products. Gross value added is the net output of an industry after adding up all outputs and subtracting intermediate inputs. Income-based GDP is the sum of the compensation of employees, mixed income, operating surplus, consumption of fixed capital, and taxes, less subsidies on production and imports. Expenditure-based GDP is the sum of final consumption expenditure of households, nonprofit institutions serving households, and the government; gross capital formation; and exports minus imports of goods and services. GDP can be measured at current prices (the prices of the current reporting period), and constant prices (obtained by expressing values in terms of a base period and chain volume measure).
GDP at PPP	Measures obtained by using PPP to convert the GDP into a common currency, and by valuing them at a uniform price level. They are the spatial equivalent of a time series of GDP for a single economy expressed at constant prices. At the level of GDP, they are used to compare the size of economies.
GDP at Current US Dollar	GDP at local currency units are obtained from the economy's official sources and are converted to US dollars using the official exchange rates from the International Monetary Fund (IMF). The exchange rates used are expressed as the average rate for a period of time (average of period), calculated as annual averages based on the monthly averages (local currency units relative to the US dollar).
GDP per Capita at PPP	GDP at PPP, divided by the midyear population.
GNI per Capita, Atlas Method	The gross national income (GNI) converted to US dollars using the World Bank Atlas method, divided by the midyear population. GNI is the sum of value added by all resident producers, plus any product taxes (less subsidies) not included in the valuation of output, plus net receipts of primary income (compensation of employees and property income) from abroad. GNI, calculated in national currency, is usually converted to US dollars at official exchange rates for comparisons across economies, although an alternative rate is used when the official exchange rate is judged to diverge by an exceptionally large margin from the rate actually applied in international transactions. To smooth fluctuations in prices and exchange rates, a special Atlas method of conversion is used by the World Bank. This applies a conversion factor that averages the exchange rate for a given year and the 2 preceding years, adjusted for differences in rates of inflation between the economy, and through 2000, the G-5 countries (France, Germany, Japan, the United Kingdom, and the US). From 2001, these countries include the Euro area, Japan, the United Kingdom, and the US.
GDP per Capita at Current US Dollar	GDP at current US dollar value, divided by the midyear population.

(continued on next page)

Indicator	Definition
Agriculture Value Added	The gross output of the agriculture sector, less the corresponding value of intermediate consumption. The industrial origin of value added is determined by ISIC revision 4, where agriculture corresponds to ISIC Section A and includes agriculture, forestry, and fishing.
Industry Value Added	The gross output of industry sectors, less the corresponding value of intermediate consumption. The industrial origin of value added is determined by ISIC revision 4, where industry corresponds to ISIC Sections B-F and includes mining and quarrying (B); manufacturing (C); electricity, gas, steam, and air-conditioning supply (D); water supply; sewerage, waste management, and remediation activities (E); and construction (F).
Services Value Added	The gross output of services sectors, less the corresponding value of intermediate consumption. The industrial origin of value added is determined by ISIC revision 4, where services corresponds to ISIC Sections G-U and includes wholesale and retail trade; repair of motor vehicles and motorcycles (G); transport and storage (H); accommodation and food service activities (I); information and communication (J); financial and insurance activities (K); real estate activities (L); professional, scientific, and technical activities (M); administrative and support service activities (N); public administration and defense; compulsory social security (O); education (P); human health and social work activities (Q); arts, entertainment, and recreation (R); other service activities (S); activities of households as employers; undifferentiated goods- and services-producing activities of households for own use (T); and activities of extraterritorial organizations and bodies (U).
Household Consumption Expenditure	Market value of all goods and services, including durable products (such as cars, washing machines, and home computers), purchased or received as income in kind by households. It excludes purchases of dwellings but includes imputed rent for owner-occupied dwellings. It also includes payments and fees to governments to obtain permits and licenses. The expenditure of nonprofit institutions serving households is generally included for most economies.
Government Consumption Expenditure	Includes all current outlays on purchases of goods and services (including wages and salaries of government employees). It also includes most expenditure on national defense and security but excludes government military expenditures that are part of public investment.
Gross Capital Formation	Total value of gross fixed capital formation, changes in inventories, and acquisitions less disposals of valuables. Gross fixed capital formation is the total value of a producer's acquisitions, less disposals, of tangible goods (such as buildings) and intangible goods (such as computer software) that are intended for use in production during several accounting periods, plus certain specified expenditure on services that adds to the value of non-produced assets. Changes in inventories are changes in stocks of produced goods and goods for intermediate consumption, and the net increase in the value of work in progress. Valuables are goods (such as precious metals and works of art) that are not used up in production but are acquired as stores of value in the expectation that they will retain or increase their value over time.
Exports of Goods and Services	Consist of sales, bartering, or gifts or grants of goods and services from residents to nonresidents. The treatment of exports in the System of National Accounts is generally identical with that in the balance of payments accounts as described in the IMF's Balance of Payments Manual.
Imports of Goods and Services	Consist of purchases, bartering, or receipts of gifts or grants of goods and services by residents from nonresidents. The treatment of imports in the System of National Accounts is generally identical with that in the balance of payments accounts as described in the IMF's Balance of Payments Manual.
Gross Domestic Saving	Difference between GDP and final consumption expenditure, where final consumption expenditure is the sum of the final consumption of household, nonprofit institutions serving households, and the government.
Production	
Agriculture Production Index	Relative level of the aggregate volume of agricultural production for each year in comparison with the base period. It is based on the sum of price-weighted quantities of different agricultural commodities produced after deductions of quantities used as seed and feed weighted in a similar manner. The resulting aggregate therefore represents disposable production for any use, except as seed and feed.

(continued on next page)

Indicator	Definition
Manufacturing Production Index	An index covering production in manufacturing. The exact coverage, the weighting system, and the methods of calculation vary from economy to economy, but the divergences are less important than, for example, in the case of price and wage indexes.
MONEY, FINANCE, AND PRICES	
Prices	
Consumer Price Index	An index that measures changes in prices against a reference period of a basket of goods and services purchased by households. Based on the purpose of the consumer price index, different baskets of goods and services can be selected. For macroeconomic purposes, a broad-based basket is used to represent the relative price movement of household final consumption expenditure.
Food and Nonalcoholic Beverages Price Index	An index that covers food and nonalcoholic beverages purchased by the household mainly for consumption or preparation at home including services for food processing for own consumption. The index corresponds to Classification of Individual Consumption by Purpose (COICOP) Version 1999 division 01. Excluded are food and nonalcoholic beverages that are provided as part of a food-serving service under hotels and restaurants (COICOP division 11).
Alcoholic Beverages, Tobacco, and Narcotics Price Index	An index that covers the purchase of alcoholic beverages, tobacco, and narcotics, regardless of where these are consumed, but not provided as part of a food-and-beverage-serving service under hotels and restaurants. Services for the production of alcohol for own consumption are also included. The index corresponds to COICOP division 02. Excluded are alcoholic beverages purchased for immediate consumption in hotels, restaurants, cafes, bars, kiosks, street vendors, automatic vending machines, etc. classified under restaurants, cafes, and the like (COICOP Group 11.1.1).
Clothing and Footwear Price Index	An index that covers all clothing materials, garments, articles and accessories, footwear and related services, including cleaning, repair, and hire of clothing and footwear, and the purchase of secondhand clothing and footwear. The index corresponds to COICOP division 03.
Housing, Water, Electricity, Gas, and Other Fuels Price Index	An index that covers goods and services for the use of the house or dwelling and its maintenance and repair; the supply of water and miscellaneous services related to the dwelling; and energy used for heating or cooling. The index corresponds to COICOP division 04.
Furnishings, Household Equipment, and Routine Household Maintenance Price Index	An index that covers a wide range of products to equip the house or dwelling and the household durables, semidurables, and nondurables as well as some household services. Includes all kinds of furniture (including lightning equipment, household textiles, glassware, tableware and household utensils), major and smaller electric household appliances, tools and equipment for house and garden, and goods for routine household maintenance. The index also includes the repair, installation, and rental services of the goods. Domestic services by paid staff in private service, supplied by enterprises or self-employed persons, window-cleaning and disinfecting services, as well as dry-cleaning and laundering of household textiles and carpets, are also included. The index corresponds to COICOP division 05.
Health Price Index	An index that covers health services provided during an overnight stay, services that do not require an overnight stay, diagnostic imaging services, medical laboratory services, patient emergency transportation, and emergency rescue services. The index also includes medicines and health products, covering all products that are separately invoiced from health services, except when administered under the direct supervision of a health care professional during an overnight stay. The index corresponds to COICOP division 06.
Transport Price Index	An index that covers four main categories of goods and services for transportation: (i) purchase of vehicles covers motor cars, motor cycles, bicycles, and animal-drawn vehicles; (ii) goods and services for the operation of the personal transport equipment cover parts and accessories for personal transport equipment, fuels and lubricants, and the repair and maintenance of personal transport equipment including expenditures for parking spaces in garages or in public places, expenditures for tolls, and expenditures to acquire a driving certificate; (iii) transport services

(continued on next page)

Indicator	Definition
	provided by the market, structured by the mode of transport; and (iv) transport services of goods covers postal and courier services, removal and storage services, and the delivery of any kinds of goods when charged separately. The index corresponds to COICOP division 07. It excludes purchases of recreational vehicles such as camper vans, caravans, trailers, aeroplanes, and boats that are classified under the Recreation and Culture Price Index.
Communication Price Index	An index that covers three main groups of goods and services: (i) information and communication equipment, including equipment for the capture, recording, and reproduction of sound and vision; software; and information and communication services; (ii) information and communication services, including telephones and other communication services; internet access services; television and radio licenses; fee and subscription services, including streaming services of films and music; and (iii) repair, maintenance, and rental of information and communication equipment. The index corresponds to COICOP division 08.
Recreation and Culture Price Index	An index that covers a wide range of goods and services for recreation, sport, and culture and is structured into eight groups: (i) recreation durables such as photographic equipment, other major durables for recreation, such as camper vans, boats, yachts, aeroplanes, and the like; (ii) nonmajor durable recreational goods such as games and toys, including video game computers, celebration articles, equipment for sport, camping, and open-air recreation; (iii) garden products and plants and flowers and purchases of pets and expenditures for pets, excluding veterinary services; (iv) recreational services cover rental, maintenance, and repair of goods, veterinary and other services for pets, recreational and leisure services, such as amusement parks, games of chance and expenditures for sporting services, both expenditures for practicing sports as well as expenditures for attendance of sport events; (v) cultural goods such as musical instruments and audio-visual media; (vi) cultural services such as cinemas, theatres, concerts, museums, and other cultural sites, and photographic services; (vii) newspapers, all kinds of books, stationery and drawing materials; and (viii) package holidays that include transportation, accommodation, food provision, or tour guide. The index corresponds to COICOP division 09.
Education Price Index	An index that covers educational services only. It includes: (i) education by radio or television broadcasting as well as e-learning and correspondence courses; (ii) admission and registration fees as well as tuition fees; and (iii) other education-related fees such as camps and/or field trips, course fees, diploma fees, examination fees, graduation fees, laboratory fees, physical education fees, etc. The index corresponds to COICOP division 10. It excludes expenditures on other education-related goods and services such as school uniforms, education support services, such as health-care services, transport services (except in the case of excursions that are part of the normal school program), text books and academic journals, stationery, catering services, and accommodation services.
Restaurants and Hotels Price Index	An index that covers services provided by restaurants, cafes, and similar facilities, either with full or limited- or self-service, or by canteens, cafeterias, or refectories at work or at school and other educational establishment's premises. It also includes catering services and accommodation services. The index corresponds to COICOP division 11.
Miscellaneous Goods and Services Price Index	An index that covers insurance and financial services. It also includes personal care, prostitution, personal effects not elsewhere classified, social protection, financial services not elsewhere classified, and other services not elsewhere classified. The index corresponds to COICOP division 12.
Wholesale Price Index	A measure that reflects changes in the prices paid for goods at various stages of distribution up to the point of retail. It can include prices of raw materials for intermediate and final consumption, prices of intermediate or unfinished goods, and prices of finished goods. The goods are usually valued at purchasers' prices.
Producer Price Index	A measure of the change in the prices of goods and services, either as they leave their place of production or as they enter the production process. A measure of the change in the prices received by domestic producers for their outputs or of the change in the prices paid by domestic producers for their intermediate inputs.

(continued on next page)

Indicator	Definition
GDP Deflator	A measure of the annual rate of price change in the economy as a whole for the period shown, obtained by dividing GDP at current prices by GDP at constant prices.
Money and Finance	
Money Supply	Refers to the total amount of money in circulation in a specific economy. Money supply can be measured in different ways: M1 (Narrow Money) is a measure of money supply that includes all coins and notes (M0) as well as personal money in current accounts. M2 (Intermediate Money) is the sum of M1 and personal money in deposit accounts. M3 (Broad Money) is the sum of M2 and government and other deposits. According to the Organisation for Economic Co-operation and Development, M3 includes currency, deposits with an agreed maturity of up to 2 years, deposits redeemable at notice of up to 3 months and repurchase agreements, money market fund shares or units, and debt securities up to 2 years. Not all economies publish the same types of aggregates, and even when aggregates are the same name (e.g., M1, M2, M3, etc.), their asset composition often differs significantly. Differences in national definitions of lowered-ordered aggregates also arise from differences in the maturity categories of nontransferable deposits included in a particular money aggregate. For example, the definition of M2 in one economy may include time deposits with maturities of 1 year or less, whereas another economy's M2 definition may include time deposits with maturities of 2 years or less. When the monetary policy strategy consists of monetary aggregate targeting, the choice of the definition of the targeted aggregate is guided mainly by two considerations. The aggregate should be sufficiently sensitive to interest rate changes for the central bank to be able to control it and display a stable relationship over time to the movement of the overall price level. Liabilities excluded from broad money are the sum of all exclusions from broad money. They may include deposits; debt securities; loans; insurance, pension, and standardized guarantee schemes; financial derivatives and employee stock options; trade credit and advances; equity; or other items.
Interest Rate on Savings Deposits	Rate paid by commercial and similar banks for savings deposits.
Interest Rate on Time Deposits	Rate paid by commercial and similar banks for time deposits.
Lending Interest Rate	Bank rate that usually meets the short- and medium-term financing needs of the private sector. This rate is normally differentiated according to creditworthiness of borrowers and objectives of financing.
Yield on Short-Term Treasury Bills	Rate at which short-term securities are issued or traded in the market.
Domestic Credit Provided by Banking Sector	Includes all credits to various sectors on a gross basis, except credit to the central government, which is net. The banking sector includes monetary authorities, deposit money banks, and other banking institutions for which data are available (including institutions that do not accept transferable deposits but do incur such liabilities as time and savings deposits). Examples of other banking institutions are savings and mortgage loan institutions and building and loan associations.
Ratio of Bank Nonperforming Loans to Total Gross Loans	Value of nonperforming loans divided by the total value of the loan portfolio (including nonperforming loans before the deduction of loan loss provisions). The amount recorded as nonperforming should be the gross value of the loan as recorded in the balance sheet, not just the amount that is overdue.
Stock Market Price Index	Index that measures changes in the prices of stocks traded in the stock exchange. The price changes of the stocks are usually weighted by their market capitalization.
Stock Market Capitalization	The share price times the number of shares outstanding (including their several classes) for listed domestic companies. Investment funds, unit trusts, and companies whose only business goal is to hold shares of other listed companies are excluded. Data are end of year values converted to US dollars using corresponding year-end foreign exchange rates. Also known as market value.

(continued on next page)

Indicator	Definition
Exchange Rates	
Official Exchange Rate	The exchange rate determined by national authorities or the rate determined in the legally sanctioned exchange market. It is calculated as an annual average based on the monthly averages (local currency units relative to the US dollar).
Purchasing Power Parity Conversion Factor	Number of units of economy B's currency that are needed in economy B to purchase the same quantity of an individual good or service, which one unit of economy A's currency can purchase in economy A.
Price Level Index	Ratio of the relevant PPP to the exchange rate. It is expressed as an index on a base of 100. A price level index (PLI) greater than 100 means that, when the national average prices are converted at exchange rates, the resulting prices tend to be higher on average than prices in the base economy (or economies) of the region (and vice versa). At the level of GDP, PLIs provide a measure of the differences in the general price levels of economies. PLIs are also referred to as comparative price levels.
GLOBALIZATION	
Balance of Payments	
Trade in Goods Balance	Difference between exports and imports of goods.
Trade in Services Balance	Difference between exports and imports of services.
Current Account Balance	Sum of net exports of goods, services, net income, and net current transfers.
Total Remittances	Sum of personal remittances and social benefits. Personal remittances include personal transfers (part of current transfers); compensation of employees less taxes, social contributions, transport, and travel; and capital transfers between households. Social benefits include benefits payable under social security funds and pension funds: they may be in cash or in kind. Includes income from individuals working abroad for short periods, income from individuals residing abroad, and social benefits from abroad.
Foreign Direct Investment	Refers to net inflows of investment to acquire a lasting management interest (10% or more of voting stock) in an enterprise operating in an economy other than that of the investor. It is the sum of equity capital, reinvestment of earnings, other long-term capital, and short-term capital as shown in the balance of payments.
External Trade	
Merchandise Exports and Imports	Covering all movable goods, with a few specified exceptions, the ownership of which changes between a resident and a foreigner. For merchandise exports, it represents the value of the goods and related distributive services at the customs frontier of the exporting economy, i.e., the free on board (FOB) value. Merchandise imports, on the other hand, are reported in cost, insurance, and freight (CIF) values.
Trade in Goods	Sum of merchandise exports and merchandise imports.
Direction of Trade	
Direction of Trade: Merchandise Exports and Imports	The direction of trade represents the value of merchandise exports and imports disaggregated according to an economy's primary trading partners. Imports are reported on a CIF basis and exports are reported on a FOB basis, with the exception of a few economies for which imports are also available in FOB. Time series data includes estimates derived from reports of partner economies for nonreporting and slow-reporting economies.
International Reserves	
International Reserves	External assets that are readily available to, and controlled by, monetary authorities for meeting balance-of-payments financing needs, for intervention in exchange markets to affect the currency exchange rate, and for other related purposes (such as maintaining confidence in the currency and the economy, and serving as a basis for foreign borrowing). Consist of monetary gold, special drawing rights holdings, reserve position in the IMF, currency and deposits, securities (including debt and equity securities), financial derivatives, and other claims (loans and other financial instruments).

(continued on next page)

Indicator	Definition
Ratio of International Reserves to Imports	International reserves outstanding at the end of the year as a proportion of imports of goods from the balance of payments during the year, where imports of goods are expressed in terms of a monthly average. It is a useful measure for reserve needs of economies with limited access to capital markets.
Capital Flows	
Net Official Development Assistance	Concessional flows to developing economies and multilateral institutions provided by official agencies, including state and local governments, or by their executing agencies, administered with the objective of promoting the economic development and welfare of developing economies, and containing a grant element of at least 25%. Net flow takes into account principal repayments for loans, offsetting entries for forgiven debt, and recoveries made on grants.
Net Other Official Flows	Official sector transactions with economies on the Development Assistance Committee List of Official Development Assistance Recipients, which do not meet the conditions for eligibility as official development assistance, either because they are not primarily aimed at development, or because they have a grant element of less than 25%. The Development Assistance Committee list of recipients of official development assistance is available at http://www.oecd.org/dac/financing-sustainable-development/development-finance-standards/daclist.htm. Net flow takes into account principal repayments for loans, offsetting entries for forgiven debt, and recoveries made on grants.
Net Private Flows	Sum of direct investment and portfolio investment. Direct investment is a category of international investment made by a resident entity in one economy (direct investor) with the objective of establishing a lasting interest in an enterprise that is resident in an economy other than that of the investor (direct investment enterprise). "Lasting interest" implies the existence of a long-term relationship between the direct investor and the enterprise and a significant degree of influence by the direct investor on the management of the direct investment enterprise. Direct investment involves both the initial transaction between the two entities and all subsequent capital transactions between them and among affiliated enterprises, both incorporated and unincorporated. Portfolio investment is the category of international investment that covers investment in equity and debt securities, excluding any such instruments that are classified as direct investment or reserve assets.
Aggregate Net Resource Flows	Sum of net official development assistance, net other official flows, and net private flows.
External Indebtedness	
Total External Debt	Debt owed to nonresidents repayable in currency, goods, or services. It is the sum of public, publicly guaranteed, and private nonguaranteed long-term debt, use of IMF credit, and short-term debt. Short-term debt includes all debt having an original maturity of 1 year or less and interest in arrears on long-term debt.
Public and Publicly Guaranteed Debt	Comprises long-term external obligations of public debtors, including the national government, political subdivisions (or an agency of either), and autonomous public bodies, and external obligations of private debtors that are guaranteed for repayment by a public entity.
External Debt as a Percentage of GNI	Total external debt as a percentage of GNI. GNI is the sum of value added by all resident producers plus any product taxes (less subsidies) not included in the valuation of output, plus net receipts of primary income (compensation of employees and property income) from abroad.
External Debt as a Percentage of Exports of Goods and Services and Primary Income	Total external debt as a percentage of exports of goods, services, and primary income. Exports of goods, services, and primary income constitute the total value of exports of goods and services, receipts of compensation of nonresident workers, and investment income from abroad.

(continued on next page)

Indicator	Definition
Total Debt Service Paid	The sum of principal repayments and interest actually paid in currency, goods, or services on long-term debt, interest paid on short-term debt, and repayments (repurchases and charges) to the IMF.
Total Debt Service Paid as a Percentage of Exports of Goods and Services and Primary Income	Total debt service paid as a percentage of exports of goods, services, and primary income.
Tourism	
International Tourist Arrivals	The number of tourists (overnight visitors) who travel to an economy other than that in which they usually reside, and outside their usual environment, for a period not exceeding 12 months, and whose main purpose of visit is other than the activity remunerated from within the economy visited. In some cases, data may also include same-day visitors when data on overnight visitors are not available separately. Data refer to the number of arrivals and not to the number of people.
International Tourism, Receipts	The receipts earned by a destination economy from inbound tourism and covering all tourism receipts resulting from expenditures made by visitors from abroad. These include lodging, food and drinks, fuel, transport in the economy, entertainment, shopping, etc. This concept includes receipts generated by overnight visits as well as by same-day trips. It does, however, exclude the receipts related to international transport by contracted residents of the other economies (for instance ticket receipts from foreigners travelling with a national company).
TRANSPORT AND COMMUNICATIONS	
Transport	
Road Network	This includes both paved and unpaved roads. Paved roads are roads surfaced with crushed stone (macadam) with hydrocarbon binder or bituminized agents, with concrete, or with cobblestones. Unpaved roads are roads surfaced with a stabilized base, but not surfaced with crushed stone, hydrocarbon binder or bituminized agents, concrete, or cobblestones.
Passenger Kilometers Traveled	A passenger-kilometer is a unit of measurement representing the transport of 1 passenger by a defined mode of transport, e.g., road, over 1 kilometer.
Freight Kilometers Traveled	A ton-kilometer is a unit of measurement representing the transport of 1 metric ton of goods (including packaging and tare weights of intermodal transport units) by a defined mode of transport, e.g., road, over a distance of 1 kilometer. Only the distance on the national territory of the reporting economy is taken into account for national, international, and transit transport.
Registered Vehicles	Mode-specific vehicle registrations refer to the number of newly (first-time) registered vehicles recorded by the authorities. This publication reports cumulative number of vehicle registrations.
Road Traffic Deaths	Death caused by a road traffic crash and occurring within 24 hours (Kiribati, the Federated States of Micronesia, Solomon Islands, Timor-Leste, Tonga); 7 days (Azerbaijan, Bhutan, the People's Republic of China, Tajikistan, Turkmenistan, Viet Nam); 30 days (Armenia, Australia, Cambodia, Fiji, India, Indonesia, Japan, Kazakhstan, the Republic of Korea, Lao PDR , Malaysia, Mongolia, Myanmar, Nepal, New Zealand, Papua New Guinea, Singapore, Sri Lanka, Uzbekistan); unlimited time period (Afghanistan, the Cook Islands, Georgia, Maldives, the Philippines, Samoa, Thailand); within a year (the Kyrgyz Republic); no definition for other economies.
Rail Lines	Rail lines are the length of railway route available for train service, irrespective of the number of parallel tracks.
Rail Network	Length of rail lines divided by the land area.
Railways, Passengers Carried	Passengers carried by railway are the number of passengers transported by rail multiplied by kilometers traveled.
Railways, Goods Transported	Goods transported by railway are the volume of goods transported by railway, measured in metric tons multiplied by kilometers traveled.
Aviation Total Passenger Kilometers	The number of aviation passengers carried, including both domestic and international aircraft passengers of air carriers registered in a given economy, multiplied by kilometers traveled.

(continued on next page)

Indicator	Definition
Aviation Freight Transport	The volume of aviation freight, express, and diplomatic bags carried on each flight stage (operation of an aircraft from takeoff to its next landing), measured in metric tons, multiplied by kilometers traveled.
Container Port Traffic	Measures the flow of containers from land to sea transport modes, and vice versa, in twenty-foot equivalent units (TEU), a standard-size container. Data refer to coastal shipping as well as international journeys. Transshipment traffic is counted as two lifts at the intermediate port (once to offload and again as an outbound lift) and includes empty units.
Liner Shipping Connectivity Index (LSCI)	The current version of the LSCI is generated from the following six components: (i) the number of scheduled ship calls per week in the economy; (ii) deployed annual capacity in TEU: total deployed capacity offered at the economy; (iii) the number of regular liner shipping services from and to the economy; (iv) the number of liner shipping companies that provide services from and to the economy; (v) the average size in TEU of the ships deployed by the scheduled service with the largest average vessel size; and (vi) the number of other economies that are connected to the economy through direct liner shipping services.
Logistics Performance Index	An interactive benchmarking tool created by the World Bank to help economies identify the challenges and opportunities they face in their performance on trade logistics and what they can do to improve their performance.
Communications	
Telephone Subscribers	Fixed-telephone subscriptions refer to the sum of active number of analogue fixed telephone lines, voice-over-IP subscriptions, fixed wireless local loop subscriptions, ISDN voice-channel equivalents, and fixed public payphones.
Mobile Phone Subscribers	The proportion of individuals who used a mobile telephone in the 3 months prior to data collection. A mobile (cellular) telephone refers to a portable telephone subscribing to a public mobile telephone service using cellular technology, which provides access to the PSTN. This includes analogue and digital cellular systems and technologies such as IMT-2000 (3G) and IMT- Advanced. Users of both postpaid subscriptions and prepaid accounts are included.
Fixed-Broadband Subscribers	Fixed-broadband subscriptions refer to fixed subscriptions to high-speed access to the public internet (a TCP/IP connection), at downstream speeds equal to, or greater than, 256 kilobits per second. This includes cable modem, DSL, fiber-to-the-home/building, other fixed (wired)- broadband subscriptions, satellite broadband and terrestrial fixed wireless broadband. This total is measured irrespective of the method of payment. It excludes subscriptions that have access to data communications (including the Internet) via mobile-cellular networks. It should include fixed WiMAX and any other fixed wireless technologies. It includes both residential subscriptions and subscriptions for organizations.
Internet Users	The frequency of internet use by individuals who used the internet from any location in the 3 months prior to data collection. Internet can be used via a computer, mobile, phone, personal digital assistant, games machine, digital TV etc.
ENERGY AND ELECTRICITY	
Energy	
GDP per Unit of Energy Use	The ratio of GDP to total energy use (measured per petajoule) with GDP converted to 2017 constant international dollars using PPP rates. An international dollar has the same purchasing power over GDP as a US dollar has in the US.

(continued on next page)

Indicator	Definition
Energy Production	Primary energy production that is the capture or extraction of fuels or energy from natural energy flows, the biosphere, and natural reserves of fossil fuels within the national territory in a form suitable for use. Inert matter removed from the extracted fuels and quantities reinjected, flared, or vented are not included. The resulting products are referred to as primary products.
Energy Use	Energy production plus imports minus exports, minus international marine bunkers, minus international aviation bunkers, minus stock changes. Also referred to as energy supply.
Energy Imports, Net	Energy imports, net estimated as energy use less production, both measured in petajoules.
Electricity	
Electricity Production	Gross production, which is the sum of the electrical energy production by all the generating units and/or installations concerned (including pumped storage), measured at the output terminals of the main generators. Also referred to as electricity generation.
Sources of Electricity	Refers to the different types of technology and/or processes for the generation or production of electricity, including: (i) electricity from combustible fuels, which refers to the production of electricity from the combustion of fuels that are capable of igniting or burning, i.e., reacting with oxygen to produce a significant rise in temperature; (ii) hydroelectricity, which refers to electricity produced from devices driven by fresh, flowing, or falling water; (iii) nuclear electricity, which refers to electricity generated by nuclear plants; and (iv) other electricity, which includes solar, wind, wave, tidal, other marine electricity, geothermal, electricity generated from chemical heat, and electricity from other sources not elsewhere specified.
Electric Power Consumption Per Capita	Total electricity consumption divided by midyear population, where consumption refers to energy-industries-own-use and final consumption. Energy-industries-own-use refers to the consumption of electricity for the direct support of the production and preparation for use of fuels and energy. Final consumption refers to the consumption of electricity by manufacturing, construction and nonfuel mining, transport, and households and other consumers (nonenergy use being irrelevant for electricity).
ENVIRONMENT	
Land	
Agricultural Land or Area	Land area that is arable, under permanent crops, and/or under permanent meadows and pastures.
Arable Land	Land under temporary agricultural crops (double-cropped areas are counted only once), temporary meadows for mowing or pasture, land under market, and kitchen gardens and land temporarily fallow (less than 5 years). The abandoned land resulting from shifting cultivation is not included. Data for arable land are not meant to indicate the amount of land that are potentially cultivable.
Permanent Cropland	Land cultivated with long-term crops that do not have to be replanted for several years (such as cocoa and coffee); land under trees and shrubs producing flowers, such as roses and jasmine; and nurseries (except those for forest trees, which should be classified under "forestry"). Permanent meadows and pastures are excluded from land under permanent crops.
Deforestation Rate	Rate of permanent conversion of natural forest area into other uses, including shifting cultivation, permanent agriculture, ranching, settlements, and infrastructure development. Deforested areas do not include areas logged but intended for regeneration or areas degraded by fuel-wood gathering, acid precipitation, or forest fires. A negative rate indicates reforestation or increase in forest area.
Pollution	

(continued on next page)

Indicator	Definition
Carbon Dioxide Emissions	Carbon dioxide emissions, largely by-products of energy production and use, account for the largest share of greenhouse gases, which are associated with global warming. Anthropogenic carbon dioxide emissions result primarily from fossil fuel combustion and cement manufacturing. In combustion, different fossil fuels release different amounts of carbon dioxide for the same level of energy used: oil releases about 50% more carbon dioxide than natural gas, while coal releases about twice as much. Cement manufacturing releases about half a metric ton of carbon dioxide for each metric ton of cement produced. Data for carbon dioxide emissions include gases from the burning of fossil fuels and cement manufacture but excludes emissions from land use such as deforestation.
Nitrous Oxide Emissions	Nitrous oxide emissions are mainly from fossil fuel combustion, fertilizers, rainforest fires, and animal waste. Nitrous oxide is a powerful greenhouse gas, with an estimated atmospheric lifetime of 114 years, compared with 12 years for methane. The per-kilogram global warming potential of nitrous oxide is nearly 310 times that of carbon dioxide within 100 years.
Methane Emissions	Methane emissions are those stemming from human activities such as agriculture and from industrial methane production. A kilogram of methane is 21 times as effective at trapping heat in the earth's atmosphere as a kilogram of carbon dioxide within 100 years.
Other Greenhouse Gases	By-product emissions of hydrofluorocarbons, perfluorocarbons, and sulfur hexafluoride. Although emissions of these artificial gases are small, they are more powerful greenhouse gases than carbon dioxide, with much higher atmospheric lifetimes and high global warming potential.
Freshwater	
Internal Renewable Water Resources	Internal renewable water resources (IRWR) refer to the long-term average annual flow of rivers and recharge of aquifers generated from endogenous precipitation. Double-counting of surface water and groundwater resources is avoided by deducting the overlap from the sum of the surface water and groundwater resources. IRWR in billion cubic meters per year refers to surface water produced internally, plus groundwater produced internally deducted by the overlap between surface water and groundwater. IRWR in cubic meters per inhabitant per year is calculated as total annual IRWR divided by total population.
Annual Freshwater Withdrawals	Sum of surface water withdrawal and groundwater withdrawal. Total water withdrawal summed by sector deducted by: desalinated water produced, direct use of treated wastewater, and direct use of agricultural drainage water.
Water Productivity	Water productivity is the ratio of the net benefits from crop, forestry, fishery, livestock, and mixed agricultural systems to the amount of water used to produce those benefits. It is calculated as GDP in constant US dollar prices, divided by annual total water withdrawal.
GOVERNMENT AND GOVERNANCE	
Government Finance	
Government Net lending/Net borrowing	Net lending (+) / net borrowing (–) is a summary measure indicating the extent to which government is either putting financial resources at the disposal of other sectors in the economy or abroad, or utilizing the financial resources generated by other sectors in the economy or from abroad. It may be viewed as an indicator of the financial impact of government activity on the rest of the economy and the rest of the world. Net lending (+) / net borrowing (–) is a balancing item calculated as the net operating balance (revenue minus expense) minus the net investment in nonfinancial assets. Net lending/net borrowing is also equal to the net acquisition of all financial assets minus the net incurrence of all liabilities from transactions. For economies following the IMF's Government Finance Statistics 1986 framework, the indicator refers to the overall budgetary surplus / deficit measured as the difference between total revenue (including grants) and total expenditure (including net lending).

(continued on next page)

Indicator	Definition
Government Taxes	Taxes are compulsory, unrequited amounts receivable by government units from institutional units. Certain compulsory receivables, such as fines, penalties, and most social security contributions are not considered taxes. For economies following the IMF's Government Finance Statistics 1986 framework, tax revenue are compulsory transfers to the central government for public purposes, which includes social security contributions.
Government Revenue	Government revenue is an increase in net worth resulting from a transaction. Revenue transactions have counterpart entries either in an increase in assets or in a decrease in liabilities - thereby increasing net worth. General government units have four types of revenue: (i) compulsory levies in the form of taxes and certain types of social contributions; (ii) property income derived from the ownership of assets; (iii) sales of goods and services; and (iv) other transfers receivable from other units. For economies following the IMF's Government Finance Statistics 1986 framework, the total revenue (including grants) consists of current and capital revenues. Current revenue is the revenue accruing from taxes as well as all current nontax revenues, except transfers received from foreign governments and international institutions. Capital revenue constitutes the proceeds from the sale of nonfinancial capital assets.
Government Expenditure	Government expenditure is the sum of expense and the net investment in nonfinancial assets. Expense is a decrease in net worth resulting from a transaction. The major types of expense are compensation of employees, use of goods and services subsidies, grants, social benefits, and other expense. The acquisition of a nonfinancial asset by purchase or barter is not an expense because it has no effect on net worth. Similarly, amounts payable on loans extended and repayments on loans incurred are not classified as expense. Nonfinancial assets are economic assets other than financial assets. Nonfinancial assets are stores of value and provide benefits either through their use in the production of goods and services or in the form of property income and holding gains. These assets are classified as fixed assets, inventories, valuables, and nonproduced assets. For economies following the IMF's Government Finance Statistics 1986 framework, total expenditure (including net lending) consists of current and capital expenditures. Current expenditure comprises purchases of goods and services by the central government, transfers to noncentral government units and to households, subsidies to producers, and interest on public debt. Capital expenditure covers outlays for the acquisition or construction of capital assets and for the purchase of intangible assets, as well as capital transfers to domestic and foreign recipients. Loans and advances for capital purposes are also included.
Government Expenditure on Education	Government expenditure on education includes expenditure on services provided to individual pupils and students and expenditure on services provided on a collective basis. Expenditure on education is allocated to pre-primary and primary education, secondary education, post-secondary nontertiary education, tertiary education, subsidiary services to education, education not definable by level, and research and development (R&D) education. For economies following the IMF's Government Finance Statistics 1986 framework, the indicator refers to government expenditure on education affairs and services.
Government Expenditure on Health	Government expenditure on health includes expenditure on services provided to individual persons and services provided on a collective basis. Expenditure on health is allocated to medical products, appliances, and equipment; outpatient services; hospital services; public health services; R&D health; and health not elsewhere classified. For economies following the IMF's Government Finance Statistics 1986 framework, the indicator refers to government expenditure on health affairs and services.

(continued on next page)

Indicator	Definition
Government Expenditure on Social Protection	Government expenditure on social protection includes expenditure on services and transfers provided to individual persons and households and expenditure on services provided on a collective basis. Expenditure on social protection is allocated to sickness and disability, old age, survivors, family and children, unemployment, housing, social exclusion not elsewhere classified, and R&D social protection. For economies following the IMF's Government Finance Statistics 1986 framework, the indicator refers to government expenditure on social security and welfare affairs and services.
Governance	
Time Required to Start Up a Business	Number of calendar days needed to complete the procedures to legally operate a business. If a procedure can be accelerated at additional cost, the fastest procedure, independent of cost, is chosen.
Score (Starting a Business)	The score for starting a business is the simple average of the scores for each of the component indicators: the procedures, time and cost for an entrepreneur to start and formally operate a business, and the paid-in minimum capital requirement.
Rank (Starting a Business)	The ranking of economies on the ease of starting a business is determined by sorting their scores for starting a business.
Corruption Perceptions Index	Ranks countries and territories based on how corrupt or otherwise their public sector is perceived to be. It is a composite index—a combination of polls—drawing on corruption-related data collected by a variety of reputable institutions. The index reflects the views of observers from around the world, including experts living and working in the countries and territories evaluated. From 2000 to 2011, scores ranged from 10 (highly clean) to 0 (highly corrupt). From 2012 onward, calculation of the score has used an updated methodology and is now presented on a 100 (very clean) to 0 (highly corrupt) scale. Due to this difference in methodology, scores from years prior to and including 2011 should not be compared with scores from 2012 onward. An economy's rank indicates its position relative to the other countries or territories included in the index. It is important to keep in mind that an economy's rank can change simply because new economies enter the index or others drop out.

Sustainable Development Goals

Goals and Targets	Statistical Indicators	Definition
Goal 1. End poverty in all its forms everywhere		
Target 1.1: By 2030, eradicate extreme poverty (currently measured as people living on less than $1.90 a day) for all people everywhere.	1.1.1.a: Proportion of the population living below the international poverty line, by sex, age, employment status, and geographical location (urban or rural)	Proportion of the population living on less than $1.90 a day, measured at 2011 international prices, adjusted for purchasing power parity (PPP). Note: The PPP conversion factor for private consumption is the number of units of an economy's currency required to buy the same amount of goods and/or services in the domestic market as a United States (US) dollar would buy in the US.
	1.1.1.b: Proportion of the employed population living below the international poverty line, by sex	Proportion of the employed population living in households with per capita consumption or income below the international poverty line of $1.90 a day. Note: The proportion of working poor in total employment (also known as the working poverty rate) combines data on household income or consumption with labor force framework variables measured at the individual level, and sheds light on the relationship between household poverty and employment. The numbers are International Labour Organization modeled estimates. Employed persons refer to all persons of working age who, during a short reference period such as a day or a week, performed work for others in exchange for pay or profit.
Target 1.2: By 2030, reduce at least by half the proportion of men, women, and children of all ages living in poverty in all its dimensions, according to national definitions.	1.2.1: Proportion of the population living below the national poverty line, by sex, age, and geographical location (urban or rural)	Percentage of the total population living below the national poverty line. Note: National poverty rates are defined at economy-specific poverty lines in local currencies, which are different in real terms across economies and different from the international poverty line of $1.90 a day. Thus, national poverty rates cannot be compared across economies or with the poverty rate of $1.90 a day.
Target 1.3: Implement nationally appropriate social protection systems and measures for all, including floors, and by 2030 achieve substantial coverage of the poor and the vulnerable	1.3.1: Proportion of population covered by social protection floors/systems, by sex, distinguishing children, unemployed persons, older persons, persons with disabilities, pregnant women, newborns, work-injury victims and the poor and the vulnerable.	Percentage of the population effectively covered by a social protection system, including social protection floors, which provide old age pensions, social security, and health insurance benefits. Effective coverage of social protection is measured by the number of people who are either actively contributing to a social insurance scheme or receiving benefits (contributory or noncontributory). Coverage is expressed as a share of the respective population. (i) Population covered by at least one social protection benefit (effective coverage): proportion of the total population receiving at least one contributory or noncontributory cash benefit, or actively contributing to at least one social security scheme. (ii) Older persons: ratio of persons above statutory retirement age receiving an old-age pension to the number of persons above statutory retirement age (including contributory and noncontributory). (iii) Poor persons covered by social assistance: ratio of social assistance recipients to the population living below the national poverty line. (iv) Vulnerable persons covered by social assistance: ratio of social assistance recipients to the total number of vulnerable persons (defined as all children plus adults not covered by contributory benefits and persons above retirement age not receiving contributory benefits, i.e., pensions). (v) Children: ratio of children or households receiving child or family cash benefits to the total number of children or households with children.

(continued on next page)

Goals and Targets	Statistical Indicators	Definition
Goal 2. End hunger, achieve food security and improved nutrition, and promote sustainable agriculture		
Target 2.1: By 2030, end hunger and ensure access by all people, in particular the poor and people in vulnerable situations, including infants, to safe, nutritious, and sufficient food all year round.	2.1.1: Prevalence of undernourishment	Proportion of the population whose habitual food consumption is insufficient to provide the dietary energy levels that are required to maintain a normal active and healthy life. Note: Undernourishment is defined as the condition by which a person has access, on a regular basis, to amounts of food that are insufficient to provide the energy required for conducting a normal, healthy, and active life, given his or her own dietary energy requirements.
Target 2.2: By 2030, end all forms of malnutrition, including achieving, by 2025, the internationally agreed targets on stunting and wasting in children under 5 years of age, and address the nutritional needs of adolescent girls, pregnant and lactating women, and older persons.	2.2.1: Prevalence of stunting—height for age <-2 standard deviation from the median of the World Health Organization (WHO) Child Growth Standards—among children under 5 years of age	Prevalence of stunting—height-for-age <-2 standard deviation from the median of WHO Child Growth Standards—among children under 5 years of age. Note: Child stunting refers to a child who is too short for his or her age as a result of chronic or recurrent malnutrition.
	2.2.2.a: Prevalence of malnutrition—weight for height >+2 standard deviation from the median of the WHO Child Growth Standards—among children under 5 years of age (overweight)	Prevalence of overweight—weight for height >+2 standard deviation from the median of WHO Child Growth Standards—among children under 5 years of age. Note: Child overweight refers to a child who is too heavy for his or her height.
	2.2.2.b: Prevalence of malnutrition—weight for height <-2 standard deviation from the median of the WHO Child Growth Standards—among children under 5 years of age (wasting)	Prevalence of wasting—weight for height <-2 standard deviation from the median of WHO Child Growth Standards—among children under 5 years of age. Note: Child wasting refers to a child who is too thin for his or her height as a result of recent rapid weight loss or the failure to gain weight.
Target 2.a: Increase investment, including through enhanced international cooperation, in rural infrastructure, agricultural research and extension services, technology development, and plant and livestock gene banks in order to enhance agricultural productive capacity in developing countries, in particular least developed countries.	2.a.1: The agriculture orientation index for government expenditures	The Agriculture Orientation Index for Government Expenditures is defined as the agriculture share of government expenditure, divided by the agriculture value-added share of gross domestic product (GDP), where "agriculture" refers to the agriculture, forestry, fishing, and hunting sector. The measure is a currency-free index, calculated as the ratio of these two shares. National governments are requested to compile government expenditures according to the Government Finance Statistics system and the Classification of Functions of Government, and agriculture value-added share of GDP according to the System of National Accounts. Note: Government Expenditure are all expenses and acquisition of nonfinancial assets associated with supporting a particular sector, as defined in the Government Finance Statistics Manual 2014 developed by the International Monetary Fund (IMF).
	2.a.2: Total official flows (official development assistance plus other official flows) to the agriculture sector	Gross disbursements of total official development assistance (ODA) and other official flows from all donors to the agriculture sector. Note: (i) The Development Assistance Committee defines ODA as those flows to countries and territories on the committee's List of ODA Recipients and to multilateral institutions which are: (ii) provided by official agencies, including state and local governments, or by their executive agencies; and

(continued on next page)

Goals and Targets	Statistical Indicators	Definition
		(iii) each transaction is administered with the promotion of the economic development and welfare of developing economies as its main objective; and is concessional in character and conveys a grant element of at least 25% (calculated at a rate of discount of 10%). Other Official Flows are defined as transactions by the official sector which do not meet the conditions for eligibility as ODA, either because they are not primarily aimed at development, or because they are not sufficiently concessional. They also exclude officially supported export credits.
Goal 3. Ensure healthy lives and promote well-being for all at all ages		
Target 3.1: By 2030, reduce the global maternal mortality ratio to less than 70 per 100,000 live births.	3.1.1: Maternal mortality ratio	Number of maternal deaths during a given time period per 100,000 live births during the same time period. Note: The term maternal deaths refers to the annual number of female deaths from any cause related to, or aggravated by, pregnancy or its management (excluding accidental or incidental causes) during pregnancy and childbirth or within 42 days of termination of pregnancy, irrespective of the duration and site of the pregnancy, expressed per 100,000 live births, for a specified time period.
	3.1.2: Proportion of births attended by skilled health personnel	Percentage of childbirths attended by professional health personnel (generally doctors, nurses, or midwives, but can refer to other health professionals providing childbirth care). These are competent maternal and newborn health professionals educated, trained, and regulated to national and international standards. They are competent to: (i) provide and promote evidence-based, human-rights based, quality, socioculturally sensitive, and dignified care to women and newborns; (ii) facilitate physiological processes during labor and delivery to ensure a clean and positive childbirth experience; and (iii) identify and manage or refer women and/or newborns with complications. Note: Having a skilled attendant at the time of delivery is an important lifesaving intervention for both mothers and babies. Not having access to this key assistance is detrimental to the health of women and newborns because it could cause the death of the women and/or the newborn or long-lasting morbidity. Achieving universal coverage for this indicator is therefore essential for reducing maternal and newborn mortality.
Target 3.2: By 2030, end preventable deaths of newborns and children under 5 years of age, with all countries aiming to reduce neonatal mortality to at least as low as 12 per 1,000 live births and under-5 mortality to at least as low as 25 per 1,000 live births.	3.2.1: Under-5 mortality rate	The probability of a child born in a specific year or period dying before reaching the age of 5 years, if subject to age specific mortality rates of that period, expressed per 1,000 live births. Note: The under-5 mortality rate as defined here is, strictly speaking, not a rate (i.e., the number of deaths divided by the number of population at risk during a certain period of time) but a probability of death derived from a life table and expressed as a rate per 1,000 live births.
	3.2.2: Neonatal mortality rate	Probability that a child born in a specific year or period will die during the first 28 completed days of life, if subject to age-specific mortality rates of that period, expressed per 1,000 live births. Note: Neonatal deaths (deaths among live births during the first 28 completed days of life) may be subdivided into early neonatal deaths, occurring during the first 7 days of life, and late neonatal deaths, occurring after the seventh day but before the 28th completed day of life.

(continued on next page)

Goals and Targets	Statistical Indicators	Definition
Target 3.3: By 2030, end the epidemics of AIDS, tuberculosis, malaria, and neglected tropical diseases; and combat hepatitis, water-borne diseases, and other communicable diseases.	3.3.1: Number of new HIV infections per 1,000 uninfected population, by sex, age, and key populations	Number of new HIV infections per 1,000 person-years among the uninfected population.
	3.3.2: Tuberculosis incidence per 100,000 population	Estimated number of new and relapse tuberculosis cases (all forms of tuberculosis, including cases in people living with HIV) arising in a given year, expressed as a rate per 100,000 population.
	3.3.3: Malaria incidence per 1,000 population	The number of new cases of malaria per 1,000 people at risk each year.
Target 3.4: By 2030, reduce by one third premature mortality from noncommunicable diseases through prevention and treatment, and promote mental health and well-being.	3.4.1: Mortality rate attributed to cardiovascular disease, cancer, diabetes, or chronic respiratory disease	Probability of dying between the ages of 30 and 70 years from cardiovascular diseases, cancer, diabetes, or chronic respiratory diseases, defined as the percentage of 30-year-old people who would die before their 70th birthday from cardiovascular disease, cancer, diabetes, or chronic respiratory disease, assuming that a person would experience current mortality rates at every age and he or she would not die from any other cause of death (e.g., injuries or HIV/AIDS). Note: Probability of dying refers to the likelihood that an individual would die between two ages given current mortality rates at each age, calculated using life table methods. The probability of death between two ages may be called a mortality rate.
	3.4.2: Suicide mortality rate	The number of suicide deaths in a year, divided by the population and multiplied by 100,000. Note: The number of suicide deaths refers to crude suicide rates (per 100,000 population).
Target 3.6: By 2020, halve the number of global deaths and injuries from road traffic accidents.	3.6.1: Death rate due to road traffic injuries	Number of road traffic fatal injury deaths per 100,000 population.
Target 3.7: By 2030, ensure universal access to sexual and reproductive health care services, including for family planning, information and education, and the integration of reproductive health into national strategies and programme	3.7.1: Proportion of women of reproductive age (15–49 years) who have their need for family planning satisfied by modern methods	The percentage of women of reproductive age (15–49 years) who desire either to have no (additional) children or to postpone the next child, and who are currently using a modern method of contraception. . The indicator is also referred to as the demand for family planning satisfied with modern methods.
	3.7.2: Adolescent birth rate (15–19 years) per 1,000 women in that age group	Annual number of births to females aged 15–19 years per 1,000 females in the respective age group.
Target 3.8: Achieve universal health coverage, including financial risk protection, access to quality essential healthcare services and access to safe, effective, quality and affordable essential medicines and vaccines for all	3.8.1 Coverage of essential health services (defined as the average coverage of essential services based on tracer interventions that include reproductive, maternal, newborn and child heath, infectious diseases, non-communicable diseases and service capacity and access, among the general and the most disadvantaged population)	The indicator is an index reported on a unitless scale of 0 to 100, which is calculated as the geometric mean of 14 tracer indicators of health service coverage. Note: The index of health service coverage is calculated as the geometric means of tracer indicators. The tracer indicators are organized by four broad categories of service coverage: (i) reproductive, maternal, newborn, and child health; (ii) infectious diseases; (iii) noncommunicable diseases; and (iv) service capacity and access.

(continued on next page)

Goals and Targets	Statistical Indicators	Definition
Target 3.9: By 2030, substantially reduce the number of deaths and illnesses from hazardous chemicals and air, water, and soil pollution and contamination.	3.9.1: Mortality rate attributed to household and ambient air pollution	Expressed as the number of deaths and death rate. Death rates are calculated by dividing the number of deaths by the total population (or indicated if a different population group is used, e.g., children under 5 years). Note: Evidence from epidemiological studies has shown that exposure to air pollution is linked to, among others, the important diseases taken into account in this estimate: - acute respiratory infections in young children (estimated under 5 years of age); - cerebrovascular diseases (stroke) in adults (estimated above 25 years of age); - ischemic heart diseases in adults (estimated above 25 years of age); - chronic obstructive pulmonary disease in adults (estimated above 25 years of age); and - lung cancer in adults (estimated above 25 years of age).
	3.9.2: Mortality rate attributed to unsafe water, unsafe sanitation, and lack of hygiene—exposure to unsafe water, sanitation, and hygiene for all (WASH) services	Number of deaths from unsafe water, unsafe sanitation, and lack of hygiene —exposure to unsafe water, sanitation and hygiene for all (WASH) services—in a year, divided by the population, and multiplied by 100,000.
Target 3.c: Substantially increase health financing and the recruitment, development, training, and retention of the health workforce in developing countries, especially in least developed countries and small island developing States	3.c.1: Health worker density and distribution	Density of medical doctors: The density of medical doctors is defined as the number of medical doctors, including generalists and specialist medical practitioners, per 10,000 population in a given national and/or subnational area. The International Standard Classification of Occupations (ISCO) unit group codes included in this category are 221, 2211, and 2212 of ISCO-08. Density of nursing and midwifery personnel: The density of nursing and midwifery personnel is defined as the number of nursing and midwifery personnel per 10,000 population in a given national and/or subnational area. The ISCO-08 codes included in this category are 2221, 2222, 3221, and 3222.
Target 3.d: Strengthen the capacity of all countries, in particular developing countries, for early warning, risk reduction, and management of national and global health risks	3.d.1: International Health Regulations (IHR) capacity and health emergency preparedness	The revised International Health Regulations (IHR) were adopted in 2005 and entered into force in 2007. Under the IHR, States Parties are obliged to develop and maintain minimum core capacities for surveillance and response, including at points of entry, in order to early detect, assess, notify, and respond to any potential public health events of international concern. Article 54 of the IHR states that: States Parties and the Director-General shall report to the Health Assembly on the implementation of these Regulations as decided by the Health Assembly. The IHR self-assessment and reporting tool captures the level of self-assessed national capacities. They are essential public health capacities that States Parties are required to have in place throughout their territories pursuant to Articles 5 and 12, and Annex 1A of the IHR (2005) requirements.
Goal 4. Ensure inclusive and equitable quality education and promote lifelong learning opportunities for all		
Target 4.1: By 2030, ensure that all girls and boys complete free, equitable, and quality primary and secondary education leading to relevant and effective learning outcomes	4.1.1.a: Proportion of children and young people in grades 2/3 achieving at least a minimum proficiency level	Percentage of children and young people achieving at least a minimum proficiency level in (i) reading and (ii) mathematics during primary education (Grade 2 or 3), at the end of primary education, and at the end of lower secondary education. The minimum proficiency level will be measured relative to new common reading and mathematics scales currently in development.

(continued on next page)

Goals and Targets	Statistical Indicators	Definition
	4.1.1.b: Proportion of children and young people at the end of primary achieving at least a minimum proficiency level 4.1.1.c: Proportion of children and young people at the end of lower secondary achieving at least a minimum proficiency level	Note: This indicator is expressed as proportion of children and/or young people at the relevant stage of education in a given year achieving or exceeding the predefined proficiency level in a given subject.
	4.1.2: Completion rate (primary education, lower secondary education, upper secondary education)	Percentage of a cohort of children or young people aged 3–5 years above the intended age for the last grade of each level of education who have completed that grade. Note: A completion rate at or near 100% indicates that all or most children and adolescents have completed a level of education by the time they are 3 to 5 years older than the official age of entry into the last grade of that level of education. A low completion rate indicates low or delayed entry into a given level of education, high drop-out, high repetition, late completion, or a combination of these factors.
Target 4.2: By 2030, ensure that all girls and boys have access to quality early childhood development, care, and preprimary education, so that they are ready for primary education.	4.2.2: Participation rate in organized learning (1 year before the official primary entry age), by sex	Percentage of children in the given age range who participate in one or more organized learning programs, including programs which offer a combination of education and care. Participation in early childhood and in primary education are both included. The age range will vary by economy depending on the official age for entry to primary education. Note: An organized learning program is one that consists of a coherent set or sequence of educational activities designed with the intention of achieving predetermined learning outcomes or the accomplishment of a specific set of educational tasks. Early childhood and primary education programs are examples of organized learning programs. The official primary entry age is the age at which children are obliged to start primary education, according to national legislation or policies.
Target 4.c: By 2030, substantially increase the supply of qualified teachers, including through international cooperation for teacher training in developing countries, especially least developed countries and small island developing states.	4.c.1.a: Proportion of teachers in preprimary education who have received at least the minimum organized teacher training 4.c.1.b: Proportion of teachers in primary education who have received at least the minimum organized teacher training 4.c.1.c: Proportion of teachers in lower secondary education who have received at least the minimum organized teacher training	Percentage of teachers by level of education taught (pre-primary, primary, lower secondary, and upper secondary education) who have received at least the minimum organized pedagogical teacher training pre-service and in-service required for teaching at the relevant level in a given economy. Note: Number of teachers in a given level of education who are trained is expressed as a percentage of all teachers in that level of education. A teacher is trained if they have received at least the minimum organized pedagogical teacher training pre-service and in-service required for teaching at the relevant level in each economy.

(continued on next page)

Goals and Targets	Statistical Indicators	Definition
	4.c.1.d: Proportion of teachers in upper secondary education who have received at least the minimum organized teacher training	
Goal 5. Achieve gender equality and empower all women and girls		
Target 5.3: Eliminate all harmful practices, such as child, early, and forced marriage, and female genital mutilation.	5.3.1: Proportion of women aged 20–24 years who were married or in a union before age 15 and before age 18	Proportion of women aged 20–24 years who were married or in a union before age 15 years and before age 18 years. Note: Both formal (i.e., marriages) and informal unions are covered under this indicator. Informal unions are generally defined as those in which a couple lives together (i.e., cohabits) for some time, intends to have a lasting relationship, but for which there has been no formal civil or religious ceremony.
Target 5.5: Ensure women's full and effective participation in, and equal opportunities for leadership at, all levels of decision-making in political, economic, and public life.	5.5.1: Proportion of seats held by women in national parliaments	The proportion of seats held by women in national parliaments, as of 1 January of reporting year, is currently measured as the number of seats held by women members in single or lower chambers of national parliaments, expressed as a percentage of all occupied seats. Note: National parliaments can be bicameral or unicameral. This indicator covers the single chamber in unicameral parliaments and the lower chamber in bicameral parliaments. It does not cover the upper chamber of bicameral parliaments. Seats are usually won by members in general parliamentary elections. Seats may also be filled by nomination, appointment, indirect election, rotation of members, and by-election. Seats refer to the number of parliamentary mandates, or the number of members of parliament.
	5.5.2: Proportion of women in managerial positions	Proportion of females in the total number of persons employed in senior and middle management. Senior and middle management correspond to major group 1 in International Standard Classification of Occupations (ISCO)-08 and ISCO-88, minus category 14 in ISCO-08 (hospitality, retail, and other services managers) and minus category 13 in ISCO-88 (general managers), since these comprise mainly managers of small enterprises. Note: The indicator provides information on the proportion of women who are employed in decision-making and managerial roles in government, large enterprises, and institutions, thus providing some insight into women's power in decision-making and in the economy (especially compared to men's power in those areas).
Goal 6. Ensure availability and sustainable management of water and sanitation for all		
Target 6.1: By 2030, achieve universal and equitable access to safe and affordable drinking water for all.	6.1.1: Proportion of population using safely managed drinking water services	Proportion of the population using safely managed drinking water services is currently being measured by the proportion of the population using an improved basic drinking water source that is located on premises, available when needed, and free of fecal (and priority chemical) contamination. Note: Improved drinking water sources include the following: piped water into a dwelling, yard, or plot; public taps or standpipes; boreholes or tubewells; protected dug wells; protected springs; packaged water; delivered water and rainwater. "Located on premises": a water source at the point of collection is within the dwelling, yard, or plot.

(continued on next page)

Goals and Targets	Statistical Indicators	Definition
		"Available when needed": households are able to access sufficient quantities of water when needed. "Free from fecal (and priority chemical) contamination": water complies with relevant national or local standards. In the absence of such standards, reference is made to the WHO Guidelines for Drinking Water Quality http://www.who.int/water_sanitation_health/dwq/guidelines/en/). E. coli or thermotolerant coliforms are the preferred indicator for microbiological quality, and arsenic and fluoride are the priority chemicals for global reporting. The WHO/UNICEF Joint Monitoring Programme (JMP) for Water Supply, Sanitation, and Hygiene estimates access to basic services for each economy, separately in urban and rural areas, by fitting a regression line to a series of data points from household surveys and censuses. This approach was used to report on use of 'improved water' sources for Millennium Development Goal monitoring. The JMP is evaluating the use of alternative statistical estimation methods as more data become available. The JMP 2017 update and SDG baselines report describes in more detail how data on availability and quality from different sources, can be combined with data on use of different types of supplies, as recorded in the current JMP database to compute the safely managed drinking water services indicator. https://washdata.org/report/jmp-2017-report-final.
Target 6.2: By 2030, achieve access to adequate and equitable sanitation and hygiene for all, and end open defecation, paying special attention to the needs of women and girls and those in vulnerable situations.	6.2.1.a: Proportion of population using safely managed sanitation services	The proportion of the population using a basic sanitation facility, including handwashing facility with soap and water, that is not shared with other households and where excreta is safely disposed in situ or treated off-site. Note: Improved sanitation facilities include flush or pour-flush toilets to sewer systems, septic tanks or pit latrines, ventilated improved pit latrines, pit latrines with a slab, and composting toilets. "Safely disposed in situ": when pit latrines and septic tanks are not emptied, the excreta may still remain isolated from human contact and can be considered safely managed. For example, with the new SDG indicator, households that use twin pit latrines or safely abandon full pit latrines and dig new facilities, a common practice in rural areas, would be counted as using safely managed sanitation services. "Treated offsite": not all excreta from toilet facilities conveyed in sewers (as wastewater) or emptied from pit latrines and septic tanks (as faecal sludge) reaches a treatment site. For instance, a portion may leak from the sewer itself or, due to broken pumping installations, be discharged directly to the environment. Similarly, a portion of the faecal sludge emptied from containers may be discharged into open drains, to open ground or water bodies, rather than being transported to a treatment plant. And finally, even once the excreta reach a treatment plant a portion may remain untreated, due to dysfunctional treatment equipment or inadequate treatment capacity, and be discharged to the environment. For the purposes of SDG monitoring, adequacy of treatment will initially be assessed based on the reported level of treatment. "A handwashing facility with soap and water": a handwashing facility is a device to contain, transport or regulate the flow of water to facilitate handwashing.

(continued on next page)

Goals and Targets	Statistical Indicators	Definition
Target 6.4: By 2030, substantially increase water-use efficiency across all sectors and ensure sustainable withdrawals and supply of freshwater to address water scarcity and substantially reduce the number of people suffering from water scarcity.	6.4.2: Level of water stress: freshwater withdrawal as a proportion of available freshwater resources	The level of water stress: freshwater withdrawal as a proportion of available freshwater resources is the ratio between total freshwater withdrawn by all major sectors and total renewable freshwater resources, after taking into account environmental water requirements. Note: Total freshwater withdrawal is the volume of freshwater extracted from its source (rivers, lakes, aquifers) for agriculture, industries, and municipalities. Freshwater withdrawal includes primary freshwater (not withdrawn before), secondary freshwater (previously withdrawn and returned to rivers and groundwater, such as discharged wastewater and agricultural drainage water) and fossil groundwater. Main sectors, as defined by International Standard Industrial Classification standards, include agriculture, forestry and fishing, manufacturing, electricity industry, and services. Environmental water requirements are the quantities of water required to sustain freshwater and estuarine ecosystems. This indicator is also known as water withdrawal intensity. Total renewable freshwater resources are expressed as the sum of internal and external renewable water resources. Internal renewable water resources are defined as the long-term average annual flow of rivers and recharge of groundwater, generated from endogenous precipitation, for a given economy. External renewable water resources refer to the flows of water entering the economy, taking into consideration the quantity of flows reserved to upstream and downstream economies through agreements or treaties.
Target 6.a: By 2030, expand international cooperation and capacity-building support to developing countries in water- and sanitation-related activities and programmes, including water harvesting, desalination, water efficiency, wastewater treatment, recycling, and reuse technologies.	6.a.1: Amount of water- and sanitation-related ODA that is part of a government-coordinated spending plan	Amount of water- and sanitation-related ODA that is part of a government-coordinated spending plan is defined as the proportion of total water- and sanitation-related ODA disbursements that are included in the government budget. Note: The amount of water- and sanitation-related ODA is a quantifiable measurement as a proxy for "international cooperation and capacity development support" in financial terms. A low value of this indicator (near 0%) would suggest that international donors are investing in water- and sanitation-related activities and programs in the economy, outside the purview of the national government. A high value (near 100%) would indicate that donors are aligned with the national government and national policies and plans for water and sanitation.
Goal 7. Ensure access to affordable, reliable, sustainable, and modern energy for all		
Target 7.1: By 2030, ensure universal access to affordable, reliable, and modern energy services.	7.1.1: Proportion of population with access to electricity	Percentage of the population with access to electricity. Note: Access to electricity addresses major critical issues in all the dimensions of sustainable development. The target has a wide range of social and economic impacts, including facilitating development of household-based income-generating activities and lightening the burden of household tasks.
	7.1.2: Proportion of population with primary reliance on clean fuels and technology	Number of people using clean fuels and technologies for cooking, heating and lighting divided by total population reporting that any cooking, heating or lighting, expressed as percentage. "Clean" is defined by the emission rate targets and specific fuel recommendations (i.e. against unprocessed coal and kerosene) included in the normative guidance WHO guidelines for indoor air quality: household fuel combustion.

(continued on next page)

Goals and Targets	Statistical Indicators	Definition
Target 7.2: By 2030, increase substantially the share of renewable energy in the global energy mix.	7.2.1: Renewable energy share in total final energy consumption	Percentage of final consumption of energy that is derived from renewable resources. Note: Renewable energy consumption includes consumption of energy derived from hydro, solid biofuels, wind, solar, liquid biofuels, biogas, geothermal, marine sources, and waste. Total final energy consumption is calculated from national balances and statistics as total final consumption minus nonenergy use.
Target 7.3: By 2030, double the global rate of improvement in energy efficiency.	7.3.1: Energy intensity measured in terms of primary energy and GDP	Energy supplied to the economy per unit value of economic output. Note: Total energy supply, as defined by the International Recommendations for Energy Statistics, is made up of production, plus net imports, minus international marine and aviation bunkers plus-stock changes. GDP is the measure of economic output. For international comparison purposes, GDP is measured in constant terms at PPP.
Goal 8. Promote sustained, inclusive, and sustainable economic growth, full and productive employment, and decent work for all		
Target 8.1: Sustain per-capita economic growth in accordance with national circumstances and, in particular, at least 7% GDP growth per annum in the least developed countries.	8.1.1: Annual growth rate of real GDP per capita	Percentage change in the real GDP per capita between 2 consecutive years. Note: Real GDP per capita is calculated by dividing GDP at constant prices by the population of a country or area. The data for real GDP is measured in constant US dollars to facilitate the calculation of economy growth rates and aggregation of the economy data.
Target 8.2: Achieve higher levels of economic productivity through diversification, technological upgrading, and innovation, including through a focus on high-value-added and labor-intensive sectors.	8.2.1: Annual growth rate of real GDP per employed person	Annual percentage change in real GDP per employed person. Note: The real GDP per employed person being a measure of labor productivity, this indicator represents a measure of labor productivity growth, thus providing information on the evolution, efficiency and quality of human capital in the production process.
Target 8.6: By 2020, substantially reduce the proportion of youth not in employment, education, or training.	8.6.1: Proportion of youth (aged 15–24 years) not in education, employment, or training	Proportion of youth (aged 15–24 years) who are not in education, employment, or training, also known as "the NEET rate". It conveys the number of young persons not in education, employment, or training as a percentage of the total youth population.
Target 8.7: Take immediate and effective measures to eradicate forced labor, end modern slavery and human trafficking, and secure the prohibition and elimination of the worst forms of child labor, including recruitment and use of child soldiers, and, by 2025, end child labor in all its forms.	8.7.1: Proportion of children aged 5–17 years engaged in child labor	The number of children aged 5–17 years reported to be in child labor during the reference period (usually the week prior to the survey). The proportion of children in child labor is calculated as the number of children in child labor, divided by the total number of children in the population.
Target 8.10: Strengthen the capacity of domestic financial institutions to encourage and expand access to banking, insurance, and financial services for all.	8.10.1: Number of commercial bank branches and ATMs per 100,000 adults	The number of commercial bank branches per 100,000 adults refers to the number of commercial banks branches reported by the central bank or the main financial regulator of the economy every year. To make it comparable, this number is presented as a reference per 100,000 adults in the respective economy.

(continued on next page)

Goals and Targets	Statistical Indicators	Definition
		The number of ATMs per 100,000 adults, refers to the number of ATMs in the economy for all types of institutions, such as commercial banks, non-deposit-taking microfinance institutions, deposit-taking microfinance institutions, credit unions, financial cooperatives, and others. This information is reported every year by the central bank or the main financial regulator of the economy. To make it comparable, this number is presented as a reference per 100,000 adults in the respective economy.
	8.10.2: Proportion of adults (aged 15 years and older) with an account at a bank or other financial institution or with a mobile-money service provider	Percentage of adults (aged 15+) who report having an account (of their own or held with someone else) at a bank or another type of financial institution or have personally used a mobile-money service in the past 12 months.
Target 8.a: Increase Aid for Trade support for developing countries, in particular least developed countries, including through the Enhanced Integrated Framework for Trade-related Technical Assistance to Least Developed Countries	8.a.1 Aid for Trade commitments and disbursements	Aid for Trade is reported here by recipient, as well as by donor economy. This is measured as total ODA allocated to aid for trade in 2015 US dollars.
Goal 9. Build resilient infrastructure, promote inclusive and sustainable industrialization, and foster innovation		
Target 9.1: Develop quality, reliable, sustainable, and resilient infrastructure, including regional and transborder infrastructure, to support economic development and human well-being, with a focus on affordable and equitable access for all.	9.1.a: Passenger volume by road transport, measured in millions of passenger-kilometers	Passenger and freight volumes are the sums of the passenger and freight volumes reported for the road and rail carriers in terms of number of people and metric tons of cargo, respectively. Note: The International Transport Forum collects data on transport (rail and road) statistics on annual basis from all its member economies. Data are collected from transport ministries, statistical offices, and other institutions designated as official data sources. Although there are clear definitions for all the terms used in this survey, economies might have different methodologies to calculate passenger-kilometers and ton-kilometers. Methods could be based on traffic or mobility surveys, using very different sampling methods and estimating techniques, which could affect the comparability of the statistics.
	9.1.b: Freight volume by road transport, measured in millions of ton-kilometers	
	9.1.c: Passenger volume by rail transport, measured in millions of passenger-kilometers	
	9.1.d: Freight volume by rail transport, measured in millions of ton-kilometers	
Target 9.2: Promote inclusive and sustainable industrialization and, by 2030, significantly raise industry's share of employment and GDP, in line with national circumstances, and double its share in least developed countries.	9.2.1: Manufacturing value added as a proportion of GDP and per capita	Manufacturing value added (MVA) as a proportion of GDP is a ratio between MVA and GDP, both reported in constant 2015 US dollars. MVA per capita is calculated by dividing MVA in constant 2015 US dollars by the population of a country or area.
	9.2.2: Manufacturing employment as a proportion of total employment	Share of manufacturing employment in total employment.

(continued on next page)

Goals and Targets	Statistical Indicators	Definition
Target 9.4: By 2030, upgrade infrastructure and retrofit industries to make them sustainable, with increased resource-use efficiency and greater adoption of clean and environmentally sound technologies and industrial processes, with all countries taking action in accordance with their respective capabilities.	9.4.1: Carbon dioxide (CO_2) emissions per unit of value-added	CO_2 emissions per unit value-added is an indicator calculated as ratio between CO_2 emissions from fuel combustion and the value added of associated economic activities. The indicator can be calculated for the whole economy (total CO_2 emissions to GDP) or for specific sectors, notably the manufacturing sector (CO_2 emissions from manufacturing industries per MVA). CO_2 emissions per unit of GDP are expressed in kilograms of CO_2 per constant 2010 US dollar PPP of GDP. CO_2 emissions from manufacturing industries per unit of MVA are measured in kilograms of CO_2 equivalent per unit of MVA in constant 2015 US dollars.
Target 9.5: Enhance scientific research and upgrade the technological capabilities of industrial sectors in all countries, in particular developing countries, including, by 2030, encouraging innovation and substantially increasing the number of research and development workers per 1 million people and public and private research and development spending.	9.5.1: Research and development expenditure as a proportion of GDP	Amount of research and development expenditure divided by the total output of the economy.
	9.5.2: Researchers (full-time equivalent) per million inhabitants	Number of research and development workers per 1 million people.
Target 9.a: Facilitate sustainable and resilient infrastructure development in developing countries through enhanced financial, technological, and technical support to African countries, least developed countries, landlocked developing countries, and small island developing States.	9.a.1: Total official international support (ODA plus other official flows) to infrastructure	Gross disbursements of total ODA and other official flows from all donors in support of infrastructure.
Target 9.b: Support domestic technology development, research, and innovation in developing countries, including by ensuring a conducive policy environment for, among other things, industrial diversification and value addition to commodities.	9.b.1: Proportion of medium- and high-tech industry value-added in total value-added	Ratio of the value added by medium- and high-tech (MHT) industry to total MVA. Note: Industrial development generally entails a structural transition from resource-based and low-tech activities to MHT activities. A modern, highly complex production structure offers better opportunities for skills development and technological innovation. MHT activities are also the high-value addition industries of manufacturing with higher technological intensity and labor productivity. Increasing the share of MHT sectors also reflects the impact of innovation.
Target 9.c: Significantly increase access to information and communications technology and strive to provide universal and affordable access to the Internet in least developed countries by 2020.	9.c.1.a: Proportion of the population covered by narrowband (2G) mobile networks 9.c.1.b: Proportion of the population covered by 3G mobile networks 9.c.1.c: Proportion of the population covered by LTE mobile networks	Proportion of the population covered by a mobile network, broken down by technology, refers to the percentage of inhabitants living within range of a mobile-cellular signal, irrespective of whether or not they are mobile-phone subscribers or users. This is calculated by dividing the number of inhabitants within range of a mobile-cellular signal by the total population and multiplying by 100. Note: Coverage refers to Long-Term Evolution (LTE), broadband (3G), and narrowband (2G) mobile-cellular technologies:

(continued on next page)

Goals and Targets	Statistical Indicators	Definition
		2G mobile population coverage refers to the percentage of inhabitants within range of a mobile networks with access to data communications (e.g. Internet) at downstream speeds below 256 Kbit/s. This includes mobile-cellular technologies such as general packet radio service (GPRS), code division multiple access (CDMA) 2000 1x and most enhanced data for GSM (global system for mobile communications) evolution (EDGE) implementations. 3G population coverage refers to the percentage of inhabitants that are within range of at least a 3G mobile-cellular signal, irrespective of whether or not they are subscribers. Long-term evolution (LTE) population coverage refers to the percentage of inhabitants that live within range of LTE/LTE-Advanced, mobile WiMAX/WirelessMAN or other more advanced mobile-cellular networks, irrespective of whether or not they are subscribers.
Goal 10. Reduce inequality within and among countries		
Target 10.1: By 2030, progressively achieve and sustain income growth of the bottom 40% of the population at a rate higher than the national average.	10.1.1.a: Growth rates of household expenditure or income per capita among the bottom 40% of the population	The growth rate in the welfare aggregate of the bottom 40% of the population is calculated as the annualized average growth rate in per capita real consumption or income of the bottom 40% of the income distribution in an economy from household surveys over a period of approximately 5 years.
	10.1.1.b: Growth rates of household expenditure or income per capita	The national average growth rate in the welfare aggregate is calculated as the annualized average growth rate in per capita real consumption or income of the total population in an economy from household surveys over a period of approximately 5 years.
Goal 11. Make cities and human settlements inclusive, safe, resilient, and sustainable		
Target 11.1: By 2030, ensure access for all to adequate, safe, and affordable housing and basic services, and upgrade slums.	11.1.1: Proportion of the urban population living in slums, informal settlements, or inadequate housing	The proportion of the urban population that lives in slums or informal settlements as well as those living in inadequate housing. Note: Most of the criteria for defining slums, informal settlements, and inadequate housing overlap. The criteria for informal settlements are essentially captured in the definition of slums, which combines both slums and informal settlements as one entity. Slums and informal settlements are therefore combined into one component of the indicator, providing some continuity with what was captured under Millennium Development Goal 7. At a later stage, a composite index will be developed that will incorporate all measures (combining slums, informal settlements, and inadequate housing) to provide one estimate.
Target 11.5: By 2030, significantly reduce the number of deaths and the number of people affected, and substantially decrease the direct economic losses relative to global GDP caused by disasters, including water-related disasters, with a focus on protecting the poor and people in vulnerable situations	11.5.2: Direct economic loss in relation to global GDP, damage to critical infrastructure, and number of disruptions to basic services, attributed to disasters	Direct economic loss is the monetary value of total or partial destruction of physical assets existing in the affected area. Direct economic loss is nearly equivalent to physical damage. Note: The original national disaster loss databases usually register physical damage value (housing unit loss, infrastructure loss, etc.), which needs conversion to a monetary value according to the United Nations International Strategy for Disaster Reduction methodology. The converted global value is divided by global GDP (inflation adjusted, constant US dollars) calculated from the World Bank Development Indicators.
Target 11.6: By 2030, reduce the adverse per capita environmental impact of cities, including by paying special attention to air quality and municipal and other waste management.	11.6.2: Annual mean levels of fine particulate matter (PM), e.g., PM2.5 and PM10, in cities, measured in total (population weighted) micrograms per cubic meter	The mean annual concentration of fine suspended particles of less than 2.5 microns in diameters (PM2.5) is a common measure of air pollution. Note: The mean is a population-weighted average for urban population in an economy and is expressed in micrograms per cubic meter

(continued on next page)

Goals and Targets	Statistical Indicators	Definition
Goal 12. Ensure sustainable consumption and production patterns		
Target 12.2: By 2030, achieve the sustainable management and efficient use of natural resources	12.2.1: Material footprint, material footprint per capita, and material footprint per GDP	Material footprint is the attribution of global material extraction to domestic final demand of an economy. The total material footprint is the sum of the material footprint for biomass, fossil fuels, metal ores, and nonmetal ores. This indicator is calculated as raw material equivalent of imports plus domestic extraction minus raw material equivalents of exports. For the attribution of the primary material needs of final demand, a global, multiregional input-output framework is employed.
	12.2.2: Domestic material consumption, domestic material consumption per capita, and domestic material consumption per GDP	Domestic material consumption (DMC) is a standard material flow accounting indicator and reports the apparent consumption of materials in a national economy. Note: DMC reports the amount of materials that are used in a national economy. DMC is a territorial (production side) indicator. DMC also presents the amount of material that needs to be handled within an economy, which is either added to material stocks of buildings and transport infrastructure or used to fuel the economy as material throughput. DMC describes the physical dimension of economic processes and interactions. It can also be interpreted as long-term waste equivalent. Per capita DMC describes the average level of material use in an economy – an environmental pressure indicator – and is also referred to as metabolic profile.
Goal 13. Take urgent action to combat climate change and its impacts		
Target 13.1: Strengthen resilience and adaptive capacity to climate-related hazards and natural disasters in all countries.	13.1.1.a: Number of persons affected by disasters	Number of people who were directly affected by disasters per 100,000 population. Note: Directly affected means people who have suffered injury, illness, or other health effects; who were evacuated, displaced, or relocated; or have suffered direct damage to their livelihoods, economic, physical, social, cultural, and/or environmental assets.
	13.1.1.b: Number of deaths due to disasters	The number of people who died during disaster, or directly after, as a direct result of the hazardous event.
	13.1.2: Number of countries that adopt and implement national disaster risk reduction strategies in line the Sendai Framework for Disaster Risk Reduction 2015–2030	Number of economies that adopt and implement local disaster risk reduction strategies in line with national disaster risk reduction strategies. Note: The score of adoption and implementation of national disaster risk reduction strategies in line with the Sendai Framework (Index) was developed to monitor progress and achievement against Indicator 13.1.2. The score of an economy indicates its compliance of alignment of national strategies with the Sendai Framework based on self-assessments of the economy using 10 criteria for monitoring the progress of national disaster risk reduction strategies.
Goal 14. Conserve and sustainably use the oceans, seas, and marine resources for sustainable development		
Target 14.5: By 2020, conserve at least 10% of coastal and marine areas, consistent with national and international law and based on the best available scientific information.	14.5.1: Coverage of protected areas in relation to marine areas	The indicator shows temporal trends in the mean percentage of each important site for marine biodiversity (i.e., those that contribute significantly to the global persistence of biodiversity) that is covered by designated protected areas and other effective area-based conservation measures. Note: The International Union for Conservation of Nature (IUCN) defines protected areas as clearly defined geographical spaces, recognized, dedicated, and managed through legal or other effective means, to achieve the long-term conservation of nature with associated ecosystem services and cultural values. Importantly, a variety of specific

(continued on next page)

Goals and Targets	Statistical Indicators	Definition
		management objectives are recognized within this definition, spanning conservation, restoration, and sustainable use. The status "designated" is attributed to a protected area when the corresponding authority, according to national legislation or common practice (e.g., by means of an executive decree or the like), officially endorses a document of designation. The designation must be made for the purpose of biodiversity conservation, not de facto protection arising because of some other activity (e.g., military).
Goal 15. Protect, restore, and promote sustainable use of terrestrial ecosystems, sustainably manage forests, combat desertification, halt and reverse land degradation, and halt biodiversity loss		
Target 15.1: By 2020, ensure the conservation, restoration, and sustainable use of terrestrial and inland freshwater ecosystems and their services, in particular forests, wetlands, mountains, and drylands, in line with obligations under international agreements.	15.1.1: Forest area as a proportion of total land area	Size of forest cover in relation to total land area. Note: Forest is defined as "land spanning more than 0.5 hectares with trees higher than 5 meters and a canopy cover of more than 10%, or trees able to reach these thresholds in situ. It does not include land that is predominantly under agricultural or urban land use". Total land area is the total surface area of an economy less the area covered by inland waters, such as major rivers and lakes.
	15.1.2: Proportion of important sites for terrestrial and freshwater biodiversity that are covered by protected areas, by ecosystem type	Proportion of important sites for terrestrial and freshwater biodiversity that are covered by protected areas shows temporal trends in the mean percentage of each important site for terrestrial and freshwater biodiversity (i.e., those that contribute significantly to the global persistence of biodiversity) that is covered by designated protected areas.
Target 15.4: By 2030, ensure the conservation of mountain ecosystems, including their biodiversity, in order to enhance their capacity to provide benefits that are essential for sustainable development	15.4.1: Coverage by protected areas of important sites for mountain biodiversity	Coverage by protected areas of important sites for mountain biodiversity shows temporal trends in the mean percentage of each important site for mountain biodiversity (i.e., those that contribute significantly to the global persistence of biodiversity) that is covered by designated protected areas. Note: Protected areas, as defined by the IUCN (IUCN; Dudley 2008), are clearly defined geographical spaces, recognized, dedicated, and managed, through legal or other effective means, to achieve the long-term conservation of nature with associated ecosystem services and cultural values. Importantly, a variety of specific management objectives are recognized within this definition, spanning conservation, restoration, and sustainable use: "(i) Category Ia: Strict nature reserve; (ii) Category Ib: Wilderness area; (iii) Category II: National park; (iv) Category III: Natural monument or feature; (v) Category IV: Habitat/species management area; (vi) Category V: Protected landscape/seascape; (vii) Category VI: Protected area with sustainable use of natural resources."
Target 15.5: Take urgent and significant action to reduce the degradation of natural habitats, halt the loss of biodiversity and, by 2020, protect and prevent the extinction of threatened species.	15.5.1: Red List Index	The Red List Index measures changes in aggregate extinction risk across groups of species. It is based on genuine changes in the number of species in each category of extinction risk on the IUCN Red List of Threatened Species (IUCN 2015), which is expressed as changes in an index ranging from 0 to 1. Note: The Red List Index value ranges from 1 (all species are categorized as "Least Concern") to 0 (all species are categorized as "Extinct"), indicating how far the set of species has moved overall toward extinction. Threatened species are those listed on The IUCN Red List of Threatened Species in the categories Vulnerable, Endangered, or Critically Endangered (i.e., species that are facing a high, very high, or extremely high risk of extinction in the wild in the medium-term future).

(continued on next page)

Goals and Targets	Statistical Indicators	Definition
Goal 16. Promote peaceful and inclusive societies for sustainable development; provide access to justice for all; and build effective, accountable, and inclusive institutions at all levels		
Target 16.1: Significantly reduce all forms of violence and related death rates everywhere.	16.1.1: Number of victims of intentional homicide per 100,000 population, by sex and age	Total count of victims of intentional homicide divided by the total population, expressed per 100,000 population. Intentional homicide is defined as the unlawful death inflicted upon a person with the intent to cause death or serious injury (International Classification of Crime for Statistical Purposes, ICCS 2015). Population refers to total resident population in a given economy in a given year. Note: This indicator is widely used at national and international levels to measure the most extreme form of violent crime, providing a direct indication of lack of security.
Target 16.3: Promote the rule of law at the national and international levels and ensure equal access to justice for all.	16.3.2: Unsentenced detainees as a proportion of the overall prison population	Total number of persons held in detention who have not yet been sentenced, as a percentage of the total number of persons held in detention, on a specified date.
Target 16.5: Substantially reduce corruption and bribery in all their forms.	16.5.2: Proportion of businesses that had at least one contact with a public official and that paid a bribe to a public official, or were asked for a bribe by those public officials during the previous 12 months	Proportion of firms that were asked for a gift or informal payment when meeting with tax officials. Note: This indicator aims to ascertain whether or not firms have been solicited for gifts or informal payments (i.e., bribes) when meeting with tax officials. Paying taxes are required of formal forms in most economies, and the rationale for this indicator is to measure the incidence of corruption during this routine interaction.
Target 16.9: By 2030, provide legal identity, including birth registration, for all.	16.9.1: Proportion of children under 5 years of age whose births have been registered with a civil authority, by age	Proportion of children under 5 years of age whose births have been registered with a civil authority.
Goal 17. Strengthen the means of implementation and revitalize the Global Partnership for Sustainable Development		
Target 17.3: Mobilize additional financial resources for developing countries from multiple sources	17.3.2: Volume of remittances (in US dollars) as a proportion of total GDP	Personal remittances comprise personal transfers and compensation of employees. Personal transfers consist of all current transfers in cash or in kind made or received by resident households to or from nonresident households. Compensation of employees refers to the income of (i) border, seasonal, and other short-term workers who are employed in an economy where they are not resident; and (ii) residents employed by nonresident entities.
Target 17.4: Assist developing countries in attaining long-term debt sustainability through coordinated policies aimed at fostering debt financing, debt relief, and debt restructuring, as appropriate, and address the external debt of highly indebted poor countries to reduce debt distress	17.4.1: Debt service as a proportion of exports of goods and services	Percentage of debt services (principle and interest payments) to the exports of goods and services. Debt services covered in this indicator refer only to public and publicly guaranteed debt.

(continued on next page)

Goals and Targets	Statistical Indicators	Definition
Target 17.9: Enhance international support for implementing effective and targeted capacity-building in developing countries to support national plans to implement all the Sustainable Development Goals, including through North-South, South-South, and triangular cooperation.	17.9.1: Dollar value of financial and technical assistance (including through North-South, South-South, and triangular cooperation) committed to developing countries	Gross disbursements of total ODA and other official flows from all donors for capacity-building and national planning. Note: ODA refers to "those flows to countries and territories on the Development Assistance Committee List of ODA Recipients and to multilateral institutions which are (i) provided by official agencies, including state and local governments, or by their executive agencies; and (ii) each transaction is administered with the promotion of the economic development and welfare of developing economies as its main objective; and is concessional in character and conveys a grant element of at least 25% (calculated at a rate of discount of 10%). Other official flows (excluding officially supported export credits) are defined as transactions by the official sector that do not meet the conditions for eligibility as ODA, either because they are not primarily aimed at development or because they are not sufficiently concessional.
Target 17.18: By 2020, enhance capacity-building support to developing countries, including for least developed countries and small island developing states, to increase significantly the availability of high-quality, timely, and reliable data disaggregated by income, gender, age, race, ethnicity, migratory status, disability, geographic location, and other characteristics relevant in national contexts.	17.18.3: Number of countries with a national statistical plan that is fully funded and under implementation, by source of funding	Count of economies that are either (i) implementing a strategy, (ii) designing a strategy, or (iii) awaiting adoption of a strategy in the current year. Note: The indicator is based on the annual Status Report on National Strategies for the Development of Statistics. In collaboration with its partners, PARIS21 reports on progress in designing and implementing national statistical plans. This indicator can be disaggregated by geographical area. Regional-level aggregates are based on the total count of national strategies.
Target 17.19: By 2030, build on existing initiatives to develop measurements of progress on sustainable development that complement GDP, and support statistical capacity-building in developing countries.	17.19.1: Dollar value of all resources made available to strengthen statistical capacity in developing countries	US dollar value of ongoing statistical support in developing economies. Note: The indicator is based on the Partner Report on Support to Statistics, which is designed and administered by PARIS21 to provide a snapshot of the US dollar value of ongoing statistical support in developing economies.
	17.19.2: Number of countries that have conducted at least one population and housing census in the past 10 years	Economies that have conducted at least one population and housing census in the past 10 years. This includes economies that compile their detailed population and housing statistics from population registers, administrative records, sample surveys, other sources, or a combination of those sources.

www.ingramcontent.com/pod-product-compliance
Lightning Source LLC
Chambersburg PA
CBHW041751220926
51847CB00014B/163
* 9 7 8 9 2 9 2 6 9 0 2 0 5 *